W9-BMS-908

Macroeconomics

8th Canadian Edition

CAMPBELL R. McCONNELL
University of Nebraska, Lincoln

STANLEY L. BRUE
Pacific Lutheran University

THOMAS P. BARBIERO
Ryerson Polytechnic University

McGraw-Hill Ryerson

Toronto Montréal New York Burr Ridge Bangkok
Bogotá Caracas Lisbon London Madrid Mexico City
Milan New Delhi Seoul Singapore Sydney Taipei

McGraw-Hill
Ryerson Limited

A Subsidiary of The **McGraw·Hill** Companies

Macroeconomics: Canada in the Global Economy
Eighth Canadian Edition

Copyright © 1999, 1996, 1993, 1990, 1987, 1984, 1981, 1978. McGraw-Hill Ryerson Limited, a Subsidiary of The McGraw-Hill Companies. All rights reserved. No part of this publication may be reproduced or transmitted in any form or by any means, or stored in a data base or retrieval system, without the prior written permission of McGraw-Hill Ryerson Limited, or in the case of photocopying or other reprographic copying, a licence from CANCOPY (the Canadian Copyright Licensing Agency), 6 Adelaide Street East, Suite 900, Toronto, Ontario, M5C 1H6.

Any request for photocopying, recording, or taping of any part of this publication shall be directed in writing to CANCOPY.

ISBN: 0-07-560459-0

2 3 4 5 6 7 8 9 10 GTC 8 7 6 5 4 3 2 1 0

Printed and bound in Canada.

Statistics Canada information is used with the permission of the Ministry of Industry, as Minister responsible for Statistics Canada. Information on the availability of the wider range of data from Statistics Canada can be obtained from Statistics Canada's Regional Offices, its World Wide Web site at *http://www.statcan.ca* and its toll-free access number 1-800-263-1136.

Care has been taken to trace ownership of copyright material contained in this text; however, the publisher will welcome any information that enables them to rectify any reference or credit for subsequent editions.

Senior Sponsoring Editor: *Lynn Fisher*
Editorial Consultant: *Joseph Gladstone*
Supervising Editor: *Jennifer Burnell*
Associate Editor: *Jenna Wallace*
Copy-editor: *Wendy Thomas*
Production Co-ordinator: *Nicla Dattolico*
Cover Design: *Liz Harasymczuk*
Cover Photo: *Mike Dobel/Masterfile*
Interior Design: *Liz Harasymczuk*
Art Director: *Dianna Little*
Typesetter: *Bookman Typesetting Co.*
Printer: *Transcontinental Printing*

Canadian Cataloguing in Publication Data
McConnell, Campbell R.
    Macroeconomics: Canada in the global economy

8th Canadian ed.
Includes index.
ISBN 0-07-560459-0

1. Macroeconomics.   I. Brue, Stanley, L., 1945– .   II. Barbiero, Thomas Paul, 1952– .   III. Title
HB172.5.M114 1999   339   C98-932825-2

This book is dedicated to Elsa, Marta, Emilia
and Robert.

About the Authors

Campbell R. McConnell earned his Ph.D. from the University of Iowa after receiving degrees from Cornell College and the University of Illinois. He taught at the University of Nebraska-Lincoln from 1953 until his retirement in 1990. He is also coauthor of *Contemporary Labor Economics*, 5th ed. (McGraw-Hill) and has edited readers for the principles and labour economics courses. He is a recipient of both the University of Nebraska Distinguished Teaching Award and the James A. Lake Academic Freedom Award, and is past-president of the Midwest Economics Association. Professor McConnell was awarded an honorary Doctor of Laws degree from Cornell College in 1973 and received its Distinguished Achievement Award in 1994. His primary areas of interest are labour economics and economic education. He has an extensive collection of jazz recordings and enjoys reading jazz history.

Stanley L. Brue did his undergraduate work at Augustana College (SD) and received his Ph.D. from the University of Nebraska-Lincoln. He teaches at Pacific Lutheran University, where he has been honoured as a recipient of the Burlington Northern Faculty Achievement Award. He has also received the national Leavey Award for excellence in economic education. Professor Brue is past president and a current member of the International Executive Board of Omicron Delta Epsilon International Economics Honorary. He is coauthor of *Economic Scenes*, 5th ed. (Prentice-Hall) and *Contemporary Labor Economics*, 5th ed. (McGraw-Hill) and author of *The Evolution of Economic Thought*, 5th ed. (HB/Dryden). For relaxation, he enjoys boating on Puget Sound and skiing trips with his family.

Thomas P. Barbiero received his Ph.D. from the University of Toronto after completing undergraduate studies at the same university. He has published papers on the role of the agricultural sector in the industrial development of northern Italy in the period 1861–1914. His research interests in the last few years have turned to economic methodology and the application of economic theory to explain social phenomena. Professor Barbiero spends part of his summer in Florence, where he teaches a European economic history course to Ryerson students. After the course is over, he and his wife search out good food and wine in the Tuscan countryside.

Contents

Preface

Welcome to the eighth Canadian edition of *Macroeconomics* and *Microeconomics*. *Macroeconomics* and *Microeconomics* continue to be leading economics texts in both Canada and the United States; about 5 million students have used this book in the two countries. It has been adapted into Australian, Italian, and Russian editions and translated into French, Spanish, and several other languages.

The resurging Canadian economy, changes in the focus of monetary policy, economic turmoil in Southeast Asia, dynamic new technologies, swings in exchange rates, capitalism in Russia—what an interesting time to teach and learn economics! Clearly, those who undertstand economic principles will have a distinct advantage in making sense of the economy and successfully participating in it.

WHAT'S NEW?

We thoroughly revised, polished, and updated this edition. (Using a software analogy, this is version 8.0, not 7.1 or 7.2.) The comments of reviewers and survey respondents motivated many of the changes and helped us create a text full of energy and innovation.

New or "Mostly New" Chapters

One chapter is totally new to this edition, and four other chapters are "mostly new."

- Chapter 11 (Macroeconomics): Aggregate Demand and Aggregate Supply. We have introduced both the short-run and long-run aggregate supply curves, and connected the long-run aggregate supply curves with potential GDP.
- Chapter 13 (Microeconomics): Technology, R&D, and Efficiency. This entirely new chapter is an explicit and cohesive discussion of the microeconomics of technological advance. We think that topics such as invention, innovation, R&D decision making, and creative destruction are exciting and simply too important to ignore or set into sidebars, so we devote an entire chapter to them. (To make room for this new content, we consolidated the discussions of monopolistic competition and oligopoly into a single chapter [Chapter 12].)
- Chapter 16 (Macroeconomics): Long-Run Macroeconomic Adjustments. In this revised chapter we use the long-run aggregate demand-aggregate supply model to analyze demand-pull inflation, cost-push inflation, and recession. In the remainder of the chapter we look at other aggregate supply topics such as the Phillips Curve and supply-side economics.
- Chapter 17 (Macroeconomics): Disputes in Macro Theory and Policy. In this nearly new chapter we broaden the ideas developed in Chapter 16 to discuss modern disputes in macro theory and policy. We now use the classic Keynesian discussion of previous editions as a historical backdrop for an examination of modern debates on (1) the sources of macro instability, (2) the extent of "self-correction" in the economy, and (3) the debate over "rules" versus "discretion." The chapter systematically examines new classical economics and introduces ideas such as misperceptions theory, coordination failures, efficiency wages, and insider-outsider relationships.

- Chapter 23 (Macroeconomics): Transition Economies: Russia and China. We added a discussion of China to the previous edition's material on Russia. We look briefly at Marxian ideology and the institutions, goals, and major problems of central planning, and then turn to the collapse of the Soviet economy, the elements of the Russian reform, and contemporary outcomes. Finally, we discuss the main features of market reform in China, including rapid economic growth and remaining difficulties.

New Pedagogy

- *Quick Quizzes.* We added four multiple-choice questions as Quick Quizzes to each of the 24 Key Graphs. Each quiz relates to the content of the specific Key Graph and is written in the same style and at the same level of difficulty as the test bank questions. The correct answers are provided upside down so students can instantly measure their understanding of key concepts.
- *Ten Key Concepts.* We have introduced the Ten Key Concepts in the first chapter of the text. These Key Concepts will help the student to better organize and understand the core materials of the text. The Ten Key Concepts are divided into three categories:

  1. those pertaining to the individual,
  2. concepts that explain the interaction among individuals; and
  3. concepts that deal with the economy as a whole.

  In Chapter 1, each concept is briefly identified with further elaboration of each of the Key Concepts provided as you progress through the text. Within a chapter, you will be notified in the "Big Picture" box each time a Key Concept is going to be discussed and an icon will be used to alert you when a Key Concept is about to be presented.
- *Chapter Learning Objectives.* We set out the learning objectives at the start of each chapter so the student can more easily organize the chapter's main concepts.
- *Internet Questions.* Each chapter contains one or two Web-Based Questions that require students to access specified Internet addresses. These questions help students apply specific

economic concepts and introduce them to relevant *Economics* Internet sites.

A Building-Block Approach to Macro

With the changes in this edition, we created a fully integrated building-block approach to macro theory, policy, and issues. Specifically, we

- Build the aggregate expenditures model (AE model)
- Derive aggregate demand from the AE model and develop the aggregate demand–aggregate supply model (AD-AS model)
- Introduce both the short-run and long-run AD-AS model.
- Use the AD-AS model to discuss fiscal policy
- Introduce monetary considerations into the AD-AS model
- Use the AD-AS model to discuss monetary policy
- Apply the long-run AD-AS model to macroeconomic instability, modern macroeconomic disputes, and economic growth

Added Content on Women, Minorities, and Discrimination

In text and vignettes, this edition includes new information on women, minorities, and discrimination. For example, in Chapter 2 we added a Last Word on the rise of women's participation in the labour force. Chapter 16 in *Microeconomics* develops the taste for discrimination model, the idea of statistical discrimination, and the theory of occupational crowding. The new Last Word in Chapter 16 in *Microeconomics* looks at the effects of "blind" auditions on the gender composition of major symphony orchestras.

Greater Emphasis on the Economic Perspective

Newly organized Chapter 1 now begins with a discussion of scarcity and choice, rational behaviour, and marginal analysis. In Chapter 2 we use the ideas of marginal benefits and marginal costs to determine the optimal position on the production possibilities curve. We continue to reinforce the economic perspective in the remainder of the book in a number of discussions, including those on investment decisions, sunk costs, rational R&D decisions, and immigration policy.

Added Directness, Reduced Formalism, Extra Human Interest Material

Our line-by-line editing adds directness and reduces formalism, but we were careful to *not* reduce the thoroughness of our explanations. Where needed, the "extra sentence of explanation" remains a distinguishing characteristic of *Macroeconomics* and *Microeconomics*. Students will especially enjoy our new Last Word in *Microeconomics*, Chapter 13, On the Path to the Personal Computer and Internet. All 40 Last Words present interesting applications.

Other New Topics and Revised Discussions

Along with the changes just discussed, there are many other revisions. Here are just a few examples in *Microeconomics*.

- ***Part 1.*** *Chapter 1:* Figure 1-1 and its discussion revised; new, livelier examples. *Chapter 2:* Improved discussion of the economic rationale for increasing costs; new applications (land-use controversies, devastation from war, and emerging technologies); consolidated discussion of economic systems. *Chapter 4:* New examples: increased demand for sports-utility vehicles; improved fuel efficiency of aircraft engines; increased demand for salsa; buyout of haddock fishing boats; the decline in the price of pink salmon. *Chapter 5:* New Global Perspective on the Index of Economic Freedom. New discussion of the principal-agent problem; new Global Perspective on government employment as a percentage of total employment for various countries. *Chapter 6:* Improved explanation of the most-favoured-nation clause.

- ***Part 2.*** *Chapter 7:* Revised discussion (based on new research) of the price elasticity of illegal drugs. *Chapter 8:* Figure 8-1 is now a Key Graph; new Figure 8-2 shows the demand curve derived from a change in product price in the utility-maximizing model. *Chapter 9:* Explicit definitions of marginal, average, and total product now precede the discussion of diminishing returns; substantially revised Table 9-1 and Figure 9-2; new example of scale economies ("extraordinarily large stamping machine"). *Chapter 10:* Figure 10-2 now includes the firm's total profit curve; the

graphical discussion of the TR-TC approach is confined to profit maximization; section on qualifications of the pure competition model is consolidated. *Chapter 11:* New Table 11-2 lays out the steps for determining profit-maximizing output, price, and profit (if any) in pure monopoly; new graphical comparison of outcomes under pure monopoly and pure competition (Figure 11-6); "discount coupons" added as an example of price discrimination. *Chapter 12:* The discussion of monopolistic competition and oligopoly is now combined into a single chapter; kinked demand model as a Key Graph added; several new examples. *Chapter 13:* New chapter on technology, R&D, and efficiency.

- ***Part 3.*** *Chapter 15:* Table 15-3 summarizes the differences between substitute resources and complementary resources; updated labour demand examples; revised discussion of least-cost and profit-maximizing combinations of resources. Chapter 16: Discussions of real wage stagnation and pitfalls of pay-for-performance plans; rewritten section on labour market imperfections.

- ***Part 4.*** *Chapter 19:* New hypothetical example (enterprising artist and his public art) to highlight the free-rider problem and public goods characteristics; new discussion of the "tragedy of the commons." *Chapter 20:* Expanded discussion of pork-barrel politics and bureaucratic inefficiency; new material on VAT and flat tax proposals, including criticisms. *Chapter 22:* We have added this chapter on international trade to *Microeconomics* for the first time.

Macroeconomics has the following revisions:

- ***Part 2.*** *Chapter 7:* Changed terminology relating to Figure 7-2 (from "expanding, static, and declining economy" to "expanding, static, and declining production capacity"); simplification of the explanation of the GDP price index (new Tables 7-5 and 7-6); fuller discussion of the CPI. *Chapter 8:* Improved discussion of structural unemployment; revision of the discussion of Okun's law; addition to Table 8-2 of unemployment rates by level of education. *Chapter 9:* Figure 9-5 (investment demand) is now a Key Graph; new Figure 9-6 shows shifts in the investment-demand curve; new Figure 9-7 links the real interest rate, the investment-demand curve, and the economy's investment schedule. *Chapter 10:* Figure 10-8 on recessionary and inflationary gaps is now a Key Graph. *Chapter 11:* Introduction of both the short-run and long-run aggregate supply curves. *Chapter 12:* Clarified discussion of the crowding-out effect of fiscal policy, including criticisms of the idea.

- *Part 3.*   *Chapter 13:* "Unit of account" replaces the term "measure of value"; new section on recent developments in money and banking (globalization of financial markets, and electronic money and smart cards). *Chapter 15:* New Global Perspective 15-1 lists the names (including nicknames) of the central banks of selected nations.
- *Part 4.*   *Chapter 16:* Extends the analysis of aggregate supply. *Chapter 17:* "New" chapter contrasts contemporary views on macro theory and policy. *Chapter 18:* Covers economic growth (Chapter 19 in the seventh edition); discusses the weak productivity gains in services; discusses the controversial idea of a "new economy."
- *Part 5.*   Chapter 20: Chapter on international trade tightened. *Chapter 21:* Improved explanation of the balance of payments; major consolidation of the discussion of past exchange-rate systems. *Chapter 22:* New world map indicating industrially advanced nations, middle-income developing nations, and low-income developing nations (Figure 22-1); revised discussion of international debt difficulties, including mention of the recent IMF bailouts of the Southeast Asian economies; entirely new policy section on development. *Chapter 23: Extensively revised chapter now includes discussion of the transition to markets in China as well as in Russia.*

Last Words

We have brought back the Last Words, which were called Applying the Theory in previous editions. Several Last Words are new; others have been revised and updated. We have placed these boxes at the ends of chapters, where they are less likely to interrupt readers' concentration.

The new Last Word topics are women and production possibilities (Chapter 2); the irrelevancy of sunk costs (*Microeconomics* Chapter 9); maximization of consumer surplus in pure competition (*Microeconomics* Chapter 10); a brief history of the personal computer and Internet (*Microeconomics* Chapter 15); the impact of blind auditions on the employment of women in major orchestras (*Microeconomics* Chapter 16); enterprise transition to capitalism in Russia (*Macroeconomics* Chapter 23).

FUNDAMENTAL GOALS

Although the eighth edition only modestly resembles the first one, our intention remains the same: to introduce beginning economics students to principles essential to understanding the basic economizing problem, specific economic issues, and policy alternatives available for dealing with them. Two fortunate by-products of this objective are an ability to reason accurately and dispassionately about economic matters and a lasting interest in economics. As always, we present the principles and problems of economics in a straightforward, logical fashion. *We continue to stress clarity of presentation, step-by-step organization, and a consistent level of analysis.*

DISTINGUISHING FEATURES

- *Comprehensive Explanations at an Appropriate Level.*   *Microeconomics* and *Macroeconomics* are comprehensive, analytical, and challenging yet accessible to a wide range of students. Their thoroughness and accessibility enable instructors to select topics for special classroom emphasis with confidence that students can read and comprehend independently other assigned material in the book.
- *Comprehensive Definition of Economics.*   Because students must first understand the fundamentals, we devote nearly all of Chapter 2 to a careful statement and development of the economizing problem and an exploration of its implications. This foundation will help put into proper perspective essential economic concepts.
- *Fundamentals of the Market System.*   Economies throughout the world are making difficult transitions from planning to markets. Our detailed description of the institutions and operation of the *market system* in Chapter 3 is even more relevant than before. We pay particular attention to property rights, freedom of

enterprise and choice, competition, and the role of profits because these concepts are poorly understood by beginning students.

- *Early Integration of International Economics.* We give the principles and institutions of the global economy early treatment. Chapter 6 examines the growth of world trade, the major participants in world trade, specialization and comparative advantage, the foreign exchange market, tariffs and subsidies, and various trade agreements. This strong introduction to international economics permits "globalization" of later macroeconomics and microeconomics discussions.

- *Early and Extensive Treatment of Government.* Government is an integral component of modern capitalism. This book introduces the economic functions of government early and systematically treats them in Chapter 5. Chapter 19 in *Microeconomics* examines government and market failure in further detail, and Chapter 20 looks at salient facets of public choice theory and public finance. Both *Macroeconomics* and *Microeconomics* include problem- and policy-oriented chapters.

- *Emphasis on Economic Growth.* This edition continues to emphasize economic growth. Chapter 2 uses the production possibilities curve to show the basic ingredients of growth. Chapter 18 in *Macroeconomics* discusses the rate and causes of growth, in addition to some of the controversies surrounding it. Chapter 22 in *Macroeconomics* focuses on the developing countries and the growth obstacles they confront. Chapter 23 in *Macroeconomics* looks at growth in the transition economies of the Soviet Union and China. Our new micro chapter on technology, R&D, and efficiency lays the micro foundation for understanding economic growth.

- *Emphasis on the Theory of the Firm.* We give much attention to microeconomics in general and to the theory of the firm in particular, for two reasons. First, the concepts of microeconomics are difficult for most beginning students; too-brief expositions usually compound these difficulties by raising more questions than they answer. Second, we wanted to couple analysis of the various market structures with a discussion of the impact of each market arrangement on price, output levels, resource allocation, and the rate of technological advance.

- *Emphasis on Economic Issues.* For many students, Part 3 in *Macroeconomics* and Part 4 in *Microeconomics* are where the action is. We sought to guide that action along logical lines through the application of appropriate analytical tools. In these parts we favour inclusiveness; instructors can effectively omit whatever chapters they choose.

ORGANIZATION AND CONTENT

Microeconomics and *Macroeconomics* reflect the challenge specific topics and concepts will likely pose for average students. For instance, the theory of the firm and macro output and price-level determination are carefully treated. Here, simplicity is correlated with comprehensiveness, not brevity.

Our experience suggests that in treating each basic topic—aggregate demand and aggregate supply, money and banking, theory of the firm, and international economics—it is desirable to couple analysis with policy. Generally, we use a three-step development of analytical tools: (1) verbal descriptions and illustrations, (2) numerical examples, and (3) graphical presentation based on these numerical illustrations.

PEDAGOGICAL AIDS

Microeconomics and *Macroeconomics* have always been student-oriented. The To the Student statement at the beginning of Part 1 details the books' many pedagogical aids. The eighth edition is also accompanied by a variety of high-quality supplements. The supplements listed here may accompany *Microeconomics and Macroeconomics, Eighth Canadian Edition.* Please contact your local McGraw-Hill Ryerson representative for details concerning policies, prices, and availability as some restrictions may apply.

The Supplements

- *Study Guide.* Torben Andersen (Ph.D. Economics, University of Washington), the current Chairperson of Humanities and Social Sciences at Red Deer College, has prepared the eighth Canadian edition of the *Study*

Guide, which many students will find indispensable. Each chapter has an introductory statement, a checklist of behavioural objectives, an outline, a list of important terms, fill-in questions, problems and projects, objective questions, and discussion questions. The answers to the end-of-chapter Key Questions appear at the end of the *Study Guide*.

- ***Instructor's Resource Manual.*** Text author Professor Tom Barbiero of Ryerson Polytechnic University has revised and updated the *Instructor's Resource Manual*. It includes chapter summaries, listings of "what's new" in each chapter, new teaching tips and suggestions, learning objectives, chapter outlines, data and visual aid sources with suggestions for classroom use, and questions and problems. Answers to the text's end-of-chapter Key Questions are also included.

Computerized Test Banks

- ***Test Bank I.*** Completely Canadianized, this test bank includes more than 5,000 questions, most of them written by the text authors.

Also available:

- ***Test Bank II.*** Written by William Walstad, one of the world's foremost experts on economic education, this U.S. test bank contains more than 5,000 questions. All Test Bank II questions are now categorized according to level of difficulty: easy, moderate, or difficult.
- ***Test Bank III.*** Also prepared by William Walstad, the U.S. Test Bank III contains "constructive response" testing to evaluate student understanding in a manner different from conventional multiple-choice and true-false questions. Suggested answers to the essay and problem questions are included.
- ***PowerPoint Presentation.*** Sam Fefferman of the Northern Alberta Institute of Technology has created our PowerPoint slides.
- ***Student Software.*** The U.S. edition of DiscoverEcon is available for *Microeconomics and Macroeconomics*. This menu-driven software, which was developed by Gerald Nelson at the University of Illinois, gives students a complete tutorial linked to the text. Each chapter features two essay questions and a multiple-choice test. Whenever relevant, interactive graphing problems let students observe how

the economic picture is altered when they select different data.

On the Web:

- **Online Learning Centre**
- **Internet Book Site**
- **McGraw-Hill Ryerson Web Communities**
  A dynamic Web site of resources, information, ideas, and opportunities, from Canadian faculty—for Canadian faculty. Instructors have the opportunity to use the Web communities to exchange ideas, news, issues, and insights on an ongoing basis. Content may include such topics as:

  - Current Events
  - Downloadables
  - Job Postings
  - Web Links
  - Lecture Suggestions
  - Site News

All linked to this text on a chapter-by-chapter basis!

Almost instantly, **current issues can be connected to this text, improving the link between theory and practice.** Classroom presentations and assignments will be enhanced by this access to the most up-to-date and relevant information related to what's being taught.

Contact your McGraw-Hill Ryerson representative for more information.

ACKNOWLEDGEMENTS

The publication of this eighth edition will extend the life of *Macroeconomics* well into its second decade. The acceptance of the parent text, *Economics*, which was generous from the outset, has expanded with each edition. This gracious reception has no doubt been fostered by the many teachers and students who have been kind enough to provide their suggestions and criticisms.

Our colleagues at the University of Nebraska-Lincoln, Pacific Lutheran University, and Ryerson Polytechnic University have generously shared knowledge of their specialties with us and have provided encouragement. We are especially indebted to Ryerson professors John Hughes, David Cape, Dagmar Rajagopal, Leo Michelis, Ingrid Bryan, Tom Tushingham, and Mark Lovewell, who have been most helpful in offsetting our comparative ignorance in their areas of specialty.

As indicated, the previous editions have benefited from a number of perceptive reviews. In both quality and quantity, they provided the richest possible source of suggestions for this revision. We wish to thank the following instructors who participated in the formal review process:

T. Andersen	Red Deer College
B. Abbott	Northern Alberta Institute of Technology
M. Benarroch	University of Winnipeg
E. Black	Brandon University
D.Box	University College of the Fraser Valley
C. Burke	Lethbridge Community College
N. Clegg	Kwantlen College
B. Cook	University of New Brunswick
K. Dawson	Conestoga College
C. Dickhoff	British Columbia Institute of Technology
S. Dodaro	St. Francis Xavier University
M. Dore	Brock University
S. Fefferman	Northern Alberta Institute of Technology
P. Fortura	Algonquin College
B. Gayle-Amyiwe	Seneca College
C. Graham	Assiniboine College
P. Jacobs	Champlain Regional College
E. Jacobson	Northern Alberta Institute of Technology
S. Law	University of New Brunswick
M. Moy	University College of Cape Breton
V. Nallainayagam	Mount Royal College
J. Newark	Athabasca University
A. Nimarko	Vanier College
D. Pepper	British Columbia Institute of Technology
R. Schwindt	Simon Fraser University
J. Skuce	Georgian College
L. Smith	University of Waterloo
L. Swanson	Lakeland College
T. Tushingham	Ryerson Polytechnic University

We also wish to thank the following instructors who participated in the formal review process of the eighth edition:

Charles Burke	Lethbridge Community College
Ibrahim Hayani	Seneca College
Ron Kessler	British Columbia Institute of Technology
Judith Skuce	Georgian College
Terry Sulyma	Northern Alberta Institute of Technology
Campion Swartout	Saskatchewan Institute of Science and Technology
Bill Thomas	Sheridan College

Throughout all editions of this text we have benefited from instructors who contributed in an informal manner their comments and suggestions to authors, editors, and McGraw-Hill Ryerson representatives we owe them a debt of gratitude. In this connection, I. Hayani of Centennial College, Sage Traviza of the International Centre for Tax Studies, Faculty of Management Studies, University of Toronto, Torben Andersen of Red Deer College, and Judith Skuce of Georgian College, were particularly helpful

We are greatly indebted to the many professionals at McGraw-Hill Ryerson—and in particular to Daphne Scriabin, Margaret Henderson, Jennifer Burnell, Jeff MacLean and Gary Bennett—for their publishing expertise. We thank Wendy Thomas for her thorough and sensitive editing.

We also strongly acknowledge the newly integrated Irwin/McGraw-Hill Ryerson sales staff, who greeted this edition with wholehearted enthusiasm.

Campbell R. McConnell
Stanley L. Brue
Thomas P. Barbiero

Economics on the World Wide Web

Part 1

Bob Parks' A Random Walk Around Economics on the Net wuecon.wustl.edu/~bob/econwalknet.html
NetEc netec.wustl.edu/local/NetEc.html
Resources for Economists on the Internet econwpa.wustl.edu/EconFAQ/EconFAQ.html
Dismal Sciences www.dismal.com/
The Mining Company economics.miningco.com/
Classroom Expernomics www.marietta.edu/~delemeeg/expernom.html
Computer Aided Instruction in Economics userwww.sfsu.edu/~bjblecha/cai.htm
Economic Education, EcEdWeb http://ecedweb.unomaha.edu/
Econ Teaching Resources woodrow.mpls.frb.fed.us/econed/class/econsite.html
AmosWorld amos.bus.okstate.edu/
Economics Working Paper Archive (EconWPA) econwpa.wustl.edu/wpawelcome.html
Journal of Economic Literature and EconLit (JEL) www.econlit.org/
CARL's UnCover uncweb.carl.org/
sci.finance.abstracts www.public.iastate.edu/~arnie/sci-finance-abstracts.htm
Economics Research Network (ERN) (part of SSRN) www.ssrn.Com/
Student Economic Review www.bess.tcd.ie/ser.html
IDEAL (Academic Press) www.apnet.com/www/ap/aboutid.htm
Applied Economics www.chapmanhall.com/ae/
B>Quest (Business Quest) www.westga.edu/~bquest/
Roland's Overview of Conferences and Meetings on Economic Theory www.wiwiss.fu-berlin.de/w3/w3bester/roland/econ_co.htm
Economics Departments, Institutes and Research Centers in the World (EDIRC)—Associations and Societies www.er.uqam.ca/nobel/r14160/economics/assocs.html
American Economic Association (AEA) www.vanderbilt.edu/AEA/

History of Economics Society cs.muohio.edu/~HisEcSoc/other_resources.shtml
History of Economics Internet References cfec.vub.ac.be/cfec/hope.htm
Regional Science Association (RSA) gopher://olymp.wu-wien.ac.at:70/11/.inst/.iir/.rsa
International Association for Feminist Economics www.bucknell.edu/~jshackel/iaffe
International Economics and Philosophy Society www.bath.ac.uk/Centres/Ethical/ieps.htm
American Law and Economics Association (ALEA) webserver.law.yale.edu/alea/alea.htm
Southern Economic Association (SEA) bubba.ucc.okstate.edu/economics/journal/south1.html
Eastern Economic Association www.iona.edu/orgs/eea.htm
Western Economic Association International www.weainternational.org/
National Association of Business Economists (NABE) www.nabe.com/
Statistics Canada www.statcan.ca/
Canadian Economic Association www.economics.ca
Organization for Economic Cooperation and Development (OECD) www.oecd.org

Part 2

Economic Science Association www.econlab.arizona.edu/esa/
Inter-university Consortium for Political and Social Research (ICPSR) www.icpsr.umich.edu/
Centre for Economic Learning and Social Evolution (ELSE) ada.econ.ucl.ac.uk/
Pool Listing Service in Game Theory fismat.dima.unige.it/citg/citg.htm
Economic Science Laboratory, Univ. of Arizona www.econlab.arizona.edu/
Center for Rationality www.ma.huji.ac.il/~ranb
The Information Economy (by Hal Varian) www.sims.berkeley.edu/resources/infoecon

Openair-Market Net: The World Wide Guide to Farmers' Markets, Street Markets, Flea Markets and Street Vendors www.openair.org/
Statistics Canada www.statcan.ca/
Canada Competition Bureau www.strategis.ic.gc.ca

Part 3

Model User Group International (CGE Modeling) watarts.uwaterloo.ca/~mug/index.html
Communications for a Sustainable Future csf.colorado.edu/
Statistics Canada www.statcan.ca
Bank of Canada www.bank-banque-canada.ca

Parts 4 and 5

Government Information Sharing Project govinfo.kerr.orst.edu/
CIA Publications and Handbooks www.odci.gov/cia/publications/pubs.html
National Transportation Statistics www.bts.gov
Energy Resources Board (DOE) www.eia.doe.gov/energy/
Integrated Public Use Microdata Sample (IPUMS) www.hist.umn.edu/~ipums
International Society for Ecological Economics kabir.umd.edu/ISEE/ISEEhome.html
Centre for Economic and Social Studies for the Environment (CESSE) www.ulb.ac.be/ceese/french/ceese.html
Getting Around the Planet www.olsen.ch/cgi-bin/exmenu/pathfinder/
International Trade & Business WWW Reference Pages pacific.commerce.ubc.ca/trade/

The Global Trade Analysis Project (GTAP) www.agecon.purdue.edu/gtap/index.htm
Global Financial Data www.globalfindata.com
QuoteCom Data Service www.quote.com/
Australian Bureau of Statistics www.statistics.gov.au/
New Zealand Treasury www.treasury.govt.nz/
InTechTra's Hong Kong Stocks Reports www.asiawind.com/pub/hksr/
Turkish Economics Page www.siue.edu/~itanris/econtr.html
Israel Central Bureau of Statistics www.cbs.gov.il/engindex.htm
Finnish Society for Economic Research www.hkkk.fi/~fecons/
The Research Institute of the Finnish Economy (ETLA) www.etla.fiEurostat europa.eu.int/eurostat.html
European Economic Association www.hec.unil.ch/prague/eea/premier.htm
Euro Internet fgr.wu-wien.ac.at/nentwich/euroint2.htm
Central European Regional Research Organization (CERRO) gopher://olymp.wu-wien.ac.at:70/11/.cerro.ind
German Federal Statistical Office www.statistik-bund.de/e_home.htm
REESweb: Russian and East European Studies-Business, Economics, and Law Resources www.pitt.edu/~cjp/rees.htm
Statistics Canada www.statcan.ca/
Environment Canada www.doe.ca
World Trade Organization (WTO) www.wto.org
Revenue Canada www.rc.gc.ca
World bank www.worldbank.org/
Organization for Economic Cooperation and Development (OECD) www.oecd.org

To the Student

Economics is concerned with efficiency—accomplishing goals using the best methods. Therefore, we offer some brief introductory comments on how to improve your efficiency—and your understanding and grade—in studying economics. Several features of this book will aid your learning.

- *Appendix on graphs*   Being comfortable with graphical analysis and a few related quantitative concepts will be a big advantage to you in understanding principles of economics. The appendix to Chapter 1 reviews graphing, line slopes, and linear equations. Be sure not to skip it!
- *The Big Picture*   The new Big Picture in each chapter is designed to stimulate interest, state the main objectives, and present an organizational overview of the chapter and its connection with previously covered chapters.
- *Terminology*   A significant portion of any introductory course is terminology. To designate key terms, we have put them in boldface type, listed them at the end of each chapter, and provided a glossary of definitions at the end of the book.
- *Reviews*   Important things should be said more than once. You will find a chapter summary at the conclusion of every chapter as well as two or three "Quick Reviews" within each chapter. These review statements will help you focus on the essential ideas of each chapter and also to study for exams. If any of these statements is unclear, you should reread the appropriate section of the text.
- *Key Graphs*   We have labelled graphs having special relevance as "Key Graphs." Your instructor may or may not emphasize each of

these figures, but pay special attention to those your instructor discusses in class. You can bet there will be exam questions on them!
- *Ten Key Concepts*   There are Ten Key Concepts we have identified that will help you to organize the core materials of the text. The Ten Key Concepts are introduced in Chapter 1 and are reinforced throughout the textbook. You will be alerted to the concepts covered in each chapter in "The Big Picture" and an icon will further identify specific coverage in the text.
- *Chapter Learning Objectives*   We set out the learning objectives at the start of each chapter so you can more easily organize the chapter's main concepts.
- *Figure legends*   Economics is known for its many graphs. The legends accompanying the diagrams in this book are self-contained analyses of the concepts shown. Study these legends carefully—they are quick synopses of important ideas.
- *Globalization*   Each nation functions increasingly in a global economy. To gain appreciation of this wider economic environment, be sure to take a look at the "Global Perspectives," which compare Canada to other selected nations.
- *The Last Word*   While it is tempting to ignore these boxes, doing so is a mistake. Some "Last Word" boxes are revealing applications of economic concepts; some are short case studies; still others present views that contrast with mainstream thinking. All will deepen and broaden your grasp of economics.
- *In the Media*   Interesting stories have been selected from the print media that show the real-world application of the economic theory

just learned. Each of these stories ends with a question to test your understanding of the chapter's materials.

• *Questions* A comprehensive list of questions is located at the end of each chapter. The old cliché that you "learn by doing" is very relevant to economics. Use of these questions will enhance your understanding. We designate several of them as "Key Questions" and answer them in the Study Guide. You can immediately turn to these particular questions when they are cited in each chapter, or later after you have read the full chapter.

• *Study Guide* We enthusiastically recommend the *Study Guide* accompanying this text.

This "portable tutor" contains not only a broad sampling of various kinds of questions, but a host of useful learning aids.

You will find in Chapter 1 that economics involves a special way of thinking—a unique approach to analyzing problems. The overriding goal of this book is to help you acquire that skill. If our cooperative efforts—yours, ours, and your instructor's—are successful, you will be able to comprehend a whole range of economic, social, and political problems that otherwise would have remained murky and elusive.

So much for the pep talk. Let's get on with the show.

Drabble reprinted by permission of United Feature Syndicate, Inc.

An Introduction to Economics and the Economy

PART 1

The Nature and Method of Economics

HUMAN BEINGS, THOSE UNFORTUNATE CREATURES, are plagued with desires. We want, among other things, love, social recognition, and the material necessities and comforts of life. Our efforts to meet our material wants, that is, to improve our well-being, are the concern of economics.

Biologically, we need only air, water, food, clothing, and shelter. But, in contemporary society, we also seek the many goods and services associated with a comfortable or affluent standard of living. Fortunately, society is blessed with productive resources—labour and managerial talent, tools and machinery, land and mineral deposits—that are used to produce goods and services. This production satisfies many of our material wants and occurs through the organizational mechanism called the *economic system* or, more simply, *the economy*.

The blunt reality, however, is that the total of all our material wants is many times greater than the productive capacity of our limited resources. Thus, the complete satisfaction of material wants is impossible. This unyielding reality provides our definition of **economics**—*the social science concerned with the efficient use of limited (scarce) resources to achieve maximum satisfaction of human material wants.*

Although it may not be evident, most of the headline-grabbing issues of our time—inflation, unemployment, health care, social security, budget deficits, discrimination, tax reform, poverty and inequality, pollution, and government regulation and deregulation of business—are rooted in the one challenge of using scarce resources efficiently.

In this first chapter we will not plunge into problems and issues; instead, we will discuss some important preliminaries. Specifically, we first introduce what we consider the "Ten Key Concepts" of economics. We believe that these concepts will help you put the main issues in economics in their proper perspective. Hopefully, you will retain the Ten Key Concepts long after you finish the course and thus continue to use them

IN THIS CHAPTER YOU WILL LEARN:

The Ten Key Concepts
to retain a lifetime.

•

About the economic
way of thinking.

•

How economists
construct theories.

•

Six widely accepted economic goals.

•

The distinction between
microeconomics and
macroeconomics.

•

The pitfalls to objective thinking.

to help understand economic events. Next, we state some of the benefits of studying economics. Then we consider the specific methods economists use to examine and explain economic behaviour and the economy, distinguishing between macroeconomics and microeconomics. Finally, we examine the problems, limitations, and pitfalls that hinder sound economic reasoning.

The
Big Picture

YOU ARE ABOUT TO EMBARK ON THE STUDY of economics, a discipline that can help you understand a vast array of human issues and problems. Economics is about *scarcity, wants,* and *choices.* Try to think of any goods or services of which there is such an abundance that *everyone* in the world has as much as he or she wants. You will not have much success! Even time must be carefully budgeted because there is less of it than we would like. As George Stigler, a Nobel Prize winner in economics, points out, "Anything that is an object of conscious desire must be scarce: One does not consciously desire the air breathed, or to hear bad jokes. Scarce things are costly. If they weren't, everyone would get so much of each that they would not be scarce anymore. So anything scarce, and worth having, has been costly for someone to obtain."*

* G.J. Stigler, *Memoirs of an Unregulated Economist* (New York: Basic Books, 1988).

If we wanted or needed very little in relation to available resources, the scarcity problem would be less pronounced. But because there are so many goods and services we need and want, we must make choices about which goods and services we most desire. Despite often being referred to as the "dismal science," economics is really about getting enjoyment out of life: getting as much enjoyment as possible out of the limited resources available to us; the study of economics may thus be your ticket to "happiness"! More realistically, you may come to better understand and appreciate the ubiquitous problem of scarcity in our daily lives.

You need to understand the scarcity problem if you are to succeed in the study of economics, particularly microeconomics. "The Big Picture" boxes have been written to continuously remind you of the raison d'être of economics, and to put the information in each chapter within the larger context of scarcity, wants, and choices. ∎

TEN KEY CONCEPTS TO RETAIN A LIFETIME

Suppose you unexpectedly meet your introductory economics professor on the street five or ten years after you complete this course. What will you be able to tell her you retained from the course? More than likely you will not be able to remember very much. To help you retain the main ideas that economics has to offer for many years after you complete it, we have come up with **Ten Key Concepts** we believe are essential to understand the world around you and help you in your chosen career. These key concepts will be reinforced throughout the textbook, and you will be alerted in the "Big Picture" box when each will be discussed. Also, an icon will alert you that a key concept is about to be discussed. The concepts will simply be listed here; elaboration on each of the key concepts will be found as we progress through the textbook. At the end of the course you should review these 10 key concepts. They will help you organize and better understand the materials you

have studied. We have divided the 10 key concepts into three categories: (a) those pertaining to the individual; (b) concepts that explain the interaction among individuals; and (c) concepts that deal with the economy as a whole and the standard of living.

The Individual

CONCEPT 1: Scarcity in relation to wants means you face **tradeoffs**; therefore you have to make **choices**.

CONCEPT 2: The **cost** of the choice you make is what you give up for it.

CONCEPT 3: Choices are usually made at the **margin**; we choose a "little" more or a "little" less of something.

CONCEPT 4: The choices you make are influenced by **incentives**.

Interaction Among Individuals

CONCEPT 5: Specialization and **trade** will make everyone better off.

CONCEPT 6: Markets usually do a good job of coordinating trade among individuals, groups, and nations.

CONCEPT 7: Governments can occasionally improve the coordinating function of markets.

The Economy as a Whole and the Standard of Living

CONCEPT 8: The **standard of living** of the average person in a particular country is dependent on its production of goods and services. A rise in the standard of living requires a rise in the output of goods and services.

CONCEPT 9: If the monetary authorities of a country annually print money in excess of the growth of output of goods and services it will eventually lead to **inflation**.

CONCEPT 10: In the short run, society faces a short-run **tradeoff** between **inflation** and its level of **unemployment**.

These concepts will be elaborated on throughout this textbook. Be sure to be on the lookout for the icon that alerts you that one of these concepts is being discussed. We now turn to our first topic, the economic way of thinking.

THE ECONOMIC PERSPECTIVE

If you lived in a world in which human and property resources were unlimited, there would be no reason to study economics. In such a world every single individual would have as many goods and services as he or she desired. It is only because resources are scarce in relation to our wants that it is necessary to spend precious time on the study of economics. Thinking in terms of scarcity gives economists a unique perspective with which to view the world. This **economic perspective** or *economic way of thinking* has several interrelated features.

Scarcity and Choice

From our definition of economics, it is easy to see why economists view the world through the lens of scarcity. Since human and property resources are scarce (limited), it follows that the goods and services we produce must also be scarce. Scarcity limits our options and necessitates that we make choices. Because we "can't have it all," we must decide what we will have.

At the core of economics is the idea that "there is no free lunch." You may get treated to lunch, making it "free" to you, but there is a cost to someone. Scarce inputs of land, equipment, farm labour, the labour of cooks and waiters, and managerial talent are required. Because these resources could be used in other production activities, they and the other goods and services they could have produced are sacrificed in making the "free" lunch available. Economists call these sacrifices *opportunity costs*.

Rational Behaviour

Economics is grounded on the assumption of "rational self-interest." That is, individuals make rational decisions to achieve the greatest satisfaction or the maximum fulfilment of their goals. For instance, they spend their incomes to get the greatest benefit from the goods and services they can afford.

Rational behaviour implies that different people will make different choices because their preferences, circumstances, and available information differ. You may have decided that it is in your best interest to attend college or university before entering the full-time labour force, while a high school classmate has chosen to forgo additional schooling and go to work. Why the different choices? Your academic abilities, along with your family's income, may be greater than your classmate's. You may also know that college- or university-educated workers have better job opportunities and lower unemployment rates than less educated workers. Thus, you opted for more education, while your former classmate—the one with less academic ability, less money, and less information—chose a job. Both choices reflect the pursuit of self-interest and are rational, but they are based on differing circumstances and information.

Of course, rational decisions may change as circumstances change. Suppose the federal government decides it is in the national interest to increase the supply of college- and university-educated workers. It might offer two years of "free" post-secondary education to all low-income students. Under these new conditions, your high school classmate might now opt for college or university rather than a job.

Rational self-interest is *not* the same as selfishness. People make personal sacrifices to help family members or friends, and they contribute to charities because they derive pleasure from doing so. Parents help pay for their children's education for the same reason. These self-interested, but unselfish, acts help maximize the givers' satisfaction as much as any personal purchase of goods or services.

Marginalism: Benefits and Costs

The economic perspective focuses largely on **marginal analysis**—comparisons of marginal benefits and marginal costs. (Used this way, "marginal" means "extra," "additional," or "a change in.") Most choices or decisions involve changes in the status quo. Should you go to school for another year or not? Should you spend more or less money on compact discs each month? Similarly, businesses regularly must decide whether to employ more or fewer workers or to produce more or less output.

Each option involves marginal benefits and, because of scarcity, marginal costs. In making choices rationally, the decision maker must compare these two amounts. Example: Your time is scarce. What will you do with two "free" hours on a Saturday afternoon? You could watch Informed University's Fighting Aardvarks play hockey on television. The *marginal benefit* to you would be the pleasure of seeing the game. The *marginal cost* would be the benefit from the other things you have to sacrifice to watch the game, including perhaps studying, jogging, or taking a nap. If the marginal benefit exceeds the marginal cost, it is rational to watch the game. But if you determine that the marginal cost of watching the game is greater than the marginal benefit, you will select one of the other options.

On the national level, government regularly makes decisions involving marginal benefits and marginal costs. More spending on health care may mean less spending on libraries, aid to the poor, or military security. In a world of scarcity, the decision to obtain the marginal benefit associated with some specific option always includes the marginal cost of forgoing something else. Again, there is no free lunch.

One surprising implication of decisions based on marginal analysis is that there can be too much of a good thing. Although certain goods and services seem inherently desirable—education, health care, a clean environment—we can in fact have too much of them. "Too much" occurs when we keep producing them beyond the point where their marginal cost (the value of the forgone options) equals their marginal benefit.

If we choose to produce so much health care that its marginal cost to society exceeds its marginal benefit, we are providing "too much" of it even though we all agree that health care is a good thing. When the marginal costs of health care exceed the marginal benefits, we are sacrificing alternative products (for example, education and pollution reduction) that are more valuable than health care *at the margin*—the place where we consider the very last units of each. *(Key Question 1)*

This chapter's In the Media and Last Word provide an everyday application of the economic perspective.

WHY STUDY ECONOMICS?

Is studying economics worth your time and effort? More than half a century ago John Maynard Keynes (1883–1946)—one of the most influential economists of this century—said:

> The ideas of economists and political philosophers, both when they are right and when they are wrong, are more powerful than is commonly understood. Indeed the world is ruled by little else. Practical men, who believe themselves to be quite exempt from any intellectual influences, are usually the slaves of some defunct economist.

Most of the ideologies of the modern world have been shaped by prominent economists of the past—Adam Smith, David Ricardo, John Stuart Mill, Karl Marx, and John Maynard Keynes. And current world leaders routinely solicit the advice and policy suggestions of today's economists.

The Government of Canada has more than a thousand economists in its various ministries and agencies—and the advice of this army of economists is essential to the functioning of modern government. The areas economists advise on include unemployment and inflation, economic growth and productivity, taxation and public expenditures, poverty and income maintenance, the balance of payments and the international monetary system, labour-management relations, health care, pollution, immigration, discrimination, competition, and industrial regulation, among others.

Economics for Citizenship

A basic understanding of economics is essential if we are to be well-informed citizens. Most of today's political problems have important economic aspects: How important is it that we balance the federal budget? How can we make the income security retirement program financially secure? How best can we reduce pollution? What must we do to keep inflation in check? What can be done to boost Canadian productivity and economic growth? Are existing welfare programs effective and justifiable? Do we need to reform our tax system? How should we respond to growing market dominance by a few firms in some high-technology sectors of the economy?

As voters, we can influence the decisions of our elected officials in responding to such questions. But intelligence at the polls requires a basic working knowledge of economics. And a sound grasp of economics is even more helpful to the politicians themselves.

Professional and Personal Applications

Economics lays great stress on precise, systematic analysis. Thus, studying economics invariably helps students improve their analytical skills, which are in great demand in the workplace. Also, the study of economics helps us make sense of the everyday activity we observe around us. How is it that so many different people, in so many different places, doing so many different things, produce exactly the goods and services we want to buy? Economics provides an answer.

Economics is also vital to business. An understanding of the basics of economic decision making and the operation of the economic system enables business managers and executives to increase profit. The executive who understands when to use new technology, when to merge with another firm, when to expand employment, and so on, will outperform the executive who is less deft at such decision making. The manager who understands the causes and consequences of recessions (downturns in the overall economy) can make more intelligent business decisions during these periods.

Economics helps consumers and workers make better buying and employment decisions. How can you spend your limited money income to maximize your satisfaction? How can you hedge against the reduction in the dollar's purchasing power that accompanies inflation? Is it more economical to buy or lease a car? Should you use a credit card or pay cash? Which occupations pay well; which are most immune to unemployment?

Similarly, an understanding of economics makes for better financial decisions. Someone who understands the relationship between budget deficits and interest rates, between foreign exchange rates and exports, between interest rates and bond prices, is in a better position to successfully allocate personal savings. So, too, is someone who understands the business implications of emerging new technologies.

In spite of these practical benefits, however, you should know that economics is *mainly* an academic, not a vocational, subject. Unlike accounting, advertising, corporate finance, and marketing, economics is not primarily a how-to-make-money area of study. Knowledge of economics and mastery of the economic perspective will help you run a business or manage your personal finances, but that is not its primary objective. Instead, economics ultimately examines problems and decisions from the *social*, rather than the *personal*, point of view. The production, exchange, and consumption of goods and services are discussed from the viewpoint of society's best interest, not strictly from the standpoint of one's own pocketbook.

1-1
QUICK REVIEW

- Economics is concerned with obtaining maximum satisfaction through the efficient use of scarce resources.
- The economic perspective stresses **a** source scarcity and the necessity of making choices, **b** the assumption of rational behaviour, and **c** comparisons of marginal benefit and marginal cost.
- Your study of economics will help you as a voting citizen as well as benefit you professionally and personally.

ECONOMIC METHODOLOGY

How do economists go about understanding economic phenomena, and how do they design economic policies that help reduce the scarcity problem? Figure 1-1 summarizes the methodology used by economists.

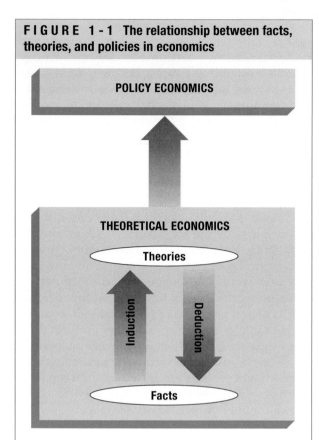

FIGURE 1-1 The relationship between facts, theories, and policies in economics

In constructing economic theories, economists may use the inductive method, through which they gather, systematically arrange, and generalize from facts. Alternatively, they may use the deductive method, in which they develop hypotheses that are then tested against facts. Generalizations derived from either method are useful not only in explaining economic behaviour but also as a basis for formulating economic policies.

Theoretical Economics

The methodology used by economists to arrive at an understanding of economic phenomena is similar to that used in other social sciences and the natural sciences. It is generally referred to as the scientific method. All sciences are based on observable and verifiable behaviour, realities, or facts. As a social science, economics examines the observable and verifiable behaviour of individuals (consumers, workers) and institutions (business, government) engaged in the production, exchange, and consumption of goods and services.

But fact gathering about economic activity and economic outcomes can be a complex process. Because the world of reality is cluttered with millions of facts, economists, like all scientists, must be highly selective in gathering information. What they are looking for are regularities in the data that can give them an understanding of the economic event under investigation.

The economist thus seeks **principles** *or* **theories**—generalizations about the behaviour of individuals and institutions. Deriving principles or theories is called **theoretical economics** (see the lower box in Figure 1-1). *The role of economic theorizing is to systematically arrange facts, interpret them, and generalize from them to find regularities that give us an understanding of economic behaviour.* Theories, or principles, bring order to facts so that we can see the relationship between them. As the economist Kenneth Boulding states: "Theories without facts may be barren, but facts without theories are meaningless."[1]

Terminology Economists speak of *laws, principles, theories,* and *models.* These terms are sometimes confusing to students, but they all mean essentially the same thing: They are generalizations about the economic behaviour of individuals and institutions. The terms *economic laws* and *principles* are useful, but they are somewhat misleading because they imply a high degree of exactness, universal application, and even moral rightness that is rare in social science. The word *theory* is often used in economics even though many people incorrectly believe theories have nothing to do with real-world applications. Economists often use the term *model* instead of the term *theory.* Both refer to a simplified picture of reality, an abstract generalization of how relevant facts actually relate to one another.

In this book we will use these four terms synonymously. Custom or convenience will determine each particular choice. Thus, the relationship between the price of a product and the amount of the product consumers purchase will be called the *law of demand,* rather than the theory or principle of demand, simply because this is the custom.

Deriving Theories

As Figure 1-1 shows, in deriving their theories economists are as likely to move from theory to facts in studying economic behaviour, as they are to move from facts to theory. That is, economists use both deductive and inductive methods.

---

[1] Kenneth Boulding, *Economic Analysis: Microeconomics,* 4th ed. (New York: Harper & Row, 1966), p. 5.

Induction moves from facts to theory, from the particular to the general. In this approach, facts are first gathered and then analyzed to derive the underlying theory. For example, suppose you collected data on the consumption and price of Pepsi at your college or university over time. As you study the data you start to see a pattern: As the price of Pepsi rises, the quantity purchased drops, and vice versa. You conclude that a generalization can be made about the relationship between the price of Pepsi and the amount of it purchased. The left upward arrow from "facts" to "theories" in the figure shows the inductive method.

More often, economists create generalization through **deduction**. They draw on casual observation, insight, logic, or intuition to frame a tentative, untested theory called a *hypothesis*. For example, they may conjecture, based on "armchair logic," that consumers will buy less of a product when its price rises. To test this hypothesis, economists collect the required data. Do real-world data confirm an inverse relationship between price and the amount purchased? If the data confirm that consumers buy less of a specific product when its price rises, we now have the basis on which to derive a theory. Of course, economists will want to subject this tentative theory to further testing before accepting it, just in case the initial testing process was flawed. The testing of a hypothesis is sometimes called *empirical economics* and is shown by the right downward arrow from "theories" to "facts" in Figure 1-1.

Deduction and induction are complementary, rather than opposing, techniques at deriving economic theories. A hypothesis formed by deduction provides a guideline for the economist in gathering and organizing data. Conversely, some understanding of factual, real-world, evidence is required to formulate meaningful hypotheses.

Derivation of economic principles requires a number of steps.

Generalizations   As we have already mentioned, economic theories are **generalizations** relating to economic behaviour or to the economy itself. They are imprecise because economic facts are usually diverse; no two individuals or institutions act in exactly the same way. *Economic theories are expressed as the tendencies of typical, or average consumers, workers, or business firms.* For example, when economists say that consumer spending rises when personal income increases, they are well aware that some households may save *all* of

an increase in their incomes. But, on average, and for the full economy, spending goes up when income increases. Similarly, economists say that consumers buy more of a particular product when its price falls. Some consumers may increase their purchases by a large amount, others by a small amount, and a few not at all. This "price-quantity" principle, however, holds for the *typical* consumer and for consumers as a group.

Abstractions   Economic principles, or theories, are *abstractions*—simplifications that omit irrelevant facts and circumstances. These models do not mirror the full complexity of the real world. The very process of sorting out and analyzing facts requires simplification and removal of clutter. Unfortunately, this "abstraction" leads some people to consider economic theory impractical and unrealistic. This is nonsense! Economic theories are practical precisely because they *are* abstractions. The full scope of economic reality itself is too complex and bewildering to be understood as a whole. Economists abstract—that is, build models—to understand an otherwise overwhelming and confusing maze of facts. Theorizing for this purpose is highly practical.

"Other-Things-Equal" Assumption   Like other scientists, economists use the *ceteris paribus*, or the **other-things-equal assumption**, to construct their theories. They assume that all other variables except those under immediate consideration are held constant for a particular analysis. For example, consider the relationship between the price of Pepsi and the amount purchased. It helps to assume that, of all the factors that might influence the amount of Pepsi purchased (for example, the price of Pepsi, the price of Coca-Cola, and consumer incomes and preferences), only the price of Pepsi varies. The economist can then focus on the "price of Pepsi–purchases of Pepsi" relationship without being confused by changes in other variables.

Natural scientists such as chemists or physicists can usually conduct controlled experiments where "all other things" are in fact held constant (or virtually so). They can test with great precision the assumed relationship between two variables. For example, they might examine the height from which an object is dropped and the length of time it takes to hit the ground. But economics is not a laboratory science. Economists test their theories using real-world data, which are generated by the actual operation of the economy. In this rather bewildering environment, "other things" *do* change. Despite the development of complex statistical techniques designed to hold other things equal, controls are less than perfect. As a result, economic principles are less certain and less precise than those of laboratory sciences.

Graphical Expression Many of the economic models in this book are expressed graphically; the most important are labelled "Key Graphs." We strongly urge you to read the appendix to this chapter as a review of graphs.

Policy Economics

Applied economics or **policy economics** is the application of theories and data to formulate policies, as shown in the upper part of Figure 1-1. Economic theories are the foundation of economic policy—a course of action based on economic theories and intended to resolve a specific problem or further a nation's economic goals. Economic policy normally is applied to problems after they arise. However, if economic analysis can predict some undesirable event such as unemployment, inflation, or an increase in poverty, then it may be possible to avoid or moderate that event through economic policy.

Formulating Economic Policy Here are the basic steps in policymaking:

1. *State the goal.* The first step is to clearly state the economic goal. If we say that we want "full employment," do we mean that everyone between, say, 16 and 65 years of age should have a job? Or do we mean that everyone who wants to work should have a job? Should we allow for some unemployment caused by inevitable changes in the structure of industry and workers voluntarily changing jobs? The goal must be specific.
2. *Determine the policy options.* The next step is to formulate alternative policies designed to achieve the goal and determine the possible effects of each policy. This requires a detailed assessment of the economic impact, benefits, costs, and political feasibility of the alternative policies. For example, to achieve full employment, should government use fiscal policy (which involves changing government spending and taxes), monetary policy (which entails

altering the supply of money), an education and training policy that enhances worker employability, or a policy of wage subsidies to firms that hire disadvantaged workers?
3. *Implement and evaluate the policy that was selected.* After implementing the policy, we need to evaluate how well it worked. Only through unbiased evaluation can we improve on economic policy. Did a specific change in taxes or the money supply alter the level of employment to the extent predicted? Did deregulation of a particular industry (for example, the airlines) yield the predicted beneficial results? If not, why not? *(Key Question 5)*

Economic Goals If economic policies are designed to achieve certain economic goals, then we need to recognize a number of goals that are widely accepted in Canada and many other countries. They include:

1. *Economic growth* Produce more and better goods and services, or, more simply, develop a higher standard of living.
2. *Full employment* Provide suitable jobs for all citizens who are willing and able to work.
3. *Economic efficiency* Achieve the maximum fulfilment of wants using the available productive resources.
4. *Price-level stability* Avoid large upswings and downswings in the general price level; that is, avoid inflation and deflation.
5. *Equitable distribution of income* Ensure that no group of citizens faces stark poverty while others enjoy extreme luxury.
6. *Balance of trade* Seek a reasonable overall balance with the rest of the world in international trade and financial transactions.

Although most of us might accept these goals as generally stated, we might also disagree substantially on their specific meanings. What are "large" changes in the price level? What is an "equitable" distribution of income? These objectives are often the subject of spirited public debate.

Also, some of these goals are complementary; when one is achieved, some other one will also be realized. For example, achieving full employment means eliminating unemployment, which is a basic cause of inequitable income distribution. But other goals may conflict or even be mutually exclusive. They may entail **tradeoffs**, meaning that to achieve one we must sacrifice another. For example, efforts to equalize the distribution of income may weaken incentives to work, invest, innovate, and take business risks, all of which promote economic growth. Taxing high-income people heavily and transferring the tax revenues to low-income people is one way to equalize the distribution of income. But then the incentives to high-income individuals may diminish because higher taxes reduce their rewards for working. Similarly, low-income individuals may be less motivated to work when government stands ready to subsidize them.

When goals conflict, society must develop a system of priorities for the objectives it seeks. Society must assess the tradeoffs and decide on the optimal (best) balance between them.

1-2
QUICK REVIEW

- Economic theories (laws, principles, or models) are generalizations relating to the economic behaviour of individuals and institutions; good theories are supported by facts.

- There are two ways economists arrive at theories. Induction observes facts and generalizes from them; deduction uses logic to create hypotheses and then tests them with factual data.

- Policy making requires a clear statement of goals, a thorough assessment of options, and an unbiased evaluation of results.

- Some of society's economic goals are complementary while others conflict; where conflicts exist, tradeoffs arise.

MACROECONOMICS AND MICROECONOMICS

Economists derive and apply theories about economic behaviour at two levels.

Macroeconomics

Macroeconomics examines either the economy as a whole or its basic subdivisions or aggregates such as the government, household, and business sectors. An **aggregate** is a collection of specific economic units treated as if they were one unit. Therefore, we might lump together the millions of con-

sumers in the Canadian economy and treat them as if they were one huge unit called "consumers."

In using aggregates, economists seek to obtain an overview, or general outline, of the structure of the economy and the relationships of its major aggregates. Macroeconomics deals with such economic measures as *total* output, *total* employment, *total* income, *aggregate* expenditures, and the *general* level of prices in analyzing various economic problems. No or very little attention is given to specific units making up the various aggregates. Macroeconomics examines the forest, not the trees.

Microeconomics

Microeconomics looks at specific economic units. At this level of analysis, the economist observes the details of an economic unit, or very small segment of the economy, under the figurative microscope. In microeconomics we talk of an individual industry, firm, or household. We measure the price of a *specific* product, the number of workers employed by a *single* firm, the revenue or income of a *particular* firm or household, or the expenditures of a *specific* firm, government entity, or family. In microeconomics, we examine the trees, not the forest.

The macro-micro distinction does not mean that economics is so highly compartmentalized that every topic can be readily labelled as either macro or micro; many topics and subdivisions of economics are rooted in both. Example: While the problem of unemployment is usually treated as a macroeconomic topic (because unemployment relates to *aggregate* spending), the decisions made by *individual* workers in searching for jobs and the way *specific* product and labour markets operate are also critical in determining the unemployment rate. *(Key Question 7)*

Positive and Normative Economics

Both macroeconomics and microeconomics involve facts, theories, and policies. Each contains elements of *positive economics* and *normative economics*. **Positive economics** focuses on facts and avoids value judgements. It tries to establish statements about economic behaviour that can be verified by facts. Positive economics deals with what the economy is actually like. Such factually based analysis is critical to good policy analysis.

In contrast, **normative economics** involves value judgements about what the economy should be like or what particular policy actions should be recommended to get it to be that way. Normative statements cannot be verified by appealing to facts to determine if they are true or false. Normative economics looks at the desirability of certain aspects of the economy. It underlies expressions of support for particular economic policies.

Positive economics concerns *what is*, while normative economics embodies subjective feelings about *what ought to be*. Examples: Positive statement: "The unemployment rate in several European nations is higher than that in Canada." Normative statement: "European nations ought to undertake policies to reduce their unemployment rates." A second positive statement: "Other things equal, if tuition is increased, enrolment at Informed University (IU) will fall." Normative statement: "Tuition should be lowered at IU so that more students can obtain an education." Whenever words such as "ought" or "should" appear in a sentence, there is a strong chance you are encountering a normative statement.

As you can imagine, most of the disagreement among economists involves normative, value-based policy questions. Of course, there is often some disagreement about which theories or models best represent the economy and its parts. But most economic controversy reflects differing opinions or value judgements about what society itself should be like. *(Key Question 8)*

1-3
QUICK REVIEW

- Macroeconomics examines the economy as a whole; microeconomics focuses on specific units of the economy.
- Positive economics deals with verifiable factual statements ("what is"); normative economics involves value judgements ("what ought to be").

PITFALLS TO OBJECTIVE THINKING

Because they affect us so personally, we often have difficulty thinking objectively about economic issues. Here are some common pitfalls to avoid in successfully applying the economic perspective.

Biases

Most people start out with a bundle of biases and preconceptions when thinking about economic issues. For example, you might think that corporate profits are excessive or that lending money is always superior to borrowing money. Perhaps you believe that government is necessarily less efficient than businesses or that more government regulation is always better than less. Biases cloud thinking and interfere with objective analysis. The student starting the study of economics must be willing to shed biases and preconceptions that are not supported by facts.

Loaded Terminology

The economic terminology used in newspapers and popular magazines is sometimes emotionally biased, or loaded. The writer or the interest group he or she represents may have a cause to promote or an axe to grind and may slant an article accordingly. High profits may be labelled "obscene"; low wages may be called "exploitive"; or self-interested behaviour may be "greed." Government workers may be referred to as "mindless bureaucrats," and those favouring stronger government regulations may be called "socialists." To objectively analyze economic issues, you must be prepared to reject or discount such terminology.

Definitions

Some of the terms used in economics have precise technical definitions that are quite different from those implied by their common usage. This is generally not a problem if everyone understands these definitions and uses them consistently. For example, "investment" to the average citizen means the purchase of stocks and bonds in security markets, as when someone "invests" in Bell Canada stock or government bonds. But to the economist, "investment" means the purchase of real capital assets such as machinery and equipment or the construction of a new factory building. It does not mean the purely financial transaction of swapping cash for securities.

Fallacy of Composition

Another pitfall in economic thinking is the assumption that what is true for one individual is necessarily true for a group of individuals. This is a logical fallacy called the **fallacy of composition**;

it is *not* correct. A statement that is valid for an individual is *not* necessarily valid for the larger group.

Consider the following example from outside of economics. You are at a football game and the home team makes an outstanding play. In the excitement, you leap to your feet to get a better view. A valid statement: "If you, *an individual*, stand, your view of the game is improved." But is this also true for the group—for everyone watching the play? Not necessarily. If *everyone* stands to watch the play, everyone—including you—will probably have a worse view than when all remain seated.

A second example comes from economics: An *individual* farmer who reaps a particularly large crop is likely to realize a sharp gain in income. But this statement cannot be generalized to farmers as a *group*. The individual farmer's large or "bumper" crop will not influence (reduce) crop prices because each farmer produces a negligible fraction of the total farm output. But for *all* farmers as a group, prices decline when total output increases. Thus, if all farmers reap bumper crops, the total output of farm products will rise, depressing crop prices. If the price declines are relatively large, total farm income will actually *fall*.

Recall our earlier distinction between macroeconomics and microeconomics: *The fallacy of composition reminds us that generalizations valid at one of these levels of analysis may or may not be valid at the other.*

Causation Fallacies

Causation is sometimes difficult to identify in economics. Two important fallacies often interfere with economic thinking.

Post Hoc Fallacy   You must think very carefully before concluding that because event A precedes event B, A is the cause of B. This kind of faulty reasoning is known as the *post hoc, ergo propter hoc*, or **after this, therefore because of this fallacy**.

Example: Suppose that early each spring the medicine man of a tribe performs a special dance. A week or so later the trees and grass turn green. Can we safely conclude that event A, the medicine man's dance, has caused event B, the landscape's turning green? Obviously not. The rooster crows before dawn, but this does not mean the rooster is responsible for the sunrise!

Informed University hires a new hockey coach and the team's record improves. Is the new coach the cause? Maybe. But perhaps the presence of more experienced players or an easier schedule is the true cause.

Correlation versus Causation   Do not confuse correlation, or connection, with causation. Correlation between two events or two sets of data indicates they are associated in some systematic and dependable way. For example, we may find that when variable X increases, Y also increases. But this correlation does not necessarily mean that there is causation—that an increase in X is the cause of an increase in Y. The relationship could be purely coincidental or dependent on some other factor, Z, not included in the analysis.

Here is an economic example: Economists have found a positive correlation between education and income. In general, people with more education earn higher incomes than people with less education. Common sense suggests education is the cause and higher incomes are the effect; more education implies a more knowledgeable and productive worker, and such workers receive larger salaries.

But causation could also partly run the other way. People with higher incomes could buy more education, just as they buy more furniture and steaks. Or is part of the relationship explainable in still other ways? Are education and income correlated because the characteristics—ability, motivation, personal habit—required to succeed in education are the same ones required to be a productive and highly paid worker? If so, then people with those traits will probably obtain more education *and* earn higher incomes. But greater education will not be the sole cause of the higher income. *(Key Question 9)*

A LOOK AHEAD

The ideas in this chapter will come into much sharper focus as you advance through Part 1, where we develop specific economic theories and models. Specifically, in Chapter 2 we build a model of the production choices facing an economy. In Chapter 3 we combine all markets in the economy to see how the so-called *market system* works. In Chapter 4 we develop a model that will help you understand how prices and quantities of goods and services are established in individual markets. Finally, in Chapters 5 and 6 we examine important sectors (components) of the economy, specifically, the private sector, the government sector, and the international sector.

In The Media

△ 4 KEY CONCEPT

Smugglers go interprovincial

Profits high, chances of getting caught low in the business of contraband cigarettes

BY PETER MOON
THE GLOBE AND MAIL

The federal government's sustained attack against the smuggling of contraband cigarettes into Canada has created a new multi-million-dollar crime problem.

Many smugglers are switching from international to interprovincial smuggling of cigarettes because the profits are high, the chances of getting caught are low, and even if they are caught the likelihood of going to prison is minimal.

"Interprovincial smuggling is costing millions and millions of dollars in lost taxes," Inspector John Ferguson, head of the RCMP's economic-crime unit in British Columbia, said in an interview. "It's a huge problem. People don't realize how serious it is."

He said British Columbia, where cigarette prices are among the highest in Canada, has been particularly hurt by the growth of interprovincial smuggling. Profits are so high it has attracted different organized-crime elements who are starting to fight among themselves for dominant positions in the trade.

"It's big business," he said. "And that's why they're in it, because it is such big business. When they get caught, they usually get fined, and that's it. They rarely go to jail."

British Columbia, because of its high tobacco taxes and large population, is a major market for smuggled cigarettes. Insp. Ferguson said it is hard to say what percentage of cigarettes reach the province through interprovincial smuggling compared to international smuggling, but added: "I sort of have the gut feeling that it is a 50–50 split."

A legal carton of cigarettes, for example, costs $26.40 in Ontario, compared with $48.55 in B.C. and $50.62 in Newfoundland. It is a problem that has captured the attention of the Auditor-General of Canada.

Source: *Globe and Mail*, July 28, 1997, p. A1 and A6. Reprinted with permission from the *Globe and Mail*.

THE STORY IN BRIEF

Smugglers of contraband cigarettes have switched from smuggling cigarettes from the United States into Canada, to interprovincial smuggling. The smugglers buy cigarettes in provinces with low taxes and sell them on the black market in provinces with high taxes.

THE ECONOMICS BEHIND THE STORY

- Economic decisions are based on marginal cost–marginal benefit considerations.
- The marginal cost–marginal benefit of smuggling cigarettes from abroad (primarily the United States) has changed. Costs have risen as the federal government crackdown intensifies.
- Compared with international cigarette smuggling, there are higher benefits and lower costs to smuggling cigarettes within Canada.
- The higher benefits to interprovincial smuggling have come about because some provinces, particularly Ontario and Quebec, lowered provincial taxes on a carton of cigarettes while others, such as British Columbia and Newfoundland, did not. The cost of interprovincial smuggling of cigarettes is lower than international smuggling because the probabilities of getting caught are much lower and the likelihood of going to prison is low.
- What should the federal and provincial governments do to stop interprovincial cigarette smuggling? ■

The Last Word

① KEY CONCEPT

FAST-FOOD LINES: AN ECONOMIC PERSPECTIVE

How can the economic perspective help us understand the behaviour of fast-food consumers?

YOU ENTER A FAST-FOOD RESTAURANT. DO YOU immediately look to see which line is the shortest? What do you do when you are in the middle of a long line and a new station opens? Have you ever gone to a fast-food restaurant, seen very long lines, and then left? Have you ever become annoyed when someone in front of you in line placed an order that took a long time to fill?

The economic perspective is useful in analyzing the behaviour of fast-food customers. These customers are at the restaurant because they expect the marginal benefit from the food they buy to match or exceed its marginal cost. When customers enter the restaurant, they scurry to the *shortest* line, believing that the shortest line will reduce their time cost of obtaining their food. They are acting purposefully; time is limited and people prefer using it in some way other than standing in line.

If one fast-food line is temporarily shorter than other lines, some people will move towards that line. These movers apparently view the time saving associated with the shorter line to exceed the cost of moving from their present line. The line changing tends to equalize line lengths. No further movement of customers between lines occurs once all lines are about equal.

Fast-food customers face another cost-benefit decision when a clerk opens a new station at the counter. Should they move to the new station or stay put? Those who shift to the new line decide that the time saving from the move exceeds the extra cost of physically moving. In so deciding, customers must also consider just how quickly they can get to the new station compared with others who may be contemplating the same move. (Those who hesitate in this situation are lost!)

Customers at the fast-food establishment select lines without having perfect information. For example, they do not first survey those in the lines to determine what they are ordering before deciding which line to enter. There are two reasons for this. First, most customers would tell them "It's none of your business," and therefore no information would be forthcoming. Second, even if they could obtain the information, the amount of time necessary to get it (a cost) would most certainly exceed any time saving associated with finding the best line (the benefit). Because information is costly to obtain, fast-food patrons select lines without perfect information. Thus, not all decisions turn out as expected. For example, you might enter a short line and find that the person in front of you is ordering hamburgers and fries for 40 people in the Greyhound bus parked out back! Nevertheless, at the time you made your decision, you thought it was optimal.

Imperfect information also explains why some people who arrive at a fast-food restaurant and observe long lines decide to leave. These people conclude that the marginal cost (monetary plus time costs) of obtaining the fast food is too large relative to the marginal benefit. They would not have come to the restaurant in the first place had they known the lines would be so long. But getting that information by, say, employing an advance scout with a cellular phone would cost more than the perceived benefit.

Finally, customers must decide what to order when they arrive at the counter. In making their choices they again compare marginal costs and marginal benefits in attempting to obtain the greatest personal satisfaction or well-being for their expenditure.

Economists believe that what is true for the behaviour of customers at fast-food restaurants is true for economic behaviour in general. Faced with an array of choices, consumers, workers, and businesses rationally compare marginal costs and marginal benefits in making decisions. ■

CHAPTER SUMMARY

1. Economics is the study of the efficient use of scarce resources in the production of goods and services to satisfy as many wants as possible.

2. The economic perspective includes three elements: scarcity and choice, rational behaviour, and marginalism. It sees individuals and institutions making rational decisions based on comparisons of marginal costs and marginal benefits.

3. A knowledge of economics contributes to effective citizenship and provides useful insights for politicians, consumers, and workers.

4. The tasks of empirical economics are (a) gathering economic facts relevant to a particular problem or specific segment of the economy, and (b) testing hypotheses against the facts to validate theories.

5. Generalizations stated by economists are called principles, theories, laws, or models. The derivation of these principles is the object of theoretical economics.

6. Induction distills theories from facts; deduction uses logic to derive hypotheses that are then tested against facts.

7. Economic principles are valuable predictors. They are the bases for economic policy, which is designed to identify and solve problems and control undesirable events.

8. Our society accepts certain shared economic goals, including economic growth, full employment, economic efficiency, price-level stability, equity in the distribution of income, and a reasonable balance in our international trade and finance. Some of these goals are complementary; others entail tradeoffs.

9. Macroeconomics looks at the economy as a whole or its major aggregates; microeconomics examines specific economic units or institutions.

10. Positive statements state facts ("what is"); normative statements express value judgements ("what ought to be").

11. In studying economics we encounter such pitfalls as biases and preconceptions, unfamiliar or confusing terminology, the fallacy of composition, and the difficulty of establishing clear cause-effect relationships.

TERMS AND CONCEPTS

economics	generalizations
tradeoff	other-things-equal assumption
inflation	policy economics
unemployment	macroeconomics
economic perspective	aggregate
marginal analysis	microeconomics
principles	positive economics
theoretical economics	normative economics
induction	fallacy of composition
deduction	after this, therefore because of this fallacy

STUDY QUESTIONS

1. **KEY QUESTION** *Use the economic perspective to explain why someone who is normally a light eater at a standard restaurant may become somewhat of a glutton at a buffet-style restaurant that charges a single price for all you can eat.*

2. Distinguish between the inductive and deductive methods for establishing economic theories. Why must both methods ultimately involve gathering facts?

3. Why is it significant that economics is not a laboratory science? What problems may be involved in deriving and applying economic principles?

4. Explain the following statements:
   a. Good economic policy requires good economic theory.
   b. Generalization and abstraction are nearly synonymous.
   c. Facts serve to sort out good and bad theories.
   d. The *other-things-equal* assumption helps isolate key economic relationships.

5. KEY QUESTION *Explain in detail the interrelationships between economic facts, theory, and policy. Critically evaluate this statement: "The trouble with economic theory is that it is not practical. It is detached from the real world."*

6. To what extent do you accept the six economic goals stated and described in this chapter? What priorities do you assign to them? It has been said that we seek simply four goals: progress, stability, justice, and freedom. Is this list of goals compatible with that given in the chapter?

7. KEY QUESTION *Indicate whether each of the following statements applies to microeconomics or macroeconomics:*
   a. *The unemployment rate in Canada was 8.4 percent in July of 1998.*
   b. *The Alpo dogfood plant in Bowser, Alberta, laid off 15 workers last month.*
   c. *An unexpected freeze in central Florida reduced the citrus crop and caused the price of oranges to rise.*
   d. *Our domestic output, adjusted for inflation, grew by about 4 percent in 1997.*
   e. *Last week the Royal Bank lowered its interest rate on business loans by one-half of 1 percentage point.*
   f. *The consumer price index rose by 1.6 percent in 1997.*

8. KEY QUESTION *Identify each of the following as either a positive or a normative statement:*
   a. *The high temperature today was 30 degrees.*
   b. *It was too hot today.*
   c. *The general price level rose by 4.4 percent last year.*
   d. *Inflation eroded living standards last year and should be reduced by government policies.*

9. KEY QUESTION *Explain and give an example of **a** the fallacy of composition, and **b** the "after this, therefore because of this" fallacy. Why are cause-and-effect relationships difficult to isolate in economics?*

10. Suppose studies show that students who study more hours receive higher grades. Does this relationship guarantee that any particular student who studies longer will get higher grades?

11. Studies indicate that married men on average earn more income than unmarried men of the same age. Why must we be cautious in concluding that marriage is the *cause* and higher income is the *effect*?

12. **(The Last Word)** Use the economic perspective to explain the behaviour of the *workers* (rather than the customers) observed at a fast-food restaurant. Why are these workers there, rather than, say, cruising around in their cars? Why do they work so diligently? Why do so many of them quit these jobs once they have graduated from high school?

13. WEB-BASED QUESTION **Economic Goals—Are They Being Achieved?** The three primary economic goals are economic growth, full employment, and price-level stability. Statistics Canada www.statcan.ca/english/Pgdb/Economy/econom.htm provides links to Canadian economic data. Visit their links for Output, Income, Expenditures (under National accounts), Prices and Employment, and Unemployment (Labour markets). How robust has economic growth (GDP) been? Has inflation remained steady? Has unemployment increased or decreased?

14. WEB-BASED QUESTION **Normative Economics—Canadian Politics.** Many economic policy statements made by the Liberal Party www.liberal.ca, the Reform Party www.reform.ca, the Progressive Conservative Party www.pcparty.ca, and the NDP www.ndp.ca can be considered normative rather than positive economic statements. Visit their Web sites and compare and contrast their views on how to achieve economic goals. How much of the rhetoric is based on positive statements and how much on normative statements?

APPENDIX TO CHAPTER 1

GRAPHS AND THEIR MEANING

If you glance quickly through this text, you will find many graphs. Some seem simple, while others seem more difficult. All are important. They are included to help you visualize and understand economic relationships. Physicists and chemists sometimes illustrate their theories by building arrangements of multicoloured wooden balls, representing protons, neutrons, and electrons, which are held in proper relation to one another by wires or sticks. Economists most often use graphs to illustrate their models. By understanding these "pictures," you can more readily comprehend economic relationships. Most of our principles or models explain relationships between just two sets of economic facts, which can be conveniently represented with two-dimensional graphs.

Construction of a Graph

A graph is a visual representation of the relationship between two variables. Table A1-1 is a hypothetical illustration showing the relationship between income and consumption for the economy as a whole. Without even studying economics, we would expect intuitively that people would buy more goods and services when their incomes go up. Thus we are not surprised to find in Table A1-1 that total consumption in the economy increases as total income rises.

The information in Table A1-1 is expressed graphically in Figure A1-1. Here is how it is done: We want to show visually or graphically how consumption changes as income changes. Since income is the determining factor, we represent it on the **horizontal axis** of the graph, as is customary. And because consumption depends on income, we represent it on the **vertical axis** of the graph, as is also customary. Actually, what we are doing is representing the *independent variable* on the horizontal axis and the *dependent variable* on the vertical axis.

Now we arrange the vertical and horizontal scales of the graph to reflect the ranges of values of consumption and income, and we mark the scales in convenient increments. As you can see, the values marked on the scales cover all the values in Table A1-1. The increments on both scales are $100 for approximately each 1.25 cm.

Because the graph has two dimensions, each point within it represents an income value and its associated consumption value. To find a point that represents one of the five income-consumption combinations in Table A1-1, we draw perpendiculars from the appropriate values on the vertical and horizontal axes. For example, to plot point *c*

TABLE A1-1 The relationship between income and consumption

Income (per week)	Consumption (per week)	Point
$ 0	$ 50	*a*
100	100	*b*
200	150	*c*
300	200	*d*
400	250	*e*

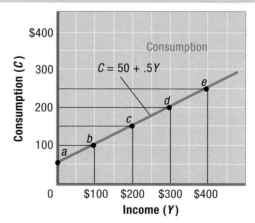

FIGURE A1-1 Graphing the direct relationship between consumption and income

Two sets of data that are positively or directly related, such as consumption and income, graph as an upsloping line.

(the $200 income–$150 consumption point), perpendiculars are drawn up from the horizontal (income) axis at $200 and across from the vertical (consumption) axis at $150. These perpendiculars intersect at point *c*, which represents this particular income-consumption combination. You should verify that the other income-consumption combinations shown in Table A1-1 are properly located in Figure A1-1. Finally, by assuming that the same general relationship between income and consumption prevails for all other incomes, we draw a line or smooth curve to connect these points. That line or curve represents the income-consumption relationship.

If the graph is a straight line, as in Figure A1-1, we say the relationship is *linear.*

Direct and Inverse Relationships

The line in Figure A1-1 slopes upward to the right, so it depicts a direct relationship between income and consumption. By a **direct relationship** (or positive relationship) we mean that two variables—in this case, consumption and income—change in the *same* direction. An increase in consumption is associated with an increase in income; a decrease in consumption accompanies a decrease in income. When two sets of data are positively or directly related, they always graph as an *upsloping* line, as in Figure A1-1.

In contrast, two sets of data may be inversely related. Consider Table A1-2, which shows the relationship between the price of basketball tickets and game attendance at Informed University. Here we have a negative or **inverse relationship** because the two variables change in *opposite* directions. When ticket prices decrease, attendance increases. When ticket prices increase, attendance decreases. The six data points in Table A1-2 are plotted in Figure A1-2. Observe that an inverse relationship always graphs as a *downsloping* line.

Dependent and Independent Variables

Although it is not always easy, economists seek to determine which variable is the "cause" and which is the "effect." Or, more formally, they seek the independent variable and the dependent variable. The **independent variable** is the cause or source; it is the variable that changes first. The **dependent variable** is the effect or outcome; it is the variable that changes because of the change in the independent variable. As noted in our income-consump-

TABLE A1-2 The relationship between ticket prices and attendance

Ticket price	Attendance (thousands)	Point
$25	0	a
20	4	b
15	8	c
10	12	d
5	16	e
0	20	f

tion example, income generally is the independent variable and consumption the dependent variable. Income causes consumption to be what it is rather than the other way around. Similarly, ticket prices determine attendance at IU hockey games; attendance does not determine ticket prices. Ticket price is the independent variable, and the quantity of tickets purchased is the dependent variable.

You may recall from your high school courses that mathematicians always put the independent variable (cause) on the horizontal axis and the dependent variable (effect) on the vertical axis.

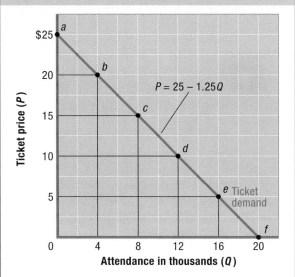

FIGURE A1-2 Graphing the inverse relationship between ticket prices and game attendance

$P = 25 - 1.25Q$

Two sets of data that are negatively or inversely related, such as ticket price and the attendance at basketball games, graph as a downsloping line.

Economists are less tidy; their graphing of independent and dependent variables is more arbitrary. Their conventional graphing of the income-consumption relationship is consistent with mathematical presentation, but economists put price and cost data on the vertical axis. Hence, economists' graphing of IU's ticket price–attendance data conflicts with normal mathematical procedure.

Other Things Equal

Our simple two-variable graphs purposely ignore many other factors that might affect the amount of consumption occurring at each income level or the number of people who attend IU basketball games at each possible ticket price. When economists plot the relationship between any two variables, they invoke the *ceteris paribus* (other things equal) assumption. Thus, in Figure A1-1 all factors other than income that might affect the amount of consumption are presumed to be constant or unchanged. Similarly, in Figure A1-2 all factors other than ticket price that might influence attendance at IU hockey games are assumed constant. In reality, "other things" are not equal; they often change, and when they do, the relationship represented in our two tables and graphs will change. Specifically, the lines we have plotted would shift to new locations.

Consider a stock market "crash." The dramatic drop in the value of stocks might cause people to feel less wealthy and therefore less willing to consume at each level of income. The result might be a downward shift of the consumption line. To see this, you should plot a new consumption line in Figure A1-1, assuming that consumption is, say, $20 less at each income level. Note that the relationship remains direct; the line merely shifts downward to reflect less consumption spending at each income level.

Similarly, factors other than ticket prices might affect IU game attendance. If a professional hockey team locates in the same city as IU, attendance at IU games might be less at each ticket price. To see this, redraw Figure A1-2, assuming that 2,000 fewer students attend IU games at each ticket price. **(Key Appendix Question 2)**

Slope of a Line

Lines can be described in terms of their slopes. The **slope of a straight line** is the ratio of the vertical change (the rise or drop) to the horizontal change (the run) between any two points of the line.

Positive Slope   Between point *b* and point *c* in Figure A1-1 the rise or vertical change (the change in consumption) is +$50 and the run or horizontal change (the change in income) is +$100. Therefore:

$$\text{Slope} = \frac{\text{vertical change}}{\text{horizontal change}} = \frac{+50}{+100} = \frac{1}{2} = .5$$

Note that our slope of $\frac{1}{2}$ or .5 is positive because consumption and income change in the same direction; that is, consumption and income are directly or positively related.

The slope of .5 tells us there will be a $1 increase in consumption for every $2 increase in income. Similarly, it indicates that for every $2 decrease in income there will be a $1 decrease in consumption.

Negative Slope   Between any two of the identified points in Figure A1-2, say, point *c* and point *d*, the vertical change is −5 (the drop) and the horizontal change is +4 (the run). Therefore:

$$\text{Slope} = \frac{\text{vertical change}}{\text{horizontal change}} = \frac{-5}{+4} = -1\frac{1}{4} = -1.25$$

This slope is negative because ticket price and attendance have an inverse relationship.

Note that on the horizontal axis attendance is stated in thousands of people. So the slope of −5/+4 or −1.25 means that lowering the price by $5 will increase attendance by 4,000 people. This is the same as saying that a $1.25 price reduction will increase attendance by 1,000 persons.

Slopes and Measurement Units   The slope of a line will be affected by the choice of units for either variable. If, in our ticket price illustration, we had chosen to measure attendance in individual people, our horizontal change would have been 4,000 and the slope would have been

$$\text{Slope} = \frac{-5}{+4000} = \frac{-1}{+800} = -.00125$$

The slope depends on the way the relevant variables are measured.

Slopes and Marginal Analysis   Recall that economics is largely concerned with changes from the status quo. The concept of slope is important in economics because it reflects marginal changes—those involving 1 more (or 1 less) unit. For example, in Figure A1-1 the .5 slope shows that $.50 of extra or marginal consumption is associated with each $1 increase in income. In this example, people collectively will consume $.50 of any $1 increase in their incomes and reduce their consumption by $.50 for each $1 decline in income.

Infinite and Zero Slopes Many variables are unrelated or independent of one another. For example, the quantity of wristwatches purchased is not related to the price of bananas. In Figure A1-3(a) we represent the price of bananas on the vertical axis and the quantity of watches demanded on the horizontal axis. The graph of their relationship is the line parallel to the vertical axis, indicating that the same quantity of watches is purchased no matter what the price of bananas. The slope of such a line is *infinite*.

Similarly, aggregate consumption is completely unrelated to the nation's divorce rate. In Figure A1-3(b) we put consumption on the vertical axis and the divorce rate on the horizontal axis. The line parallel to the horizontal axis represents this lack of relatedness. This line has a slope of *zero*.

Vertical Intercept

A line can be located on a graph (without plotting points) if we know its slope and its **vertical intercept**. The vertical intercept of a line is the point where the line meets the vertical axis. In Figure A1-1 the intercept is $50. This intercept means that if current income were zero, consumers would still spend $50. They might do this through borrowing or by selling off some of their assets. Similarly, the

vertical intercept in Figure A1-2 shows that at a $25 ticket price, IU's hockey team would be playing in an empty arena.

Equation of a Linear Relationship

If we know the vertical intercept and slope, we can describe a line succinctly in equation form. In its general form, the equation of a line is

$$y = a + bx$$

where y = dependent variable
a = vertical intercept
b = slope of the line
x = independent variable.

For our income-consumption example, if C represents consumption (the dependent variable) and Y represents income (the independent variable), we can write $C = a + bY$. By substituting the known values of the intercept and the slope, we get

$$C = 50 + .5Y$$

This equation also allows us to determine the amount of consumption C at any specific level of income. You should use it to confirm that at the $250 income level, consumption is $175.

When economists reverse mathematical convention by putting the independent variable on the vertical axis and the dependent variable on the horizontal axis, then y stands for the independent variable, rather than the dependent variable in the general form. We noted previously that this case is relevant for our IU ticket price-attendance data. If P represents the ticket price (independent vari-

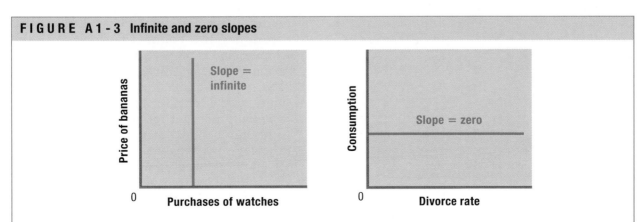

FIGURE A1-3 Infinite and zero slopes

(a) A line parallel to the vertical axis has an infinite slope. Here, purchases of watches remain the same no matter what happens to the price of bananas. (b) A line parallel to the horizontal axis has a slope of zero. Here, consumption remains the same no matter what happens to the divorce rate. In both (a) and (b), the two variables are totally unrelated to one another.

able) and Q represents attendance (dependent variable), their relationship is given by

$$P = 25 - 1.25Q$$

where the vertical intercept is 25 and the negative slope is $-1\frac{1}{4}$ or -1.25. Now, knowing the value of P let's solve for Q, our dependent variable. You should use this equation to predict IU ticket sales when the ticket price is $7.50. *(Key Appendix Question 3)*

Slope of a Nonlinear Curve

We now move from the simple world of linear relationships (straight lines) to the more complex world of nonlinear relationships. The slope of a straight line is the same at all its points. The slope of a line representing a nonlinear relationship changes from one point to another. Such lines are referred to as curves. (It is also permissible to refer to a straight line as a "curve.")

Consider the downsloping curve in Figure A1-4. Its slope is negative throughout, but the curve flattens as we move down along it. Thus, its slope constantly changes; the curve has a different slope at each point.

To measure the slope at a specific point, we draw a straight line that is tangent to the curve at

that point. A line is *tangent* at a point if it touches, but does not intersect, the curve at that point. Thus line *aa* is tangent to the curve in Figure A1-4 at point A. The slope of the curve at that point is equal to the slope of the tangent line. Specifically, the total vertical change (drop) in the tangent line *aa* is –20 and the total horizontal change (run) is +5. Because the slope of the tangent line *aa* is –20/+5, or –4, the slope of the curve at point A is also –4.

Line *bb* in Figure A1-4 is tangent to the curve at point B. Following the same procedure, we find the slope at B to be –5/+15, or –1/3. Thus, in this flatter part of the curve, the slope is less negative. *(Key Appendix Question 6)*

APPENDIX SUMMARY

1. Graphs are a convenient and revealing way to represent economic relationships.
2. Two variables are positively or directly related when their values change in the same direction. The line (curve) representing two directly related variables slopes upward.
3. Two variables are negatively or inversely related when their values change in opposite directions. The curve representing two inversely related variables slopes downward.
4. The value of the dependent variable (the "effect") is determined by the value of the independent variable (the "cause").
5. When the "other factors" that might affect a two-variable relationship are allowed to change, the graph of the relationship will likely shift to a new location.
6. The slope of a straight line is the ratio of the vertical change to the horizontal change between any two points. The slope of an upsloping line is positive; the slope of a downsloping line is negative.
7. The slope of a line or curve depends on the units used in measuring the variables. It is especially relevant for economics because it measures marginal changes.
8. The slope of a horizontal line is zero; the slope of a vertical line is infinite.
9. The vertical intercept and slope of a line determine its location; they are used in expressing the line—and the relationship between the two variables—as an equation.
10. The slope of a curve at any point is determined by calculating the slope of a straight line tangent to the curve at that point.

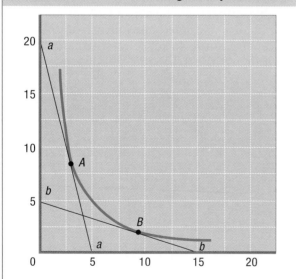

FIGURE A1-4 Determining the slopes of curves

The slope of a nonlinear curve changes from point to point on the curve. The slope at any point (say, *B*) can be determined by drawing a straight line tangent to that point (line *bb*) and calculating the slope of that line.

APPENDIX TERMS AND CONCEPTS

horizontal axis

vertical axis

direct relationship

inverse relationship

independent variable

dependent variable

slope of a straight line

vertical intercept

APPENDIX STUDY QUESTIONS

1. Briefly explain the use of graphs as a way to represent economic relationships. What is an inverse relationship? How does it graph? What is a direct relationship? How does it graph? Graph and explain the relationships you would expect to find between **a** the number of millimetres of rainfall per month and the sale of umbrellas, **b** the amount of tuition and the level of enrolment at a university, and **c** the size of a university's athletic scholarships and the number of games won by its football team.

In each case cite and explain how variables other than those specifically mentioned might upset the expected relationship. Is your graph in part (b) consistent with the fact that, historically, enrolments and tuition have both increased? If not, explain any difference.

2. KEY APPENDIX QUESTION *Indicate how each of the following might affect the data shown in Table A1-2 and Figure A1-2 of this appendix:*
   a. *IU's athletic director schedules higher-quality opponents.*
   b. *IU's Fighting Aardvarks experience three losing seasons.*
   c. *IU contracts to have all its home games televised.*

3. KEY APPENDIX QUESTION *The following table contains data on the relationship between saving and income. Rearrange these data into a meaningful order and graph them on the accompanying grid. What is the slope of the line? The vertical intercept? Interpret the meaning of both the slope and the intercept. Write the equation that represents this line. What would you predict saving to be at the $12,500 level of income?*

Income (per year)	Saving (per year)
$15,000	$1,000
0	−500
10,000	500
5,000	0
20,000	1,500

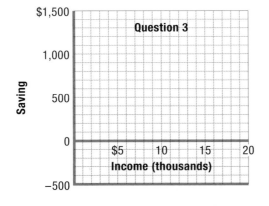

4. Construct a table from the data shown on the graph below. Which is the dependent variable and which the independent variable? Summarize the data in equation form.

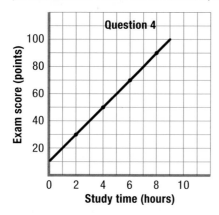

5. Suppose that when the interest rate that must be paid to borrow funds is 16 percent, businesses find it unprofitable to invest in machinery and equipment. However, when the interest rate is 14 percent, $5 billion worth of investment is profitable. At 12 percent interest, a total of $10 billion of investment is profitable. Similarly, total investment increases by $5 billion for each successive 2-percentage-point decline in the interest rate. Describe the relevant relationship between the interest rate and investment in words, in a table, graphically, and as an equation. Put the interest rate on the vertical axis and investment on the horizontal axis. In your equation use the form $i = a + bI$, where i is the interest rate, a is the vertical intercept, b is the slope of the line (which is negative), and I is the level of investment. Comment on the advantages and disadvantages of the verbal, tabular, graphical, and equation forms of description.

6. **KEY APPENDIX QUESTION** *The accompanying graph shows curve XX and tangents at points A, B, and C. Calculate the slope of the curve at these three points.*

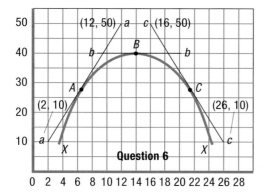

7. In the accompanying graph, is the slope of curve *AA'* positive or negative? Does the slope increase or decrease as we move along the curve from *A* to *A'*? Answer the same two questions for curve *BB'*.

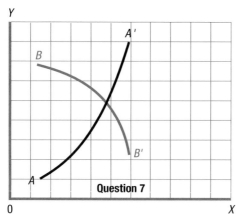

The Economic Problem: Scarcity, Wants, and Choices

YOU MAKE DECISIONS EVERY DAY THAT CAPTURE the essence of economics. Suppose you have $40 and are deciding how to spend it. Should you buy a pair of new jeans? Two or three compact discs? A ticket for a music concert?

Similarly, what should you do with your time between 3 and 6 o'clock on, say, a Thursday afternoon? Should you work extra hours at your part-time job? Do research on a term project? Prepare for an economics quiz? Watch TV? Take a nap?

Money and time are both scarce, and making decisions in the context of scarcity always means there are costs. If you choose the jeans, the cost is the forgone CDs or concert. If you nap or watch TV, the cost might be a low score on your quiz.

Scarcity, wants, and choices—these are the key elements of this chapter. Here we introduce and explore the fundamentals of economic science. We first illustrate, extend, and modify our definition of economics and explore the so-called *economizing problem* by means of a model. Next, we briefly survey the ways diverse economies respond to the economizing problem. Finally, we develop an overview of the market system in the form of the circular flow model.

IN THIS CHAPTER YOU WILL LEARN:

That economics is about choosing among alternative ends.

•

The distinction between allocative and productive efficiency.

•

What a production possibility curve is.

•

The meaning of opportunity cost.

•

The four different economic systems society can choose to coordinate production and consumption decisions.

•

What the circular model is.

The Big Picture

THE ECONOMIZING PROBLEM ARISES FROM scarcity (or limited) resources and human unlimited wants. As a consequence, individuals and societies must make choices about what they want to produce and consume.

Consider the following scenario. Fall term has just ended and one weekend remains before the Christmas holiday begins. You must study for a final exam but you also need to do your Christmas shopping. Also, it just snowed and you are itching to ski for the first time of the season. Moreover, your friends have invited you to a Christmas party Friday night of the same weekend.

You need to make choices since it would be impossible for you to do all the things you want. And whatever choices you make entails giving something up. That, in short, captures the economizing problem, the result of limited resources and many wants.

As you read this chapter, keep the following points in mind:

- **Key Concepts 1, 2, 4,** and **8** are discussed.
- Resources to produce the goods and services we want are limited in relation to our wants.
- Even if a few very wealthy individuals have all the material things they desire, the vast majority of the human race certainly does not.
- In the face of limited resources, choices about what to produce and consume must be made.
- Limited resources imply that choosing more of one good or service means giving up some quantity of another good or service. ■

THE FOUNDATION OF ECONOMICS

Two fundamental facts together constitute the **economizing problem** and provide a foundation for the field of economics:

1. *Society's material wants, that is, the material wants of its citizens and institutions, are virtually unlimited and insatiable.*
2. *Economic resources—the means of producing goods and services—are limited or scarce.*

You must fully understand these two facts because all that follows depends directly on them.

Unlimited Wants

In stating the first fact, what do we mean by "material wants"? We mean, first, the desires of consumers to obtain and use various goods and services that provide **utility**, meaning pleasure or satisfaction.[1] An amazingly wide range of products accomplishes this, from houses and automobiles to toothpaste, pizzas, sweaters, and hamburgers. Innumerable products sometimes classified as *necessities* (food, shelter, and clothing) and *luxuries* (perfumes, yachts, racecars) can satisfy human desires. Of course, what is a luxury to Smith may be a necessity to Jones, and what is a necessity today may have been a luxury a few years ago.

Services satisfy our wants as much as products do. Repair work on a car, the removal of an inflamed appendix, legal and accounting advice, and haircuts and hairstyling all satisfy human wants. Actually, we buy many goods—for example, automobiles and washing machines—for the services they render. Thus, the differences between goods and services are often smaller than they would appear to be.

"Wants" also include the desires of businesses and units of government to satisfy material goals. Businesses want factory buildings, machinery, trucks, warehouses, communication systems, and other things that help them achieve their production goals. Government, reflecting the collective wants of its citizenry or goals of its own, seeks highways, mass transit systems, schools, and military equipment.

We say that, as a group, these wants are *insatiable*, or *unlimited*, meaning that our desires for

---

[1] This definition leaves a variety of wants—recognition, status, love, and so forth—for the other social sciences to examine and study.

goods and services cannot be completely satisfied. Our desires for a *particular* good or service can be satisfied; over a short period of time we can surely get enough toothpaste or pasta. And one appendicitis operation is plenty.

But goods *in general* are another story. We do not, and presumably cannot, get enough. A simple mental experiment can help verify this: Suppose all members of society were asked to list the goods and services they would buy if they had unlimited income. Do you imagine that their list would ever end?

Furthermore, over time, wants multiply. As we fill some of the wants on the list, new ones pop up. Material wants have a high reproduction rate. The rapid introduction of new products whets our appetites, and extensive advertising persuades us that we need items we might not otherwise have desired. Not long ago, we did not want personal computers, Internet service, video recorders, fax machines, and compact discs because they did not exist. Also, we often cannot stop with simple satisfaction: The acquisition of an Escort or Geo has been known to whet the appetite for a Porsche or Mercedes.

At any specific time the individuals and institutions constituting society have innumerable unfulfilled material wants. Some wants—food, clothing, shelter—have biological roots. But some are also influenced by the conventions and customs of society. The specific kinds of food, clothing, and shelter we seek are frequently determined by the general social and cultural environment in which we live. Over time, wants change and multiply, fuelled by the development of new products and extensive promotion.

The overall objective of all economic activity is to satisfy these diverse material wants.

Scarce Resources

In stating the second fundamental fact—*economic resources are limited or scarce*—what do we mean by **economic resources**? In general, we mean all natural, human, and manufactured resources that go into the production of goods and services. This covers a lot of ground: all the factory and farm buildings and all the equipment, tools, and machinery used to produce manufactured goods and agricultural products; all transportation and communication facilities; the innumerable types of labour; and land and mineral resources of all kinds. Economists broadly classify these as either *property* resources—land or raw materials and capital—or *human* resources—labour and entrepreneurial ability.

Resource Categories Let's examine four specific categories of resources.

LAND Land means much more to the economist than to most people. Land is all natural resources— all "gifts of nature"—usable in the production process. Such resources as arable land, forests, mineral and oil deposits, and water resources come under this classification.

CAPITAL Capital (or *capital goods* or *investment goods*) includes all manufactured aids to production, that is, all tools, machinery, equipment, and factory, storage, transportation, and distribution facilities used in producing goods and services and getting them to the ultimate consumer. The process of producing and purchasing capital goods is known as **investment**.

Two other points are pertinent. First, *capital goods* differ from *consumer goods* since the latter satisfy wants directly, while the former do so indirectly by aiding production of consumer goods. Second, the term "capital" as here defined does not refer to money. True, business executives and economists often talk of "money capital," meaning money available to purchase machinery, equipment, and other productive facilities. But money, as such, produces nothing, so it is not an economic resource. *Real capital*—tools, machinery, and other productive equipment—is an economic resource; *money* or *financial capital* is not.

LABOUR Labour is a broad term for all the physical and mental talents of individuals available and usable in producing goods and services. (This *excludes* a special set of talents—entrepreneurial ability—which, because of its special significance in a market economy, we consider separately.) The services of a logger, retail clerk, machinist, teacher, professional football player, and nuclear physicist all fall under the general heading "labour."

ENTREPRENEURIAL ABILITY Finally, there is the special human resource we label **entrepreneurial ability** or, simply, *enterprise*. The entrepreneur performs four related functions.

1. The entrepreneur *takes the initiative* in combining the resources of land, capital, and labour to produce a good or service. Both a sparkplug and a catalyst, the entrepreneur is the driving

force behind production and the agent who combines the other resources in what is hoped will be a successful business venture.

2. The entrepreneur *makes basic business-policy decisions*, that is, those nonroutine decisions that set the course of a business enterprise.

3. The entrepreneur *is an innovator*—the one who attempts to introduce on a commercial basis new products, new productive techniques, or even new forms of business organization.

4. The entrepreneur *is a risk taker*. This is apparent from a close examination of the other three entrepreneurial functions. The entrepreneur in a market economy has no guarantee of profit. The reward for his or her time, efforts, and abilities may be profits *or* losses and eventual bankruptcy. The entrepreneur risks not only time, effort, and business reputation but his or her invested funds and those of associates or stockholders.

Since these four resources—land, labour, capital, and entrepreneurial ability—are combined to *produce* goods and services, they are called the **factors of production**.

Resource Payments   The income received from supplying raw materials and capital equipment (the property resources) is called *rental income* and *interest income*, respectively. The income accruing to those who supply labour is called *wages*, which includes salaries and all wage and salary supplements such as bonuses, commissions, and royalties. Entrepreneurial income is called *profits*, which may be negative—that is, losses.

Relative Scarcity

The four types of economic resources, or factors of production, or *inputs*, have one fundamental characteristic in common: *They are scarce or limited in supply*. Our "spaceship earth" contains only limited amounts of resources to use in producing goods and services. Quantities of arable land, mineral deposits, capital equipment, and labour (time) are all limited; they are available only in finite amounts. Because of the scarcity of productive resources and the constraint that this scarcity puts on productive activity, output itself is limited. Society is not able to produce and consume all the goods and services it wants. Thus, in Canada—one of the most affluent nations—output per person was limited to $26,355 in 1997. In the poorest

nations, annual output per person is as low as $200 or $300!

ECONOMICS: GETTING THE MOST OUT OF AVAILABLE RESOURCES

The economizing problem is thus at the heart of the definition of economics, first stated in Chapter 1: *Economics is the social science concerned with the problem of using scarce resources to attain the maximum fulfilment of society's unlimited wants.* Economics is concerned with "doing the best with what we have." Because our resources are scarce, we cannot satisfy all our unlimited wants. The next best thing is to achieve the greatest possible satisfaction of those wants. Society wants to use its limited resources efficiently; it desires to produce as many goods and services as possible from its available resources, so that it maximizes total satisfaction. To realize this outcome, it must achieve both full employment and full production.

Full Employment: Using Available Resources

By **full employment** we mean the use of all available resources. No workers should be involuntarily out of work; the economy should provide employment for all who are willing and able to work. Nor should capital equipment or arable land sit idle. But note that we say all *available* resources should be employed. Each society has certain customs and practices that determine what particular resources are available for employment. For example, in most countries legislation and custom provide that children and the very aged should not be employed. Similarly, to maintain productivity, it is desirable to allow farmland to lie fallow periodically. And it is desirable to "conserve" some resources for use by future generations.

Full Production: Using Resources Efficiently

The employment of all available resources is not enough to achieve efficiency. Full production must also be realized. By **full production** we mean that all employed resources should be used so that they provide the maximum possible satisfaction of our material wants. If we fail to realize full production, economists say our resources are *under-employed*.

Full production implies two kinds of efficiency—productive and allocative efficiency:

1. **Productive efficiency** is the production of *any particular mix of goods and services in the least costly way*. When we produce, say, compact discs at the lowest achievable unit cost, we are expending the smallest amount of resources to produce CDs and therefore making available the largest amount of resources to produce other desired products. Suppose society has only $100 of resources available. If we can produce a CD for only $5 of resources, then $95 of resources will be available to produce other goods. This is clearly better than producing the CD for $10 and having only $90 of resources for alternative uses.

   In real-world terms, productive efficiency requires that Ford pickups and Dodge vans be produced with computerized and roboticized assembly techniques. It would be wasteful of scarce resources—that is, inefficient—to use the primitive assembly lines of the 1920s. Similarly, it would be inefficient to have farmers harvesting wheat with scythes or picking corn by hand since mechanical harvesting equipment is available to do the job at a much lower cost per unit.

2. **Allocative efficiency** is the production of *that particular mix of goods and services most wanted by society*. For example, society wants resources allocated to compact discs and cassettes, not to 45 rpm records. We want personal computers (PCs), not manual typewriters. Furthermore, we do not want to devote *all* our resources to producing CDs and PCs; we want to assign some of them to producing automobiles and office buildings. Allocative efficiency requires that the "right" mix of goods and services be produced—each item at the least unit cost. It means apportioning limited resources among firms and industries in such a way that society obtains the combination of goods and services that it wants the most. *(Key Question 5)*

2-1
QUICK REVIEW

- Human material wants are virtually unlimited.
- Economic resources—land, capital, labour, and entrepreneurial ability—are scarce.
- Economics is concerned with the efficient allocation of scarce resources to achieve the maximum fulfilment of society's material wants.
- Economic efficiency requires full employment and full production; the latter requires both productive and allocative efficiency.

Production Possibilities Table

Because resources are scarce, a full-employment, full-production economy cannot have an unlimited output of goods and services. Therefore, people must choose which goods and services to produce and which to forgo. The necessity and consequences of these choices can best be understood through a production possibilities model. Let's examine the model first as a table, then as a graph.

Assumptions We begin our discussion with four simplifying assumptions:

1. **FULL EMPLOYMENT AND PRODUCTIVE EFFICIENCY** The economy is employing all its available resources (full employment) and producing goods and services at least cost (productive efficiency). We will consider allocative efficiency later.

2. **FIXED RESOURCES** The available supplies of the factors of production are fixed in both quantity and quality. Nevertheless, they can be reallocated, within limits, among different uses; for example, land can be used for factory sites or for food production.

3. **FIXED TECHNOLOGY** The state of technology—the methods used to produce output—does not change during our analysis. This assumption and the previous one imply that we are looking at an economy at one specific time or over a very short period of time. Later in the analysis, we will examine the situation over a longer period.

4. **TWO GOODS** The economy is producing only two goods: pizzas and industrial robots. Pizza symbolizes **consumer goods**: products that satisfy our wants *directly*; industrial robots symbolize **capital goods**: products that satisfy our wants *indirectly* by enabling more efficient production of consumer goods.

The Need for Choice From our assumptions, we see that society must choose among alternatives. Limited resources mean limited outputs of pizza and robots. And since all available resources are fully employed, to increase the production of robots we must shift resources away from the production of pizza. The reverse is also true: To increase the production of pizza, we must take resources from the production of robots. There is no such thing as a free pizza. This, recall, is the essence of the economizing problem.

A **production possibilities table** lists the different combinations of two products that can be produced with a specific set of resources (and with full employment and productive efficiency). Table 2-1 is such a table for a pizza-robot economy; the data are, of course, hypothetical. At alternative A, this economy would be devoting all its available resources to the production of robots (capital goods); at alternative E, all resources would go to pizza production (consumer goods). Those alternatives are unrealistic extremes; an economy typically produces both capital and consumer goods, as in B, C, and D. As we move from alternative A to E, we increase the production of pizza at the expense of robot production.

Because consumer goods satisfy our wants directly, any movement towards E looks tempting. In producing more pizzas, society increases the current satisfaction of its wants. But there is a cost: fewer robots. This shift of resources to consumer goods catches up with society over time as the stock of capital goods dwindles—or at least ceases to expand at the current rate—with the result that some potential for greater production is lost. By moving towards alternative E, society chooses "more now" at the expense of "much more later."

By moving towards A, society chooses to forgo current consumption. The sacrifice of current consumption frees resources that can be used to increase the production of capital goods. By building up its stock of capital this way, society will have greater future production and, therefore, greater future consumption. By moving towards A, society is choosing "more later" at the cost of "less now."

Generalization: *At any point in time, an economy that is achieving full employment and productive efficiency must sacrifice some of one good to obtain more of another good. Scarce resources prohibit such an economy from having more of both goods.*

Production Possibilities Curve

The data and ideas of a production possibilities table can also be shown graphically. We use a simple two-dimensional graph, arbitrarily representing the output of capital goods (here, robots) on the vertical axis and the output of consumer goods (here, pizza) on the horizontal axis, as shown in *Figure 2-1 (Key Graph)*. Following the procedure given in the appendix to Chapter 1, we graph a **production possibilities curve**.

Each point on the production possibilities curve represents some maximum output of the two products. The curve is a production *frontier* because it shows the limit of attainable outputs. To obtain the various combinations of pizza and robots that fall *on* the production possibilities curve, society must achieve both full employment and productive efficiency. Points lying *inside* (to the left of) the curve are also attainable but not as desirable as points on the curve. Points inside the curve imply that the economy could have more of both robots and pizza if it achieved full employment and productive efficiency. Points lying *outside* (to the right of) the production possibilities curve, like point *W*, would represent a greater output than that at any point on the curve, but such points are unattainable with the current supplies of resources and technology.

Law of Increasing Opportunity Cost

Because resources are scarce relative to the virtually unlimited wants that these resources can be used to satisfy, people must choose among alternatives. More of pizza means less of robots. The amount of other products that must be forgone or sacrificed to obtain 1 unit of a specific good is called the **opportunity cost** of that good. In our case, the amount of robots that must be given up to get another unit of pizza is the *opportunity cost*, or simply the *cost*, of that unit of pizza.

TABLE 2-1 Production possibilities of pizza and robots with full employment and productive efficiency

Type of product	PRODUCTION ALTERNATIVES				
	A	B	C	D	E
Pizza (in hundred thousands)	0	1	2	3	4
Robots (in thousands)	10	9	7	4	0

In moving from alternative A to B in Table 2-1, we find that the cost of 1 additional unit of pizza is 1 less unit of robots. But as we now pursue the concept of cost through the additional production possibilities—B to C, C to D, and D to E—an important economic principle is revealed: The opportunity cost of each additional unit of pizza is greater than that of the previous one. When we move from A to B, just 1 unit of robots is sacrificed for 1 more unit of pizza; but going from B to C sacrifices 2 additional units of robots for 1 more unit of pizza; then 3 more of robots for 1 more of pizza; and finally 4 for 1. Conversely, you should confirm that as we move from E to A, the cost of each additional robot is $\frac{1}{4}$, $\frac{1}{3}$, $\frac{1}{2}$, and 1 unit of pizza, respectively, for the four successive moves.

Note two points about these opportunity costs:

1. Our costs are measured in *real* terms, that is, in actual goods rather than money. We will shift to monetary comparisons in a moment.
2. We are discussing *marginal* (meaning "extra") opportunity costs, rather than cumulative or total opportunity costs. For example, the marginal opportunity cost of the third unit of pizza in Table 2-1 is 3 units of robots (= 7 − 4). But the *total* opportunity cost of 3 units of pizza is 6 units of robots (= 1 unit of robots for the first unit of pizza *plus* 2 units of robots for the second unit of pizza *plus* 3 units of robots for the third unit of pizza).

The **law of increasing opportunity costs** generalizes our example: The more of a product that is produced, the greater is its opportunity cost ("marginal" being implied).

Concavity   The law of increasing opportunity costs is reflected in the shape of the production possibilities curve: The curve is *concave*, or bowed out, from the origin. In Figure 2-1, you can see that when the economy moves from A to E, it must give up successively larger amounts of robots (1, 2, 3, and 4) to acquire equal increments of pizza (1, 1, 1, and 1). This reality is shown by the slope of the production possibilities curve that becomes steeper as we move from A to E. A curve that gets steeper as you move down along it is always concave as viewed from the origin.

Economic Rationale   What is the economic rationale for the law of increasing opportunity costs? Why does the sacrifice of robots increase as we produce more pizza? The answer is that *economic resources are not completely adaptable to alternative uses.* Many resources are better at producing one good than at producing others. Fertile farmland is highly conducive to producing the ingredients needed to make pizza, while land containing rich mineral deposits is highly suited to producing the materials needed to make robots. As we step up pizza production, resources that are less and less adaptable to making pizza must be "pushed" into pizza production. If we start at *A* and move to *B*, we can shift the resources whose productivity of pizza is greatest in relation to their productivity of robots. But as we move from *B* to *C*, *C* to *D*, and so on, resources highly productive of pizza become increasingly scarce. To get more pizza, resources whose productivity in robots is great in relation to their productivity in pizza will be needed. It will take more and more of such resources—and hence a greater sacrifice of robots—to achieve each increase of 1 unit in the production of pizza. This lack of perfect flexibility, or interchangeability, on the part of resources is the cause of increasing opportunity costs. **(Key Question 6)**

Allocative Efficiency Revisited

Our analysis has assumed full employment and productive efficiency, both of which are necessary to produce at *any point* on an economy's production possibilities curve. We now turn to allocative efficiency, which requires that the economy produce at the most valued, or *optimal*, point on the production possibilities curve. Of all the attainable combinations of pizza and robots on the curve in Figure 2-1, which is best? That is, what specific quantities of resources should be allocated to pizza and what specific quantities to robots?

Our discussion of the *economic perspective* in Chapter 1 puts us on the right track. Recall that economic decisions centre on comparisons of marginal benefits and marginal costs. Any economic activity—for example, production or consumption—should be expanded as long as marginal benefits exceed marginal costs and should be reduced if marginal costs are greater than marginal benefits. The optimal amount of the activity occurs where MB = MC.

Consider pizza. We already know from the law of increasing opportunity costs that the marginal cost (MC) of additional units of pizza will rise as

KEY GRAPH

FIGURE 2-1 The production possibilities curve

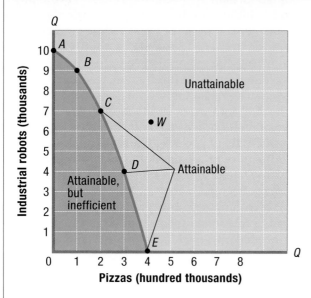

Each point on the production possibilities curve represents some maximum combination of two products that can be produced if full employment and full production are achieved. When operating on the curve, more robots mean less pizza, and vice versa. Limited resources and a fixed technology make any combination of robots and pizza lying outside the curve (such as at *W*) unattainable. Points inside the curve are attainable, but they indicate that full employment and productive efficiency are not being realized.

2-1

QUICK QUIZ

1. Production possibilities curve *ABCDE* is concave because:
    (a) the marginal benefit of pizza declines as more pizza is consumed.
    (b) the curve gets steeper as we move from *E* to *A*.
    (c) it reflects the law of increasing opportunity costs.
    (d) resources are scarce.

2. The *marginal* opportunity cost of the second unit of pizza is:
    (a) 2 units of robots.
    (b) 3 units of robots.
    (c) 7 units of robots.
    (d) 9 units of robots.

3. The *total* opportunity cost of 7 units of robots is:
    (a) 1 unit of pizza.
    (b) 2 units of pizza.
    (c) 3 units of pizza.
    (d) 4 units of pizza.

4. All points on this production possibilities curve necessarily represent:
    (a) allocative efficiency.
    (b) less than full use of resources.
    (c) unattainable levels of output.
    (d) productive efficiency.

Answers: 1. (c); 2. (a); 3. (b); 4 (d).

more units are produced. This can be shown with an upsloping MC curve, as in Figure 2-2. We are also aware that we obtain extra or marginal benefits (MB) from additional units of pizza. However, although material wants in the aggregate are insatiable, the second unit of a particular product yields less additional utility or benefit to you than the first. And a third will provide even less MB than the second. So it is for society as a whole. Therefore, we can portray the marginal benefits from pizza with a downsloping MB curve, as in Figure 2-2.

The optimal quantity of pizza production is indicated by the intersection of the MB and MC curves: 200,000 units in Figure 2-2. Why is this the optimal quantity? If only 100,000 pizzas were pro-

duced, the marginal benefit of pizza would exceed its marginal cost. In money terms, MB might be $15, while MC is only $5. This suggests that society would be *underallocating* resources to pizza production; more of it should be produced.

How do we know? Because society values an additional pizza as being worth $15, while the alternative products that the required resources could produce are worth only $5. Society benefits—it is better off in the sense of having a higher-valued output to enjoy—whenever it can gain something worth $15 by forgoing something worth only $5. A reallocating of resources from other products to pizza would mean society is using its resources more efficiently. Each addi-

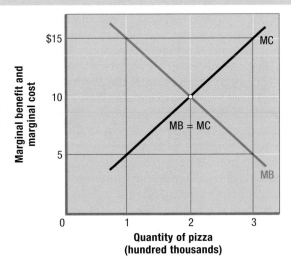

FIGURE 2-2 Allocative efficiency: MB = MC

Resources are being allocated efficiently to a product when its output quantity is such that its marginal benefit (MB) equals its marginal cost (MC). Here, the optimal quantity of pizza is 200,000.

2-2

QUICK REVIEW

- The production possibilities curve illustrates four concepts: **a** *scarcity* of resources is implied by the area of unattainable combinations of output lying outside the production possibilities curve; **b** *choice* among outputs is reflected in the variety of attainable combinations of goods lying along the curve; **c** *opportunity cost* is illustrated by the downward slope of the curve; **d** the law of *increasing opportunity costs* is implied by the concavity of the curve.

- Full employment and productive efficiency must be realized for the economy to operate on its production possibilities curve.

- A comparison of marginal benefits and marginal costs is needed to determine allocative efficiency—the best or optimal output-mix on the curve.

tional pizza up to 200,000 would provide such a gain, indicating that allocative efficiency would be improved by this production. But when MB = MC, the benefits of producing pizza or alternative products with the available resources are equal. Allocative efficiency is achieved where MB = MC.

The production of 300,000 pizzas would represent an *overallocation* of resources to their production. Here the MC of pizza is $15 and its MB is only $5. This means 1 unit of pizza is worth only $5 to society, while the alternative products that the required resources could otherwise produce are valued at $15. By producing 1 less unit, society loses a pizza worth $5. But by reallocating the freed resources, it gains other products worth $15. When society gains something worth $15 by forgoing something worth only $5, it is better off. In Figure 2-2, such net gains can be realized until pizza production has been reduced to 200,000.

Generalization: *Resources are being efficiently allocated to any product when its output is such that its marginal benefit equals its marginal cost (MB = MC).* Suppose that by applying the above analysis to robots, we find their optimal (MB = MC) output is 7,000. This would mean that alternative *C* on our production possibilities curve—200,000 pizzas and 7,000 robots—would result in allocative efficiency for our hypothetical economy. *(Key Question 9)*

UNEMPLOYMENT, GROWTH, AND THE FUTURE

Let's now drop the first three assumptions underlying the production possibilities curve to see what happens.

Unemployment and Productive Inefficiency

The first assumption was that our economy was achieving full employment and productive efficiency. Our analysis and conclusions change if some resources are idle (unemployment) or if least-cost production is not realized. The five alternatives in Table 2-1 represent maximum outputs; they illustrate the combinations of robots and pizzas that can be produced when the economy is operating at full capacity—with full employment and productive efficiency. With unemployment or inefficient production, the economy would produce less than each alternative shown in the table.

Graphically, situations of unemployment or productive inefficiency are represented by points *inside* the original production possibilities curve (reproduced in Figure 2-3). Point *U* is one such point. Here the economy is falling short of the various maximum combinations of pizza and robots

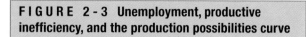

FIGURE 2-3 Unemployment, productive inefficiency, and the production possibilities curve

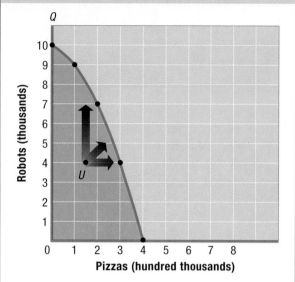

Any point inside the production possibilities curve, such as *U*, represents unemployment or a failure to achieve productive efficiency. The arrows indicate that, by realizing full employment and productive efficiency, the economy could operate on the curve. This means it could produce more of one or both products than it is producing at point *U*.

reflected by the points *on* the production possibilities curve. The arrows in Figure 2-3 indicate three possible paths back to full employment and least-cost production. A move towards full employment and productive efficiency would yield a greater output of one or both products.

A Growing Economy

When we drop the assumptions that the quantity and quality of resources and technology are fixed, the production possibilities curve shifts positions; that is, the potential maximum output of the economy changes.

Increases in Resource Supplies Let's first abandon the assumption that total supplies of land, labour, capital, and entrepreneurial ability are fixed in both quantity and quality. Common sense tells us that over time a nation's growing population will bring about increases in the supplies of labour and entrepreneurial ability. Also, labour quality usually improves over time. Historically, our stock of capital has increased at a sig-

nificant, though unsteady, rate. And although we are depleting some of our energy and mineral resources, new sources are being discovered. The drainage of swamps and the development of irrigation programs add to our supply of arable land.

The net result of these increased supplies of the factors of production is the ability to produce more of both pizza and robots. Thus 20 years from now, the production possibilities in Table 2-1 may be superseded by those shown in Table 2-2. The greater abundance of resources would result in a greater potential output of one or both products at each alternative. Economic growth in the sense of an expanded potential output will have occurred.

But such a favourable change in the production possibilities data does not *guarantee* that the economy will actually operate at a point on its new production possibilities curve. Some 15 million jobs will give Canada full employment now, but 10 or 20 years from now its labour force will be larger, and 15 million jobs will not be sufficient for full employment. The production possibilities curve may shift, but at the future date the economy may fail to produce at a point on that new curve.

Advances in Technology Our second assumption is that we have constant or unchanging technology. Actually, though, technology has progressed greatly over time. An advancing technology involves both new and better goods *and* improved ways of producing them. For now, let's think of technological advances as being only improvements in capital facilities—more efficient machinery and equipment. Such technological advances alter our previous discussion of the economizing problem by improving productive efficiency, allowing society to produce more goods with fixed resources. As with increases in resource supplies, technological advances enable the production of more robots *and* more pizza.

TABLE 2-2 Production possibilities of pizza and robots with full employment and productive efficiency

Type of product	PRODUCTION ALTERNATIVES				
	A′	B′	C′	D′	E′
Pizza (in hundred thousands)	0	2	4	6	8
Robots (in thousands)	14	12	9	5	0

Thus, when either supplies of resources increase or an improvement in technology occurs, the production possibilities curve in Figure 2-3 shifts outward and to the right, as illustrated by curve A', B', C', D', E' in Figure 2-4. Such an outward shift of the production possibilities curve represents growth of economic capacity or, simply, **economic growth**—*the ability to produce a larger total output*. This growth is the result of (1) increases in supplies of resources, (2) improvements in resource quality, and (3) technological advance.

The consequence of growth is that our full-employment economy can enjoy a greater output of both robots and pizza. *While a static, no-growth economy must sacrifice some of one product to get more of another, a dynamic, growing economy can have larger quantities of both products.*

Economic growth does *not* typically mean proportionate increases in a nation's capacity to produce all its products. Note in Figure 2-4 that at the maximums, the economy can produce twice as much pizza as before but only 40 percent more robots. You should sketch in two new production possibilities curves: one showing the situation where a better technique for producing robots has been developed while the technology for producing pizza is unchanged, and the other illustrating an improved technology for pizza while the technology for producing robots remains constant.

Present Choices and Future Possibilities An economy's current choice of positions on its production possibilities curve is a basic determinant of the future location of that curve. Let's designate the two axes of the production possibilities curve as *goods for the future* and *goods for the present*, as in Figure 2-5. Goods for the future are such things as capital goods, research and education, and preventive medicine. They increase the quantity and quality of property resources, enlarge the stock of technological information, and improve the quality of human resources. As we have already seen, goods for the future, like industrial robots, are the ingredients of economic growth. Goods for the present are pure consumer goods such as pizza, clothing, soft drinks, and boom boxes.

Now suppose there are two economies, Alta and Zorn, which are initially identical in every respect except one: Alta's current choice of positions on its production possibilities curve strongly favours present goods rather than future goods. Point A in Figure 2-5a indicates this choice. It is located quite far down the curve to the right, indicating a high priority for goods for the present, at the expense of fewer goods for the future. Zorn, in contrast, makes a current choice that stresses larger amounts of future goods and lesser amounts of present goods, as shown by point Z in Figure 2-5b.

Now, other things equal, we can expect the future production possibilities curve of Zorn to be farther to the right than Alta's curve. By currently choosing an output more favourable to technological advance and to increases in the quantity and quality of resources, Zorn will achieve greater economic growth than Alta. In terms of capital goods, Zorn is choosing to make larger current additions to its "national factory"—to invest more of its current output—than Alta. The payoff from this choice for Zorn is more rapid growth—greater future production capacity. The opportunity cost is fewer consumer goods in the present for Zorn to enjoy. *(Key Questions 10 and 11)*

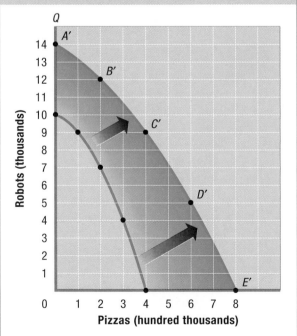

FIGURE 2-4 Economic growth and the production possibilities curve

The expanding resource supplies, improved resource quality, and technological advances that occur in a dynamic economy move the production possibilities outward and to the right, allowing the economy to have larger quantities of both types of goods.

FIGURE 2-5 An economy's present choice of positions on its production possibilities curve helps determine the curve's future location

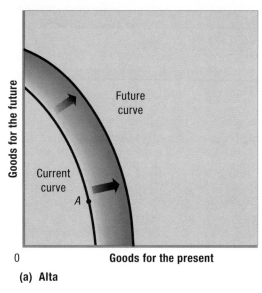

(a) Alta

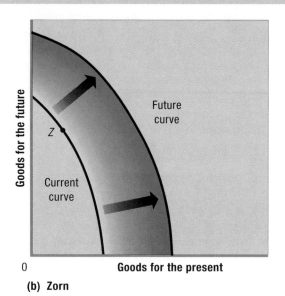

(b) Zorn

A nation's current choice favouring "present goods," as made by Alta in (a), will cause a modest outward shift of the curve in the future. A nation's current choice favouring "future goods," as made by Zorn in (b), will result in a greater outward shift in the curve in the future.

A Qualification: International Trade

The message of the production possibilities curve is that an individual nation is limited to the combinations of output indicated by its production possibilities curve. *But this message must be modified when there is international specialization and trade.*

You will see in later chapters that a nation can avoid the output limits imposed by its domestic production possibilities curve through international specialization and trade. *International specialization* means directing domestic resources to output that a nation is highly efficient at producing. *International trade* involves the exchange of these goods for goods produced abroad. Specialization and trade enable a nation to get more of a desired good at less sacrifice of some other good. Rather than sacrifice 3 robots to get a third unit of pizza, as in Table 2-1, a nation might be able to obtain the third unit of pizza by trading only 2 units of robots for it. Specialization and trade have the same effect as having more and better resources or discovering improved production techniques; both increase the quantities of capital and consumer goods available to society. The output gains from greater international specialization and trade are the equivalent of economic growth.

2-3
QUICK REVIEW

- Unemployment and the failure to achieve productive efficiency cause the economy to operate at a point inside its production possibilities curve.

- Increases in resource supplies, improvements in resource quality, and technological advance cause economic growth, depicted as an outward shift of the production possibilities curve.

- An economy's present choice of output—particularly of capital and consumer goods—helps determine the future location of its production possibilities curves. (See Global Perspective 2-1.)

- International specialization and trade enable a nation to obtain more goods than indicated by its production possibilities curve.

Applications

There are many possible applications of production possibilities analysis.

1. **GOING TO WAR** At the beginning of World War II (1939–45), Canada had considerable

2-1

GLOBAL PERSPECTIVE

Investment and economic growth, selected countries

Nations that invest large portions of their national outputs tend to enjoy high growth rates, measured here by output per person. Additional capital goods make workers more productive and this means greater output per person.

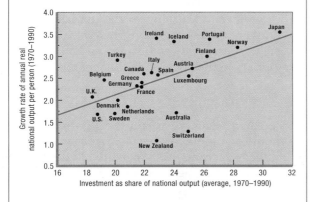

Source: International Monetary Fund data, as reported in *Economic Report of the President, 1994*, p. 37.

unemployment. By quickly employing its idle resources, the Canadian economy was able to produce an almost unbelievably large quantity of war goods and at the same time increase the output of consumer goods (as shown in Figure 2-3). The Soviet Union, in contrast, entered World War II at almost capacity production; it was operating close to full employment. An attempt to achieve simultaneously more pizza and more robots—or more guns and more butter—in a full-employment economy was doomed to failure. Its military preparations required considerable shifting of resources from the production of civilian goods, and its standard of living dropped substantially.

2. **DISCRIMINATION** Discrimination based on race, gender, age, sexual orientation, or ethnic background impedes the efficient employment of human resources, keeping the economy operating at some point inside its production possibilities curve. Discrimination prevents visible minorities, women, and others from obtaining jobs in which society can use their skills and talents efficiently. Elimination of discrimination would help move the economy from some point inside the production possibilities curve towards a point on the curve.

3. **LAND-USE CONTROVERSIES** The tradeoffs portrayed in the production possibilities curve are part of many controversies relating to alternative uses of publicly owned land.

   One example is the conflict between the logging industry in the U.S. Pacific Northwest and environmentalists trying to save that area's spotted owls. Envision a production possibilities curve with "lumber production" on one axis and "spotted owls" on the other. It so happens that the spotted owl depends on the mature trees in national forests for nests and survival. Increasing the output of lumber limits the owl's habitat, destroys the species, and thus reduces environmental quality. Maintaining the mature forests preserves the owl but destroys thousands of jobs in the logging and lumber industry.

   A second land-use example is the continuing debate over inclusion of more land in Canada's system of national parks. Some of these lands contain sizable oil, natural gas, and mineral deposits, and no drilling or mining is usually allowed. Here, the relevant production possibilities curve has "national parks" on one axis and "minerals" on the other. The concepts of resource scarcity, opportunity costs, and the necessity of choice again become quite apparent.

4. **MORE WOMEN IN THE WORKFORCE** An increase in the number of women who work outside the home has shifted the Canadian production possibilities curve outward. In 1970 about 35 percent of women worked in full-time or part-time jobs, compared to 68 percent today. As recently as 1980, only about 50 percent of married women were in the paid workforce. Today, that share is about 65 percent. This rise in the *quantity of labour* has contributed greatly to economic growth in Canada.

5. **FAMINE IN AFRICA** Modern industrial societies take economic growth—rightward shifts of the production possibilities curve—for granted. But periodic catastrophic famines in sub-Saharan nations of Africa show that in some circumstances the production possibilities curve may shift leftward. In addition to

drought, a cause of African famines is ecological degradation—poor land-use practices. Land has been deforested, overfarmed, and overgrazed, causing the production possibilities of these highly agriculturally oriented countries to diminish. In fact, the per-capita domestic outputs of most of these nations declined in the past decade or so.

6. **EMERGING TECHNOLOGIES**   The world economies are experiencing a spurt of new technologies relating to computers, communications, and biotechnology. Technological advances have dropped the prices of computers and greatly enhanced their speed. Cellular phones, the Internet, and fax machines have increased communication capability, enhancing production and improving the efficiency of markets. Advances in biotechnology, specifically genetic engineering, have resulted in important agricultural and medical discoveries. Some observers believe that these new technologies are of such significance that they will ultimately contribute to faster economic growth than has occurred in the recent past (faster rightward shifts in nations' production possibilities curves).

ECONOMIC SYSTEMS

A society needs to select an **economic system**—*a particular set of institutional arrangements and a coordinating mechanism*—to respond to the economizing problem. Economic systems can differ as to (1) who owns the factors of production and (2) the method used to coordinate and direct economic activity.

Pure Capitalism

The private ownership of resources and the use of a system of markets and prices to coordinate and direct economic activity characterize *laissez-faire capitalism*, or **pure capitalism**. In such **market systems** each participant acts in his or her own self-interest; each individual or business seeks to maximize its satisfaction or profit through its own decisions regarding consumption or production. The system allows for the private ownership of capital, communicates through prices, and coordinates economic activity through *markets*—places where buyers and sellers come together. Goods and services are produced and resources are sup-

plied by whomever is willing and able to do so. The result is competition among many small, independently acting buyers and sellers of each product and resource. Thus, economic power is widely dispersed.

Advocates of pure capitalism argue that such an economy promotes efficiency in the use of resources, stability of output and employment, and rapid economic growth. Hence, there is little or no need for government planning, control, or intervention. The term *laissez-faire* means "let it be," that is, keep government from interfering with the economy. The idea is that such interference will disturb the efficient working of the market system. Government's role is therefore limited to protecting private property and establishing an environment appropriate to the operation of the market system.

The Command Economy

The polar alternative to pure capitalism is the **command economy**, or *communism*, characterized by public (government) ownership of virtually all property resources and economic decision making through central economic planning. All major decisions concerning the level of resource use, the composition and distribution of output, and the organization of production are determined by a central planning board appointed by government. Business firms are governmentally owned and produce according to government directives. The planning board determines production goals for each enterprise, and the plan specifies the amounts of resources to be allocated to each enterprise so that it can reach its production goals. The division of output between capital and consumer goods is centrally decided, and capital goods are allocated among industries on the basis of the central planning board's long-term priorities.

Mixed Systems

Pure capitalism and the command economy are extremes; real-world economies fall between the two. The Canadian economy leans towards pure capitalism, but with important differences. Government actively participates in the economy by promoting economic stability and growth, providing certain goods and services that would be underproduced or not produced at all by the market system, and modifying the distribution of income. In contrast to wide dispersion of economic power among many small units, as implied by pure capitalism, the Canadian economy has spawned a number of very powerful economic organizations in the form of large corporations and labour unions. The ability of these power blocs to manipulate some markets to their advantage is a further reason for government involvement in the economy.

While the former Soviet Union historically approximated the command economy, it relied to some extent on market-determined prices and had some private ownership. Recent reforms in the former Soviet Union, China, and most of the eastern European nations have moved these economies toward more market-oriented systems. North Korea and Cuba are the best remaining examples of centrally planned economies.

But private ownership and reliance on the market system do not always go together, nor do state ownership and central planning. For example, the fascism of Hitler's Nazi Germany has been dubbed *authoritarian capitalism* because the economy had a high degree of governmental control and direction but property was privately owned. In contrast, the present economic system of China might be called *market socialism*. It has extensive government ownership of natural resources and capital coupled with considerable reliance on free markets to organize and coordinate some parts of economic activity. The Swedish economy is also a hybrid system. Although more than 90 percent of Sweden's business activity is in private hands, government is deeply involved in redistributing income. Similarly, the market-dominated Japanese economy involves much planning and coordination between government and the business sector.

The Traditional Economy

Some developing countries have customary or **traditional economies**, in which production methods, exchange of goods, and distribution of income are all sanctioned by custom. Heredity and caste dictate the economic roles of individuals, and changes in socioeconomic status are rare. Technological change may also be constrained because it clashes with tradition and threatens the social fabric. Economic activity is often secondary to religious and cultural values and society's desire to perpetuate the status quo.

The main point here is that there is no unique or universally accepted way to respond to the economizing problem. Various societies, having different cultural and historical backgrounds, different mores and customs, and contrasting ideological frameworks—not to mention a great diversity of resources—use different institutions to deal with the reality of scarcity. The best method for responding to this reality in one society may or may not be appropriate in another society.

THE CIRCULAR FLOW MODEL

Because market systems now dominate the world economy, our focus in the remainder of this chapter, and the two that follow, is on how nations use markets to respond to the economizing problem. Our goal in this last section is modest: We want to identify the major groups of decision makers and the major markets in the market system. Our tool is the circular flow diagram.

Resource and Product Markets

Figure 2-6 (Key Graph) shows two groups of decision makers—households and businesses. (Government will be added as a third decision maker in Chapter 5.) The coordinating mechanism that aligns the decisions of households and businesses is the market system, in particular resource and product markets.

The upper half of the diagram portrays the **resource market**—*the place where resources or the services of resource suppliers are bought and sold.* Households (that is, people) either own all economic resources directly or own them indirectly through their ownership of business corporations. These households *supply* their resources to businesses. Businesses *demand* resources because resources are necessary for producing goods and services. The interaction of the demand for and supply of the immense variety of human and property resources establishes the price of each resource. The payments that businesses make to obtain resources are costs to businesses, but those payments simultaneously are flows of wage, rent, interest, and profit income to the households supplying the resources. Thus resources flow from households to businesses, and money flows from businesses to households.

Now consider the **product market**—*the place where goods and services of businesses are bought and sold*—represented in the bottom half of the dia-

KEY GRAPH

FIGURE 2-6 The circular flow of output and income

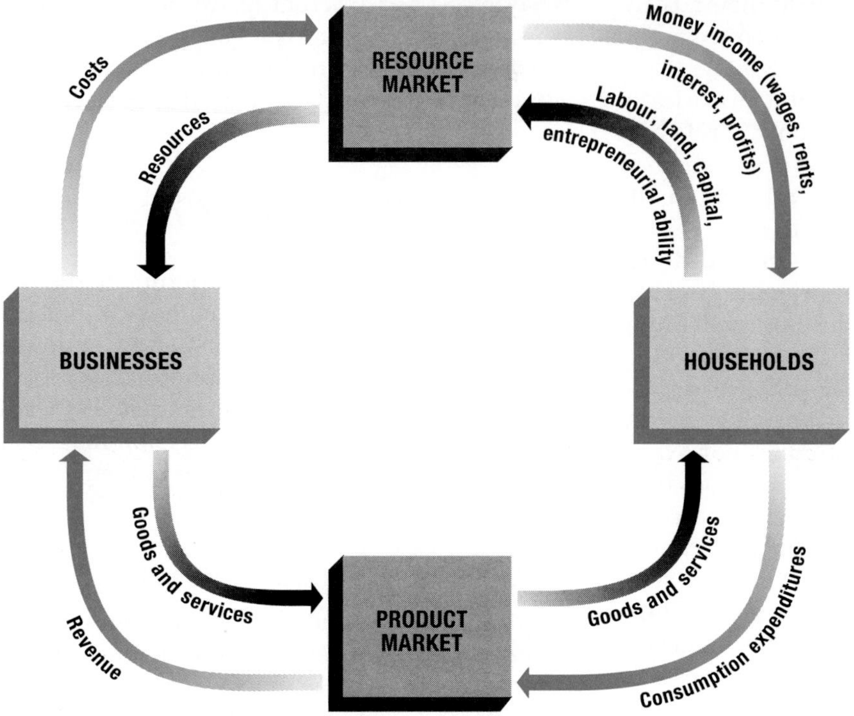

The prices paid for the use of labour, land, capital, and entrepreneurial ability are determined in the resource market shown in the upper loop. Businesses are on the demand side and households are on the supply side of this market. The prices of finished goods and services are determined in the product market shown in the lower loop. Households are on the demand side and businesses are on the supply side of this market.

2-6
QUICK QUIZ

1. The resource market is where:
   (a) households sell products and businesses buy products.
   (b) businesses sell resources and households sell products.
   (c) households sell resources and businesses buy resources (or the services of resources).
   (d) businesses sell resources and households buy resources (or the services of resources).

2. Which of the following would be determined in the product market?
   (a) a manager's salary.
   (b) the price of equipment used in a bottling plant.
   (c) the price of 80 hectares of farmland.
   (d) the price of a new pair of athletic shoes.

3. In this circular flow diagram:
   (a) money flows counterclockwise.
   (b) resources flow counterclockwise.
   (c) goods and services flow clockwise.
   (d) households are on the supply side of the product market.

4. In this circular flow diagram:
   (a) households spend income in the product market.
   (b) firms supply resources to households.
   (c) households receive income through the product market.
   (d) households produce goods.

Answers: 1. (c); 2. (d); 3. (b); 4. (a).

gram. The money income received by households from the sale of resources does not, as such, have real value. Consumers cannot eat or wear coins and paper money. But they can spend their money for goods and services. And by their willingness to spend money income, households express their *demand* for a vast variety of goods and services. Simultaneously, businesses combine the resources they have obtained to produce and *supply* these goods and services. The interaction of consumer demand and business supply decisions determines product prices. The flow of consumer expenditures for goods and services constitutes sales revenues for businesses.

This **circular flow model** suggests a complex, interrelated web of decision making and economic activity. Note that households and businesses participate in both basic markets, but on different sides of each. Businesses are on the buying or demand side of resource markets, and households (as resource owners and suppliers) are on the selling or supply side. In the product market, these positions are reversed; households are on the buying or demand side, and businesses on the selling or supply side. Each group of economic units both buys and sells.

Moreover, the spectre of scarcity haunts these transactions. Because households have only limited amounts of resources to supply to businesses, the money incomes of consumers are limited. This means that each consumer's income will go only so far. A limited amount of money income clearly will not permit the purchase of all the goods and services the consumer might like to buy. Similarly, because resources are scarce, the output of finished goods and services is also necessarily limited.

To summarize: In a monetary economy, households, as resource owners, sell their resources to businesses and, as consumers, spend the resource income by buying goods and services. Businesses must buy resources to produce goods and services; their finished products are then sold to households in exchange for consumption expenditures or, as business sees it, revenues. These revenues are used to purchase additional resources to maintain the circular flow. The net result is, in Figure 2-6, a counterclockwise *real flow* of economic resources and finished goods and services, and a clockwise *money flow* of income and consumption expenditures. These flows are simultaneous and repetitive.

Limitations

Our model simplifies in many ways. Transactions between households and between businesses are concealed. Government and the "rest of the world" are ignored as decision makers. The model implies constant flows of output and income, while in fact these flows vary over time. Nor is the circular flow a perpetual-motion machine; production exhausts human energies and absorbs physical resources, the latter creating potential problems of environmental pollution. Finally, our model does not explain how product and resource prices are actually determined. We turn to this last topic in Chapter 4.

In The Media

Down's Transplant Bid Poses Dilemma: Lung Recipients Face Long Odds

BY ALANNA MITCHELL

CALGARY—Terry Urquhart's request for a new lung has created a moral dilemma for the doctors and ethicists who decide who gets organ transplants.

Mr. Urquhart, 17, who has been placed on a waiting list and who reports for his medical assessment next week, is the first person with Down's syndrome in Canada, perhaps in the world, to be actively considered for a new lung, and the decision to put him on the list has raised an ethical storm that has shaken Alberta.

Some call it a moral victory and others say it is a waste of a scarce resource. To Mr. Urquhart, the medical miracle of a new lung means simply the chance to live out his last few years without gasping for air.

The people who run Canada's transplant programs say that since lung transplants became an option in Canada in the late 1980s, Mr. Urquhart is the first person with Down's to request one, despite the fact that severe lung problems are a common feature of that genetic disorder.

The case poses a problem for those who decide who gets which scarce organs, especially since costly transplant programs need to show success in order to survive. They also have a duty to use the scarce donated lungs in the best way possible.

In all of Canada, just 28 single-lung transplants were performed in 1993, the last year for which statistics are available. Between 20 per cent and 40 per cent of those who await a lung die during the wait.

Those who survive the operation face long odds. Roughly 14 per cent die within 30 days of the operation. About half are alive three years later. Doctors cannot offer recipients a guarantee of longer life, only the possibility of a life of better quality.

SOURCE: *Globe and Mail*, April 28, 1995, p. A1. Reproduced with permission from the *Globe and Mail*.

THE STORY IN BRIEF

Scarcity often causes difficult moral dilemmas. There are not enough human organ donors to satisfy the need for organs. In this story, the issue is whether a person with Down's syndrome should receive one of the "scarce donated lungs."

THE ECONOMICS BEHIND THE STORY

- The number of patients who want a lung transplant is greater than the number of donated lungs.

- A person with Down's syndrome has requested one of the scarce donated lungs. But giving a donated lung to one person necessarily means denying another patient one.
- The "moral" dilemma arises because of scarcity. If there were enough donated lungs to satisfy the demand for them, the "moral" dilemma would be resolved.
- Think of some other examples where "moral dilemmas" could be resolved by having more of any good or service so that painful tradeoffs are avoided. Is there a direct relationship between scarcity and moral dilemmas? ■

The Last Word
△ 4 KEY CONCEPT

WOMEN AND EXPANDED PRODUCTION POSSIBILITIES

A large increase in the number of employed women has shifted the Canadian production possibilities curve outward.

ONE OF THE MORE REMARKABLE CANADIAN trends of the past half-century has been the substantial rise in the number of women working in the paid workforce. Today, nearly 70 percent of women work full- or part-time in paid jobs, compared to only 31 percent in 1965. There are many reasons for this increase.

1. **Rising Wage Rates of Women**   Women have acquired more education and skill training, which have greatly increased their productivity in the workplace. As a result, the wages that women can earn in the labour market have increased rapidly over time. These higher wages have boosted women's

opportunity costs—the forgone wage earnings—of staying at home. In response, women have substituted labour market employment for now more "expensive" home activities. This substitution has been particularly pronounced for married women.

Higher wages for women have produced other reallocations of time and purchasing patterns to facilitate labour market work. Day-care services have partly replaced personal childcare. Restaurant meals, fast food, prepared take-home meals, and pizza delivery now substitute for elaborate home-made family meals. Convenience stores and catalogue sales have proliferated, as have lawn-care and in-home cleaning services. Shorter family vacations by airplane have replaced longer cross-country trips by car. Microwave ovens, dishwashers, automatic washers and dryers, and other household "capital goods" are now commonly used to enhance productivity in the home. These and similar household adjustments have helped make labour force participation more attractive for women.

2. **Expanded Job Accessibility**   Greater accessibility to jobs, as distinct from higher pay, is a second factor boosting the employment of women. Service industries that traditionally have employed mainly women have expanded both absolutely and relatively in the past several decades. A growing demand for teachers, nurses, secretarial workers, salesclerks, and other service jobs has attracted many women to the labour market. Also, population has shifted from farms and rural regions to urban areas, where jobs for women are more abundant and geographically accessible. Finally, the decline in the average length of the workweek, together with an increased availability of part-time jobs, has made it easier for women to combine labour market employment with child-rearing and household activities.

3. **Changing Preferences and Attitudes**   Women as a group have changed their preferences from household activities in favour of labour market employment. An increasing number of women have found personal fulfilment in jobs, careers, and earnings. More broadly, most industrial societies now widely accept and encourage labour force participation by married women, including women with preschool children. Today about 60 percent of Canadian mothers with preschool children participate in the labour force, compared to only 30 percent in 1970. More than half of today's employed mothers return to work before their youngest child is two years old.

4. **Declining Birthrates**   While there were 3.8 lifetime births per woman in 1957 at the peak of the baby boom, that number is less than 2 today. This marked decline in the typical family size has freed up time for greater labour force participation since child rearing and associated homemaking activities are time-consuming. Not only do women now have

fewer children, but these children are also spaced closer together in age. Thus, women who leave their jobs during their children's early years can return to the labour force sooner.

The decline in birthrates has resulted from the widespread availability and use of birth control methods, coupled with changing lifestyles. But higher wage rates have also been at work. Women with relatively high wage earnings, on average, have fewer children than women with lower earnings. The opportunity cost of children—the income sacrificed by not being employed—rises as wage earnings rise. In the language of economics, the higher "price" associated with children has reduced the "quantity of children demanded."

5. **Rising Divorce Rates**   Marital instability, as evidenced by high divorce rates in the 1970s and 1980s, may have motivated many women to establish and maintain labour-market ties. The economic impact of divorce on nonworking women is often disastrous because alimony and child support are not always forthcoming. Most previously nonworking women enter the labour force following divorce. And married women—perhaps even women contemplating marriage—may have increasingly participated in the labour force to protect themselves against the financial difficulties of potential divorce.

6. **Stagnating Male Earnings**   A final factor explaining the rise in women's labour force participation rate is that men's real earnings have risen very slowly in the past two decades, particularly for men without university degrees. This stagnation has motivated many wives to enter the labour force to maintain family living standards. If wives had not entered the labour force in record numbers in the past two decades, many households would have suffered absolute or relative declines in their real incomes.

Together, these factors have produced a rapid rise in the availability of women workers in Canada. This increase in the *quantity of resources* has helped push the Canadian production possibilities curve outward. That is, it has greatly contributed to Canadian economic growth. ■

CHAPTER SUMMARY

1. Economics is grounded on two basic facts: **a** human material wants are virtually unlimited; **b** economic resources are scarce.

2. Economic resources may be classified as property resources—raw materials and capital—or as human resources—labour and entrepreneurial ability. These resources (land, capital, labour, and entrepreneurial ability) are the factors of production.

3. Economics is concerned with the problem of using or managing scarce resources to produce goods and services that fulfil the material wants of society. Both full employment and efficient use of available resources are essential to maximize want satisfaction.

4. Efficient use of resources consists of productive efficiency (producing all output combinations in the least costly way) and allocative efficiency (producing the specific output mix most desired by society).

5. An economy that is achieving full employment and productive efficiency—that is, operating on its production possibilities curve—must sacrifice the output of some types of goods and services to achieve increased production of others. Because resources are not equally productive in all possible uses, shifting resources from one use to another brings the law of increasing opportunity costs into play. The production of additional units of a product entails the sacrifice of *increasing* amounts of the other product.

6. Allocative efficiency means operating at the optimal point on the production possibilities curve. That point represents the highest-valued mix of goods and is determined by expanding the production of each good until its marginal benefit (MB) equals its marginal cost (MC).

7. Over time, technological advance and increases in the quantity and quality of resources allow the economy to produce more of all goods and services—to experience economic growth. Society's choice as to the mix of consumer goods and capital goods in current output is a major determinant of the future location of the production possibilities curve and thus of economic growth.

8. The various economic systems of the world differ in their ideologies and also in their responses to the economizing problem. Basic differences centre on **a** whether most resources are owned by government or held privately and **b** whether economic activity is coordinated mainly by a market system or by central planning.

9. The circular flow model provides an overview of the operation of the market system. This simple model locates the product and resource markets and shows the major income-expenditure flows and resource-output flows that constitute the lifeblood of the market economy.

TERMS AND CONCEPTS

economizing problem

utility

economic resources

land

capital

investment

labour

entrepreneurial ability

factors of production

full employment

full production

productive efficiency

allocative efficiency

consumer goods

capital goods

production possibilities table and curve

opportunity cost

law of increasing opportunity costs

economic growth

economic system

pure capitalism

market systems

command economy

traditional economies

resource market

product market

circular flow model

STUDY QUESTIONS

1. Explain this statement: "If resources were unlimited and freely available, there would be no subject called *economics.*"

2. Comment on the following statement from a newspaper article: "Our junior high school serves a splendid hot meal for $1 without costing the taxpayers anything, thanks in part to a government subsidy."

3. Critically analyze: "Wants aren't insatiable. I can prove it. I get all the coffee I want to drink every morning at breakfast." Explain: "Goods and services are scarce because resources are scarce." Analyze: "It is the nature of all economic problems that absolute solutions are denied to us."

4. What are economic resources? What are the major functions of the entrepreneur?

5. KEY QUESTION *Why is the problem of unemployment part of the subject matter of economics? Distinguish between productive efficiency and allocative efficiency. Give an illustration of achieving productive, but not allocative, efficiency.*

6. KEY QUESTION *Here is a production possibilities table for war goods and civilian goods:*

TYPE OF PRODUCTION	PRODUCTION ALTERNATIVES				
	A	**B**	**C**	**D**	**E**
Automobiles	0	2	4	6	8
Rockets	30	27	21	12	0

   a. *Show these data graphically. Upon what specific assumptions is this production possibilities curve based?*
   b. *If the economy is at point C, what is the cost of one more automobile? One more rocket? Explain how the production possibilities curve reflects the law of increasing opportunity costs.*
   c. *What must the economy do to operate at some point on the production possibilities curve?*

7. What is the opportunity cost of attending college or university?

8. Suppose you arrive at a store expecting to pay $100 for an item but learn that a store two kilometres away is charging $50 for it. Would you drive there and buy it? How does your decision benefit you? What is the opportunity cost of your decision? Now suppose that you arrive at a store expecting to pay $6,000 for an item but learn that it costs $5,950 at the other store. Do you make the same decision as before? Perhaps surprisingly, you should! Explain why.

9. KEY QUESTION *Specify and explain the shapes of the marginal-benefit and marginal-cost curves. How are these curves used to determine the optimal allocation of resources to a particular product? If current output is such that marginal cost exceeds marginal benefit, should more or fewer resources be allocated to this product? Explain.*

10. KEY QUESTION *Label point G inside the production possibilities curve you drew in question 6. What does it indicate? Label point H outside the curve. What does that point represent? What must occur before the economy can attain the level of production shown by point H?*

11. KEY QUESTION *Referring again to question 6, suppose improvement occurs in the technology of producing rockets but not in the production of automobiles. Draw the new production possibilities curve. Now assume that a technological advance occurs in producing automobiles but not in producing rockets. Draw the new production possibilities curve. Now draw a production possibilities curve that reflects technological improvement in the production of both products.*

12. Explain how, if at all, each of the following affects the location of the production possibilities curve:
   a. Standardized examination scores of high school, university and college students decline.
   b. The unemployment rate falls from 9 to 6 percent of the labour force.
   c. Defence spending is reduced to allow government to spend more on health care.
   d. Society decides it wants compact discs rather than long-playing records.
   e. A new technique improves the efficiency of extracting copper from ore.
   f. A new baby boom increases the size of the nation's workforce.

13. Explain: "Affluence tomorrow requires sacrifice today."

14. Suppose that, based on a nation's production possibilities curve, an economy must sacrifice 10,000 pizzas domestically to get the one additional industrial robot it desires but that it can get the robot from another country in exchange for 9,000 pizzas. Relate this information to the following statement: "Through international specialization and trade, a nation can reduce its opportunity cost of obtaining goods and thus 'get outside its production possibilities curve.'"

15. Contrast how pure capitalism and a command economy try to cope with economic scarcity.

16. Explain this statement: "Although Canada has a capitalist economy, not a traditional economy, *traditions* (for example, weddings, Christmas, and Halloween) play an important role in determining what goods are produced."

17. Portray the major features of the circular flow model. In what way are businesses and households both *suppliers* and *demanders* in this model? Explain how scarcity enters the model.

18. **(The Last Word)** Which *two* of the six reasons listed in the Last Word do you think are the *most important* in explaining the rise of women's participation in the workplace? Explain your reasoning.

19. WEB-BASED QUESTION **Different Geographical Areas and Outputs—Japan and Canada** Compared to Japan, Canada has 26 times the geographical area and about 19 percent of its population. Other things equal, Canada should have approximately 19 percent of Japan's output. Visit the Web site of the OECD (Organization for Economic Cooperation and Development) www.oecd.org/std/gdp.htm and calculate the ratio of Canada's gross domestic product (a measure of national output) to the gross domestic product of Japan. Is the ratio above or below 19 percent? What might explain this difference?

20. WEB-BASED QUESTION **Increasing Productivity in Hong Kong** The Hong Kong Productivity Council hkpcms.hkpc.org/ was established in 1967 to promote increased productivity. Its mission is "to achieve a more effective utilization of available resources and to enhance the value-added content of products and services. The aim is to increase efficiency and competitiveness, thereby contributing to raising the standard of living of people in Hong Kong." How does the Council define productivity, and how does it try to increase it?

Overview of the Market System

IN THE PAST FEW YEARS THE MEDIA HAVE inundated us with stories of how Russian and other centrally planned economies are trying to alter their systems in the direction of capitalism, otherwise referred to as the market system or market economy. What are the features and institutions of a market system that these nations are trying to emulate?

Our initial task is to describe and explain how a pure market system, or laissez-faire capitalism, functions. Although a pure market system has never existed, a description of such an economy provides a useful approximation of how the economies of Canada and many other industrially advanced nations function. We will modify this approximation in later chapters to correspond more closely to the reality of modern economies.

In examining pure capitalism, we first discuss its basic assumptions and institutions. We then consider certain other institutions common to all advanced-industrial economies. Finally, we explain how a market system coordinates economic activity and contributes to the efficient use of scarce resources.

IN THIS CHAPTER YOU WILL LEARN:

The basic institutions required for a market economy.

•

The benefits of specialization and trade.

•

The Five Fundamental Questions any economy faces.

•

How the "invisible hand" helps to close the gap between private and public interests.

•

About the structure of the Canadian economy.

The
Big Picture

THE SCARCITY PROBLEM IS CONFRONTED BY all societies. Each society must choose a coordinating system that will determine how much of each product is produced, how it will be produced, and how output is divided among its population. This chapter offers an overview of one way to coordinate production and distribution: the market system—sometimes referred to as the capitalist system. A familiarity with the main features of a market system will greatly help you put the materials of this textbook in their proper perspective.

As you read this chapter, keep the following points in mind:

- **Key Concepts 4, 5,** and **6** are discussed.

- A market system does not arise automatically; it needs the proper institutions, such as private property.
- The driving force of the market system is "self-interest," not to be confused with selfishness. In a world of limited resources in relation to wants, competition follows automatically. In competing for the available resources, all participants in a market system—businesses and households—try to do the best they can for themselves.
- The distinguishing characteristics of the market system are **a** autonomous decision making by each participant, and **b** spontaneous coordination of production and consumption. ∎

THE MARKET SYSTEM

Let's begin by examining in some detail the basic tenets that define the market system of capitalism: (1) private property, (2) freedom of enterprise and choice, (3) self-interest as the dominant motive, (4) competition, (5) reliance on self-regulating markets, and (6) a limited role for government.

Private Property

In a pure market system, property resources (land, capital) are usually owned by private individuals and firms, not by government. In fact, the private ownership of capital is what gives capitalism its name. This right of **private property**, coupled with the freedom to negotiate binding legal contracts, allows private persons or businesses to obtain, control, employ, and dispose of property resources as they see fit. The right to bequeath—the right of a property owner to designate who receives his or her property at the time of death—sustains the institution of private property.

Property rights are important because they encourage investment, innovation, exchange, and economic growth. Why would anyone stock a store, construct a factory, or clear land for farming if someone else, including government, could take that property for his or her own benefit?

Property rights also apply to intellectual property via patents and copyrights. These long-term protections encourage people to write books, music, and computer programs and to invent new products and production processes without fear that others will steal them and the rewards they may bring.

Another important role of property rights is that they facilitate exchange. A title to an automobile or deed to a cattle ranch assures the buyer that the seller is the legitimate owner. Finally, with property rights, people can spend their time, energy, and resources producing more goods and services, rather than using them to protect and retain the property they have already produced and acquired.

There are broad legal limits to this right of private ownership. For example, the use of private property to produce illegal drugs is prohibited. And even in pure capitalism, government ownership of certain property resources may be essential to produce "public goods": national defence, basic education, and courtrooms and prisons, for instance.

Freedom of Enterprise and Choice

Closely related to private ownership of property is freedom of enterprise and choice. Capitalism requires that economic units make choices, which are expressed and implemented through the free markets of the economy.

Freedom of enterprise means that private businesses are free to obtain economic resources, to organize those resources in the production of goods and services of the firm's own choosing, and to sell them in the markets of their choice. In pure capitalism no artificial obstacles or restrictions imposed by government or other producers block an entrepreneur's decision to enter or leave a particular industry.

Freedom of choice means that owners can employ or dispose of their property and money as they see fit. It also means that workers are free to enter any lines of work for which they are qualified. Finally, it means that consumers are at liberty, within the limits of their incomes, to buy that collection of goods and services that best satisfies their wants.

Freedom of *consumer* choice in a capitalist economy is perhaps the most profound of these freedoms. The consumer is in a particularly strategic position; in a sense, the consumer is sovereign. Consumers ultimately decide via their choices what the market economy should produce. Businesses and resource suppliers then make their free choices within these constraints. They are not really "free" to produce goods and services consumers do not desire because producing such items would be unprofitable.

Again, all these choices are free only within broad legal limitations. Illegal choices are punished through fines and imprisonment. (The degree of economic freedom varies greatly from nation to nation, as indicated in Global Perspective 3-1.)

Self-Interest

The primary driving force of capitalism is **self-interest**. Each economic unit strives to do what is best for itself. Entrepreneurs aim to maximize their firm's profit or, in adverse circumstances, minimize losses. Property owners attempt to get the highest price for the sale or rent of their resources. Workers attempt to maximize their satisfaction by finding jobs that offer the best combination of wages, fringe benefits, and working conditions. Consumers, in purchasing a specific product, seek to obtain it at the lowest possible price. Consumers also apportion their expenditures to maximize their satisfaction. In brief, capi-

3-1
GLOBAL PERSPECTIVE

Index of economic freedom, selected nations

The Index of Economic Freedom measures economic freedom using 10 broad categories such as trade policy, property rights, and government intervention—with more than 50 specific economic criteria in each category. It then ranks 150 nations as to degree of economic freedom. Below are selected rankings for 1997.

FREE
| 1 Hong Kong |
| 4 New Zealand |
| 5 United States |

MOSTLY FREE
| 11 Japan |
| 15 Canada |
| 20 Germany |

MOSTLY UNFREE
| 78 Colombia |
| 85 Poland |
| 94 Brazil |

REPRESSED
| 133 Haiti |
| 143 Iran |
| 148 Cuba |

Source: Heritage Foundation and *Wall Street Journal.*

talism presumes self-interest as the *modus operandi* for the various economic units as they express their free choices. The motive of self-interest gives direction and consistency to what might otherwise be an extremely chaotic economy.

Pursuit of self-interest should not be confused with selfishness. A stockholder may invest to receive the best available corporate dividends but then donate much of it to the United Way or give it to grandchildren. A worker may take a second job to help pay college or university tuition for her or his children. An entrepreneur may make a fortune and donate much of it to a charitable foundation.

Competition

Freedom of choice exercised in promotion of one's own monetary returns is the basis for competition. In its pure form, **competition** requires:

1. Large numbers of independently acting buyers and sellers operating in the market for any particular product or resource.
2. Freedom of buyers and sellers to enter or leave any particular market, based on their economic self-interest.

Large Numbers The essence of competition is the widespread diffusion of economic power within the two major aggregates—businesses and households—that make up the economy. When many buyers and many sellers are in a particular market, no one buyer or seller is able to demand or supply a quantity of the product sufficiently large to affect its price. Let's examine this statement in terms of the supply side of the product market.

When a product becomes unusually scarce, its price rises. An unseasonable frost in Florida may seriously reduce the supply of citrus crops and sharply increase the price of oranges. Similarly, if a single producer or a small group of producers acting together can somehow restrict the total output of a product, then it can raise the price to the seller's advantage. By controlling supply, a firm can "rig the market" on its own behalf. In its purest form, competition means there are so many independently acting firms that each has virtually no influence over the market supply or, therefore, over price *because it is contributing an almost negligible fraction of the total output.*

Suppose there are 10,000 farmers, each producing and selling 100 bushels of corn in the Winnipeg grain market when the price of corn is $4 per bushel. Could a single farmer who is dissatisfied with that price cause an artificial scarcity of corn to boost the price above $4? The answer is no. Even if Farmer Jones withheld his output completely, he would reduce the total amount supplied only from 1,000,000 to 999,900 bushels. This is not much of a shortage! Supply would be virtually unchanged, and the $4 price would persist.

Competition means that each seller is providing a minuscule amount of the market supply. Individual sellers can make no noticeable impact on total output; thus a seller cannot as an individual producer manipulate product price, which is why economists say that an individual competitive seller is "at the mercy of the market."

The same reasoning applies to the demand side of the market. Buyers are plentiful and act independently. Thus single buyers cannot manipulate the market to their advantage by refusing to buy at the market price.

The widespread diffusion of economic power underlying competition controls the use and limits the potential abuse of that power. A producer charging more than the equilibrium price will lose sales to other producers. An employer paying less than the equilibrium wage rate will lose workers to other employers. Competition is the basic regulatory force in a market economy.

Easy Entry and Exit Competition also implies that it is simple for producers to enter or leave an industry; there are no artificial barriers to the expansion or contraction of specific industries. This freedom of an industry to expand or contract provides a competitive economy with the flexibility needed to remain efficient over time. Freedom of entry and exit allows the economy to adjust to changes in consumer tastes, technology, and resource availability.

Markets and Prices

The basic coordinating mechanism of a capitalist economy is the market system. Without a market economy, there is no capitalism. Decisions made by buyers and sellers of products and resources become effective through a system of markets. A market is a mechanism or arrangement that brings buyers (demanders) and sellers (suppliers) into contact with one another. The preferences of sellers and buyers are registered on the supply and demand sides of various markets, and the outcome of these choices is a set of product and resource prices. These prices are guideposts on which resource owners, entrepreneurs, and consumers make and revise their free choices as they pursue their self-interests.

Just as competition is the controlling mechanism, so a system of markets and prices is the basic organizing force. The market system is an elaborate communication system through which innumerable individual free choices are recorded, summarized, and balanced against one another. Those who obey the dictates of the market system are rewarded; those who ignore them are penalized by the system. Through this communication system, society decides what the economy should produce, how production can be efficiently organized, and how the fruits of productive effort are distributed among the individual economic units that make up capitalism.

Not only is the market system the mechanism through which society decides how it allocates its resources and distributes the resulting output, but it is through the market system that these decisions are carried out.

Limited Government

A competitive market economy promotes a high degree of efficiency in the use of its resources. There is little need for governmental intervention in the operation of such an economy beyond its role of imposing broad legal limits on the exercise of individual choices and the use of private property. The concept of pure capitalism as a self-regulating and self-adjusting economy precludes any extensive economic role for government. However, as you will find in Chapter 5, a number of limitations and potentially undesirable outcomes associated with the market system have resulted in active government participation in the economy.

3-1
QUICK REVIEW

- Pure capitalism rests on the private ownership of property and freedom of enterprise and choice.
- Pure capitalism permits economic entities—businesses, resource suppliers, and consumers—to pursue and further their own self-interests. Competition prevents any single economic entity from dictating product or resource prices.
- The coordinating mechanism of capitalism is a system of markets and prices.
- The efficient operation of the pure market system allegedly makes significant government intervention unnecessary.

OTHER CHARACTERISTICS

Private property, freedom of enterprise and choice, self-interest as a motivating force, competition, and reliance on a market system are more or less exclusively associated with a pure market system.

But there are certain institutions and practices that are characteristic of all modern economies, including those with much central command: (1) the use of advanced technology and large amounts of capital goods, (2) specialization, and (3) the use of money. Advanced technology and specialization are prerequisites to efficient employment of an economy's resources. The use of money helps society specialize and use advanced technology.

Extensive Use of Technology and Capital Goods

All advanced industrial economies are based on state-of-the-art technology and the extensive use of capital goods. In a market economy the opportunity and motivation for technological advance are created by competition, freedom of choice, self-interest, and the fact that monetary rewards for new products or production techniques accrue directly to the innovator. Pure capitalism therefore encourages extensive use and rapid development of complex capital goods: tools, machinery, large-scale factories, and facilities for storage, communication, transportation, and marketing. In the command economy, in contrast, the motivation for technological advance is weak; it must come through the directive of the central plan.

Why are advanced technology and capital goods important? Because the most direct method of producing a product is usually the least efficient. The inefficiencies of direct production can be avoided through **roundabout production**—the construction and use of capital to aid in the production of consumer goods. It would be ridiculous for a farmer to go at production with bare hands. There are huge benefits in the form of more efficient production and, therefore, a more abundant output, from creating tools of production (capital equipment) and using them in the production process. The farmer's output will increase with the use of a plough, a tractor, storage bins, and so on. There is a better way for the farmer to get water out of a well than to dive in after it!

But there is a hitch. Recall the main message of the production possibilities curve: For an economy operating on its production possibilities curve, resources used to produce capital goods must be diverted from the production of consumer goods. Society must sacrifice some consumer goods today to produce the capital goods that will give it more consumer goods tomorrow. Greater abundance tomorrow requires sacrifices today. *(Key Question 2)*

Specialization

The extent to which society relies on **specialization** is astounding. The majority of consumers produce virtually none of the goods and services they consume, and they consume little or nothing of what they produce. The worker who spends most of a lifetime machining parts for marine engines may never "consume" an ocean cruise. The worker who devotes eight hours a day to installing windows in Fords may own a Honda. Few households seriously consider producing their own food, shelter, and clothing. Many farmers sell their milk to the local dairy and then buy margarine at the local general store. Society learned long ago that self-sufficiency breeds inefficiency. The jack-of-all-trades may be a very colourful individual but is certainly not efficient.

Division of Labour

In what ways does human specialization—called the **division of labour**—enhance a society's output?

1. **MAKES USE OF ABILITY DIFFERENCES** Specialization enables individuals to take advantage of existing differences in their abilities and skills. If caveman A is strong, swift, and accurate with a spear, and caveman B is weak and slow but patient, their distribution of talents can be most efficiently used if A hunts and B fishes.

2. **ALLOWS LEARNING BY DOING** Even if the abilities of A and B are identical, specialization may be advantageous. By devoting all your time to a single task, you are more likely to develop the appropriate skills and to discover improved techniques than by apportioning your time among a number of diverse tasks. You learn to be a good hunter by hunting!

3. **SAVES TIME** Specialization—devoting all one's time to, say, a single task—avoids the loss of time involved in shifting from one job to another.

   For all these reasons the division of labour results in greater total output from society's limited human resources.

Geographic Specialization

Specialization also works on a regional and international basis. Apples could be grown in Saskatchewan, but because of the unsuitability of the land, rainfall, and temperature, the costs would be very high. British Columbia could achieve some success in the production of wheat, but for similar reasons such production would be costly. That's why the farmers of Saskatchewan produce those products—wheat in particular—for which their resources are best adapted, and British Columbians (in the Okanagan valley) produce apples. In specializing, both produce more than is needed locally. Then, very sensibly, they swap some of their surpluses—wheat for apples. Specialization thus enables each area to make the goods it can most efficiently produce and it permits both to enjoy a larger amount of all goods than would otherwise be available.

Similarly, on an international basis Canada specializes in such items as telecommunication equipment and small commercial aircraft that it sells abroad in exchange for video recorders from Japan, bananas from Honduras, and woven baskets from Thailand. Both human specialization and geographical specialization are essential in achieving efficiency in the use of resources.

Use of Money

Virtually all economies, advanced or primitive, use money. Money performs several functions, but first and foremost it is a **medium of exchange**; it makes trade easier.

In our example, Saskatchewan must exchange wheat for British Columbia's apples if both provinces are to share in the benefits of specialization. If trade were highly inconvenient or prohibited for some reason, the gains from their specialization would be lost. Saskatchewan and British Columbia would then be forced to be more self-sufficient—to produce both wheat and apples and whatever else their consumers desire. *A convenient means of exchanging goods is a prerequisite of specialization.*

Exchange can, and sometimes does, occur on the basis of **barter**, that is, swapping goods for goods, say, wheat for apples. But barter can pose serious problems for the economy because it requires a *coincidence of wants* between the two transactors. In our example, we assumed that Saskatchewan had excess wheat to trade and wanted apples. And we assumed British Columbia had excess apples to swap and wanted wheat. So exchange occurred. But if this coincidence of wants does not exist, trade is stymied.

Suppose Saskatchewan does not want any of B.C.'s apples but is interested in buying potatoes from Prince Edward Island. Ironically, Prince Edward Island wants B.C.'s apples but not Saskatchewan's wheat. And, to complicate matters, suppose that British Columbia wants some of Saskatchewan's wheat but none of Prince Edward Island's potatoes. The situation is summarized in Figure 3-1.

In no case do we find a coincidence of wants. Trade by barter clearly would be difficult. To overcome such a stalemate, economies use **money**, which is simply a convenient social invention to facilitate exchanges of goods and services. Historically, cattle, cigarettes, shells, stones, pieces of metal, and many other commodities have been used, with varying degrees of success, as a medium for facilitating exchange. But to be money, an item needs to pass only one test: *It must be generally acceptable to sellers in exchange for goods and services.* Money is socially defined; whatever society accepts as a medium of exchange *is* money.

Most economies use pieces of paper as money. This is true with the Saskatchewan–B.C.–P.E.I. economy; they use dollars as money. The use of dollars as a medium of exchange allows them to overcome their trade stalemate, as demonstrated in Figure 3-1.

Specifically:

1. British Columbia exchanges money for some of Saskatchewan's wheat.
2. Saskatchewan exchanges the money earned from the sale of wheat for some of Prince Edward Island's potatoes.
3. Prince Edward Island then exchanges the money received from the sale of potatoes for some of B.C.'s surplus apples.

The willingness to accept paper money (or any other kind of money) as a medium of exchange has permitted a three-way trade that allows each province to specialize in one product and obtain the other product(s) its residents desire, despite the absence of a coincidence of wants between any two of the parties. Barter, resting as it does on a coincidence of wants, would not have permitted this exchange and so would not have allowed the three provinces to specialize. The efficiencies of specialization would then have been lost to those provinces.

On a global basis the fact that different nations have different currencies complicates international specialization and exchange. However, foreign exchange markets permit Canadians, Japan-

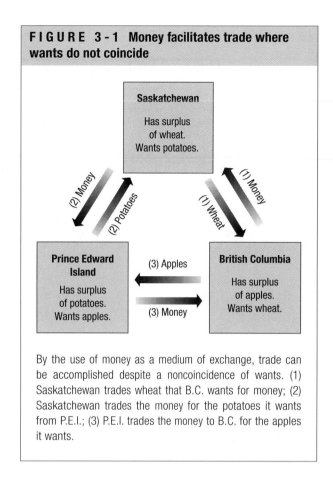

FIGURE 3-1 Money facilitates trade where wants do not coincide

By the use of money as a medium of exchange, trade can be accomplished despite a noncoincidence of wants. (1) Saskatchewan trades wheat that B.C. wants for money; (2) Saskatchewan trades the money for the potatoes it wants from P.E.I.; (3) P.E.I. trades the money to B.C. for the apples it wants.

ese, Germans, Britons, and Mexicans to exchange dollars, yen, marks, pounds, and pesos for one another to complete international exchanges of goods and services.

A final example: Imagine an Oshawa, Ontario, labourer producing crankshafts for Oldsmobiles. At the end of the week, instead of receiving a piece of paper endorsed by the company comptroller, or a few pieces of the paper we widely accept as money, the worker receives from the company paymaster four Oldsmobile crankshafts. With no desire to hoard crankshafts, the worker ventures into the Oshawa business district to spend this income on a bag of groceries, a pair of jeans, and a movie. Obviously, the worker is faced with some inconvenient and time-consuming trading, and may not be able to negotiate any exchanges at all. Finding a clothier with jeans who happens to be in the market for an Oldsmobile crankshaft can be a formidable task. And if the jeans do not trade evenly for crankshafts, how do the transactors "make change"? It is fair to say that money is one of the great social inventions of civilization.

3-2
QUICK REVIEW

- Advanced economies achieve greater efficiency in production through the use of large quantities of technologically advanced capital goods.

- Specialization enhances efficiency by allowing individuals, regions, and nations to produce those goods and services for which their resources are best suited.

- The use of money facilitates the exchange of goods and services, which specialization requires.

THE COMPETITIVE MARKET SYSTEM

There are two primary *decision makers* in a market economy: **households** (consumers) and **firms** (businesses). Households are the ultimate suppliers of all economic resources and simultaneously the major spending group in the economy. Firms provide goods and services to the economy.

Consumers are at liberty to buy what they choose; firms to produce and sell what they choose; and resource suppliers to make their resources available in whatever endeavours or occupations they choose. We may wonder why such an economy does not collapse in chaos. If consumers want breakfast cereal, businesses choose to produce aerobic shoes, and resource suppliers want to offer their services in manufacturing computer software, production would be deadlocked because of the apparent inconsistency of these free choices.

In reality, the millions of decisions made by households and firms are highly consistent. Firms *do* produce those particular goods and services that consumers want. Households *do* provide the kinds of labour that businesses want to hire. What we want to explain is how a competitive market system constitutes a coordinating mechanism that overcomes the potential chaos of freedom of enterprise and choice. The competitive market system is a mechanism both for communicating the decisions of consumers, producers, and resource suppliers to one another and for synchronizing those decisions towards consistent production objectives.

THE FIVE FUNDAMENTAL QUESTIONS

To understand the operation of a market economy, we must first recognize that every economy must respond to these **Five Fundamental Questions**:

1. *How much of a society's resources should be used?* What total amount of available resources should be used in producing goods and services?
2. *What is to be produced?* What collection of goods and services will best satisfy society's material wants?
3. *How is that output to be produced?* How should production be organized? What firms should do the producing, and what production techniques should they use?
4. *Who is to receive the output?* How should households share the output of the economy?
5. *Can the system adapt to change?* Can it adjust to changes in consumer wants, resource supplies, and technology?

The Five Fundamental Questions are merely an elaboration of the economic choices underlying Chapter 2's production possibilities curve. These questions would be irrelevant were it not for the economizing problem: scarce resources in a world of unlimited wants.

THE MARKET SYSTEM AT WORK

Chapter 2's circular flow diagram (Figure 2-6) provides the setting for our discussion.

What Is To Be Produced?

With product and resource prices established by competing buyers and sellers in both the product and resource markets, how would a market economy decide the types and quantities of goods to be produced? Since businesses seek profits and want to avoid losses, we can generalize that those goods and services that can be produced at a profit will be produced and those whose production leads to a loss will not. Those industries that are profitable usually expand, those that incur losses usually contract.

Consumers register their preferences on the demand side of the product market; producers and resource suppliers respond appropriately in seeking to further their own self-interests. The market system communicates the wants of consumers to businesses and resource suppliers and elicits appropriate responses.

Organizing Production

How is production to be organized in a market economy? This Fundamental Question is composed of three subquestions:

1. How should resources be allocated among specific industries?
2. What specific firms should do the producing in each industry?
3. What combinations of resources—what technology—should each firm employ?

The market system steers resources to those industries whose products consumers want—simply because those industries survive, are profitable, and pay for resources. It simultaneously deprives unwanted industries of profits and hence of scarce resources.

The second and third subquestions are closely intertwined. In a competitive market economy, the firms that survive to do the producing are the ones willing and able to employ the most economically efficient technique of production. And the most efficient technique depends on:

1. The available technology, that is, the alternative combinations of resources that will produce the desired results
2. The prices of the needed resources.

Distributing Total Output

The market system enters the picture in two ways in solving the problem of distributing total output. Generally, any specific product will be distributed to consumers on the basis of their ability and willingness to pay the existing market price for it. If the price of some product, say, a pocket calculator, is $15, then those buyers who are able and willing to pay that price will get a pocket calculator; those who are not, will not. This is the rationing function of equilibrium prices.

The sizes of consumers' money incomes determines their ability to pay the equilibrium prices for pocket calculators and other products. And consumers' money incomes depend on the quantities of the various property and human resources they supply and on the prices in the resource market. Resource prices are key in determining the size of each household's claim against the total output of society. Within the limits of a consumer's money income, however, it is a person's willingness to pay the equilibrium price for a pocket calculator that determines whether a unit of this product is distributed to her or him. And this willingness to buy the calculator depends on that consumer's preference for it compared with other available products and their relative prices. Thus, product price is not only key in determining how output is distributed, it also is central in determining the spending patterns of consumers.

There is nothing particularly ethical about the market system as a mechanism for distributing output. Households that accumulate large amounts of property resources by inheritance, through hard work and frugality, through business acumen, or by illegal activities will receive large incomes and thus command large shares of the economy's total output. Others, offering unskilled and relatively unproductive labour resources that elicit low wages, will receive meagre money incomes and small portions of total output.

Accommodating Change

Industrial societies are dynamic: Consumer preferences, technology, and supplies of resources all change. This means that the particular allocation of resources that is *now* the most efficient for a *specific* pattern of consumer tastes, for a *specific* range of technological alternatives, and for *specific* supplies of resources will become obsolete and inefficient as consumer preferences change, new techniques of production are discovered, and resource supplies change over time. The market economy adjusts to these changes so that resources are still used efficiently.

COMPETITION AND THE "INVISIBLE HAND"

In capitalism the market system is the organizational mechanism, and competition is the mechanism of control. Supply and demand communicate the wants of consumers (society) to businesses and, through businesses, to resource suppliers. It is competition, however, that forces businesses and resource suppliers to make appropriate responses.

But competition does more than guarantee responses appropriate to the wishes of society. It also forces firms to adopt the most efficient production techniques, keeping costs and prices at their lowest levels. In a competitive market, more efficient firms will eventually eliminate a firm that fails to use the least-costly production technique. And competition provides an environment conducive to such technological advance.

In 1776 Adam Smith, in his book *The Wealth of Nations*, first noted that the operation of a competitive market system creates a curious and important unity between private and social interests. Firms and resource suppliers, seeking to further their own self-interests and operating within the framework of a highly competitive market system, will simultaneously, as though guided by an **invisible hand**, promote the public or social interest. For example, we have seen that in a competitive environment, businesses use the least-costly combination of resources to produce a specific output because it is in their private self-interests to do so. To act otherwise would be to forgo profit or even to risk business failure. But, at the same time, it is clearly also in the social interest to use scarce resources in the least-costly (most efficient) way.

It is self-interest, awakened and guided by the competitive market system, that induces responses appropriate to the change in society's wants. Businesses seeking to make higher profits and to avoid losses, and resource suppliers pursuing greater monetary awards, negotiate changes in the allocation of resources and end up with the output that society demands. The force of competition controls or guides self-interest in such a way that it automatically, and quite unintentionally, furthers the best interests of society. The "invisible hand" tells us that when firms maximize their profits, society's domestic output is also maximized.

The virtues of the market system are thus implicit in our discussion. Three merit emphasis:

1. **EFFICIENCY** The basic economic argument for the market system is that it promotes the efficient use of resources. The competitive market system guides resources into the production of those goods and services most wanted by society. It forces the use of the most efficient techniques in organizing resources for production, and it leads to the development and adoption of new and more efficient production techniques.

2. **INCENTIVES** The market system provides incentives for improvement and innovation. Greater work effort means higher money incomes that can be translated into a higher standard of living. Similarly, the assuming of risks by entrepreneurs can result in substantial profit incomes. Successful innovations may also generate economic rewards.

3. **FREEDOM** The major noneconomic argument for the market system is its great emphasis on personal freedom. In contrast to central planning, the market system can coordinate economic activity without coercion. The market system permits—indeed, it thrives on—freedom of enterprise and choice. Entrepreneurs and workers are not herded from industry to industry by government directives to meet production targets established by some governmental agency. On the contrary, they are free to further their own self-interest, subject to the rewards and penalties imposed by the market system itself. *(Key Question 9)*

3-3
QUICK REVIEW

- The output mix of the market system is determined by profits, which in turn depend heavily on consumer preferences. Profits cause preferred, efficient industries to expand; losses cause inefficient industries to contract.

- Competition forces industries to use the least-costly (most efficient) production methods.

- Consumer incomes and product prices determine the distribution of output among households in a market economy.

- Competitive markets reallocate resources in response to changes in consumer tastes, technological advances, and changes in supplies of resources.

- The "invisible hand" of the market system channels the pursuit of self-interest to the good of society.

THE STRUCTURE OF THE CANADIAN ECONOMY AND ITS EVOLUTION OVER TIME

Table 3-1 sets out the contribution to Canadian domestic output (GDP) by each sector and industry. The major sectors of any economy are **primary,**

TABLE 3-1 Production shares by sector, selected years 1870-1997

	% OF GROSS DOMESTIC PRODUCT AT FACTOR COST							
	1870	**1911**	**1926**	**1960**	**1970**	**1980**	**1986**	**1997**
PRIMARY	46.2	39.4	23.4	10.4	8.3	11.2	10.0	7.4
Agriculture	34.3	30.8	18.1	4.9	3.3	3.3	3.3	1.8
Forestry*	9.9	4.6	1.3	1.3	0.8	0.9	0.7	1.5
Fishing and trapping	1.1	1.5	0.8	0.2	0.2	0.2	0.2	0.1
Mining, quarrying, oil wells	0.9	2.5	3.2	4.0	4.0	6.8	5.8	4.0
SECONDARY	22.6	29.7	38.7	44.8	41.4	38.3	36.7	34.0
Manufacturing	na	18.8	21.7	26.4	23.3	20.6	19.5	17.2
Construction	na	10.3	4.1	6.0	6.3	5.9	7.0	5.4
Transportation and communication	na	na	12.9	9.6	8.9	8.3	7.3	7.7
Electric power, gas, and water utilities	na	0.6		2.8	2.9	3.5	2.9	3.7
TERTIARY	31.2[a]	30.8[a]	37.9	44.8	50.2	50.5	53.3	58.6
Trade (wholesale, retail)	na	na	11.6	12.8	12.4	11.0	11.7	11.2
Finance, insurance, real estate	na	na	10.0	11.6	11.3	11.3	14.1	16.1
Public administration, defence	na	na	3.4	6.9	7.3	7.4	7.2	6.2
Service	na	na	12.9	13.5	19.2	20.8	20.3	25.1
Total	100.0	100.0	100.0	100.0	100.0	100.0	100.0	100.0

[a] Includes income generated by the railway and telephone industries.
* Figure for Forestry calculated as a residual.
Source: Data for 1870 to 1986 from C. Green, *Canadian Industrial Organization and Policy* (Toronto: McGraw-Hill Ryerson Ltd., 1990), p. 4. Data for 1997 calculated from Statistics Canada, *Canadian Economic Observer*, Statistical Summary, July 1998.

secondary, and **tertiary** (which is more commonly referred to as the service sector). Table 3-1 also breaks each sector into sub-sectors or industries.

The service sector has come to dominate in terms of its contributing share to Canadian domestic output, followed by the secondary sector, in which manufacturing dominates. The primary sector has experienced an almost continuous decline in GDP share over the last century.

Table 3-2, which shows employment shares by each sector and industry, reflects contribution to domestic output. For example, agriculture's employment share fell from about a quarter of the workforce in 1947 to just over 3 percent in 1997. Manufacturing has also experienced a decline in employment share, but a much less steep decline. The service sector, on the other hand, has almost doubled its employment share of the economy.

We noted earlier in this chapter that industries expand and contract on their profitability. The inter-sectoral shifts are due to a number of factors, of which technological improvements and accompanying productivity increases are dominant. For example, while there has been a continuous decline in agriculture's employment share, it has come about because of large labour (and land) productivity improvements. A large improvement in labour productivity means fewer people are needed in that sector, unless there is an accompanying increase in the demand for foodstuffs. Since there is a limit to our capacity to increase our food intake, the excess labour had to find work elsewhere. Throughout the nineteenth and early twentieth centuries, excess agricultural workers found jobs in the secondary sector, primarily in manufacturing.

Since World War II, the secondary sector has been losing employment share as productivity in that sector rose. Manufacturing in particular has seen a significant drop in its employment share.

T A B L E   3 - 2   Employment shares (%) by economic sector and industry

	1891[a]	1921[a]	1947	1960	1970	1980	1987	1997
PRIMARY	49	36	27.5	14.3	9.3	7.3	6.4	6.5
Agriculture			24.1	11.3	6.5	4.5	4.0	3.1
Forestry			1.2	1.1	0.9	0.7	0.6 ⎫	
Fishing and trapping			0.7	0.4	0.3	0.3	0.3 ⎬	2.1
Mining, quarrying, oil wells			1.5	1.5	1.6	1.8	1.5	1.3
SECONDARY	31	34	40.3	40.7	37.5	34.0	30.4	29.1
Manufacturing			26.7	24.9	22.7	19.7	17.1	16.0
Construction			5.2	7.2	6.0	5.8	5.7	5.5
Transportation and communication			7.7	7.5	7.7	7.3	6.6 ⎫	
Public utilities			0.7	1.1	1.1	1.2	1.0 ⎬	7.6
TERTIARY	20	30	32.1	45.0	53.2	58.7	63.2	64.4
Trade (wholesale, retail)			12.3	16.2	16.7	17.2	17.7	17.6
Finance, insurance, real estate			2.7	3.8	4.6	5.7	5.8	5.9
Community, business, personal services (including health, education)			} 17.1 {	} 25.0	25.7	28.9	32.9	35.1
Public administration					6.2	6.9	6.8	5.8
Total	100.0	100.0	100.0	100.0	100.0	100.0	100.0	100.0

[a] Based on occupational data in which all clerical workers are allocated to the tertiary sector and all nonprimary sector labourers are allocated to the secondary sector.
Source: Data for 1891 to 1987 from C. Green, *op. cit.* (Toronto: McGraw-Hill Ryerson Ltd., 1990), p. 6. Data for 1997 calculated from Statistics Canada, *Canadian Economic Observer*, Statistical Summary, July 1998.

Table 3-1 shows manufacturing's GDP share dropped from a high of 26 percent in 1960, to just over 17 percent by 1997. Table 3-2 shows the employment share of manufacturing has fallen steadily since 1945 from over a quarter of the Canadian labour force to 16 percent in the late 1990s.

While it is true that natural resources are important to Canada's economy, the output and employment share of the primary sector continues to fall. Only the mining, quarrying, and oil wells category has maintained a relatively steady employment share, but a decreasing GDP share.

There is good evidence to suggest that some Canadian industries are highly concentrated in their market power. More will be said about this topic in Chapter 14. For now it will suffice to say that compared with the U.S. economy, many of our industries are dominated by a few firms that control a significant percentage of the market.

Foreign Ownership

Another distinguishing characteristic of the Canadian economy is that a high percentage is **foreign owned**, particularly by Americans. The term "foreign owned" generally means outright ownership of a firm or at least owning 51 percent of the stocks, which means control of a firm.

Foreign ownership has costs and benefits. These have been extensively debated. Given the difficulties of measuring costs and benefits, it is not surprising that the issue of foreign ownership often arouses strong emotions. Perhaps the most serious accusation against foreign ownership is that it jeopardizes Canada's political autonomy. However, such an accusation is difficult to prove or disprove.

There are various explanations of the high incidence of foreign direct investment in Canada. Some attribute it to the relatively high Canadian tariffs instituted with the implementation of the National Policy in 1879. Since foreign firms, particularly American firms, couldn't compete by exporting here, they established production facilities. Our patent laws in the past, which allowed no protection to their foreign owner, also helped to stimulate foreign ownership as firms not wanting to have their technologies imitated quickly established themselves in Canada. Our country's proximity to the United States also has stimulated foreign ownership, as American firms often viewed Canada as an extension of their domestic market.

All these explanations have some merit. However, all that can be said with certainty is that if foreign firms decided to establish productive capacities in Canada, it must have been because it was the most profitable alternative.

In The Media

4 KEY CONCEPT

Rush for riches in Temagami

Prospectors raced across wild terrain yesterday, hoping for a toehold on mineral wealth as they staked claims in a vast region of northeastern Ontario

By Patrick Brethour
The Globe and Mail
Shining Tree, Ont.

It was a race for gold—or copper, or zinc or diamonds—Christmas and the Olympics rolled into 15 adrenalin-packed minutes.

Except that these sprints were run across slippery forest floors, through bogs and across lakes. And many of the racers carried axes, using them to notch trees and mark the line of their claims.

One of them, red-faced and wheezing, scrambled south through the bush toward Mitch Lavery—who greeted him with a grin.

The axe-carrying runner had just secured a mining claim for Strike Minerals Inc., which came out of yesterday's giant staking rush in the Temagami region of northeastern Ontario with 50 prime sites.

The rush may have been the province's largest ever, but the total number of claims staked won't be known for about a month. Earlier estimates put the number of prospectors at 600, and Strike Minerals alone spent $100,000 on its staking effort for the day.

However big it is, the rush is mining history in the making, said Mr. Lavery, vice-president of the Kirkland Lake, Ont., company. "This is a very unique situation that we won't ever likely see again."

Strike Minerals' red-faced runner was just one of the hundreds who swarmed over the vast tract that was opened up for staking after a 23-year land freeze.

Ontario's Progressive Conservative government, aiming to bring more economic development to the rural region, decided in June to allow mining and expanded logging.

The decision has elicited controversy as the area is also famed for its old-growth pines. Environmental groups did not disrupt the staking rush, but several people were arrested this week in protests against logging.

Still, environmentalists will target mining companies if large-scale exploration or exploitation occur, said Tim Gray, executive director of the Toronto-based Wildlands League. "We'll be there to make sure [big-scale mining is] not a good investment or a good business decision," he said on Sunday after an information session for prospectors in the town of Temagami before the rush.

The 617,500 hectares in 103 townships is the largest area in Ontario ever made available at one time for staking.

Mr. Lavery said he hopes Strike Minerals' sites—in Tyrell and Knight townships, about 120 kilometres northwest of Temagami—contain gold deposits that the junior gold explorer can exploit with the help of larger mining outfits.

For the prospectors—some working for themselves, some for industry giants—the rush is the chance of a lifetime. "There's no 10 per cent or anything else," Mr. Lavery said. "It's all or nothing."

The race for riches began yesterday at 9 a.m. Fifteen minutes later, winners were celebrating.

In between, the prospectors, including high-school track runners hired by the mining companies, raced around the 1.6-kilometre perimeter of each claim. One runner said he was being paid $100 a day and expenses plus a $100 bonus for each claim successfully staked.

To stake a claim, runners had to erect posts at the four corners of the claim, starting at the northeast and proceeding counterclockwise. Along the way, slipping across forest floors and through bogs, they had to mark trees with axes and inscribe the stakes to identify the claim.

As helicopters buzzed overhead just before the start, 18-year-old Derek Didyk braced himself for his run around a claim just off of Highway 560, in the northwestern tip of the staking area.

The terrain "is worse than I've ever seen it," Mr. Didyk said. He runs the 1,500-metre track event at his high school near Timmins, Ont.

Asked about the writing scrawled on his forearm and shirt, he explained that it was the information he would need to mark the posts of the claim. "You get the adrenalin pumping and you don't want to forget," he said.

At 9 a.m., he erected the first corner post and then ran off to the south, trailed by a second man who helped to notch trees.

Three minutes later, the red-faced runner from the claim to the north puffed his way to the corner post.

At 9:14, Mr. Didyk was back, muddy, huffing and jubilant, along with Mr. Lavery and the rest of the Strike Minerals prospectors.

Unexpectedly for the Strike Minerals crew, there was no competition for the four adjacent claims.

A few kilometres south, other Strike Minerals prospectors beat out teams from larger mining outfits for several hotly contested spots, pushing the company's total claims for the day to 50.

Sitting the night before in the crowded Lakeview Motel & Restaurant in Gowganda, a hamlet about 100 kilometres northwest of Temagami, Mr. Lavery explained the appeal of staking, which has changed little in the last 100 years.

"It is the last way the little guy can get a toehold onto the exploration business," he said, speaking over loud country music and louder strings of expletives. "It doesn't matter if you're big or small, everyone's on the same level playing field."

For Monday night at least, the more than 150 prospectors gathered at the Lakeview motel were anything but competitive as they recounted takes of past rushes —and the fervent hope that the Temagami one would be the richest.

Motel owners Erich and Inge Knies struck rich days before the rush. The couple, who have operated the Lakeview for 18 years, said they've never had a busier day than Monday.

They normally have room for 80 guests, and temporary quarters had to be set up in an elementary school.

Source: Globe and Mail, September 18, 1996, p. B5. Reprinted with permission from the *Globe and Mail*.

THE STORY IN BRIEF

Ontario's government decided to allow mining and expanded logging in rural regions after a 23-year freeze. Many prospectors rushed to the Temagami area to try to stake claims.

THE ECONOMICS BEHIND THE STORY

- Self-regulating markets work on the basis of self-interest. But by pursuing one's own individual self-interest, one is also serving the interest of society.

- Prospectors rushed out to stake their claim in the hope of "striking it rich." But such claims would be worthless unless there are people who want the commodities. Thus by an "invisible hand" the prospectors are serving the needs of society.

- While markets bring the interests of the individual and society closer to each other, it does not bring together the interests of the individual and every other individual of which society is composed. Environmental groups protested the development of the region.

- What drives markets? Explain in terms of producers and consumers. ■

The
Last Word

6 KEY CONCEPT

THE MAGIC OF THE MARKET

MOST PEOPLE FIND IT HARD TO BELIEVE THAT self-regulating markets provide most of the goods and services we purchase every day. Our minds seem to be wired to believe that some authority is coordinating output and consumption. In a market economy, consumers are not forced to buy any particular product or service. Certainly, most producers are not told by anyone what to produce and in what quantities. By an "invisible hand" producers of goods and services come up with what consumers want.

Markets coordinate the decisions of consumer and producers. The signals used are prices. Consumers are constantly looking for lower prices, while producers hope for higher prices to add to their profit. Through the decisions of many buyers and sellers, a "market price" is arrived at. Some prices, such as those of stocks, can change every minute, while others, such as housing prices, change a lot less often.

One of the amazing attributes of the market is that it brings closer together the interest of the individual and the interest of other members of a society. The baker may bake bread to sell at a profit, but in doing so she is providing fellow citizens with bread that would not otherwise have been made available.

Prices transmit information about relative scarcities. If the price of wheat flour skyrockets, the baker will likely use less of it and more of a less costly flour. Consumers respond to higher prices of wheat flour by buying less wheat bread, and more of a less expensive bread, say rye.

The market system facilitates specialization and trade. Each person can specialize in producing a good and service and exchange some of it for other goods and service he or she needs. You may have a job selling popcorn at the local movie theatre. You then use your earnings to exchange for other goods and services, say a CD or music lessons. In a mature market economy, we often exchange with persons we do not know. You may travel to another country and rent a car from a complete stranger, except that the person happens to work for one of the large international car rental companies.

While it can appear a very complex system, the market is simply an institution through which individuals exchange the things each produces in return for goods and services that are desired. The complexity arises because there are billions of people engaged in exchange, each individual representing an extremely small part of the whole market system.

Not everyone finds the market a "magical" institution. Self-regulating markets can bring about an "unfair" distribution of income. Critics argue that one individual may become fabulously rich, such as Bill Gates of Microsoft, while others beg on street corners. Defenders of the market system point out that in the western industrialized nations where self-regulating markets dominate, most individuals are neither fabulously rich nor dirt poor, and the average person is materially much better off than citizens in countries with alternative economic systems.

Market economies need a central government to provide the institutional background for self-regulating markets to function efficiently. In the next chapter we will see that self-regulating markets do not work where collective decisions have to be made about providing certain goods and services, such as roads and airports, that no private company would find profitable to produce. ∎

CHAPTER SUMMARY

1. The capitalist, or market, system is characterized by private ownership of resources, including capital, and the freedom of individuals to engage in economic activities of their choice to advance their own material well-being. Self-interest is the driving force of such an economy, and competition functions as a regulatory or control mechanism.

2. In the capitalist system, markets and prices organize and make effective the many millions of individual decisions that determine what is produced, the methods of production, and the sharing of output. The pure market system assumes government plays a minor and relatively passive economic role.

3. Specialization and an advanced technology based on the extensive use of capital goods are common to all advanced industrial economies.

4. Functioning as a medium of exchange, money circumvents problems of bartering and thus permits easy trade and greater specialization, both domestically and internationally.

5. Every economy faces Five Fundamental Questions: **a** How much of available resources should be employed to produce goods? **b** What goods and services are to be produced? **c** How should they be produced? **d** To whom should the output be distributed? **e** Can the system adapt to changes in consumer tastes, resource supplies, and technology?

6. Consumer sovereignty means that both businesses and resource suppliers channel their efforts in accordance with the wants of consumers.

7. The competitive market system can communicate changes in consumer tastes to resource suppliers and entrepreneurs, prompting appropriate adjustments in the allocation of the economy's resources. The competitive market system also provides an environment conducive to technological advance and capital accumulation.

8. Competition, the primary mechanism of control in the market economy, promotes a unity of private and social interests; as though directed by an "invisible hand," competition harnesses the self-interest motives of businesses and resource suppliers to simultaneously further the social interest in using scarce resources efficiently.

9. In terms of both employment share and contribution to domestic production, the service sector dominates in the Canadian economy.

10. Compared to the U.S. economy, many of our industries are highly concentrated; a relatively few firms represent a high percentage of output and sales. A high proportion of our industries are foreign owned.

TERMS AND CONCEPTS

private property	barter
freedom of enterprise	money
freedom of choice	households
self-interest	firms
competition	Five Fundamental Questions
roundabout production	invisible hand
specialization	primary, secondary, tertiary sectors
division of labour	foreign owned
medium of exchange	

STUDY QUESTIONS

1. Explain each of these statements:
   a. "Capitalism not only *accepts* self-interest as a fact of human existence; it *relies* on self-interest to achieve society's material goals."
   b. "Where there is private property, property rights, and economic freedom, there will be capitalism; unlike the command economy, capitalism emerges spontaneously."

2. **KEY QUESTION** *What advantages result from "roundabout" production? What problem is involved in increasing a full-employment economy's stock of capital goods? Illustrate this problem using the production possibilities curve. Does an economy with unemployed resources face the same problem?*

3. What are the advantages of specialization in the use of human and material resources? Explain: "Exchange is the necessary consequence of specialization."

4. What problems does barter entail? Indicate the economic significance of money as a medium of exchange. "Money is the only commodity that is good for nothing but to be gotten rid of. It will not feed you, clothe you, shelter you, or amuse you unless you spend or invest it. It imparts value only in parting." Explain this statement.

5. Briefly describe how the market system answers the Fundamental Questions. Why must economic choices be made?

6. Evaluate and explain the following statements:
   a. "The market system is a profit and loss economy."
   b. "Competition is the indispensable disciplinarian of the market economy."
   c. "Production methods that are inferior in the engineering sense may be the most efficient methods in the economic sense."

7. Explain the meaning and implications of the following quotation.

   > The beautiful consequence of the market is that it is its own guardian. If output prices or certain kinds of remuneration stray away from their socially ordained levels, forces are set into motion to bring them back to the fold. It is a curious paradox which thus ensues: the market, which is the acme of individual economic freedom, is the strictest taskmaster of all. One may appeal the ruling of a planning board or win the dispensation of a minister; but there is no appeal, no dispensation, from the anonymous pressures of the market mechanism. Economic freedom is thus more illusory than at first appears. One can do as one pleases in the market. But if one pleases to do what the market disapproves, the price of individual freedom is economic ruination.[1]

8. Suppose the demand for bagels dramatically rises while the demand for breakfast cereal plummets. Explain how the competitive market economy will make the needed adjustments to reestablish an efficient allocation of society's scarce resources.

9. **KEY QUESTION** *Some large hardware stores such as Canadian Tire boast of carrying as many as 20,000 different products in each store. What motivated the producers of these particular items—everything from screwdrivers to ladders to water heaters—to make them and offer them for sale? How did producers decide on the best combinations of resources to use? Who made these resources available, and why? Who decides whether these specific hardware products should continue to get produced and offered for sale?*

10. In a single sentence, describe the meaning of the phrase "invisible hand."

11. **(The Last Word)** Describe how the market brings together public and private interest.

12. **WEB-BASED QUESTION** **The United Nations' Virtual Marketplace** The United Nations urgento.gse.rmit.edu.au/untpdc/eto has set up an Electronic Trade Opportunity (ETO), a large-scale virtual marketplace for trade offers (ETOs) from around the world. ETOs are received by millions of companies every week in one of several electronic forms. How does this new virtual marketplace improve the efficient use of resources and increase the freedom of enterprise and choice? Does it increase competition? How does it help firms in developing countries? Why would the United Nations set up such a virtual marketplace?

13. **WEB-BASED QUESTION** **Barter and Revenue Canada** Bartering occurs when goods or services are exchanged without the exchange of money. For some, barter's popularity is that it enables them to avoid paying taxes to the government. How might such avoidance occur? Does Revenue Canada www.rc.gc.ca/E/pub/tp/it490et/it490e.txt.html treat barter as taxable or nontaxable income? How is the value of a barter transaction determined? What are some of Revenue Canada's barter examples? What does Revenue Canada require of so-called barter exchanges with regard to their members?

---

[1] Robert L. Heilbroner, *The Worldly Philosophers*, 3d ed. (New York: Simon & Schuster, Inc., 1967), p. 42.

Demand and Supply

ACCORDING TO AN OLD JOKE, IF YOU TEACH A parrot to say "Demand and supply," you have an economist. There is an element of truth in this quip. The tools of demand and supply can take us far in understanding not only specific economic issues but also how the entire economy works.

Our circular flow model in Chapter 2 identified the participants in the product and resource markets. There, we asserted that prices were determined by the "interaction" between demand and supply in these markets. In this chapter we examine that interaction in detail, explaining how prices and output quantities are determined.

IN THIS CHAPTER YOU WILL LEARN:

What demand is and what factors affect it.

•

What supply is and what factors affect it.

•

How demand and supply together determine price and quantity bought and sold.

•

How prices allocate scarce resources in a market economy.

The
Big Picture

IN A WORLD OF SCARCITY IN RELATION TO unlimited wants, there is constant competition for the available goods and services. The supply and demand curves represent the self-interest of the producers and consumers respectively. Firms are willing to supply more of a specific product at successively higher prices, but consumers actually want less at successively higher prices. What quantities of a particular good or service and at what price it is exchanged are determined by the interaction of these two opposing forces. The price mechanism is at the heart of the market system because prices adjust in response to choices made by consumers, suppliers, and other actors in the economy. Price changes mediate the effects of these various choices, leading to a more or less coherent allocation of resources in our society.

As you read this chapter, keep the following points in mind:

- **Key Concepts 4** and **6** are discussed.

- Think of the supply and demand curves as independent of each other. Each of these curves shifts for different reasons. Remember that suppliers of goods and services and the consumers have diverging interests.
- Make sure you understand the distinction between movement along the curves and shifts of the curves.
- The supply and demand curves shift only when certain conditions change. It is imperative that you learn the causes of the demand and supply curve shifts, reproduced in Tables 4-4 and 4-7.
- Supply and demand analysis can appear deceptively easy at first glance. Whenever applying supply and demand analysis, be sure to use graphs; trying to figure out a problem in your head can quickly lead to errors. Supply and demand analysis is mastered by getting "your hands dirty"; you need lots of practice applying it, and graphing is an important part. ■

MARKETS

Recall from Chapter 2 that a **market** *is an institution or mechanism that brings together buyers ("demanders") and sellers ("suppliers") of particular goods, services, or resources.* Markets exist in many forms. The corner gas station, the fast-food outlet, the local music store, a farmer's roadside stand—all are familiar markets. The Toronto Stock Exchange and the Chicago Board of Trade are markets where buyers and sellers of stocks and bonds and farm commodities from all over the world communicate with one another and buy and sell. Auctioneers bring together potential buyers and sellers of art, livestock, used farm equipment, and, sometimes, real estate. The professional hockey player and his agent bargain with the owner of an NHL team. A graduating finance major interviews with the Royal Bank or the Canadian Imperial Bank of Commerce at the university placement office.

All these situations that link potential buyers with potential sellers are markets. As our examples imply, some markets are local, while others are national or international. Some are highly personal, involving face-to-face contact between demander and supplier; others are impersonal, with buyer and seller never seeing or knowing each other.

To keep things simple, this chapter focuses on markets made up of large numbers of independently acting buyers and sellers exchanging a standardized product. These are the highly competitive markets such as a central grain exchange, a stock market, or a market for foreign currencies in which the equilibrium price is "discovered" by the interacting decisions of buyers and sellers. They are *not* the markets in which one or a handful of producers "set" prices, such as the markets for commercial airplanes or greeting cards.

DEMAND

Demand *is a schedule or a curve showing the various amounts of a product consumers are willing and able to purchase at each of a series of possible prices during a* specified period of time.[1] Demand, therefore, shows the quantities of a product that will be purchased at various possible prices, *other things equal*. Demand can easily be shown in table form. Table 4-1 is a hypothetical **demand schedule** for a single consumer purchasing bushels of corn.

The portrayal of demand in Table 4-1 reflects the relationship between the possible prices of corn and the quantity of corn the consumer would be willing and able to purchase at each of these prices. We say willing and *able*, because willingness alone is not effective in the market. You may be willing to buy a Porsche, but if this willingness is not backed by the necessary dollars, it will not be effective and, therefore, not be reflected in the market. In Table 4-1, if the price of corn were $5 per bushel, our consumer would be willing and able to buy 10 bushels per week; if it were $4, the consumer would be willing and able to buy 20 bushels per week; and so forth.

The table showing demand does not tell us which of the five possible prices will actually exist in the corn market. This depends on demand *and supply*. Demand is simply a statement of a buyer's plans, or intentions, with respect to the purchase of a product.

To be meaningful, the quantities demanded at each price must relate to a specific period—a day, a week, a month. Saying "A consumer will buy 10 bushels of corn at $5 per bushel" is meaningless. Saying "A consumer will buy 10 bushels of corn *per week* at $5 per bushel" is clear and meaningful. Without a specific time period we would not know whether demand for a product was large or small.

Law of Demand

A fundamental characteristic of demand is this: *All else equal, as price falls, the quantity demanded rises; and as price rises, the corresponding quantity demanded falls*. In short, there is a negative or *inverse* relationship between price and quantity demanded. Economists call this inverse relationship the **law of demand**.

The "other things equal" assumption is critical here. Many factors other than the price of the product being considered affect the amount purchased. The quantity of Nikes purchased will depend not

---

[1] This definition obviously is worded to apply to product markets. To adjust it to apply to resource markets, substitute the word "resource" for "product" and "businesses" for "consumers."

TABLE 4-1 An individual buyer's demand for corn

Price per bushel	Quantity demanded per week
$5	10
4	20
3	35
2	55
1	80

only on the price of Nikes but also on the prices of such substitutes as Reeboks, Adidas, and Filas. The law of demand in this case says that fewer Nikes will be purchased if the price of Nikes rises *and the prices of Reeboks, Adidas, and Filas all remain constant*. In short, if the *relative price* of Nikes increases, fewer Nikes will be bought. However, if the price of Nikes and all other competing shoes increases by some amount—say, $5—consumers might buy more, less, or the same amount of Nikes.

What is the foundation for the law of demand? Why is it that as price falls, the quantity demanded of a good rises, and vice versa? There are several levels of analysis on which to argue the case. Let's look at two of them:

1. In any specific time period, each buyer of a product will derive less satisfaction (or benefit or utility) from each successive unit of the good consumed. The second Big Mac will yield less satisfaction to the consumer than the first, and the third still less satisfaction than the second. That is, consumption is subject to **diminishing marginal utility**. And because successive units of a particular product yield less and less marginal utility, consumers will buy additional units only if the price of those units is reduced.

2. The law of demand can also be explained in terms of income and substitution effects. The **income effect** indicates that a lower price increases the purchasing power of a buyer's money income, enabling the buyer to purchase more of the product than she or he could buy before. A higher price has the opposite effect.

   The **substitution effect** suggests that at a lower price, buyers have the incentive to substitute the now cheaper good for similar goods that are now relatively more expensive. Consumers tend to substitute less expensive products for dear products.

For example, a decline in the price of beef will increase the purchasing power of consumer incomes, enabling them to buy more beef (the income effect). At a lower price, beef is relatively more attractive and is substituted for pork, mutton, chicken, and fish (the substitution effect). The income and substitution effects combine to make consumers able and willing to buy more of a product at a low price than at a high price.

The Demand Curve

The inverse relationship between price and quantity demanded for any product can be represented on a simple graph, in which, by convention, we measure *quantity demanded* on the horizontal axis and price on the vertical axis. In Figure 4-1 we have plotted the five price-quantity data points in Table 4-1 and connected them with a smooth curve, labelled *D*. Such a curve is called a **demand curve**. It slopes downward and to the right because the relationship it portrays between price and quantity demanded is inverse. The law of demand—people buy more at a low price than at a high price—is reflected in the downward slope of the demand curve.

Table 4-1 and Figure 4-1 contain exactly the same data and reflect the same relationship between price and quantity demanded. But the advantage of a graph is that it shows the relationship more simply and clearly than a table or a description in words. Moreover, graphs allow us to very easily show the effects of *changes* in variables. Graphs are thus valuable tools in economic analysis.

Individual and Market Demand

Until now we have concentrated on just one consumer. But usually there are many buyers in each market. We can get from *individual* demand to *market* demand by adding the quantities demanded by all consumers at each of the various possible prices. If there are just three buyers in the market, as represented in Table 4-2, it is relatively easy to determine the total quantity demanded at each price. Figure 4-2 shows the graphical summing procedure: At each price we add the individual quantities demanded to obtain the total quantity demanded for that price; we then plot the price and total quantity as one point of the market demand curve.

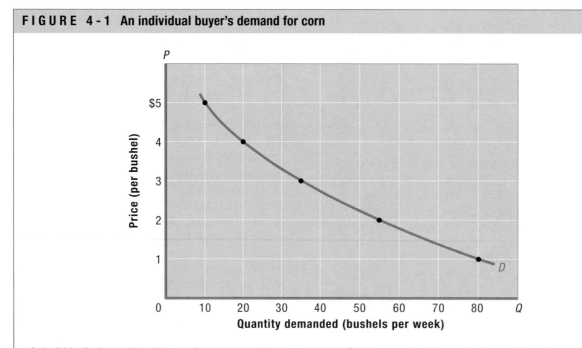

F I G U R E   4 - 1   An individual buyer's demand for corn

An individual's demand schedule graphs as a downsloping curve such as *D*, because price and quantity demanded are inversely related. Specifically, the law of demand generalizes that, other things equal, consumers will buy more of a product as its price declines. Here and in later figures, *P* stands for price, and *Q* stands for quantity (either demanded or supplied).

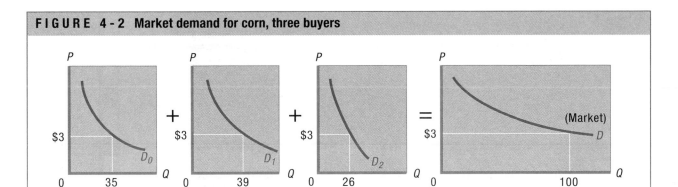

FIGURE 4-2 Market demand for corn, three buyers

The market demand curve D (market) is found by adding horizontally the individual demand curves (D_0, D_1, and D_2) of all consumers in the market. At the price of $3, for example, the three individual curves yield a total quantity demanded of 100 bushels.

Of course, there are usually many more than three buyers of a product. To avoid hundreds or thousands or millions of additions, we suppose that all the buyers in a market are willing and able to buy the same amounts at each of the possible prices. Then we just multiply those amounts by the number of buyers to obtain the market demand. Curve D_0 in Figure 4-3 was obtained this way, for a market with 200 corn buyers whose demand is that in Table 4-1. Table 4-3 shows the calculations.

Determinants of Demand

An economist constructing a demand curve such as D_0 in Figure 4-3 assumes that price is the most important influence on the amount of any product purchased. But the economist knows that other factors can and do affect purchases. These factors are called **determinants of demand**, and they are assumed to be constant when a demand curve like D_0 is drawn. They are the "other things equal" in the relationship between price and quantity demanded. When any of these determinants changes, the location of the demand curve will shift to the right or left. For this reason, determinants of demand are sometimes referred to as *demand shifters*.

The basic determinants of demand are (1) consumers' tastes and preferences, (2) the number of consumers in the market, (3) consumers' money incomes, (4) the prices of related goods, and (5) consumer expectations about future prices and incomes.

Change in Demand

A change in one or more of the determinants of demand will change the demand data (the *demand schedule*) of Table 4-3 and therefore the location of the demand curve in Figure 4-3. A change in the demand schedule or, graphically, a shift in the location of the demand curve is called a *change in demand*.

If consumers become willing and able to buy more corn at each possible price than is reflected in column 4 of Table 4-3, this *increase in demand* means a shift of the demand curve to the *right*, say, from D_0 to D_1. Conversely, *a decrease in demand* occurs when consumers buy less corn at each possible price than is indicated in column 4, Table 4-3. Graphically, a decrease in demand is shown as a shift of the demand curve to the *left*, say, from D_0 to D_2 in Figure 4-3.

Let's now examine how changes in each determinant affect demand.

TABLE 4-2 Market demand for corn, three buyers

Price per bushel	QUANTITY DEMANDED			Total quantity demanded per week
	First buyer	Second buyer	Third buyer	
$5	10 +	12 +	8 =	30
4	20 +	23 +	17 =	60
3	35 +	39 +	26 =	100
2	55 +	60 +	39 =	154
1	80 +	87 +	54 =	221

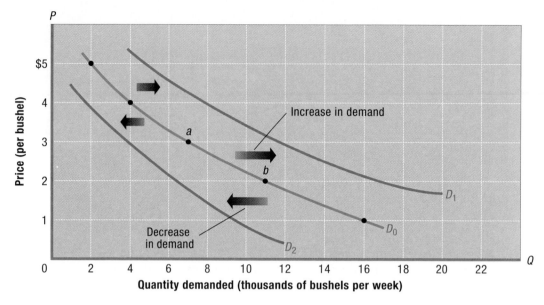

FIGURE 4-3 Changes in the demand for corn

A change in one or more of the determinants of demand causes a change in demand. An increase in demand is shown as a shift of the demand curve to the right, as from D_0 to D_1. A decrease in demand is shown as a shift of the demand curve to the left, as from D_0 to D_2. These changes in demand are distinguished from a change in quantity demanded, which is caused by a change in the price of the product, as shown by a movement from, say, point *a* to point *b* on fixed demand curve D_0.

Tastes A favourable change in consumer tastes or preferences for a product—one that makes the product more desirable—means that more of it will be demanded at each price. Demand will increase; the demand curve will shift rightward. An unfavourable change in consumer preferences will decrease demand, shifting the demand curve to the left.

New products can affect consumer tastes; for example, the introduction of compact discs has greatly decreased the demand for cassette tapes. Consumer concern about the health hazards of cholesterol and obesity have increased the demand for broccoli, low-calorie sweeteners, and fresh fruit while decreasing the demands for beef, veal, eggs, and whole milk. Over the past several years, the demands for light trucks and sports utility vehicles have greatly increased, driven by a change in tastes. So, too, has the demand for bagels.

Number of Buyers An increase in the number of consumers in a market increases demand. A decrease in the number of consumers decreases demand. For example, improvements in communications have given financial markets international range, increasing demand for stocks and bonds. And the baby boom after World War II increased demand for diapers, baby lotion, and the services of obstetricians. When the baby boomers reached their 20s in the 1970s, the demand for housing increased. Conversely, the aging of the baby boomers in the 1980s and 1990s has been a factor in the relative "slump" in housing demand.

TABLE 4-3 Market demand for corn, 200 buyers

(1) Price per bushel	(2) Quantity demanded per week, single buyer		(3) Number of buyers in the market		(4) Total quantity demanded per week
$5	10	×	200	=	2,000
4	20	×	200	=	4,000
3	35	×	200	=	7,000
2	55	×	200	=	11,000
1	80	×	200	=	16,000

Also, increasing life expectancy has increased demands for medical care, retirement communities, and nursing homes. And international trade agreements such as the North American Free Trade Agreement (NAFTA) and the General Agreement on Tariffs and Trade (GATT) have reduced foreign trade barriers to Canadian farm products, increasing the demands for those products.

Income How changes in money income affect demand is more complex. For most commodities, a rise in income causes an increase in demand. Consumers typically buy more steaks, sunscreen, and stereos as their incomes increase. Conversely, the demands for such products decline as incomes fall. Commodities whose demand varies *directly* with money income are called *superior*, or **normal, goods**.

Although most products are normal goods, there are a few exceptions. As incomes increase beyond some point, the amount of bread or lard or cabbages purchased at each price may diminish because higher incomes allow consumers to buy more high-protein foods, such as dairy products and meat. Rising incomes may also decrease the demands for used clothing and third-hand automobiles. Similarly, rising incomes may cause demands for hamburger and charcoal barbecues to decline as wealthier consumers switch to T-bones and gas barbecues. Goods whose demand varies *inversely* with money income are called **inferior goods**.

Prices of Related Goods A change in the price of a related good may increase or decrease the demand for a product, depending on whether the related good is a substitute or a complement. A **substitute good** is one that can be used in place of another good. A **complementary good** is one used together with another good.

SUBSTITUTES Beef and chicken are examples of substitute goods. When the price of beef rises, consumers buy less beef, increasing the demand for chicken. Conversely, as the price of beef falls, consumers buy more beef, decreasing the demand for chicken. *When two products are substitutes, the price of one and the demand for the other move in the same direction.* So it is with Nikes and Reeboks, sweaters and jackets, Toyotas and Hondas, and Coke and Pepsi.

COMPLEMENTS Complementary goods are used together and are usually demanded together. If the price of gasoline falls and, as a result, you drive your car more, this extra driving increases your demand for motor oil. Thus gas and oil are jointly demanded; they are complements. So it is with ham and eggs, movies and popcorn, and cameras and film. *When two products are complements, the price of one good and the demand for the other good move in opposite directions.*

UNRELATED GOODS Many goods are not related to one another; they are *independent goods*. Examples are such pairs of goods as butter and golf balls, potatoes and automobiles, bananas and wristwatches. A change in the price of one has little or no impact on the demand for the other.

Expectations Consumer expectations about future product prices, product availability, and future income can shift demand. Consumer expectations of higher future prices may prompt them to buy now to "beat" anticipated price rises, thus increasing today's demand. Similarly, the expectations of rising incomes may induce consumers to be freer in current spending. In contrast, the expectation of falling prices or falling income will decrease current demand for products.

First example: If freezing weather destroys much of Florida's citrus crop, consumers may reason that the price of orange juice will rise. Forthcoming shortages of frozen orange juice will escalate its price. They may stock up on orange juice by purchasing large quantities now.

Second example: A first-round NHL draft choice might splurge for a new Mercedes in anticipation of a lucrative professional hockey contract.

In summary, an *increase* in demand—the decision by consumers to buy larger quantities of a product at each possible price—can be caused by:

1. A favourable change in consumer tastes
2. An increase in the number of buyers
3. Rising incomes if the product is a normal good
4. Falling incomes if the product is an inferior good
5. An increase in the price of a substitute good
6. A decrease in the price of a complementary good
7. Consumer expectations of higher future prices and incomes

Be sure you can "reverse" these generalizations to explain a *decrease* in demand. Table 4-4 provides additional illustrations to reinforce your understanding of the determinants of demand. *(Key Question 2)*

TABLE 4-4 Determinants of demand: factors that shift the demand curve

1 **Change in buyer tastes** Example: Physical fitness increases in popularity, increasing the demand for jogging shoes and bicycles

2 **Change in number of buyers** Examples: Japanese reduce import quotas on Canadian telecommunications equipment, increasing the demand for it; a birthrate decline reduces the demand for education

3 **Change in income** Examples: An increase in incomes increases the demand for such normal goods as butter, lobster, and filet mignon, while reducing the demand for such inferior goods as cabbage, turnips, retreaded tires, and used clothing

4 **Change in the prices of related goods** Examples: A reduction in airfares reduces the demand for bus transportation (substitute goods); a decline in the price of compact disc players increases the demand for compact discs (complementary goods)

5 **Change in expectations** Example: Inclement weather in South America causes the expectation of higher future coffee prices, thereby increasing the current demand for coffee

Changes in Quantity Demanded

A *change in demand* must not be confused with a *change in quantity demanded*. A **change in demand** is a shift of the entire curve to the right (an increase in demand) or to the left (a decrease in demand). A change in demand occurs because the consumer's state of mind about purchasing the product has been altered. The cause is a change in one or more of the determinants of demand. Recall that *demand* is a schedule or curve; therefore, a *change in demand* means a change in the entire schedule and a shift of the entire curve.

In contrast, a **change in quantity demanded** is a movement from one point to another point—from one price-quantity combination to another—on a fixed demand schedule or demand curve. The cause of such a change is an increase or decrease in the price of the product being considered. In Table 4-3, for example, a decline in the price from $5 to $4 will increase the quantity of corn demanded from 2,000 to 4,000 bushels.

In Figure 4-3 the shift of the demand curve D_0 to either D_1 or D_2 is a change in demand. But the movement from point *a* to point *b* on curve D_0 rep-

resents a change in quantity demanded. Demand has not changed; it is the entire curve, and it remains fixed in place.

4-1
QUICK REVIEW

- A market is any arrangement that facilitates the purchase and sale of goods, services, and resources.

- Demand is a schedule or a curve showing the amount of a product buyers are willing and able to purchase at each potential price in a series of prices.

- The law of demand states that, other things equal, the quantity of a good purchased varies inversely with its price.

- The demand curve shifts because of changes in **a** consumer tastes, **b** the number of buyers in the market, **c** incomes, **d** the prices of substitute or complementary goods, and **e** expectations.

- A change in demand is a shift of the entire demand curve; a change in quantity demanded is a movement from one point to another on a stable demand curve.

SUPPLY

Supply *is a schedule or curve showing the amounts of a product a producer is willing and able to produce and make available for sale at each of a series of possible prices during a specific period.*[2] Table 4-5 is a hypothetical **supply schedule** for a single producer of corn. It shows the quantities of corn that will be supplied at various prices, other things equal.

Law of Supply

Table 4-5 shows a positive or direct relationship between price and quantity supplied. *As price rises, the quantity supplied rises; as price falls, the quantity supplied falls.* This particular relationship is called the **law of supply**. A supply schedule tells us that firms will produce and offer for sale more of their product at a high price than at a low price. This, again, is basically common sense.

---

[2] This definition is worded to apply to product markets. To adjust it to apply to resource markets, substitute "resource" for "product," and "owner" for "producer."

TABLE 4-5 An individual producer's supply of corn

Price per bushel	Quantity supplied per week
$5	60
4	50
3	35
2	20
1	5

Price is an obstacle from the standpoint of the consumer, who is on the paying end. The higher the price, the less the consumer will buy. But the supplier is on the receiving end of the product's price. To a supplier, price represents *revenue* and thus is an incentive to produce and sell a product. The higher the price, the greater this incentive and the greater the quantity supplied.

Consider a farmer who can shift resources among alternative products. As price moves up in Table 4-5, the farmer finds it profitable to take land out of wheat, oats, and soybean production and

put it into corn. And the higher corn prices allow the farmer to cover the increased costs associated with more intensive cultivation and the use of more seed, fertilizer, and pesticides. The overall result is more corn.

Now consider a manufacturer. Beyond some production quantity, manufacturers usually encounter increasing costs per added unit of output. Certain productive resources—in particular, the firm's plant and machinery—cannot be expanded quickly. So the firm uses more of the other resources, such as labour, to produce more output. But at some point the existing plant becomes increasingly crowded and congested, meaning that each added worker produces less added output. As a result, the cost of successive units of output rises. The firm will not produce these more costly units unless it receives a higher price for them. Again, price and quantity supplied are directly related.

The Supply Curve

As with demand, it is convenient to represent supply graphically. In Figure 4-4, curve S_0 is a graph of the market supply data in Table 4-6. Those data assume there are 200 suppliers in the market, each

FIGURE 4-4 Changes in the supply of corn

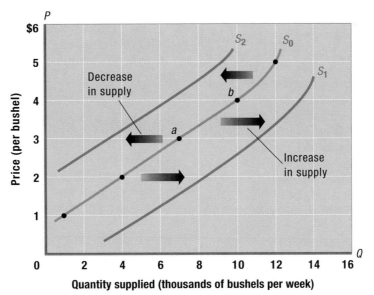

A change in one or more of the determinants of supply causes a change in supply. An increase in supply is shown as a rightward shift of the supply curve, as from S_0 to S_1. A decrease in supply is depicted as a leftward shift of the curve, as from S_0 to S_2. In contrast, a change in the quantity supplied is caused by a change in the product's price and is shown by a movement from one point to another—as from *a* to *b*—on a fixed supply curve.

TABLE 4-6 Market supply of corn, 200 producers

(1) Price per bushel	(2) Quantity supplied per week, single producer		(3) Number of sellers in the market		(4) Total quantity supplied per week
$5	60	×	200	=	12,000
4	50	×	200	=	10,000
3	35	×	200	=	7,000
2	20	×	200	=	4,000
1	5	×	200	=	1,000

willing and able to supply corn according to Table 4-5. That is, we obtain the market **supply curve** by horizontally adding the supply curves of the individual producers. Note that the axes in Figure 4-4 are the same as those used in our graph of market demand, except for the change of "quantity demanded" to "quantity supplied" on the horizontal axis.

Determinants of Supply

In constructing a supply curve, the economist assumes that price is the most significant influence on the quantity supplied of any product. But other factors (the *other things equal*) can and do affect supply. The supply curve is drawn assuming that these other things are fixed and do not change. If any of them does change, a *change in supply* will occur—the entire supply curve will shift.

The basic **determinants of supply** are (1) resource prices, (2) the technique of production, (3) taxes and subsidies, (4) prices of other goods, (5) price expectations, and (6) the number of sellers in the market. A change in any one or more of these determinants of supply, or *supply shifters*, will move the supply curve for a product either to the right or to the left. A shift to the *right*, as from S_0 to S_1 in Figure 4-4, is an *increase* in supply: Producers supply larger quantities of the product at each possible price. A shift to the *left*, as from S_0 to S_2, indicates a *decrease* in supply: Suppliers offer less output at each price.

Changes in Supply

Let's consider how changes in each of the determinants affect supply. As our discussion proceeds,

remember that costs are a major factor underlying supply curves; anything that affects costs (other than changes in output itself) usually shifts the supply curve.

Resource Prices The prices of the *resources* used in the production process help determine the costs of production incurred by firms. Higher *resource* prices raise production costs and, assuming a particular *product* price, squeeze profits. This reduction in profits reduces the incentive for firms to supply output at each product price. In contrast, lower resource prices induce firms to supply more output at each product price since production costs fall and profits expand.

It follows that a decrease in resource prices will increase supply, shifting the supply curve to the right. If prices of seed and fertilizer decrease, we can expect the supply of corn to increase. Conversely, an increase in resource prices will raise production costs and reduce supply, shifting the supply curve to the left. Increases in the prices of iron ore and coke will increase the cost of producing steel and reduce its supply.

Technology Improvements in technology enable firms to produce units of output with fewer resources. Because resources are costly, using fewer of them lowers production costs and increases supply. Example: Recent improvements in the fuel efficiency of aircraft engines have reduced the cost of providing passenger air service. Thus, airlines now offer more air service than previously at each ticket price; the supply of air service has increased.

Taxes and Subsidies Businesses treat most taxes as costs. An increase in sales or property taxes will increase production costs and reduce supply. In contrast, subsidies are "taxes in reverse." If government subsidizes the production of a good, it in effect lowers production costs and increases supply.

Prices of Other Goods Firms producing a particular product, say, soccer balls, can sometimes use their plant and equipment to produce alternative goods, say, basketballs and volleyballs. Higher prices of these "other goods" may entice soccer ball producers to switch production to them in order to increase profits. This *substitution in production* results in a decline in the supply of soccer balls. Alternatively, lower prices of basketballs and volleyballs may entice producers of these goods to produce more soccer balls, increasing their supply.

Expectations   Expectations about the *future* price of a product can affect the producer's *current* willingness to supply that product. It is difficult, however, to generalize about how the expectation of higher prices affects the present supply of a product. Farmers anticipating a higher corn price in the future might withhold some of their current corn harvest from the market, which would cause a decrease in the current supply of corn. Similarly, if the price of Air Canada stock is expected to rise significantly in the near future, the supply offered for sale today might decrease. In contrast, in many types of manufacturing industries, expected price increases may induce firms to add another shift of workers or expand their production facilities, causing current supply to increase.

Number of Sellers   Other things equal, the larger the number of suppliers, the greater the market supply. As more firms enter an industry, the supply curve shifts to the right. Conversely, the smaller the number of firms in the industry, the less the market supply. This means that as firms leave an industry, the supply curve shifts to the left. Example: Canada and the United States have imposed restrictions on haddock fishing to replenish dwindling stocks. As part of that policy, the federal government has bought the boats of some of the haddock fishermen as a way of putting them out of business and decreasing the catch. The result has been a decline in the market supply of haddock.

Table 4-7 is a checklist of the determinants of supply, along with further illustrations. **(Key Question 5)**

Changes in Quantity Supplied

The distinction between a *change in supply* and *change in quantity supplied* is the same as that between a change in demand and a change in quantity demanded. Because supply is a schedule or curve, a **change in supply** means a change in the entire schedule and a shift of the entire curve. An increase in supply shifts the curve to the right; a decrease in supply shifts it to the left. The cause of a change in supply is a change in one or more of the determinants of supply.

In contrast, a **change in quantity supplied** is a movement from one point to another on a fixed supply curve. The cause of such a movement is a change

TABLE 4-7 Determinants of supply: factors that shift the supply curve

1   **Change in resource prices**   Examples: A decline in the price of fertilizer increases the supply of wheat; an increase in the price of irrigation equipment reduces the supply of corn

2   **Change in technology**   Example: The development of a more effective insecticide for corn rootworm increases the supply of corn

3   **Changes in taxes and subsidies**   Examples: An increase in the excise tax on cigarettes reduces the supply of cigarettes; a decline in subsidies to colleges and universities reduces the supply of higher education

4   **Change in prices of other goods**   Example: A decline in the prices of mutton and pork increases the supply of beef

5   **Change in expectations**   Example: Expectations of substantial declines in future oil prices cause oil companies to increase current supply

6   **Change in number of suppliers**   An increase in the number of firms producing personal computers increases the supply of personal computers; formation of women's professional basketball leagues increases the supply of women's professional basketball games

in the price of the specific product being considered. In Table 4-6, a decline in the price of corn from $5 to $4 decreases the quantity of corn supplied from 12,000 to 10,000 bushels. This is a change in quantity supplied, not a change in supply. Supply is the full schedule of prices and quantities shown, and this schedule does not change when price changes.

4-2
QUICK REVIEW

- A supply schedule or curve shows that, other things equal, the quantity of a good supplied varies directly with its price.
- The supply curve shifts because of changes in **a** resource prices, **b** technology, **c** taxes or subsidies, **d** prices of other goods, **e** expectations of future prices, and **f** the number of suppliers.
- A change in supply is a shift of the supply curve; a change in quantity supplied is a movement from one point to another on a fixed supply curve.

SUPPLY AND DEMAND: MARKET EQUILIBRIUM

We can now bring together supply and demand to see how the buying decisions of households and the selling decisions of businesses interact to determine the price of a product and the quantity actually bought and sold. In Table 4-8, columns 1 and 2 repeat the market supply of corn (from Table 4-6), and columns 2 and 3 repeat the market demand for corn (from Table 4-3). Note that column 2 lists a common set of prices. We assume competition—a large number of buyers and sellers.

Surpluses

We have limited our examples to only five possible prices. Of these, which will actually prevail as the market price for corn? We can find an answer through trial and error; for no particular reason, let's start with $5. We immediately see that this cannot be the prevailing market price. At the $5 price, producers are willing to produce and offer for sale 12,000 bushels of corn, but buyers are willing to buy only 2,000 bushels. The $5 price encourages farmers to produce lots of corn but discourages most consumers from buying it. The result is a 10,000-bushel **surplus** or *excess supply* of corn. This surplus, shown in column 4 in Table 4-8, is the excess of quantity supplied over quantity demanded at $5. Corn farmers would find themselves with 10,000 unsold bushels of output.

A price of $5—even if it existed temporarily in the corn market—could not persist over a period of time. The very large surplus of corn would prompt

competing sellers to lower the price to encourage buyers to take the surplus off their hands.

Suppose the price goes down to $4. The lower price encourages consumers to buy more corn and, at the same time, induces farmers to offer less of it for sale. The surplus diminishes to 6,000 bushels. Nevertheless, since there is still a surplus, competition among sellers will once again reduce the price. Clearly, then, the prices of $5 and $4 are unstable—they will not survive—because they are "too high." The market price of corn must be less than $4.

Shortages

Let's jump now to $1 as the possible market price of corn. Observe in column 4 in Table 4-8 that at this price, quantity demanded exceeds quantity supplied by 15,000 units. The $1 price discourages farmers from devoting resources to corn production and encourages consumers to buy more than is available. The result is a 15,000-bushel **shortage** of, or *excess demand* for, corn. The $1 price cannot persist as the market price. Many consumers who are willing and able to buy at this price will not get corn. They will express a willingness to pay more than $1 to get some of the available output. Competition among these buyers will drive up the price to something greater than $1.

Suppose the competition among buyers boosts the price to $2. This higher price reduces, but does not eliminate the shortage of corn. For $2, farmers devote more resources to corn production, and some buyers who were willing to pay $1 per bushel choose not to buy corn at $2. But a shortage of 7,000 bushels still exists at $2. This shortage will push the market price above $2.

Equilibrium Price and Quantity

By trial and error we have eliminated every price but $3. At $3, *and only at this price*, the quantity of corn that farmers are willing to produce and supply is identical with the quantity consumers are willing and able to buy. There is neither a shortage nor a surplus of corn at that price.

With no shortage or surplus at $3, there is no reason for the price of corn to change. Economists call this price the *market-clearing* or **equilibrium price**, equilibrium meaning "in balance" or "at rest." At $3, quantity supplied and quantity demanded are in balance at the **equilibrium quantity** of 7,000 bushels. So $3 is the only stable price of corn under the supply and demand conditions shown in Table 4-8.

TABLE 4-8 Market supply of and demand for corn

(1) Total quantity supplied per week	(2) Price per bushel	(3) Total quantity demanded per week	(4) Surplus (+) or shortage (−) (arrows indicate effect on price)
12,000	$5	2,000	+10,000↓
10,000	4	4,000	+ 6,000↓
7,000	3	7,000	0
4,000	2	11,000	− 7,000↑
1,000	1	16,000	−15,000↑

The price of corn—or of any other product bought and sold in competitive markets—will be established where the supply decisions of producers and the demand decisions of buyers are mutually consistent. Such decisions are consistent only at the equilibrium price (here, $3) and equilibrium quantity (here, 7,000 bushels). At a higher price, suppliers want to sell more than consumers want to buy and a surplus results; at any lower price, consumers want to buy more than producers make available for sale and a shortage results. Such discrepancies between the supply and demand intentions of sellers and buyers then prompt price changes that bring the two sets of intentions into accord.

A graphical analysis of supply and demand yields these same conclusions. *Figure 4-5 (Key Graph)* shows the market supply and demand curves for corn on the same graph. (The horizon-

KEY GRAPH

FIGURE 4-5 Equilibrium price and quantity

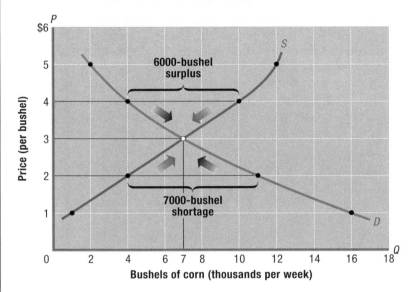

The intersection of the downsloping demand curve *D* and the upsloping supply curve *S* indicates the equilibrium price and quantity, here $3 and 7,000 bushels of corn. The shortages of corn at below-equilibrium prices—for example, 7,000 bushels at $2—drive up price. These higher prices increase the quantity supplied and reduce the quantity demanded until equilibrium is achieved. The surpluses caused by above-equilibrium prices—for example, 6,000 bushels at $4—push price down. As price drops, the quantity demanded rises and the quantity supplied falls until equilibrium is established. At the equilibrium price and quantity, there are neither shortages nor surpluses of corn.

4-5
QUICK QUIZ

1. Demand curve *D* is downsloping because:
   (a) producers offer less of a product for sale as the price of the product falls.
   (b) lower prices of a product create income and sub-stitution effects that lead consumers to purchase more of it.
   (c) the larger the number of buyers in a market, the lower the product price.
   (d) price and quantity demanded are directly (posi-tively) related.

2. Supply curve *S*:
   (a) reflects an inverse (negative) relationship between price and quantity supplied.
   (b) reflects a direct (positive) relationship between price and quantity supplied.
   (c) depicts the collective behaviour of buyers in this market.
   (d) shows that producers will offer more of a product for sale at a low product price than at a high product price.

3. At the $3 price:
   (a) quantity supplied exceeds quantity demanded.
   (b) quantity demanded exceeds quantity supplied.
   (c) the product is abundant and a surplus exists.
   (d) there is no pressure on price to rise or fall.

4. At price $5 in this market:
   (a) there will be a shortage of 10,000 units.
   (b) there will be a surplus of 10,000 units.
   (c) quantity demanded will be 12,000 units.
   (d) quantity demanded will equal quantity supplied.

Answers: 1. (b); 2. (b); 3. (d); 4. (b)

tal axis now measures both quantity demanded and quantity supplied.)

Graphically, the intersection of the supply curve and demand curve for a product indicates the market equilibrium. Here, equilibrium price and quantity are $3 per bushel and 7,000 bushels. At any above-equilibrium price, quantity supplied exceeds quantity demanded. This surplus of corn causes price reductions by sellers who are eager to rid themselves of their surplus. The falling price causes less corn to be offered and simultaneously encourages consumers to buy more. The market moves to its equilibrium.

Any price below the equilibrium price creates a shortage; quantity demanded now exceeds quantity supplied. Buyers try to obtain the product by offering to pay more for it; this drives the price upward towards its equilibrium level. The rising price simultaneously causes producers to increase the quantity supplied and many buyers to leave the market, eliminating the shortage. Again the market moves to its equilibrium.

Rationing Function of Prices

The ability of the competitive forces of supply and demand to establish a price at which selling and buying decisions are consistent is called the **rationing function of prices**. In our case, the equilibrium price of $3 clears the market, leaving no burdensome surplus for sellers and no inconvenient shortage for potential buyers. And it is the combination of freely made individual decisions that sets this market-clearing price. In effect, the market mechanism of supply and demand says that any buyer willing and able to pay $3 for a bushel of corn will be able to acquire one; those who are not, will not. Similarly, any seller willing and able to produce bushels of corn and offer them for sale at $3 will be able to do so; sellers who are not, will not. *(Key Question 7)*

Changes in Supply, Demand, and Equilibrium

We know that demand might change because of fluctuations in consumer tastes or incomes, changes in consumer expectations, or variations in the prices of related goods. Supply might change in response to changes in resource prices, technology, or taxes. What effects will such changes in supply and demand have on equilibrium price and quantity?

Changes in Demand Suppose that supply is constant and demand increases, as shown in Figure 4-6a. As a result, the new intersection of the supply and demand curves is at higher values on both the price and quantity axes. Clearly, an increase in demand raises both equilibrium price and equilibrium quantity. Conversely, a decrease in demand—such as that shown in Figure 4-6b—reduces both equilibrium price and equilibrium quantity. (The value of graphical analysis is now apparent: We need not fumble with columns of figures to determine the outcomes, but only compare the new and the old points of intersection on the graph.)

The explanation of the dynamics of how a shift in demand results in a new equilibrium price and quantity is similar to the shortage-surplus story in Figure 4-5. In the case of an increase in demand, there would be a shortage at the original equilibrium price, leading to a higher price. A higher price to producers results in more output offered for sale. To better understand the dynamics of an equilibrium change, draw a diagram with an equilibrium price and quantity and shift the demand curve to the right. Now, do an analysis of the dynamics. Go through the same exercise for a fall in demand. The key to understanding the dynamics of a change in equilibrium is to understand the shortage or surplus that occurs when there is excess demand or excess supply at a given price.

Changes in Supply Let's now suppose demand is constant but supply increases, as in Figure 4-6c. The new intersection of supply and demand is located at a lower equilibrium price but at a higher equilibrium quantity. An increase in supply reduces equilibrium price but increases equilibrium quantity. In contrast, if supply decreases, as in Figure 4-6d, the equilibrium price rises while the equilibrium quantity declines.

As in the case of a shift in demand, the explanation of the dynamics of a change in equilibrium when the supply curve shifts is the existence of a surplus or a shortage at the original equilibrium price. For example, if the supply curve shifts to the right, at the original equilibrium price there would be a surplus, therefore price drops. Draw a diagram and do the analysis of a change in equilibrium when the supply curve shifts to the right, and then repeat the analysis for a shift of the supply curve to the left.

As you do the above analysis, keep in mind that equilibrium price and quantity cannot spontaneously change; price and quantity change only as a result of a shift in demand and supply.

Complex Cases When both supply and demand change, the effect is a combination of the individ-

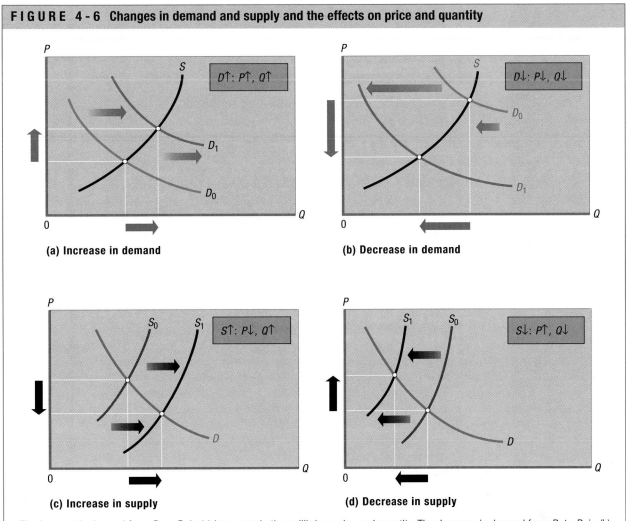

FIGURE 4-6 Changes in demand and supply and the effects on price and quantity

(a) Increase in demand

(b) Decrease in demand

(c) Increase in supply

(d) Decrease in supply

The increase in demand from D_0 to D_1 in (a) increases both equilibrium price and quantity. The decrease in demand from D_0 to D_1 in (b) decreases both equilibrium price and quantity. The increase in supply from S_0 to S_1 in (c) decreases equilibrium price and increases equilibrium quantity. The decline in supply from S_0 to S_1 in (d) increases equilibrium price and reduces equilibrium quantity. The boxes in the top right corners summarize the respective changes and outcomes. The upward arrows in the boxes signify increases in demand (D), supply (S), equilibrium price (P), and equilibrium quantity (Q); the downward arrows signify decreases in these items.

ual effects. There are four possibilities: (1) supply increases and demand decreases; (2) supply decreases and demand increases; (3) supply increases and demand decreases; and (4) supply decreases and demand decreases.

Table 4-9 summarizes these four cases. To understand them fully you should draw supply and demand diagrams for each case to confirm the effects listed in the table.

Special cases might arise where a decrease in demand and a decrease in supply, or an increase in demand and an increase in supply, exactly cancel out. In both cases, the net effect on equilibrium price will be zero; price will not change. *(Key Question 8)*

A Reminder: "Other Things Equal"

We stress once again that specific demand and supply curves—such as those in Figure 4-6—show relationships between prices and quantities demanded and supplied, *other things equal*. The downsloping demand curves tell us that price and quantity demanded are inversely related, other things equal. The upsloping supply curves imply that price and quantity supplied are directly related, *other things equal*.

If you forget the other-things-equal assumption, you can encounter situations that *seem* to be in conflict with these basic principles. For example,

TABLE 4-9   Effects of changes in both supply and demand

Change in supply	Change in demand	Effect on equilibrium price	Effect on equilibrium quantity
1 increase	decrease	decrease	indeterminate
2 decrease	increase	increase	indeterminate
3 increase	increase	indeterminate	increase
4 decrease	decrease	indeterminate	decrease

suppose salsa manufacturers sell 1 million bottles of salsa at \$4 a bottle in one year; 2 million bottles at \$5 in the next year; and 3 million at \$6 in the year thereafter. Price and quantity purchased vary directly, and these data seem to be at odds with the law of demand. But there is no conflict here; these data do *not* refute the law of demand. The catch is that the law of demand's other-things-equal assumption has been violated over the three years in the example. Specifically, because of changing tastes and growing incomes, the demand for salsa has increased sharply, as in Figure 4-6a. The result is higher prices *and* larger quantities purchased.

As another example, the price of coffee occasionally has shot upward at the same time that the quantity of coffee produced has declined. These events seemingly contradict the direct relationship between price and quantity denoted by supply. The catch again is that the other-things-equal assumption underlying the upsloping supply curve was violated. Poor coffee harvests decreased supply, as in Figure 4-6d, increasing the equilibrium price of coffee and reducing the equilibrium quantity.

These examples also emphasize the importance of our earlier distinction between a change in quantity demanded (or supplied) and a change in demand (supply). In Figure 4-6a a change in demand caused a change in the quantity supplied. In Figure 4-6d a change in supply caused a change in quantity demanded.

Application: Pink Salmon

To reinforce the concepts we just discussed, let's briefly examine the real-world market for pink salmon—a market in which price has dramatically changed.

In the early 1970s, fishermen earned today's equivalent of \$1.20 for each kilogram of pink

salmon delivered to the docks. This equilibrium price is shown in Figure 4-7 at the intersection of supply curve S_0 and demand curve D_0. The corresponding equilibrium quantity of pink salmon—the type most often used for canning—was Q_0 kilograms. (The actual "quantity numbers" are unimportant to our analysis.)

Between the early 1970s and late 1990s, changes in supply and demand occurred in the market for pink salmon. On the supply side, improved technology in the form of larger, more efficient fishing boats greatly increased the catch and lowered the cost of obtaining the fish. Also, the then-high profits at the \$1.20 price encouraged many new fishermen to enter the industry. As a result of these changes, the supply of pink salmon greatly increased and the supply curve shifted to the right, as from S_0 to S_1 in Figure 4-7.

Over the same years, the demand for pink salmon declined, as represented by the shift from demand curve D_0 to D_1 in Figure 4-7. The decline in demand resulted mainly from changes in consumer tastes, together with increases in consumer income: Buyers shifted their preferences away from canned fish and towards higher-quality fresh or frozen fish, including higher-quality species of salmon such as Chinook and Coho.

These supply and demand changes had a sizable effect on the price of pink salmon, as shown in

FIGURE 4-7   The market for pink salmon

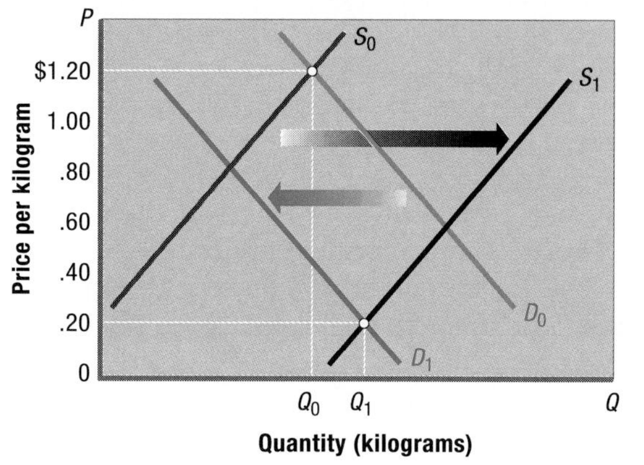

Since the early 1970s, the supply of pink salmon has increased and the demand for pink salmon has decreased. As a result, the price of pink salmon has declined, here from \$1.20 to \$.20 a kilogram. Since supply has increased more than demand has declined, the equilibrium quantity of pink salmon has increased, here from Q_0 to Q_1.

Figure 4-7. By 1997 the equilibrium price had fallen to just $.20 per kilogram—over 80 percent below the price in the early 1970s. Both the increase in supply and the decrease in demand helped reduce the equilibrium price. However, the equilibrium *quantity* of pink salmon increased, as represented by the increase from Q_0 to Q_1. This change in quantity occurred because the increase in the supply of pink salmon exceeded the decline in demand.

4-3
QUICK REVIEW

- In competitive markets, prices adjust to the equilibrium level at which quantity demanded equals quantity supplied.

- The equilibrium price and quantity are those indicated by the intersection of the supply and demand curves for any product or resource.

- An increase in demand increases equilibrium price and quantity; a decrease in demand decreases equilibrium price and quantity.

- An increase in supply reduces equilibrium price but increases equilibrium quantity; a decrease in supply increases equilibrium price but reduces equilibrium quantity.

- Over time, equilibrium price and quantity may change in directions that seem at odds with the laws of demand and supply because the other-things-equal assumption is violated.

In The Media

London trader takes huge cocoa delivery

Holds 212,500 tonnes after squeeze attempt

BY JALIL HAMID
REUTERS NEWS AGENCY

LONDON—A major commodity trader had to take virtually all the 212,500 tonnes of cocoa delivered on a London futures market yesterday after an attempt to squeeze the market failed.

The London Commodity Exchange said 21,250 original tenders representing 212,500 tonnes were registered, the largest delivery yet in one day. The LCE provided no further details, but market sources said a single large trader was believed to have received almost all the cocoa and has additional long positions of 8,000 to 9,000 10-tonne lots.

"It is an attempt to squeeze which didn't work because they underestimated the size of the crop and they underestimated the strength of other commodity traders," one trader said. "They never thought there would be enough cocoa that could be put on the market and they've been proved wrong."

The trader's position of about 300,000 tonnes of cocoa is equivalent to one-third of the crop produced by the world's top cocoa grower, Ivory Coast.

Yesterday's delivery marked the climax of a five-month war of nerves over the London September cocoa futures contract.

Although the tonnage came as no surprise, traders said the market is now watching the major trader's next move.

Traders estimated that it would cost the trader at least £1.25-million a year to store the cocoa.

"I don't suppose there's much else they can do in this moment in time," another trader said. "The market has given them cocoa ... and they have to carry [it] for the time being. There's nothing else they can do."

Any move to sell the cocoa—a fine, dark-brown powder made from pulverizing chocolate that's used to prepare beverages and as a flavouring ingredient—would put further pressure on a sliding market amid ample crops from producers and slack demand from the chocolate industry.

Cocoa delivered on the LCE has to have a grading certificate proving it is of acceptable quality. The certificate is valid for six months.

Source: Globe and Mail, September 3, 1996, p. B6. Copyright Reuters Limited 1998.

THE STORY IN BRIEF

A commodity exchange is a market in which a trader can buy or sell a commodity to be delivered at a specified future date. A trader that tried to corner the cocoa market ended up having to take delivery of a very large quantity.

THE ECONOMICS BEHIND THE STORY

- Commodity prices are determined by supply and demand. There is a futures market in which one can buy or sell a particular commodity. Buyers are those who need the commodity at some future time, sellers are the producers of a commodity who may wish to sell even before they produce the commodity. There are traders (speculators) who buy and sell commodities in the hope of making a profit by correctly predicting their prices at some future date. Such traders do not normally take delivery of commodities they trade.
- One trader bought large quantities of cocoa for future delivery in the expectation that there would be a shortage, thus the trader could sell the cocoa at a higher price than it was bought for.
- The trader was wrong. The crop was larger than expected, driving the supply curve for cocoa to the right.
- The trader in question could have sold the large position, but such a move would have driven the market supply curve further to the right, bringing the price down further. Thus the trader was left with the option of taking delivery of the cocoa and selling at a future date at possibly better prices, or taking an immediate very large loss.
- Can you explain why understanding supply and demand analysis will not easily make you rich? ■

The Last Word

TICKET SCALPING: A BUM RAP?

Some market transactions get a bad name that's not warranted.

TICKETS TO ATHLETIC AND ARTISTIC EVENTS are sometimes resold at higher-than-original prices—a market transaction known by the unsavoury term "scalping." For example, a $40 ticket to an NHL hockey game may be resold by the original buyer for $200, $250, or more. The media often denounce scalpers for "ripping off" buyers by charging "exorbitant" prices. Scalping and extortion are synonymous in some people's minds.

But is scalping really sinful? We must first recognize that such ticket resales are voluntary—not coerced—transactions. This implies that both buyer and seller expect to gain from the exchange or it would not occur. The seller must value the $200 more than seeing the game, and the buyer must value seeing the game more than the $200. So there are no losers or victims here: Both buyer and seller benefit from the transaction. The "scalping" market simply redistributes assets (game tickets) from those who value them less to those who value them more.

Does scalping impose losses or injury on other parties—in particular, the sponsors of the event? If the sponsors are injured, it is because they initially priced tickets below the equilibrium level. In so doing they suffer an economic loss in the form of less revenue and profit than they might have otherwise received. But the loss is self-inflicted because of their pricing error. That mistake is quite separate and distinct from the fact that some tickets were later resold at a higher price.

What about spectators? Does scalping somehow impose losses by deteriorating the quality of the game's audience? No! People who most want to see the game—generally those with the greatest interest in and understanding of the game—will pay the scalper's high prices. Ticket scalping also benefits the athletic teams and performing artists—they will appear before more dedicated and perhaps more appreciative audiences.

So, is ticket scalping undesirable? Not on economic grounds. Both seller and buyer of a "scalped" ticket benefit, and a more interested and appreciative audience results. Game sponsors may sacrifice revenue and profits, but that stems from their own misjudgement of the equilibrium price. ■

CHAPTER SUMMARY

1. A market is any institution or arrangement that brings together buyers and sellers of a product, service, or resource.

2. Demand is a schedule or curve representing the willingness of buyers in a specific period to purchase a particular product at each of various prices. The law of demand says that consumers will buy more of a product at a low price than at a high price. Therefore, other things equal, the relationship between price and quantity demanded is negative or inverse and is graphed as a downsloping curve. Market demand curves are found by adding horizontally the demand curves of the many individual consumers in the market.

3. Changes in one or more of the determinants of demand—consumer tastes, the number of buyers in the market, the money incomes of consumers, the prices of related goods, and consumer expectations—shift the market demand curve. A shift to the right is an increase in demand; a shift to the left is a decrease in demand. A change in demand is different from a change in the quantity demanded, the latter being a movement from one point to another point on a fixed demand curve because of a change in the product's price.

4. Supply is a schedule or curve showing the amounts of a product that producers are willing to offer in the market at each possible price during a specific period. The law of supply states that, other things equal, producers will offer more of a product at a high price than at a low price. Thus, the relationship between price and quantity supplied is positive or direct, and supply is graphed as an upsloping curve. The market supply curve is the horizontal summation of the supply curves of individual producers of the product.

5. Changes in one or more of the determinants of supply—a change in resource prices, production techniques, taxes or subsidies, the prices of other goods, price expectations, or the number of sellers in the market—shift the supply curve of a product. A shift to the right is an increase in supply; a shift to the left is a decrease in supply. In contrast, a change in the price of the product being considered causes a change in the quantity supplied, which is shown as a movement from one point to another point on a fixed supply curve.

6. The equilibrium price and quantity are those indicated by the intersection of the supply and demand curves. The interaction of market demand and market supply adjusts the price to the point at which quantity demanded and quantity supplied are equal. This is the equilibrium price. The corresponding quantity is the equilibrium quantity.

7. The ability of market forces to synchronize selling and buying decisions to eliminate potential surpluses and shortages is known as the rationing function of prices.

8. A change in either demand or supply changes the equilibrium price and quantity. Increases in demand raise both equilibrium price and equilibrium quantity; decreases in demand reduce both equilibrium price and equilibrium quantity. Increases in supply reduce equilibrium price and increase equilibrium quantity; decreases in supply raise equilibrium price and reduce equilibrium quantity.

9. Simultaneous changes in demand and supply affect equilibrium price and quantity in various ways, depending on their direction and relative magnitudes.

TERMS AND CONCEPTS

market
demand
demand schedule
law of demand
diminishing marginal utility
income and substitution effect
demand curve
substitution effect
demand curve
determinants of demand
normal good
inferior good
substitute good

complementary good
change in demand (or supply) versus change in quantity
    demanded (or supplied)
supply
supply schedule
law of supply
supply curve
determinants of supply
surplus
shortage
equilibrium price and quantity
rationing function of prices

STUDY QUESTIONS

1. Explain the law of demand. Why does a demand curve slope downward? What are the determinants of demand? What happens to the demand curve when each of these determinants changes? Distinguish between a change in demand and a change in the quantity demanded, noting the cause(s) of each.

2. **KEY QUESTION** *What effect will each of the following have on the demand for product B?*
   a. *Product B becomes more fashionable.*
   b. *The price of substitute product C falls.*
   c. *Income declines and B is an inferior good.*
   d. *Consumers anticipate the price of B will be lower in the near future.*
   e. *The price of complementary product D falls.*
   f. *Foreign tariff barriers on B are eliminated.*

3. Explain the following news dispatch from Hull, England: "The fish market here slumped today to what local commentators called 'a disastrous level'—all because of a shortage of potatoes. The potatoes are one of the main ingredients in a dish that figures on almost every café-menu—fish and chips."

4. Explain the law of supply. Why does the supply curve slope upward? What are the determinants of supply? What happens to the supply curve when each of these determinants changes? Distinguish between a change in supply and a change in the quantity supplied, noting the cause(s) of each.

5. **KEY QUESTION** *What effect will each of the following have on the supply of product B?*
   a. *A technological advance in the methods of producing B.*
   b. *A decline in the number of firms in industry B.*
   c. *An increase in the prices of resources required in the production of B.*
   d. *The expectation that the equilibrium price of B will be lower in the future than it is currently.*
   e. *A decline in the price of product A, a good whose production requires substantially the same techniques and resources as does the production of B.*
   f. *The levying of a specific sales tax on B.*
   g. *The granting of a 50-cent per-unit subsidy for each unit of B produced.*

6. "In the corn market, demand often exceeds supply and supply sometimes exceeds demand." "The price of corn rises and falls in response to changes in supply and demand." In which of these two statements are the terms "supply" and "demand" used correctly? Explain.

7. **KEY QUESTION** *Suppose the total demand for wheat and the total supply of wheat per month in the Winnipeg grain market are as follows:*

Thousands of bushels demanded	Price per bushel	Thousands of bushels supplied	Surplus (+) or shortage (−)
85	$3.40	72	_____
80	$3.70	73	_____
75	$4.00	75	_____
70	$4.30	77	_____
65	$4.60	79	_____
60	$4.90	81	_____

   a. *What is the equilibrium price? What is the equilibrium quantity? Fill in the surplus-shortage column and use it to explain why your answers are correct.*
   b. *Graph the demand for wheat and the supply of wheat. Be sure to label the axes of your graph correctly. Label equilibrium price P and equilibrium quantity Q.*
   c. *Why will $3.40 not be the equilibrium price in this market? Why not $4.90? "Surpluses drive prices up; shortages drive them down." Do you agree?*

d. *Now suppose that the government establishes a ceiling (maximum legal) price of, say, $3.70 for wheat. Explain carefully the effects of this ceiling price. Demonstrate your answer graphically. What might prompt government to establish a ceiling price?*

8. **KEY QUESTION** *How will each of the following changes in demand and/or supply affect equilibrium price and equilibrium quantity in a competitive market; that is, do price and quantity rise, fall, or remain unchanged, or are the answers indeterminate because they depend on the magnitudes of the shifts? You should use supply and demand diagrams to verify the answers.*
   a. *Supply decreases and demand is constant.*
   b. *Demand decreases and supply is constant.*
   c. *Supply increases and demand is constant.*
   d. *Demand increases and supply increases.*
   e. *Demand increases and supply is constant.*
   f. *Supply increases and demand decreases.*
   g. *Demand increases and supply decreases.*
   h. *Demand decreases and supply decreases.*

9. "Prices are the automatic regulator that tends to keep production and consumption in line with each other." Explain.

10. Explain: "Even though parking meters may yield little or no net revenue, they should nevertheless be retained because of the rationing function they perform."

11. Critically evaluate: "In comparing the two equilibrium positions in Figure 4-6a, I note that a larger amount is actually purchased at a higher price. This refutes the law of demand."

12. Suppose you go to a recycling centre and are paid $.25 per kilogram for your aluminum cans. However, the recycler charges you $.20 per bundle to accept your old newspapers. Use demand and supply diagrams to portray both markets. Explain how different government policies with respect to the recycling of aluminum and paper might account for these different market outcomes.

13. **Advanced analysis:** Assume that demand for a commodity is represented by the equation $P = 10 - .2Q_d$ and supply by the equation $P = 2 + .2Q_s$, where Q_d and Q_s are quantity demanded and quantity supplied, respectively, and P is price. Using the equilibrium condition $Q_s = Q_d$, solve the equations to determine equilibrium price. Now determine equilibrium quantity. Graph the two equations to substantiate your answers.

14. **(The Last Word)** Discuss the economic aspects of ticket scalping, specifying gainers and losers.

15. **WEB-BASED QUESTION** **Changes in Demand—Baby Diapers and Retirement Villages** Other things equal, an increase in the number of buyers for a product or service will increase demand. Baby diapers and retirement villages are two products designed for different population groups. The U.S. Census www.census.gov/ipc/www/idbpyr.html provides population pyramids (graphs which show the distribution of population by age and sex) for countries for the current year, 2025, and 2050. View the population pyramids for Mexico, Japan, and the United States. Which country would you expect to have the greatest percentage increase in demand for baby diapers in the year 2050? For retirement villages? Which country would you expect to have the greatest absolute increase in demand for baby diapers? For retirement villages?

APPENDIX TO CHAPTER 4

THE MATHEMATICS OF MARKET EQUILIBRIUM

A market equilibrium is the price and the quantity, denoted as the pair (Q*, P*), of a commodity bought or sold at price P*. The following mathe-matical note provides an introduction of how a market equilibrium (Q*, P*) is derived.

The market equilibrium is found by using the market demand (buyers' behaviour), the market supply (sellers' behaviour), and the negotiating process (to find the agreed upon price and quantity, namely P* and Q*, on which to transact). The market equilibrium is identified by the condition reached at the end of the negotiating process that at the price they negotiated, P*, the quantity of the commodity that buyers are willing to buy, denoted as Q_D, and the quantity sellers are willing to sell, denoted as Q_S, matches exactly.

The equation describing the downward sloping demand, in which Q_D represents the quantity demanded by buyers and P the price, is

$$P = a - bQ_d$$

The demand tells us that if the price is higher than *a* then the buyers will not buy; thus, for a transaction to occur the price must be lower. The demand also tells us that at a price lower than *a* the quantity demanded by the buyers increases. Buyers' behaviour, as described by the demand equation, is that at lower prices buyers buy more quantity.

The equation describing the upward sloping market supply function, in which Q_S represents the quantity supplied by sellers and P the price is

$$P = c + dQ_s$$

For the sellers if the price is lower than *c* then they will sell nothing. If the price is *c* or higher, then the supply equation states that sellers facing higher prices sell more quantity. Sellers' behaviour, as described by the supply equation, is that at higher prices sellers sell more quantity.

The negotiating process (in which price and quantity or both adjust) provides the mechanism by which, eventually, buyers and sellers agree upon a price, P*, and a quantity, Q*, at which they can buy and sell and thus complete the transaction. At the end of the negotiating process, the quantity demanded by the buyers, Q_D, is equal to the quantity supplied by the sellers, Q_S (at the agreed upon price), and thus the market is in equilibrium. The mathematical representation of such a negotiating process is described in the following paragraphs.

At the agreed price, P*, the equilibrium condition of the negotiating process, the equality in the quantity demanded and supplied, is

$$D_d = Q_s$$

Having denoted Q* as the equilibrium quantity, then it must be that $Q^* = Q_d = Q_s$. To solve for the equilibrium quantity Q* and the equilibrium price

P* the demand and supply functions are used. With Q* the equilibrium quantity, for the buyers

$$P^* = a - bQ^*,$$

and for the sellers

$$P^* = c + dQ^*.$$

Now, since P* is the same agreed upon price by both buyer and seller, then

$$a - bQ^* = c + dQ^*,$$

giving the equilibrium quantity, Q*, as

$$Q^* = (a - c)/(b + d).$$

To find P* substitute $(a - c)/(b + d)$ in the supply (or demand) function.

$$P^* = c + d(a - c)/(b + d), \text{ thus}$$

$$P^* = (ad + bc)/(a + d).$$

The equilibrium is $(Q^*, P^*) = [(a - c)/(b + d), (ad + cb)/(a + d)]$.

The market equilibrium may also be represented diagrammatically, as follows:

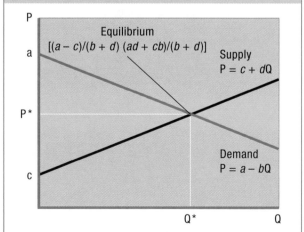

FIGURE A4-1

- Increase (decrease) in demand, *a* increases (decreases) and both Q* and P* increase (decrease)
- Increase (decrease) in supply, *c* decreases (increases) and Q* increases (decreases) and P* decreases (increases)

The Public Sector

WE NOTED IN CHAPTER 2 THAT A SOCIETY CAN choose various ways to deal with the economizing problem. A pure market system is one possibility; at the other extreme is a command economy, in which a central government makes the decisions as to what to produce, how much to produce, by what method to produce it, and how that production is distributed.

In fact, all economies are "mixed" to some extent; government and the market system share the responsibility of responding to the Five Fundamental Questions. In Canada, we have an economy dominated by markets, but government has played a significant role in the economic system of this country from the time of Confederation.

In this chapter we investigate several economic functions of the public sector in a market economy. Much emphasis is put on the crucial role of government when markets fail to fulfil their function of coordinating economic activity. The chapter ends with a discussion of the growth of government in recent decades and the ongoing debate on the extent of government involvement in self-regulating markets.

IN THIS CHAPTER YOU WILL LEARN:

The five main economic functions of government in a market economy.

●

What spillover benefits and costs are.

●

What a public good is.

●

The source of government revenues and expenditures in Canada.

The
Big Picture

PRIVATE MARKETS ARE VERY GOOD AT GETTING the most out of available resources. Markets also produce those goods and services that people with income to spend want most. But the market system does not arise instantaneously on its own. It requires certain institutions to function well. Among the most important of these is a central government that provides an environment conducive to a market economy.

Sometimes the market system fails to do its job of coordinating production and consumption decisions, or does it badly. We call these instances "market failures," and they require government intervention.

As you read this chapter, keep the following points in mind:
- **Key Concepts 1, 4,** and **7** are discussed.
- At times market participants have an effect on individuals not involved in market transactions. These effects can be negative, as in the case of a firm polluting the water supply of a village, or positive, as when a neighbour undertakes to beautify her house.
- Sometimes the market system does not produce enough of a specific good that is economically or socially justified. In such instances the government either produces the good itself or gives subsidies to private firms to supply it. ∎

ECONOMIC FUNCTIONS OF GOVERNMENT

All economies in the real world are "mixed": Government and the market system share the responsibility of responding to the Five Fundamental Questions. The Canadian economy is predominantly a market economy, yet the economic activities of government are of great significance.

In the next several sections we discuss the major economic functions of government—the public sector—in our economy. These functions are: (1) providing a legal and social framework; (2) maintaining competition within markets, (3) redistributing income as necessary for equity, (4) reallocating resources, and (5) stabilizing the economy.

The first two of these economic functions strengthen and facilitate the working of the market system; the last three modify pure capitalism to achieve economic and social goals.

LEGAL AND SOCIAL FRAMEWORK

Government provides the legal framework and the services needed for a market economy to operate effectively. The legal framework sets the legal status of business enterprises, ensures the rights of private ownership, and allows the making and enforcement of contracts. Government also establishes the legal "rules of the game" governing the relationships of businesses, resource suppliers, and consumers with one another. Units of government can referee economic relationships, seek out foul play, and exercise authority in imposing appropriate penalties.

Services provided by government include police powers to maintain internal order, a system of standards for measuring the weight and quality of products, and a system of money to facilitate exchanges of goods and services.

The Food and Drug Act and Regulations of 1920 is an example of how government has strengthened the market system. This act sets rules of conduct governing producers in their relationships with consumers. It prohibits the sale of adulterated and misbranded foods and drugs, requires net weights and ingredients of products to be specified on their containers, establishes quality standards that must be stated on labels of packaged foods, and prohibits deceptive claims on patent-medicine labels. These measures are designed to prevent fraudulent activities by producers and to increase the public's confidence in the integrity of the market system. Similar legislation pertains to labour-management relations and relations of business firms to one another.

This type of government activity is presumed to improve resource allocation. Supplying a medium of exchange, ensuring product quality, defining ownership rights, and enforcing contracts increase the volume and safety of exchange. This widens markets and permits greater specialization in the use of property and human resources. Such specialization means a more efficient allocation of resources. However, some argue that government overregulates the interactions of businesses, consumers, and workers and say that this stifles economic incentives and impairs efficiency.

MAINTAINING COMPETITION

Competition is the basic regulatory mechanism in a market economy. It is the force that subjects producers and resource suppliers to the dictates of consumer sovereignty. With competition, buyers are the boss, the market is their agent, and businesses are their servants.

It is a different story where there is only a single seller—a **monopoly**—or a small handful of sellers with *monopoly power*. Monopolists are not regulated by competition. When the number of sellers becomes so small that each seller can influence total supply, the seller or sellers have the power to set the product price. By restricting supply, these firms can charge above-competitive prices. Also, because entry to these industries is blocked, monopolists can enjoy persistent economic profits. The restricted output and the high prices and profits directly conflict with the interests of consumers. In fact, producer sovereignty supplants consumer sovereignty, and monopoly supplants competition. Where there is monopoly, the pursuit of self-interest does *not* lead to the social good. Rather, society's economic resources are *underallocated* to the monopolized product.

In Canada, government has attempted to control monopoly primarily in two ways:

1. **REGULATION AND OWNERSHIP** In a few situations, industries are *natural monopolies*—industries in which technology is such that only a single seller can achieve the lowest possible costs. Government has allowed these monopolies to exist but has also created public commissions to regulate their prices and set their service standards. Some aspects of transportation, communications, electricity, and other utilities are natural monopolies that government regulates in varying degrees. Some-

times, especially at the local level of government, public ownership replaces regulation.

2. **ANTI-MONOPOLY LAWS** In nearly all markets, efficient production can best be attained with a high degree of competition. The federal government has therefore enacted a series of anti-combines (anti-monopoly) laws, to maintain and strengthen competition.

REDISTRIBUTION OF INCOME

The market system is impersonal. It may distribute income with more inequality than society desires. The market system yields very large incomes to those whose labour, by virtue of inherent ability and acquired education and skills, commands high wages. Similarly, those who—through hard work or easy inheritance—possess valuable capital and land receive large property incomes.

But others in society have less productive ability, have received only modest amounts of education and training, and have accumulated or inherited no property resources. Moreover, many of the aged, the physically and mentally handicapped, and female-headed families earn only very small incomes, or, like the unemployed, no incomes at all. Thus, in the market system there is considerable inequality in the distribution of income and therefore in the distribution of output among individual households. Poverty amidst overall plenty in the economy persists.

Thus, society chooses to redistribute income through a variety of government policies and programs:

1. **TRANSFERS** *Transfer payments,* for example, in the form of welfare cheques, provide relief to the destitute, the dependent, the handicapped, and older citizens; employment insurance payments provide aid to the unemployed.

2. **MARKET INTERVENTION** Government also alters the distribution of income by *market intervention,* that is, by acting to modify the prices that are or would be established by market forces. Providing farmers with above-market prices for their outputs and requiring that firms pay minimum wages are illustrations of government price fixing designed to raise incomes of specific groups.

3. **TAXATION** The personal income tax has been used historically to take a larger proportion of

the incomes of the rich than of the incomes of the poor, thus narrowing the after-tax income gap between high- and low-income earners.

The *extent* to which government should redistribute income is subject to many debates. Redistribution involves both benefits and costs. The alleged benefits are greater "fairness," or "economic justice"; the alleged costs are reduced incentives to work, save, invest, and produce, and therefore less total output and income.

REALLOCATION OF RESOURCES

Market failure occurs when the competitive market system (1) produces the "wrong" amounts of certain goods and services or (2) fails to allocate any resources whatsoever to the production of certain goods and services whose output is economically justified. The first type of failure results from what economists call *spillovers*, and the second type involves *public goods*. Both kinds of market failure can be corrected by government action.

Spillovers or Externalities

When we say that competitive markets automatically bring about efficient resource use, we assume that all the benefits and costs for each product are fully reflected in the market demand and supply curves. This is not always so in real markets; certain benefits or costs may escape the buyer or seller.

A spillover occurs when some of the costs or the benefits of a good are passed on to or "spill over to" parties other than the immediate buyer or seller. Spillovers are also called *externalities* because they are benefits or costs accruing to some third party that is external to the market transaction.

Spillover Costs
Production or consumption costs that are inflicted on a third party without compensation are called **spillover costs**. Many spillover costs are in the form of environmental pollution. When a chemical manufacturer or meat-packing plant dumps its wastes into a lake or river, swimmers, fishermen, and boaters—and perhaps drinking-water supplies—suffer spillover costs. When a petroleum refinery pollutes the air with smoke or a paper mill creates distressing odours, the community bears spillover costs for which it is not compensated.

What are the economic effects? Recall that costs determine the position of the firm's supply curve. When a firm avoids some costs by polluting, its supply curve lies farther to the right than it does when the firm bears the full costs of production. This results in a larger output than is socially desirable—a market failure in the form of an *overallocation* of resources to the production of the good.

Correcting for Spillover Costs
Government can do two things to correct the overallocation of resources. Both solutions are designed to internalize the external costs, that is, to make the offending firm pay the costs rather than shift them to others:

1. **LEGISLATION** In our examples of air and water pollution, the most direct action is legislation prohibiting or limiting pollution. Such legislation forces potential polluters to pay for the proper disposal of industrial wastes—here, by installing smoke-abatement equipment or water-purification facilities. The idea is to force potential offenders, under the threat of legal action, to bear all the costs associated with production.

2. **SPECIFIC TAXES** A less direct action is based on the fact that taxes are a cost and therefore a determinant of a firm's supply curve. Government might levy a *specific tax*—a tax confined to a particular product—on each unit of the polluting firm's output. The amount of this tax would roughly equal the estimated amount of the spillover cost arising from the production of each unit of output. Through this tax, government would pass back to the offending firm a cost equivalent to the spillover cost that the firm is avoiding. This would shift the firm's supply curve to the left, reducing equilibrium output and eliminating the overallocation of resources.

Spillover Benefits
But spillovers may also appear as benefits. Production or consumption of certain goods and services may confer spillover or external benefits on third parties or on the community at large without compensating payment. Measles and polio immunization result in direct benefits to the immediate consumer of those vaccines. But immunization against contagious diseases yields widespread and substantial spillover benefits to the entire community. Discovery of an

AIDS vaccine would benefit society far beyond the persons vaccinated. Unvaccinated individuals would clearly benefit by the slowing of the spread of the disease.

Education is another example of **spillover benefits**. Education benefits individual consumers: "More educated" people generally achieve higher incomes than "less educated" people. But education also provides benefits to society. The economy as a whole benefits from a more versatile and more productive labour force, on the one hand, and smaller outlays for crime prevention, law enforcement, and welfare programs, on the other. There is evidence indicating that any worker with a *specific* educational or skill level will be more productive if associated workers have more education. In other words, worker Smith becomes more productive simply because coworkers Jones and Green are more educated.

Spillover benefits mean that the market demand curve, which reflects only private benefits, understates total benefits. The demand curve for the product lies farther to the left than it would if all benefits were taken into account by the market. This means that a smaller amount of the product will be produced or, alternatively, that there will be an *underallocation* of resources to the product—again a market failure.

Correcting for Spillover Benefits
How might the underallocation of resources associated with spillover benefits be corrected? The answer is to either subsidize consumers (to increase demand), subsidize producers (to increase supply), or, in the extreme, have government produce the product.

1. **SUBSIDIZE CONSUMERS** To correct the underallocation of resources to higher education, the Canadian government provides low-interest loans to students so that they can afford more education. These loans increase the demand for higher education.
2. **SUBSIDIZE SUPPLIERS** In some cases government might find it more convenient and administratively simpler to correct an underallocation by subsidizing producers. This is done in higher education, where provincial governments provide substantial portions of the budgets of colleges and universities. These subsidies lower the costs of producing higher education and increase its supply. Publicly subsidized immunization programs, hospitals, and medical research are other examples.
3. **PROVIDE GOODS VIA GOVERNMENT** A third policy option may be used where spillover benefits are extremely large: Government may finance or, in the extreme, own and operate all industries that are involved.

Public Goods and Services

Private goods, which are produced through the competitive market system, are said to be *divisible* because they are produced in units small enough to be purchased and used by individual buyers. Private goods are also subject to the **exclusion principle**. Buyers who are willing and able to pay the equilibrium price of the product obtain it, but those who are unable or unwilling to pay are *excluded* from the product and its benefits.

Certain other goods and services called **public goods** are not produced by the market system because they have the opposite characteristics. Public goods are indivisible; they must be produced in such large units that they cannot ordinarily be sold to individual buyers. Individuals can buy hamburgers, computers, and automobiles through the market, but not aircraft carriers, highways, space telescopes, and air-traffic control.

More important, *the exclusion principle does not apply to public goods*; there is no effective way of excluding individuals from their benefits once those goods come into existence. Obtaining the benefits of private goods requires that they be *purchased*; obtaining benefits from public goods requires only that they be *available*.

The classic public goods example is a proposed lighthouse on a treacherous coast. The construction of the lighthouse would be economically justified if its benefits (fewer shipwrecks) exceeded its cost. But the benefits accruing to one user would not be great enough to justify the purchase of such an indivisible product. Moreover, once it was in operation, the warning light would be a guide to all ships; there would be no practical way to exclude any captain from using the light. Economists call this the **free-rider-problem**: people receiving benefits from a good without contributing to its cost.

Because the exclusion principle does not apply to the lighthouse, private enterprises have no economic incentive to supply it. Since the services of the lighthouse cannot be priced and sold, it would be unprofitable for a private firm to devote resources to it. So here we have a service that could yield substantial benefits but to which the market would allocate no resources. It is a public good, much like national defence, flood control, public health, satellite navigation systems, and insect-abatement programs. If society requires such goods, they must be provided by the public sector and financed by compulsory charges in the form of taxes.

Quasi-Public Goods

The applicability of the exclusion principle distinguishes private from public goods, and government may provide the latter. However, many other goods and services are provided by government even though they could be made exclusive. Such goods, called **quasi-public goods**, include education, streets and highways, police and fire protection, libraries and museums, preventive medicine, and sewage disposal. These goods or services could be produced and delivered in such a way that the exclusion principle applied. All could be priced and provided by private firms through the market system. But, as noted earlier, these services have substantial spillover benefits, so they would be underproduced by the market system. Therefore, government may provide them to avoid the underallocation of resources that would otherwise occur.

Since quasi-public goods can be produced in either the private or the public sector—and because spillover benefits are difficult to measure—we can understand the continuing controversy surrounding the status of medical care and low-income housing. Are these private goods to be produced through the market system, or are they quasi-public goods to be provided by government?

Allocation of Resources to Public and Quasi-Public Goods

The market system fails to allocate resources for public goods and underallocates resources for quasi-public goods. What then is the mechanism by which such goods get produced?

Public and quasi-public goods are purchased through the government on the basis of group, or collective, choices. (Contrast this with private goods, which are purchased from private enterprises on the basis of individual choices.) The types and qualities of goods to be produced by government are determined in a democracy by political voting. That is, the members of a society vote for particular political candidates. Each candidate represents certain public policies, and those policies determine the quantities of the various public and quasi-public goods to be produced and consumed. The group choices made in the political arena supplement the choices of households and businesses in answering the Five Fundamental Questions.

How are resources reallocated from the production of private goods to the production of public and quasi-public goods? In an economy whose resources are fully employed, government must free resources from private goods production to make them available for production of public and quasi-public goods. The means of releasing resources from private uses is to reduce private demand for them. This is accomplished by levying taxes on households and businesses, taking some of their income out of the circular flow. With lower incomes and hence less purchasing power, households and businesses must curtail their consumption and investment spending. Taxes diminish the private demand for goods and services, which in turn reduce the private demand for resources. So by diverting purchasing power from private spenders to government, taxes remove resources from private uses. (Global Perspective 5-1 shows the extent to which various countries divert labour from private sector to public sector employment.)

Government expenditures of tax proceeds can then reallocate the resources to the provision of public and quasi-public goods and services. Personal and corporate income taxation releases resources from the production of consumer goods (food, clothing, television sets) and investment goods (printing presses, boxcars, warehouses). Government expenditures shift these resources to the production of public and quasi-public goods (post offices, submarines, parks). Government purposely reallocates resources to bring about significant changes in the composition of the economy's total output. *(Key Questions 3 and 4)*

STABILIZATION

Historically, the most recent function of government is that of stabilizing the economy—helping the private economy achieve full employment of resources and stable prices. Here we will only outline (rather than fully explain) how government tries to do this.

5-1
GLOBAL PERSPECTIVE

Government employment as a percentage of total employment, selected nations

The ratio of government employment to total employment measures the extent to which government diverts labour resources from the private sector in order to produce public goods and quasi-public goods. The ratio, or percentage, varies greatly among nations.

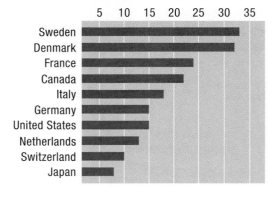

Government employment as a percentage of total employment, 1996

Source: Organization for Economic Cooperation and Development.

An economy's level of output depends directly on total or aggregate expenditure. A high level of total spending means it is profitable for industries to produce large outputs, which in turn ensures that both property and human resources will be employed at high levels. But aggregate spending may either fall short of or exceed the particular level necessary for full employment and price stability. Either of two possibilities, unemployment and inflation, may then occur:

1. **UNEMPLOYMENT**   The level of total spending in the private sector may be too low to employ all available resources. Then government may choose to augment private spending so that total spending—private *plus* public—will be sufficient to generate full employment. Government can do this by adjusting government spending and taxation. Specifically, it might increase its own spending on public goods and services or reduce taxes to stimulate private spending. It might also reduce interest rates to promote more private borrowing and spending.

2. **INFLATION**   Inflation is a rising general level of prices and is undesirable because it makes goods and services less attainable for many households. Prices of goods and services rise when the economy attempts to spend more than its capacity to produce. If aggregate spending exceeds the economy's output, prices will rise as consumers bid for available goods. That is, excessive aggregate spending is inflationary. Government's appropriate response is to eliminate the excess spending. It can do this by cutting its own expenditures, raising taxes to curtail private spending, or by increasing interest rates to reduce private borrowing and spending.

5-1
QUICK REVIEW

- Government enhances the operation of the market system by providing an appropriate legal foundation and promoting competition.

- Transfer payments, direct market intervention, and taxation are ways government can lessen income inequality.

- Government can correct for the overallocation of resources associated with spillover costs through legislation or specific taxes; the underallocation of resources associated with spillover benefits can be offset by government subsidies.

- Government (rather than private firms) must provide desired public goods because they are indivisible and the exclusion principle does not apply to them; government also provides many quasi-public goods because of their large spillover benefits.

- Government spending, tax revenues, and interest rates can be manipulated to stabilize the economy.

THE CIRCULAR FLOW REVISITED

Government is thoroughly integrated into the real and monetary flows that make up the economy. In Figure 5-1 we have integrated government into the circular flow model of Chapter 2. In that figure flows (1) through (4) restate Figure 2-6. Flows (1) and (2) show business expenditures for the resources pro-

FIGURE 5-1 The circular flow and the public sector

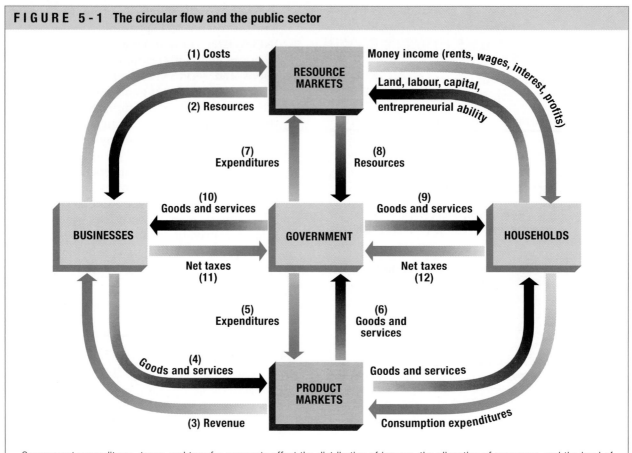

Government expenditures, taxes, and transfer payments affect the distribution of income, the allocation of resources, and the level of economic activity.

vided by households. These expenditures are costs to businesses but represent wage, rent, interest, and profit income to households. Flows (3) and (4) portray households' consumer expenditures for the goods and services produced by businesses.

Now consider the modifications resulting from the addition of government. Flows (5) through (8) tell us that government makes purchases in both product and resource markets. Specifically, flows (5) and (6) represent government purchases of such things as paper, computers, and military hardware from private businesses. Flows (7) and (8) reflect government purchases of resources. The federal government employs and pays salaries to members of Parliament, the armed forces, lawyers, meat inspectors, and so on. Provincial and municipal governments hire and pay teachers, bus drivers, police, and firefighters. The federal government might also lease or purchase land to expand a military base; a city may buy land on which to build a new elementary school.

Government then provides public goods and services to both households and businesses as shown by flows (9) and (10). Financing public goods and services requires tax payments by businesses and households as reflected in flows (11) and (12). These flows are labelled as *net* taxes to acknowledge that they also include "taxes in reverse" in the form of transfer payments to households and subsidies to businesses. Thus, flow (11) entails not merely corporate income, sales, and excise taxes flowing from businesses to government but also various subsidies to farmers, shipbuilders, and some airlines. Most business subsidies are "concealed" in the form of low-interest loans, loan guarantees, tax concessions, or public facilities provided at prices below their cost. Similarly, flow (12) includes both taxes (personal income taxes, payroll taxes) collected by government directly from households and transfer payments, for example, welfare payments and social insurance benefits, paid to households.

Our circular flow model shows how government can alter the distribution of income, reallocate resources, and change the level of economic activity. The structure of taxes and transfer payments can have a significant impact on income distribution. In flow (12) a tax structure that draws tax revenues primarily from well-to-do households, combined with a system of transfer payments to low-income households, will result in greater equality in the distribution of income.

Flows (6) and (8) imply an allocation of resources different from that of a purely private economy. Government buys goods and labour resources that differ from those purchased by households.

Finally, all the governmental flows suggest ways government might try to stabilize the economy. If the economy were experiencing unemployment, an increase in government spending with taxes and transfers held constant would increase total spending, output, and employment. Similarly, with the level of government expenditures constant, a decline in taxes or an increase in transfer payments would increase spendable incomes and boost private spending and employ-

ment. To fight inflation, the opposite policies would be in order: reduced government spending, increased taxes, and reduced transfers.

THE SIZE OF GOVERNMENT

The size of governments has increased significantly since the end of World War II. Not only have the number of employees of the federal, provincial, and municipal governments increased, but the shares of the total output of goods and services governments take in taxes and spend have also risen significantly. In 1997 the expenditures of all three levels of governments in Canada collectively represented about 45 percent of the annual production of the country; this is more than double what it was in 1945. Figure 5-2 shows the growth of government expenditures and revenues of all three levels of governments in Canada since 1970. Expenditures have risen more rapidly than revenues, giving rise to persistent deficits. This trend reversed beginning in the mid-1990s as all levels of government cut back their expenditures.

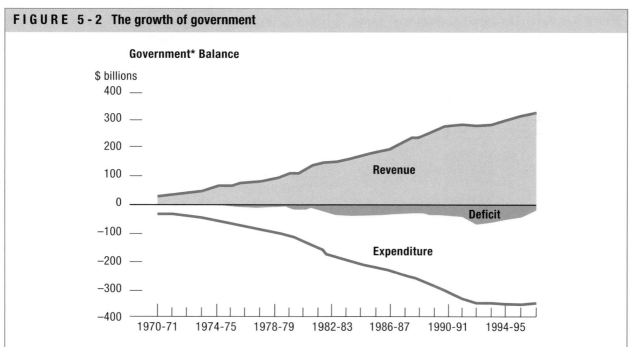

FIGURE 5-2 The growth of government

Government* Balance

An indication of the increasing growth of government is the expanding combined expenditures and revenues of the federal, provincial, and municipal governments. Both government revenues and expenditures have increased rapidly since 1970, but levelled off in the mid-1990s.

*Consolidated federal, provincial, territorial and municipal governments.
Source: Data for 1970–71, adapted from Statistics Canada, *Canada Yearbook, 1994*, Catalogue No. 11-402; "Canadian Economic Observer," Catalogue No. 11-010; for the remaining years computed from data in Statistics Canada. CANSIM, Matrix 3315 and 3776.

Growth of Government Outlays

We can get a general impression of the size and growth of government's economic role by examining government purchases of goods and services and government transfer payments. The distinction between these two types of outlays is significant.

1. **Government purchases** are "exhaustive"; they directly absorb or employ resources. For example, the purchase of a car absorbs the labour of engineers along with steel, plastic, and a host of other inputs.

2. **Transfer payments** are "nonexhaustive"; they do not directly absorb resources or account for production. Social and health benefits, welfare payments, veterans' benefits, and unemployment insurance payments are examples of transfer payments. Their key characteristic is that those who receive them make no current contribution to output in return for these payments.

Figure 5-3 shows the changing pattern of government expenditures between the mid-1980s and mid-1990s. The areas in which there have been sig-

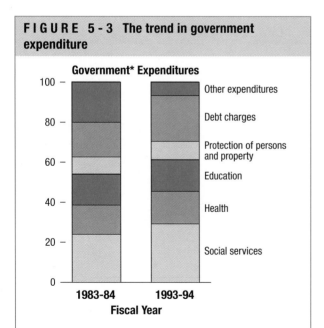

FIGURE 5-3 The trend in government expenditure

The two main changes in the pattern of government expenditures have been the increase in debt payment and spending on social services.

*Consolidated federal, provincial, territorial and municipal governments.
Source: Statistics Canada, *Canada Yearbook, 1997.*

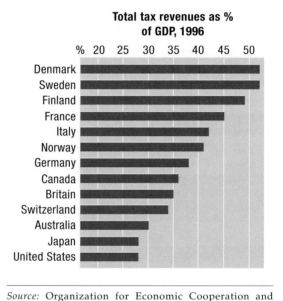

5-2
GLOBAL PERSPECTIVE

Total tax revenues as a percentage of domestic output

The ratio of tax revenues to domestic output is one measure of a country's tax burden (level of taxes). Among the world's industrialized nations, Canada's tax burden is closer to those in western Europe, such as Italy and Germany, than those of our immediate neighbour to the south, the United States.

Source: Organization for Economic Cooperation and Development.

nificant changes are debt charges and spending on social services. Debt charges have doubled, while expenditure on social services has reached about a third of all government expenditure. Global Perspective 5-2 shows that total revenues as a percentage of GDP for the federal government are about 35 percent, closer to European countries than to the United States.

SOURCES OF GOVERNMENT EXPENDITURES AND REVENUES

Now let's disaggregate the public sector into federal, provincial, and municipal units of govern-

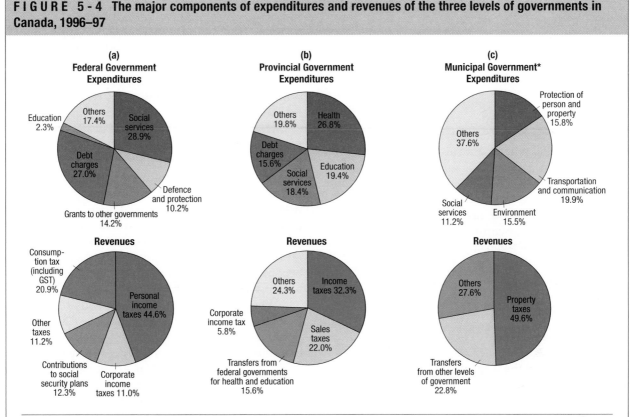

FIGURE 5-4 The major components of expenditures and revenues of the three levels of governments in Canada, 1996–97

Source: Statistics Canada, CANSIM, Matrix 3315, 3776, and 7093. More recent data are available from Statistics Canada www. statcan. ca/english/Pgdb/State/govern.htm.
*Municipal government data are for 1996.

ment to compare their expenditures. Figure 5-4a tells the story for the federal government.

Federal Expenditures and Revenues

Figure 5-4a shows that three important areas of federal spending stand out: (1) social services, (2) protection of persons and property, and (3) interest on the public debt. The social services category, representing almost 30 percent of total expenditures, reflects the myriad income-maintenance programs for the aged, the disabled, the unemployed, the handicapped, and families with no breadwinner. *Transfers to other governments* constitute about 14 percent of the federal budget and underscore the fact that provinces and municipalities have constitutional responsibilities but inadequate sources of revenues. *Interest on the public debt* has risen steeply in recent years because the public debt itself has grown.

On the revenue side, **personal income taxes** continue to contribute the largest share of federal government revenues at about 45 percent; **corporate income taxes** represent 11 percent, while contributions to social security plans account for 12 percent. The remaining revenues are raised by a variety of taxes, including the Goods and Services Tax (GST), which contributes about 21 percent.

Provincial Expenditures and Revenues

Health is the largest provincial and territorial outlay at an estimated 27 percent of total expenditures in 1996–97. Education was the second largest outlay at about 19 percent, and social services, the third largest expenditure, accounted for about the same percentage (18.4 percent).

Figure 5-4b shows that income taxes, general sales taxes, and transfers from other levels of governments represented the main generators of revenues at 32.3 percent, 22 percent, and 15.6 percent respectively.

Municipal Government Expenditures and Revenues

Transportation and communication is the largest component of municipal government spending at almost 20 percent of total expenditures, as Figure 5-4c shows. The other main categories of expenditures are environmental, person and property protection, and social services outlays.

Municipal government revenues come primarily from **property taxes** (50 percent of the total); provincial government transfers make up about a quarter of the rest.

THE DEBATE OVER THE SIZE OF GOVERNMENT

The debate over the appropriate size of government is a long-standing one, but it has received considerable attention in the last decade as government debt has spiralled upwards.

There are those who argue passionately for reducing government expenditure as a way of bringing down government deficits and reducing the size of government itself. Others maintain the government debt problem has been exaggerated and that if it is, or becomes, a problem the government ought to raise revenues by taxing corporations and well-off Canadians at a higher rate.

These differing views arise because of the different perceptions of the effectiveness of government policies in the past. Those in favour of reducing the size of government argue that instances of government success at alleviating social and economic problems are rare. Those who favour increasing taxes to deal with the mounting debt point out how much worse the social and economic problems would have been and are likely to become if drastic government expenditure cutbacks were implemented.

Whichever side of the debate you are on, there is no dispute over the fact that in the last 20 years the public debt in Canada has risen steeply, and more so than the OECD average. Figure 5-5 shows the steep rise in the Canadian public net debt compared with the OECD average between the mid-1980s and mid-1990s. Since then the growth of the public debt has levelled off and actually begun to fall.

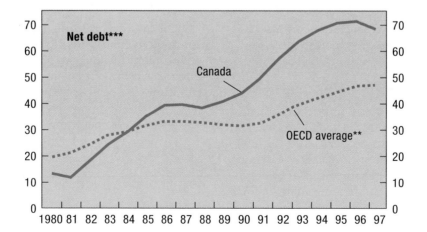

FIGURE 5 - 5   Public debt* as a percentage of GDP

Since the mid-1980s, Canada's public debt has grown much more rapidly than the OECD average. Recently the public debt has levelled off and begun to fall compared to the OECD average.

*General government: National Accounts definitions. 1997 data are OECD projections.
**Weighted average using 1991 GDP weights and exchange rates.
***Financial liabilities less financial assets.
Source: OECD, National Accounts: Secretariat estimates.

In
The Media

Blue-box Program not Huge Success*

Leaked memo shows recycling cost far greater than disposal in landfills

By Gay Abbate
The Globe and Mail

TORONTO—The blue-box recycling program in Toronto is far from the financial success that has been claimed, with 85 per cent of all residential garbage ending up at landfill sites, according to a leaked municipal works department document.

The document, leaked to The Globe and Mail and some Toronto city councillors, shows how poorly the blue-box program is doing 11 years after it was implemented.

The figures on the recycling program are on a one-page spreadsheet that Art Smith, a senior engineer in the waste reduction division of the former municipality of Metro Toronto, sent to a colleague in the old city of Toronto works department this month. The departments have since merged as part of the amalgamation of Toronto and other municipalities.

The data show that Torontonians produce about 859,262 tonnes of garbage annually, costing $89.8-million to collect and recycle or dump.

Among the details outlined in the document:

- About 39.5 per cent of the 5,818 tonnes of plastic containers used are deposited into blue boxes, but only 22 per cent of the total consumption ends up being recycled.
- About 25.8 per cent of the 6,654 tonnes of high-density polyethylene products are discarded into blue boxes but only 20 per cent is recycled.
- Only 23.31 per cent of the 6,620 tonnes of aluminum cans used are put into blue boxes, but only 22 per cent is recycled.
- About 112,600 tonnes of cardboard and corrugated products are generated, of which only 12.65 per cent is deposited in blue boxes, but all is recycled.

The figures are outrageous and shocking, said Councillor Judy Sgro, a strong advocate of recycling in the former municipality of North York, where she also was a councillor.

"It's costing us a fortune in dollars [to recycle], and most of the material is still ending up in landfill sites."

Ms. Sgro, who also received a copy of the document, said in an interview last night that the numbers are "significantly different from figures [Metro] staff gave me six weeks ago."

She said she was told that it cost about $55 a tonne to collect and recycle items in the blue boxes and $60 a tonne to put them into a dump site.

And last month, the group Corporations Supporting Recycling produced similar figures in a news release: $52 a tonne for recycling, compared with $87 a tonne for disposal in a landfill.

But according to the leaked figures, the net recycling cost per tonne is $136.89 and the cost for landfill disposal is $96.90 a tonne.

"Staff is telling us a major success story, but the numbers show otherwise," Ms. Sgro said.

Last year, Metro Toronto councillors approved construction of a recycling plant in the Dufferin Street and Allan Road area to sort all recyclable materials. The cost, between $4 million and $7 million, was approved because politicians believed the blue-box program was a success.

In light of the new figures, Toronto Council should halt the project immediately, Ms. Sgro said. She plans to demand that works department staff prepare a report for Mayor Mel Lastman, a strong advocate of recycling when he was mayor of North York.

---

*Source: Globe and Mail, January 27, 1998, pp. A1 and A12. Reprinted with permission from the Globe and Mail. *Subsequent stories on this subject suggested that recycling costs are not as high as this article reports.*

THE STORY IN BRIEF

The blue-box program in one large Canadian city seems to have failed. Most of the plastic containers, aluminum cans, and cardboard and corrugated products still end up in landfill sites, and the cost of recycling what is collected is much higher than dumping it in landfill sites.

THE ECONOMICS BEHIND THE STORY

- Garbage can cause negative externalities by polluting landfill sites or taking up valuable farmland or potential residential building sites around urban areas. One way to reduce these negative externalities is to recycle some of the refuse.

- According to the report, many people are not separating their garbage; most of the recyclable refuse such as newspaper and plastic containers is thrown out with the rest of the garbage. This suggests that the marginal benefit of recycling to most people is less than the marginal cost associated with separating the garbage. It also appears that the cost of recycling is significantly higher than putting it in landfill sites.

- Can you think of a way to get households to reduce the amount of garbage they generate? ■

The
Last Word

MARKET FAILURE AND THE NEED FOR GOVERNMENT

Private markets fulfil individual desires very well, but where there is a need for collective action, they often fail.

SUPPOSE A MUNICIPALITY REQUIRES NEW ROADS. In the absence of a government request that a private firm build it, it is unlikely that a private firm will build the required road on its own initiative. Or, to express it in another way, private markets will not make available public goods. The citizens of the municipality have to elect a government to either direct a private firm to build the road, or hire people to buy the capital equipment needed to construct the road on its own.

Why would a private firm not undertake to build a road on its own? The obstacle is common property rights. The land on which the road is to be built must be owned by the firm before it would consider building the road. Lands used by all citizens are most often held publicly. The firm would thus need to get the consent of all the citizens affected. Such unanimity would be difficult to achieve. Indeed, it is the difficulty of making collective decisions that makes governments essential to the creation of an infrastructure—such as roads and airports—necessary to facilitate the functioning of markets. Not only must a decision be made to build the road, but then the decision must be made as to who should bear the cost. The free-rider problem arises here. Every individual hopes someone will pay for the needed road. This way he or she can have the benefits without contributing to its cost. The free-rider problem can potentially arise in all situations where collective action must be taken. Unless we have a central authority—government—with the monopoly power to impose costs on all members of a society, many socially useful projects will not be undertaken.

In a pathbreaking book, *The Logic of Collective Action*,[1] Mancur Olson pointed out some 30 years ago that contrary to popular belief, groups of individuals with common interest do not necessarily attempt to further those common interests. In many instances group members attempt to further their own personal interests. A few years later, the political scientist Garrett Hardin popularized the term "the tragedy of the commons"[2] to describe the problems that arise when there are common property rights. For example, where there are common property rights to a natural resource, it is typically overexploited. The cod stocks on Canada's east coast have suffered just that fate.

Where collective action is required, or where there are common property rights, governments are needed because markets fail to bring together the interests of the individual and those of society. The federal government has had to impose mandatory fishing restrictions to save the cod stocks from dwindling further. Governments must make decisions to construct a road, otherwise the road might never get built. Clearly, markets work best where there are private property rights. ■

---

[1] Mancur Olson, *The Logic of Collective Action* (Cambridge: Cambridge University Press, 1965).
[2] Garret Hardin, "The Tragedy of the Commons," *Science* 162 (1968):1243–48.

CHAPTER SUMMARY

1. Government enhances the operation of the market system by **a** providing an appropriate legal and social framework, and **b** acting to maintain competition.

2. Government alters the distribution of income through the tax-transfer system and market intervention.

3. Spillovers or externalities cause the equilibrium output of certain goods to vary from the socially efficient output. Spillover costs result in an overallocation of resources that can be corrected by legislation or specific taxes. Spillover benefits are accompanied by an underallocation of resources that can be corrected by subsidies to consumers or producers.

4. Only government is willing to provide public goods, because such goods are indivisible and entail benefits from which nonpaying consumers (free-riders) cannot be excluded; private firms will not produce these goods. Quasi-public goods have some characteristics of public goods and some of private goods; they are provided by government because the private sector would underallocate resources to their production.

5. Government can reduce unemployment or inflation by altering its taxation, spending, and interest-rate policies.

6. Government purchases use up or absorb resources; transfer payments do not. Government purchases have been rising as a percentage of domestic output since 1950. Transfers also have grown significantly, so that total government spending is now over 40 percent of domestic output.

7. The main categories of federal spending are for employment insurance, health, and interest on the public debt; revenues come primarily from personal income, payroll, and corporate income taxes.

8. The primary sources of revenue for the provinces are sales and excise taxes; public welfare, education, highways, and health and hospitals are their major expenditures.

9. At the local level, most revenue comes from property tax, and education is the largest expenditure.

10. Under our system of fiscal federalism, provincial and municipal tax revenues are supplemented by sizable revenue transfers from the federal government.

TERMS AND CONCEPTS

monopoly
spillover costs
spillover benefits
exclusion principle
public goods
free-rider problem

quasi-public goods
government purchases
transfer payments
personal income taxes
corporate income taxes
property taxes

STUDY QUESTIONS

1. List and briefly discuss the main economic functions of government. Which of these functions do you think is the most controversial? Explain your reasoning.

2. What divergences arise between equilibrium and an efficient output when **a** spillover costs and **b** spillover benefits are present? How might government correct for these discrepancies? "The presence of spillover costs suggests underallocation of resources to that product and the need for governmental subsidies." Do you agree? Why or why not? Explain how zoning and seat belt laws might be used to deal with a problem of spillover costs.

3. **KEY QUESTION** *What are the basic characteristics of public goods? Explain the significance of the exclusion principle. By what means does government provide public goods?*

4. **KEY QUESTION** *Draw a production possibilities curve with public goods on the vertical axis and private goods on the horizontal axis. Assuming the economy is initially operating on the curve, indicate how the production of public goods might be increased. How might the output of public goods be increased if the economy is initially operating at a point inside the curve?*

5. Use your understanding of the characteristics of private and public goods to determine whether the following should be produced through the market system or provided by government: **a** bread; **b** street lighting; **c** bridges; **d** parks; **e** swimming pools; **f** medical care; **g** mail delivery; **h** housing; **i** air-traffic control; **j** libraries. State why you answered as you did in each case.

6. Explain how government can manipulate its expenditures and tax revenues to reduce **a** unemployment and **b** the rate of inflation.

7. "Most government actions affect the distribution of income, the allocation of resources, and the levels of unemployment and prices." Use the circular flow model to confirm this assertion for each of the following: **a** the construction of a new high school in Huron County; **b** a 2 percent reduction in the corporate income tax; **c** an expansion of preschool programs for disadvantaged children; **d** a $50-million increase in spending for space research; **e** the levying of a tax on air polluters; and **f** a $1 increase in the legally required minimum wage.

8. What is the most important source of revenue and the major type of expenditure for the federal government? For provincial governments? For municipal governments?

9. **(The Last Word)** Why do private markets fail? In your answer, refer to the dwindling cod stocks on Canada's east coast.

10. **WEB-BASED QUESTION** **Federal Revenues and Expenditures** Look at Statistics Canada's Web site at www.statcan.ca/english/Pgdb/State/Government/govt02a.htm and locate the federal government revenues and expenditures tables for the last five years. What has been the trend for expenditures? Revenues? What is the trend in the annual deficit or surplus?

Canada in the Global Economy

BACKPACKERS IN THE WILDERNESS LIKE TO THINK they are "leaving the world behind." Ironically, like Atlas, they carry the world on their shoulders. Much of their backpacking equipment is imported—knives from Switzerland, rain gear from South Korea, cameras from Japan, aluminum pots made in England, miniature stoves from Sweden, sleeping bags from China, and compasses from Finland. Some backpackers wear hiking boots from Italy, sunglasses made in France, and watches from Japan or Switzerland. Moreover, they may drive to the trailheads in Japanese-made Toyotas or Swedish-made Volvos, sipping coffee from Brazil or snacking on bananas from Honduras.

International trade and the global economy affect all of us daily, whether we are hiking in the wilderness, driving our cars, listening to music, or working at our jobs. We cannot "leave the world behind." We are enmeshed with the rest of the world in a complex web of economic relationships—trading of goods and services, multinational corporations, cooperative ventures among the world's firms, and ties among the world's financial markets. This web is so complex that it is difficult to determine just what is—or isn't—a Canadian product! Japanese auto companies have set up factories in Ontario, while many "Canadian" manufacturers have factories or outlets in other countries, particularly in the United States.

This chapter introduces the basic principles underlying the global economy. (A more advanced discussion of international economics is found in the last part of this book.) Here, we first look at world trade today, Canada's role in it, and some factors that have caused it to grow. Next, we modify Chapter 5's circular flow diagram to account for international trade flows, explore the basis for world trade, and look at the system of exchange rates that facilitates it. Finally, we describe several restrictive trade practices and discuss major efforts to implement freer trade.

IN THIS CHAPTER YOU WILL LEARN:

That trade is crucial to Canada's economic well-being.

•

The distinction between absolute advantage and comparative advantage.

•

That comparative advantage explains the gains from specialization and trade.

•

How the value of a currency is established on foreign exchange markets.

•

The economic costs of trade barriers.

•

About Canada's participation in the North American Free Trade Agreement (NAFTA), and the world's other trading blocs.

The Big Picture

THE SCARCITY PROBLEM CAN BE LESSENED IF a society can produce more goods and services from its limited resources. One powerful way for all societies to produce more from the limited resources available to them is to specialize in producing specific goods. If all nations specialized in producing what each was especially good at, each could get its other needs by trading. If all nations specialized, the whole world would be materially better off since we would increase the total goods and services we could produce from available resources. As the twentieth century is coming to a close, this lesson is being followed by more and more nations. Not surprisingly, trade among nations is growing, and Canada is no exception in this trend.

As you read this chapter, keep the following points in mind:

- **Key Concept 5** is discussed.

- Opportunity cost plays a central role in specialization, and determines what products a nation ought to specialize in. Keep asking yourself what a particular good would cost to produce domestically compared to purchasing it from another nation. We could grow bananas in Canada (in greenhouses, of course), but could we purchase bananas at a lower price from a nation better suited to grow bananas?
- Specialization necessarily implies trade. Since nations have different currencies, there is a market for them called the foreign exchange market. As with any market, there are suppliers and those that demand a particular currency. The exchange rate is determined by supply and demand conditions at any given time period.
- Trade is reciprocal in nature: one nation's exports are another's imports, and a nation cannot import unless it also exports. ■

GROWTH OF WORLD TRADE

The volume of world trade is so large and its characteristics so unique that it is difficult to describe except in some general terms.

Volume and Pattern

Figure 6-1 provides a rough index of the importance of world trade for several selected countries. Many nations, such as Canada, with limited domestic markets cannot efficiently produce the variety of goods they want to consume. Such countries must import the goods they desire from other nations, which in turn means they must export, or sell abroad, some of their own products. In Canada exports make up about 38 percent of our national output. Other countries, the United States, for example, have rich and diversified resource bases and vast internal markets and are less dependent on world trade.

Volume   For Canada and the world, the volume of international trade has been increasing both absolutely and relatively. A comparison of the

boxed data within Figure 6-2 reveals the substantial growth in the absolute dollar volume of both Canadian exports and imports over the past several decades. The lines in the figure show the growth of exports and imports as a percentage of gross domestic product (GDP)—the dollar value of all goods and services produced within Canadian borders. Exports and imports currently are 38 and 37 percent of GDP respectively, up substantially from 1960.

Dependence   Canada depends heavily on the world economy. Canada is almost entirely dependent on other countries for bananas, cocoa, coffee, spices, tea, raw silk, and natural rubber. Imported goods compete strongly in many of our domestic markets—for example, French and Italian wines, and Japanese autos. Foreign cars now account for about a third of the total automotive sales in Canada. Even the great Canadian pastime—hockey—relies heavily on imported equipment.

But world trade is a two-way street, and many Canadian industries are highly dependent on foreign markets. Almost all segments of agriculture rely heavily on foreign markets—wheat exports vary from one-fourth to more than one-half of

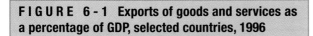

FIGURE 6-1 Exports of goods and services as a percentage of GDP, selected countries, 1996

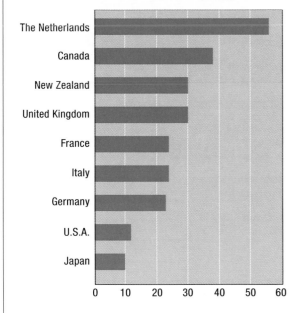

Canada's exports make up almost 40 percent of domestic output of goods and services.

Source: IMF, International Financial Statistics, 1997.

have either an overall trade surplus or deficit. How does a nation—or a person—obtain more goods from others than it provides to them? The answer is either by borrowing or selling assets.

Rapid Trade Growth

Several factors have facilitated the rapid growth of international trade since World War II.

Transportation Technology   High transportation costs are a barrier to any type of trade, particularly trade between distance places. But improvements in transportation have shrunk the globe, fostering world trade. Airplanes now transport low-weight, high-value items such as diamonds and semiconductors quickly from one nation to another. We now routinely transport oil in massive tankers, greatly reducing the cost of transportation per barrel. Grain is loaded onto ocean-going ships at

total output. The chemical, aircraft, automobile, machine tool, and forest industries are only a few of many Canadian industries that sell significant portions of their output in international markets. Figure 6-3 shows some of Canada's major commodity exports and imports.

Trade Patterns   Figure 6-4 provides an overview of the pattern of Canada's international trade.

1. The bulk of our export and import trade is with other industrially advanced nations, not with the less developed nations or the countries of Eastern Europe.
2. The United States is our most important trading partner quantitatively. Over 80 percent of our exports are sold to Americans, who in turn provide us with three-quarters of our imports.
3. Canada imports some of the same categories of goods that it exports—specifically, automobiles, industrial machinery and materials, chemicals, and telecommunications equipment.

Linkages   International trade means complex financial linkages among nations. A nation can

FIGURE 6-2 Canada's imports and exports as a percentage of GDP

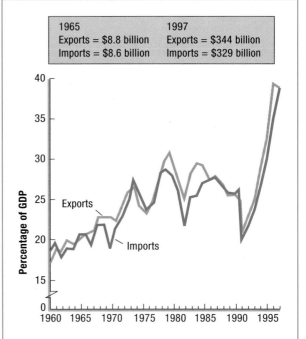

1965	1997
Exports = $8.8 billion	Exports = $344 billion
Imports = $8.6 billion	Imports = $329 billion

Canada's imports and exports have expanded since 1965, but have fluctuated over this period.

Source: Statistics Canada, CANSIM, Matrix 6548. Adapted from "Canadian International Merchandise Trade," Catalogue No. 65-001. More recent data are available from Statistics Canada www. statcan.ca/english/Pgdb/Economy/Economic/econ04.htm.

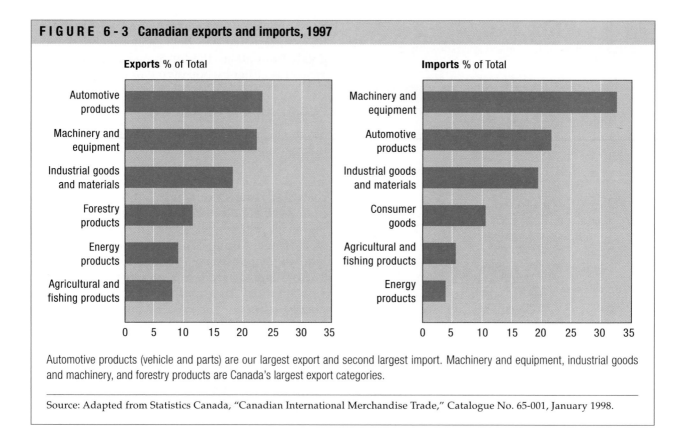

FIGURE 6-3 Canadian exports and imports, 1997

Automotive products (vehicle and parts) are our largest export and second largest import. Machinery and equipment, industrial goods and machinery, and forestry products are Canada's largest export categories.

Source: Adapted from Statistics Canada, "Canadian International Merchandise Trade," Catalogue No. 65-001, January 1998.

modern, efficient grain silos located at Great Lakes ports and the coastal ports of Vancouver and Halifax. Container ships transport self-contained railroad boxes directly to foreign ports, where cranes place the containers onto railroad cars for internal shipment. Natural gas flows through large diameter pipelines from exporting to importing countries—for instance, from Russia to Germany and from this country to the United States. Workers clean fish on large processing ships located

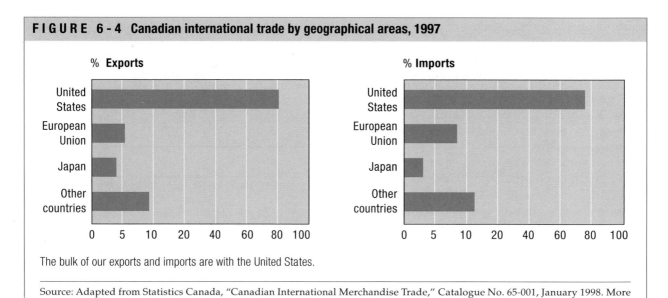

FIGURE 6-4 Canadian international trade by geographical areas, 1997

The bulk of our exports and imports are with the United States.

Source: Adapted from Statistics Canada, "Canadian International Merchandise Trade," Catalogue No. 65-001, January 1998. More recent data are available from Statistics Canada www. statcan.ca/english/Pgdb/Economy/International/gblec02a.htm.

directly on the fishing grounds. Refrigerated vessels then transport the fish to overseas ports.

Communications Technology   World trade has expanded because of dramatic improvements in communications technology. Telephones, fax (facsimile) machines, and computers now directly link traders around the world, allowing exporters to assess overseas markets and to complete trade deals. New communications enable us to move money around the world in the blink of an eye. Exchange rates, stock prices, and interest rates flash onto computer screens nearly simultaneously in Vancouver, Toronto, London, and Lisbon.

In short, exporters and importers in today's world can as easily communicate between Sweden and Australia as between Calgary and Winnipeg. A distributor in Calgary can get a price quote on 1,000 thatched baskets in Thailand just as quickly as a quotation on 1,000 tonnes of steel in Hamilton.

General Decline in Tariffs   Tariffs—excise taxes (duties) on imported products—have had their ups and downs, but since 1940 have generally fallen worldwide. A glance ahead to Figure 6-8 shows that Canada's tariff duties as a percentage of dutiable imports are now about 5 percent, down substantially from the highs of 1930. Many nations still have barriers to free trade, but on average, tariffs have fallen greatly, increasing international trade.

Peace   World War II matched powerful industrial countries against one another and thus disrupted commercial international trade. Not only has trade been restored since World War II, but it has been greatly bolstered by peaceful relations and by trade agreements. In particular, Japan and Germany—two defeated World War II powers—now are major participants in world trade.

Participants

All nations of the world participate to some extent in international trade.

Canada, United States, Japan, and Western Europe   As implied in Global Perspective 6-1, the top participants in world trade are the United States, Germany, and Japan. In 1996 these three nations had combined exports of over U.S. $1.5 trillion. Along with Germany, other Western European nations such as France, Britain, and Italy are

6-1
GLOBAL PERSPECTIVE

Comparative exports in billions of U.S. dollars

The United States, Germany, and Japan are the world's largest exporters. Canada ranks seventh.

Merchandise exports, 1996
(billions of dollars)

Source: World Trade Organization.

major exporters and importers. In fact, Canada, the United States, Japan, and the Western European nations now dominate world trade. These areas also are at the heart of the world's financial system and headquarter most of the world's large **multinational corporations**, which have sizable foreign production and distribution activities in other countries. Among the world's top 25 multinationals are Royal Dutch Shell and Unilever (Britain and the Netherlands); Ford Motor, General Motors, and IBM (United States); British Petroleum (Britain); Nestlé (Switzerland); Fiat (Italy); Siemens and Bayer Chemicals (Germany); Mitsubishi and Mitsui (Japan); and Elf Aquitaine (France).

New Players   New, important participants have arrived on the world trade scene. One group of such nations is the newly industrializing Asian economies of Hong Kong (now part of China), Singapore, South Korea, and Taiwan. These "**Asian**

tigers" have expanded their share of world exports from about 3 percent in 1972 to more than 10 percent today. Together they export as much as Japan and much more than either France, Britain, or Italy. Other countries in Southeast Asia, particularly Malaysia and Indonesia, have also expanded their international trade.

China is another emerging trading power. Since initiating market reforms in 1979, its annual growth of output has averaged 9 percent (compared to 2 to 3 percent annually in Canada). At this remarkable rate of growth, China's total output nearly doubles every eight years! An upsurge of exports and imports has accompanied this expansion of output. In 1989 Chinese exports and imports each were about $50 billion. In 1996 they each topped $151 billion, with about a third of the exports going to Canada and the United States. Also, China has been attracting much foreign investment (more than $600 billion since 1990). Experts predict that China will eventually become one of the world's leading trading nations.

The collapse of communism in Eastern Europe and the former Soviet Union has also altered world trade patterns. Before this collapse, the Eastern European nations of Poland, Hungary, Czechoslovakia, and East Germany traded mainly with the Soviet Union and such political allies as North Korea and Cuba. Today, East Germany is reunited with West Germany, and Poland, Hungary, and the Czech Republic have established new trade relationships with Western Europe and America.

Russia itself has initiated far-reaching market reforms, including widespread privatization of industry, and has consummated major trade deals with firms from across the globe. Although its transition to capitalism has been far from smooth, there is no doubt that Russia has the potential to be a major trading power. Other former Soviet republics—now independent nations—such as Ukraine and Estonia also are opening their economies to international trade and finance.

BACK TO THE CIRCULAR FLOW MODEL

We can easily add "the rest of the World" to Chapter 5's circular flow model. We do so in Figure 6-5 via two adjustments.

1. Our previous "Resource Markets" and "Product Markets" now become "Canadian Resource Markets" and "Canadian Product Markets." Similarly, we add the modifier "Canadian" to the "Businesses," "Government," and "Households" sectors.

2. We place the foreign sector—the "Rest of the World"—so that it interacts with Canadian Product Markets. This sector designates all foreign nations that we deal with and the individuals, businesses, and governments that make them up.

Flow (13) in Figure 6-5 shows that people, businesses, and governments abroad buy Canadian products—our exports—from our product market. This goods and services flow of Canadian exports to foreign nations is accompanied by an opposite monetary revenue flow (14) from the rest of the world to us. In response to these revenues from abroad, Canadian businesses demand more domestic resources (flow 2) to produce the goods for export; they pay for these resources with revenues from abroad. Thus, the domestic flow (1) of money income (rents, wages, interest, and profits) to Canadian households rises.

But our exports are only half the picture. Flow (15) shows that Canadian households, businesses, and government spend some of their income on foreign products. These products, of course, are our imports (flow 16). Purchases of imports, say, autos and electronic equipment, contribute to foreign output and income, which in turn provides the means for foreign households to buy Canadian exports.

Our circular flow model is a simplification that emphasizes product market effects, but a few other Canada–Rest of the World relationships also require comment. Specifically, there are linkages between the Canadian resource markets and the rest of the world.

Canada imports and exports not only products, but also resources. For example, we import some crude oil and export raw logs. Moreover, some Canadian firms choose to engage in production abroad, which diverts spending on capital from our domestic resource market to resource markets in other nations. For instance, Nortel might build an assembly plant in Germany. Or flowing the other direction, Sony might construct a plant for manufacturing CD players in Canada.

There are also international flows of labour. About 250,000 immigrants enter Canada each year. These immigrants expand the availability of labour resources in Canada, raising our total output and income. On the other hand, immigration tends to increase the labour supply in certain Canadian labour markets, reducing wage rates for some types of Canadian labour.

The expanded circular flow model also demonstrates that a nation engaged in world trade faces potential sources of instability that would not affect a "closed" nation. Recessions and inflation can be highly contagious among nations. Suppose the nations of Western Europe experienced a rather severe recession. As their income declines, they curtail purchases of Canadian exports. As a result flows (13) and (14) in Figure 6-5 decline and inventories of unsold Canadian goods rise. Canadian firms would respond by limiting their production and employment, reducing the flow of money income to Canadian households (flow 1). Recession in Europe in this case contributed to a recession in Canada.

FIGURE 6-5 The circular flow with the foreign sector

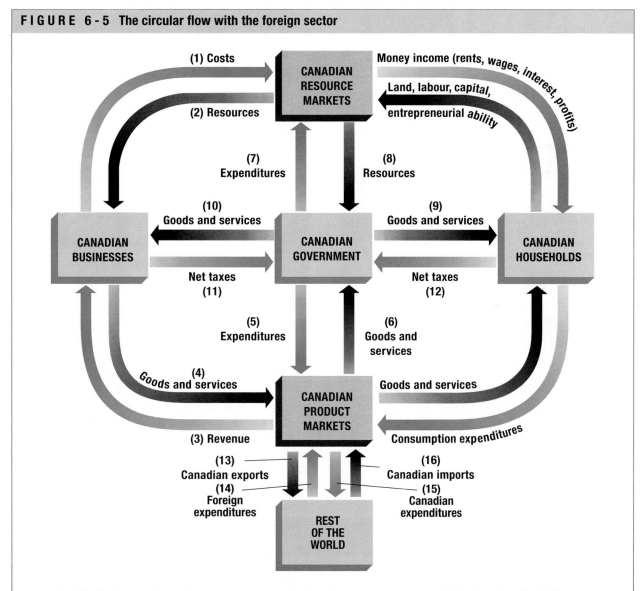

Flows 13-16 in the lower portion of the diagram show how the Canadian economy interacts with "The Rest of the World." People abroad buy Canadian exports, contributing to our business revenue and money income. Canadians, in turn, spend part of their incomes to buy imports from abroad. Income from a nation's exports helps pay for its imports.

Figure 6-5 also helps us to see that the foreign sector alters resource allocation and incomes in the Canadian economy. With a foreign sector, we produce more of some goods (our exports) and fewer of others (our imports) than we would otherwise. Thus, Canadian labour and other resources are shifted towards export industries and away from import industries. We use more of our resources to manufacture autos and telecommunication equipment. So we ask: "Do these shifts of resources make economic sense? Do they enhance our total output and thus our standard of living?" We look at some answers next. *(Key Question 3)*

6-1

QUICK REVIEW

- World trade has increased globally and nationally. Canada is a leading international trader, with exports and imports about 38 percent and 37 percent of GDP.

- Advances in transportation and communications technology, declines in tariffs, and peaceful relations among major industrial countries all have helped to expand world trade.

- World trade is dominated by the United States, Japan, Canada, and the Western European nations, but has recently been bolstered by new participates such as the "Asian tigers" (Hong Kong, Singapore, South Korea, and Taiwan), China, the Eastern European nations, and the newly independent states formerly making up the Soviet Union.

- The circular flow model with foreign trade includes flows of exports from our domestic product market, imports to our domestic product market, and the corresponding flows of spending.

SPECIALIZATION AND COMPARATIVE ADVANTAGE

Specialization and trade increase the productivity of a nation's resources and allow for larger total output than otherwise. This notion is not new! According to Adam Smith in 1776:

It is the maxim of every prudent master of a family, never to attempt to make at home what it will cost him more to make than to buy. The taylor does not attempt to make his own shoes, but buys them from the shoemaker. The shoemaker does not attempt to make his own clothes, but employs a taylor. The farmer attempts to make neither the one or the other, but employs those different artificers....

What is prudence in the conduct of every private family, can scarce be folly in that of a great kingdom. If a foreign country can supply us with a commodity cheaper than we can make it, better buy it of them with some part of the produce of our own industry, employed in a way in which we have some advantage.[1]

Nations specialize and trade for the same reasons as individuals: Specialization and exchange among individuals, regions, and nations result in greater overall output and income.

Basic Principle

In the early 1800s British economist David Ricardo expanded Smith's idea, observing that it pays for a person or a country to specialize and exchange even if that person or nation is more productive than a potential trading partner in *all* economic activities.

Consider an example of a chartered accountant (CA) who is also a skilled house painter. Suppose the CA can paint her house in less time than the professional painter she is thinking of hiring. Also suppose the CA can earn $50 per hour doing her accounting and must pay the painter $15 per hour. Let's say that it will take the accountant 30 hours to paint her house; the painter, 40 hours.

Should the CA take time from her accounting to paint her own house or should she hire the painter? The CA's opportunity cost of painting her house is $1,500 (= 30 hours × $50 per hour of sacrificed income). The cost of hiring the painter is only $600 (40 hours × $15 per hour paid to the painter). The CA is better at both accounting and painting— she has an **absolute advantage** in both accounting and painting. But her relative or comparative advantage lies in accounting (more will be said about comparative advantage below). She will *lower the cost of getting her house painted* by specializing in accounting and using some of the earnings from accounting to hire a house painter.

---

[1] Adam Smith, *The Wealth of Nations* (New York: Modern Library, Inc., 1937), p. 424. [Originally published in 1776.]

Similarly, the house painter can reduce his cost of obtaining accounting services by specializing in painting and using some of his income to hire the CA to prepare his income tax forms. Suppose that it would take the painter ten hours to prepare his tax return, while the CA could handle this task in two hours. The house painter would sacrifice $150 of income (= 10 hours × $15 per hour of sacrificed time) to accomplish a task that he could hire the CA to do for $100 (= 2 hours × $50 per hour of the CA's time). By using the CA to prepare his tax return, the painter lowers *his cost of getting the tax return completed*.

What is true for our CA and house painter is also true for nations. Countries can reduce their cost of obtaining desirable goods by specializing.

Comparative Costs

Our simple example clearly shows that specialization is economically desirable because it results in more efficient production. To understand the global economy, let's now put specialization in the context of trading nations, employing the familiar concept of the production possibilities table for our analysis. Suppose production possibilities for two products in Mexico and Canada are as shown in Tables 6-1 and 6-2. In these tables we assume constant costs. Each country must give up a constant amount of one product to secure a particular increment of the other product. (This assumption simplifies our discussion without impairing the validity of our conclusions.)

Specialization and trade are mutually beneficial or "profitable" to the two nations if the comparative costs of the two products within the two nations differ. What are the comparative costs of corn and soybeans in Mexico? By comparing production alternatives A and B in Table 6-1, we see that 5 tonnes of soybeans (= 15 − 10) must be sacrificed to produce 20 tonnes of corn (= 20 − 0). Or

TABLE 6-1 Mexico's production possibilities table (in tonnes)

Product	A	B	C	D	E
			PRODUCTION ALTERNATIVES		
Corn	0	20	24	40	60
Soybeans	15	10	9	5	0

TABLE 6-2 Canada's production possibilities table (in tonnes)

Product	R	S	T	U	V
			PRODUCTION ALTERNATIVES		
Corn	0	30	33	60	90
Soybeans	30	20	19	10	0

more simply, in Mexico it costs 1 tonne of soybeans (*S*) to produce 4 tonnes of corn (*C*); that is, $1S \equiv 4C$. Because we assumed constant costs, this domestic *comparative-cost ratio* will not change as Mexico expands the output of either product. This is evident from looking at production possibilities B and C, where we see that 4 more tonnes of corn (= 24 − 20) cost 1 unit of soybeans (= 10 − 9).

Similarly, in Table 6-2, comparing Canadian production alternatives R and S reveals that in Canada it costs 10 tonnes of soybeans (= 30 − 20) to obtain 30 tonnes of corn (= 30 − 0). That is, the domestic comparative-cost ratio for the two products in Canada is $1S \equiv 3C$. Comparing production alternative S and T reinforces this; an extra 3 tonnes of corn (= 33 − 30) comes at the direct sacrifice of 1 tonne of soybeans (= 20 − 19).

The comparative costs of the two products within the two nations are clearly different. Economists say that Canada has a domestic comparative advantage or, simply, a **comparative advantage** over Mexico in soybeans. Canada must forgo only 3 tonnes of corn to get 1 tonne of soybeans, but Mexico must forgo 4 tonnes of corn to get 1 tonne of soybeans. In terms of domestic opportunity costs, soybeans are relatively cheaper in Canada. *A nation has a comparative advantage in some product when it can produce that product at a lower domestic opportunity cost than can a potential trading partner.* Mexico, in contrast, has a comparative advantage in corn. While 1 tonne of corn costs $\frac{1}{3}$ tonne of soybeans in Canada, it costs only $\frac{1}{4}$ tonne of soybeans in Mexico. Comparatively speaking, corn is cheaper in Mexico.

Because of these differences in domestic comparative costs, if both nations specialize, each according to its comparative advantage, each can achieve a larger total output with the same total input of resources. Together they will be using their scarce resources more efficiently.

Terms of Trade

Canada can shift production between soybeans and corn at the rate of 1S for 3C. Thus, Canadians would specialize in soybeans only if they could obtain *more than* 3 tonnes of corn for 1 tonne of soybeans by trading with Mexico. Similarly, Mexico can shift production at the rate of 4C for 1S. So it would be advantageous to Mexico to specialize in corn if it could get 1 tonne of soybeans for *less than* 4 tonnes of corn.

Suppose that through negotiation the two nations agree on an exchange rate of 1 tonne of soybeans for $3\frac{1}{2}$ tonnes of corn. These **terms of trade** are mutually beneficial to both countries since each can "do better" through such trade than via domestic production alone. Canadians can get $3\frac{1}{2}$ tonnes of corn by sending 1 tonne of soybeans to Mexico, while they can get only 3 tonnes of corn by shifting resources domestically from soybeans to corn. Mexicans can obtain 1 tonne of soybeans at a lower cost of $3\frac{1}{2}$ tonnes of corn through trade with Canada, compared to the cost of 4 tonnes if Mexicans produce 1 tonne of corn themselves.

Gains from Specialization and Trade

Let's pinpoint the size of the gains in total output from specialization and trade. Suppose that before specialization and trade, production alternative C in Table 6-1 and alternative T in Table 6-2 were the optimal product mixes for the two countries. These outputs are shown in column 1 of Table 6-3. That is, Mexicans preferred 24 tonnes of corn and 9 tonnes of soybeans (Table 6-1) and Canadians preferred 33 tonnes of corn and 19 tonnes of soybeans (Table 6-2) to all other alternatives available within their respective domestic economies.

Now assume both nations specialize according to comparative advantage, Mexico producing 60 tonnes of corn and no soybeans (alternative E) and Canada producing no corn and 30 tonnes of soybeans (alternative R). These outputs are reflected in column 2 of Table 6-3. Using our $1S = 3\frac{1}{2}$ C terms of trade, assume Mexico exchanges 35 tonnes of corn for 10 tonnes of Canadian soybeans. Column 3 of Table 6-3 shows the quantities exchanged in this trade. As indicated in Column 4, after trade Mexicans have 25 tonnes of corn and 10 tonnes of soybeans, while Canadians have 35 tonnes of corn and 20 tonnes of soybeans. Compared with their optimum product mixes before specialization and trade (column 1), *both* nations now enjoy more corn and more soybeans! Specifically, Mexico has gained 1 tonne of corn and 1 tonne of soybeans. Canada has gained 2 tonnes of corn and 1 tonne of soybeans. These gains are shown in column 5 where we have subtracted the *before*-specialization outputs of column (1) from the *after*-specialization outputs in column (4).

Specialization based on comparative advantage improves resource allocation. The same total inputs of world resources result in a larger global output. If Mexico and Canada allocate all their resources to corn and soybeans respectively, the same total inputs of resources can produce more output between them, indicating that resources are being used or allocated more efficiently.

We noted in Chapter 2 that through specialization and international trade a nation can overcome the production constraints imposed by its domestic production possibilities table and curve. Table 6-3 and its discussion show just how this is done. The domestic production possibilities data of the two countries have not changed, meaning that neither nation's production possibilities curve

TABLE 6-3 Specialization according to comparative advantage and the gains from trade (in tonnes)

Country	(1) Outputs before specialization	(2) Outputs after specialization	(3) Amounts traded	(4) Outputs available after trade	(5) Gains from specialization and trade (4) − (1)
Mexico	24 corn	60 corn	−35 corn	25 corn	1 corn
	9 soybeans	0 soybeans	+10 soybeans	10 soybeans	1 soybeans
Canada	33 corn	0 corn	+35 corn	35 corn	2 corn
	19 soybeans	30 soybeans	−10 soybeans	20 soybeans	1 soybeans

has shifted. But specialization and trade mean that citizens of both countries have enjoyed increased consumption. *Thus, specialization and trade have the same effect as an increase in resources or technological progress: they make more goods available to an economy.* **(Key Question 4)**

FOREIGN EXCHANGE MARKET

People, firms, or nations that specialize in the production of specific goods or services exchange those products for money and then use the money to buy other products or to pay for the use of resources. Within the economy, prices are stated in the domestic currency and buyers use that currency to purchase domestic products. In Mexico, for example, buyers possess pesos, exactly the currency that sellers want.

International markets are different. How many dollars does it take to buy a truckload of Mexican corn selling for 3,000 pesos, a German automobile selling for 90,000 marks, or a Japanese motorcycle priced at 300,000 yen? Producers in Mexico, Germany, and Japan want payment in pesos, marks, and yen, respectively, so they can pay their wages, rent, interest, dividends, and taxes. A **foreign exchange market**, a market in which various national currencies are exchanged for one another, serves this need. The equilibrium prices in these markets are called **exchange rates**—the rate at which the currency of one nation is exchanged for the currency of another nation. (See Global Perspective 6-2.) Two points about the foreign exchange market are particularly noteworthy:

1. **A COMPETITIVE MARKET** Real-world foreign exchange markets conform closely to the markets discussed in Chapter 4. They are competitive markets characterized by large numbers of buyers and sellers dealing in standardized products such as the Canadian dollar, the German mark, the British pound, the Swedish krona, and the Japanese yen.

2. **LINKAGES TO ALL DOMESTIC AND FOREIGN PRICES** The market price or exchange rate of a nation's currency is an unusual price; it links all domestic (say, Canadian) prices with all foreign (say, Japanese or German) prices. Exchange rates enable consumers in one country to translate prices of foreign goods into units of their own currency: They

6-2

GLOBAL PERSPECTIVE

Exchange rates: foreign currency per Canadian dollar

The amount of foreign currency that a dollar will buy varies greatly from nation to nation. These amounts are for May 1998 and fluctuate in response to supply and demand changes in the foreign exchange market.

One Canadian dollar bought:

1.25 German marks
.42 British pounds
.70 U.S. dollars
5.9 Mexican pesos
1.0 Swiss francs
4.1 French francs
91 Japanese yen
949 South Korean won
2.36 Polish zloty

need only multiply the foreign product price by the exchange rate. If the dollar-yen exchange rate is $.01 (1 cent) per yen, a Sony television set priced at ¥20,000 will cost a Canadian $200 (= 20,000 × $.01) in the United States. If the exchange rate is $.02 (2 cents) per yen, it will cost a Canadian $400 (= 20,000 × $.02). Similarly, all other Japanese products would double in price to Canadian buyers. As you will see, a change in exchange rates has important implications for a nation's level of domestic production and employment.

Dollar-Yen Market

How does the foreign exchange market work? Let's look briefly at the market for dollars and yen, leaving details to a later chapter. Canadian firms exporting to Japan want payment in dollars, not yen; but Japanese importers of Canadian goods possess yen, not dollars. So the Japanese importers are willing to supply their yen in exchange for dollars in the foreign exchange market. At the same time, there are Canadian importers of Japanese goods who need to pay Japanese exporters with yen, not dollars. These Canadians go to the foreign exchange market as demanders of yen. We then have a market in which the "price" is in dollars and the "product" is yen.

Figure 6-6 shows the supply of yen (by Japanese importers) and the demand for yen (by Canadian importers). The intersection of demand curve D_y and supply curve S_y establishes the equilibrium dollar price of yen. Here the equilibrium price of 1 yen—the dollar-yen exchange rate—is 1 cent per yen, or $.01 = ¥1. At this price, the market for yen clears; there is neither a shortage nor a surplus of yen. The equilibrium $.01 price of 1 yen means that $1 will buy 100 yen or ¥100 worth of Japanese goods. Conversely, 100 yen will buy $1 worth of Canadian goods.

Changing Rates: Depreciation and Appreciation

What might cause the exchange rate to change? The determinants of the demand for and supply of yen are similar to the determinants of demand and supply for almost any product. In Canada, several things might increase the demand for—and therefore the dollar price of—yen. Incomes might rise in Canada, enabling Canadians to buy not only more domestic goods but also more Sony televi-

sions, Nikon cameras, and Nissan automobiles from Japan. So Canadians would need more yen and the demand for yen would increase. Or a change in Canadian tastes might enhance their preferences for Japanese goods. When gas prices soared in the 1970s, many Canadian auto buyers shifted their demands from gas-guzzling domestic cars to gas-efficient Japanese compact cars. The result was an increased demand for yen.

The point is that an increase in the Canadian demand for Japanese goods will increase the demand for yen and raise the dollar price of yen. Suppose the dollar price of yen rises from $.01 = ¥1 to $.02 = ¥1. When the dollar price of yen increases, we say a **depreciation** of the dollar relative to the yen has occurred: It then takes more dollars (pennies in this case) to buy a single unit of the foreign currency (a yen). Alternatively stated, the *international value of the dollar* has declined. A depreciated dollar buys fewer yen and therefore fewer Japanese goods; the yen and all Japanese goods have become more expensive to Canadians. Result: Canadian consumers shift their expenditures from Japanese goods to now less expensive Canadian goods. The Ford Taurus becomes relatively more attractive than the Honda Accord to Canadian consumers. Conversely, because each yen buys more dollars—that is, because the international value of the yen has increased—Canadian goods become cheaper to people in Japan and Canadian exports to them rise.

If the opposite event occurred—if the Japanese demanded more Canadian goods—then they would supply more yen to pay for these goods. The increase in the supply of yen relative to the demand for yen would decrease the equilibrium price of yen in the foreign exchange market. For example, the dollar price of yen might decline from $.01 = ¥1 to $.005 = ¥1. A decrease in the dollar price of yen is called an **appreciation** of the dollar relative to the yen. It means that the international value of the dollar has increased. It then takes fewer dollars (or pennies) to buy a single yen; the dollar is worth more because it can purchase more yen and therefore more Japanese goods. Each Sony Walkman becomes less expensive in terms of dollars, so Canadians purchase more of them. In general, Canadian imports rise. Meanwhile, because it takes more yen to get a dollar, Canadian exports to Japan fall.

We summarize these currency relationships in Figure 6-7, which you should examine closely. *(Key Question 6)*

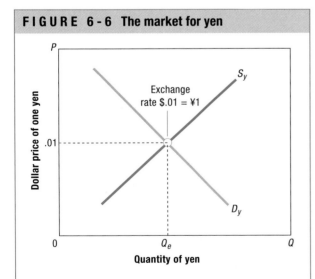

FIGURE 6-6   The market for yen

P — Dollar price of one yen (vertical axis)

Exchange rate $.01 = ¥1

.01

S_y

D_y

0   Q_e Q

Quantity of yen (horizontal axis)

Canadian imports from Japan create a demand D_y for yen, while Canadian exports to Japan create a supply S_y of yen. The dollar price of one yen—the exchange rate—is determined at the intersection of the supply and demand curves. In this case the equilibrium price is $.01, meaning that 1 cent will buy 1 yen.

FIGURE 6-7 Currency appreciation and depreciation

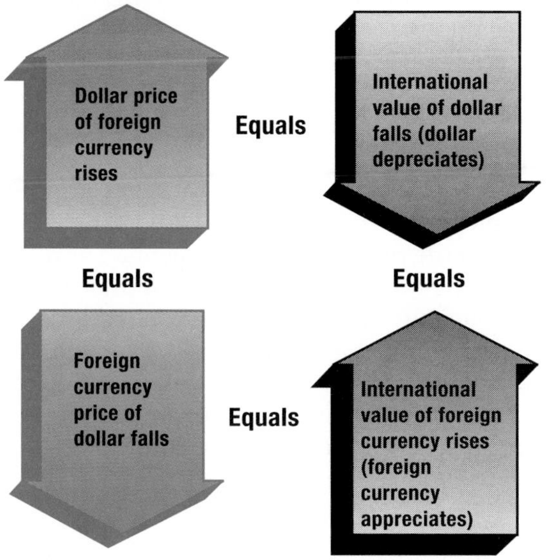

An increase in the dollar price of foreign currency is equivalent to a decline in the international value of the dollar (dollar depreciation). An increase in the dollar price of foreign currency also implies a decline in the foreign currency price of dollars. That is, the international value of foreign currency rises relative to the dollar (the foreign currency appreciates).

6-2
QUICK REVIEW

- A country has a comparative advantage in some product when it can produce it at a lower domestic opportunity cost than can a potential trading partner.

- Specialization based on comparative advantage increases the total output available for nations that trade with one another.

- The foreign exchange market is the market where the currencies of nations are exchanged for each other.

- An appreciation of the dollar is an increase in the international value of the dollar relative to the currency of some other nation; a dollar now buys more units of that currency. A depreciation of the dollar is a decrease in the international value of the dollar relative to another currency; a dollar now buys fewer units of that currency.

GOVERNMENT AND TRADE

If people and nations benefit from specialization and international exchange, why do governments sometimes try to restrict the free flow of imports or to bolster exports? What kinds of world-trade barriers can governments erect, and why would they do so?

Trade Impediments and Subsidies

There are four usual means by which governments might interfere with free trade:

1. **Protective tariffs** are excise taxes or duties placed on imported goods. Most are designed to shield domestic producers from foreign competition. They impede free trade by increasing the prices of imported goods, shifting demand towards domestic products. An excise tax on imported shoes, for example, would make domestically made shoes more attractive to consumers.

2. **Import quotas** are limits on the quantities or total value of specific items that may be imported. Once a quota is "filled," it chokes off imports of that product. Import quotas can be more effective than tariffs in retarding international commerce. A particular product could be imported in large quantities despite high tariffs; a low import quota completely prohibits imports once the quota is filled.

3. **Nontariff barriers** (and, implicitly, *nonquota* barriers) include licensing requirements, unreasonable standards pertaining to product quality, or simply unnecessary bureaucratic red tape in customs procedures. Some nations require their domestic importers of foreign goods to obtain licences. By restricting the issuance of licences, imports can be effectively impeded. Great Britain bars coal importation in this way. Also, some nations impede imports of fruit by insisting that *each* crate be inspected for worms and insects.

4. **Export subsidies** consist of governmental payments to domestic producers of export goods. The payments reduce their production costs, permitting them to charge lower prices and thus sell more exports in world markets. Two examples: Participating European governments have heavily subsidized Airbus Industries, which produces commercial aircraft. These subsidies have helped Airbus

compete against Boeing, an American firm with plants in Canada. Canada and other nations have subsidized domestic farmers, boosting domestic food supply. This has reduced the market price of food, artificially decreasing export prices on agricultural produce.

Why Government Trade Interventions?

Why would a nation want to send more of its output for consumption abroad than it gains as imported output in return? Why the impulse to impede imports or boost exports through government policy when free trade is beneficial to a nation? There are several reasons—some legitimate, most not. We will look at two here, and examine others in a later chapter.

Misunderstanding of the Gains from Trade   It is a commonly accepted myth that the fundamental benefit of international trade is greater domestic employment in the export sector. This suggests that exports are "good" because they increase domestic employment, whereas imports are "bad" because they deprive people of jobs at home. In reality, the true benefit from international trade is the *overall* increase in output obtained through specialization and exchange. A nation can fully employ its resources, including labour, with or without international trade. International trade, however, enables society to use its resources in ways that increase its total output and therefore its overall well-being.

A nation does not need international trade to locate *on* its production possibilities curve. A closed (nontrading) national economy can have full employment without international trade. But through world trade an economy can reach a point *beyond* its domestic production possibilities curve. The gain from trade is the extra output obtained from abroad—the imports got for less cost than if they were produced using domestic resources. The only valid reason for exporting part of our domestic output is to obtain imports that are of greater value to us. Specialization and international exchange make this possible.

Political Considerations   While a nation as a whole gains from trade, trade may harm particular domestic industries and groups of resource suppliers. In our earlier comparative-advantage example, specialization and trade adversely affected the Canadian corn industry and the Mexican soybean industry. Those industries might seek to preserve their economic positions by persuading their respective governments to protect them from imports—perhaps with tariffs or import quotas.

Policymakers often see little public opposition to demands for *protectionism* because tariffs and quotas are buried in the prices of goods. Indeed, the public may be won over by the apparent plausibility ("Cut imports and prevent domestic unemployment") and patriotic ring ("Buy Canadian!") of the protectionist arguments. The alleged benefits of tariffs are immediate and clear-cut to the public, but the adverse effects cited by economists are obscure and dispersed over the entire economy. When political deal making is added in, the sum can be a network of protective tariffs, import quotas, and export subsidies.

Costs to Society

Tariffs and quotas benefit domestic producers of the protected products, but they harm domestic consumers, who must pay higher than world prices for the protected goods. They also hurt those domestic firms that use the protected goods as inputs in their production processes. For example, a tariff on imported steel would boost the price of steel girders, hurting firms that construct large buildings. Also, tariffs and quotas reduce competition in the protected industries. With less competition from foreign producers, domestic firms may be slow to design and implement cost-saving production methods and introduce new and improved products.

Study after study has shown that the cost of trade protection to consumers and adversely affected input buyers exceeds the benefit to the protected firms. That is, there is a *net cost* (cost *minus* benefit) to society from trade protection. In Canada this net cost was as much as $5 billion a couple of decades ago but has dropped significantly in recent years along with declines in Canadian tariffs and quotas.

MULTILATERAL TRADE AGREEMENTS AND FREE-TRADE ZONES

When one nation enacts barriers against imports, the nations whose exports suffer may retaliate with trade barriers of their own. In such a *trade war*, tariffs escalate, choking off world trade and reducing everyone's economic well-being. The raising of tariffs by many nations in the early 1930s to fight domestic unemployment is a classic example. Although Canada's action was meant to reduce imports and stimulate Canadian production, its high tariffs prompted affected nations to retaliate with equally high tariffs. International trade across the globe fell, lowering the output, income, and employment levels of all nations. Economic historians generally agree that the high tariffs were a contributing cause of the Great Depression. In view of this fact, the world's nations have worked to lower tariffs worldwide. Their pursuit of free trade has been aided by powerful domestic interest groups. Specifically, exporters of goods and services, importers of foreign components used in "domestic" products, and domestic sellers of imported products all strongly support lower tariffs worldwide.

Figure 6-8 makes clear that Canada has been a high-tariff nation over much of its history. But it also demonstrates that, in general, Canadian tariffs have declined during the past half-century.

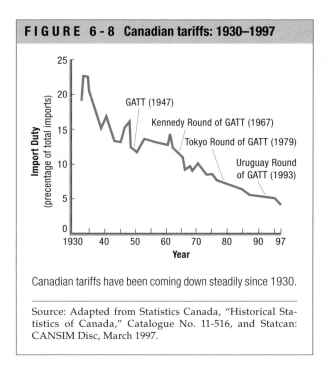

FIGURE 6-8 Canadian tariffs: 1930–1997

GATT (1947)
Kennedy Round of GATT (1967)
Tokyo Round of GATT (1979)
Uruguay Round of GATT (1993)

Canadian tariffs have been coming down steadily since 1930.

Source: Adapted from Statistics Canada, "Historical Statistics of Canada," Catalogue No. 11-516, and Statcan: CANSIM Disc, March 1997.

BILATERAL AGREEMENTS AND GATT

The specific tariff reductions negotiated between Canada and any particular nation became generalized through **most-favoured-nation clauses**, which often accompanied these agreements. These clauses stipulate that any subsequently reduced Canadian tariff, resulting from negotiation with any other nation would apply equally to the nation signing the original agreement. So if Canada negotiates a reduction in tariffs with, say, France, the lower Canadian tariffs on French imports would also apply to the imports of other nations having the most-favoured-nation status, say, Sweden and Switzerland. This way, a new reduction in Canadian tariffs automatically applies to many other nations.

This approach was broadened in 1947 when 23 nations, including Canada, signed a **General Agreement on Tariffs and Trade (GATT).** GATT is based on three cardinal principles: (1) equal, nondiscriminatory trade treatment for all member nations; (2) the reduction of tariffs by multilateral negotiations; and (3) the elimination of import quotas.

Basically, GATT is a forum to negotiate reductions in trade barriers on a multilateral basis among nations. One hundred and twenty-five nations now belong to GATT, and there is little doubt that it has been a positive force in the trend towards liberalized world trade. Under its sponsorship, member nations have completed eight "rounds" of negotiations to reduce trade barriers in the post-World War II period.

GATT's Uruguay Round The eighth and most recent "round" of GATT negotiations began in Uruguay in 1986. After seven years of wrangling, in 1993 the participant nations reached a new agreement. The agreement took effect on January 1, 1995, and its provisions will be phased in through 2005.

Under this latest GATT agreement, tariffs will be eliminated or reduced on thousands of products, with tariffs dropping overall by 33 percent. The agreement will also liberalize government rules that in the past have impeded the global market for such services as advertising, legal services, tourist services, and financial services. Quotas on imported textiles and apparel will be phased out, to be replaced with tariffs. (Tariffs are preferable to quotas, since tariffs let in an unlimited amount of imported goods; in contrast, quotas block all imports beyond a specified quantity.)

Other important provisions will reduce agricultural subsidies paid to farmers and protect intellectual property (patents, trademarks, copyrights) against piracy. Finally, the Uruguay Round of GATT created the **World Trade Organization (WTO)** as GATT's successor. The WTO has judicial powers to mediate among members and rule on disputes involving the trade rules.

When fully implemented, the most recent GATT agreement is expected to boost the world's GDP by about $6 trillion, or 8 percent. Consumers in Canada will gain about $3 billion annually.

European Union

Countries have also sought to reduce tariffs by creating regional free-trade zones or trade blocs. The most dramatic example is the **European Union (EU)**, formerly called the European Economic Community. Initiated as the Common Market in 1958, the EU now comprises 15 western European nations—France, Germany, Italy, Belgium, the Netherlands, Luxembourg, Denmark, Ireland, United Kingdom, Greece, Spain, Portugal, Austria, Finland, and Sweden.

Goals　The original Common Market called for (1) gradual abolition of tariffs and import quotas on all products traded among the participating nations; (2) establishment of a common system of tariffs applicable to all goods received from nations outside the EU; (3) free movement of capital and labour within the Common Market; and (4) creation of common policies in other economic matters of joint concern, such as agriculture, transportation, and restrictive business practices. The EU has achieved most of these goals and is now a strong **trade bloc**: a group of countries having a common identity, set of economic interests, and trade rules.

Results　The motives for creating the EU were political and economic. The main economic motive was liberalized trade for members. While it is difficult to determine how much of EU prosperity and growth has resulted from economic integration, that integration clearly has created large markets for EU industries. The resulting economies of large-scale production have enabled European industries to achieve much lower costs than they could in their small, single-nation markets.

The effects of EU success on nonmember nations, such as Canada, are mixed. A peaceful and increasingly prosperous EU makes its members better customers for Canadian exports. But Canadian and other nonmember firms encounter tariffs that make it difficult to compete against firms within the EU trade bloc. For example, before the establishment of the EU, North American, German, and French automobile manufacturers all faced the same tariff selling their products in, say, Belgium. However, with the establishment of free internal trading among EU members, Belgian tariffs on German Volkswagens and French Renaults fell to zero, but an external tariff still applies to North American Chevrolets and Fords. This puts Canadian and American firms at a serious disadvantage. Similarly, EU trade restrictions hamper Eastern European exports of metals, textiles, and farm products, goods that the Eastern Europeans produce in abundance.

By giving preferences to countries within their free-trade zone, trade blocs such as the EU tend to reduce their trade with nonbloc members. Thus, the world loses some of the benefits of a completely open global trading system. Eliminating this disadvantage has been one of the motivations for liberalizing global trade through the World Trade Organization.

North American Free Trade Agreement

In 1993 Canada, Mexico, and the United States formed a trade bloc. The **North American Free Trade Agreement (NAFTA)** established a free-trade zone having about the same combined output of the EU, but covering a much larger geographical area. A 1989 free-trade agreement between Canada and the United States—the **Canada-U.S. Free Trade Agreement**—preceded NAFTA. NAFTA will eliminate tariffs and other trade barriers between Canada, Mexico, and the United States over a 15-year period.

Critics of the agreement fear that one result will be a loss of Canadian jobs as firms move to Mexico to take advantage of lower wages and weaker regulations on pollution and workplace safety. Also, there is concern that Japan and South Korea will build plants in Mexico to transport goods tariff-free to Canada and the United States, further hurting Canadian and American firms and workers.

Defenders of NAFTA reject these concerns. They contend that specialization according to comparative advantage will enable each nation to obtain more total output from its scarce resources. They also argue that NAFTA's free-trade zone will encourage worldwide investment in Mexico, enhancing Mexican productivity and national income. Mexican consumers will use some of that increased income to buy Canadian and American exports. Any loss of jobs, say defenders of NAFTA, most likely would have occurred anyway to other low-wage countries such as China.

Hostile Trade Blocs or Further Integration?

With the formation of NAFTA, it may appear that the world's nations are separating into potentially hostile trade blocs. But NAFTA is also a means for negotiating reductions in trade barriers with the EU, Japan, and other trading countries. Access to the vast North American market is as important to the EU and Japan as is access to their markets by Canada, Mexico, and the United States. NAFTA gives its members leverage in future trade negotiations with the EU and Japan. Eventually, direct negotiations between the EU and NAFTA might link the two free-trade zones. Japan and other major trading nations, not wishing to be left out of the world's wealthiest trade markets, would be forced to eliminate their trade barriers—to open their domestic markets to additional imports. Nor do other nations and trade blocs want to be excluded from free-trade zones. Examples:

1. **APEC** Canada and several other nations have agreed to liberalize trade and open investment over the next few decades through the Asian-Pacific Economic Cooperation (APEC) forum. APEC members are Australia, Brunei, Canada, Chile, China (Hong Kong), Indonesia, Japan, Malaysia, Mexico, New Zealand, the Philippines, Papua New Guinea, Singapore, South Korea, Taiwan, Thailand, and the United States.
2. **CHILE'S POTENTIAL INCLUSION IN NAFTA** Canada, Mexico, and the United States are negotiating with Chile to become the fourth partner in NAFTA.
3. **MERCOSUR** The free-trade group encompassing Brazil, Argentina, Uruguay, and Paraguay—called Mercosur—has expressed interest in eventually linking up with NAFTA.

Economists generally agree that the ideal free-trade area would encompass the entire world. *(Key Question 10)*

6-3
QUICK REVIEW

- Governments promote exports and reduce imports through tariffs, quotas, nontariff barriers, and export subsidies.
- The various "rounds" of the General Agreement on Tariffs and Trade (GATT) have established multinational reductions in tariffs and import quotas among the 125 member nations.
- The Uruguay Round of GATT, which went into effect in 1995 and will be fully implemented by 2005, **a** reduces tariffs worldwide; **b** liberalizes rules impeding barriers to trade in services; **c** reduces agricultural subsidies; **d** creates new protections for intellectual property; **e** phases out quotas on textiles and apparel; and **f** sets up the World Trade Organization.
- The European Union (EU) and the North American Free Trade Agreement (NAFTA) have reduced internal trade barriers among their members by establishing large free-trade zones.

CANADIAN FIRMS IN THE WORLD ECONOMY

Freer international trade has brought with it intense competition in Canada and the world. Not long ago three large North American producers dominated the North American automobile industry. Imported autos were an oddity, accounting for a tiny portion of auto sales. But General Motors, Ford, and Chrysler now face intense competition as they struggle for sales against Nissan, Honda, Toyota, Hyundai, BMW, and others. Similarly, imports have gained major shares of the North American markets for automobile tires, clothing, sporting goods, electronics, motorcycles, outboard motors, and toys.

Nevertheless, thousands of Canadian firms—large and small—have thrived and prospered in the global marketplace. Nortel, Bombardier, Newbridge Networks, and Corel are just a few of them. These and many other firms have continued to retain high market shares at home and have dramatically expanded their sales abroad. Of course, not all firms have been so successful. Some corporations simply have not been able to compete; their international competitors make better-quality products, have lower production costs, or both. Not surprisingly, the Canadian firms that have been hurt most by foreign competition are precisely those that have long enjoyed the protection of tariffs and quotas. These barriers to imports have artificially limited competition, removing the incentive to improve production methods and products. Also, trade barriers have shielded some domestic firms from the gradual changes in output and employment resulting from national shifts in comparative advantage over time. As trade protection declines under WTO and NAFTA, some Canadian firms will surely discover that they are producing goods for which Canada clearly has a comparative *dis*advantage (perhaps some types of apparel, for example).

Is the greater competition that accompanies the global economy a good thing? Although some domestic producers and their workers do not like it, foreign competition clearly benefits consumers. Imports break down the monopoly power of existing firms, reducing product prices and providing consumers with a greater variety of goods. Foreign competition also forces domestic producers to become more efficient and to improve product quality; this has already happened in several Canadian industries, including steel and autos. Evidence shows that most—but clearly not all—Canadian firms *can* and *do* compete successfully in the global economy.

What about Canadian firms that cannot successfully compete in open markets? The harsh reality is that they should go out of business, much like an unsuccessful corner boutique. Persistent economic losses mean scarce resources are not being used efficiently. Shifting these resources to alternative, profitable uses will increase total Canadian output.

In
The Media

Dollar Closes at Lowest Level Since 1858

Bank of Canada appears reluctant to defend currency by raising rates

By Marian Stinson
Money Markets Reporter

The Canadian dollar ended trading yesterday at its lowest level since its creation in 1858, nine years before Confederation.

The 140-year low—69.20 cents (U.S.)—came despite buying efforts by the Bank of Canada to steady its value.

The dollar was hammered by hints from senior deputy Bank of Canada governor Bernard Bonin that interest rates may head lower because of turmoil in Asian markets.

"It could be less tightening or it could be more easing," he told reporters after a luncheon speech to financial analysts in Montreal.

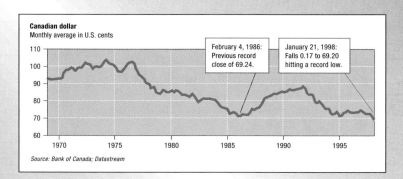

Source: Bank of Canada; Datastream

Such dismal days for the currency are a sharp departure from most of its history, when it traded above 90 cents (U.S.), and even above par with the U.S. dollar for brief periods, such as during the U.S. Civil War when the United States abandoned the gold standard, and during the 1970s, until a separist government was first elected in Quebec.

The only other time the dollar has traded as low as its current level was early 1986, when it fell as low as 69.13 cents (U.S.) on Feb. 3, but edged up to end that day at 69.24 cents.

The dollar first appeared in 1858 when a decimal currency system was introduced in Upper and Lower Canada to replace the mixture of coins and notes in circulation. After Confederation, the dollar became the currency in the new territories of the Dominion.

From 1870 to the beginning of the First World War in 1914, the dollar traded at par with the U.S. dollar, but depreciated sharply to 90 cents after the war and in the 1920s and during the Great Depression.

In 1940, it was pegged at 90.9 cents (U.S.) and was revalued at parity with the U.S. dollar in 1946. In October of 1950 it moved above

par, but weakened again to 92.50 cents in 1961—and became known as the Diefenbuck—when then prime minister John Diefenbaker was in conflict with central bank governor James Coyne.

Source: Globe and Mail, January 22, 1998, p. A1. Reprinted with permission from the Globe and Mail.

THE STORY IN BRIEF

In early 1998 the Canadian dollar reached its lowest level against the American dollar since the middle of the nineteenth century. (By August 1998 the Canadian dollar dropped below U.S.$ .64).

THE ECONOMICS BEHIND THE STORY

- The value of a currency against other currencies is determined by supply and demand for that currency.
- In early 1998 the demand for the American dollar rose. As the demand for the U.S. dollar shifted to the right, the Canadian dollar price for one American dollar rose, at one point during the day in question reaching Can $ 1.445 for one U.S. dollar. (Later in 1998 the Canadian dollar declined to as low as $1.59 for one U.S. dollar.) The strong demand for the U.S. currency is partly explained by the turmoil on Asian equity and foreign exchange markets at the time. Investors were seeking the "safety" of the American currency.
- The Bank of Canada intervened in the foreign exchange market to slow the fall of the Canadian dollar. To achieve this end the Bank of Canada sold American dollars, thereby shifting the supply of the U.S. currency to the right.
- How would you expect Canadian imports and exports to the United States to be affected by a depreciating Canadian dollar? What about the effect on the number of American tourists to Canada? ■

The Last Word

PETITION OF THE CANDLEMAKERS, 1845

The French economist Frédéric Bastiat (1801–1850) devastated the proponents of protectionism by satirically extending their reasoning to its logical and absurd conclusions.

PETITION OF THE MANUFACTURERS OF CANDLES, Waxlights, Lamps, Candlesticks, Street Lamps, Snuffers, Extinguishers, and of the Producers of Oil Tallow, Rosin, Alcohol, and, Generally, of Everything Connected with Lighting.

TO MESSIEURS THE MEMBERS OF THE CHAMBER OF DEPUTIES.

Gentlemen—You are on the right road. You reject abstract theories, and have little consideration for cheapness and plenty. Your chief care is the interest of the producer. You desire to emancipate him from external competition, and reserve the national market for national industry.

We are about to offer you an admirable opportunity of applying your—what shall we call it? your theory? No; nothing is more deceptive than theory; your doctrine? your system? your principle? but you dislike doctrines, you abhor systems, and as for principles, you deny that there are any in social economy: we shall say, then, your practice, your practice without theory and without principle.

We are suffering from the intolerable competition of a foreign rival, placed, it would seem, in a condition so far superior to ours for the production of light, that he absolutely inundates our national market with it at a price fabulously reduced. The moment he shows himself, our trade leaves us—all consumers apply to him; and a branch of native industry, having countless ramifications, is all at once rendered completely stagnant. This rival ... is no other than the Sun.

What we pray for is, that it may please you to pass a law ordering the shutting up of all windows, skylights, dormerwindows, outside and inside shutters, curtains, blinds, bull's-eyes; in a word, of all openings, holes, chinks, clefts, and fissures, by or through which the light of the sun has been in use to enter houses, to the prejudice of the meritorious manufactures with which we flatter ourselves we have accommodated our country,— a country which, in gratitude, ought not to abandon us now to a strife so unequal.

If you shut up as much as possible all access to natural light, and create a demand for artificial light, which of our French manufactures will not be encouraged by it?

If more tallow is consumed, then there must be more oxen and sheep; and, consequently, we shall behold the multiplication of artificial meadows, meat, wool, hides, and, above all, manure, which is the basis and foundation of all agricultural wealth.

The same remark applies to navigation. Thousands of vessels will proceed to the whale fishery; and, in a short time, we shall possess a navy capable of maintaining the honor of France, and gratifying the patriotic aspirations of your petitioners, the undersigned candlemakers and others.

Only have the goodness to reflect, Gentlemen, and you will be convinced that there is, perhaps, no Frenchman, from the wealthy coalmaster to the humblest vender of lucifer matches, whose lot will not be ameliorated by the success of this our petition. ■

Source: Frédéric Bastiat, *Economic Sophisms* (Edinburgh: Oliver and Boyd, Tweeddale Court, 1873), pp. 49–53, abridged.

CHAPTER SUMMARY

1. International trade is growing in importance globally and for Canada. World trade is vital to Canada in two respects. **a** Canadian imports and exports as a percentage of national output are significant. **b** Canada is completely dependent on trade for certain commodities and materials that cannot be obtained domestically.

2. Principal Canadian exports include automotive products, machinery and equipment, and grain; major Canadian imports are general machinery and equipment, automobiles, and industrial goods and machinery. Quantitatively, the United States is our most important trading partner.

3. Global trade has been greatly facilitated by **a** improvements in transportation technology; **b** improvements in communications technology; **c** general declines in tariffs; and **d** continuing peaceful relations among major industrial nations. Canada and the United States, Japan, and the Western European nations dominate the global economy. But the total volume of trade has been increased by several new trade participants, including the "Asian tigers" (Hong Kong, Singapore, South Korea, and Taiwan), China, the Eastern European countries, and the newly independent countries of the former Soviet Union.

4. The open economy circular flow model connects the domestic Canadian economy to the rest of the world. Customers from abroad enter our product market to buy some of our output. These Canadian exports create business revenues and generate income in Canada. Canadian households spend some of their money income on products made abroad and imported to Canada.

5. Specialization based on comparative advantage enables nations to achieve higher standards of living through exchange with other countries. A trading partner should specialize in products and services for which its domestic opportunity costs are lowest. The terms of trade must be such that both nations can get more of some output via trade than they can obtain by producing it at home.

6. The foreign exchange market sets exchange rates between nations' currencies. Foreign importers are suppliers of their currencies and domestic importers are demanders of foreign currencies. The resulting supply-demand equilibrium sets an exchange rate; these exchange rates link the price levels of all nations. Depreciation of a nation's currency reduces its imports and increases its exports; appreciation increases its imports and reduces exports.

7. Governments shape trade flows through **a** protective tariffs; **b** quotas; **c** nontariff barriers; and **d** export subsidies. These are impediments to free trade; they result from misunderstandings about the gains to be had from trade and also from political considerations. By increasing product prices, trade barriers cost Canadian consumers billions of dollars annually.

8. The post-World War period has seen a trend towards lower Canadian tariffs. In 1947 the General Agreement on Tariffs and Trade (GATT) was formed to **a** encourage nondiscriminatory treatment for all trading nations; **b** reduce tariffs; and **c** eliminate import quotas.

9. The Uruguay Round of GATT negotiations, completed in 1993 and to be implemented through 2005, **a** reduces tariffs, **b** liberalizes trade in services, **c** reduces agricultural subsidies, **d** reduces pirating of intellectual property, **e** phases out import quotas on textiles and apparel, and **f** establishes the World Trade Organization.

10. Free-trade zones (trade blocs) may liberalize trade within regions but may also impede trade with nonbloc members. Two examples of free-trade arrangements are the European Union (EU), formerly the European Community or "Common Market," and the North American Free Trade Agreement (NAFTA), comprising Canada, Mexico, and the United States.

11. The global economy has created intense foreign competition in many Canadian product markets, but most Canadian firms can compete well both at home and in global markets.

TERMS AND CONCEPTS

multinational corporations	import quotas
"Asian tigers"	nontariff barriers
absolute advantage	export subsidies
comparative advantage	most-favoured-nation clauses
terms of trade	General Agreement on Tariffs and Trade (GATT)
foreign exchange market	World Trade Organization
exchange rates	European Union (EU)
depreciation	trade bloc
appreciation	North American Free Trade Agreement (NAFTA)
protective tariffs	Canada-U.S. Free Trade Agreement (FTA)

STUDY QUESTIONS

1. How important is international trade to the Canadian economy? Who is Canada's most important trade partner? How can persistent trade deficits be financed? "Trade deficits mean we get more merchandise from the rest of the world than we provide them in return. Therefore, trade deficits are economically desirable." Do you agree? Why or why not?

2. What factors account for the rapid growth of world trade since World War II? Who are the major players in international trade today? Who are the "Asian tigers" and how important are they in world trade?

3. KEY QUESTION *Use the circular flow model (Figure 6-5) to explain how an increase in exports would affect the revenues of domestic firms, the money income of domestic households, and imports from abroad. Use Figure 6-2 to find the amounts (in 1997) of Canada's exports (flow 13) and imports (flow 16) in the circular flow model. What do these amounts imply for flows 14 and 15?*

4. KEY QUESTION *The following are production possibilities tables for South Korea and Canada. Assume that before specialization and trade the optimal product mix for South Korea is alternative B and for Canada alternative D.*

PRODUCT	SOUTH KOREA'S PRODUCTION ALTERNATIVES					
	A	**B**	**C**	**D**	**E**	**F**
Radios (in thousands)	30	24	18	12	6	0
Chemicals (in tonnes)	0	6	12	18	24	30

PRODUCT	CANADA'S PRODUCTION ALTERNATIVES					
	A	**B**	**C**	**D**	**E**	**F**
Radios (in thousands)	10	8	6	4	2	0
Chemicals (in tonnes)	0	4	8	12	16	20

a. *Are comparative-cost conditions such that the two areas should specialize? If so, what product should each produce?*

b. *What is the total gain in radio and chemical output that results from this specialization?*

c. *What are the limits of the terms of trade? Suppose actual terms of trade are 1 unit of radios for $1\frac{1}{2}$ units of chemicals and that 4 units of radios are exchanged for 6 units of chemicals. What are the gains from specialization and trade for each area?*

d. *Can you conclude from this illustration that specialization according to comparative advantage results in more efficient use of world resources? Explain.*

5. Suppose that the comparative-cost ratios of two products—baby formula and tuna fish—are as follows in the hypothetical nations of Canswicki and Tunata.

   Canswicki: 1 can baby formula ≡ 2 cans tuna fish
   Tunata: 1 can baby formula ≡ 4 cans tuna fish

In what product should each nation specialize? Explain why terms of trade of 1 can baby formula = $2\frac{1}{2}$ cans tuna fish would be acceptable to both nations.

6. KEY QUESTION *"Canadian exports create a demand for foreign currencies; foreign imports of our goods generate supplies of foreign currencies." Do you agree? Other things being equal, would a decline in Canadian incomes or a weakening of Canadian preferences for foreign products cause the dollar to depreciate or appreciate? What would be the effects of that depreciation or appreciation on our exports and imports?*

7. If the French franc declines in value (depreciates) in the foreign exchange market, will it be easier or harder for the French to sell their wine in Canada? If you were planning a trip to Paris, how would the depreciation of the franc change the dollar cost of this trip?

8. True or false? "An increase in the Canadian dollar price of the German mark implies that the German mark has depreciated in value." Explain.

9. What tools do governments use to promote exports and restrict imports? Who benefits and who loses from protectionist policies? What is the net outcome for consumers?

10. KEY QUESTION *What is GATT? How does it affect nearly every person in the world? What were the major outcomes of the Uruguay Round of GATT? How is GATT related to the European Union (EU), the Canada-U.S. Free Trade Agreement (FTA), and the North American Free Trade Agreement (NAFTA)?*

11. Explain: "Free trade zones such as the EU and NAFTA lead a double life: They can promote free trade among members, but pose serious trade obstacles for nonmembers." Do you think the net effects of these trade blocs are good or bad for world trade? Why?

12. What do you see as the competitive strengths of Canadian firms? Competitive weaknesses? Explain: "Even if Japan captured the entire worldwide auto market, that simply would mean that Japan would have to buy a whole lot of other products from abroad. Thus, Canada and other industrial nations would necessarily experience an increase in exports to Japan."

13. **(The Last Word)** What point is Bastiat trying to make with his petition of the candlemakers?

14. WEB-BASED QUESTION **Trade Balances With Partner Countries.** Statistics Canada www.statcan.ca/english/Pgdb/Economy/International/gblec02a.htm sets out Canadian imports and exports to major trading partners and areas for the last five years. Do we have a trading surplus or deficit with the United States? What about with Japan and the European Union?

15. WEB-BASED QUESTION **Foreign Exchange Rates—the U.S. for Canadian Dollar.** Statistics Canada provides the exchange rate of the Canadian dollar against the U.S. dollar for the last five years at www.statcan.ca/english/Pgdb/Economy/Economic/econ07.htm. Assume you visited New York City every summer for the last five years and bought a Coney Island hotdog for U.S. $5. Convert this amount to Canadian dollars using the exchange rate for each year and plot the Canadian dollar price of the Coney Island hotdog. Has the Canadian dollar appreciated or depreciated against the U.S. dollar? What was the least amount in Canadian dollars your Coney Island hotdog cost? The most?

National Income, Employment, and Fiscal Policy

Measuring Domestic Output and the Price Level

"DISPOSABLE INCOME FLAT"; "PERSONAL Consumption Surges"; "Net Investment Stagnates"; "Russia's GDP Slide Halted"; "GDP Price Index Rises Less Rapidly Than CPI."

These are typical headlines in the business and economics news. They look like gibberish—unless you know the language of macroeconomics and national income accounting. This chapter will help you learn that language and the ideas it communicates. After studying it, you will have a basic understanding of how government statisticians and accountants measure and record the levels of domestic output, national income, and prices for the economy.

In this chapter we first explain why it is important to measure the performance of an economy. Then we define the key measure of total output—gross domestic product (GDP)—and show how it is actually calculated. We also derive and explain several other important measures of output and income. Next, we turn to the measurement of the overall level of prices—the price level. We then demonstrate how GDP is adjusted for inflation or deflation so that it more accurately reflects the physical amount of a nation's production. Finally, we list and explain some limitations of the measures of domestic output and national income.

IN THIS CHAPTER YOU WILL LEARN:

What gross domestic product is and what it measures

•

Two ways to calculate a nation's production of goods and services (GDP): (a) the expenditure approach; (b) the income approach.

•

The distinction between nominal GDP and real GDP.

•

What the Consumer Price Index (CPI) is and how it is constructed.

•

That the output of goods and services, or GDP, is only one measure of a country's overall well-being.

The Big Picture

YOU ARE ABOUT TO EMBARK ON THE STUDY of macroeconomics—the study of the whole economy (the aggregation of individual markets) and its major components. You would be well advised to review Chapter 2, particularly the production possibility curve and what it represents: the economizing problem, brought about by scarcity of resources in relation to our wants, and thus the necessity of making choices. Macroeconomics in its broadest sense is concerned with understanding how the overall economy works so we can devise effective macroeconomic policies. In the short to medium term these policies aim to get the most out of available resources (getting on the production possibility curve) and in the long run they aim to promote the growth of the economy's productive capacity. These goals should be achieved with stable prices, equitable distribution of income, and a long-run balance in our international trade and financial transactions. This chapter deals with measurement of the output and the price level of the economy.

As you read this chapter, keep the following points in mind:

- **Key Concept 8** is discussed.
- We need a way to measure the output performance of the economy to determine how well or badly it is doing. The output of the economy is measured in dollars and the time period is one year.
- We can measure what is produced in a given year either by adding up all the expenditures during that year, or all the income earned by the factors of production (land, labour, capital, and entrepreneurial talent) in producing total output.
- The fluctuation of the value of money makes it necessary to have a measurement for that change. Inflation and disinflation measure, respectively, a general increase and a general decrease in the price level of all goods.
- If we know the amount by which the value of money has changed, it is easier to get a true measure of what is produced in an economy in a given year. ∎

MACROECONOMIC MEASUREMENT

Our first goal is to explain the ways the overall production performance of the economy is measured. This is part of *national income accounting*, which does for the economy as a whole what private accounting does for the individual business enterprise or, for that matter, for the household.

A firm measures its flows of income and expenditures to assess its operations over some time period, usually three months or a year. With this information, the firm can gauge its economic health. If things are going well, the accounting data can be used to explain this success. Costs might be down or output or prices up, resulting in large profit. If things are going badly, accounting measures can help discover why. And by comparing the accounts over several periods, the firm can detect the growth or decline of profit and what caused the change. All this information helps the firm's managers make intelligent business decisions.

National income accounting operates in much the same way for an economy.

1. It allows us to keep a finger on the economic pulse of a nation. A national income accounting system permits us to measure the level of production in an economy in some particular year and explain why it is at that level.
2. By comparing national accounts over a number of years, we can track the long-run course of the economy and see whether it has grown, been steady, or stagnated.
3. Information supplied by national accounts provides a basis for designing and applying public policies to improve the performance of the economy. Without national accounts, economic policy would be based on guesswork. *National income accounting allows us to assess the health of an economy and formulate policies to maintain and improve that health.*

GROSS DOMESTIC PRODUCT

There are many measures of an economy's economic performance. The best available measures, however, are based on the economy's annual total output of goods and services or, as it is sometimes called, its *aggregate output*. An economy's aggregate output is measured by its **gross domestic product** (GDP): *the total market value of all final goods and services produced within a country in one year.* GDP is also sometimes referred to as *national income* (NI). GDP includes goods and services produced by citizen-supplied *and* foreign-supplied resources within a particular nation's geographical boundaries. Thus, Canadian GDP includes not only the value of Fords produced at a Canadian-owned factory in Ontario, but also the value of Honda autos produced at a Japanese-owned factory in the same province of Ontario.

A Monetary Measure

GDP measures the market value of annual output; *it is a monetary measure.* Indeed it must be if we are to compare the heterogeneous collection of goods and services produced in different years and get a meaningful idea of their relative worth.

If the economy produces three sofas and two computers in year 1 and two sofas and three computers in year 2, in which year is output greater? We cannot answer that question until price tags are attached to the various products as indicators of society's evaluation of their relative worth.

In Table 7-1, the money price of sofas is $500 and the price of computers is $2,000. Year 2's output of $7,000 is greater than year 1's output of $5,500 because society values year 2's output more highly; society is willing to pay $1,500 more for the collection of goods produced in year 2 than in year 1.

Avoidance of Multiple Counting

To measure total output accurately, all goods and services produced in any specific year must be counted once, but not more than once. Most products go through a series of production stages before reaching a market. As a result, parts of some products may be bought and sold many times. To avoid multiple counting of parts that are sold and resold, GDP includes only the market value of *final goods* and ignores transactions involving *intermediate goods*.

By **final goods** we mean goods and services being purchased for final use by the purchaser, and not for resale or further processing or manufacturing. *They are "purchases" not resold.* **Intermediate goods** are goods and services that are purchased for further processing and manufacturing or for resale.

The value of final goods is included in GDP, and the value of intermediate goods is excluded. Why? Because the value of final goods already includes the value of all intermediate goods involved in producing the final goods. Counting intermediate goods separately would be **double counting**, which would exaggerate the value of GDP.

To clarify this, suppose there are five stages in manufacturing a wool suit and getting it to the consumer—the ultimate or final user. As Table 7-2 indicates, firm A, a sheep ranch, provides $120 worth of wool to firm B, a wool processor. Firm A receives $120 from B and pays it out in wages, rent, interest, and profit. Firm B processes the wool and sells it to firm C, a suit manufacturer, for $180. What does firm B do with the $180 it receives? As noted, $120 goes to firm A, and the remaining $60 is used by B to pay wages, rent, interest, and profit for the resources needed in processing the wool. The manufacturer sells the suit to firm D, a clothing wholesaler, who sells it to firm E, a retailer, and then, at last, a consumer, the final user, buys it for $350.

At each stage, the difference between what a firm has paid for the product and what it receives for selling the product is paid out as wages, rent, interest, and profit for the resources used by that firm to produce and distribute the suit.

How much of this should we include in GDP to account for the production of the suit? We should include just $350, the value of the final product. This amount includes all the intermedi-

TABLE 7-1 Comparing heterogeneous outputs by using money prices		
Year	Annual output	Market value
1	3 sofas and 2 computers	3 at $500 + 2 at $2000 = $5500
2	2 sofas and 3 computers	2 at $500 + 3 at $2000 = $7000

TABLE 7-2   Value added in a five-stage production process

(1) Stage of production	(2) Sales value of materials or product	(3) Value added
	0	
Firm A, sheep ranch	$ 120	$120 (= $120 – $ 0)
Firm B, wool processor	180	60 (= 180 – 120)
Firm C, suit manufacturer	220	40 (= 220 – 180)
Firm D, clothing wholesaler	270	50 (= 270 – 220)
Firm E, retail clothier	350	80 (= 350 – 270)
Total sales values	$1140	
Value added (total income)		$350

ate transactions leading up to the product's final sale. It would be a gross distortion to include the sum of all the intermediate sales, $1,140, in GDP. This would be multiple counting: counting the final product *and* the sale and resale of its various parts in the multistage production process. The production and sale of the suit have generated $350, *not* $1,140, worth of output and income.

To avoid multiple counting, national income accountants are careful to calculate only the *value added* by each firm. **Value added** is the market value of a firm's output *less* the value of the inputs which it has purchased from others. For example, column 3, Table 7-2, shows that the value added by firm B is $60, the difference between the $180 value of its output and the $120 it paid for the inputs provided by firm A. By adding the values added by the five firms in Table 7-2, the total value of the suit can be accurately determined. Similarly, by calculating and summing the values added by all firms in the economy, we can determine the GDP—the market value of total output.

Exclusion of Nonproduction Transactions

GDP measures the annual production of the economy. Although many monetary transactions in the economy are for currently produced final goods and services, many other transactions are not. These nonproduction transactions must be ex-

cluded. *Nonproduction transactions* are of two major types: (1) purely financial transactions and (2) secondhand sales.

Financial Transactions   Purely financial transactions are of three general kinds:

1. **PUBLIC TRANSFER PAYMENTS**   These are the social insurance payments, welfare payments, and veterans' benefits that government makes to particular households. The basic characteristic of public transfer payments is that recipients make no contribution to *current* production in return for them. To include them in GDP would be to overstate this year's production.
2. **PRIVATE TRANSFER PAYMENTS**   These payments—for example, a university student's monthly subsidy from home or an occasional gift from a wealthy relative—do not entail production but simply the transfer of funds from one private individual to another.
3. **SECURITY TRANSACTIONS**   Buying and selling of stocks and bonds are also excluded from GDP. Stock market transactions involve swapping paper assets. The amount spent on these assets does not directly create current production. Only the services provided by the security broker are included in GDP. However, sales of *new* issues of stocks and bonds

transfer money from savers to businesses that often spend the proceeds on capital goods. Thus, these transactions may *indirectly* contribute to spending, which does account for output and hence add to GDP.

Secondhand Sales

Secondhand sales are excluded from GDP because they either reflect no *current* production or involve multiple counting. Suppose you sell your 1965 Ford Mustang to a friend; this transaction should be excluded in determining this year's GDP because it does not represent any current production. Including sales of goods produced some years ago in this year's GDP would exaggerate this year's output. Similarly, if you purchased a brand new Mustang but resold it a week later to your neighbour, the sale to your neighbour would be excluded from current GDP. *(Key Question 3)*

Two Sides to GDP: Spending and Income

Let's consider how the market value of total output—or for that matter, any single unit of output—is measured. Returning to Table 7-2, how can we measure the market value of a suit?

We can determine how much a consumer, the final user, pays for it; that will tell us the value of the final product. Or we can add up all the wage, rent, interest, and profit incomes created in producing it. This second approach is the value-added technique discussed in Table 7-2.

The final-product and value-added approaches are two ways of looking at the same thing. *What is spent on a product is received as income by those who helped produce it.* Chapter 2's circular flow model demonstrated this. If $350 is spent on the suit, then $350 is the total amount of income derived from its production. You can verify this by looking at the incomes generated by firms A, B, C, D, and E in Table 7-2—$120, $60, $40, $50, and $80—which total $350.

This equality of the expenditure for a product and the income derived from its production is guaranteed, because profit balances the two. Profit —or loss—is the income remaining after wage, rent, and interest incomes have been paid by the producer. If the wage, rent, and interest incomes the firm must pay in getting the suit produced are less than the $350 expenditure for the suit, the difference will be the firm's profit. Conversely, if wage, rent, and interest incomes exceed $350, profit will be negative. That is, losses will be incurred, balancing the expenditure on the product and the income derived from its production.

It is the same for the total output of the economy. There are two ways of looking at GDP: One is to see GDP as the sum of all the expenditures in buying that total output. This is the **expenditures approach**. The other views GDP in terms of the income derived or created from producing it. This is the **income approach**.

This year's GDP can be determined either by adding up all that is spent to buy this year's total output or by summing up all the incomes derived from the production of this year's total output. That is,

$$
\left.\begin{array}{l}
\text{Dollar value} \\
\text{of this year's} \\
\text{total output}
\end{array}\right\} = \left\{\begin{array}{l}
\text{money income derived} \\
\text{from producing this} \\
\text{year's total output}
\end{array}\right.
$$

This relationship is an *identity*: an equation whose variables are defined and measured such that one side of the equation always equals the other side. Buying (spending money) and selling (receiving money income) are two aspects of the same transaction. *What is spent on a product is income to those who have contributed their human and property resources to getting that product produced and to the market.*

We can expand this identity to read as in Figure 7-1. On the output side of GDP, all final goods produced in an economy are purchased by the three domestic sectors (households, businesses, and government) and by foreign buyers. On the income side of GDP (and aside from a few complicating factors, discussed later in this chapter), the total receipts of businesses acquired from the sale of total output are allocated among resources suppliers as wage, rent, interest, and profit income.

GDP: THE EXPENDITURES APPROACH

To determine GDP through expenditures, we add up all spending on final goods and services. But national income accountants have more precise terms for the different types of spending than those listed in the left panel in Figure 7-1.

Personal Consumption Expenditures (*C*)

What we have called "consumption expenditures by households" is **personal consumption expenditures** to national income accountants. It includes expenditures by households on *durable consumer*

FIGURE 7-1 The expenditures and income approaches to GDP

Expenditures Approach   **Income Approach**

Consumption expenditures by households		Wages
plus		plus
Investment expenditures by government and businesses	= GDP =	Rents
plus		plus
Government purchases of goods and services		Interest
plus		plus
Expenditures by foreigners		Profits
		plus
		Statistical adjustment

There are two general approaches to measuring gross domestic product. We can determine the value of output by summing all expenditures on that output. Alternatively, with some modifications, we can determine GDP by adding up the components of income arising from the production of that output.

---

goods (automobiles, refrigerators, video recorders), *nondurable consumer goods* (bread, milk, vitamins, pencils, toothpaste), and *consumer expenditures for services* (of lawyers, doctors, mechanics, barbers). We will use the symbol C to designate this part of GDP.

Gross Investment (I_g)

Under the heading **gross investment** (I_g), national income accountants combine:

1. All final purchases of machinery, equipment, and tools by governments and business enterprises
2. All construction
3. Changes in inventories

This is more than we have meant by "investment" thus far. The first item simply restates our definition of investment spending as the purchase of tools, machinery, and equipment.

The second item includes such construction as building a new factory, warehouse, or store. But "all construction" also includes residential construction. Why is that investment rather than consumption? Because apartment buildings are investment goods that, like factories and stores, are income-earning assets when they are rented or leased. Other residential units that are rented or leased are, for the same reason, investment goods. And owner-occupied houses are investment

goods because they *could be* rented out to yield a money-income return, even though the owners may choose not to do so. For these reasons all residential construction is considered investment.

Finally, changes in inventories are counted as investment because an increase in inventories is, in effect, "unconsumed output." And, as we know from production possibilities analysis, that is what investment is.

Inventory Changes: A Part of Investment   Let's look at inventory changes more carefully. Because GDP measures total current (this year's) output, we must include within it any products produced this year even though they are *not sold* this year. GDP must include the market value of any additions to inventories accruing during the year. A laptop computer produced in 1999 must be counted as GDP in 1999, even though it remains unsold as of February 2000. If we excluded an increase in inventories, GDP would understate the current year's total production. If businesses have more goods on their shelves and in warehouses at year's end than they had at the start, the economy has produced more than was purchased during the year. This increase in inventories must be included in GDP as part of current production, along with the value of goods that were manufactured *and sold* during the year.

What about a decline in inventories? This must be subtracted in figuring GDP. The economy can sell a total output that exceeds its production by dipping into, and thus reducing, its inventories. Then some of this year's purchases reflect not current production but a drawing down of inventories on hand at the beginning of this year. And inventories on hand at the start of any year's production represent the production of previous years. The laptop computer produced in 1999 but sold in 2000 cannot be counted as part of 2000 GDP. Because GDP is a measure of the *current* year's output, we must omit any purchases of past production, that is, any drawing down of inventories, in determining GDP. We do this by subtracting inventory decreases in determining investment expenditures.

Noninvestment Transactions   We have discussed what investment is. Now we need to emphasize what it is not. Investment does *not* include the transfer of financial assets (stocks, bonds) or resale of physical assets. Economists exclude the buying of stocks and bonds from their definition of investment because such purchases merely transfer the ownership of existing assets. The same is true of the resale of existing physical assets.

Investment is the construction or manufacture of *new* capital assets. The production of these assets creates jobs and income; the transfer (sale) of claims to existing capital goods does not.

Gross versus Net Investment   Our category **gross investment**, or **gross capital formation**, includes purchases of machinery and equipment, all construction, and changes in inventories. Gross investment includes the production of *all* investment goods—both those that replace machinery, equipment, and buildings used up to produce the current year's output *and* any net additions to the economy's stock of capital. Gross investment includes both investment in replacement capital *and* investment in added capital. **Net investment**, however, refers only to investment in added capital.

To make the distinction clear: In 1997 the Canadian economy produced about $165.8 billion of capital goods. However, in producing that GDP, the economy used up $110.7 billion of machinery and equipment. Thus, the Canadian economy added $55.1 (or $165.8 minus $110.7) billion to its stock of capital in 1997. Gross investment in 1997 was $165.8 billion; net investment was $57.8 billion. The difference is the value of the capital used up in producing 1997's GDP.

Net Investment and Economic Growth

The amount of a nation's capital worn out or used up in a particular year is called **capital consumption allowance**, or simply **depreciation**. The relationship between gross investment and depreciation indicates whether an economy's production capacity is expanding, static, or declining. Figure 7-2 illustrates these cases.

1. **EXPANDING PRODUCTION CAPACITY**   When gross investment exceeds depreciation (Figure 7-2a), the economy's productive capacity is expanding; its stock of capital is growing. *Positive net investment expands the production capacity of the economy.* As indicated previously, this was true for the Canadian economy in 1997. It added $55.1 billion to the size of its "national factory" that year. This increase in capital helped shift the Canadian production possibilities curve outward.

2. **STATIC PRODUCTION CAPACITY**   *When gross investment and depreciation are equal, a nation's production capacity is static* (Figure 7-2b). The production capacity is standing pat; the economy produces just enough capital to replace what is consumed in producing the year's output—no more, no less. Example: In World War II, the federal government purposely restricted private investment to free resources for the production of war goods. In 1942, gross private investment and depreciation were each about $1.2 billion. Thus net investment was roughly zero. At the end of 1942, our stock of capital was about the same as it was at the start of that year. The Canadian economy's production capacity was stationary; its production facilities did not expand.

3. **DECLINING PRODUCTION CAPACITY**   *When gross investment is less than depreciation, an economy's production capacity declines.* The economy uses up more capital in a year than it produces (Figure 7-2c). When this situation occurs, net investment is negative—the economy is *disinvesting*. Depressions foster such circumstances. During bad times, when production and employment are low, the nation has a greater production capacity than it is currently using. There is no incentive to replace depreciated capital equipment, much less add to the existing stock. Depreciation is likely to exceed gross investment, with the result that the

FIGURE 7-2

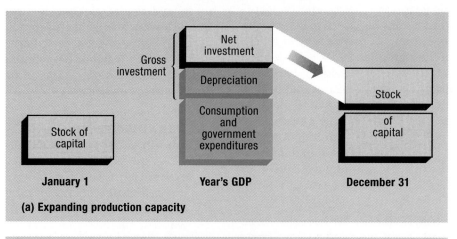

(a) Expanding production capacity

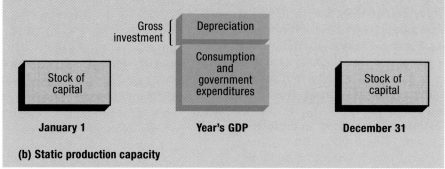

(b) Static production capacity

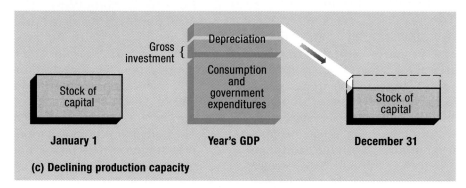

(c) Declining production capacity

(a) In an expanding economy, gross investment exceeds depreciation, which means that the economy is making a net addition to its stock of capital facilities. (b) In a static economy, gross investment precisely replaces the capital facilities depreciated in producing the year's output, leaving the stock of capital goods unchanged. (c) In a declining economy, gross investment is insufficient to replace the capital goods depreciated by the year's production. As a result, the economy's stock of capital declines.

nation's stock of capital is less at the end of each year than it was at the start.

This was the case during the Great Depression. In 1933 gross investment was about $208 million, while the capital consumed during that year was $532 million. Net disinvestment was therefore $324 million.

That is, net investment was a minus $324 million, indicating that the size of our "national factory" shrunk during that year.

We use the letter I for domestic investment spending, attaching the subscript g to mean gross investment and the subscript n to mean net investment. It is gross investment I_g that is used in determining GDP. *(Key Question 6)*

Government Purchases (*G*)

Government purchases (of consumption goods) include all government spending (federal, provincial, and municipal) on the finished products of businesses and all direct purchases of resources, including labour. It excludes all government transfer payments because such outlays reflect no current production but merely transfers of government receipts to some households. We use the letter *G* to indicate government purchases, the third part of GDP.

Net Exports (*X_n*)

A country's international trade transactions enter into national income accounting. Let's use the Canadian economy to show how: On the one hand, we want to include in GDP all spending that accounts for the production of goods and services in Canada. Spending by people abroad on Canadian goods accounts for Canadian output, just as does spending by Canadian citizens in Canadian markets. Thus, we must include what the rest of the world spends on Canadian goods and services—Canadian exports—when determining GDP by the expenditures approach.

On the other hand, we know that part of the money spent for consumption, investment, and government purchases is spent on imports: goods and services produced abroad. This spending does not reflect production in Canada. It is some other nation's GDP. So we must subtract the value of imports to avoid overstating total production in Canada.

Rather than add exports and subtract imports separately, national income accountants add to GDP the difference "exports less imports." This difference, called **net exports**, is the amount by which foreign spending on a nation's goods and services exceeds that nation's spending on foreign goods and services. It is designated by X_n.

If people abroad buy \$45 billion of Canadian exports, and Canadians buy \$35 billion of foreign imports in a year, Canada's net exports are *plus* \$10 billion. If the rest of the world spends \$30 billion on Canadian exports and Canadians spend \$40 billion on foreign imports, Canada's net exports are *minus* \$10 billion.

The left side of Table 7-3 shows the computation of Canadian GDP for 1997 via the expenditures approach. Note that in 1997 the rest of the world spent \$14.3 billion more on Canadian goods and services than Canadians spent on goods and services from abroad.

TABLE 7-3 The income statement for the economy, 1997 (in billions of dollars)

Receipts: expenditure approach		Allocations: income approach	
Personal consumption expenditure (*C*)	505.9	Wages, salaries, and supplementary labour income	\$445.8
Gross investment (*I_g*)	165.8	Corporation profits before taxes	85.7
Government current purchases of goods and services (*G*)	168.5	Interest and miscellaneous investment income	46.2
Net exports (*X_n*)	14.3	Accrued net income of farm operators from farm production	1.4
Statistical discrepancy	.6	Net income of nonfarm unincorporated business, including rent	53.0
		Inventory valuation adjustment	−1.6
		Net domestic income at factor cost	\$630.5
		Indirect taxes less subsidies	114.5
		Capital consumption allowances	110.7
		Statistical discrepancy	−.6
Gross domestic product at market prices	\$855.1	Gross domestic product at market prices	\$855.1

Source: Statistics Canada, National Income and Expenditure Accounts, First Quarter 1998. These data and updates may be retried from Statistics Canada's Web site at www.statcan.ca/english/Pgdb/Economy/econom.htm.

The GDP Equation: $C + I_g + G + X_n$

These four categories of expenditures—personal consumption expenditures (C), gross private domestic investment (I_g), government purchases (G), and net exports (X_n)—include all possible types of spending. Added together, they measure the market value of the year's output or, in other words, the GDP. That is,

$$C + I_g + G + X_n = GDP$$

For Canada in 1997, in billions (Table 7-3):

$$505.9 + 165.8 + 168.5 + 14.3 + 0.6* = 855.1$$

Global Perspective 7-1 compares GDPs for selected nations.

GDP: THE INCOME APPROACH[1]

The allocations side of Table 7-3 shows how 1997's $855.1 billion of expenditure was distributed as income. It would be simple if we could say that all expenditures on the economy's annual output flowed to Canadian households as wage, rent, interest, and profit incomes. But the picture is complicated by two adjustments necessary to balance the expenditures and income sides of the national accounting statement. Let's first look at the various items of *national income* shown on the right side of Table 7-3. Then we will turn to the two complications.

There are five categories of factor income payments in our national accounts: (1) wages, salaries, and supplementary labour income, (2) corporate profits before taxes, (3) interest and miscellaneous investment income, (4) farmers' income, and (5) income of nonfarm unincorporated businesses.

Wages, Salaries, and Supplementary Labour Income

The largest income category is made up primarily of the wages and salaries paid by businesses and government to suppliers of labour. It also includes wage and salary supplements, in particular pay-

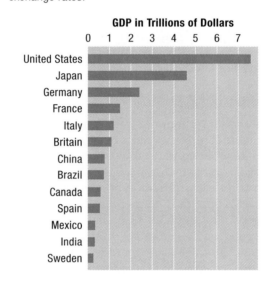

7-1

GLOBAL PERSPECTIVE

Comparative GDPs in trillions of U.S. dollars, 1996

Canada has the world's ninth highest GDP. These GDP data have been converted to dollars via international exchange rates.

GDP in Trillions of Dollars

Source: International Monetary Fund data.

ments by employers of employment insurance premiums, workers' compensation premiums, and employer contributions to a variety of private and public pension and welfare funds for workers. These wage and salary supplements (or "fringe benefits") are a part of the employer's cost of obtaining labour and therefore are treated as a component of the firm's total wage payments.

Corporation Profits Before Taxes

Corporate profits are distributed three ways.

1. A part is claimed by government as **corporate income taxes**.
2. A part of the remaining corporate profits is paid out to stockholders as **dividends**. Such payments flow to households, the ultimate owners of all corporations.
3. What remains of corporate profits is **undistributed corporate profits**. These retained corporate earnings, will be invested—currently or in the future—in new plants and equip-

---

*Statistical discrepancy. For an explanation see page 140.
[1] Some instructors may choose to omit this section, because the expenditures approach is more relevant for the analysis of Chapters 9 to 12.

ment, increasing the real assets of the business doing the investing.

Interest and Miscellaneous Investment Income

Interest refers to money income payments that flow from private businesses to the suppliers of money capital. It is the firm's cost of borrowing funds supplied to it by lenders (either individuals, other businesses, or governments). Miscellaneous investment income includes such smaller categories as royalties received by individuals.

Farmers' Income

The net income of farmers includes the sales of farm products, plus the imputed value of farm output consumed by the farm family, plus the value of the physical change in farm inventories, less farm operating expenses and capital consumption allowances on farm buildings and equipment.

Net Income of Nonfarm Unincorporated Business, Including Rent

This is the earnings of working proprietors from their own businesses, excluding farms and corporations. Like the previous category, this one represents a mixture of labour income and investment income that is impossible to segregate. Farm and nonfarm proprietors supplying their own capital earn profits (or losses), interest, and rents mixed in with their labour income. Rents cover the net income received by persons, other than farms and corporations, for the rental of property.

The last two categories represent factor of production payment: wages, rent, interest, and profits. A small business with one owner may supply her own labour, capital, and land, therefore it is not easy to divide the income earned into the four conventional categories.

Note that since we want to measure current production, a small adjustment must be made that reflects changes in the price of inventories during the current year. Inventory prices are averaged out during the year rather than using end-of-the-year prices. Suppose a widget was produced in January, its price 1 cent at the time, and became part of inventory. If in December the price of a widget were 3 cents, for national accounting purposes the average price, say 1.5 cents, is used.

This adjustment is referred to as "inventory valuation adjustment."

When we add wages, salaries and supplementary labour income, corporate profits, interest and miscellaneous investment income, farmers' income, income of nonfarm unincorporated business, and make the appropriate inventory valuation adjustment, we get **net domestic income at factor costs** (NDI)—all the income earned by Canadian-supplied resources. But Table 7-3 reveals that net domestic income, shown on the right-hand side of the account, is less than the sum of the expenditures, shown on the left-hand side.

Two Adjustments We can balance both sides of the account by adding two items to net domestic income:

1. **INDIRECT TAXES** The first adjustment is to add to net domestic income certain taxes, called **indirect taxes**, which firms treat as costs of production and therefore add to the prices of the products they sell. Such taxes include general sales taxes, excise taxes, business property taxes, licence fees, and custom duties.

   To see why we must add indirect business taxes to net domestic income in balancing expenditures and income, assume that a firm produces a good selling at $1. Production of this item creates $1 of wage, rent, interest, and profit income. But now government imposes a 5 percent sales tax on all products sold at retail. The retailer adds this 5 percent to the price of the product, raising its price from $1 to $1.05, and thus shifts the sales tax to consumers. This $.05 is *not* earned income, because government contributes nothing directly to the production of the good in return for the tax receipt. The value of the output is $1.05, but only $1 of this value is paid to households as wage, rent, interest, and profit income. Therefore, we must add the $.05 to the $1 of net domestic income in calculating GDP—the total value of output. In Table 7-3 we make this adjustment for the entire economy.

2. **DEPRECIATION: CAPITAL CONSUMPTION ALLOWANCE** The second adjustment is depreciation. The useful life of capital equipment extends far beyond the year of purchase. Capital may be purchased in one year and used productively for many years after that. To avoid gross understatement of profit and therefore of total income in the year of pur-

chase, and overstatement of profit and total income in succeeding years, the total cost of such goods must be allocated over their lives. The annual charge that estimates the amount of capital equipment used up in each year's production is called *depreciation*. Depreciation is a bookkeeping entry designed to yield a more accurate statement of profit and hence total income for a firm in each year.

If profits and total income for the economy are to be stated accurately, a gigantic depreciation charge must be made against the economy's private and public stock of capital. (Public capital includes government buildings, port facilities, and so on.) This depreciation charge is called *capital consumption allowance*—the allowance for capital goods "consumed" in producing this year's GDP. It is the portion of this year's GDP that must be set aside to replace the capital goods used up in production. That part of this charge is the difference between gross private investment, I_g, and net investment, I_n.

For present purposes, the significance of this charge is that this part of the business sector's receipts is not available for income payments to resource suppliers. This part of receipts—this portion of the value of production—is a cost of production that reduces business profits. But, unlike other costs of production, depreciation *does not add to anyone's income*. We must therefore add consumption of fixed capital to net domestic income in balancing an economy's expenditures and income, as in Table 7-3.

Statistical Discrepancy

Despite their best efforts, when statisticians at Statistics Canada have finished rechecking their estimate of GDP through both approaches, they often find that the figures do not quite add up. Should they find, for example, that their expenditure estimate is $1.2 billion less than their income estimate, they will split the difference. They will add $0.6 billion from the expenditure estimate and subtract $0.6 billion to the income estimate. That is what they did in 1997, as shown in Table 7-3.

Table 7-3 summarizes our discussions of both the expenditure and income approaches to GDP. This is a gigantic income statement for the economy. The left-hand side tells us what the economy produced in 1997 and the total receipts derived from that production. The right-hand side indicates how the income derived from the production of 1997's GDP was allocated.

7-1
QUICK REVIEW

- Gross domestic product (GDP) measures the total market value of all final goods and services produced within a nation in a specific year.

- The expenditures approach to GDP sums total spending on final goods and services: GDP = C + I_g + G + X_n.

- When net investment is positive, the economy's production capacity expands; when net investment is negative, the economy's production capacity erodes.

- The income approach to GDP sums the total income earned by a nation's resource suppliers, then adds in indirect taxes, and capital consumption allowance.

OTHER INCOME MEASUREMENTS

Our discussion has centred on GDP as a measure of the economy's annual output. But there are related national accounts of equal importance that can help you understand the components of the economy.

Gross National Product (GNP)

Until 1986, **gross national product (GNP)** was the main aggregate in the national accounts published by Statistics Canada. The change came about because in a country such as Canada in which foreign investment is significant, GDP would give us a better indication of both output *produced in* Canada, and the total income derived from that output. GNP measures output by Canadians here and abroad, but excludes the contribution to Canadian output from investments of nonresidents, which yields *net investment income from nonresidents*.

Personal Income (PI)

Personal income (PI) includes all income *received* by households, earned or unearned. It is likely to differ from net domestic income (NDI) because some income that is earned—corporate income taxes, undistributed corporate profits, government investment income, and social insurance contributions—is not actually received by households, and conversely, some income that is received—transfer payments—is not currently earned. Transfer payments, you will recall, are made up of such items as (1) Canada and Quebec Pension Plan payments, old age security pension payments, and unemployment insurance benefits; (2) welfare payments; (3) a variety of veterans' payments. Thus, we must subtract from domestic income income that is earned but not received and add in income received but not currently earned.

Disposable Income (DI)

Disposable income is personal income less personal taxes and other personal transfers to government. *Personal taxes* are made up of personal income taxes and personal property taxes, the first of which is the most important. The other personal transfers to government include contributions to employment insurance, Canada and Quebec Pension Plans, and public service pensions.

Households apportion their disposable income in two ways. The bulk of it is spent on consumer goods. Another significant portion is saved.

Personal saving is the amount remaining after consumption has been deducted from disposable income.

7-2
QUICK REVIEW

We have derived three additional national accounting concepts:

- Gross national product is derived by subtracting from GDP net investment income from nonresidents;
- Personal income (PI) is income *received* by households before personal taxes;
- Disposable income (DI) is income received by households less personal taxes.

The Circular Flow Revisited

Figure 7-3 combines the expenditure and income approaches to GDP. As a more realistic and more complex expression of the circular flow model of

the economy (discussed in Chapters 2 and 5), this figure merits your careful study.

Starting at the GDP rectangle in the upper left, the expenditure side of GDP is shown by the large arrow. Immediately to the right of the GDP rectangle are the nine components of GDP and the additions and subtractions needed to derive NDI and PI. All allocations or income flows are depicted by arrows. Note the flow of personal taxes out of PI and the division of DI between consumption and personal saving in the household sector. In the government sector the flows of revenue in the form of four basic types of taxes are denoted on the right; on the left, government disbursements take the form of purchases of goods and services and transfers. The position of the business sector emphasizes, on the left, investment expenditures and, on the right, the three major sources of funds for business investment.

Observe the role of the rest of the world in Figure 7-3. Spending by people abroad on our exports adds to our GDP, but our consumption, government, and investment expenditures buy imported products as well as domestically produced goods. The flow emanating from "Rest of the World" shows that we handle this complication by calculating *net* exports (exports minus imports). This may be a positive or negative amount.

The major virtue of Figure 7-3 is that it simultaneously portrays the expenditure and income aspects of GDP, fitting the two approaches to one another. These flows of expenditure and income are part of a continuous, repetitive process. Cause and effect are intermingled: expenditures create income, and out of this income arise expenditures that again flow to resource owners as income.

The table at the back of this book contains a historical summary of the national income accounts and related statistics since 1926.

NOMINAL VERSUS REAL GDP

Recall that GDP is the market value of all final goods and services produced in a year. So money or *nominal* values are used as a common denominator to sum a heterogeneous output into a meaningful total. But this raises a problem: The value of different years' outputs (GDPs) can be usefully compared only if the value of money itself does not change because of inflation (rising overall prices) or deflation (falling overall prices).

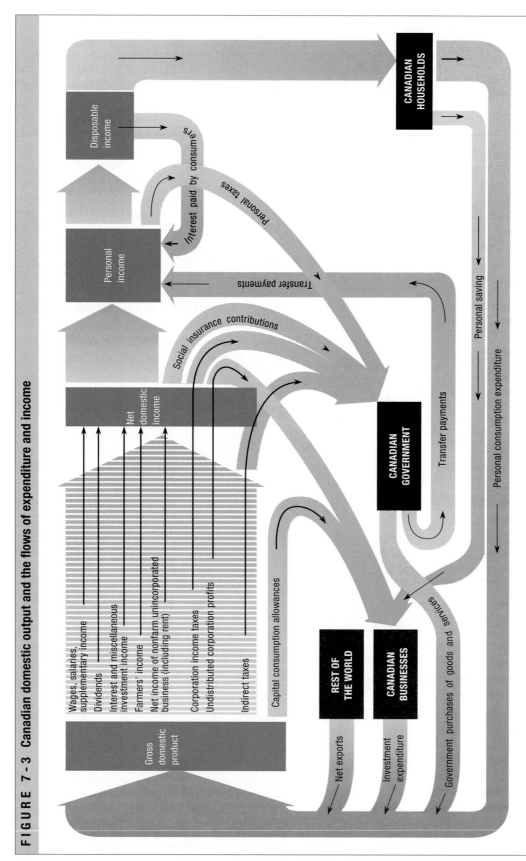

FIGURE 7-3 Canadian domestic output and the flows of expenditure and income

This figure is an elaborate circular flow diagram that fits the expenditures and allocations sides of GDP to one another. The income or allocations flows are shown in green; the expenditure flows, in grey. You should trace through the income and expenditures flows, relating them to the five basic national income accounting measures.

Inflation or deflation complicates GDP because GDP is a price-times-quantity figure. The direct data used to measure GDP are the total sales revenues of business firms, but these revenues include both output quantities and the level of prices, which means that a change in either the quantity of output or the level of prices will affect the size of the GDP. Identical changes in GDP will occur if there is, say, a 5 percent increase in output with no change in prices *or* a 5 percent increase in prices with no change in output. But it is the quantity of goods produced and distributed to households that affects their standard of living, not the price tags on these goods. The hamburger selling for $2 in 1997 yields the same satisfaction as an identical hamburger of 1970 that sold for 50 cents, *not* four times as much satisfaction, as the nominal value might imply.

Fortunately, we can resolve this difficulty by *deflating* GDP for rising prices and *inflating* it when prices are falling. These adjustments give us a picture of GDP for various years as if prices and the value of the dollar were the same as those in some reference period (or year). A GDP figure that reflects the prices prevailing when the output is produced is called unadjusted GDP, or **nominal GDP**. In contrast, a GDP figure that is deflated or inflated for price-level changes is called adjusted GDP, or **real GDP**.

Adjustment Process in a One-Good Economy

There are two ways we can adjust nominal GDP figures for price changes. Let's consider each using a simplified example. Assume an economy produces only one good, pizza, and in the amounts indicated in Table 7-4 for years 1, 2, and 3. An examination of columns 1 and 2 tells you that the nominal GDPs for years 2 and 3, as shown in column 4, greatly overstate the increases in real output occurring in those two years. *That is, the monetary measure of production (nominal GDP) does not accurately reflect the actual changes that have occurred in output (real GDP).* Considerable proportions of the sharp increases in nominal GDP in years 2 and 3 are due to the rather drastic inflation shown in column 2, the remainder owing to the changes in output shown in column 1. Both increases in output and price increases are reflected in the nominal GDP.

Let's first suppose that we have directly gathered data from financial reports of businesses to derive nominal GDP in various years. In this approach, we will not know *directly* to what extent changes in price and changes in quantity of output have accounted for the observed increases in GDP. At this stage, we do not have before us the data in column 1, but only the data in column 4.

GDP Price Index So how can we determine real GDP in our pizza-only economy? One method is to determine price changes and then adjust the nominal GDP figures. Once the price changes (as shown in column 2) are discovered, we can derive a price index that compares prices between years and estimates overall changes in the price level. Generally defined, a **price index** *measures the combined price of a particular collection of goods and services, called a "market basket," in a specific period relative to the combined price of an identical (or highly similar) group of goods and services in a reference period.* This point of reference, or benchmark, is called the base period or *base year.* More formally,

---

TABLE 7-4 Calculating real GDP

Year	(1) Units of output	(2) Price of Pizza per unit	(3) Price index, (year 1 = 100)	(4) Unadjusted, or nominal, GDP (1) × (2)	(5) Adjusted, or real, GDP
1	5	$10	100	$ 50	$50
2	7	20	200	140	70
3	8	25	250	200	80
4	10	30	_____	_____	_____
5	11	28	_____	_____	_____

$$\text{Price index in a given year} = \frac{\text{Price of market basket in a specific year}}{\text{Price of the same market basket in the base year}} \times 100 \quad (1)$$

By convention, the price ratio between the specific year and the base year is multiplied by 100. For example, a price ratio of 2/1 (= 2) is expressed as an index number of 200. Similarly, the price ratio of 1/3 (= .33) is expressed as 33.

In our simple example, our market basket consists of only one product: pizza. We see in column 2 in Table 7-4 that the price of pizza was $10 in year 1, $20 in year 2, $25 in year 3, and so on. Selecting year 1 as the base year, we can express the prices of the pizza "market basket" in, say, years 2 and 3 relative to the price of the market basket in year 1 as follows:

$$\text{Price index, year 2} = \frac{\$20}{\$10} \times 100 = 200$$

$$\text{Price index, year 3} = \frac{\$25}{\$10} \times 100 = 250$$

For year 1 the index must be 100 since the specific year and the base year are identical ($10).

These index numbers tell us that the price of pizza increased from year 1 to year 2 by 100 percent {=[(200 − 100)/100] × 100} and from year 1 to year 3 by 150 percent {=[(250 − 100)/100] × 100}.

We can now use the index number in column 3 to deflate the nominal GDP figures in column 4. The simplest and most direct method of deflating is to express these index numbers as hundredths, that is, in decimal form, and divide them into the corresponding nominal GDP. This procedure yields real GDP:

$$\text{Real GDP} = \frac{\text{Nominal GDP}}{\text{Price index (in hundredths)}} \quad (2)$$

Column 5 shows the results. These real GDP figures measure the value of total output in years 1, 2, and 3 as if the price of pizza had been constant at $10 throughout the three-year period. So real GDP shows the market value of each year's output measured in terms of dollars that have the same purchasing power as in the base year.

To ensure you understand the deflating process, you should complete Table 7-4 for years 4

and 5, using equation (2). Second, you should rework the entire deflating procedure, using year 3 as the base period. You will find that in this case you must *inflate* some of the nominal GDP data, using the same procedure as used in our examples.

An Alternative Method We could more directly establish real GDP by initially gathering *separate* data on physical outputs (as in column 1) and their prices (as in column 2). Let's again consider our pizza-only economy in Table 7-4. If we first determine the physical outputs for each year, as shown in column 2, we can then see what each of those actual outputs would have sold for *if the base year price (here $10) had prevailed*. In year 2, the 7 units of pizza would be valued at $70 (= 7 units of output *times* the $10 price in the base year). As confirmed in column 5, this $70 of output *is* year 2's real GDP. Similarly, the real GDP of $80 for year 3 is found by multiplying the 8 units of output in year 3 by the $10 price in the base year.

When we determine real GDP through this method, the price index for a specific year is *implied*; it is simply the nominal GDP divided by the real GDP for that year:

$$\frac{\text{Price index}}{\text{(in hundredths)}} = \frac{\text{Nominal GDP}}{\text{Real GDP}} \quad (3)$$

Example: In year 2 in Table 7-4, the price index of 200, or, in hundredths, 2.00, equals the nominal GDP of $140 divided by the real GDP of $70. You should note that equation (3) is simply a rearrangement of equation (2). Table 7-5 summarizes the two methods we have used to determine real GDP in our assumed single-good economy. *(Key Question 11)*

Real-World Considerations and Data

In the real world of many goods and services, the government's determination of real GDP and its actual price index are *much* more complex than in our pizza-only economy. The government accountants must assign "weights" to various categories of goods and services based on their relative proportions of total output. In Canada, accountants update these weights as expenditure patterns change.

Nevertheless, once real GDP and the GDP price index are established, the relationship between nominal GDP, real GDP, and the GDP

TABLE 7-5 Steps for deriving real GDP from nominal GDP

Method 1

1. Find nominal GDP for each year.
2. Compute a GDP price index.
3. Divide each year's nominal GDP by that year's price index (in hundredths) to determine real GDP.

Method 2

1. Break down nominal GDP into physical quantities of output and prices for each year.
2. Find real GDP for each year by determining the dollar amount that each year's physical output would have sold for if base-year prices had prevailed. (The GDP price index can then be found by dividing nominal GDP by real GDP.)

price index is clear. Table 7-6 provides some Canadian illustrations of these relationships. Note that the point of reference for the price index is 1992, the base year Statistics Canada is currently using, where the index value is set at 100. Because the

TABLE 7-6 Nominal GDP, real GDP, and GDP price index, selected years

(1) Year	(2) Nominal GDP	(3) Real GDP	(4) GDP price index 1992 = 100
1965	57.5	277.7	20.7
1970	89.1	347.6	——
1975	171.5	448.5	38.2
1980	309.9	——	57.0
1985	478.0	627.0	76.2
1990	667.8	721.3	92.6
1992	690.1	690.1	100.0
1993	724.9	716.1	——
1994	762.3	744.2	102.4
1995	799.1	——	105.1
1996	820.3	769.7	106.6
1997	855.1	798.2	107.1

Source: Statistics Canada, National Economic Accounts, various years. For updates on nominal and real GDP visit Statistics Canada Website at www.statcan.ca/english/Pgdb/Economy/econom.htm.

long-run trend has been for the price level to rise, the pre-1992 values of real GDP (column 3) are higher than the nominal values (column 2). This upward adjustment acknowledges that prices were lower in the years before 1992. As a result, nominal GDP understated the real output of those years and must be inflated.

The rising price level has caused nominal GDP figures for the post-1992 years to overstate real output. The government accountants therefore reduce, or deflate, these figures to gauge what GDP would have been in 1994, 1996, and so on, if 1992 prices had prevailed. So, since the 1992 reference year, real GDP has been less than nominal GDP.

By inflating the nominal pre-1992 GDP data and deflating the post-1992 data, government accountants determine annual real GDP, which can then be compared to any other year in the series. That is, the real GDP values in column 3 are directly comparable with one another in a meaningful way since they reflect changes in physical output.

Table 7-6 also reminds us that once nominal GDP and real GDP are known, the price index can be calculated, or, alternatively, if nominal GDP and the price index are known, real GDP can be calculated. Example: For 1994 nominal GDP was $762.3 billion and real GDP was $744.2. So the price level was 102.4 (= $762.3/$744.2 × 100), or 2.4 percent higher than in 1992. Alternatively, to find real GDP for 1994 we could express the 1994 GDP price index in hundredths (102.4) and divide it into the nominal GDP of $762.3.

To test your understanding of the relationships between nominal GDP, real GDP, and the price level, you should (1) determine the price-index values for years 1970 and 1993, and (2) determine real GDP for years 1980 and 1995. For each of these years we have purposely left out data in Table 7-6. *(Key Question 12)*

THE CONSUMER PRICE INDEX

The GDP price index in Table 7-6 is *not* the same as the **consumer price index** (CPI), which government uses to report the rate of inflation each month. The CPI measures the prices of a market basket of some 600 consumer goods and services purchased by a typical urban consumer in 64 urban centres across Canada. The GDP index in Table 7-6 is much broader; it includes not only consumer goods and services but also capital goods, goods and services purchased by government, and goods and services entering world trade.

The present composition of the market basket used in the CPI was determined from a survey of the spending patterns of urban consumers in 1992. Thus the CPI in any specific year is as follows:

$$CPI = \frac{\text{Price of the 1992 market basket in a specific year}}{\text{Price of same market basket in base period (1992)}} \times 100$$

Unlike the GDP price index, in which the weights (relative purchases) of various goods and services are adjusted continuously, the CPI is a historical, *fixed-weight price index*. If 20 percent of consumer spending was on housing in 1992, the assumption is that 20 percent of spending is still on housing in 1999. The base period is changed roughly every 10 years. The idea behind the historical, fixed-weight approach is to measure changes in the *cost* of a *constant* standard of living. Changes in the CPI thus allegedly measure the rate of inflation facing consumers. For example, the CPI increased from 105.9 in 1996 to 107.6 in 1997, indicating that 1997's rate of inflation was 1.6 percent [= (107.6 − 105.9)/105.9]. However, many economists believe that the CPI overstates actual inflation. We address this issue in this chapter's Last Word.

7-3

QUICK REVIEW

- Nominal GDP is output valued at current prices; real GDP is output valued at constant prices (base-year prices).
- The GDP price index compares the price (cost) of goods and services constituting GDP in a specific year to the price of the same market basket in a reference year.
- A year's nominal GDP can be adjusted to real GDP by dividing the nominal GDP by the GDP price index (expressed in hundredths).
- The consumer price index (CPI) measures changes in the prices of a fixed market basket of some 600 goods bought by the typical Canadian consumer.

GDP AND ECONOMIC WELL-BEING

GDP is a reasonably accurate and extremely useful measure of domestic economic performance. It is not, and was never intended to be, an index of society's overall well-being—its total satisfaction. GDP is merely a measure of the annual volume of goods and services produced. Many things could make a country better off without necessarily raising GDP, such as reduction of crime and violence, greater equality of opportunity, improved racial harmony, better understanding between parents and children, and reductions of drug and alcohol abuse.

Nevertheless, it is widely held that there should be a strong positive correlation between real GDP and economic well-being; that is, greater production should move society towards economic well-being, "the good life." Thus, we must understand some of the shortcomings of GDP—why it might understate or overstate real output, and why more output will not necessarily make society better off.

Nonmarket Transactions

Certain production transactions do not take place in markets. Thus, GDP as a measure of the market value of output fails to include them. Examples include the production services of a homemaker and the work of the carpenter who repairs his or her own home. Such transactions are not reflected in the profit and loss statements of business firms and therefore escape the national income accountants, causing GDP to be understated.

Leisure

The Canadian workweek has declined significantly over the 20th century, from about 53 hours at the turn of the century to about 36 hours now. Also, the expanded availability of paid vacations, holidays, and leave time has reduced the work year, which has given us increased leisure time and, thus, has had a positive effect on our well-being. Our system of national income accounting understates our well-being by not directly recognizing the benefits of increased leisure. Nor do national accounts reflect the satisfaction—the "psychic income"—that many people derive from their work.

Improved Product Quality

GDP is a quantitative, not a qualitative, measure. It does not accurately reflect improvements in product quality. There is a fundamental qualitative difference between a $3,000 personal computer purchased today and a computer costing the same amount just a few years ago. Today's $3,000 computer has far more speed and storage capacity as well as a clearer monitor and improved multimedia capabilities.

Failure to account adequately for quality improvement is a shortcoming of GDP accounting. Quality improvement clearly affects economic well-being as much as does the quantity of goods. Because product quality has improved over time, GDP understates the resulting improvement in our material well-being.

Composition and Distribution of Output

Changes in the composition of total output and its allocation among specific households may influence economic well-being. GDP, however, reflects only the size of output and tells us nothing about whether this collection of goods is "right" for society. A handgun and a set of encyclopedias, both selling for $350, are weighted equally in the GDP. Distribution is also ignored by GDP. Some economists believe that a more equal distribution of total output would increase national economic well-being. If they are correct, a future trend towards a less unequal distribution of GDP would enhance the economic well-being of society. A more unequal distribution—which appears to be occurring—would have the reverse effect.

Per-Capita Output

For many purposes the most meaningful measure of economic well-being is *per-capita output*, found by dividing real GDP by population. Because GDP measures the size of total output, it may conceal or misrepresent changes in the standard of living of individuals and households. GDP may rise, but if population is also growing rapidly, the per-person standard of living may be constant or even declining.

This is the plight of some developing countries. Madagascar's domestic output grew approximately 1 percent per year from 1985 to 1995. But annual population growth was 3 percent, resulting in a yearly decrease in per-capita output slightly above 2 percent.

GDP and the Environment

Undesirable and much publicized "gross domestic by-products," such as dirty air and water, toxic waste, automobile junkyards, congestion, and noise, accompany production and the growth of GDP. The costs of pollution reduce our economic well-being. These spillover costs are associated with production and hence with the GDP but are not deducted from total output; thus GDP overstates our national economic well-being.

Ironically, the final physical product of economic production and consumption is garbage. A rising GDP means more garbage, and it may mean more pollution and a greater divergence between GDP and economic well-being. In fact, under existing accounting procedures, when a manufacturer pollutes a river and government spends to clean it up, the cleanup expense is added to the GDP while the pollution is not subtracted!

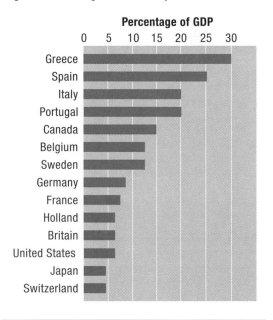

7-2
GLOBAL PERSPECTIVE

The underground economy as a percentage of GDP, selected nations

Several nations have relatively larger underground economies than Canada. In general, the higher the tax rates and the greater the number of regulations, the larger is the underground economy.

Source: *The Economist* August 14, 1993, p. 55. Estimate for Canada reported in "Tax Revolt," *Globe and Mail*, Report on Business, January 28, 1995, p. B19.

The Underground Economy

Economists agree there is a large underground sector in our economy. Some participants in this sector engage in illegal activities such as gambling, loan-sharking, prostitution, and the narcotics trade. These may well be "growth industries." Obviously, persons receiving income from illegal businesses choose to conceal their incomes.

However, most participants in the underground economy are in *legal* activities but do not fully report their incomes to Revenue Canada. A bell captain at a hotel or a waiter at a restaurant may underreport tips from customers. A business person may record only a portion of sales receipts for the tax collector. A worker who wants to retain employment insurance benefits may obtain an "off-the-books" or "cash-only" job so there is no record of his or her work activities. A brick mason may agree to remodel a neighbour's fireplace in exchange for the neighbour's doing off-the-books repair work on the mason's boat engine. None of these underground transactions, obviously, are included in GDP.

Although there is no consensus on the size of the underground economy, estimates suggest it is between 5 and 15 percent of the recorded GDP. In 1997, that meant GDP was understated by between $37 and $112 billion. If this additional income had been taxed at a 30 percent average tax rate, the federal budget deficit for 1994 would have declined from $29 billion to between an $18 billion deficit and a surplus of almost $4 billion.

Global Perspective 7-2 indicates the relative sizes of underground economies in selected nations.

In
The Media

Economic Growth Slows

Consumers, businesses cool spending pace in fourth quarter

BY BRUCE LITTLE
ECONOMICS REPORTER

Canada's economic growth slowed during the final quarter of 1997, as the two big drivers of growth cooled and major strikes took another slice off the expansion.

Statistics Canada reported that gross domestic product increased 0.7 per cent during the fourth quarter—3 per cent at annual rates—as consumer and business spending suddenly slowed. Growth in the first three quarters had been an annualized average of 4.6 per cent.

Household and corporate spending had powered the economy's growth for most of the previous year, but suddenly shifted into lower gear as 1997 drew to a close.

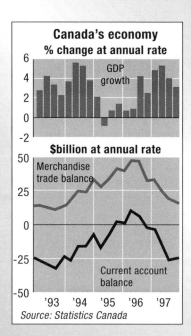

Canada's economy
% change at annual rate

GDP growth

$billion at annual rate

Merchandise trade balance

Current account balance

'93 '94 '95 '96 '97
Source: Statistics Canada

As a whole, 1997 turned in the country's second-strongest economic performance of the 1990s. GDP grew 3.8 per cent from 1996, just shy of the 3.9-per-cent growth rate in 1994, but better than any other year since 1988.

But forecasters said the fourth-quarter slowdown may be a hint of what Canadians can expect as 1998 unfolds.

"It seems to me that the message is one of caution this year," said Warren Jestin, chief economist at Bank of Nova Scotia. He thinks his own forecast of 3-per-cent growth in 1998 may turn out to be a little optimistic.

"The figures are healthy, but not stunning," said John McCallum, his counterpart at Royal Bank of Canada. "The trend is down from the [third] quarter, which was down from the previous quarter."

He said he's still comfortable with his prediction that the economy will grow 3.2 per cent this year, but said that figure implies a slowdown in the second half of the year to an annualized growth rate of less than 3 per cent.

Statscan's quarterly GDP report was one of three major indicators released yesterday.

• The current account deficit in the balance of payments narrowed slightly to $6.2-billion in the fourth quarter from $6.6-

billion in the third. The usual surplus in the trade of goods fell to $4.1-billion from $4.7-billion, but the deficit in investment income also dropped—to $7.9-billion from $9.2-billion.

• The monthly measure of GDP showed that output increased 1 per cent in December alone as two industries affected by strikes returned to normal. Ontario teachers were off the job for two weeks in October and November, while postal workers shut down Canada Post Corp. for two weeks in November and early December. GDP

had contracted 0.3 per cent in November.

The fourth-quarter slowdown in consumer spending and business investment was substantial. Consumer outlays, which had expanded at annual rates of almost 5 per cent in the first three quarters of the year, decelerated to a 2.3-per-cent pace in the fourth quarter. Auto purchases soared, but spending on everything else actually fell compared with the third quarter.

Source: Globe and Mail, March 3, 1998, p. B1. Reprinted with permission from the Globe and Mail.

THE STORY IN BRIEF

The economy slows down in the fourth quarter of 1997.

THE ECONOMICS BEHIND THE STORY

• This article is about Statistics Canada's use of the expenditure approach to measure economic growth in Canada. It reports that during the fourth quarter

of 1997 output of goods and services expanded 0.7 percent. For the entire year GDP grew 3.8 percent.

• But the growth rate slowed in the fourth quarter. In the first three-quarters of 1997, the economy had been growing at 4.6 percent, at an annualized rate. The two components of expenditures that slowed were consumption (C) and business investment (I).

• On the basis of the fourth-quarter data, economic forecasters were predicting that the Canadian economy would grow at about 3 percent in 1998.

• What were net exports in the fourth quarter of 1997? ∎

The Last Word

THE CPI: DOES IT OVERSTATE INFLATION?

THE CONSUMER PRICE INDEX IS THE MOST widely reported measure of inflation; therefore, we should become familiar with its characteristics and limitations.

The consumer price index (CPI) measures changes in the prices of a "market basket" of 600 goods and services purchased by a typical Canadian consumer in 64 urban centres across Canada. The present composition

of the market basket was determined from a survey of the spending patterns of urban consumers in 1992. Unlike the GDP deflator, the CPI is a historical, fixed-weight price index. In each year, the composition or "weight" of the items in the market basket remains the same as in the base period (1992). If 20 percent of consumer spending was on housing in 1992, it is assumed that 20 percent of consumer spending is still spent on housing in 1996 and 2001. The base period is changed roughly every 10 years—a new CPI index appeared in 1995. The idea behind the historical, fixed-weight approach is to measure changes in the cost of a constant standard of living. These changes supposedly measure the rate of inflation facing consumers.

But here are four problems with the CPI that cause it to overstate the true rate of inflation, according to critics.

1. Changed spending patterns.   Although the composition of the market basket is assumed to remain unchanged, in fact, consumers do change their spending patterns, particularly in response to changes in relative prices. When the price of beef rises while fish and chicken prices are steady, consumers move away from beef and buy fish or chicken instead. Over time consumers are buying a market basket that contains more of the relatively low-priced and less of the relatively high-priced goods and services. The fixed-weight CPI assumes that these substitutions have not occurred. Therefore the index overstates the actual cost of living.

2. New products.   Many new consumer goods and services such as fax machines, multimedia computers, and cellular phone services either are not included or are severely underweighted in the market basket used to construct the CPI. Often prices of new products drop following their introductions. The CPI, with its historical, fixed-weight market basket, fails to pick up these price changes and thus overstates inflation.

3. Quality improvements.   The CPI does not take quality improvements into account. To the extent that product quality has improved since the base year, prices should be higher. We ought to pay more for televisions today than a decade ago because they are generally of higher quality. In general, it's the same for automobiles, automobile tires, electronic equipment, and many other items. But the CPI assumes that all the increases in the nominal value of the market basket arise solely from inflation, not quality improvements. Again the CPI overstates the rate of inflation.

4. Price discounting.   In calculating the CPI, Statistics Canada continually rotates the stores it checks for prices. But once a set of stores is selected, the price survey picks up price changes only on a same-store basis. If Hudson Bay department stores raise their price on footwear, then this price increase is picked up in the CPI. But the CPI survey does not fully account for price discounts on footwear that The Bay may have offered during a particular period. If people increasingly shop for discounts and special sales to buy footwear—and other products—the CPI will overstate the true increase in the cost of living.

In general, economists conclude that the CPI overstates the rate of inflation, perhaps by as much as 0.5 percentage points a year. So what? The problem is that the CPI affects nearly everyone. Examples abound: Government payments to social insurance receivers are indexed to the CPI; when the CPI rises, social security payments automatically rise in lockstep. Millions of unionized workers have cost-of-living adjustment clauses (COLAs) in their labour contracts. Moreover, the wage demands of virtually all workers—union or non-union, blue- or white-collar—are linked to the rate of inflation as measured by the CPI. Also, interest rates are often linked to the rate of inflation, as measured by the CPI. When the CPI rises, lenders raise their nominal interest rates to keep their real interest rates constant.

Another consequence of an overstated CPI stems from the indexing of personal income tax brackets. This adjusting of tax brackets upward to account for the rate of inflation was begun in the mid-1970s to resolve an inequity in the personal income tax. The intent of indexing is to prevent inflation from pushing households into higher tax brackets even though their real incomes have not increased. For example, a 10 percent increase in your *nominal* income might put you in a higher marginal tax bracket and increase the proportion of your income paid in taxes. But if product prices are also rising by 10 percent, your *real* or inflation-adjusted income has remained constant. The result would be an unintended redistribution of real income from taxpayers to the federal government. The purpose of indexing tax brackets was to prevent this redistribution. However, to the extent that the CPI *overstates* inflation, indexing will reduce government's tax share. The federal government will be deprived of substantial tax revenues and real income will be redistributed from government to taxpayers. ∎

CHAPTER SUMMARY

1. Gross domestic product (GDP), a basic measure of an economy's economic performance, is the market value of all final goods and services produced within the borders of a nation in a year.

2. Intermediate goods, nonproduction transactions, and secondhand sales are purposely excluded in calculating GDP.

3. GDP may be calculated by summing total expenditures on all final output or by summing the income derived from the production of that output.

4. By the expenditures approach, GDP is determined by adding consumer purchases of goods and services, gross investment spending by businesses, government purchases, and net exports: GDP $C + I_g + G + X_n$.

5. Gross investment can be divided into **a** replacement investment (required to maintain the nation's stock of capital at its existing level) and **b** net investment (the net increase in the stock of capital). Positive net investment is associated with an expanding production capacity; negative net investment with a declining production capacity.

6. By the income approach, GDP is calculated as the sum of wages and salaries, dividends, interest, net income of farmers, net income of nonfarm unincorporated business (including rent), corporation income taxes, undistributed corporation profits, and the two nonincome charges (indirect taxes less subsidies and capital consumption allowances).

7. Other national income accounting measures are derived from the GDP. Net domestic income (NDI) is total income earned by resource suppliers; it is found by subtracting indirect taxes and capital consumption allowances from GNP. Personal income (PI) is the total income paid to households prior to any allowance for personal taxes. Disposable income (DI) is personal income after personal taxes have been paid. DI measures the amount of income households have available to consume or save.

8. Price indexes are computed by comparing the price of a specific collection or "market basket" or output in a particular period with the price (cost) of the same market basket in a base period and multiplying the outcome (quotient) by 100. The GDP deflator is the price index associated with adjusting nominal GDP to account for inflation and thereby to obtain real GDP.

9. Nominal (current dollar) GDP measures each year's output valued in terms of the prices prevailing in that year. Real (constant dollar) GDP measures each year's output in terms of the prices that prevailed in a selected base year. Because it is adjusted for price level changes, real GDP measures the level of productive activity.

10. The consumer price index (CPI) measures changes in the price of a market basket of some 600 goods and services purchased by typical Canadian consumers. Unlike the GDP price index, in which the weights of the goods change annually with spending patterns, the CPI is a fixed-weight price index, meaning that each year the items in the market basket remain the same as those in the base period (currently 1992).

11. National income accounting measures exclude nonmarket and illegal transactions, changes in leisure and in product quality, the composition and distribution of output, and the environmental effects of production. Nevertheless, these measures are reasonably accurate and very useful indicators of a nation's economic performance.

TERMS AND CONCEPTS

national income accounting
gross domestic product (GDP)
final and intermediate goods
double counting
value added
expenditure and income approaches
personal consumption expenditure
gross and net investment
gross capital formation
capital consumption allowances (depreciation)
depreciation
government current purchases of goods and services
net exports

corporate income taxes
dividends
undistributed corporate profits
net domestic income at factor costs
indirect taxes
gross national product (GNP)
personal income
disposable income
personal saving
nominal GDP
real GDP
price index
consumer price index

STUDY QUESTIONS

1. In what ways are national income statistics useful?

2. Explain why an economy's output, in essence, is also its income.

3. **KEY QUESTION** *Why do national income accountants include only final goods in measuring GDP for a particular year? Why don't they include the value of the stocks and bonds bought and sold? Why don't they include the value of the used furniture bought and sold?*

4. What is the difference between gross investment and net investment?

5. Why are changes in inventories included as part of investment spending? Suppose inventories declined by $1 billion during 2000. How would this affect the size of gross investment and gross domestic product in 2000? Explain.

6. **KEY QUESTION** *Use the concepts of gross and net investment to distinguish between an expanding, a static, and a declining economy. "In 1933 net investment was minus $324 million. This means in that particular year the economy produced no capital goods at all." Do you agree? Explain: "Though net investment can be positive, negative, or zero, it is quite impossible for gross investment to be less than zero."*

7. Define net exports. Explain how Canadian exports and imports each affect domestic production. Suppose foreigners spend $117 billion on Canadian exports in a given year and Canadians spend $105 billion on imports from abroad in the same year. What is the amount of Canada's net exports? Explain how net exports might be a negative amount.

8. **KEY QUESTION** *Below is a list of national income figures for a given year. All figures are in billions. Determine the major national income measures by both the expenditure and income methods. The answers derived by each approach should be the same.*

Personal consumption expenditures	$120
Accrued net income of farmers	5
Capital consumption allowances (depreciation)	20
Interest and miscellaneous investment income	10
Net income of nonfarm unincorporated business (including rent)	12
Net exports	+5
Corporation profits before taxes	34
Wages, salaries, and supplementary labour income	113
Indirect taxes (less subsidies)	21
Undistributed corporate profits	8
Government current purchases of goods and services	40
Net investment (net capital formation)	30

    a. *Using the above data, determine GDP by both the expenditure and income methods.*
    b. *Determine NDI.*

9. Given the following national income accounting data, compute **a** GDP and **b** NDI. All figures are in billions.

Wages, salaries, and supplementary labour income	$194.2
Canadian exports of goods and services	13.4
Capital consumption allowances	11.8
Government current purchases of goods and services	59.4
Indirect taxes	12.2
Net investment (net capital formation)	52.1
Government transfer payments	13.9
Canadian imports of goods and services	7.5
Personal taxes	40.5
Personal consumption expenditures	219.1

10. Why do national income accountants compare the market value of the total outputs in various years rather than actual physical volumes of production? Explain. What problem is posed by any comparison, over time, of the market values of various total outputs? How is this problem resolved?

11. KEY QUESTION *Suppose that in 1984 the total output in a single-good economy was 7,000 buckets of chicken. Also suppose that in 1984 each bucket of chicken was priced at $10. Finally, assume that in 1992 the price per bucket of chicken was $16 and that 22,000 buckets were purchased. Determine the GDP price index for 1984, using 1992 as the base year. By what percentage did the price level, as measured by this index, rise between 1984 and 1992? Use the two methods listed in Table 7-5 to determine real GDP for 1984 and 1992.*

12. KEY QUESTION *The table below shows nominal GDP and an appropriate price index group of selected years. Compute real GDP. Indicate in each calculation whether you are inflating or deflating the nominal GDP data.*

Year	Nominal GDP (billions)	Price level index (percent) (1992 = 100)	Real GDP (billions)
1929	$ 6.400	11.9	$_____
1933	3.723	9.7	$_____
1962	44.408	23.7	$_____
1974	152.111	43.0	$_____
1984	444.735	72.1	$_____
1994	762.3	102.4	$_____
1996	820.3	106.6	$_____

13. Which of the following are actually included in deriving this year's GDP? Explain your answer in each case.
   a. Interest on a Bell Canada bond.
   b. Canada Pension payments received by a retired factory worker.
   c. The services of a painter in painting the family home.
   d. The income of a dentist.
   e. The money received by Smith when she resells her economics textbook to a book buyer.
   f. The monthly allowance a college student receives from home.
   g. Rent received on a two-bedroom apartment.
   h. The money received by Mac when he resells this year's Plymouth Prowler to Stan.
   i. Interest received on government bonds.
   j. A two-hour decline in the length of the workweek.
   k. The purchase of a Quebec Hydro bond.
   l. A $2-billion increase in business inventories.
   m. The purchase of 100 shares of CP Ltd. common stock.
   n. The purchase of an insurance policy.

14. (The Last Word) What is the CPI? What are its shortcomings in accurately measuring inflation?

15. WEB-BASED QUESTION **Latest Short-Term Indicators—Rank the Economies** The OECD (Organization for Economic Cooperation and Development) www.oecd.org/std/indksti.htm provides the latest short-term indicators of their member countries for the previous year. Of the following six countries (Canada, United States, Germany, Japan, France, and Italy), rank them from first to sixth for best to worst in the following categories: GDP (percentage change), CPI (percentage change), unemployment rate, and interest rate (assume lowest is best). Which economy received the greatest number of total points? Which received the lowest?

16. WEB-BASED QUESTION **Per-Capita Gross Domestic Product** The OECD (Organization for Economic Cooperation and Development) www.oecd.org/std/nahome.htm provides an annual comparison of levels of GDP per capita based on both exchange rates and on purchasing power parities (PPPs). Rank the current top 10 countries using each method. How do the rankings differ, and which method is a more realistic indicator of "output per person"? What explains the difference in Japan's per-capita income when calculated using exchange rates and when calculated using PPPs?

Macroeconomic Instability: Unemployment and Inflation

IN AN IDEAL ECONOMY, REAL GDP WOULD EXPAND over time at a brisk, steady pace and the price level, as measured by the GDP deflator or the consumer price index, would remain constant or only rise slowly. The result would be neither significant unemployment nor inflation. Several periods of Canadian history fit this pattern, but experience shows that steady economic growth, full employment, and a stable price level are not always achieved. Recent evidence: (1) The inflation rate skyrocketed to 10.2 percent in 1980. (2) During 1982, real GDP fell by 3.2 percent. (3) Over half a million more people were unemployed in 1983 than in 1980. (4) In 1990, output in the Canadian economy turned downward for its fifth time since 1945 and unemployment has remained stubbornly high throughout the 1990s.

In this and the next several chapters we explore the problem of achieving macroeconomic stability, which means steady economic growth, full employment, and price stability. The present chapter proceeds as follows: First, we establish an overview of the business cycle—the periodic fluctuations in output, employment, and price levels characterizing market economics. Then we look in more detail at unemployment: What are the various types of unemployment? How is unemployment measured? Why is unemployment undesirable? Finally, we examine inflation—a problem that plagued Canada throughout the 1970s and into the early 1980s. What are inflation's causes and consequences?

IN THIS CHAPTER YOU WILL LEARN:

The nature and cause of the business cycle.

•

The nature of unemployment and its measurement.

•

The definition of inflation and how it is measured.

•

The potential redistributive and output effects of inflation.

The Big Picture

IN A PERFECT WORLD EVERYONE WOULD HAVE as many goods and services as he or she desired. In an imperfect world not only are there limited resources, but these limited resources (land, labour, capital, and entrepreneurial talent) are often not fully employed; we fail to get the most out of the limited resources we do have. The one resource we are particularly interested in is labour. Quite often in Canada we have had unacceptably high unemployment. People want to work but can't find a job. Moreover, the economy can build inflationary pressures that can, if not checked, impede the efficient functioning of a market economy. In recent decades there have been periods when the Canadian economy has suffered from both high unemployment and inflation at the same time.

Market economies are prone to a certain amount of instability—unemployment and inflation. In this chapter we take a first glance at this instability—also referred to as the business cycle—and its causes. Understanding the nature of economic instability will allow us to devise better macroeconomic policies to maintain healthy economic growth, and low levels of unemployment and inflation.

As you read this chapter, keep the following points in mind:

- **Key Concept 9** is discussed.
- In a market economy "full employment" does not mean zero unemployment.
- There is a difference between what the economy could produce if all its available resources were utilized and what the economy actually produces. Applying this to the production possibility curve, it means the economy is functioning inside the curve. In a world of scarcity, this is a paradox. This is a major challenge for macroeconomists to explain and attempt to rectify.
- Inflation is an increase in the general price level. High inflation can potentially diminish a nation's output as households and firms become preoccupied with minimizing the negative effect of inflation or profiting from inflation rather than striving to improve their economic positions by producing more output ■

THE BUSINESS CYCLE

Nations seek economic growth, full employment, and price-level stability as their major macroeconomic goals. For the most part, the history of the industrial nations, including Canada, is one of remarkable economic growth. Technological progress, rapid increases in capital, increased skill levels of labour, and other factors have interacted to raise real GDP and real GDP per capita.

But long-run economic growth has not always been steady; it is sometimes interrupted by periods of economic instability, as revealed for Canada in Figure 8-1. In various countries at various times, rapid economic growth has been marred by inflation. At other times, growth has given way to recession and depression, that is, to declines in employment and real output. In short, both unemployment and inflation have interrupted and complicated the long-term trend of economic growth. These difficulties often are associated with *business cycles*.

Phases of the Cycle

The term **business cycle** refers to alternating increases and decreases in the level of economic activity, sometimes extending over several years. Individual business cycles (one "up" and one "down" period) vary substantially in duration and intensity. Yet all display common phases that are variously labelled by different economists. Figure 8-2 shows the four phases of a stylized business cycle.

1. **PEAK** We begin our description with a **peak** at which business activity has reached a temporary maximum, such as the middle peak shown in Figure 8-2. Here the economy is at full employment and the level of real output is at or very close to its capacity. The price level is likely to rise during this phase.
2. **RECESSION** The peak is followed by a **recession**—a period of decline in total output, income, employment, and trade, lasting six months or longer. This downturn is marked

FIGURE 8-1 Canadian business-cycle experience

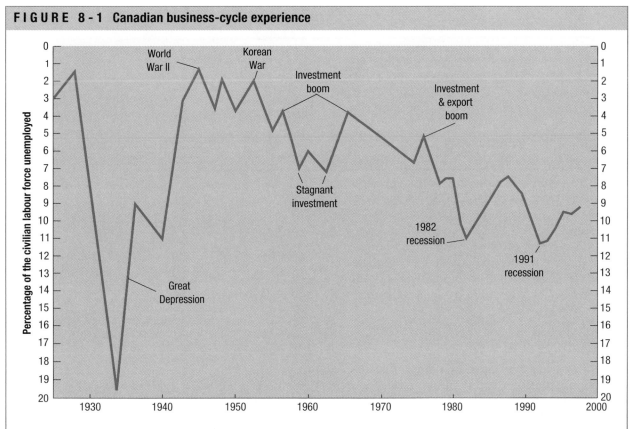

The Canadian economy has encountered periods of prosperity and recession. Until 1981, only minor slowdowns had occurred since World War II.

FIGURE 8-2 The business cycle

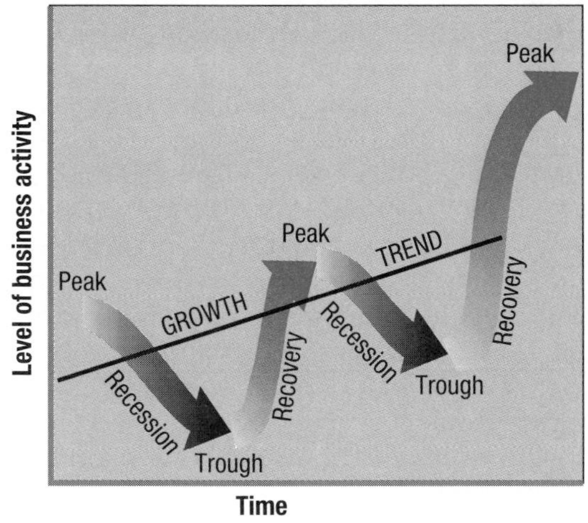

Economists distinguish four phases of the business cycle, with the duration and strength of each phase being highly variable.

by the widespread contraction of business in many sectors of the economy. But because many prices are downwardly inflexible, the price level is likely to fall only if the recession is severe and prolonged—that is, if a depression occurs.

3. **TROUGH** The **trough** of the recession or depression is the phase in which output and employment "bottom out" at their lowest levels. The trough phase of the cycle may be short-lived or quite long.

4. **RECOVERY** In the expansion or **recovery** phase, output and employment increase towards full employment. As recovery intensifies, the price level may begin to rise before there is full employment and full capacity production.

Despite all having the same phases, business cycles vary greatly in duration and intensity. Many economists therefore prefer to talk of business *fluctuations* rather than cycles because cycles imply regularity while fluctuations do not. The Great Depression of the 1930s resulted in a 40 percent decline in real GDP over a three-year period in Canada and seriously impaired business activity for a decade. By comparison, more recent Canadian recessions—detailed in Table 8-1—were relatively minor in both intensity and duration.

Provincial Variations

National GDP data for Canada do not reveal significant differences in economic fluctuations among Canada's 10 provinces. Table 8-2 gives a provincial breakdown of economic growth. In 1997, for example, GDP grew by 6.0 percent in Alberta, but only 0.7 percent in New Brunswick. Thus, the national growth rates in Canada can be misleading; in 1997 Alberta's economy was booming, while those of Newfoundland and New Brunswick were barely growing.

Causation: A First Glance

Economists have suggested many theories to explain fluctuations in business activity. Some contend that major innovations, such as the railroad, the automobile, and synthetic fibres, have great impact on investment and consumption spending and therefore on output, employment, and the price level. These major innovations occur irregularly and thus contribute to the variability of economic activity.

Other economists have explained the business cycle in terms of political and random events, as suggested by some of the labelling in Figure 8-1. Wars, for example, can be economically disruptive. A virtually insatiable demand for war goods during hostilities can generate a period of overfull employment and sharp inflation, which is fol-

TABLE 8-2 Provincial real GDP (percent change)

	1995	1996	1997
CANADA	1.9	1.6	4.0
Newfoundland	0.2	−1.1	1.7
P.E.I.	4.2	3.1	1.9
Nova Scotia	1.2	0.5	2.0
New Brunswick	2.3	1.0	0.7
Quebec	0.7	0.9	2.4
Ontario	2.7	1.7	4.4
Manitoba	2.6	2.9	4.5
Saskatchewan	0.5	3.7	6.0
Alberta	1.9	2.5	7.5
British Columbia	1.5	1.0	2.3

Real GDP: Real Gross Domestic Product in 1986 dollars
Source: Statistics Canada, Provincial Gross Domestic Product by Industry, 1984–1997, Table 1, Cat. 15-203.

lowed by an economic slump when peace returns and military spending plummets.

Still other economists view the business cycle as a purely monetary phenomenon. When government creates too much money, they say, an inflationary boom occurs. In contrast, too little money precipitates a decline in output and employment.

Despite these diverse opinions, most economists see changes in the level of total spending as the immediate cause of cyclical changes in the levels of real output and employment. In a market economy, businesses produce goods or services only if they can sell them profitably. If total spending sinks, many businesses find that it is no longer profitable to produce their usual volume of goods and services. Therefore, output, employment, and incomes will fall. In contrast, a higher level of spending means that more production is profitable, and output, employment, and incomes will rise. Once the economy nears full employment, further gains in real output become more difficult to achieve. Still more spending may raise the price level as consumers bid for the limited amount of available goods.

Noncyclical Fluctuations

Not all changes in business activity result from business cycles. For example, there can be

TABLE 8-1 Canadian recessions since 1945

Year	Depth (decline in real GDP)
1945	−2.4%
1946	−2.2
1954	−1.1
1982	−3.2
1991	−1.7

Source: Statistics Canada

seasonal variations in business activity. Pre-Christmas and pre-Easter buying surges cause considerable fluctuations in the tempo of business activity each year, particularly in the retail industry. Agriculture, the automobile industry, and construction are also subject to some degree of seasonality.

Business activity also displays a **secular trend**—expansion or contraction over a long period of years, say, 25, 50, or 100 years. The long-run secular trend for the Canadian economy has been remarkable expansion. For present purposes, the importance of this long-run expansion is that the business cycle fluctuates around a long-run growth trend.

Cyclical Impact: Durables and Nondurables

The business cycle is felt in every sector of the economy. The parts of the economy are related in such a way that few, if any, escape the negative effects of depression or surging inflation. However, the business cycle affects various individuals and segments of the economy in different ways and degrees.

With regard to production and employment, service industries and industries producing non-durable consumer goods are somewhat insulated from the most severe effects of recession. And, of course, recession actually helps some firms, such as pawnbrokers and law firms specializing in bankruptcies! Who is hit hardest by recession? The firms and industries producing capital goods and consumer durables. The construction industry is particularly vulnerable. Industries and workers producing housing and commercial buildings, heavy capital goods, farm implements, automobiles, refrigerators, gas ranges, and similar products bear the brunt of bad times. Conversely, these "hard-goods" industries benefit most from expansion.

Two facts help explain the vulnerability of these industries to the business cycle.

Postponability   Within limits, a purchase of hard goods can be postponed. As the economy slips into bad times, producers frequently delay the purchase of more modern production facilities and the construction of new plants. The business outlook simply does not warrant increases in the stock of capital goods. The firm's present capital

facilities and buildings will likely see it through the recession. In good times, capital goods are usually replaced before they completely depreciate. When recession strikes, however, business firms patch up their outmoded equipment and make it do. As a result, investment in capital goods declines sharply. Some firms, having excess plant capacity, may not even bother to replace all the capital they are currently consuming. Net investment for them may be negative.

It is much the same for consumer durables. When recession occurs and the household must trim its budget, plans for the purchase of such durables as major appliances and automobiles feel the axe first. People repair their old appliances and cars rather than buy new ones. Purchases of many consumer nondurables—food and clothing, for instance—are not so easily postponed; people must clothe themselves and eat. The quantity and quality of purchases of nondurables will decline to some extent, but not so much as will purchases of capital goods and consumer durables.

Monopoly Power   Many industries producing capital goods and consumer durables are industries of *high concentration*, in which a small number of large firms dominate the market. These firms have monopoly power—the ability to set above-competitive prices to increase their profit. When recession hits, each of these firms is very reluctant to lower its price because doing so would upset the industry price structure. Specifically, each firm fears that its price cut would spark a *price war*—successive rounds of deeper and deeper price cuts by rivals. This reluctance to lower price means that, at least for a time, the effects of a drop in demand are primarily a decline in production and a decrease in employment.

The reverse pattern is true in nondurables, or *low-concentration* "soft-goods" industries, in which prices are established in competitive markets. Firms in such industries are unable to resist the price declines dictated by the market, so their *prices* decline more rapidly than their levels of production and employment.

During the Great Depression this was especially serious for Canada, for we exported mostly raw materials, including agricultural commodities, whose prices fell considerably, while we imported mostly manufactured and highly processed goods, whose prices dropped very little. *(Key Question 1)*

8-1

QUICK REVIEW

- The long-term secular trend of real domestic output has been upward in Canada.
- The typical business cycle has four phases: peak, recession, trough, and recovery.
- Industries producing capital goods and consumer durables normally suffer greater output and employment declines during recession than do service and nondurable consumer goods industries. The latter suffer greater price declines, however.

UNEMPLOYMENT

"Full employment" is hard to define. A person might think it means that everyone in the labour market—100 percent of the labour force—is employed. But that is not so; some unemployment is normal or warranted.

Types of Unemployment

Before defining full employment, let's first introduce three types of unemployment: frictional, structural, and cyclical.

Frictional Unemployment

At any time some workers will be "between jobs." With freedom to choose occupations and jobs, some workers will be voluntarily moving from one job to another. Others will have been fired and will be seeking reemployment. Still others will be temporarily laid off from their jobs because of seasonality, for example, bad weather in the construction industry. And there will be some particularly young workers searching for their first jobs.

As these unemployed people find jobs or are called back from temporary layoffs, other job seekers and temporarily laid-off workers will replace them in the "unemployment pool." Therefore, even though the specific individuals who are unemployed for these reasons change from month to month, this type of unemployment persists.

Economists use the term **frictional unemployment**—consisting of *search unemployment* and *wait* unemployment—for workers who are either searching for jobs or waiting to take jobs in the near future. "Frictional" correctly implies that the labour market does not operate perfectly or instantaneously—without friction—in matching workers and jobs.

Frictional unemployment is inevitable and, at least in part, desirable. Many workers who are voluntarily between jobs are moving from low-paying, low-productivity jobs to higher-paying, higher-productivity positions. This means greater income for workers and a better allocation of labour resources—and therefore a larger real output—for the economy as a whole.

Structural Unemployment

Frictional unemployment blurs into a category called **structural unemployment.** Here, economists use "structural" in the sense of "compositional." Changes over time in consumer demand and in technology alter the "structure" of the total demand for labour, both occupationally and geographically.

Occupationally, some skills will be less in demand or may even become obsolete; demand for other skills, including skills not existing earlier, will expand. Unemployment results because the composition of the labour force does not respond quickly or completely to the new structure of job opportunities. Some workers thus find that they have no marketable talents; their skills and experience have become obsolete or unneeded. They are structurally unemployed due to a *mismatch between their skills and the skills required by employers who are hiring workers*.

Geographically, the demand for labour also changes over time. The migration of industry and thus of employment opportunities from the Snow Belt to the Sun Belt over the past few decades is an example. Another example is the movement of jobs from inner-city factories to suburban industrial parks. These shifting job opportunities mean that some workers become structurally unemployed; there is a *mismatch between their location and the location of job openings*.

The following list presents several illustrations of structural unemployment:

1. Many years ago, highly skilled glassblowers were thrown out of work by the invention of bottle-making machines.
2. Historically, mechanization of agriculture dislodged thousands of low-skilled, poorly educated people from their jobs. Many migrated to cities and suffered prolonged unemployment because of racial bias and insufficient skills.

3. Many oil-field workers in Alberta found themselves structurally unemployed when the world price of oil nosedived in the 1980s. Less drilling and oil-related activity took place, resulting in widespread layoffs.

4. Recently, "corporate downsizing" has occurred in several major Canadian manufacturing industries. Many people losing their jobs have been corporate managers who have found it difficult to find new work.

5. Recent closures of military bases and other defence cutbacks have displaced many workers, adding them to the roles of the structurally unemployed.

6. The depletion of the cod stock off Canada's eastern seaboard has put thousands of fishermen without other skills out of work.

7. The decline of coal-mining and steel-making in Cape Breton has resulted in endemic unemployment there, already higher than the national average.

The distinction between frictional and structural unemployment is hazy. The key difference is that frictionally unemployed workers have salable skills and either are located where jobs exist or are able to move to where jobs exist. Structurally unemployed workers cannot easily be reemployed without retraining, additional education, or geographic relocation. Frictional unemployment is short-term; structural unemployment is more long-term and therefore is regarded as more serious.

Cyclical Unemployment

Cyclical unemployment occurs in the recession phase of the business cycle. It is caused by a deficiency of total spending. As the overall demand for goods and services decreases, employment falls and unemployment rises. For this reason, cyclical unemployment is sometimes called *deficient-demand unemployment*. During the recession year 1983, for example, the unemployment rate rose to 11.9 percent. This compares with a 11.3 percent unemployment rate in the recession year 1992. Cyclical unemployment at the depth of the Great Depression in 1933 was about 30 percent of the labour force.

Definition of "Full Employment"

Full employment does *not* mean zero unemployment. Economists regard frictional and structural unemployment as essentially unavoidable in a dynamic economy. Thus, "full employment" is something less than 100 percent employment of the labour force. Specifically, the **full-employment unemployment rate** is equal to the total frictional and structural unemployment. Stated differently, the full-employment unemployment rate is achieved when cyclical unemployment is zero.

The full-employment rate of unemployment is also referred to as the **natural rate of unemployment**. The real level of domestic output associated with the natural rate of unemployment is called the economy's **potential output**. The economy's potential output is the real output produced when the economy is "fully employed."

From a slightly different vantage point the full-employment or natural rate of unemployment results when labour markets are in balance in the sense that the number of job seekers equals the number of job vacancies. The natural rate of unemployment is some positive amount because it takes time for frictionally unemployed job seekers to find open jobs they can fill. Also, it takes time for the structurally unemployed to achieve the skills and geographic relocation needed for reemployment. If the number of job seekers exceeds available vacancies, labour markets are not in balance; there is a deficiency of total spending and cyclical unemployment is present. But if total spending is excessive, a shortage of labour will arise; the number of job vacancies will exceed the number of workers seeking employment. Here, the actual rate of unemployment will be below the natural rate. Such unusually "tight" labour markets are normally associated with inflation.

The concept of the natural rate of unemployment merits elaboration in two respects:

1. **NOT AUTOMATIC** "Natural" does not mean the economy will always operate at the natural rate and thus realize its potential output. Our brief discussion of the business cycle demonstrated that the economy sometimes operates at an unemployment rate higher than the natural rate—due to cyclical unemployment. In contrast, the economy may on some occasions achieve an unemployment rate below the natural rate. For example, during World War II, when the natural rate was about 4 percent, the pressure of wartime production resulted in an almost unlimited demand for labour. Overtime work was common, as was "moonlighting" (working at more than one job). And the government mandated that some people working in essential industries

remain in these jobs, which helped reduce frictional unemployment. As a result, the actual rate of unemployment was below 2 percent in 1944 and 1945. The economy was producing beyond its potential output, but it was building up considerable inflationary pressure in the process.

2. **NOT IMMUTABLE**   The natural rate of unemployment is not forever fixed. It can change when demographics change or when there are changes in society's laws and customs. In the 1960s this unavoidable minimum of frictional and structural unemployment was about 4 percent of the labour force. That is, full employment meant that 96 percent of the labour force was employed. Today, the consensus is that the rate is between 7 and 8 percent.

Why these changes? First, the demographic makeup of the labour force has changed since the 1960s. In the 1970s and 1980s, younger workers became a larger part of the labour force. Because they traditionally have high unemployment rates, their greater relative numbers increased the natural unemployment rate. Second, laws and customs have changed. For example, the employment insurance program in Canada has been expanded both in the number of workers covered and in the size of benefits. By cushioning the economic impact of joblessness, employment insurance permits unemployed workers to engage in a more deliberate, lengthy job search, thereby increasing frictional unemployment and the natural unemployment rate.

The natural rate may be falling mainly because the growing proportion of younger workers has reversed itself as the baby-boom generation has aged. The labour force now has a larger proportion of middle-aged workers, who traditionally have lower unemployment rates. Also, increased competition in product and labour markets has limited price and wage increases. A decade ago, a 7 or 8 percent rate of unemployment might have boosted the inflation rate; today, this unemployment rate appears to be consistent with a stable, low rate of inflation.

Measurement of Unemployment

Determining the unemployment rate means first determining who is eligible and available to work. Figure 8-3 is a helpful starting point. It shows the

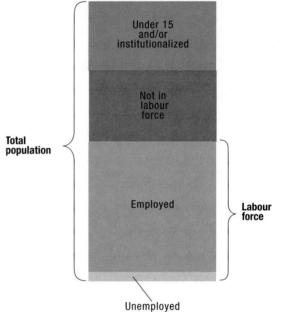

FIGURE 8 - 3   The labour force, employment, and unemployment, 1997

The labour force consists of persons 15 years of age or older who are not in institutions or the armed forces, and who are employed or unemployed.

Total population	30,000,000
Less: Under 15 and/or institutionalized	6,313,500
Less: Not in labour force	8,333,500
Equals: Labour force	15,354,000
Employed	13,940,500
Unemployed	1,413,500

Source: Statistics Canada. For updates, visit Statistics Canada's Web site at www.statcan/english/Pgdb/Economy/economic/econ10.htm.

total Canadian population as being divided into three groups. One group is made up of people under 15 years of age and/or institutionalized— for example, in correctional institutions.

A second group, labelled "Not in labour force," are adults who are potential workers but for some reason—they are homemakers, in school, or retired —are not employed and are not seeking work.

The third group is the **labour force**, which constituted about 50 percent of the total population in 1997. The labour force is all people who are able and willing to work. *Both those who are employed and those who are unemployed but actively seeking work are counted as being in the labour force.* The **unemployment rate** is the percentage of the labour force that is unemployed:

$$\text{Unemployment rate} = \frac{\text{unemployed}}{\text{labour force}} \times 100$$

The statistics in Figure 8-3 show that in 1997 the unemployment rate was

$$9.2\% = \frac{1,413,500}{15,354,000} \times 100$$

Unemployment rates for select years between 1929 and 1997 are provided at the end of this book.

Statistics Canada (StatsCan) determines who is employed and who is not by conducting its nationwide random Labour Force Survey of some 59,000 representative households each month. A series of questions is asked regarding what members of the household are working, unemployed and looking for work, not looking for work, and so on. Despite the very sophisticated sampling and interview techniques used, the data collected from this survey are subject to two criticisms.

1. **PART-TIME EMPLOYMENT** The official data include all part-time workers as fully employed. Many part-timers want to work full-time, but can't find suitable full-time work or worked fewer hours because of a temporary lapse in consumer demand. These workers are really partially employed and partially unemployed. By counting them as fully employed, the official StatsCan data tend to *understate* the unemployment rate. In 1997 2.6 million workers were employed part-time.

2. **DISCOURAGED WORKERS** You must be actively seeking work to be counted as unemployed. An unemployed individual who is not actively seeking employment is classified as "not in the labour force." The problem is that many workers, after unsuccessfully seeking employment for a time, become discouraged and drop out of the labour force. Although the number of such **discouraged workers** is larger during recession than prosperity, estimates suggest several hundred thousand fall into this category. By not counting discouraged workers as unemployed, say critics, official data

understate the unemployment rate. **(Key Question 3)**

Economic Cost of Unemployment

Unemployment above the natural rate involves great economic and social costs.

GDP Gap and Okun's Law The basic economic cost of unemployment is forgone output. *When the economy fails to create enough jobs for all who are able and willing to work, potential production of goods and services is irretrievably lost.* In terms of Chapter 2's analysis, unemployment means that society is located at some point inside its production possibilities curve. Economists measure this sacrificed output as the **GDP gap**—the amount by which *actual GDP* falls short of *potential GDP*.

Potential GDP is determined by assuming that the natural rate of unemployment exists. The growth of potential GDP is simply projected forward on the basis of the economy's "normal" growth rate of real GDP. Figure 8-4 shows the GDP gap for recent years in Canada. It also indicates the close correlation between the actual unemployment rate (Figure 8-4b) and the GDP gap (Figure 8-4a). The higher the unemployment rate, the larger the GDP gap.

Macroeconomist Arthur Okun quantified the relationship between the unemployment rate and the GDP gap. **Okun's law**, based on recent estimates, indicates that *for every 1 percentage point that the actual unemployment rate exceeds the natural rate, a GDP gap of about 2 percent occurs.* With this information, we can calculate the absolute loss of output associated with any above-natural unemployment rate. For example, in 1993 the unemployment rate was 11.2 percent, or 3.7 percentage points above the 7.5 percent natural rate of unemployment then existing. Multiplying this 3.7 percent by Okun's 2 indicates that 1993's GDP gap was 7.4 percent of potential GDP (in real terms). Then, by applying this 7.4 percent loss to 1993's potential GDP of $769.1 billion, we find that the economy sacrificed about $53 billion of real output because the natural rate of unemployment was not achieved. **(Key Question 5)**

Sometimes the economy's actual output will exceed its potential output. (We already noted that this happened during World War II when unemployment rates fell below 2 percent. Extra shifts of workers were employed, capital equipment was

FIGURE 8-4 (a) Potential and actual GDP and (b) the unemployment rate

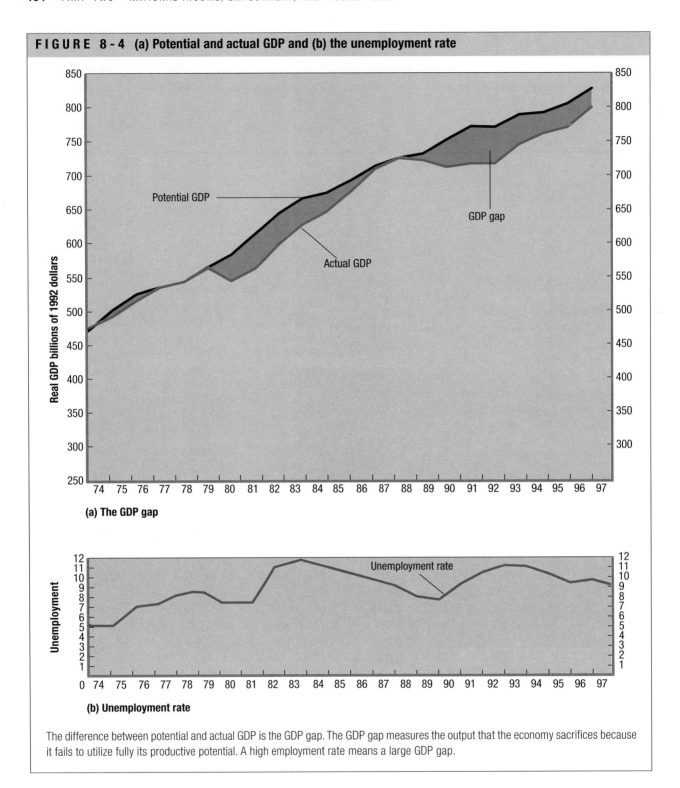

(a) The GDP gap

(b) Unemployment rate

The difference between potential and actual GDP is the GDP gap. The GDP gap measures the output that the economy sacrifices because it fails to utilize fully its productive potential. A high employment rate means a large GDP gap.

used beyond its designed capacity, and overtime work and moonlighting were common.) Potential GDP can occasionally be exceeded, but the excess of actual over potential GDP eventually causes inflation and cannot be sustained indefinitely.

Unequal Burdens An increase in the unemployment rate from 9 to 12 percent might be more tolerable to society if every worker's hours of work and wage income were reduced proportionally. But this is not the case. Part of the burden of unemployment is that its cost is unequally distributed.

Table 8-3 examines unemployment rates for various labour market groups for two years. The 1991–92 recession pushed the 1992 unemployment rate to 11.3 percent. In contrast, the economy achieved full employment in 1989, with a 7.5 percent unemployment rate. By observing the large variance in unemployment rates for the different groups *within each year* and comparing the rates *between the two years*, we can generalize as follows:

1. **OCCUPATION** White-collar workers enjoy lower unemployment rates than blue-collar workers. White-collar workers generally are employed in less cyclically vulnerable industries (such as services and nondurable goods) or are self-employed. Also, white-collar workers are usually less subject to unemployment during recession than blue-collar workers. Businesses want to retain their more skilled white-collar workers, in whom they have invested the expense of training. But it is not always this way. During the 1990–91 recession, many firms "downsized" their management structures, discharging more white-collar workers than ever before. The unemployment rate of white-collar workers increased more rapidly than for blue-collar labourers. Never-

theless, the unemployment rate of white-collar workers remained far below that of blue-collar workers.

2. **AGE** Teenagers incur much higher unemployment rates than adults. Teenagers have low skill levels, more frequently quit their jobs, are more frequently discharged from jobs, and have little geographic mobility. Many unemployed teenagers are new in the labour market, searching for their first job.

3. **GENDER** Male and female unemployment rates are highly similar. The lower unemployment rate for women in 1992 occurred because there are more male than female workers in such cyclically vulnerable hard-goods industries as automobile, steel, and construction.

4. **EDUCATION** Less educated workers, on average, have higher unemployment rates than workers with more education. Less education is usually associated with lower-skilled, less permanent jobs, more time in between jobs, and jobs that are more vulnerable to cyclical layoff.

5. **DURATION** The number of persons unemployed for long periods—15 weeks or more—as a percentage of the labour force is much less than the overall unemployment rate. But this percentage rises significantly during recessions. The "long-term" unemployed were only 4.0 percent of the labour force in 1989 compared with the overall 7.5 percent unemployment rate. A large proportion of unemployment is of relatively short duration. But also observe that the long-term unemployed were 6.6 percent of the labour force in 1992, implying more economic hardship when recessions occur.

6. **REGIONAL VARIATIONS** The national unemployment rate in Canada does not reveal the significant diversity in regional unemployment. Table 8-4 gives both the national unemployment rate and a provincial breakdown. For 1997 the national rate was 9.2 percent but as high as 18.6 in Newfoundland and as low as 6 percent in Alberta and Saskatchewan.

Noneconomic Costs

Severe cyclical unemployment is more than an economic malady; it is a social catastrophe. Depression means idleness. And idleness means loss of skills, loss of self-respect, a plummeting of morale, family disintegration, and sociopolitical unrest.

TABLE 8-3 Unemployment by demographic group and duration as unemployment increases

Demographic group	Unemployment rate, March 1989	Unemployment rate, March 1992
Overall	7.5%	11.1%
Occupation		
Manufacturing	7.2	12.7
Services	6.8	9.2
Age		
15–24 years	10.6	19.1
25 years and over	6.7	11.1
Sex		
Male	7.2	13.9
Female	7.9	10.8
Duration		
14 weeks +	4.0	6.6

Source: Statistics Canada, adapted from *The Labour Force, Catalogue No. 71-001, March 1989* and *March 1992*.

TABLE 8-4 Provincial breakdown of the unemployment rate (per cent)

	1995	1996	1997
CANADA	9.5	9.7	9.2
Newfoundland	18.3	19.4	18.8
Prince Edward Island	14.7	14.5	14.9
Nova Scotia	12.1	12.6	12.2
New Brunswick	11.5	11.7	12.8
Quebec	11.3	11.8	11.4
Ontario	8.7	9.1	8.5
Manitoba	7.5	7.5	6.6
Saskatchewan	6.9	6.6	6.0
Alberta	7.8	7.0	6.0
British Columbia	9.0	8.9	8.7

Data are seasonally adjusted.
Source: Statistics Canada, *Canadian Economic Observer*, August 1998.

History demonstrates that severe unemployment leads to rapid and sometimes violent social and political change. The shift of Canadian political philosophy towards the left during the Depression of the 1930s is an example. Witness also Hitler's ascent to power against a background of unemployment. At the individual level, research links increases in suicide, homicide, cardiovascular mortality, and mental illness to high unemployment.

International Comparisons

Unemployment rates vary greatly among nations at any specific time. One reason for the differences is that nations have different natural rates of unemployment. Another explanation is that nations may be in different phases of their business cycles. Global Perspective 8-1 shows unemployment rates for five industrialized nations in recent years. Historically, Canada has had higher unemployment rates than most industrially advanced nations.

8-1

GLOBAL PERSPECTIVE

Unemployment rates in five industrial nations, 1987–1997

The unemployment rate in Canada has been above average compared with that in the United States, the United Kingdom, Japan, and Germany in the past 11 years.

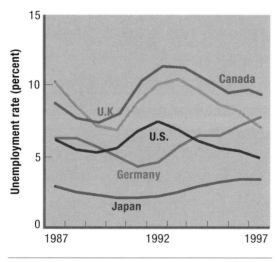

Source: OECD

8-2

QUICK REVIEW

- Unemployment is of three general types: frictional, structural, and cyclical.
- The natural unemployment rate (frictional plus structural) is presently estimated to be about 7.5 percent.
- Society loses real GDP when cyclical unemployment occurs; according to Okun's law, for each 1-percentage point of unemployment above the natural rate, the Canadian economy suffers a 2 percent decline in real GDP below potential.
- Blue-collar workers, teenagers, and less educated workers bear a disproportionate burden of unemployment.

INFLATION DEFINED AND MEASURED

We now turn to inflation as an aspect of macroeconomic instability. The problems inflation poses are more subtle than those of unemployment.

Meaning of Inflation

Inflation *is a rising general level of prices.* This does not mean that all prices are rising. Even during periods of rapid inflation, some prices may be relatively constant and others falling. For example, although Canada experienced high rates of inflation in the 1970s and early 1980s, the prices of video recorders, digital watches, and personal computers declined. As you will see, one troublesome aspect of inflation is that prices rise unevenly. Some streak upward; others ascend leisurely; still others do not rise at all.

Measurement of Inflation

Inflation is measured by price-index numbers such as those introduced in Chapter 7. Recall that a price index measures the general level of prices in any year relative to prices in a base period.

To illustrate, the consumer price index (CPI) now uses 1992 as the base period, meaning that period's price level is set equal to 100. The 1997 price index was about 107.6. Thus consumer prices were 7.6 percent higher in 1997 than in 1992, so a set of goods that cost $100 in 1992 cost $107.60 in 1997.

The *rate* of inflation can be calculated for any specific year (say, 1997) by subtracting the previous year's (1996) price index from that year's (1997) index, dividing by the previous year's index, and multiplying by 100 to express the result as a percentage. As an example, the CPI was 105.9 in 1996 and 107.6 in 1997, so the rate of inflation for 1997 is calculated as follows:

$$\text{Rate of inflation} = \frac{107.6 - 105.9}{105.9} \times 100 = 1.6 \text{ percent}$$

The so-called **rule of 70** provides a quantitative grasp of inflation's effect. If we divide the number 70 by the annual rate of inflation, the quotient is the number of years it takes for inflation to double the price level:

$$\begin{array}{c}\text{Approximate number}\\ \text{of years required to}\\ \text{double price level}\end{array} = \frac{70}{\begin{array}{c}\text{annual percentage}\\ \text{rate of inflation}\end{array}}$$

Examples: A 3 percent annual rate of inflation will double the price level in about 23 (= 70 ÷ 3) years. Inflation of 8 percent per year will double the price level in about 9 (= 70 ÷ 8) years. The rule of 70 is generally applicable. You can use it, for example, to estimate how long it will take for real GDP *or* your savings account to double. (*Key Question 7*)

Facts of Inflation

Figure 8-5 shows inflation in Canada since 1926. The curve represents annual values of the consumer price index, relative to the base year 1992. That is, the CPI for 1992 is arbitrarily set at 100.

Although most of you have grown up in an "age of inflation," our economy has not always been inflation-prone. The price level declined—*deflation* occurred—during the late 1920s and during the early years of the Great Depression of the 1930s. Prices then rose in the immediate years after World War II (1945–48) and in 1950. Overall price stability characterized the 1951–65 period, when the average annual increase in the price levels was less than 1.5 percent. But the price increases that began in the late 1960s and that then surged in the 1970s introduced Canadians to double-digit inflation. In 1981 and 1982 the price level rose at 11 percent to 12 percent annually. However, by the late of the 1990s, the rate had fallen to under 2%. Historical national annual rates of inflation can be found in the tables at the back of this textbook.

Regional Variations

Just as there are significant differences in unemployment rates among the provinces, there are also differences in the rates of inflation. Table 8-5 shows both the national and provincial annual percentage change in the CPI. In 1997, for example, the national rate was 1.6 percent but provincial rates varied from a low of 0.7 percent in British Columbia to a high of 2.2 percent in Manitoba.

Inflation is not unique to Canada; all industrial nations have experienced this problem. Global Perspective 8-2 traces the post-1986 annual inflation rates of Canada, the United States, the United Kingdom, Japan, and Germany. Observe that inflation in Canada has been coming down steadily since the late 1980s. Canada now has one of the lowest inflation rates among the industrialized nations.

Some nations have had double-digit, triple-digit, or even higher annual rates of inflation in recent years. In 1996, for example, the annual

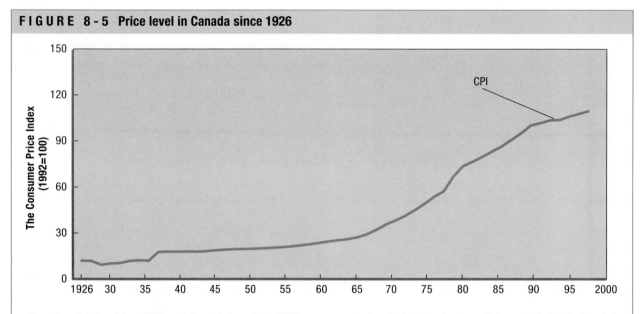

FIGURE 8-5 Price level in Canada since 1926

The price stability of the 1920s and the deflation of the 1930s gave way to sharp inflation in the immediate post-World War II period. The 1951–65 period was characterized by a reasonably stable price level, but the period since 1965 has been an age of inflation.

Sources: Statistics Canada, *National Income and Expenditures Accounts 1926–1986* (Ottawa, 1988) and Statistics Canada, *Canadian Economic Observer*, various years. Updates can be retrieved from Statistics Canada Web site at www.statcan.ca/english/Pgdb/Economy/Economic/econ46.htm

inflation rate in Turkey was 82 percent; in Venezuela, 120 percent; and in Bulgaria, 123 percent. A few nations experienced astronomical rates of inflation in 1996: Turkmenistan, 992 percent; and Angola, 4145 percent!

TABLE 8-5 Consumer Price Index (Percent change)

	1994	1995	1996	1997
CANADA	0.2	2.2	1.6	1.6
Newfoundland	1.2	1.5	1.5	2.1
Prince Edward Island	−0.2	1.6	1.8	1.2
Nova Scotia	1.1	1.5	1.7	2.1
New Brunswick	0.5	1.6	1.5	1.9
Quebec	−1.4	1.8	1.6	1.5
Ontario	0.0	2.5	1.5	1.9
Manitoba	1.4	2.7	2.2	2.2
Saskatchewan	1.8	1.9	1.9	1.3
Alberta	1.4	2.3	2.2	2.1
British Columbia	1.9	2.3	0.9	0.7

Source: Statistics Canada. For updates visit Statistics Canada at http://www.statcan.ca/english/Pgdb/Economy/econom.htm.

Causes of Inflation: A First Glance

Economists distinguish between two types of inflation: *demand-pull inflation* and *cost-push inflation*.

Demand-Pull Inflation Traditionally, changes in the price level are attributed to an excess of total spending beyond the economy's capacity to produce. Because resources are fully employed, the business sector cannot respond to this excess demand by expanding output, so the excess demand bids up the prices of the limited real output, causing **demand-pull inflation**. The essence of this type of inflation is "too much spending chasing too few goods."

Cost-Push or Supply-Side Inflation Inflation may also arise on the supply or cost side of the market. During several periods in our economic history the price level has risen even though aggregate demand was not excessive. These were periods when output and employment were both *declining* (evidence of a deficiency of total demand), while at the same time the general price level was *increasing*.

8-2
GLOBAL PERSPECTIVE

Inflation rates in five industrial nations, 1987–1997

Inflation rates in Canada have been coming down steadily over the last 10 years. Its inflation rate is now low relative to rates in other industrial nations.

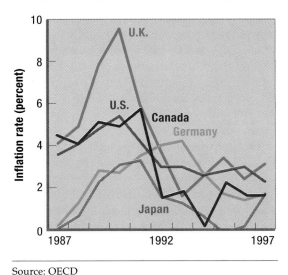

Source: OECD

We will look at demand-pull and cost-push inflation more closely in Chapter 16.

8-3
QUICK REVIEW

- Inflation is a rising general level of prices and is measured as a percentage change in a price index such as the CPI.

- Canada's inflation rate during the 1990s was one of the lowest among advanced industrial nations. Inflation varies among Canada's regions.

- Demand-pull inflation occurs when total spending exceeds the economy's ability to provide goods and services at the existing price level; total spending *pulls* the price level upward.

- Cost-push inflation occurs when factors such as excessive wage increases and rapid increases in raw-material prices drive up per-unit production costs; higher costs *push* the price level upward.

The theory of **cost-push inflation** explains rising prices in terms of factors that raise **per-unit production cost**. A per-unit production cost is the average cost of a particular level of output. This average cost is found by dividing the total cost of all resource inputs by the amount of output produced. That is,

$$\text{Per-unit production cost} = \frac{\text{total input cost}}{\text{units of output}}$$

Rising per-unit production costs squeeze profits and reduce the amount of output firms are willing to supply at the existing price level. As a result, the economy-wide supply of goods and services declines. This decline in supply drives up the price level. Under this scenario, costs are *pushing* the price level upward, rather than demand *pulling* it upward, as with demand-pull inflation.

Two potential sources of cost-push inflation are increases in nominal wages and increases in the prices of nonwage inputs such as raw materials and energy.

REDISTRIBUTION EFFECTS OF INFLATION

We now turn from the causes of inflation to its effects. In this section we consider how inflation can redistribute income if it is unanticipated; in the next section, we examine the possible effects of rising prices on domestic output.

The historical relationship between the price level and domestic output is ambiguous. Until recently, real output and the price level have risen and fallen together. In the past two decades, however, there have been times when real output has fallen while prices have continued to rise. We will dodge this difficulty by assuming here that real output is constant and at the full-employment level. Holding real output and income constant will allow us to isolate the effects of inflation on the distribution of that income: With a fixed national income pie, how does inflation affect the size of the slices going to different income receivers? Before we can answer, we need to discuss some terminology.

Nominal and Real Income You must first be clear about the difference between money income or nominal income and real income. *Money in-*

come or **nominal income** is the number of dollars received as wages, rent, interest, or profits. **Real income** measures the amount of goods and services nominal income can buy.

If your nominal income increases faster than the price level, your real income will rise. If the price level increases faster than your nominal income, your real income will decline. We can determine approximately how real income changes with this formula:

$$
\begin{array}{ccc}
\text{Percentage} & \text{percentage} & \text{percentage} \\
\text{change in} = & \text{change in} & - \text{change in} \\
\text{real income} & \text{nominal income} & \text{price level}
\end{array}
$$

If your nominal income rises by 10 percent and the price level rises by 6 percent in the same period, your real income will *increase* by about 4 percent. Conversely, a 6 percent increase in nominal income accompanied by 10 percent inflation will *decrease* your real income by approximately 4 percent.[1]

The main point is this: While inflation reduces the purchasing power of the dollar—the amount of goods and services each dollar will buy—it does not necessarily decrease a person's real income. Your real income (or standard of living) drops only when your nominal income fails to keep pace with inflation.

Anticipations   The redistribution effects of inflation depend on whether or not it is expected. With fully expected, or **anticipated inflation**, an income receiver *may* be able to avoid or lessen the adverse effects inflation would otherwise have on real income. The generalizations that immediately follow assume **unanticipated inflation**—inflation whose full extent was not expected.

---

[1] A more precise calculation follows Chapter 7's process for changing nominal GDP to real GDP. Thus,

$$
\text{Real income} = \frac{\text{nominal income}}{\text{price index (in hundredths)}}
$$

In our first illustration, if nominal income rises by 10 percent from $100 to $110 and the price level (index) increases by 6 percent from 100 to 106, then real income has increased as follows:

$$
\frac{\$110}{1.06} = \$103.77
$$

The 4 percent increase in real income shown by the simple formula in the text is a good approximation of the 3.77 percent yielded by our more precise formula.

Fixed-Nominal-Income Receivers

Our distinction between nominal and real incomes shows that *inflation penalizes people who receive fixed nominal incomes*. Inflation redistributes real income away from fixed-income receivers and towards others in the economy. The classic case is the elderly couple living on a private pension or annuity providing a fixed amount of nominal income each month. They may have retired in, say, 1984 on what appeared to be an adequate pension. However, by 1999 they will discover that the purchasing power of that pension has been cut by one-half.

Similarly, landlords who receive lease payments of fixed dollar amounts will be hurt by inflation as they receive dollars of declining value over time. To a lesser extent some white-collar workers, some public sector employees whose incomes are dictated by fixed pay scales, and families living on fixed levels of welfare will also be victims of inflation. Note, however, that Canada has partially *indexed* social insurance benefits. For example, the old-age security pension is partially indexed. This means that these payments increase when the consumer price index increases, preventing or lessening erosion from inflation.

Some people living on flexible incomes *may* benefit from inflation. The nominal incomes of such people may spurt ahead of the price level, with the result that their real incomes are enhanced. As an example, workers in expanding industries who are represented by strong unions may keep their nominal wages apace with, or ahead of, the rate of inflation.

Some wage earners are hurt by inflation. Those in declining industries or without strong unions may find that the price level jumps ahead of their money incomes.

Business executives and other profit receivers may benefit from inflation. If product prices rise faster than resource prices, business receipts will grow at a faster rate than costs. Thus some—but not necessarily all—profit incomes will outdistance the rising tide of inflation.

Savers

Inflation hurts savers, if it is unanticipated. *As prices rise, the real value, or purchasing power, of a nest egg of savings deteriorates*. Savings accounts, insurance policies, annuities, and other fixed-value paper assets once adequate to meet rainy-day contingencies or provide for a comfortable retirement decline in real value during inflation. The simplest case is the individual who hoards money as a cash balance. A $1,000 cash balance would have lost one-half its real value between 1980 and 1995. Of course, most forms of savings earn interest. But the value of savings will still decline if the rate of inflation exceeds the rate of interest.

Example: A household may save $1,000 in a chartered bank or credit union at 6 percent annual interest. But if inflation is 12.5 percent (as in 1981), the real value or purchasing power of that $1,000 will be cut to about $942 by the end of the year. The saver will receive $1,060 (equal to $1,000 plus $60 of interest), but deflating that $1,060 for 12.5 percent inflation means that its real value is only about $942 (= $1,060 divided by 1.125).

Debtors and Creditors

Inflation redistributes real income between debtors and creditors. *Unanticipated inflation benefits debtors (borrowers) at the expense of creditors (lenders).* Suppose you borrow $1,000 from a bank, to be repaid in two years. If in that time the general level of prices doubles, the $1,000 you repay will have only half the purchasing power of the $1,000 originally borrowed. True, if we ignore interest charges, the same number of dollars will be repaid as was borrowed. But because of inflation, each of these dollars will buy only half as much as it did when the loan was negotiated. As prices go up, the value of the dollar comes down. Thus, the borrower is loaned "dear" dollars but, because of inflation, pays back "cheap" dollars.

The inflation of the past several decades has been a windfall to those who purchased homes in earlier periods with low, fixed-interest-rate mortgages. Inflation has greatly reduced the real burden of their mortgage indebtedness. They have also benefited because the nominal value of housing has increased more rapidly than the overall price level.

Anticipated Inflation

The redistribution effects of inflation are less severe or are eliminated if people (1) anticipate inflation and (2) can adjust their nominal incomes to reflect expected price-level changes. The prolonged inflation which began in the late 1960s prompted many unions in the 1970s to insist on labour contracts with **cost-of-living adjustment** (COLA) clauses; such agreements automatically raise workers' nominal incomes when inflation occurs.

Similarly, the redistribution of income from lender to borrower might be altered if inflation is anticipated. Suppose a lender (perhaps a commercial bank or savings and loan institution) and a borrower (a household) both agree that 5 percent is a fair rate of interest on a one-year loan *provided* the price level is stable. But assume inflation has been occurring and is expected to be 6 percent over the next year. If the bank lends the household $100 at 5 percent interest, the bank will be paid back $105 at the end of the year. But if 6 percent inflation does occur during that year, the purchasing power of the $105 will have been reduced to about $99. The *lender* will in effect have paid the *borrower* $1 to use the lender's money for a year.

The lender can avoid this subsidy by charging an **inflation premium**, that is, by increasing the interest rate by 6 percent, the amount of the anticipated inflation. By charging 11 percent, the lender will receive back $111 at the end of the year. Adjusted for the 6 percent inflation, that amount will have purchasing power of today's $105. The result then will be a mutually agreeable transfer of purchasing power from borrower to lender of $5, or 5 percent, for the use of $100 for one year. Financial institutions have also developed variable-interest-rate mortgages to protect themselves from the adverse effects of inflation. (Incidentally, this example points out that, rather than being a cause of inflation, high nominal interest rates are a consequence of inflation.)

Our illustration shows the difference between the real rate of interest and the money or nominal rate of interest. The **real interest rate** *is the percentage increase in purchasing power that the lender receives from the borrower*. In our example the real interest rate is 5 percent. The **nominal interest rate** *is the percentage increase in money that the lender receives*. In our example, the nominal rate of interest is 11 percent. The difference in these two concepts is that the real interest rate is adjusted or deflated for the rate of inflation while the nominal interest rate is not. The nominal interest rate is the sum of the real interest rate plus the premium paid to offset the expected rate of inflation. These distinctions are illustrated in Figure 8-6.

Addenda

Three final points must be mentioned:

1. **DEFLATION** The effects of unanticipated deflation are substantially the reverse of those of

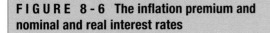

FIGURE 8-6 The inflation premium and nominal and real interest rates

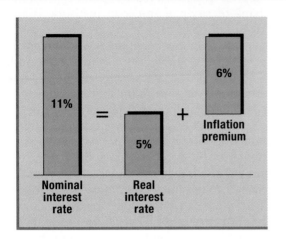

The inflation premium—the expected rate of inflation—gets built into the nominal interest rate. Here, the nominal interest rate of 11 percent is made up of the real interest rate of 5 percent plus the inflation premium of 6 percent.

inflation. *Assuming no change in total output*, people with fixed money incomes will find their real incomes enhanced. Creditors will benefit at the expense of debtors. And savers will discover the purchasing power of their savings has grown because of the falling prices.

2. **MIXED EFFECTS** The fact that any person may be an income earner, a holder of financial assets, and an owner of real assets simultaneously will likely cushion the redistribution impact of inflation. If the individual owns fixed-value monetary assets (savings accounts, bonds, and insurance policies), inflation will lessen their real value. But that same inflation may increase the real value of any property assets (a house, land) that the person owns.

In short, many individuals are simultaneously hurt and benefit by inflation. All these effects must be considered before we can conclude that any particular person's net position is better or worse because of inflation.

3. **ARBITRARINESS** The redistribution effects of inflation are arbitrary; they occur regardless of society's goals and values. Inflation lacks a social conscience and takes from some and gives to others, whether they be rich, poor, young, old, healthy, or infirm.

8-4
QUICK REVIEW

• Inflation arbitrarily "taxes" those who receive relatively fixed nominal incomes and it "subsidizes" some people who receive flexible nominal incomes.

• Unanticipated inflation penalizes savers, and it benefits debtors at the expense of creditors.

• The nominal interest rate exceeds the real interest rate by the expected rate of inflation.

OUTPUT EFFECTS OF INFLATION

We assumed in the last section that the economy's real output is fixed at the full-employment level. In that situation, the redistribution effects of inflation and deflation are that some groups gain real income at the expense of others. *If the size of the pie is fixed and inflation causes some groups to get larger slices, other groups must get smaller slices.* But, in fact, the level of domestic output—the size of the pie—may vary as the price level changes.

There is uncertainty and disagreement as to whether inflation will be accompanied by a rising or a falling real output. We will consider three scenarios, one associating inflation with an expanding output and two associating it with a declining output.

Stimulus of Demand-Pull Inflation

Some economists argue that full employment can be achieved only if some modest amount of inflation is tolerated. This perspective has been criticized in recent years. Many economists feel that any tradeoff between the inflation rate and the unemployment rate is transitory and that there is no such tradeoff in the long run. This controversy will be explored in Chapter 16.

Cost-Push Inflation and Unemployment

There is an equally plausible set of circumstances in which inflation might reduce both output and employment. Suppose the level of total spending is initially such that the economy is enjoying full employment *and* price-level stability. If cost-push inflation occurs, the existing level of total spending will now buy less real output because of the higher price level. Thus, real output will soon fall and unemployment will rise.

Economic events of the 1970s provide an example of how inflation can reduce real output. In late 1973 the Organization of Petroleum Exporting Countries (OPEC) became very effective in exerting its market power and was able to quadruple the price of oil. The cost-push inflationary effects generated rapid price-level increases in the 1973–75 period. At the same time the Canadian unemployment rate rose from slightly less than 5.6 percent in 1973 to 6.9 percent in 1975. Similar outcomes occurred in 1979–80 in response to a second OPEC oil supply shock.

Hyperinflation and Breakdown

Some economists express anxiety over our first scenario. They are fearful that the mild, "creeping" inflation that might initially accompany an economic recovery phase can snowball into severe **hyperinflation**. This is an extremely rapid inflation whose impact on real output and employment can be devastating. Their contention is that as prices persist in creeping upward, households and businesses will expect them to rise further. So, rather than let their idle savings and current incomes depreciate, people will "spend now" to beat anticipated price rises. Businesses will do the same by buying capital goods. Actions based on this "inflationary psychosis" will then intensify the pressure on prices, and inflation will feed on itself.

Wage-Price Inflationary Spiral   Furthermore, as the price level rises, labour will demand and get higher nominal wages. Unions may seek wage increases sufficient not only to cover last year's price increases but also to compensate for inflation anticipated during the future life of their new collective bargaining agreements. Prosperity is not a good time for firms to risk strikes by resisting such demands, so they will agree, expecting to recoup their rising labour costs by boosting their prices. And for good measure, businesses may jack prices up an extra notch to be sure their profits keep up with the inflationary parade. As such price increases raise the general price level further, labour finds it once again has an excellent reason to demand and obtain substantial wage increases. But this triggers another round of price increases. And so on. The net effect is a cumulative *wage-price inflationary spiral*. Nominal wage and price rises feed on each other and transform creeping inflation into galloping inflation.

Potential Economic Collapse   Aside from its disruptive redistribution effects, hyperinflation can cause economic collapse. Severe inflation encourages speculative activity. Businesses may find it increasingly profitable to hoard both materials and finished products, anticipating further price increases. But restricting the availability of materials and products intensifies the inflationary pressure. Also, rather than invest in capital equipment, businesses and individual savers may purchase nonproductive wealth—jewels, gold and other precious metals, real estate, and so forth—as a hedge against inflation.

In the extreme, as prices shoot up sharply and unevenly, normal economic relationships are disrupted. Business owners do not know what to charge for their products. Consumers do not know what to pay. Resource suppliers want to be paid with actual output, rather than with rapidly depreciating money. Creditors avoid debtors to escape the repayment of debts with cheap money. Money eventually becomes almost worthless and ceases to do its job as a medium of exchange. The economy may be thrown into a state of barter. Production and exchange drop dramatically, and the net result is economic, social, and possibly political chaos. The hyperinflation has precipitated monetary collapse, depression, and sociopolitical disorder.

Examples   History reveals a number of examples that fit this scenario. Consider the effects of World War II on price levels in Hungary and Japan:

> The inflation in Hungary exceeded all known records of the past. In August 1946, 828 octillion (1 followed by 27 zeros) depreciated pengös equaled the value of 1 prewar pengö. The price of the American dollar reached a value of 3×10^{22} (3 followed by 22 zeros) pengös. Fishermen and farmers in 1947 Japan used scales to weigh currency and change, rather than bothering to count it. Prices rose some 116 times in Japan, 1938 to 1948.[2]

---

[2] Theodore Morgan, *Income and Employment*, 2nd ed. (Englewood Cliffs, N.J.: Prentice-Hall, Inc., 1952), p. 361.

The German inflation of the 1920s was also catastrophic:

> The German Weimar Republic is an extreme example of a weak government which survived for some time through inflationary finance. On April 27, 1921, the German government was presented with a staggering bill for reparations payments to the Allies of 132 billion gold marks. This sum was far greater than what the Weimar Republic could reasonably expect to raise in taxes. Faced with huge budget deficits, the Weimar government simply ran the printing press to meet its bills.
>
> During 1922, the German price level went up 5,470 percent. In 1923, the situation worsened; the German price level rose 1,300,000,000,000 times. By October of 1923, the postage on the lightest letter sent from Germany to the United States was 200,000 marks. Butter cost 1.5 million marks per pound, meat 2 million marks, a loaf of bread 200,000 marks, and an egg 60,000 marks. Prices increased so rapidly that waiters changed the prices on the menu several times during the course of a lunch. Sometimes customers had to pay double the price listed on the menu when they ordered.[3]

A closing word of caution: Dramatic hyperinflations like these are almost invariably the consequence of imprudent expansion of the money supply by government. Such expansions result in excessive spending and thus demand-pull inflation. With appropriate public policies, however, mild inflation need not become hyperinflation.

---

[3] Raburn M. Williams, *Inflation! Money, Jobs, and Politicians* (Arlington Heights, Ill.: AHM Publishing Corporation, 1980), p. 2.

In The Media

Unemployment Rate Dips to Seven-Year Low

Surge of new jobs pushes it down to 8.6 per cent

BY BRUCE LITTLE
AND SUSAN BOURETTE
THE GLOBE AND MAIL

It's been a long time coming, but Canada's unemployment rate dropped in December below 9 per cent for the first time in more than seven years as a strong surge in job creation pushed it down to 8.6 per cent.

The decline ended a string of 86 months in which the rate was 9 per cent or higher, the longest such stretch since Statistics Canada began recording monthly job data 51 years ago.

The main reason for the lower unemployment rate was simple: The economy created 62,000 new jobs in December, more than double the average monthly gains in the first 11 months of the year.

Better yet, the number of full-time jobs grew 111,000—the second-largest such increase on record—while part-time employment fell 49,000. Full-time jobs generally offer better wages and benefits than part-time ones.

Lisa Rixon of St. John's exemplifies the trend. After holding down a part-time bookkeeping job at Zellers for 10 years while she finished a commerce degree, she was hired three days before Christmas to head the human-resources department at Stratos Global Corp., a satellite-communications company.

"A full-time job, a pay cheque, a permanent position—life is just grand. I couldn't ask for a single thing more," Ms. Rixon said.

Neither could analysts who examined the Statscan job report. "This is the best postholiday present the economy could ever get," said economist John Clinkard of the Canadian Imperial Bank of Commerce.

Sherry Cooper, chief economist at Nesbitt Burns Inc., said it was a "wonderful" report. "The doomsayers were wrong in 1997, and they will be wrong again in 1998. The jobless rate is headed below 8 per cent before the end of the year."

The December job gains brought Canada's total employ-ment to 14.12 million on a season-ally adjusted basis, up 363,000 jobs from a year earlier. Full-time employment was up 377,000 while the number of part-time jobs fell 14,000. It was the biggest annual increase since 1994, which was the best year of the 1990s.

Source: Globe and Mail, January 10, 1998, pp. A1 and A4. Reprinted with permission from the *Globe and Mail.*

THE STORY IN BRIEF

The unemployment rate in Canada dips below 9 percent for the first time in over seven years.

THE ECONOMICS BEHIND THE STORY

- As a result of very strong job growth in the final month of 1997, the unemployment rate finally fell below 9 percent for the first time in 86 months. The good news was attributable to strong economic growth. In 1997 the Canadian economy grew at almost 4 percent per annum.
- The story implies both frictional and cyclical unem-ployment fell, contributing to the positive results. Full-time employment rose during the year, while part-time jobs fell.
- Will a strong economy bring down structural un-employment? ∎

The
Last Word

THE STOCK MARKET AND MACROECONOMIC INSTABILITY

How, if at all, do changes in stock prices relate to the macroeconomy?

FINANCIAL INVESTORS DAILY BUY AND SELL the stock (ownership shares) of thousands of corpora-tions. These corporations pay dividends—a portion of their profits—to the owners of their shares. The price of a particular company's stock is determined by supply and demand. Individual stock prices generally rise and fall in concert with the collective expectations for each firm's profits. Greater profits normally result in higher dividends to the owners of the stock, and in anticipation of these higher dividends, financial investors are willing to pay more for the stock.

Stock market averages such as the Toronto Stock Exchange industrial average—the weighted-average price of the stocks of major Canadian industrial firms—are closely watched and reported. It is common for these price averages to change over time, or even to rise or fall sharply during a single day. On "Black Monday," October 19, 1987, the TSE industrial average experienced a record one-day drop of 20 percent.

The volatility of the stock market raises this ques-tion: Do changes in stock price averages *cause* macro-economic instability? There are linkages between the stock market and the economy that might lead us to think the answer is yes. Consider a sharp decline in stock prices. Feeling poorer, owners of stock may respond by reducing their spending on goods and services. Firms may react by cutting back on their purchases of new cap-ital goods because that is more attractive than raising funds by issuing new shares of stock.

Studies find, however, that the consumption and investment impacts of stock price changes are relatively mild. Therefore, although stock price averages do influ-ence total spending, the stock market is *not* a major cause of recession or inflation.

A related question emerges: Even though changes in stock prices do not *cause* significant changes in domestic output and the price level, might they predict such changes? That is, if stock market values are based on expected profits, wouldn't we expect rapid changes in stock price averages to forecast changes in future busi-ness conditions? Indeed, stock prices often *do* fall prior to recessions and rise prior to expansions. For this reason stock prices are among a group of 11 variables that constitute an index of leading indicators (Last Word, Chapter 12). Such an index often provides a useful clue to the future direction of the economy. But taken alone, stock market prices are not a reliable predictor of changes in GDP. Stock prices have fallen rapidly in some instances with no recession following. Black Monday itself did not produce a recession during the following two years. In other instances, recessions have occurred with no prior decline in stock market prices. ■

CHAPTER SUMMARY

1. Canada and other industrial economies have gone through periods of fluctuations in domestic output, employment, and the price level. Although they have common phases—peak, recession, trough, recovery—business cycles vary greatly in duration and in intensity.

2. Although economists explain the business cycle in terms of such ultimate causal factors as major innovations, political events, and money creation, they generally agree that the level of total spending is the immediate determinant of real output and employment.

3. The business cycle affects all sectors of the economy, but in varying ways and degrees. The cycle has greater output and employment effects in the capital goods and durable consumer goods industries than in the services and non-durable goods industries. Over the cycle, price fluctuations are greater in competitive than in monopolistic industries.

4. Economists distinguish between frictional, structural, and cyclical unemployment. The full-employment or natural rate of unemployment, composed of frictional and structural unemployment, is currently about 7.5 percent. Part-time and discouraged workers complicate the accurate measurement of unemployment.

5. The economic cost of unemployment, as measured by the GDP gap, consists of the goods and services forgone by society when its resources are involuntarily idle. Okun's law suggests that every 1 percentage point increase in unemployment above the natural rate causes a 2 percent GDP gap.

6. Unemployment rates and inflation rates vary widely among nations. Unemployment rates differ because nations have different natural rates of unemployment and often are in different phases of their business cycles. Inflation and unemployment rates in Canada recently have been in the middle range compared with rates in other industrial nations.

7. Economists discern both demand-pull and cost-push (supply-side) inflation. Two variants of cost-push inflation are wage-push inflation and inflation caused by supply shocks.

8. Unanticipated inflation arbitrarily redistributes real income at the expense of fixed-income receivers, creditors, and savers. If inflation is anticipated, individuals and businesses may be able to take steps to lessen or eliminate adverse redistribution effects.

9. The demand-pull theory of inflation suggests that some inflation may be necessary for the economy to realize high levels of output and employment. However, the cost-push theory of inflation indicates that inflation may be accompanied by declines in real output and employment. Hyperinflation, usually associated with injudicious government policy, might undermine the monetary system and cause economic collapse.

TERMS AND CONCEPTS

business cycle
peak
recession
trough
recovery

seasonal variations
secular trend
frictional unemployment
structural unemployment
cyclical unemployment

full-employment unemployment rate
natural rate of unemployment
potential output
labour force
unemployment rate
discouraged workers
GDP gap
Okun's law
inflation
rule of 70
demand-pull inflation

cost-push inflation
per-unit production costs
nominal income
real income
anticipated inflation
unanticipated inflation
cost-of-living adjustment
inflation premium
real interest rate
nominal interest rate
hyperinflation

STUDY QUESTIONS

1. **KEY QUESTION** *What are the four phases of the business cycle? How long do business cycles last? How do seasonal variations and secular trends complicate measurement of the business cycle? Why does the business cycle affect output and employment in capital goods industries and consumer durable goods industries more severely than in industries producing consumer nondurables?*

2. What factors make it difficult to determine the unemployment rate? Why is it difficult to distinguish between frictional, structural, and cyclical unemployment? Why is unemployment an economic problem? What are the consequences of a GDP gap? What are the noneconomic effects of unemployment?

3. **KEY QUESTION** *Use the following data to calculate* **a** *the size of the labour force and* **b** *the official unemployment rate: total population, 500; population under 15 years of age or institutionalized, 120; not in labour force, 150; unemployed, 23; part-time workers looking for full-time jobs, 10.*

4. Since there is an employment insurance program that provides income for those out of work, why worry about unemployment?

5. **KEY QUESTION** *Assume that in a particular year the natural rate of unemployment is 5 percent and the actual rate of unemployment is 9 percent. Use Okun's law to determine the size of the GDP gap in percentage-point terms. If the nominal GDP is $500 billion in that year, how much output is being forgone because of cyclical unemployment?*

6. Explain how an *increase* in your nominal income and a *decrease* in your real income might occur simultaneously. Who loses from inflation? Who loses from unemployment? If you had to choose between **a** full employment with a 6 percent annual rate of inflation and **b** price stability with an 8 percent unemployment rate, which would you select? Why?

7. **KEY QUESTION** *If the price index was 110 last year and is 121 this year, what is this year's rate of inflation? What is the "rule of 70"? How long would it take for the price level to double if inflation persisted at* **a** *2,* **b** *5, and* **c** *10 percent per year?*

8. Describe the relationship between total spending and the levels of output and employment. Explain what happens to the price level as increases in total spending move the economy from substantial unemployment to moderate unemployment, to full employment, and finally to full-capacity output.

9. Explain how hyperinflation might lead to a depression.

10. Evaluate as accurately as you can how each of the following individuals would be affected by unanticipated inflation of 10 percent per year:
    a. A pensioned railroad worker
    b. A department store clerk
    c. A unionized assembly line worker
    d. A heavily indebted farmer
    e. A retired business executive whose current income comes entirely from interest on government bonds
    f. The owner of an independent small-town department store

11. A noted television comedian once defined inflation as follows: "Inflation? That means your money today won't buy as much as it would have during the Depression when you didn't have any." Is his definition accurate? Explain.

12. **(The Last Word)** Suppose that stock prices fall by 10 percent in the stock market. All else equal, are these lower stock prices likely to cause a decrease in real GDP? How might these lower prices forecast a decline in real GDP?

13. **WEB-BASED QUESTION** **The Employment Situation—Write the News Release** Visit Statistics Canada www.statcan.ca/english/econoind/lfsadj.htm and look at the current national employment situation summary for the latest month. Then rewrite the following paragraph.

    Employment in Canada (rose/fell/remained unchanged), and the unemployment rate edged (up/down/stayed unchanged) to (?) percent in the latest month. The unemployment rate had (risen/ fallen/stayed unchanged) from (?) percent in (previous month) to (?) percent in (latest month). The number of jobs (increased/decreased/ were unchanged) by (? thousand) in the latest month

14. **WEB-BASED QUESTION** **Inflation and the "Official CPI"** Each month, Statistics Canada releases thousands of detailed CPI numbers to the press. However, the press generally focuses on the broadest, most comprehensive CPI, called the official CPI. Go to www.statcan.ca/english/econoind/cpia.htm and find the figures for the official CPI: **a** index level for all items for the current month (for example, March 1998 = 108.4 for all items); **b** 12-month percentage change (for example, March 1997 to March 1998 = 0.9 percent for all items); **c** 1-month percentage change (for example, from February 1998 to March 1998 = 0.1 for all items); and **d** the annual percentage rate of change so far this year for all items. Click on the "List of Tables" and look at the CPI for the provinces; which province had the highest/lowest change in the CPI for the last 12 months?

Building the Aggregate Expenditures Model

TWO OF THE MOST CRITICAL QUESTIONS IN macroeconomics are these: (1) What determines the level of GDP, given a nation's production capacity? (2) What factors can cause real GDP to expand in one period and fall in another? To answer these questions, we construct the *aggregate expenditures model*. Recall that to economists "aggregate" means "total" or "combined," so "aggregate expenditures" refers to the economy's total spending. The model is based on the general equality between total spending and output described in Chapter 7. One of its primary uses is in clarifying the occurrence of business fluctuations discussed in Chapter 8.

We begin this chapter with a brief review of the economic thinking and events leading to the development of the aggregate expenditures model. Next we examine the relations between income and consumption and between income and saving, both aspects of the model. Then we focus on investment—specifically how businesses choose the amounts of capital goods to buy. Finally, we combine consumption, saving, and investment into a model that can be used to determine the equilibrium level of GDP for an economy.

The model developed in this chapter applies only to a private (no government), closed (no foreign trade) economy. In the next, chapter we complete the model by adding government and the foreign sector.

IN THIS CHAPTER YOU WILL LEARN:

How aggregate expenditures determine the short-run output and employment in an economy.

•

The factors that determine consumption expenditure and saving.

•

The factors that determine investment spending.

•

How equilibrium GDP is determined in a closed economy without a government sector.

The Big Picture

WE NOTED IN THE LAST CHAPTER THAT A market economy is prone to a certain amount of instability, also referred to as the business cycle. We need to understand how GDP and the price level are determined so that we can devise the appropriate macroeconomic policies to counteract macroeconomic fluctuations. Remember, the goal is to employ all of the economy's available factors of production—particularly labour—and get the most output out of them. We put aside the issue of the price level until Chapter 11, to concentrate on how GDP is determined.

We already know that the main immediate determinant of GDP in an economy is the level of expenditures. From Chapter 7 we also learned there are four expenditure categories: consumption, investment, government, and net export. Here we begin with the simplest expenditure model of an economy—one with only two categories of expenditure: consumption and investment. In doing so, we also investigate the main determinants of consumption and investments.

As you read this chapter, keep the following points in mind:

- Our simple expenditure model has no foreign sector (thus, a closed economy), and no government sector. These will be added in the next chapter.
- The main determinant of the level of consumption is disposable income; the main determinant of investments is interest rates.
- The expenditure model assumes a fixed price level. The price level will be considered in another model (the aggregate supply-aggregate demand model) to be introduced in Chapter 11. ■

HISTORICAL BACKDROP

A bit of historical background will help you see how and why the aggregate expenditures model came about.

Classical Economics and Say's Law

Until the Great Depression of the 1930s, many economists of the nineteenth and early twentieth centuries—now called classical economists[1]—believed the market system would ensure full employment of the economy's resources. They acknowledged that now and then abnormal circumstances such as wars, political upheavals, droughts, speculative crises, and gold rushes would occur, deflecting the economy from full-employment status (as seen in Figure 8-1). But when these deviations did occur, automatic adjustments in prices, wages, and interest rates within the market would soon restore the economy to the full-employment level of output. A slump in output and employment would reduce prices, wages, and interest rates. Lower prices would increase consumer spending, lower wages would increase employment, and lower interest rates would boost investment spending. Any excess supply of goods and workers soon would be eliminated.

Classical macroeconomists denied the possibility of long-term underspending—a level of spending insufficient to purchase the entire full-employment output. This denial was based in part on **Say's law**, attributed to the nineteenth-century French economist J. B. Say. Say's law is the seemingly simple notion that the very act of producing goods generates an amount of income equal to the value of the goods produced. The production of any output automatically provides the income needed to take that output off the market—the income needed to buy what's produced. In other words, *supply creates its own demand*.

Say's law can best be understood in terms of a barter economy. A shoemaker, for example, produces or *supplies* shoes as a means of buying or *demanding* the shirts and stockings produced by other workers. The shoemaker's supply of shoes is his income, which he will "spend" to satisfy his demand for other goods. The goods he buys (demands) will be exactly equal in value to the

---

[1] The most prominent classical economists were David Ricardo, John Stuart Mill, F.Y. Edgeworth, Alfred Marshall, and A.C. Pigou.

goods he produces (supplies). And so it allegedly is for other producers and for the entire economy. Demand must be the same as supply! The circular flow model of the economy and national income accounting both suggest something of this sort. Income generated from the production of any level of output would, when spent, be just sufficient to provide a matching total demand. Assuming the composition of output is in accord with consumer preferences, all markets would be cleared of their outputs. It would seem that what all business owners need to do to sell a full-employment output is to produce that output; Say's law guarantees there will be sufficient consumption spending to buy it all.

Say's law and classical macroeconomics are not simply historical curiosities. A few modern economists have reformulated, revitalized, and extended the work of the nineteenth- and early twentieth-century economists to generate a "new" classical economics. (We will examine this modern reincarnation in later chapters.)

The Great Depression and Keynes

Two events weakened the theory that supply creates its own demand (Say's law) and led to the realization that underspending or overspending can occur:

The Great Depression
The Depression of the 1930s was worldwide. In Canada, it cut real GDP by about a third and raised the unemployment rate to nearly 20 percent. Much the same occurred in other industrial nations. The negative effects of the Depression lingered for a decade. There is, obviously, a blatant inconsistency between a theory that says unemployment is virtually impossible and the actual occurrence of a 10-year siege of very substantial unemployment.

Keynes and Keynesian Economics
In 1936 British economist John Maynard Keynes (pronounced "Caines") explained why there was cyclical employment in capitalistic economies. In his *General Theory of Employment, Interest, and Money*, Keynes attacked the foundations of classical theory and touched off a major revolution in economic thinking on macroeconomic questions. Keynes disputed Say's law, pointing out that in some periods not all income will get spent on the output that is produced. When widespread under-

spending occurs, unsold goods will accumulate in producers' warehouses. Producers will respond to rising inventories by reducing their output and cutting their employment. A recession or depression will follow.

Because Keynes developed the ideas underlying the aggregate expenditures model, this kind of analysis is referred to as **Keynesian economics**. But the model reflects contributions of numerous other economists since Keynes. In the aggregate expenditures model, the macroeconomy is inherently unstable; it is subject to periods of recession and inflation. Keynesian economics says that the market economy is not a self-regulating system capable of uninterrupted prosperity. While a market economy is an excellent engine of long-term economic growth, we cannot always depend on it to "run itself."

Furthermore, economic fluctuations are not associated exclusively with external forces such as wars, droughts, and similar abnormalities. Rather, the Keynesian view sees the causes of unemployment and inflation as the failure of certain fundamental economic decisions—in particular, saving and investment decisions—to be completely synchronized. In addition, product prices and wages are downwardly inflexible, meaning that significant declines in prices and wages will occur only after extended and costly periods of recession or depression. Internal factors, in addition to external forces (wars and droughts), contribute to economic instability.

SIMPLIFICATIONS

Four assumptions will help us build the aggregate expenditures model:

1. Initially we will assume a "closed economy" where there are no international trade transactions. Complications arising from exports and imports in the "open economy" will be deferred to Chapter 10.
2. We will also ignore government until Chapter 10. This will permit us first to demonstrate that at times laissez-faire capitalism may not achieve and maintain full employment. For now we will deal with a "private" closed economy.
3. Although both businesses and households save, we will for convenience speak as if all saving were personal saving.

4. To keep things simple, we will assume that depreciation is zero.

We should note two implications of these assumptions. First, recall from Chapter 7 that aggregate spending has four components: consumption, investment, government purchases, and net exports. Assumptions 1 and 2 mean that, for now, we are concerned only with consumption and investment.

Second, assumptions 2 through 4 permit us to treat gross domestic product (GDP), net domestic income (NDI), personal income (PI), and disposable income (DI) as being equal to each other. All the items that in practice distinguish them from one another result from depreciation, government (taxes and transfer payments), and business saving. Our assumptions mean that if $500 billion of goods and services is produced as GDP, exactly $500 billion of DI is received by households to use as either consumption or saving.

TOOLS OF THE AGGREGATE EXPENDITURES MODEL

The aggregate expenditures model embodies the following basic theory regarding the macroeconomy: *The amount of goods and services produced and therefore the level of employment depend directly on the level of total or aggregate expenditures.* Businesses will produce a level of output they can profitably sell. Workers and machinery are idled when there are no markets for the goods and services they can produce. Total output and employment decrease when the level of aggregate expenditures decreases, and they increase when it increases.

Our strategy in this chapter is to analyze the consumption and investment components of aggregate expenditures and derive a private sector model of equilibrium GDP and employment. Chapter 10 examines changes in real GDP and adds net exports and government expenditures (along with taxes) to the model.

As we begin our discussion, be sure you understand that we are assuming the economy has substantial excess production capacity and unemployed labour (unless specified otherwise). An increase in aggregate expenditures will thus increase real output and employment but *not* the price level.

9-1

QUICK REVIEW

• Classical macroeconomics was grounded in Say's law, which asserted that supply creates its own demand and therefore underspending leading to recessions was unlikely.

• The Great Depression and Keynes's development of an alternative model of the macroeconomy undermined classical macroeconomics and led to the modern aggregate expenditures theory.

• In the aggregate expenditures model, the level of total or aggregate expenditures determines the amount of output produced that in turn establishes the level of employment.

CONSUMPTION AND SAVING

In terms of absolute size, consumption is the largest component of aggregate expenditures. We therefore need to understand the determinants of consumption spending. Recall that economists define personal saving as "not spending" or "that part of disposable income (DI) not consumed." In other words, saving equals disposable income less consumption. Thus, in examining the determinants of consumption we are also exploring the determinants of saving.

Income-Consumption and Income-Saving Relationships

Many factors influence the level of consumer spending. But the most significant determinant is income—in particular, disposable income. And, since saving is that part of disposable income not consumed, DI is also the basic determinant of personal saving.

Consider some recent historical data. In Figure 9-1 each black dot represents consumption and disposable income for one year since 1973. The green line, fitted to these points, shows that consumption is directly related to disposable income; moreover, households clearly spend most of their incomes.

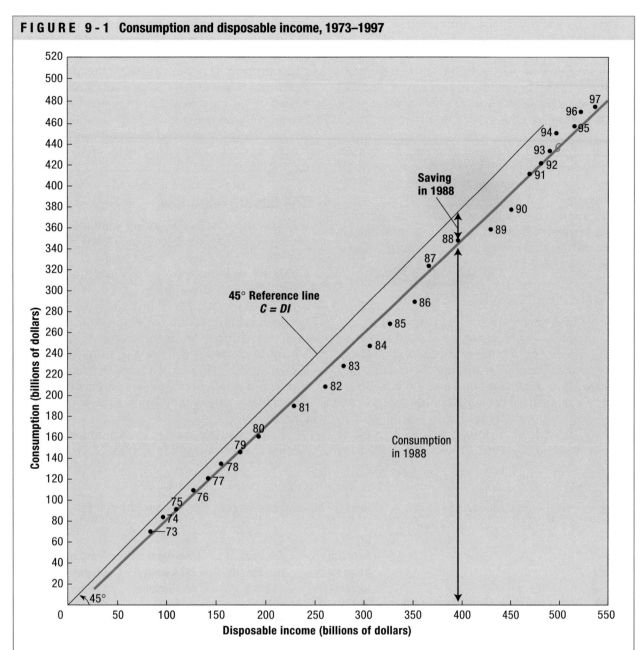

FIGURE 9-1 Consumption and disposable income, 1973–1997

Each dot in this figure shows consumption and disposable income in a specific year. The *C* line generalizes the relationship between consumption and disposable income. It indicates a direct relationship and that households consume the bulk of their incomes.

Source: Statistics Canada, *National Income and Expenditure Accounts, various years.*

But we can say more. The black 45-degree line is added to the diagram as a reference line. Because this line bisects the 90-degree angle formed by the vertical and horizontal axes of the graph, each point on the line must be equidistant from the two axes. That is, each point on the line represents a sit-

uation in which consumption equals disposable income, or *C* = DI. We can therefore regard the vertical distance from any point on the horizontal axis to the 45-degree line as measuring either consumption *or* disposable income. If we regard it as measuring disposable income, then the vertical distance by which actual consumption in any year falls short of the 45-degree line represents the amount of saving in that year. For example, in 1988 consumption was $350 billion, and disposable income was $394 billion; hence, saving in 1988 was $44 billion. Disposable income less consumption equals saving, or DI – C = S. By observing these vertical distances as we move to the left or to the right in Figure 9-1, we see that saving also varies directly with the level of disposable income: As DI increases, saving increases; as DI decreases, saving decreases.

Figure 9-1 thus suggests that (1) households consume most of their disposable incomes, and (2) both consumption and saving are directly related to the income level.

The Consumption Schedule

The dots in Figure 9-1 represent historical data— how much households *actually had as DI* and *actually did consume* (and save) over a period of years. Those data are useful for finding the relationship between DI and consumption and saving. But to build our model, we need a schedule that tells us the various amounts households would *plan* to consume at each of various levels of disposable income that could prevail at *some specific time*. A

hypothetical **consumption schedule** of the type we require is shown in columns 1 and 2, Table 9-1, and is plotted in *Figure 9-2a (Key Graph)*. This consumption schedule reflects the direct consumption-disposable income relationship suggested by the empirical data in Figure 9-1, and it is consistent with many empirical household budget studies. Households tend to spend a *larger proportion* of a small disposable income than of a large disposable income.

The Saving Schedule

It is simple to derive a **saving schedule**. Because saving equals disposable income *less* consumption (S = DI – C), we need only subtract consumption (Table 9-1, column 2) from disposable income (column 1) to find the amount saved (column 3) at each DI. Thus, columns 1 and 3 in Table 9-1 are the saving schedule, plotted in Figure 9-2b. Note that there is a direct relationship between saving and DI but that saving is a smaller proportion (fraction) of a small DI than of a large DI. If households consume a smaller and smaller proportion of DI as DI increases, then they must save a larger and larger proportion.

Remembering that at each point on the 45-degree line consumption equals DI, we see that

TABLE 9-1 Consumption and saving schedules (in billions) and propensities to consume and save

(1) Level of output and income (GDP = DI)	(2) Consumption (C)	(3) Saving (S) (1) – (2)	(4) Average propensity to consume (APC) (2)/(1)	(5) Average propensity to save (APS) (3)/(1)	(6) Marginal propensity to consume (MPC) Δ(2)/Δ(1)*	(7) Marginal propensity to save (MPS) Δ(3)/Δ(1)*
(1) $370	$375	$–5	1.01	–.01		
					.75	.25
(2) 390	390	0	1.00	.00		
					.75	.25
(3) 410	405	5	.99	.01		
					.75	.25
(4) 430	420	10	.98	.02		
					.75	.25
(5) 450	435	15	.97	.03		
					.75	.25
(6) 470	450	20	.96	.04		
					.75	.25
(7) 490	465	25	.95	.05		
					.75	.25
(8) 510	480	30	.94	.06		
					.75	.25
(9) 530	495	35	.93	.07		
					.75	.25
(10) 550	510	40	.93	.07		

* The Greek letter Δ, delta, means "the change in."

KEY GRAPH

FIGURE 9-2 (a) Consumption and (b) saving schedules

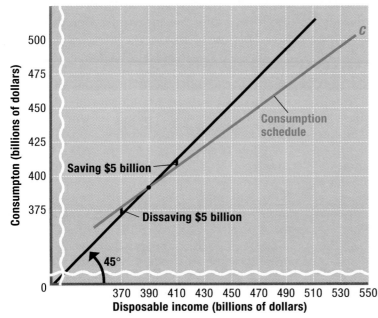

(a) Consumption schedule

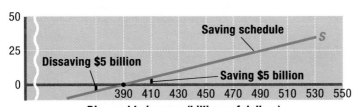

(b) Saving schedule

The two parts of this figure show the income-consumption and income-saving relationships in Table 9-1 graphically. The saving schedule in (b) is found by subtracting the consumption schedule in (a) vertically from the 45-degree line. Consumption equals disposable income (and saving thus equals zero) at $390 billion for these hypothetical data.

9-2
QUICK QUIZ

1. The slope of the consumption schedule in this figure is .75. Thus, the
    (a) slope of the saving schedule is 1.33.
    (b) marginal propensity to consume is .75.
    (c) average propensity to consume is .25.
    (d) slope of the saving schedule is also .75.

2. In this figure, when consumption is a positive amount, saving
    (a) must be a negative amount.
    (b) also must be a positive amount.
    (c) can be either a positive or a negative amount.
    (d) is zero.

3. In this figure,
    (a) the marginal propensity to consume is constant at all levels of income.
    (b) the marginal propensity to save rises as disposable income rises.
    (c) consumption is inversely (negatively) related to disposable income.
    (d) saving is inversely (negatively) related to disposable income.

4. When consumption equals disposable income,
    (a) the marginal propensity to consume is zero.
    (b) the average propensity to consume is zero.
    (c) consumption and saving must be equal.
    (d) saving must be zero.

Answers: 1. (b); 2. (c); 3. (a); 4. (d).

dissaving (consuming in excess of after-tax income) will occur at relatively low DIs like $370 billion (row 1, Table 9-1), where consumption is actually $375 billion. Households can consume more than their incomes by liquidating (selling for cash) accumulated wealth or by borrowing. Graphically, dissaving is shown as the vertical distance of the consumption schedule *above* the 45-degree line or as the vertical distance of the saving schedule *below* the horizontal axis. Dissaving at the $370 billion level of income is marked in Figure 9-2a and b. Each of the two vertical distances measures the $5 billion of dissaving occurring at the $370 billion income level.

In our example, the **break-even income** is $390 billion (row 2). This is the income level where households plan to consume their entire incomes (C = DI). Graphically, the consumption schedule cuts the 45-degree line, and the saving schedule cuts the horizontal axis (saving is zero) at the break-even income level.

At all higher incomes, households plan to save part of their incomes. Graphically, the vertical distance of the consumption schedule *below* the 45-degree line measures this saving, as does the vertical distance of the saving schedule *above* the horizontal axis. For example, at the $410 billion level of income (row 3), both these distances indicate $5 billion worth of saving (see Figure 9-2a and b).

Average and Marginal Propensities

Columns 4 to 7 in Table 9-1 show additional characteristics of the consumption and saving schedules.

APC and APS

The fraction, or percentage, of any total income that is consumed is called the **average propensity to consume** (APC). The fraction of any total income that is saved is the **average propensity to save** (APS). That is,

$$APC = \frac{consumption}{income}$$

and

$$APS = \frac{saving}{income}$$

For example, at the $470 billion level of income (row 6) in Table 9-1, the APC is $\frac{450}{470} = \frac{45}{47}$, or about 96 percent, while the APS is $\frac{20}{470} = \frac{2}{47}$, or about 4 percent.

Columns 4 and 5 in Table 9-1 show the APC and APS at each of the 10 levels of DI; note there that the APC falls and the APS rises as DI increases. This is another way of stating a point we just made: The fraction of total DI that is consumed declines as DI rises, and the fraction of DI that is saved rises as DI increases.

Because disposable income is either consumed or saved, the fraction of any DI consumed plus the fraction saved (not consumed) must exhaust that income. Mathematically, APC + APS = 1 at any level of disposable income. Columns 4 and 5 in Table 9-1 illustrate this.

Global Perspective 9-1 shows APCs for several countries.

MPC and MPS

The fact that households consume a certain proportion of some total income— for example, $\frac{45}{47}$ of a $470 billion disposable income —does not guarantee they will consume the same proportion of any *change* in income they might receive. The proportion, or fraction, of any change

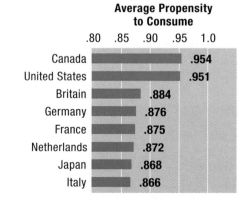

9-1

GLOBAL PERSPECTIVE

Average propensities to consume, selected nations, 1996

There are surprisingly large differences in average propensities to consume (APCs) among nations. Canada and the United States in particular have substantially higher APCs, and thus lower APSs, than other advanced economies.

Average Propensity to Consume

Canada	.954
United States	.951
Britain	.884
Germany	.876
France	.875
Netherlands	.872
Japan	.868
Italy	.866

Source: *Statistical Abstract of the United States 1997*, p. 840.

in income consumed is called the **marginal propensity to consume** (MPC), marginal meaning "extra" or "a change in." Equivalently, the MPC is the ratio of a *change* in consumption to the change in income that caused that change in consumption:

$$\text{MPC} = \frac{\text{change in consumption}}{\text{change in income}}$$

Similarly, the fraction of any change in income saved is the **marginal propensity to save** (MPS). The MPS is the ratio of a *change* in saving to the *change* in income bringing it about:

$$\text{MPS} = \frac{\text{change in saving}}{\text{change in income}}$$

If disposable income is $470 billion (row 6 in Table 9-1) and household incomes rise by $20 billion to $490 billion (row 7), households will consume $\frac{15}{20}$, or $\frac{3}{4}$, and save $\frac{5}{20}$, or $\frac{1}{4}$, of that *increase in income*. In other words, the MPC is $\frac{3}{4}$ or .75, and the MPS is $\frac{1}{4}$ or .25, as shown in columns 6 and 7.

The sum of the MPC and the MPS for any change in disposable income must always be 1. Consuming and saving out of extra income is an either-or proposition; the fraction of any change in income not consumed is, by definition, saved. Therefore the fraction consumed (MPC) plus the fraction saved (MPS) must exhaust the whole change in income:

$$\text{MPC} + \text{MPS} = 1$$

In our example .75 plus .25 equals 1.

MPC and MPS as Slopes

The MPC is the numerical value of the slope of the consumption schedule, and the MPS is the numerical value of the slope of the saving schedule. We know from the appendix to Chapter 1 that the slope of any line is the ratio of the vertical change to the horizontal change involved in moving from one point to another on that line.

In Figure 9-3 we measure the slopes of the consumption and saving lines, using enlarged portions of Figures 9-2a and 9-2b. Observe that consumption changes by $15 billion (vertical change) for each $20 billion change in disposable income (horizontal change); the slope of the consumption line is thus .75 (= $15/$20)—the value of the MPC. Saving changes by $5 billion (vertical

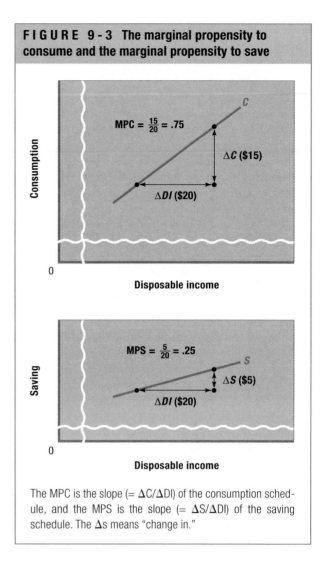

FIGURE 9-3 The marginal propensity to consume and the marginal propensity to save

The MPC is the slope (= ΔC/ΔDI) of the consumption schedule, and the MPS is the slope (= ΔS/ΔDI) of the saving schedule. The Δs means "change in."

change) for every $20 billion change in disposable income (horizontal change). The slope of the saving line therefore is .25 (= $5/$20), which is the value of the MPS. *(Key Question 6)*

Nonincome Determinants of Consumption and Saving

The level of disposable income is the basic determinant of the amounts households will consume and save, just as price is the basic determinant of the quantity demanded of a single product. Recall that changes in determinants other than price, such as consumer tastes and incomes, will shift the demand curve for a product. Similarly, certain determinants other than income might cause households to consume more or less at each possible level of income and thereby change the locations of the consumption and saving schedules. These other determinants are wealth, expectations, indebtedness, and taxation.

Wealth

Generally, the greater the wealth households have accumulated, the larger the amount of consumption and the smaller the amount of saving out of any level of current income. By *wealth* we mean both real assets (a house, automobiles, television sets, and other durables) and financial assets (cash, savings accounts, stocks, bonds, insurance policies, pensions) that households own. Households save—refrain from consumption—to accumulate wealth. The more wealth households have accumulated, the weaker the incentive to save in order to accumulate additional wealth. An increase in wealth thus shifts the saving schedule downward and the consumption schedule upward.

Examples: The dramatic stock market crash of 1929 significantly decreased the financial wealth of many families almost overnight and was a factor in the low levels of consumption in the depressed 1930s. More recently, the general decline in real estate values during 1989 and 1990 eroded household wealth and contributed to a reduction of consumer spending.

For the most part, however, the amount of wealth held by households changes only modestly from year to year and therefore does not account for large shifts in the consumption and saving schedules.

Expectations

Household expectations about future prices, money incomes, and the availability of goods may significantly affect current spending and saving. Expectations of rising prices and product shortages tomorrow may trigger more spending and less saving today. This shifts the consumption schedule upward and the saving schedule downward.

Household Debt

In drawing a particular consumption schedule, we assume that household debt as a percentage of DI is constant. When consumers as a group increase their household debt, they can increase current consumption. Increased borrowing enables consumers to increase consumption at each level of DI; it shifts the consumption schedule upward. However, when levels of household debt get abnormally high, households may elect to reduce their consumption

to pay off some of their loans. At that time, the consumption schedule shifts downward.

Taxation

When we add government to our analysis (Chapter 10), the convenient equality between GDP and DI breaks down. At that stage, we plot consumption and saving against GDP (not DI). You will then see that changes in taxes will shift the consumption and saving schedules. Taxes are paid partly at the expense of consumption and partly at the expense of saving. Therefore, an increase in taxes will shift both the consumption *and* saving schedules downward. Conversely, a tax reduction will be partly consumed and partly saved by households. A tax decrease will shift both the consumption *and* saving schedules upward.

Shifts and Stability

Three final points regarding the consumption and saving schedules are relevant:

1. **TERMINOLOGY** The movement from one point to another on a stable consumption schedule (for example, from *a* to *b* on C_0 in Figure 9-4a) is called a *change in the amount consumed*. The sole cause of this change in consumption is a change in disposable income (or, later, GDP). On the other hand, a *change in the consumption schedule* refers to an upward or downward shift of the entire schedule—for example, a shift from C_0 to C_1 or C_2 in Figure 9-4a. A shift of the consumption schedule is caused by changes in any one or more of the four nonincome determinants just discussed.

    A similar distinction in terminology applies to the saving schedule in Figure 9-4b.

2. **SCHEDULE SHIFTS** The first three nonincome determinants of consumption (wealth, expectations, and household debt) will shift the consumption schedule in one direction and the saving schedule in the opposite direction. If households decide to consume more at each possible level of disposable income, they want to save less, and vice versa. (Even when they spend more by borrowing, they are, in effect, reducing their current saving by the amount borrowed.) Graphically, if the consumption schedule shifts upward from C_0 to C_1 in Figure 9-4, the saving schedule will shift downward, from S_0 to S_1. Similarly, a downshift in the consumption schedule from C_0 to

FIGURE 9-4 Shifts in the (a) consumption and (b) saving schedules

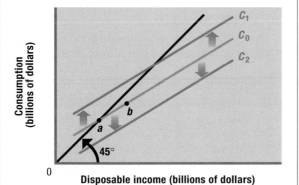

(a) Consumption schedule

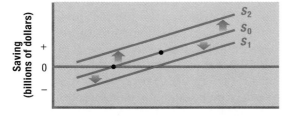

(b) Saving schedule

Normally, if households consume more at each level of DI, they are necessarily saving less. Graphically this means that an upshift of the consumption schedule (C_0 to C_1) entails a downshift of the saving schedule (S_0 to S_1). If households consume less at each level of DI, they are saving more. A downshift of the consumption schedule (C_0 to C_2) is reflected in an upshift of the saving schedule (S_0 to S_2). (This pattern breaks down, however, when increases in consumption result from increased borrowing or when a shift in the consumption schedule results from a change in taxes.)

are quite stable. Only significant increases or decreases in taxes have a major impact on the location of the schedules. Their stability may be because consumption-saving decisions are strongly influenced by *long-term* considerations such as saving to meet emergencies or saving for retirement. It may also be because changes in the nonincome determinants frequently work in opposite directions and therefore may be self-cancelling.

9-2
QUICK REVIEW

- Consumption spending and saving both rise when disposable income increases; they fall when disposable income decreases.

- The average propensity to consume (APC) is the fraction of any specific level of disposable income that is spent on consumer goods; the average propensity to save (APS) is the fraction of any specific level of disposable income that is saved. The APC falls and the APS rises as disposable income increases.

- The marginal propensity to consume (MPC) is the fraction of any change in disposable income that is consumed and is the slope of the consumption schedule; the marginal propensity to save (MPS) is the fraction of any change in disposable income that is saved and is the slope of the saving schedule.

- Changes in consumer wealth, consumer expectations, household debt, and taxes can shift the consumption and saving schedules.

C_2 means an upshift in the saving schedule from S_0 to S_2.

The exception to the above generalization involves the fourth nonincome determinant: taxation. We have seen that households will consume less *and* save less when they must pay higher taxes. Thus, a tax increase will lower both the consumption *and* saving schedules, while a tax cut will shift both schedules upward.

3. **STABILITY** Although changes in nonincome determinants can shift the consumption and saving schedules, in practice these schedules

INVESTMENT

We now turn to investment, the second component of private spending. Recall that investment consists of expenditures on new plants, capital equipment, machinery, and so on. The investment decision is a marginal benefit-marginal cost decision: The marginal benefit from investment is the expected rate of return businesses hope to realize. The marginal cost is the interest rate that must be paid for borrowing funds. We will see that businesses will invest in all projects for which the expected rate of return exceeds the interest rate. Expected returns (profits) and the interest rate therefore are the two basic determinants of investment spending.

Expected Rate of Return

Investment spending is guided by the profit motive; businesses buy capital goods only when they expect such purchases to be profitable. Suppose the owner of a small cabinetmaking shop is considering investing in a new sanding machine costing $1,000 and having a useful life of only one year. The new machine will presumably increase the firm's output and sales revenue. Suppose the *net* expected revenue from the machine (that is, after such operating costs as power, lumber, labour, and certain taxes have been subtracted) is $1,100. Then, after operating costs have been accounted for, the remaining expected net revenue is sufficient to cover the $1,000 cost of the machine and leave a profit of $100. Comparing this $100 profit with the $1,000 cost of the machine, we find that the **expected rate of return**, r, on the machine is 10 percent (= $100/$1,000).

The Real Interest Rate

One important cost associated with investing that our example has so far ignored is interest—the financial cost of borrowing the *money* capital required to purchase the *real* capital (the sanding machine).

To include the interest cost, we note that it is computed by applying the interest rate, i, to the amount borrowed—the cost of the machine. The cost of the machine is the same amount that we used to compute the rate of return, r. Thus, we can generalize as follows: If the expected rate of return (say, 10 percent) exceeds the interest rate (say, 7 percent), the investment will be profitable. But if the interest rate (say, 12 percent) exceeds the expected rate of return (10 percent), the investment will be unprofitable. The firm should undertake all profitable investments projects. That means it should invest to the point where r = i, since then it has undertaken all investment for which r exceeds i.

But what if the firm does *not* borrow, instead financing the investment internally out of funds saved from past profits? The role of the interest rate in investing in real capital does not change. When the firm uses money from savings to invest in the sander, it incurs an opportunity cost because it forgoes the interest income it could have earned by lending the funds to someone else.

The *real* rate of interest, rather than the nominal rate, is crucial in making investment decisions. Recall from Chapter 8 that the nominal interest rate is expressed in dollars of current value, while the real interest rate is stated in dollars of constant or inflation-adjusted value. The real interest rate is the nominal rate less the rate of inflation. In our sanding machine illustration we have implicitly assumed a constant price level so that all our data, including the interest rate, are in real terms.

But what if inflation *is* occurring? Suppose a $1,000 investment is expected to yield a real (inflation-adjusted) rate of return of 10 percent and the nominal interest rate is 15 percent. At first, we would say the investment will be unprofitable. But assume there is ongoing inflation of 10 percent per year. This means the investing firm will pay back dollars with approximately 10 percent less in purchasing power. While the nominal interest rate is 15 percent, the real rate is only 5 percent (= 15 percent − 10 percent). Comparing this 5 percent real interest rate with the 10 percent expected real rate of return, we find that the investment *is* profitable and should be undertaken.

Investment Demand Curve

We now move from a single firm's investment decision to total demand for investment goods by the entire business sector. Assume every firm has estimated the expected rates of return from all investment projects and these data have been collected. The data can be *cumulated*—successively summed—by asking: How many dollars' worth of investment projects have an expected rate of return of, say, 16 percent or more? Of 14 percent or more? Of 12 percent or more? And so on.

Suppose there are no prospective investments yielding an expected return of 16 percent or more. But there are $5 billion of investment opportunities with expected rates of return between 14 and 16 percent; an *additional* $5 billion yielding between 12 and 14 percent; still an *additional* $5 billion yielding between 10 and 12 percent; and an *additional* $5 billion in each successive 2 percent range of yield down to and including the 0 to 2 percent range.

To cumulate these figures for each rate of return, r, we add the amounts of investment that will yield *that particular rate of return* r *or higher*. This way we obtain the data in Table 9-2, shown

TABLE 9-2 Rates of expected return and investment

Expected rate of return, r, (in percent)	Cumulative amount of investment having this rate of return or higher, (billions of dollars per year)
16%	$ 0
14	5
12	10
10	15
8	20
6	25
4	30
2	35
0	40

graphically in *Figure 9-5 (Key Graph)*. In Table 9-2 the number opposite 12 percent, for example, tells us there are $10 billion of investment opportunities that yield an expected rate of return of 12 percent *or more*. The $10 billion includes the $5 billion of investment expected to yield a return of 14 percent or more *plus* the $5 billion expected to yield between 12 and 14 percent.

We know from our example of the sanding machine that an investment project will be profitable, and will be undertaken, if its expected rate of return, r, exceeds the real interest rate, i. Let's first suppose i is 12 percent. Businesses will undertake all investments for which r exceeds 12 percent. That is, they will invest until the 12 percent rate of return equals the 12 percent interest rate. Figure 9-5 reveals that $10 billion of investment spending will be undertaken at a 12 percent interest rate; that means $10 billion of investment projects have an expected rate of return of 12 percent or more.

Put another way: At a financial "price" of 12 percent, $10 billion of investment goods will be demanded. If the interest rate is lower, say, 8 percent, the amount of investment for which r equals or exceeds i is $20 billion. Thus, firms will demand $20 billion of investment goods at an 8 percent real interest rate. At 6 percent, they will demand $25 billion of investment goods.

By applying the marginal-benefit–marginal-cost rule that investment projects should be undertaken up to the point where $r = i$, we see that we can add the real interest rate to the vertical axis in Figure 9-5. The curve in Figure 9-5 not only shows rates of return, it shows the quantity of investment demanded at each "price" i of investment. Various possible real interest rates are shown on the vertical axis in Figure 9-5 and the corresponding quantities of investment demanded on the horizontal axis. The inverse (downsloping) relationship between the interest rate (price) and dollar quantity of investment demanded is consistent with the *law of demand* discussed in Chapter 4. The curve labelled *ID* in Figure 9-5 is the economy's **investment demand curve**. It shows the amount of investment forthcoming at each real interest rate.

This analysis of investment allows us to anticipate an important aspect of macroeconomic policy. You will find in our discussion of monetary policy (Chapter 15) that by changing the supply of money, government can change the interest rate. It does this primarily to change the level of investment spending. At any time, firms have a variety of investment projects under consideration. If real interest rates are high, only projects with the highest expected rates of return will be undertaken. The level of investment will be low. As the real interest rate is lowered, projects whose expected rates of return are less will also become potentially profitable and investment in them will rise. To fight recession, government reduces interest rates; to fight inflation, government increases interest rates. *(Key Question 8)*

Shifts in the Investment Demand Curve

Figure 9-5 portrays the interest-rate–amount-of-investment relationship, *other things equal*. When these other things change, the investment-demand curve shifts to the right or to the left. In general, any factor that leads businesses collectively to expect greater rates of return on their investments will increase investment demand; that factor will shift the investment demand curve to the right, as from ID_0 to ID_1 in Figure 9-6. Any factor that leads businesses collectively to expect lower rates of return on their investments will shift the curve to the left, as from ID_0 to ID_2. What are these non-interest-rate determinants of investment demand?

Acquisition, Maintenance, and Operating Costs

As the sanding machine example revealed, the initial costs of capital goods, and the estimated costs

KEY GRAPH

FIGURE 9-5 The investment demand curve

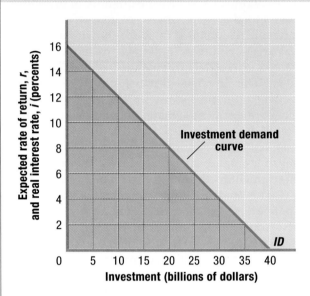

The investment demand curve is constructed by arraying all potential investment projects in descending order of their expected rates of return. The curve is downsloping, reflecting an inverse relationship between the real interest rate (the financial "price" of each dollar of investing) and the quantity of investment demanded.

9-5

QUICK QUIZ

1. The investment demand curve:
   (a) reflects a direct (positive) relationship between the real interest rate and investment.
   (b) reflects an inverse (negative) relationship between the real interest rate and investment.
   (c) shifts to the right when the real interest rate rises.
   (d) shifts to the left when the real interest rate rises.

2. In this figure:
   (a) greater cumulative amounts of investment are associated with lower expected rates of return on investment.
   (b) lesser cumulative amounts of investment are associated with lower expected rates of return on investment.
   (c) higher interest rates are associated with higher expected rates of return on investment, and therefore greater amounts of investment.
   (d) interest rates and investment move in the same direction.

3. In this figure, if the real interest rate falls from 6 to 4 percent:
   (a) investment will increase from 0 to $30 billion.
   (b) investment will decrease by $5 billion.
   (c) the expected rate of return will rise by $5 billion.
   (d) investment will increase from $25 billion to $30 billion.

4. In this figure, investment will be:
   (a) zero if the real interest rate was zero.
   (b) $40 billion if the real interest rate was 16 percent.
   (c) $30 billion if the real interest rate was 4 percent.
   (d) $20 billion if the real interest rate was 12 percent.

Answers: 1. (b); 2. (a); 3. (d); 4. (c)

of operating and maintaining those goods, affect the expected rate of return on investment. When costs fall, the expected rate of return from prospective investment projects will rise, shifting the investment demand curve to the right. Example: Lower electricity costs associated with running equipment would shift the investment demand curve to the right. Higher costs, in contrast, will shift the curve to the left.

Business Taxes   Business owners look to expected returns *after taxes* in making their invest-

ment decisions. An increase in business taxes will lower the expected profitability of investments and shift the investment demand curve to the left; a tax reduction will shift it to the right.

Technological Change   Technological progress—the development of new products, improvements in existing products, and the creation of new machinery and production processes—stimulates investment. The development of a more efficient machine, for example, will lower production costs or improve product quality, increasing the expected

FIGURE 9-6 Shifts in the investment demand curve

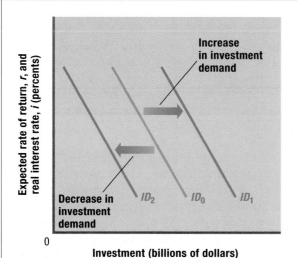

Increases in investment demand are shown as rightward shifts in the investment demand curve; decreases in investment demand are shown as leftward shifts in the investment demand curve.

Expectations We noted that business investment is based on *expected* returns (expected additions to profit). Capital goods are durable; they have a life expectancy of 10 or 20 years. Thus, the expected rate of return on any capital investment will depend on the firm's expectations of *future* sales, *future* operating costs, and *future* profitability of the product that the capital helps to produce. These expectations are based on forecasts of future business conditions as well as on such elusive and difficult-to-predict factors as changes in the domestic political climate, the thrust of foreign affairs, population growth, and consumer tastes. If executives become more optimistic about future sales, costs, and profits, the investment demand curve will shift to the right; a pessimistic outlook will shift it to the left.

Global Perspective 9-2 compares investment spending relative to GDP for several nations in a recent year. Domestic interest rates and investment demand determine the levels of investment relative to GDP.

rate of return from investing in the machine. Profitable new products—mountain bikes, sports utility vehicles, high-resolution televisions, cellular phones, and so on—induce a flurry of investment as firms tool up for expanded production. A rapid rate of technological progress shifts the investment demand curve to the right.

Stock of Capital Goods on Hand The stock of capital goods on hand, relative to output and sales, influences investment decisions by firms. When the economy is *overstocked* with production facilities and firms have excessive inventories of finished goods, the expected rate of return on new investment declines. Firms with excess production capacity have little incentive to invest in new capital. Therefore, less investment is forthcoming at each real interest rate; the investment demand curve shifts to the left.

When the economy is *understocked* with production facilities and firms are selling their output as fast as it can be produced, the expected rate of return on new investment increases. Firms add to their production facilities to meet the growing demand for their products and services. So the investment demand curve shifts to the right.

9-2

GLOBAL PERSPECTIVE

Gross investment expenditures as a percentage of GDP, selected nations

As a percentage of GDP, investment varies widely by nations. These differences, of course, can change from year to year.

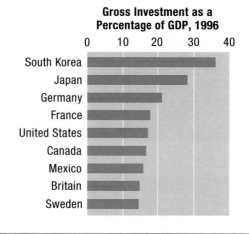

Source: Organization for Economic Cooperation and Development.

9-3

QUICK REVIEW

- A specific investment will be undertaken if the expected rate of return, r, equals or exceeds the real interest rate, i.

- The investment demand curve shows the total monetary amounts that will be invested by an economy at various possible real interest rates.

- The investment demand curve shifts when changes occur in **a** the costs of acquiring, operating, and maintaining capital goods, **b** business taxes, **c** technology, **d** the stock of capital goods on hand, and **e** business expectations.

Investment Schedule

To add the investment decisions of businesses to the consumption plans of households, we must express investment plans in terms of the level of disposable income (DI) or gross domestic product (GDP). That is, we need to construct an **investment schedule** showing the amounts business firms collectively intend to invest at each possible level of GDP. Such a schedule represents the investment plans of businesses in the same way the consumption and saving schedules represent the consumption and saving plans of households. In developing the investment schedule, we will assume that investment is *independent* of the level of current disposable income or real output.

Suppose the investment demand curve is as shown in Figure 9-7a and the current real interest rate is 8 percent. This means that firms will find it profitable to spend $20 billion on investment goods. Our assumption tells us that this $20 billion of investment will occur at both low and high levels of GDP. The line I_g (*gross* investment) in Figure 9-7b shows this graphically; it is the economy's *investment schedule*. You should not confuse this investment schedule I_g with the investment demand curve *ID* in Figure 9-7a. The investment schedule shows the amount of investment forthcoming at each level of GDP. As indicated in Figure 9-7, this amount ($20 billion) is determined by the interest rate together with the location of the investment demand curve. Table 9-3 shows the investment schedule in tabular form for the GDP levels in Table 9-1.

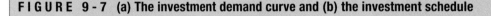

FIGURE 9-7 (a) The investment demand curve and (b) the investment schedule

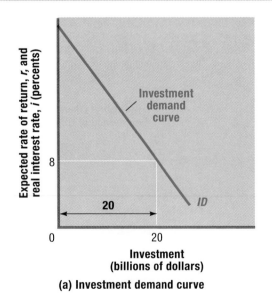
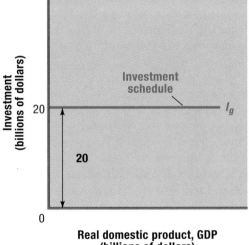

(a) Investment demand curve

(b) Investment schedule

(a) The level of investment spending (here, $20 billion) is determined by the real interest rate (here, 8 percent), together with the investment demand curve *ID*. (b) The investment schedule I_g relates the amount of investment ($20 billion) determined in (a) to the various levels of GDP.

TABLE 9-3 The investment schedule (in billions)

(1) Level of real output and income	(2) Investment (I_g)
$370	$20
390	20
410	20
430	20
450	20
470	20
490	20
510	20
530	20
550	20

The assumed independence of investment and income is admittedly a simplification. A higher level of business activity may *induce* additional spending on capital facilities for at least two reasons:

1. Investment is related to profit; much investment is financed internally out of business profits. Therefore, it is plausible that as GDP rises, so will business profits and therefore the level of investment.
2. At low levels of income and output, the business sector has excess production capacity; many industries have idle machinery and equipment and therefore little incentive to purchase additional capital goods. But, as the level of domestic income and output rises, this excess capacity disappears and firms are inclined to add to their stock of capital goods.

Instability of Investment

In contrast to the consumption schedule, the investment schedule is unstable; it shifts significantly upward or downward quite often. Investment, in fact, is the most volatile component of total spending. Figure 9-8 shows just how volatile investment has been. Note that its swings are much greater than are those of GDP. The figure also suggests that our simplified treatment of investment as independent of GDP (Figure 9-7b) is essentially realistic; investment does not closely follow GDP.

Factors explaining the variability of investment follow:

Durability Because of their durability, capital goods have an indefinite useful life. Within limits, purchases of capital goods are discretionary and therefore postponable. Older equipment and buildings can be scrapped and replaced, or they can be patched up and used for a few more years. Optimism about the future may prompt firms to replace their older facilities; modernizing their plants will call for a high level of investment. A less optimistic view, however, may lead to very small amounts of investment as older facilities are repaired and kept in use.

Irregularity of Innovation We know that technological progress is a major determinant of investment. New products and processes stimulate investment. But history suggests that major innovations—railroads, electricity, automobiles, fibre optics, and computers—occur quite irregularly. When they do occur they induce a vast upsurge or "wave" of investment spending that in time recedes.

A classic illustration is the widespread acceptance of the automobile in the 1920s. This event not only substantially increased investment in the automobile industry itself but also induced tremendous investment in such related industries as steel, petroleum, glass, and rubber as well as public investment in streets and highways. But when investment in these related industries was ultimately "completed"—when enough capital facilities had been created to meet the needs of the automobile industry—total investment levelled off.

Variability of Profits Businesses invest only when they think it will be profitable, and to a significant degree, the expectation of future profitability is influenced by the size of current profits. Current profits, however, are themselves highly variable (line 16 of the table at the back of this book provides information on undistributed corporate profits). Thus, the variability of profits contributes to the volatile nature of the incentive to invest.

The instability of profits may also cause investment fluctuations in a second way. Profits are a major source of funds for business investment. Canadian businesses often prefer this internal source of financing to increases in external debt or stock issue.

FIGURE 9-8 The volatility of investment

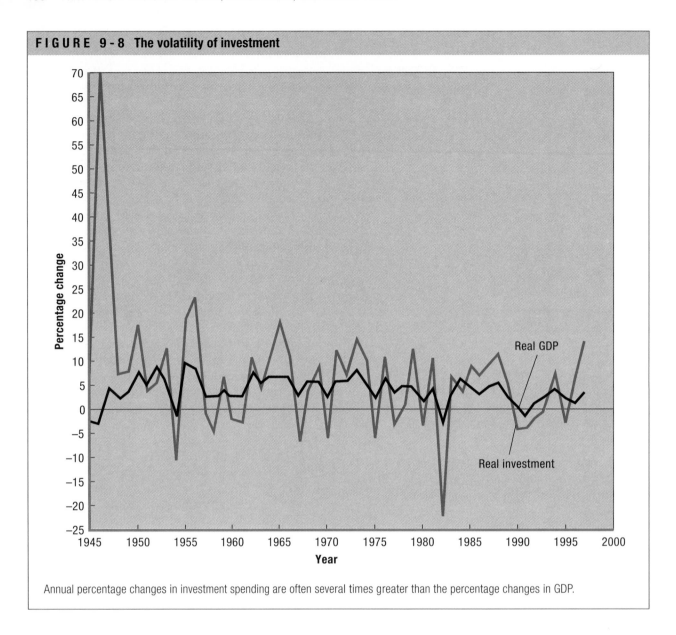

Annual percentage changes in investment spending are often several times greater than the percentage changes in GDP.

In short, expanding profits give firms both greater *incentives* and greater *means* to invest; declining profits have the reverse effects. The fact that actual profits are variable thus adds doubly to the instability of investment.

Variability of Expectations Firms tend to project current business conditions into the future. But their expectations can change radically and quickly when some event suggests a possible dramatic change in future business conditions. Changes in the domestic political climate, changes in exchange rates, changes in the outlook for international peace, court decisions in key labour or antitrust cases, legislative actions, changes in trade barriers, changes in governmental economic policies, and a host of similar considerations may cause substantial shifts in business optimism or pessimism.

The stock market requires specific comment in this regard. Firms frequently look to the stock market as an indicator of society's overall confidence in future business conditions. Rising stock prices signify public confidence in the business future, while falling stock prices imply a lack of confidence. The stock market, however, is highly speculative. Participants who jump in and buy when stock prices begin to rise, or sell as soon as prices start to fall, can seriously magnify initially modest changes in stock prices. The volatility of this market can produce swings in optimism and pessimism, thus adding to the instability of investment spending. This stock market effect on investment, however, has proved to be relatively mild in the past several decades.

For the reasons we just discussed, changes in investment cause most fluctuations in output and employment. We can think of the volatility of investment shown in Figure 9-8 as being reflected in occasional and substantial upward and downward shifts of the investment schedule in Figure 9-7b, caused by occasional and substantial rightward and leftward shifts of the *investment demand curve* in Figure 9-7a.

EQUILIBRIUM GDP: EXPENDITURES-OUTPUT APPROACH

In this and the next section, we use the consumption, saving, and investment schedules to explain the equilibrium levels of output, income, and employment. We will do so first by taking the

aggregate expenditures-domestic output (or $C + I_g$ = GDP) **approach**.

Tabular Analysis

Columns 2 through 5 in Table 9-4 repeat the consumption and saving schedules in Table 9-1 and the investment schedule in Table 9-3.

Real Domestic Output Let's look again at column 2, Table 9-4. It lists the various possible levels of total output—of real GDP—that the business sector might produce. *Producers are willing to offer any of these 10 levels of output if they can expect to receive an identical level of income from the sale of that output.* For example, the business sector will produce $370 billion of output, incurring $370 billion of costs (wages, rents, interest, and profit) only if firms believe they can sell this output for $370 billion. Some $390 billion of output will be offered for sale if firms think they can sell this output for $390 billion. And so it is for all the other possible levels of output.

Aggregate Expenditures In our assumed closed economy in Table 9-4, aggregate expenditures consist of consumption (column 3) plus investment

TABLE 9-4 Determination of the equilibrium levels of employment, output, and income: a closed private economy

(1) Possible levels of employment, millions	(2) Real domestic output (and income) (GDP = DI),* billions	(3) Consumption (C), billions	(4) Saving (S), billions	(5) Investment (I_g), billions	(6) Aggregate expenditures (C + I_g), billions	(7) Unintended investment (+) or disinvestment (−) in inventories	(8) Tendency of employment, output, and incomes
(1) 40	$370	$375	$−5	$20	$395	$−25	Increase
(2) 45	390	390	0	20	410	−20	Increase
(3) 50	410	405	5	20	425	−15	Increase
(4) 55	430	420	10	20	440	−10	Increase
(5) 60	450	435	15	20	455	−5	Increase
(6) 65	470	450	20	20	470	0	Equilibrium
(7) 70	490	465	25	20	485	+5	Decrease
(8) 75	510	480	30	20	500	+10	Decrease
(9) 80	530	495	35	20	515	+15	Decrease
(10) 85	550	510	40	20	530	+20	Decrease

*If depreciation is zero, government is ignored, and it is assumed that all saving occurs in the household sector of the economy, GDP as a measure of domestic output is equal to PI and DI. This means that households receive a DI equal to the value of total output.

(column 5). Their sum is shown in column 6, which with column 2 makes up the **aggregate expenditures schedule** for the economy. This schedule shows the amount $(C + I_g)$ that will be spent at each possible output or income level.

At this point we are working with *planned investment*—the data in column 5, Table 9-4. These data show the amounts firms intend to invest, not the amounts which *actually will be invested* if there are unplanned changes in inventories.

Equilibrium GDP

Of the 10 possible levels of GDP in Table 9-4, which will be the equilibrium level? Which total output will the economy be capable of sustaining?

The equilibrium output is that output whose production will create total spending just sufficient to purchase that output. So the equilibrium level of GDP is the level where the total quantity of goods produced (GDP) equals the total quantity of goods purchased $(C + I_g)$. Look at the domestic output levels in column 2 and the aggregate expenditures levels in column 6 and you will see that this equality exists only at $470 billion of GDP (row 6). That is the only output at which spending precisely equals the amount necessary to take that output from the shelves. There, the annual rates of production and spending are in balance. There is no overproduction, which would result in a piling up of unsold goods and therefore cutbacks in the production rate. Nor is there an excess of total spending, which would draw down inventories of goods and prompt increases in the rate of production. In short, there is no reason for businesses to alter this rate of production; $470 billion is therefore the **equilibrium GDP**.

Disequilibrium

To better understand the meaning of the equilibrium level of GDP, let's examine other levels of GDP to see why they cannot be sustained.

If businesses produced $410 billion of GDP (row 3 in Table 9-4), they would find that this output yields $405 billion in consumer spending. Supplemented by $20 billion of planned investment, total expenditures $(C + I_g)$ would be $425 billion, as shown in column 6. The economy would provide an annual rate of spending more than sufficient to purchase the $410 billion of annual production. Because buyers would be taking goods off the shelves faster than firms could produce them, an unintended decline in business inventories of $15 billion would occur (column 7)

if this situation continued. But businesses can adjust to such an imbalance between aggregate expenditures and real output by stepping up production. Greater output will increase employment and total income. In brief, if aggregate expenditures exceed the domestic output, those expenditures will drive domestic output upward.

We can make a similar comparison of GDP (column 2) and $C + I_g$ (column 6) at any other level of GDP *below* the $470 billion equilibrium level. In each case we will find that spending is in excess of the level at which businesses are willing to produce. The excess of total spending at all these levels of GDP will drive GDP upward to the $470 billion equilibrium level.

The reverse is true at all levels of GDP *above* the $470 billion equilibrium level. Businesses will find that these total outputs fail to generate the spending needed to clear the shelves of goods. Being unable to recover their costs, businesses will cut back on production.

To illustrate: At the $510 billion output (row 8), business managers would find there is insufficient spending to permit the sale of all that output. Of the $510 billion of income that this output creates, $480 billion would be received back by businesses as consumption spending. Though supplemented by $20 billion of planned investment spending, total expenditures ($500 billion) would fall $10 billion short of the $510 billion quantity produced. If this imbalance persisted, $10 billion of inventories would pile up (column 7). But businesses can adjust to this unintended accumulation of unsold goods by cutting back on the rate of production. The resulting decline in output would mean fewer jobs and a decline in total income. You should verify that all other levels of GDP above the $470 billion equilibrium level would also result in insufficient spending.

The equilibrium level of GDP occurs where the total output, measured by GDP, and aggregate expenditures, $C + I_g$ are equal. Any excess of total spending over total output will drive GDP upward. Any deficiency of total spending will pull GDP downward.

Graphical Analysis

The same analysis can be shown in a graph. In *Figure 9-9 (Key Graph)* the **45-degree line** now takes on increased significance. Recall that the special property of this line is that at any point on it, the value of what is being measured on the horizontal

KEY GRAPH

FIGURE 9-9 The aggregate expenditures-domestic output approach to equilibrium GDP

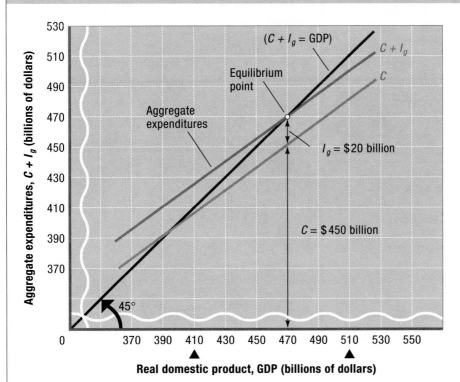

The aggregate expenditures schedule, $C + I_g$, is determined by adding the investment schedule I_g to the upsloping consumption schedule C. Since investment is assumed to be the same at each level of GDP, the vertical distances between C and $C + I_g$ do not change. Equilibrium GDP is determined where the aggregate expenditures schedule intersects the 45-degree line, in this case at $470 billion.

9-9
QUICK QUIZ

1. In this figure, the slope of the aggregate expenditures schedule $C + I_g$:
   (a) increases as real GDP increases.
   (b) falls as real GDP increases.
   (c) is constant and equals the MPC.
   (d) is constant and equals the MPS.

2. At all points on the 45 degree line:
   (a) equilibrium GDP is possible.
   (b) aggregate expenditures exceed real GDP.
   (c) consumption exceeds investment.
   (d) aggregate expenditures are less than real GDP.

3. The $490 billion level of real GDP is *not* at equilibrium because:
   (a) investment exceeds consumption.
   (b) consumption exceeds investment.
   (c) planned $C + I_g$ exceeds real GDP.
   (d) planned $C + I_g$ is less than real GDP.

4. The $430 billion level of real GDP is *not* at equilibrium because:
   (a) investment exceeds consumption.
   (b) consumption exceeds investment.
   (c) planned $C + I_g$ exceeds real GDP.
   (d) planned $C + I_g$ is less than real GDP.

Answers: 1. (c); 2. (a); 3. (d); 4. (c).

axis (in this case GDP) is equal to the value of what is being measured on the vertical axis (here, aggregate expenditures or $C + I_g$). Having discovered in our tabular analysis that the equilibrium level of domestic output is determined where $C + I_g$ equals GDP, we can say that the 45-degree line in

Figure 9-9 is a graphical statement of this equilibrium condition.

Now we must graph the aggregate expenditures schedule onto Figure 9-9. One way to do this is to duplicate the consumption schedule C in Figure 9-2a and add to it *vertically* the constant $20 bil-

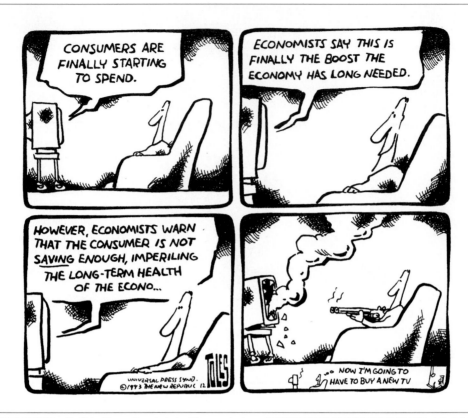

Source: TOLES © 1993 The Buffalo News. Reprinted with permission of UNIVERSAL PRESS SYNDICATE. All rights reserved.

lion amount of investment I_g from Figure 9-7b. This $20 billion is the amount we assumed firms plan to invest at all levels of GDP. Or, more directly, we can plot the $C + I_g$ data in column 6, Table 9-4.

Observe in Figure 9-9 that the aggregate expenditures line $C + I_g$ shows that total spending rises with income and output (GDP), but not as much as income rises, because the marginal propensity to consume—the slope of line C—is less than 1. A part of any increase in income will not be spent; it will be saved. And because the aggregate expenditures line $C + I_g$ is parallel to the consumption line C, the slope of the aggregate expenditures line also equals the MPC for the economy and is less than 1. For our particular data, aggregate expenditures rise by $15 billion for every $20 billion increase in real output and income because $5 billion of each $20 billion increment is saved. Therefore, in numerical terms the slope of the aggregate expenditures line is .75 (= Δ $15/Δ$20).

The equilibrium GDP is the GDP that corresponds to the intersection of the aggregate expenditures sched- *ule and the 45-degree line.* This intersection locates the only point at which aggregate expenditures (on the vertical axis) are equal to GDP (on the horizontal axis). Because Figure 9-9 is based on the data in Table 9-4, we once again find that equilibrium output is $470 billion. Observe that consumption at this output is $450 billion and investment is $20 billion.

It is evident from Figure 9-9 that no levels of GDP above the equilibrium level are sustainable because at those levels $C + I_g$ falls short of GDP. Graphically, the aggregate expenditures schedule lies *below* the 45-degree line in those situations. At the $510 billion GDP level, for example, $C + I_g$ is only $500 billion. This underspending causes inventories to rise, prompting firms to readjust production downward in the direction of the $470 billion output level.

Conversely, at levels of GDP below $470 billion, spending is in excess of what businesses are producing. Then $C + I_g$ exceeds total output. Graphically, the aggregate expenditures schedule lies *above* the 45-degree line. At the $410 billion GDP level, for example, $C + I_g$ totals $425 billion. This overspending causes inventories to decline, prompting firms to raise production towards the $470 billion GDP. Unless there is some change in the location of the aggregate expenditures line, the $470 billion level of GDP will be sustained indefinitely.

EQUILIBRIUM GDP: LEAKAGES-INJECTIONS APPROACH

The expenditures-output approach to determining GDP spotlights aggregate expenditures as the immediate determinant of the levels of output and income. Though the **leakages-injections** ($S = I_g$) **approach** is less direct, it does have the advantage of underscoring the *reason* $C + I_g$ and GDP are unequal at all levels of output except the equilibrium level.

The idea of the leakages-injections approach is this: Under our simplifying assumptions we know that the production of any level of real output will generate an identical amount of disposable income. But we also know a part of that income may be saved—*not* consumed—by households. Saving therefore represents a **leakage** or withdrawal of spending from the income-expenditures stream. Saving is what keeps consumption short of total output or GDP; as a result of saving, consumption by itself is insufficient to take all domestic output off the shelves, setting the stage, it would seem, for a decline in total output.

However, the business sector does not intend to sell its entire output to consumers; some domestic output will consist of capital goods sold within the business sector. Investment can therefore be thought of as an **injection** of spending into the income-expenditures stream; investment is a supplement to consumption. Investment is thus a potential replacement for the leakage of saving.

If, at a certain level of GDP, the leakage of saving exceeds the injection of investment, then $C + I_g$ will fall short of GDP and that level of GDP is too high to be sustained. Any GDP for which saving exceeds investment is an above-equilibrium GDP. Conversely, if the injection of investment exceeds the leakage of saving, then $C + I_g$ will be greater than GDP and GDP will be driven upward. Any GDP for which investment exceeds saving is a below-equilibrium GDP.

Only where $S = I_g$—where the leakage of saving is exactly offset by the injection of investment—will aggregate expenditures equal real output. And that equality is what defines the equilibrium GDP.

In the closed economy assumed here, there is a single leakage (saving) and a single injection (investment). In more general terms, a *leakage* is any use of income other than to purchase domestically produced output. In the expanded models that follow (in Chapter 10), we will need to incorporate the additional leakages of imports and taxes into our analysis.

Similarly, an *injection* is any supplement to consumer spending on domestic production. Again, in later models we will add injections of exports and government purchases to our discussion. But for now we need only compare the single leakage of saving with the sole injection of investment to obtain the equilibrium GDP.

Tabular Analysis

Our $C + I_g$ = GDP approach has led us to conclude that, in our example, all levels of GDP less than $470 billion are unstable. That is true because then $C + I_g$ exceeds GDP, which drives GDP upward. Now let's look at the saving schedule (columns 2 and 4) and the investment schedule (columns 2 and 5) in Table 9-4. Comparing the amounts households and firms want to save and invest at GDP levels *below* $470 billion explains the excesses of total spending. At each of these lower GDP levels, firms plan to invest more than households want to save.

For example, at a GDP of $410 billion (row 3), households will save only $5 billion but businesses will invest $20 billion. Hence, investment exceeds saving by $15 billion (= $20 – $5). Columns 6 and 2 show that aggregate expenditures exceed GDP by that same $15 billion (= $425 – $410). The small leakage of saving at this relatively low income level is more than compensated for by the larger injection of investment spending, which causes $C + I_g$ to exceed GDP and drives GDP higher.

In contrast, all levels of GDP *above* $470 billion are unstable because they exceed $C + I_g$. The reason for this insufficient spending is that at all GDP levels above $470 billion, households want to save more than firms plan to invest. The saving leakage is not compensated for by the injection of investment.

For example, households will save $30 billion at a GDP of $510 billion (row 8). Firms, however, will plan to invest only $20 billion. This $10 billion excess of saving over planned investment will reduce total spending to $10 billion below the value of total output. Specifically, aggregate expenditures will be $500 billion and real GDP is $510 billion. This spending deficiency will reduce GDP.

Again we verify that the equilibrium GDP is $470 billion. At this level of GDP, the saving desires of households and the investment plans of businesses are the same ($20 billion each). When firms and households attempt to invest and save the same amounts—where leakages equal injections—aggregate expenditures will equal GDP. Here, there will be no unplanned changes in inventories.

Graphical Analysis

The leakages-injections approach to determining equilibrium GDP is demonstrated in Figure 9-10, in which we have again graphed the saving schedule in Figure 9-2b and the investment schedule in 9-7b. The numerical data for these schedules are in columns 2, 4, and 5, Table 9-4. The two lines S and I_g intersect at the equilibrium GDP, $470 billion. Only here do businesses and households plan to invest and save the same amounts; only here will GDP and $C + I_g$ be the same.

At higher levels of GDP, households will save more than businesses plan to invest. Because the saving leakage will exceed the investment injection, $C + I_g$ will fall short of GDP, driving GDP downward. At the $510 billion GDP, for example, saving of $30 billion will exceed investment of $20 billion by $10 billion, with the result that $C + I_g$ will be $10 billion short of GDP.

At all levels of GDP below the $470 billion equilibrium level, businesses will plan to invest more than households save. Because the injection of investment will exceed the leakage of saving, $C + I_g$ will exceed GDP, driving GDP upward. To illustrate: At the $410 billion level of GDP the $5 billion leakage of saving is more than compensated for by the $20 billion that businesses plan to invest. The result is that $C + I_g$ will exceed GDP by $15 billion. *(Key Question 10)*

PLANNED VERSUS ACTUAL INVESTMENT

We have seen that differences between saving and investment can occur and bring about changes in the equilibrium GDP. Now we must emphasize that, in another sense, saving and investment are always equal. This apparent contradiction concerning the equality of saving and investment is resolved when we distinguish between **planned investment** and saving (which need not be equal) and **actual investment** and saving (which by definition must be equal). The catch is that *actual investment consists of planned investment and*

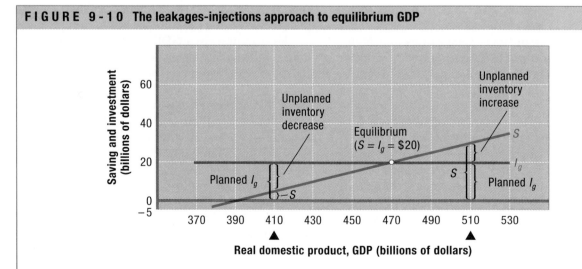

FIGURE 9-10 The leakages-injections approach to equilibrium GDP

In this approach, the equilibrium GDP is determined by the intersection of the saving (S) and planned investment (I_g) schedules. Only at that point will households plan to save the amount businesses want to invest. At other, nonequilibrium GDPs, overspending or underspending will result in unplanned inventory changes.

unplanned investment (unplanned changes in inventory investment). Unplanned investment acts as a balancing item that equates the actual amounts saved and invested in any period.

Disequilibrium and Inventories

Consider, as an example, the $490 billion above-equilibrium GDP (row 7 in Table 9-4). What happens if businesses produce this output, thinking they can sell it? At this level, households save $25 billion of their $490 billion DI, so consumption is only $465 billion. *Planned* investment (column 5) is $20 billion; businesses intend to buy $20 billion worth of capital goods. This means aggregate expenditures $(C + I_g)$ are $485 billion, and sales therefore fall short of production by $5 billion. This extra $5 billion of goods is retained by businesses as an *unintended* or *unplanned* increase in inventories (column 7). It is unintended because it results from the failure of total spending to take total output off the shelves. Remembering that, by definition, changes in inventories are a part of investment, we note that *actual* investment is $25 billion ($20 planned *plus* $5 unintended or unplanned). It exactly equals the saving of $25 billion, even though saving exceeds *planned* investment by $5 billion. Since firms cannot earn profits by accumulating unwanted inventories, they will cut back production.

Now look at the below-equilibrium $450 billion output (row 5, Table 9-4). Because households save only $15 billion of their $450 billion DI, consumption is $435 billion. Planned investment by firms is $20 billion, so aggregate expenditures are $455 billion. Sales exceed production by $5 billion. This is so only if an unplanned decrease in business inventories occurs. Firms must unintentionally *dis*invest $5 billion in inventories (column 7). Note again that actual investment is $15 billion ($20 planned minus $5 unplanned) and equal to saving of $15 billion, even though planned investment exceeds saving by $5 billion. The decline in inventories from the excess of sales over production will induce firms to expand production.

Once again: At all *above-equilibrium* GDPs (where saving exceeds planned investment), actual investment and saving are made equal by unintended increases in inventories that are added to planned investment. In Figure 9-9, the vertical distance of the saving schedule above the (planned) investment schedule I_g represents an unintended inventory increase.

At all *below-equilibrium* GDPs (where planned investment exceeds saving), actual investment is made equal to saving by unintended decreases in inventories, which are subtracted from planned investment. An unintended inventory decrease is shown graphically as the vertical distance of the (planned) investment schedule above the saving schedule.

Attainment of Equilibrium

These distinctions are important because they mean that it is the equality of planned investment and saving that determines the equilibrium level of GDP. We can think of the process by which equilibrium is achieved as follows:

1. A difference between saving and planned investment creates a difference between the production and spending plans of the economy as a whole.

2. The difference between production plans and spending plans results in unintended investment or disinvestment in inventories.

3. As long as unintended investment in inventories persists, firms will revise their production plans downward and reduce GDP. Conversely, as long as unintended disinvestment in inventories exists, firms will revise their production plans upward and increase GDP. Both GDP movements are towards equilibrium because they bring about the equality of planned investment and saving.

4. GDP will reach equilibrium when planned investment and saving are equal. At that GDP, there is no unintended investment or disinvestment in inventories to drive GDP upward or downward. *(Key Question 11)*

9-4
QUICK REVIEW

- In a private closed economy, equilibrium GDP occurs where aggregate expenditures equal real domestic output $(C + I_g = GDP)$.

- Alternatively, equilibrium GDP is established where saving equals planned investment $(S = I_g)$.

- Actual investment consists of planned investment plus unplanned changes in inventories and is always equal to saving in a private closed economy.

- At equilibrium GDP, changes in inventories are zero; no unintended investment or disinvestment occurs.

In The Media

Consumer confidence at nine-year high

From Alberta's oil patch to Newfoundland's Hibernia, the economy is humming and people are spending—on homes, cars and sheer pleasure. But in B.C., the recovery's already a memory.

BY MIRO CERNETIG,
VANCOUVER
BRUCE LITTLE, TORONTO
BRIAN LAGHI, EDMONTON

Need proof that the national economy is sizzling this Christmas? Go no farther than Bloor Street West, Toronto's chi-chi shopping district, where the good times are rolling and conspicuous consumption is most definitely back in vogue.

In Secrett, the custom jeweller catering to high-end indulgences, the rich are on a spending spree. The store's $10,000 sapphire-and-diamond bracelets, sets of $15,000 diamond earrings and $8,000 onyx panther sculptures—and things worth much, much more—are leaving the glass display cases faster than they have since, well, the greedy eighties.

"I'm pretty confident our sales will exceed the Christmas of '89," owner Terry Wilson said.

"What's been selling is the high-end things."

However, diamond sales on Toronto's Bloor Street are by no means an indicator of prosperity in every pocket of the country. Ask the residents of Prince Rupert, B.C., who are watching their pulp mill close and the fishing plants go belly-up, and people in other parts of British Columbia, where the boom is now a memory.

Nevertheless, wherever you happen to live, there is no escaping that Ontario still represents 40 per cent of the national economy. And after years of trying to get back on its feet after the battering it took in the early 1990s, it is finally beginning to run again. The auto industry is heading for its best production year, and Ontarians are beginning to spend the money they got from provincial income-tax cuts.

So when the gemstones start moving this quickly on Bloor

Street, it's a sign that the country's larger economic turbine is humming—at least for now. Indeed, there's no sign of a Canada-wide recession on the horizon.

Many sectors of the disparate economy seem to be faring well going into 1998: Calgary's oil patch is awash in petrobucks; Alberta's real estate, even Edmonton's, is finally coming back as billions of dollars are pumped into the tarsands projects to the north. Newfoundlanders are brimming with renewed confidence, with the dream of Hibernia crude now a reality, gushing out at the rate of 45,000 barrels a day.

It boils down to one fact: Money is on the move at a terrific clip mainly because consumer and business spending has been on a tear for the past year.

Source: *Globe and Mail*, December 20, 1997, A1. Reprinted with permission from the *Globe and Mail*.

THE STORY IN BRIEF

Canadians are optimistic about the economy and are showing it by spending more on goods and services.

THE ECONOMICS BEHIND THE STORY

- We know that as income rises, consumers spend more—we move along the consumption schedule.
- But the story also suggests that the consumption schedule is shifting up in many parts of Canada. In

Ontario, a provincial income-tax cut has spurred consumption. Expectations about the future performance of the Canadian economy are positive, leading many Canadians to open their wallets and spend.

- Not every part of the Canadian economy is doing well. British Columbia's economy is not expanding at the same rate as in many other parts of Canada, and consumers in that province are not spending at the same levels as other Canadians.
- Increased consumption is helping the Canadian economy grow. What other expenditures category does the article mention is also increasing? ∎

The
Last Word

JOHN MAYNARD KEYNES (1883–1946)

The English economist John Maynard Keynes is regarded as the originator of modern macroeconomics.

IN 1935 GEORGE BERNARD SHAW RECEIVED A letter from John Maynard Keynes in which Keynes asserted, "I believe myself to be writing a book on economic theory which will largely revolutionize ... the way the world thinks about economic problems." And, in fact, Keynes's *The General Theory of Employment, Interest, and Money* did revolutionize economic analysis and established Keynes as one of the most influential economists of all time.

The son of an eminent English economist, Keynes was educated at Eton and Cambridge. While his early interests were in mathematics and probability theory, Keynes ultimately turned to economics.

Keynes was far more than an economist: He was an incredibly active, many-sided man who also played such diverse roles as principal representative of the Treasury at the World War I Paris Peace Conference, deputy for the Chancellor of the Exchequer, a director of the Bank of England, trustee of the National Gallery, chairman of the Council for the Encouragement of Music and the Arts, bursar of King's College, Cambridge, editor of the *Economic Journal*, chairman of the *Nation* and later the *New Statesman* magazines, and chairman of the National Mutual Life Assurance Society. He also ran an investment company, organized the Camargo Ballet (his wife, Lydia Lopokova, was a renowned star of the Russian Imperial Ballet), and built (profitably) the Arts Theatre at Cambridge.*

*E. Ray Canterbery, *The Making of Economics*, 3d ed. (Belmont, Calif.: Wadsworth Publishing Company, 1987), p. 126.

In addition, Keynes found time to amass a $2-million personal fortune by speculating in stocks, international currencies, and commodities. He was also a leading figure in the "Bloomsbury group," an *avant-garde* group of intellectual luminaries who greatly influenced the artistic and literary standards of England.

Most importantly, Keynes was a prolific scholar. His books encompassed such widely ranging topics as probability theory, monetary economics, and the economic consequences of the World War I peace treaty. His *magnum opus*, however, was the *General Theory*, which has been described by John Kenneth Galbraith as "a work of profound obscurity, badly written and prematurely published." Yet the *General Theory* attacked the classical economists' contention that recession will automatically cure itself. Keynes's analysis suggested that recession could easily spiral downward into a depression. Keynes claimed that modern capitalism contained no automatic mechanism that would propel the economy back towards full employment. The economy might languish for many years in depression. Indeed, the massive unemployment of the worldwide depression of the 1930s seemed to provide sufficient evidence that Keynes was right. His basic policy recommendation—a startling one in view of the balanced-budget sentiment at the time—was for government in these circumstances to increase its spending to induce more production and put the unemployed back to work. ■

CHAPTER SUMMARY

1. Classical economists argued that because supply creates its own demand (Say's law), general underspending was improbable. Thus the economy would provide virtually continuous full employment. Even if temporary declines in total spending occurred, these declines would be compensated for by downward price and wage adjustments that would boost spending and employment, restoring the economy to its full-employment level of output.

2. The Great Depression and Keynes's *General Theory of Employment, Interest, and Money* undermined classical macroeconomics. The Great Depression challenged the classical precept that full employment was the norm in a capitalist economy. Keynes's aggregate expenditures analysis showed how periods of underspending or overspending could occur.

3. The basic tools of the aggregate expenditures model are the consumption, saving, and investment schedules, which show the various amounts households intend to consume and save and firms plan to invest at the various income and output levels, assuming a fixed price level.

4. The *average* propensities to consume and save show the fractions of any *total* income that are consumed and saved; APC + APS = 1. The *marginal* propensities to consume and save show the fractions of any *change* in total income that are consumed and saved; MPC + MPS = 1.

5. The locations of the consumption and saving schedules are determined by **a** the amount of wealth owned by households; **b** expectations of future income, future prices, and product availability; **c** the relative size of household debt; and **d** taxation. The consumption and saving schedules are relatively stable.

6. The immediate determinants of investment are **a** the expected rate of return and **b** the real rate of interest. The economy's investment demand curve can be found by cumulating investment projects, arraying them in descending order according to their expected rates of return, graphing the result, and applying the rule that investment will be profitable up to the point at which the real interest rate, *i*, equals the expected rate of return, *r*. The investment demand curve reveals an inverse relationship between the interest rate and the level of aggregate investment.

7. Shifts in the investment demand curve can occur as the result of changes in **a** the acquisition, maintenance, and operating costs of capital goods; **b** business taxes; **c** technology; **d** the stocks of capital goods on hand; and **e** expectations.

8. For simplicity we assume that the level of investment determined by the current interest rate and the investment demand curve does not vary with the level of real GDP.

9. The durability of capital goods, the irregular occurrence of major innovations, profit volatility, and the variability of expectations all contribute to the instability of investment spending.

10. For a closed economy the equilibrium level of GDP occurs when aggregate expenditures and real output are equal or, graphically, where the $C + I_g$ line intersects the 45-degree line. At any GDP greater than equilibrium GDP, real output will exceed aggregate spending, resulting in unintended investment in inventories, and eventual declines in output and income (GDP). At any below-equilibrium GDP, aggregate expenditures will exceed real output, resulting in unintended disinvestment in inventories and eventual increases in GDP.

11. The leakages-injections approach determines equilibrium GDP at the point where the amount households save and the amount businesses plan to invest are equal. This is the point where the saving and planned investment schedules intersect. Any excess of saving over planned investment will cause a shortage of total spending, forcing GDP to fall. Any excess of planned investment over saving will cause an excess of total spending, inducing GDP to rise. The change in GDP will in both cases correct the discrepancy between saving and planned investment.

12. Actual investment consists of planned investment plus unplanned changes in inventories. When planned investment diverges from saving, an unintended investment or disinvestment in inventories occurs that equates actual investment and saving. At equilibrium GDP, planned investment equals saving; inventory levels are then constant (there is no unplanned investment or disinvestment).

TERMS AND CONCEPTS

Say's law
Keynesian economics
consumption schedule
saving schedule
break-even income
average propensity to consume
average propensity to save
marginal propensity to consume
marginal propensity to save
expected rate of return
investment demand curve

investment schedule
aggregate expenditures—domestic output approach
aggregate expenditures schedule
equilibrium GDP
45-degree line
leakages-injections approach
leakage
injection
planned investment
actual investment

STUDY QUESTIONS

1. Relate Say's law to the view held by classical economists that the economy generally will operate at a position *on* its production possibilities curve (Chapter 2). Use production possibilities analysis to demonstrate the Keynesian view on this matter.

2. Explain what relationships are shown by **a** the consumption schedule, **b** the saving schedule, **c** the investment demand curve, and **d** the investment schedule.

3. Precisely how are the APC and the MPC different? Why must the sum of the MPC and the MPS equal 1? What are the basic determinants of the consumption and saving schedules? Of your own level of consumption?

4. Explain how each of the following will affect the consumption and saving schedules or the investment schedule:
   a. A decline in the amount of government bonds that consumers are holding
   b. The threat of limited, non-nuclear war, leading the public to expect future shortages of consumer durables
   c. A decline in the real interest rate
   d. A sharp decline in stock prices
   e. An increase in the rate of population growth
   f. The development of a cheaper method of manufacturing pig iron from ore
   g. The announcement that the social insurance program is to be restricted as to size of benefits
   h. The expectation that mild inflation will persist in the next decade
   i. An increase in the federal personal income tax

5. Explain why an upshift in the consumption schedule typically involves an equal downshift in the saving schedule. What are the exceptions to this relationship?

6. **KEY QUESTION** *Complete the following table:*

Level of output and income (GDP = DI)	Consumption	Saving	APC	APS	MPC	MPS
$240	$_____	$–4	_____	_____		
260	_____	0	_____	_____	_____	_____
280	_____	4	_____	_____	_____	_____
300	_____	08	_____	_____	_____	_____
320	_____	12	_____	_____	_____	_____
340	_____	16	_____	_____	_____	_____
360	_____	20	_____	_____	_____	_____
380	_____	24	_____	_____	_____	_____
400	_____	28	_____	_____	_____	_____

   a. *Show the consumption and saving schedules graphically.*
   b. *Find the break-even level of income. Explain how it is possible for households to dissave at very low income levels.*
   c. *If the proportion of total income consumed (APC) decreases and the proportion saved (APS) increases as income rises, explain both verbally and graphically how the MPC and MPS can be constant at various levels of income.*

7. What are the basic determinants of investment? Explain the relationship between the real interest rate and the level of investment. Why is the investment schedule less stable than the consumption and saving schedules?

8. **KEY QUESTION** *Assume there are no investment projects in the economy that yield an expected rate of return of 25 percent or more. But suppose there are $10 billion of investment projects yielding expected returns of between 20 and 25 percent; another $10 billion yielding between 15 and 20 percent; another $10 billion between 10 and 15 percent; and so forth. Cumulate these data and present them graphically, putting the expected rate of return on*

the vertical axis and the amount of investment on the horizontal axis. What will be the equilibrium level of aggregate investment if the real interest rate is **a** 15 percent, **b** 10 percent, and **c** 5 percent? Explain why this curve is the investment demand curve.

9. Explain graphically the determination of the equilibrium GDP by **a** the aggregate expenditures–domestic output approach and **b** the leakages-injections approach for a private closed economy. Why must these two approaches always yield the same equilibrium GDP? Explain why the intersection of the aggregate expenditures schedule and the 45-degree line determines the equilibrium GDP.

10. KEY QUESTION *Assuming the level of investment is $16 billion and independent of the level of total output, complete the following table and determine the equilibrium levels of output and employment that this private closed economy would provide. What are the sizes of the MPC and MPS?*

Possible levels of employment, millions	Real domestic output (GDP = DI), billions	Consumption, billions	Saving, billions
40	$240	$244	$_____
45	260	260	_____
50	280	276	_____
55	300	292	_____
60	320	308	_____
65	340	324	_____
70	360	340	_____
75	380	356	_____
80	400	372	_____

11. KEY QUESTION *Using the consumption and saving data in question 10 and assuming investment is $16 billion, what are saving and planned investment at the $380 billion level of domestic output? What are saving and actual investment at that level? What are saving and planned investment at the $300 billion level of domestic output? What are the levels of saving and actual investment? Use the concept of unplanned investment to explain adjustments towards equilibrium from both the $380 and $300 billion levels of domestic output.*

12. "Planned investment is equal to saving at all levels of GDP; actual investment equals saving only at the equilibrium GDP." Do you agree? Explain. Critically evaluate: "The fact that households may save more than firms want to invest is of no consequence, because events will in time force households and firms to save and invest at the same rates."

13. **Advanced Analysis:** Linear equations for the consumption and saving schedules take the general form $C = a + bY$ and $S = -a + (1 - b) Y$, where C, S, and Y are consumption, saving, and national income, respectively. The constant a represents the vertical intercept, and b the slope of the consumption schedule.
   a. Use the following data to substitute numerical values for a and b in the consumption and saving equations:

National income (Y)	Consumption (C)
$ 0	$ 80
100	140
200	200
300	260
400	320

   b. What is the economic meaning of b? Of $(1 - b)$?
   c. Suppose the amount of saving that occurs at each level of national income falls by $20, but that the values of b and $(1 - b)$ remain unchanged. Restate the saving and consumption equations for the new numerical values, and cite a factor that might have caused the change.

14. **Advanced Analysis:** Suppose that the linear equation for consumption in a hypothetical economy is $C = 40 + .8Y$. Also suppose that income (Y) is \$400. Determine **a** the marginal propensity to consume, **b** the marginal propensity to save, **c** the level of consumption, **d** the average propensity to consume, **e** the level of saving, and **f** the average propensity to save.

15. **Advanced Analysis:** Assume that the linear equation for consumption in a hypothetical closed economy is $C = 10 + .9Y$, where Y is total real income (output). Also suppose that the equation for investment is $I_g = I_{g0} = 40$, meaning that I_g is 40 at all levels of total real income. Using the equation $Y = C + I_g$, determine the equilibrium level of Y. What are the total amounts of consumption, saving, and investment at equilibrium Y?

16. **(The Last Word)** What is the significance of John Maynard Keynes's book, *General Theory of Employment, Interest, and Money*, published in 1936?

17. WEB-BASED QUESTION **Consumption Expenditure** Statistics Canada www.statcan.ca/english/econoind/gdp86.htm reports the expenditure components of GDP. Look at "personal expenditure on consumer goods and services." By what percentage did this category change this quarter from the last quarter? What is the change from the last quarter last year? What is the largest component of personal expenditures: durable goods, semi-durable, non-durable, or services?

18. WEB-BASED QUESTION **Investment Expenditures** Visit Statistics Canada www.statcan.ca/english/Pgdb/Economy/Economic/econ04.htm and look at "Business gross fixed capital formation." What has been the trend of gross investment? Which components of gross investment have changed most? Compare gross private investment with gross government investment; has their growth rate been significantly different?

Aggregate Expenditures: The Multiplier, Net Exports, and Government

YOU HAVE SEEN WHY A PARTICULAR EQUILIBRIUM level of real GDP exists, specifically in a closed economy. But recall from Chapter 8 that the GDP in Canada is seldom stable; instead, it experiences long-run growth and is punctuated by cyclical fluctuations. We now turn our attention to why and how the equilibrium real GDP fluctuates. And since the public sector and the foreign sector *do* influence real GDP, later in this chapter we make the aggregate expenditures model more realistic by bringing these two sectors into the model.

We first analyze changes in investment spending and how they affect output, income, and employment. You will discover that a change in investment creates a multiple change in GDP. Then we "open" our simplified "closed" economy to show how exports and imports affect it. Next, we bring government—with its expenditures and taxes—into the model. Finally, we apply our extended model to two historical periods and consider some of the model's deficiencies.

IN THIS CHAPTER YOU WILL LEARN:

What the multiplier is and how it works.

•

The factors that determine the level of imports and exports, and how they affect a nation's aggregate expenditures and GDP.

•

The effect of government expenditure and taxation on aggregate expenditures and GDP.

•

To distinguish between equilibrium GDP and full employment GDP.

•

How a recessionary gap and an inflationary gap come about.

The Big Picture

WE NOW COMPLETE THE EXPENDITURE MODEL with the addition of the government and foreign sectors. You are reminded that we are trying to understand how GDP is determined to help us devise macroeconomic policies that lessen fluctuations and attain full employment and price stability—to keep us on the production possibility curve. We will see that government expenditures can be used to stabilize the economy in the short to medium term.

As you read through this chapter, keep the following points in mind:
- **Key Concept 7** is discussed.
- Imports take away from aggregate expenditures and exports add to them. The volume of imports into Canada depends primarily on domestic economic growth; exports depend primarily on economic growth in the economies of our major trading partners.
- Full employment is not zero unemployment. A market economy will always have some frictional and structural unemployment.
- Think of government as both reducing consumer expenditures by levying taxes, and adding to expenditures through its own purchases of goods and services.
- An economy can be at equilibrium at either above or below the economy's potential (full employment) output. ■

CHANGES IN EQUILIBRIUM GDP AND THE MULTIPLIER

In the closed economy, the equilibrium GDP will change in response to changes in the investment schedule or the saving and consumption schedules. Because the investment schedule is much less stable than the consumption and saving schedules, we will assume that the investment schedule is what changes.

Figure 10-1 shows the effect of changes in investment. Suppose the expected rate of return on investment rises (shifting the investment demand curve in Figure 9-7a to the right) or the interest rate falls (now the investment demand curve in Figure 9-7a does not shift; we instead move down the curve). As a result, investment spending increases by, say, $5 billion. This is indicated in Figure 10-1a by an upward shift of the aggregate expenditures schedule from $(C + I_g)_0$ to $(C + I_g)_1$ and in Figure 10-1b by an upward shift in the investment schedule from I_{g0} to I_{g1}. In each graph the result is a rise in the equilibrium GDP from $470 to $490 billion.

If the expected rate of return on investment decreases or the interest rate rises, the result is a decline in investment spending of, say, $5 billion.

This is shown by the downward shift of the investment schedule from I_{g0} to I_{g2} in Figure 10-1b and the downward shift of the aggregate expenditures schedule from $(C + I_g)_0$ to $(C + I_g)_2$ in Figure 10-1a. In each case, the shift reduces the equilibrium GDP from the original $470 billion to $450 billion.

You should verify these conclusions in Table 9-4 by substituting first $25 billion and then $15 billion for the $20 billion planned investment amount in column 5. If you do, you will see that $C + I_g$ becomes equal to GDP first at $490 billion (row 7) and then at $450 billion (row 5), the values indicated in Figure 10-1.

At the risk of getting ahead of ourselves, we note that the $5 billion changes in investment may be the direct result of economic policy. Looking back at Figure 9-7a, we see that the initial $20 billion of investment is associated with an 8 percent interest rate. If the economy is in recession at that investment level, monetary authorities may purposely reduce the interest rate to 6 percent (by increasing the supply of money). This will cause a $5 billion increase in investment and in aggregate expenditures to expand the economy's GDP.

Conversely, suppose the initial $20 billion of investment is "too great" and thus is causing demand-pull inflation. The monetary authorities may increase the interest rate (by reducing the

FIGURE 10-1 Changes in the equilibrium GDP caused by shifts in (a) the aggregate expenditures schedule and (b) the investment schedule

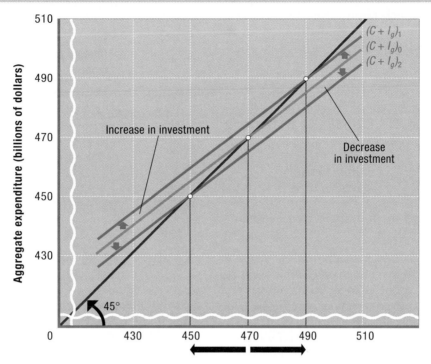

(a) Change in aggregate expenditures schedule

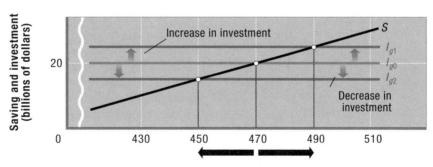

(b) Change in investment schedule

An upshift in the aggregate expenditures schedule from $(C + I_g)_0$ to $(C + I_g)_1$ will increase the equilibrium GDP. Conversely, a downshift in the aggregate expenditures schedule from $(C + I_g)_0$ to $(C + I_g)_2$ will lower the equilibrium GDP. In the saving-investment figure an upshift in the investment schedule (I_{g0} to I_{g1}) will raise, and downshift (I_{g0} to I_{g2}) will lower, the equilibrium GDP.

money supply), causing a reduction in investment and aggregate expenditures to constrain the inflation. Monetary policy—changing the money supply to alter interest rates and aggregate expenditures—is the subject of Chapter 15.

The Multiplier Effect

You may have noticed above that a $5 billion change in investment spending led to a $20 billion change in output and income. This surprising result is called the *multiplier effect:* a change in a component of aggregate expenditures leads to a larger change in equilibrium GDP. The **multiplier** determines how much larger; it is the ratio of a change in equilibrium GDP to the change in investment. Stated generally,

$$\text{Multiplier} = \frac{\text{Change in real GDP}}{\text{Initial change in spending}}$$

Here the multiplier is 4 ($20/$5). By rearranging the above equation, we can also say that

$$\text{Change in GDP} = \text{Multiplier} \times \text{Initial change in spending}$$

Three points about the multiplier must be made here:

1. The "initial change in spending" is usually associated with investment spending because of its volatility. But changes in consumption, net exports, and government purchases also lead to the multiplier effect.
2. The "initial change in spending" refers to an upshift or downshift of the aggregate expenditures schedule due to an upshift or downshift of one of its components. In Figure 10-1b we find that real GDP has increased by $20 billion because the investment schedule has shifted upward by $5 billion from I_{g0} to I_{g1}.
3. Implicit in this second point is that the multiplier works in both directions. An increase in initial spending can create a multiple increase in GDP, or a decrease in spending can be multiplied into a larger decrease in GDP.

Rationale   The multiplier effect follows from two facts. First, the economy supports repetitive, continuous flows of expenditures and income through which dollars spent by Smith are received as income by Chin, then spent by Chin and received as income by Gonzales, and so on. Second, any change in income will cause both consumption and saving to vary in the same direction as, and by a fraction of, the change in income.

It follows that an initial change in the rate of spending will cause a spending chain through the economy. That chain of spending, although of diminishing importance at each successive step, will cumulate to a multiple change in GDP.

The rationale underlying the multiplier effect is illustrated numerically in Table 10-1. Suppose a

TABLE 10-1 The multiplier: a tabular illustration (in billions)

	(1) Change in income	(2) Change in consumption (MPC = .75)	(3) Change in saving (MPS = .25)
Increase in investment of $5.00	$ 5.00	$ 3.75	$1.25
Second round	3.75	2.81	0.94
Third round	2.81	2.11	0.70
Fourth round	2.11	1.58	0.53
Fifth round	1.58	1.19	0.39
All other rounds	4.75	3.56	1.19
Totals	$20.00	$15.00	$5.00

$5 billion increase in investment spending occurs. This is the upshift of the aggregate expenditures schedule by $5 billion in Figure 10-1a and the upshift of the investment schedule from $20 to $25 billion in Figure 10-1b. Because we are still using the data in Table 9-1, we assume that the MPC is .75 and the MPS is .25. Also, we suppose that the economy is initially in equilibrium at $470 billion.

The initial increase in investment spending generates an equal amount of wage, rent, interest, and profit income because spending income and receiving income are two sides of the same transaction. How much consumption will be induced by this $5 billion increase in the incomes of households? The answer is found by applying the marginal propensity to consume of .75 to this change in income. Thus, the $5 billion increase in income initially raises consumption by $3.75 (= .75 × $5) billion and saving by $1.25 (= .25 × $5) billion, as shown in columns 2 and 3 in Table 10-1.

The $3.75 billion of consumption spending is received by other households as income (second round). These households consume .75 of this $3.75 billion, or $2.81 billion, and save .25 of it, or $0.94 billion. The $2.81 billion that is consumed flows to still other households as income to be spent or saved (third round). And the process continues.

Figure 10-2, derived from Table 10-1, shows the cumulative effects of this process. Each round *adds* the pale green blocks to national income and GDP. The cumulation of the additional income in

FIGURE 10-2 The multiplier process (MPC = .75)

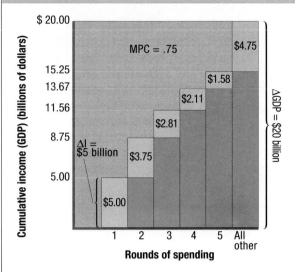

An initial change in investment spending of $5 billion creates an equal $5 billion of new income in round 1. Households spend $3.75 (= .75 × $5) billion of this new income, creating $3.75 of added income in round 2. Of this $3.75 of new income, households spend $2.81 (= .75 × $3.75) billion and income rises by that amount in round 3. The cumulation of such income increments over the entire process eventually results in a total change of income and GDP of $20 billion. The multiplier therefore is 4 (= $20 billion/$5 billion).

each round—the sum of the pale green blocks—is the total change in income or GDP. Though the spending and respending effects of the increase in investment diminish with each successive round of spending, the cumulative increase in output and income will be $20 billion. The $5 billion increase in investment will therefore increase the equilibrium GDP by $20 billion, from $470 to $490 billion. Thus, the multiplier is 4 (= $20 billion ÷ $5 billion).

It is no coincidence that the multiplier effect ends at the point where exactly enough saving has been generated to offset the initial $5 billion increase in investment spending. Only then will the disequilibrium created by the investment increase be corrected. In other words, GDP and total incomes *must* rise by $20 billion to create $5 billion in additional saving to balance the $5 billion increase in investment spending. Income must increase by four times the initial excess of investment over saving, because households save one-fourth of any increase in their incomes (that is, the MPS is .25).

The Multiplier and the Marginal Propensities

You may have sensed from Table 10-1 a relationship between the MPS and the multiplier. The fraction of an increase in income saved—the MPS—determines the cumulative respending effects of any initial change in spending and therefore determines the multiplier. *The MPS and the multiplier are inversely related.* The smaller the fraction of any change in income saved, the greater the respending at each round and, therefore, the greater the multiplier. If the MPS is .25, as in our example, the multiplier is 4. If the MPS were .33, the multiplier would be 3. If the MPS were .2, the multiplier would be 5. Let's see why.

Look again at Table 9-4 and Figure 10-1b. Initially the economy is in equilibrium at the $470 billion level of GDP. Now businesses increase investment by $5 billion so that planned investment of $25 billion exceeds saving of $20 billion at the $470 billion level. This means $470 billion is no longer the equilibrium GDP. By how much must output and income rise to restore equilibrium? By enough to generate $5 billion of additional saving to offset the $5 billion increase in investment. Because households save $1 out of every $4 of additional income they receive (MPS = .25), GDP must rise by $20 billion—four times the increase in investment—to create the $5 billion of extra saving necessary to restore equilibrium. Thus, the multiplier is 4.

If the MPS were .33, GDP would have to rise by only $15 billion (three times the increase in investment) to generate $5 billion of additional saving and restore equilibrium, and the multiplier therefore would be 3. But if the MPS were .20, GDP would have to rise by $25 billion for people to save an extra $5 billion and equilibrium to be restored; then the multiplier would be 5.

Also, recall that the MPS measures the slope of the saving schedule. In the leakages-injections ($S = I_g$) approach, this means that if the MPS is relatively large (say, .5) and the slope of the saving schedule is therefore relatively steep (.5), any upward shift in investment spending will be subject to a relatively small multiplier. A $5 billion increase in investment will entail a new point of intersection of the S and I_g schedules only $10 billion to the right of the original equilibrium GDP. The multiplier is only 2.

But if the MPS is relatively small (say, .10), the slope of the saving schedule will be relatively gentle (.10). Therefore, the same $5 billion upward shift in the investment schedule will provide a new intersection point $50 billion to the right of the original equilibrium GDP. The multiplier is 10 in this case. You should verify these two examples by drawing appropriate saving and investment diagrams.

We can summarize by saying *the multiplier is equal to the reciprocal of the MPS*. The reciprocal of any number is the quotient you obtain by dividing 1 by that number:

$$\text{Multiplier} = \frac{1}{\text{MPS}}$$

This formula is a quick way to determine the multiplier. To do so, all you need to know is the MPS.

Recall, too, from Chapter 9 that MPC + MPS = 1; it follows, then, that MPS = 1 – MPC. Therefore, we can also write the multiplier formula as

$$\text{Multiplier} = \frac{1}{1 - \text{MPC}}$$

Significance of the Multiplier The significance of the multiplier is that a small change in the investment plans of businesses or the consumption and saving plans of households can trigger a larger change in the equilibrium GDP. The multiplier magnifies the fluctuations in business activity initiated by changes in spending.

As illustrated in Figure 10-3, the larger the MPC (the smaller the MPS), the greater the multiplier. If the MPC is .75, the multiplier is 4; a $10 billion decline in planned investment will reduce the equilibrium GDP by $40 billion. But if the MPC is only .67, the multiplier is 3; the same $10 billion drop in investment will reduce the equilibrium GDP by only $30 billion. This makes sense intuitively: A large MPC means the succeeding rounds of consumption spending shown in Figure 10-2 diminish slowly and thereby cumulate to a large change in income. Conversely, a small MPC (a large MPS) causes the increases in consumption to decline quickly so the cumulative change in income is small.

Generalizing the Multiplier The multiplier we presented above is called the *simple multiplier* because it is based on a simple model of the economy. When it is computed as 1/MPS, the simple multiplier reflects only the leakage of income into saving. In the real world successive rounds of

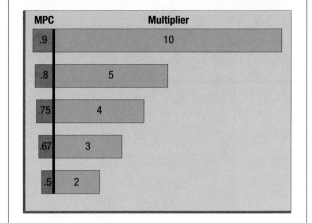

FIGURE 10-3 **The MPC and the multiplier**

The larger the MPC (the smaller the MPS), the greater the size of the multiplier.

income and spending can also be diminished by leakages into imports and taxes. As with the leakage into saving, some part of income at each round would be siphoned off as additional taxes, and another part would be used to purchase additional goods from abroad. The result of these added leakages is that the $\frac{1}{\text{MPS}}$ statement of the multiplier can be generalized. Specifically, we can change the denominator to read "fraction of the change in income that is not spent on domestic output" or "fraction of the change in income that leaks, or is diverted, from the income-expenditures stream." The more realistic multiplier that results when all leakages—saving, taxes, and imports—are included is called the *complex multiplier*. The complex multiplier for Canada is estimated to be about 1.6. *(Key Question 2)*

INTERNATIONAL TRADE AND EQUILIBRIUM OUTPUT

Our aggregate expenditures model has ignored international trade by assuming a closed economy. We now acknowledge the existence of exports and imports and note that **net exports** (exports minus imports) may be either positive or negative. Item 4 on the National Income Statistics pages at the back of this book reveals that net exports in some years have been positive (exports > imports) and in other years negative (imports > exports). In 1997, for example, net exports were a *positive* $14.3 billion, while in 1991 they were a *negative* $8 billion.

Net Exports and Aggregate Expenditures

Like consumption and investment, exports (X) create domestic production, income, and employment for a nation. Even though Canadian goods and services produced for export are sent abroad, foreign spending on those goods and services increases production and creates jobs and incomes in Canada. Exports must therefore be added as a component of each nation's aggregate expenditures.

Conversely, when an economy is open to international trade, part of its consumption and investment spending will be for imports (M)—goods and services produced abroad rather than in domestic industries. To avoid overstating the value of domestic production, we must reduce the sum of consumption and investment expenditures by the amount spent on imported goods. In measuring aggregate expenditures for domestic goods and services, we must subtract expenditures on imports.

In short, for a closed economy, aggregate expenditures are $C + I_g$. But for an open economy with international trade, aggregate spending is $C + I_g + (X - M)$. Or, recalling that net exports (X_n)

equal ($X - M$), we can say that aggregate expenditures for a private open economy are $C + I_g + X_n$.

The Determinants of Imports and Exports and the Net Export Schedule

What are the determinants of exports and imports? Note that in Table 10-2 exports are constant at all levels of GDP. This is because the GDP in other countries is the main determinant of our exports. *If the GDP in other countries is growing, we can expect the demand for our exports to increase.* If GDP in the United States increases, we can expect that the U.S. will purchase more goods and services from Canada. For example, housing construction expands with the economy and, thus, if that sector were to expand in the United States, it would translate into higher sales of Canadian lumber. If the United States experiences a recession, our exports will decrease.

Our imports are dependent on our own GDP. When the Canadian economy expands, imports also rise. For example, as the business sector expands and GDP rises, it will require machines and materials from abroad. Likewise, as consumer spending rises, some of it will go to imports.

Another determinant of imports and exports is the exchange rate, the rate at which the Canadian dollar can be exchanged for other currencies.

TABLE 10-2 Net export schedule

(1) Domestic output (and income) (GDP = DI) (billions)	(2) Exports (billions) (X)	(3) Imports (billions) (M)	(4) Net exports (billions) (X_n) (2) – (3)	(5) Marginal propensity to import (MPM) Δ(3)/Δ(1)
$370	$40	$15	$25	0.25
390	40	20	20	0.25
410	40	25	15	0.25
430	40	30	10	0.25
450	40	35	5	0.25
470	40	40	0	0.25
490	40	45	–5	0.25
510	40	50	–10	0.25
530	40	55	–15	0.25
550	40	60	–20	0.25

A **depreciation** of the Canadian dollar occurs when our currency buys fewer units of another currency or currencies. An **appreciation** of the Canadian dollar is the opposite: when the value of the Canadian dollar rises against other currencies, fewer Canadian dollars are required to purchase a unit of a foreign currency.

Generally, an appreciation of the Canadian dollar will lead to a rise of imports and a decrease in exports,[1] thus a decrease of net exports and aggregate expenditure. A depreciation of the Canadian dollar will have the opposite result.

A hypothetical **net export schedule** is shown in columns 1 to 4 of Table 10-2. Note that while exports are constant at all levels of GDP, imports, and therefore *net* exports $(X - M)$, change by $5 billion for every $20 billion change in GDP. The change in imports to a given change in GDP is called the **marginal propensity to import** (MPM). In our example the marginal propensity to import is 0.25 (= $5 billion/$20 billion). Just as the mar-

ginal propensity to consume was the slope of the consumption schedule, so the marginal propensity to import is the slope of the net export schedule.

Net Exports and Equilibrium GDP

Let's now add exports and imports to our discussion of income determination. Columns 1 and 2 of Table 10-3 repeat columns 2 and 6 from Table 9-4, where the equilibrium GDP for a closed economy was $470 billion. Columns 3 to 5 of Table 10-3 repeat columns 2 to 4 of Table 10-2. In column 6, we have adjusted the domestic aggregate expenditures of column 2 for net exports, giving us aggregate expenditures for an open economy.

The export and import figures we have selected are such that foreign trade leaves the equilibrium GDP unchanged. Net exports are zero at the closed economy's equilibrium GDP of $470 billion, so aggregate expenditures for the open economy (column 6) equal domestic output (column 1) at $470 billion.

Figure 10-4 shows these results. The $C + I_g$ schedule is aggregate expenditures for the closed economy, plotted from column 2 of Table 10-2. The

---

[1] As well, price and income elasticity of demand for particular imports and exports will influence their demand.

TABLE 10-3 Determination of the equilibrium levels of output and income in an open economy (without government)

(1) Domestic output (and income) (GDP = DI) (billions)	(2) Aggregate expenditures for closed economy, without government $(C + I_g)$ (billions)	(3) Exports (billions) (X)	(4) Imports (billions) (M)	(5) Net exports (billions) (3) − (4) (X_n)	(6) Aggregate expenditures for open economy, without government $(C + I_g + X_n)$ (billions) (2) + (5)
$370	$395	$40	$15	$25	$420
390	410	40	20	20	430
410	425	40	25	15	440
430	440	40	30	10	450
450	455	40	35	5	460
470	470	40	40	0	470
490	485	40	45	−5	480
510	500	40	50	−10	490
530	515	40	55	−15	500
550	530	40	60	−20	510

FIGURE 10-4   Net exports and the equilibrium GDP

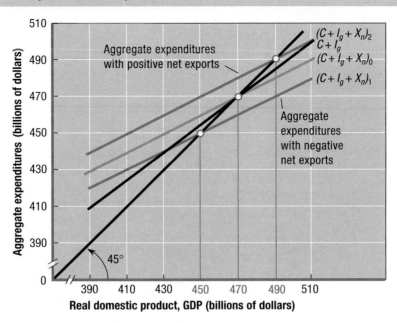

(a) Aggregate expenditures schedule

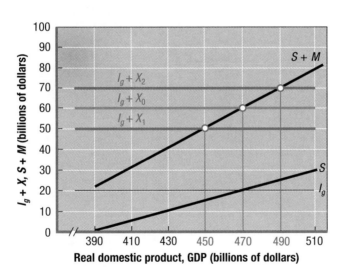

(b) Investment/export schedule

An increase in net exports raises the aggregate expenditures schedule as from $(C + I_g + X_n)_0$ to $(C + I_g + X_n)_2$ and increases the equilibrium GDP. Conversely, a decrease in net exports shifts the aggregate expenditures schedule downward as from $(C + I_g + X_n)_0$ to $(C + I_g + X_n)_1$ and lowers the equilibrium GDP. Note also that net exports in (a) reduce the slope of the aggregate expenditures schedule and that in (b) imports increase the slope of the "leakages" $(S + M)$ schedule.

$(C + I_g + X_n)_0$ schedule is aggregate expenditures for the open economy and reflects the figures of column 6. Observe that, *in this case*, aggregate expenditures for the open economy intersect domestic output at the same point as do aggregate expenditures for the closed economy, and therefore the $470 billion equilibrium GDP is unchanged by world trade.

Negative Net Exports   But there is no reason why net exports will have a neutral effect on equilibrium GDP. For example, by *either* reducing exports by $10 billion (from $40 to $30 billion) or increasing imports by $10 billion at each level of GDP, net exports are *minus* $10 billion at the $470 billion GDP. Recalculating aggregate expenditures in column 6 of Table 10-3, the resulting net equilibrium GDP will be $450 billion.

Graphically, the new open-economy aggregate expenditures schedule is shown by $(C + I_g + X_n)_1$ in Figure 10-4a. This schedule lies $10 billion below $(C + I_g + X_n)_0$, reflecting the $10 billion decline in net exports. Thus, at the original $470 billion equilibrium GDP, a spending gap of $10 billion exists, which causes the equilibrium GDP to *decline* to $450 billion.

Figure 10-4b shows the same result. Note that the $I_g + X_0$ schedule intersects the "leakages," $S + M$, schedule at the equilibrium GDP of $470 billion. The new $I_g + X_1$ schedule (denoting a $10 billion drop in exports: $I_g + X$ decreases from $60 to $50 billion) intersects the $S + M$ schedule at the new equilibrium GDP of $450 billion. The same result would be obtained by raising the $S + M$ schedule a vertical distance of $10 billion, indicating an increase in imports of $10 billion at all income levels.

Positive Net Exports   Conversely, by *either* increasing exports by $10 billion (from $40 to $50 billion) or decreasing imports by $10 billion at each GDP level, we discover that net exports are now *plus* $10 billion at the original $470 billion GDP. Again, the recalculation of aggregate expenditures in column 6 of Table 10-3 reveals that the equilibrium GDP will shift from $470 to $490 billion.

In Figure 10-4a, the new open-economy aggregate expenditures line is $(C + I_g + X_n)_2$, which lies $10 billion above $(C + I_g + X_n)_0$ because of the assumed $10 billion increase in net exports. This creates a $10 billion gap at the original $470 equilibrium GDP, and as a result the equilibrium GDP *increases* to $490 billion.

Figure 10-4b shows the same result. The new $I_g + X_2$ schedule (a $10 billion increase in exports: $I_g + X$ increases from $60 to $70 billion) intersects the $S + M$ schedule at the new equilibrium GDP of $490 billion. The same result would be obtained by dropping the $S + M$ schedule a vertical distance of $10 billion, indicating a decrease in imports of $10 billion at all income levels.

The generalizations that follow from these examples are these: *A decline in net exports decreases aggregate expenditures and reduces a nation's GDP; conversely, a rise in net exports increases aggregate expenditures and raises a nation's GDP.*

Net exports vary greatly among the major industrial nations, as is shown in Global Perspective 10-1. *(Key Question 5)*

International Economic Linkages

Our analysis of net exports and real GDP reveals how circumstances or policies abroad can affect our GDP.

Prosperity Abroad   A rising level of real output and thus income among our trading partners permits us to sell more goods abroad, thus raising our net exports and increasing our GDP. We should be interested in the prosperity of our trading partners because their good fortune enables them to buy more of our exports and transfer some of their prosperity to us.

Tariffs   Suppose our trading partners impose high tariffs on Canadian goods to reduce their imports and stimulate production in their economies. But their imports are our exports. So when they restrict their imports to stimulate *their* economies, they are reducing our exports and depressing *our* economy. We may retaliate by imposing trade barriers on

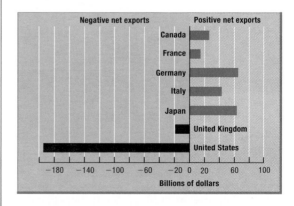

10-1
GLOBAL PERSPECTIVE

Merchandise net exports, selected nations

Some nations, such as Canada, Japan, and Germany, have positive net exports; other countries, such as the United States and the United Kingdom, have negative net exports.

Source: Organization for Economic Cooperation and Development. Data are for 1996.

their products. If so, their exports will decline and their net exports to us may fall. In the Great Depression of the 1930s various nations, including Canada, imposed trade barriers as a way to reduce domestic unemployment. But rounds of retaliation simply throttled world trade, worsened the depression, and increased unemployment.

Exchange Rates   Depreciation of the dollar relative to other currencies enables people abroad to obtain more dollars per unit of their currencies. The price of Canadian goods in terms of these currencies will fall, stimulating purchases of our exports. Also, Canadian consumers will find they need more dollars to buy foreign goods and, consequently, will reduce their spending on imports. The increased Canadian exports and decreased imports will increase Canada's net exports and expand the nation's GDP.

Whether depreciation of the dollar will actually raise real GDP or produce inflation depends on the initial position of the economy relative to its full-employment output. If the economy is operating below its full employment level, depreciation of the dollar and the resulting rise in net exports will increase aggregate expenditures and thus expand real GDP. But if the economy is already fully employed, the increase in net exports and aggregate expenditures will cause demand-pull inflation. Because resources are already fully employed, the increased spending cannot expand real output, but it can and does increase the prices of the existing output.

Finally, this last example has been cast only in terms of *depreciation* of the dollar. You should now think through the impact that *appreciation* of the dollar would have on net exports and equilibrium GDP.

Open-Economy Multiplier

The slope of the aggregate expenditures schedule in Figure 10-4 is reduced by international trade. The lower slope means a smaller multiplier. Expressed differently, note in Figure 10-4b that the leakages, $S + M$, schedule has an *increased* slope. In the above illustrations we noted that a $10 billion change in net exports would cause a $20 billion change in equilibrium GDP, indicating a multiplier of 2 (= $20/$10). Why does this new **open-economy multiplier** differ from the multiplier of 4 in the closed economy?

Recall that for the closed economy the multiplier is 1/MPS or, for our data, 1/0.25 or 4. The

multiplier is the reciprocal of the MPS, where the MPS is the fraction of any change in national income that "leaks" into saving. Moving to an open economy we add a second leakage—expenditures on imports. Saving and imports are similar because both are ways of disposing of income other than spending it on *domestically* produced goods. Since the *marginal propensity to import* (MPM) is the fraction of any change in disposable income spent on imports, we must add the MPM to the MPS in the denominator of the multiplier formula. The multiplier for an open economy becomes

$$\frac{1}{\text{MPS} + \text{MPM}}$$

For the data of Table 10-1, the MPM is 5/20, or 0.25, and the open-economy multiplier is

$$\frac{1}{\text{MPS} + \text{MPM}} = \frac{1}{0.25 + 0.25} = \frac{1}{0.5} = 2$$

10-1
QUICK REVIEW

- The multiplier effect reveals that an initial change in spending can cause magnified changes in domestic income and output. The multiplier is the factor by which the initial change is magnified: multiplier = change in real GDP/initial change in spending.

- The higher the marginal propensity to consume (the lower the marginal propensity to save), the larger is the simple multiplier; multiplier = 1/MPS.

- The main determinant of exports is the GDP in other countries, particularly our trading partners.

- The main determinant of imports is our own GDP.

- An appreciation of the Canadian dollar will decrease net exports, while a depreciation will increase net exports.

- Positive net exports increase aggregate expenditures on domestic output and increase equilibrium GDP; negative net exports decrease aggregate expenditures on domestic output and reduce equilibrium GDP.

- The open economy multiplier is smaller than the multiplier for a closed economy. The higher the marginal propensity to import, the smaller is the open economy multiplier.

ADDING THE PUBLIC SECTOR

Our final step in constructing the aggregate expenditures model is to move the analysis from that of a private (no government) open economy to a mixed open economy that has a public sector. This means adding government spending and taxes to the model.

Simplifying Assumptions

For clarity and simplicity, the following simple assumptions are made.

1. We continue to use the simplified investment schedule, where the level of investment is independent of the level of GDP.
2. We suppose government purchases neither depress nor stimulate private spending. They do not cause any upward or downward shifts in the consumption, investment, and net export schedules.
3. We assume the government's net tax revenues—total tax revenues less "negative taxes" in the form of transfer payments—are derived entirely from personal taxes. Although DI will

fall short of PI by the amount of government's tax revenues, GDP and PI will remain equal.

4. We assume that a fixed amount of taxes is collected regardless of the level of GDP.
5. We continue to suppose that, unless otherwise indicated, the price level is constant.

These assumptions will give us a simple and uncluttered view of how government spending and taxes fit within the aggregate expenditures model. Most of these assumptions will be dropped in Chapter 12 when we discuss how government uses changes in its expenditures and taxes to alter equilibrium GDP and the rate of inflation.

Government Purchases and Equilibrium GDP

Suppose that government decides to purchase $40 billion of goods and services regardless of the level of GDP.

Tabular Example   Table 10-4 shows the impact of this purchase on the equilibrium GDP. Columns 1 to 7 are carried over from Tables 9-4 and 10-3 for the private, open economy in which the equilib-

TABLE 10-4   The impact of government purchases on equilibrium GDP

(1) Domestic output (and income) (GDP = DI) (billions)	(2) Consumption (billions) (C)	(3) Savings (billions) (S)	(4) Investment (billions) (I_g)	(5) Exports (billions) (X)	(6) Imports (billions) (M)	(7) Net exports (billions) (5) – (6) (X_n)	(8) Government purchases (billions) (G)	(9) Aggregate expenditures ($C + I_g + X_n + G$) (billions) (2) + (4) + (7) + (8)
(1) $370	$375	$–5	$20	$40	$15	$25	$40	$460
(2) 390	390	0	20	40	20	20	40	470
(3) 410	405	5	20	40	25	15	40	480
(4) 430	420	10	20	40	30	10	40	490
(5) 450	435	15	20	40	35	5	40	500
(6) 470	450	20	20	40	40	0	40	510
(7) 490	465	25	20	40	45	–5	40	520
(8) 510	480	30	20	40	50	–10	40	530
(9) 530	495	35	20	40	55	–15	40	540
(10) 550	510	40	20	40	60	–20	40	550

rium GDP was $470 billion. The only new items are exports and imports in columns 5 and 6, and government purchases in column 8. By adding government purchases to private spending ($C + I_g + X_n$), we get a new, higher level of aggregate expenditures, as shown in column 9. Comparing columns 1 and 9, we find that aggregate expenditures and real output are equal at a higher level of GDP. Without government spending, equilibrium GDP was $470 billion (row 6); with government spending, aggregate expenditures and real output are equal at $550 billion (row 10). *Increases in public spending, like increases in private spending, shift the aggregate expenditures schedule upward and result in a higher equilibrium GDP.*

Note, too, that government spending is subject to the open-economy multiplier. A $40 billion increase in government purchases has increased equilibrium GDP by $80 billion (from $470 billion to $550 billion). We have implicitly assumed the $40 billion in government expenditure has all gone to purchase domestic output. This $40 billion increase in government spending is *not* financed by increased taxes. Soon we will find that increased taxes *reduce* equilibrium GDP.

In the leakages-injections approach, government expenditures are an injection of spending. Leakages of saving and imports cause consumption of real output to fall short of income, creating a potential spending gap. This gap may be filled by injections of any or all of investment, exports, and government purchases. In Table 10-4, the $550 billion equilibrium level of GDP (row 10) occurs when leakages equal injections or where $S + M = I_g + X + G$. That is, when taxes are zero, 40 + 60 = 20 + 40 + 40.

Graphical Analysis In Figure 10-5a we add $40 billion of government purchases, G, vertically to the level of private spending, $C + I_g + X_n$. That increases the aggregate expenditures schedule (private plus public) to $C + I_g + X_n + G$, resulting in the $80 billion increase in equilibrium GDP shown from $470 to $550 billion.

Figure 10-5b shows the same change in equilibrium GDP via the leakages-injections approach. Like investment and exports, government spending is an injection that offsets the leakage of saving and imports. It therefore raises the "injections" schedule as shown. Assuming no taxes, the equilibrium GDP is determined by the intersection of the $S + M$ schedule and the $I_g + X + G$ schedule.

Both the aggregate expenditures and leakages-injections approaches indicate the same $550 billion equilibrium GDP. This is $80 billion more than the $470 billion equilibrium GDP of the private closed economy.

A decline in government spending G will lower the aggregate expenditures schedule in Figure 10-5a and lower the $I_g + X + G$ schedule in Figure 10-5b. In either case, the result is a multiplied decline in the equilibrium GDP. You should verify in Table 10-4 that if government spending were to decline from $40 billion to $20 billion, the equilibrium GDP would fall by $40 billion, that is, from $550 to $510 billion.

Taxation and Equilibrium GDP

Government also collects taxes. Suppose government imposes a **lump-sum tax**, which *is a tax of a constant amount or, more precisely, a tax yielding the same amount of tax revenue at each level of GDP.* Also, assume this lump-sum tax is $40 billion, so government obtains $40 billion of tax revenue at each level of GDP.

Tabular Example Table 10-5 continues our example. In it we now find taxes in column 2, and we see in column 3 that disposable (after-tax) income is lower than GDP (column 1) by the $40 billion amount of the tax. Because disposable income is used for consumer spending and saving, the tax lowers both consumption and saving relative to what they would be in the private economy. But by how much will each decline as a result of the $40 billion in taxes? The MPC and MPS hold the answer: The MPC tells us what fraction of a decline in disposable income will come out of consumption, and the MPS indicates what fraction will come out of saving. Since the MPC is .75, if government collects $40 billion in taxes at each possible level of GDP, the amount of consumption at each level of GDP will drop by $30 billion (= .75 × $40 billion). Since the MPS is .25, the amount of saving at each level of GDP will fall by $10 billion (= .25 × $40 billion).

But there is one more refinement we must make to the new lower consumption level brought about by the tax increase. In an open economy such as Canada's, consumption consists of both domestic and imported commodities. Of the $30 billion drop in total consumption, there will be a $10 billion decrease in M since the MPM equals $\frac{1}{4}$.

FIGURE 10-5 Government spending and the equilibrium GDP

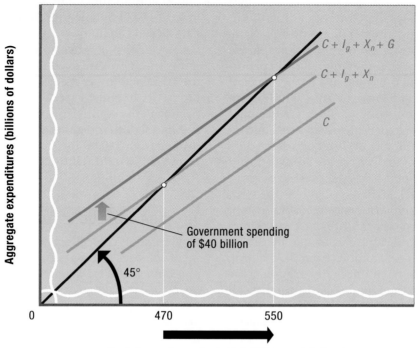

(a) Aggregate expenditures-domestic output approach

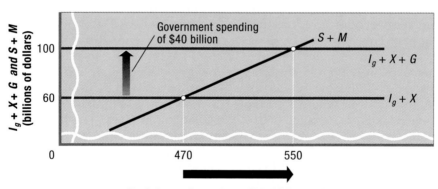

(b) Leakages-injections approach

(a) The aggregate expenditures-domestic output approach. The addition of government purchases, G, raises the aggregate expenditures $(C + I_g + X_n + G)$ schedule and increases the equilibrium level of GDP, as would an increase in C, I_g or X_n. (b) Leakages-injections approach. Government spending is an injection that adds to investment and export spending, raising the injection $(I_g + X + G)$ schedule and increasing the equilibrium GDP.

The remaining $20 billion, therefore, comes out of domestic consumption.

Columns 4 and 5 of Table 10-5 list the amounts of consumption and saving *at each level of GDP*, which are $30, $20 and $10 billion smaller, respec-

tively, than those in Table 10-4. Before the taxes, where GDP equalled DI, for example, consumption was $435 billion, saving $15 billion, and imports $35 billion at the $450 billion level of GDP (row 5 of Table 10-4). After taxes are imposed, DI

TABLE 10-5 Determination of the equilibrium levels of employment, output, and income (in billions): private and public sectors

(1) Real domestic output and income (GDP = PI)	(2) Taxes (T)	(3) Disposable income (DI) (1) − (2)	(4) Consumption (C_a)	(5) Saving (S_a) (3) − (4)	(6) Investment (I_g)	(7) Net exports (X_n) X	M_a	X_{na}	(8) Government purchases (G)	(9) Aggregate expenditures ($C_a + I_g + X_{na} + G$) (4) + (6) + (8) + (9)
(1) $370	$40	$330	$345	$−15	$20	$40	$ 5	$35	$40	$440
(2) 390	40	350	360	−10	20	40	10	30	40	450
(3) 410	40	370	375	−5	20	40	15	25	40	460
(4) 430	40	390	390	0	20	40	20	20	40	470
(5) 450	40	410	405	5	20	40	25	15	40	480
(6) 470	40	430	420	10	20	40	30	10	40	490
(7) 490	40	450	435	15	20	40	35	5	40	500
(8) 510	40	470	450	20	20	40	40	0	40	510
(9) 530	40	490	465	25	20	40	45	−5	40	520
(10) 550	40	510	480	30	20	40	50	−10	40	530

is $410 billion, $40 billion short of the $450 billion GDP, with the result that consumption is only $405 billion, saving is $5 billion, and imports $25 billion (row 5 of Table 10-5).

Taxes cause disposable income to fall short of GDP by the amount of the taxes. This decline in DI reduces consumption, saving, and imports at each level of GDP. The sizes of the declines in C, S, and M are determined by the MPC, the MPS, and the MPM, respectively.

What is the effect of taxes on equilibrium GDP? To find out, we calculate aggregate expenditures once again, as shown in column 9 of Table 10-5. Note there that aggregate spending is $20 billion less at each level of GDP than it was in Table 10-4. The reason is that after-tax consumption, C_a, is $30 billion less, and M_a is $10 billion less (therefore, X_{na} is $10 billion more) at each level of GDP. Comparing real output and aggregate expenditures, in columns 1 and 9, we see that the aggregate amounts produced and purchased are equal only at the $510 billion level of GDP (row 8). The imposition of a $40 billion lump-sum tax has caused equilibrium GDP to fall from $550 billion (row 10 in Table 10-4) to $510 billion (row 8).

The leakages-injections approach confirms this result. Taxes, like saving and imports, are a leakage from the domestic income-expenditures stream. Consumption will now fall short of

domestic output—creating a potential spending gap—in the amount of imports and after-tax saving *plus* taxes. This gap may be filled by planned investment, exports, and government purchases.

Thus, our new equilibrium condition for the leakages-injections approach is this: After-tax saving, S_a, plus imports plus taxes equal planned investment plus exports plus government purchases. Symbolically,

$$S_a + M_a + T = I_g + X + G$$

$$(20 + 40 + 40 = 20 + 40 + 40)$$

You should verify, in Table 10-5, that this equality of leakages and injections is fulfilled *only* at the $510 billion level of GDP (row 8).

Graphical Analysis In Figure 10-6a the $40 billion *increase* in taxes shows up as a $20 (*not* $40) billion *decline* in the aggregate expenditures ($C_a + I_g + X_{na} + G$) schedule. Under our assumption that all taxes are personal income taxes, this decline in aggregate expenditures results solely from a decline in the consumption C component of the aggregate expenditures schedule = $(MPC)(\Delta T) = (\frac{3}{4})$ ($40 billion) = $30 billion, of which $20 billion is domestic consumption and $10 billion is import

FIGURE 10-6 Taxes and the equilibrium GDP

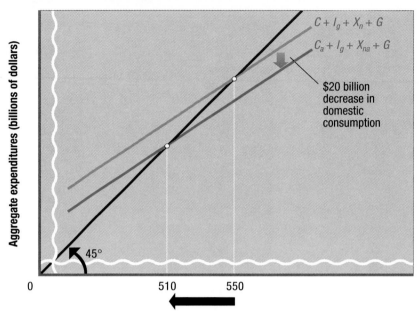

(a) Aggregate expenditures–domestic output approach

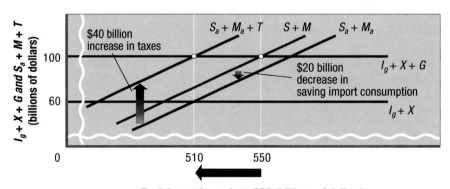

(b) Leakages-injections approach

(a) Aggregate expenditures-domestic output approach. If the MPC is 3/4, the imposition of $40 billion of taxes will lower the aggregate domestic expenditures schedule by $20 billion and cause a decline in the equilibrium GDP. (b) Leakages-injections approach. Here, taxes have a twofold effect. First, with an MPS of 1/4, the imposition of taxes of $40 billion will reduce disposable income by $40 billion and saving by $10 billion at each level of GDP. Also imports fall by $10 billion because some of the reduction of aggregate consumption reduces the consumption good component of imports. This is shown by a shift from $(S + M)$ (savings before taxes plus imports) to $(S_a + M_a)$ (savings after taxes plus imports). Second, the $40 billion of taxes constitute an additional $40 billion leakage at each GDP level, giving us $S_a + M_a + T$. By adding government, the equilibrium condition changes from $S + M = I_g + X$ to $S_a + M_a + T = I_g + X + G$.

consumption. The equilibrium GDP changes from $550 billion to $510 billion because of this tax-induced drop in consumption. *Increases in taxes lower the aggregate expenditures schedule relative to the 45-degree line and reduce the equilibrium GDP.*

Consider now the leakages-injections approach. The analysis here is more complex because the $40 billion in taxes has a twofold effect in Figure 10-6b.

1. The taxes reduce DI by $40 billion and, with the MPS at .25, cause saving to fall by $10 billion at each level of GDP. Also, the import component of consumption falls by $10 billion. In Figure 10-6b, this is shown as a shift from $S + M$ (saving before taxes and imports) to $S_a + M_a$ (saving after taxes and reduction in import consumption).
2. The $40 billion in taxes is a $40 billion additional leakage at each GDP level, which must be added to $S_a + M_a$ (not $S + M$), giving us $S_a + M_a + T$.

Equilibrium now exists at the $510 billion GDP, where the total amount that households save and the economy imports, plus the amount of taxes government intends to collect, are equal to the total amount businesses both export and plan to invest plus the amount of government purchases. The equilibrium condition for the leakages-injection approach now is $S_a + M_a + T = I_g + X + G$. Graphically, it is the intersection of the $S_a + M_a + T$ and the $I_g + X + G$ schedules that determines the equilibrium GDP.

In contrast to our previous case, *decrease* in existing taxes will raise aggregate expenditures schedule in Figure 10-6a as a result of an increase in the consumption at all GDP levels. In Figure 10-6b, a tax cut will lower the $S_a + M_a + T$ schedule. The result is a magnified *increase* in the equilibrium GDP.

You should use both the expenditures-output and the leakages-injections approaches to confirm that a tax reduction of $20 billion (from the present $40 billion to $20 billion) will increase the equilibrium GDP from $510 billion to $530 billion. *(Key Question 8)*

Balanced-Budget Multiplier

There is a curious thing about our tabular and graphical illustrations. *Equal increases in government spending and taxation increase the equilibrium GDP. If G and T are each increased by a particular amount, the*

equilibrium level of domestic output will rise by that same amount. In our example the $40 billion increases in G and T cause the equilibrium GDP to increase $40 billion (from $470 to $510 billion).

The rationale for this **balanced-budget multiplier** is revealed in our example. A change in government spending affects aggregate expenditures more powerfully than a tax change of the same size.

Government spending has a *direct* impact on aggregate expenditures. Government spending is a direct component of aggregate expenditures. So, when government purchases increase by $40 billion as in our example, the aggregate expenditures schedule shifts upward by the entire $40 billion.

But a change in taxes affects aggregate expenditures *indirectly* by changing disposable income and thereby changing both the domestic and import components of consumption. Specifically, our $40 billion lump-sum tax increase shifts the domestic aggregate expenditures schedule downward by $20 billion. While there has been a $30 billion decrease in total consumption (since MPC = .75), $10 billion of it represents the decrease in the consumption of imported goods. Thus, there is an overall $20 billion decrease in domestic consumption.

The overall result is a *net* upward shift of the domestic aggregate expenditures schedule of $20 billion (i.e., $40 billion *more* government spending, but $20 billion *less* spending on domestic consumption), which, subject to a multiplier of 2, boosts GDP by $40 billion. This $40 billion increase in GDP is equal to the size of the initial increase in government expenditures and taxes. *Thus, the balanced budget multiplier is 1.*

The fact that the balanced budget multiplier is 1 is clarified in Figure 10-7. With an MPC of .75, the tax increase of $40 billion reduces disposable income by $40 billion and decreases total consumption expenditures by $30 billion. The $30 billion decline in consumption results in a $20 billion drop in domestic consumption, and $10 billion in import consumption and the fall in domestic expenditures *reduces* GDP by $40 billion (= $20 billion × the multiplier of 2). However, observe in Figure 10-7 that the increase in government expenditures of $40 billion *increases* GDP by $80 billion (= $40 billion × the multiplier of 2). The equal increases of taxes and government expenditures of $40 billion thus yield a net increase of GDP of $40 billion (= $80 billion − $40 billion). *Equal increases*

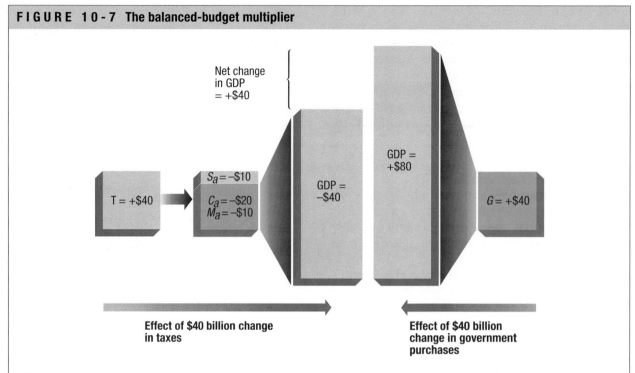

FIGURE 10-7 The balanced-budget multiplier

The balanced-budget multiplier is 1. An equal increase in taxes and government expenditures will increase GDP by an amount equal to the increase in the amount of government expenditures and taxes. Given an MPC of .75, a tax increase of $40 billion will reduce disposable income by $40 billion and lower consumption expenditures by $20 billion. Because the multiplier is 2, GDP will therefore decline by $40 billion. The $40 billion increase in government expenditures, however, will produce an increase in GDP of $80 billion. The net increase in GDP will be $20 billion, which equals the amount of the increase in government expenditures and taxes.

in G and T increase real GDP by an amount equal to those increases.

This balanced-budget multiplier effect is not limited to situations in which the multiplier is 2. It holds no matter what the multiplier is, a fact you should verify by experimenting with different MPCs and MPSs. The balanced-budget multiplier is always 1.

EQUILIBRIUM VERSUS FULL-EMPLOYMENT GDP

Now that we have the full aggregate expenditures model at our disposal, we can use it to evaluate the equilibrium GDP.

The $510 billion equilibrium GDP in our complete analysis (Table 10-5 and Figure 10-6) may or may not provide full employment. Indeed, our assumption thus far has been that the economy is operating at less than full employment.

Recessionary Gap

Assume in *Figure 10-8a (Key Graph)* that the full-employment level of GDP is $530 billion and the aggregate expenditures schedule is $(C + I_g + X_n + G)_1$. This schedule intersects the 45-degree line to the left of the full-employment output, so the economy's aggregate production falls $20 billion short of its full employment output of $530 billion. According to column 1 in Table 9-4, employment at full-employment GDP is 15 million workers. But the economy depicted in Figure 10-8a is employing only 13 million workers; 2 million workers are not employed. For that reason, the economy is sacrificing $20 billion of output.

The amount by which GDP falls short of the full-employment level of GDP (also called potential GDP) is called the **recessionary gap**. In Table 10-5, assuming the full-employment GDP to be $530 billion, the corresponding recessionary gap is $20 billion. The aggregate expenditures schedule would have to shift upward to realize the full-employment GDP. Because the multiplier is 2, the

KEY GRAPH

FIGURE 10-8 Recessionary and inflationary gaps

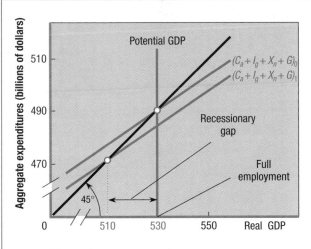

(a) Recessionary gap

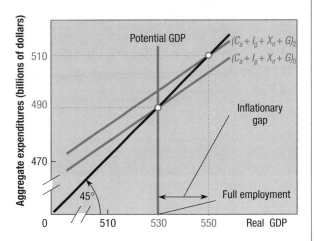

(b) Inflationary gap

The equilibrium and full-employment GDPs may not coincide. (a) A recessionary gap is the amount by which equilibrium GDP falls short of full-employment GDP. Here, the recessionary gap is $20 billion, caused by a $10 billion shortfall of aggregate expenditures. (b) An inflationary gap is the amount by which equilibrium GDP exceeds full-employment GDP. Here, the inflationary gap is $20 billion; this overspending brings about demand-pull inflation.

10-8

QUICK QUIZ

1. In the economy depicted
   (a) the MPS is .50.
   (b) the multiplier is 2.
   (c) the full-capacity level of real GDP is $510 billion.
   (d) nominal GDP always equals real GDP.

2. The inflationary gap depicted will cause
   (a) demand-pull inflation.
   (b) cost-push inflation.

   (c) cyclical unemployment.
   (d) frictional unemployment.

3. The recessionary gap depicted will cause
   (a) demand-pull inflation.
   (b) cost-push inflation.
   (c) cyclical unemployment.
   (d) frictional unemployment.

4. In the economy depicted, the $20 billion inflationary gap
   (a) expands real GDP to $550 billion.
   (b) leaves real GDP at $530 billion, but causes inflation.
   (c) could be remedied by equal $20 billion increases in taxes and government spending.
   (d) implies that real GDP exceeds nominal GDP.

Answers: 1. (b); 2. (a); 3. (c); 4. (b)

expenditure shortfall is $10 billion; an increase in any of the expenditure components by $10 billion would raise GDP by $20 billion to the full-employment GDP.

Inflationary Gap

If aggregate expenditures are at $(C_a + I_g + X_n + G)_2$ in Figure 10-8b, a demand-pull inflationary

gap exists. The amount by which GDP exceeds the full-employment level of GDP is called an **inflationary gap**. In this case, there is a $20 billion inflationary gap.

The effect of this inflationary gap—an excess aggregate demand of $10 billion—will be to pull up output prices. Businesses cannot respond to the $10 billion excessive spending by expanding their real outputs, so demand-pull inflation will occur.

Nominal GDP will rise because of a higher price level, but real GDP will not. *(Key Question 10)*

HISTORICAL APPLICATIONS

Let's see how these concepts of recessionary and inflationary gaps apply to two economic events.

The Great Depression

In October of 1929 the stock market collapsed, marking the beginning of the most severe and prolonged depression of modern times. Real GDP (in 1992 dollars) plummeted from $68 billion in 1929 to a low of $49 billion in 1933. The unemployment rate rose from 2.9 percent in 1929 to 19.1 percent in the same period. As late as 1939, real GDP was only 6 percent above its level of 10 years earlier and the unemployment rate still was 11.4 percent!

A sagging level of investment spending was the major weight that pulled the Canadian economy to the economic chaos of the 1930s. In real terms, gross investment spending shrank from $1.24 billion in 1929 to $.187 billion in 1933—an 85 percent decline. In Figure 10-8, we would depict this decline in investment as a dramatic downward shift in the nation's aggregate expenditure schedule, causing a severe recessionary (depressionary) gap and a historic decline in real GDP.

Several factors caused this steep decline in investment.

Overcapacity and Business Indebtedness   Flush with the prosperity of the 1920s, businesses had overexpanded their productive capacity. In particular, there was tremendous expansion of the automobile industry—and the related petroleum, rubber, steel, glass, and textile industries—which ended as the market for new autos became saturated. Business indebtedness also increased rapidly during the twenties. Furthermore, by the late 1920s much of the income of businesses was committed for the payment of interest and principal on past capital purchases, and thus was not available for sustaining expenditures on new capital.

Decline in Residential Construction   The 1920s experienced a boom in residential construction in response to population growth and to housing

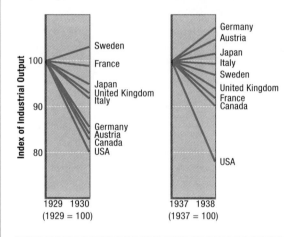

10-2
GLOBAL PERSPECTIVE

Changes in industrial production, selected countries, 1929–1930 and 1937–1938

The Great Depression of the 1930s was global, with large declines in industrial output occurring in most countries. The Depression began in 1929–30 for many countries. Between 1933 and 1937 industrial output partially recovered. Precipitous declines in industrial output again occurred in some nations in 1937–38.

Source: League of Nations, *World Economic Survey*, 1938–1939, p. 107.

demand that was deferred because of World War I. This investment spending began to level off as early as 1926, and by the late 1920s the construction industry had virtually collapsed.

Stock Market Crash   The most striking aspect of the Great Depression was the stock market crash of October 1929. The optimism of the prosperous 1920s had elevated stock market speculation to something of a national pastime. This speculation had bid up stock prices to the point where they did not reflect financial reality, and stock prices rose far beyond the profit-making potentials of the firms they represented. A downward adjustment was necessary and it came suddenly and quickly in 1929.

The stock market crash had significant secondary effects. Most important was the psychological repercussions. The buoyant optimism of the 1920s gave way to a wave of crippling pessimism, and the crashing of stock prices created highly unfavourable conditions for acquiring additional money for investment.

Shrinking Money Supply The nation's money supply plummeted in the early years of the Great Depression, from $2.27 billion in 1929 to $1.99 billion by 1933. This shrinkage resulted from forces operating both at home and abroad. The reduction of the money supply contributed to a sharp decline in aggregate expenditures, including investment, that occurred in the early 1930s.

Impact of American Economic Growth

The 1960s was a period of prolonged expansion or real GDP, fuelled by increases in consumption spending and investment. One factor in this long expansion was the rapid economic growth in our main trading partner, the United States. American policy called for government to manipulate its tax collections and expenditures in such a way as to increase aggregate demand, increasing employment and real GDP. For example, in 1962 legislation was enacted that provided for a 7 percent tax credit on investment in new machinery and equipment, thus strengthening the incentives of businesses to invest. In 1964 the government cut personal and corporate income taxes, boosting consumption spending and further increasing investment spending. The American unemployment rate fell from 5.2 percent in 1964 to 4.5 percent in 1965.

At this time another expansionary force came into play. The escalation of American participation in the Vietnam war resulted in a 40 percent increase in U.S. government spending on national defence between 1965 and 1967. There was another 15 percent increase in war-related spending in 1968.

Remarkably, the American unemployment rate fell below 4 percent during the entire 1966–69 period. But the increased government expenditures, imposed on an already booming economy, also brought about the worst inflation in two decades. Inflation jumped from 1.6 percent in 1965 to 5.7 percent by 1970. In terms of Figure 10-8, the booming investment expenditures and the added government expenditures shifted the aggregate expenditures schedule sharply upward, creating an inflationary gap. The rapid economic growth in the United States spilled over into Canada through our increased exports to them, creating an inflationary gap in Canada as well. Real GDP expanded at almost 7 percent per annum in a number of years during the 1960s, reaching a high of 7.7 percent in 1971. Inflation also rose, but did not become serious until 1973.

10-2

QUICK REVIEW

- Government purchases shift the aggregate expenditures schedule upward and raise the equilibrium GDP.

- Taxes reduce disposable income, lower consumption spending on domestically produced goods and saving, shift the imported and aggregate expenditures schedules downward, and reduce the equilibrium GDP.

- The balanced budget multiplier is 1.

- A recessionary gap is the amount by which GDP must increase for the economy to achieve full employment GDP; the inflationary gap is the amount by which GDP must decrease for the economy to eliminate inflationary pressures and still achieve the full-employment GDP.

- The Great Depression of the 1930s was a period having a large recessionary (depressionary) gap; the late 1960s and early 1970s represent a period characterized by an inflationary gap.

CRITIQUE AND PREVIEW

Our analysis and examples demonstrate the power of the aggregate expenditures model to help us understand how the economy works, how recessions or depressions can occur, and how demand-pull inflation can arise. But models are approximations of reality—they have shortcomings. The aggregate expenditures theory has two limitations.

1. **DOES NOT SHOW PRICE LEVEL CHANGES** The model can account for demand-pull inflation, as in Figure 10-8b, but it does not indicate how *much* the price level will rise when aggregate expenditures are excessive relative to the economy's capacity. Will the $10 billion inflationary gap of Figure 10-8b cause a 3 percent, 5 percent, 10 percent, or some other rate of inflation? By how much will the GDP price index of Chapter 7 rise for each $1 billion of

the inflationary gap? The aggregate expenditures model does not include the price level; it has no way of measuring the rate of inflation.

2. **OMITS COST-PUSH INFLATION**   We know from Chapter 8 that there are two general types of inflation: demand-pull inflation and cost-push inflation. The aggregate expenditures model does not address cost-push inflation.

In Chapter 11 we remedy these deficiencies, while preserving the insights of the aggregate expenditures model. We use the model to derive aggregate demand—a schedule or curve relating various price levels to the amounts of real GDP that will be demanded at those price levels. When this aggregate demand curve is combined with an aggregate supply curve, we obtain an aggregate expenditures-based model that overcomes the shortcomings just discussed. The better you understand the aggregate expenditures model, the easier it will be for you to grasp Chapter 11's aggregate demand-aggregate supply model.

In The Media

U.S. Shoppers Head North for Bargains

ASSOCIATED PRESS

With the U.S. dollar worth $1.40, U.S. shoppers are making a run for the border to hunt for bargains.

The 40-per-cent exchange rate makes shopping in Canada worthwhile to Americans—even after taxes and tunnel or bridge tolls, shoppers and merchants say.

"It's always been questionable till the past year," Peter Brain, general manager of the Windsor-Detroit Tunnel Duty Free Shop, told *The Detroit News* in a story published yesterday. "If you do your homework, you can save quite a bit of money."

Clothing, china and giftware are particularly hot for U.S. shoppers, said Hans Geenan of the Station Mall Merchants Association in Sault Ste. Marie, Ont.

"The word I'm getting is they're noticing a sizable increase in U.S. customers," he said yesterday, citing reports from the mall's more than 100 merchants.

In Windsor, Ont., merchants say goods such as furs and crystal are pulling in U.S. customers.

Gene Nori, general manager of the Sault Ste. Marie, Ont., Chamber of Commerce, credited the exchange rate with bringing in more U.S. shoppers in recent months.

Besides saving on the exchange rate, U.S. shoppers save on sales taxes when they buy items such as furs and jewelry. Most stores ship the merchandise directly to their U.S. customers. The North American free-trade agreement means customers don't have to pay sales tax on those items.

Source: *Globe and Mail*, December 31, 1997, p. B3. Reprinted with permission—Associated Press.

THE STORY IN BRIEF

A lower Canadian dollar attracts American shoppers to Canada.

THE ECONOMICS BEHIND THE STORY

• In 1998, the Canadian dollar fell below $.65 U.S. At this level, Canadian goods and services became relatively cheap for Americans. Adding to the attrac-tion of Canadian goods is that under the North American Free Trade Agreement, U.S. customers don't have to pay duty on certain items.

• The lower Canadian dollar is a stimulus to the Canadian economy. One of the main effects is higher exports and lower imports, thus higher net exports. This stimulus would shift the aggregate expenditure curve upward, helping raise Canadian GDP.

• How do you explain the old adage "When the U.S. economy sneezes, the Canadian economy gets pneumonia?" ∎

The Last Word

SQUARING THE ECONOMIC CIRCLE

American humorist Art Buchwald examines the multiplier.

WASHINGTON—THE RECESSION HIT SO FAST that nobody knows exactly how it happened. One day we were the land of milk and honey and the next day we were the land of sour cream and food stamps.

This is one explanation.

Hofberger, the Chevy salesman in Tomcat, Va., a suburb of Washington, called up Littleton, of Littleton Menswear & Haberdashery, and said, "Good news, the new Novas have just come in and I've put one aside for you and your wife."

Littleton said, "I can't, Hofberger, my wife and I are getting a divorce.

"I'm sorry," Littleton said, "but I can't afford a new car this year. After I settle with my wife, I'll be lucky to buy a bicycle."

Hofberger hung up. His phone rang a few minutes later.

"This is Bedcheck the painter," the voice on the other end said. "When do you want us to start painting your house?"

"I changed my mind," said Hofberger. "I'm not going to paint the house."

"But I ordered the paint," Bedcheck said. "Why did you change your mind?"

"Because Littleton is getting a divorce and he can't afford a new car."

That evening when Bedcheck came home his wife said, "The new color television set arrived from Gladstone's TV Shop."

"Take it back," Bedcheck told his wife.

"Why?" she demanded.

"Because Hofberger isn't going to have his house painted now that the Littletons are getting a divorce."

The next day Mrs. Bedcheck dragged the TV set in its carton back to Gladstone. "We don't want it."

Gladstone's face dropped. He immediately called his travel agent, Sandstorm. "You know that trip you had scheduled for me to the Virgin Islands?"

"Right, the tickets are all written up."

"Cancel it. I can't go. Bedcheck just sent back the color TV set because Hofberger didn't sell a car to Littleton because they're going to get a divorce and she wants all his money."

Sandstorm tore up the airline tickets and went over to see his banker, Gripsholm. "I can't pay back the loan this month because Gladstone isn't going to the Virgin Islands."

Gripsholm was furious. When Rudemaker came in to borrow money for a new kitchen he needed for his restaurant, Gripsholm turned him down cold. "How can I loan you money when Sandstorm hasn't repaid the money he borrowed?"

Rudemaker called up the contractor, Eagleton, and said he couldn't put in a new kitchen. Eagleton laid off eight men.

Meanwhile, General Motors announced it was giving a rebate on its new models. Hofberger called up Littleton immediately. "Good news," he said, "even if you are getting a divorce, you can afford a new car."

"I'm not getting a divorce," Littleton said. "It was all a misunderstanding and we've made up."

"That's great," Hofberger said. "Now you can buy the Nova."

"No way," said Littleton. "My business has been so lousy I don't know why I keep the doors open."

"I didn't realize that," Hofberger said.

"Do you realize I haven't seen Bedcheck, Gladstone, Sandstorm, Gripsholm, Rudemaker or Eagleton for more than a month? How can I stay in business if they won't patronize my store?" ∎

Source: Art Buchwald, "Squaring the Economic Circle," *Cleveland Plain Dealer,* February 22, 1975. Reprinted by permission.

CHAPTER SUMMARY

1. A shift in the saving and consumption schedules or in the investment schedule will change the equilibrium output-income level by several times the amount of the initial change in spending. This multiplier effect accompanies both increases and decreases in aggregate expenditures.

2. The simple multiplier is equal to the reciprocal of the marginal propensity to save. The higher the marginal propensity to save, the lower is the size of the simple multiplier. The higher the marginal propensity to consume, the greater is the simple multiplier. The complex multiplier includes all the leakages—saving, imports, and taxes.

3. The net export schedule relates net exports (exports minus imports) to levels of GDP. In our aggregate expenditures model, we assume that the level of net exports is the same at all levels of real GDP.

4. Positive net exports increase aggregate expenditures above their level in a closed economy, raising Canadian real GDP by a multiple amount; negative net exports decrease aggregate expenditures below their level, decreasing Canadian real GDP by a multiple amount. Increases in exports or decreases in imports have an expansionary effect on real GDP, while decreases in exports or increases in imports have a contractionary effect. The open economy multiplier is smaller than the simple multiplier for a closed economy.

5. Government purchases shift the aggregate expenditures schedule upward and raise equilibrium GDP.

6. Taxation reduces disposable income; reduces consumption spending, imports, and saving; shifts the aggregate expenditures schedule downward; and reduces equilibrium GDP.

7. The equilibrium level of real GDP and the full-employment GDP need not coincide. The amount by which equilibrium GDP falls short of the full-employment GDP (potential GDP) is called the recessionary gap. The amount by which equilibrium GDP exceeds full-employment GDP (potential GDP) is the inflationary gap; it causes demand-pull inflation.

8. The Great Depression of the 1930s resulted from a precipitous decline in aggregate expenditures that produced a severe and long-lasting recessionary gap. The late 1960s and early 1970s provide a good example of an inflationary gap with its accompanying demand-pull inflation.

9. The aggregate expenditures model provides many insights about the macroeconomy, but does not show price level changes or account for cost-push inflation. The aggregate demand-aggregate supply model—the subject of Chapter 11—addresses these shortcomings.

TERMS AND CONCEPTS

multiplier	open-economy multiplier
net exports	lump-sum tax
depreciation	balanced-budget multiplier
appreciation	recessionary gap
net export schedule	inflationary gap
marginal propensity to import	

STUDY QUESTIONS

1. What effect will each of the changes listed in question 4 of Chapter 9 have on the equilibrium level of GDP? Explain your answers.

2. **KEY QUESTION** *What is the multiplier effect? What relationship does the MPC bear to the size of the simple multiplier? The MPS? What will the multiplier be when the MPS is 0, .4, .6, and 1? What will it be when the MPC is 1, .90, .67, .50, and 0? How much of a change in GDP will result if firms increase their level of investment by $8*

billion and the MPC in the economy is .80? If the MPC is .67? Explain the difference between the simple and the complex multiplier.

3. Graphically depict the aggregate expenditures model for a private closed economy. Now, show a decrease in the aggregate expenditures schedule and explain why the decline in real GDP in your diagram is greater than the initial decline in aggregate expenditures. What would be the ratio of the decline in real GDP to the initial drop in aggregate expenditures if the slope of your aggregate expenditures schedule were .8?

4. Speculate on why a planned increase in saving (an upshift of the saving schedule) by households, accompanied by an increase in investment spending by firms might instead result in a decline in real GDP and *no* increase in actual saving. Demonstrate this point graphically using the leakage-injection approach to equilibrium real GDP. Now assume in your diagram that planned investment instead increases to match the initial increase in desired saving. Using your knowledge from Chapter 2, explain why these *joint* increases in planned saving and planned investment might be desirable for a society.

5. **KEY QUESTION** *The data in columns 1 and 2 of the table below are for a private closed economy.*

(1) Real domestic output (GDP = DI), billions	(2) Aggregate expenditures, private closed economy, billions	(3) Exports, billions	(4) Imports, billions	(5) Net exports, billions	(6) Aggregate expenditures, private open economy (billions)
$200	$240	$20	$18	$_____	$_____
250	280	20	22	_____	_____
300	320	20	26	_____	_____
350	360	20	30	_____	_____
400	400	20	34	_____	_____
450	440	20	38	_____	_____
500	480	20	42	_____	_____
550	520	20	46	_____	_____

   a. *Use columns 1 and 2 to determine the equilibrium GDP for this hypothetical economy.*
   b. *Now open this economy to international trade by including the export and import figures of columns 3 and 4. Fill in columns 5 and 6 and determine the equilibrium GDP for the open economy. Explain why this equilibrium GDP differs from that of the closed economy.*
   c. *Given the original $20 billion level of exports, what would be the equilibrium GDP if imports were $14 billion greater at each level of GDP? Or $14 billion less at each level of GDP? What generalizations concerning the level of imports and the equilibrium GDP do these examples illustrate?*
   d. *What is the open economy multiplier in these examples?*

6. Assume that, without taxes, the consumption schedule for an economy is as shown below:

GDP, billions	Consumption, billions
$100	$120
200	200
300	280
400	360
500	440
600	520
700	600

    a. Graph this consumption schedule and determine the size of the MPC.

    b. Assume now that a lump-sum tax system is imposed such that the government collects $10 billion in taxes at all levels of GDP. Graph the resulting consumption schedule and compare the MPC and the multiplier with that of the pretax consumption schedule.

    c. Now suppose a proportional tax system with a 10 percent tax rate is imposed instead. Calculate the new consumption schedule, graph it, and note the MPC and the multiplier.

    d. Finally, impose a progressive tax system such that the tax rate is 0 percent when GDP is $100, 5 percent at $200, 10 percent at $300, 15 percent at $400, and so forth. Determine and graph the new consumption schedule, noting the effect of this tax system on the MPC and the multiplier.

7. Explain graphically the determination of equilibrium GDP for an economy through the aggregate expenditures approach. Now add government spending and taxation, showing the impact of each on the equilibrium GDP. Finally, add taxation (any amount of a lump-sum tax that you choose) to your graph and show its effect on equilibrium GDP. Looking at your graph, determine whether equilibrium GDP has increased, decreased, or stayed the same, in view of the sizes of the government spending and taxes that you selected.

8. KEY QUESTION *Refer to columns 1 and 6 of the table for question 5. Incorporate government into the table by assuming that it plans to tax and spend $100 billion at each possible level of GDP. Also assume that all taxes are personal taxes and that government spending does not induce a shift in the private aggregate expenditures schedule. Compute and explain the change in equilibrium GDP caused by the addition of government.*

9. What is the balanced-budget multiplier? Demonstrate the balanced-budget multiplier in terms of your answer to question 8. Explain: "Equal increases in government spending and tax revenues of *n* dollars will increase the equilibrium GDP by *n* dollars." Does this hold true regardless of the size of the MPS?

10. KEY QUESTION *Refer to the accompanying table in answering the questions that follow.*

(1) Possible levels of employment, millions	(2) Real domestic output, billions	(3) Aggregate expenditures, $C + I_g + X_n + G$, billions
9	$500	$520
10	550	560
11	600	600
12	650	640
13	700	680

    a. *If full employment in this economy is $13 million, will there be an inflationary or a recessionary gap? What will be the consequences of this gap? By how much would aggregate expenditures in column 3 have to change to eliminate the inflationary or recessionary gap? Explain.*

    b. *Will there be an inflationary or recessionary gap if the full-employment level of output is $500 billion? Explain the consequences. By how much would aggregate expenditures in column 3 have to change to eliminate the inflationary or recessionary gap? Explain.*

    c. *Assuming that investment, net exports, and government expenditures do not change with changes in real GDP, what are the sizes of the MPC, the MPS, and the multiplier?*

11. **Advanced Analysis** Assume the consumption schedule for an open economy is such that consumption $C = 50 + 0.8Y$. Assume further that I_g investment and net exports planned independent of the level of real GDP and constant at $I_g = 30$ and $X_n = 10$. Recall also that in equilibrium the amount of real output produced (Y) is equal to the aggregate expenditures: $Y = C + I_g + X_n$.

    a. Calculate the equilibrium level of income or real GDP for this economy. Check your work by putting the consumption, investment, and net export schedules in tabular form and determining the equilibrium GDP.

    b. What happens to equilibrium Y if $I_g = 10$? What does this reveal about the size of the multiplier?

12. **Advanced Analysis** We can add the public sector to the private economy of question 12 as follows. Assume $G = 28$ and $T = 30$ at all levels of real output Y. Because of the taxes, the consumption schedule, $C = 50 + 0.8Y$, must be modified to read $C_a = 50 + 0.8(Y - T)$, where the term $(Y - T)$ is disposable (after-tax) income. If we assume that all taxes are levied on personal income, investment remains $I_g = 30$. Net exports are again independent of the level of income, that is, $X_n = 10$. Using the equilibrium condition $Y = C_a + I_g + X_n + G$, determine the equilibrium level of income. Explain why the addition of a public budget with a slight surplus increases the equilibrium income.

13. **(The Last Word)** What is the central economic idea humorously illustrated in Art Buchwald's piece, "Squaring the Economic Circle"?

14. WEB-BASED QUESTION **The Multiplier—Calculate a Change in GDP** The Bureau of Economic Analysis has current data on national income and product accounts at www.statcan.ca/english/Pgdb/Economy/Economic/econ04.htm. Find the most current values for GDP $= C + I + G + (X - M)$. Assume a MPC of .75, and that for each of the following, the values of the initial variables are those you just discovered. What would be the new value of GDP if **a** investment increased by 5 percent? **b** imports increased by 5 percent and exports increased by 5 percent? **c** consumption increased by 5 percent? **d** government spending increased by 5 percent? Which 5 percent increase caused GDP to change the most in absolute dollars?

15. WEB-BASED QUESTION **Net Exports—What Is the Current Economic Impact?** Positive net exports have an expansionary effect on domestic GDP; negative net exports have a contractionary effect. Check the latest figures at Statistics Canada www.statcan.ca/english/Pgdb/Economy/Economic/econ04.htm for exports and imports of goods and services. Assume a multiplier of 4. Compared to the previous period, how much is GDP increased or decreased by a change in **a** net exports of goods, **b** net exports of services, and **c** net exports of goods and services? Which has the greatest impact? Should services be included or excluded from net exports?

Aggregate Demand and Aggregate Supply

THE AGGREGATE EXPENDITURES MODEL DEVELOPED in Chapters 9 and 10 is a *fixed-price-level model*—its focus is on changes in real GDP, not on changes in the price level. Moving closer to the real world, we now develop a *variable-price-level model* so that we can simultaneously analyze changes in real GDP *and* the price level. To do this, we need to aggregate all the individual product markets of the economy into a single market. We must combine the thousands of individual equilibrium prices—of pizzas, robots, corn, computers, crankshafts, doughnuts, new houses, perfume, and legal services—into an aggregate price level. Similarly, we must merge the equilibrium quantities of all the individual products and services into a real GDP. Our new graphical model measures the price level on the vertical axis and real domestic output, or real GDP or real output, on the horizontal axis.

Specifically, in this chapter we introduce the concepts of *aggregate* demand and *aggregate* supply. We explain the shapes of the *aggregate* demand and short- and long-run *aggregate* supply curves and the forces causing the short-run aggregate supply curve to shift. Next, we consider the equilibrium levels of prices and real GDP. Finally, we explore the difference between equilibrium GDP and full-employment GDP, and the distinction between a *recessionary gap* and an *inflationary gap*.

What you learn in this chapter will help organize your thinking about equilibrium GDP, the price level, and government macroeconomic policies. The tools you acquire here will also help you in later chapters, where we contrast differing views on macroeconomic theory and policy.

IN THIS CHAPTER YOU WILL LEARN:

Why the aggregate demand curve is downward sloping, and what factors shift the entire curve.

•

What determines the shape of the aggregate supply curve in the short and long run, and what factors shift the short-run aggregate supply curve.

•

How the price level and equilibrium real GDP are determined.

•

The distinction between equilibrium GDP and full-employment GDP.

•

The nature and causes of recessionary and inflationary gaps.

The Big Picture

THOSE OF YOU WHO HAVE STUDIED THE expenditure model will recall that it assumed a fixed price level. Also, the expenditure model deals only with aggregate demand; the aggregate supply in an economy is ignored. In this chapter you will study a model of the macroeconomy that explains both the price level and GDP—the aggregate demand and aggregate supply model. If you have previously studied demand and supply analysis, you will discern similarities. But there are many differences. For those who have covered the aggregate expenditure model, there is a section that links it to the aggregate demand curve.

The purpose of studying the aggregate demand-aggregate supply model is the same as for the aggregate expenditure model. We aim to understand how the macroeconomy functions, so we can devise policies that will stabilize the economy and promote growth. The aggregate demand–aggregate supply model is a powerful theoretical model that allows us to better understand the main macroeconomic issues: economic growth, inflation, and unemployment.

As you read this chapter, keep the following points in mind:

- **Key Concept 10** is discussed.
- Distinguish between factors that shift the aggregate demand and the short-run aggregate supply curves and movements along each curve. Each of the curves is independent of the other; each shifts for different reasons.
- We are focusing on the short run. For the most part, the short-run aggregate supply curve is upward-sloping. The short run in macroeconomics can last many years.
- In the short run, the economy may be at equilibrium at a level of GDP below full employment (potential GDP). This means the economy is not fully employing all its available resources, particularly its labour force. If such is the case, the economy is in a recession. If the short-run equilibrium GDP is above full-employment GDP, inflationary pressures appear.
- In the long run, equilibrium GDP and potential GDP are the same. This means the long-run aggregate supply curve is vertical. ∎

AGGREGATE DEMAND

Aggregate demand *is a schedule or a curve showing the various amounts of goods and services—the amounts of real output—that domestic consumers, businesses, government, and foreign buyers collectively desire to purchase at each possible price level.* Other things equal, the lower the price level, the larger the real GDP these buyers will purchase. Conversely, the higher the price level, the smaller the real GDP they will buy. Thus, the relationship between the price level and the amount of real GDP demanded is inverse or negative.

Aggregate Demand Curve

The inverse relationship between the price level and real output is shown in Figure 11-1 where the aggregate demand curve AD slopes downward as does the demand curve for an individual product.

Why the downward slope? The rationale is *not* the same as for a single product. That explanation centred on income and substitution effects. When the price of an individual product falls, the consumer's (constant) nominal income will enable him or her to purchase more of the product (the income effect). And, as price falls, the consumer wants to buy more of the product because it becomes relatively less expensive than other goods (the substitution effect).

But these explanations do not work for aggregates. In Figure 11-1, when the economy moves down its aggregate demand curve, it moves to lower price levels. But our circular flow model tells us that when consumers pay lower prices for goods and services, less income is likely to flow to resource suppliers in the form of wages, rents, interest, and profits. As a result, a decrease in the price level does *not* necessarily mean an increase in the nominal income of the economy as a whole. Thus, a decline in the price level need not produce an income effect (more of a product is purchased because a decline in its price leaves buyers with more real income).

Similarly, in Figure 11-1 prices in general are falling as we move down the aggregate demand

FIGURE 11-1 The aggregate demand curve

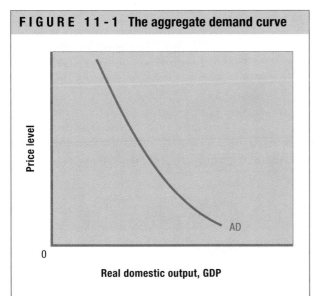

The downsloping aggregate demand curve AD indicates an inverse relationship between the price level and the amount of real domestic output purchased.

curve, so the rationale for the substitution effect (more of a product is purchased because it becomes cheaper relative to all other products) is not applicable. There is no overall substitution effect when the price level falls.

If the substitution and income effects do not explain the downsloping aggregate demand curve, what does? The rationale rests on the following three factors.

Wealth Effect
The first reason for the downsloping aggregate demand curve involves the **wealth effect**. A higher price level reduces the real value or purchasing power of the public's accumulated financial assets. In particular, the real value of assets with fixed money values, such as savings accounts or bonds, diminishes. Because of the erosion of purchasing power of such assets, the public is poorer in real terms and will reduce its spending. A household might buy a new car or a sailboat if the purchasing power of its financial asset balances is, say, $50,000. But if inflation erodes the purchasing power of the asset balances to $30,000, the family may defer its purchase.

Conversely, a decline in the price level will increase the real value or purchasing power of a household's wealth and increase consumption spending.

Interest-Rate Effect
The **interest-rate effect** tells us that the aggregate demand curve is

downsloping because of the impact of price-level changes on interest rates and, in turn, on consumption and investment spending. As the price level rises, so do interest rates, and rising interest rates reduce certain kinds of consumption and investment spending.

Elaboration: *The aggregate demand curve assumes the supply of money in the economy is fixed.* When the price level increases, consumers need more money for purchases, and businesses similarly require more money to meet their payrolls and to buy other needed resources. In short, a higher price level increases the demand for money.

With a fixed supply of money, this increase in the demand for money drives up the price paid for its use. That price is the interest rate. Higher interest rates curtail interest-sensitive expenditures by businesses and households. A firm expecting a 10 percent return on a potential purchase of capital will find that purchase profitable when the interest rate is, say, only 7 percent. But the purchase is unprofitable and will not be made when the interest rate has risen to, say, 12 percent. Similarly, some consumers will decide *not* to purchase houses or automobiles when the interest rate rises.

Conclusion: A higher price level—by increasing the demand for money and the interest rate—reduces the amount of real output demanded.

Foreign-Trade Effect
We found in Chapter 7's discussion of national income accounting that imports and exports are components of total spending. The volumes of our imports and exports depend on, among other things, relative price levels here and abroad. If the price level rises in Canada relative to the levels in other countries, Canadian buyers will purchase more imports and fewer Canadian goods. Similarly, the rest of the world will buy fewer Canadian goods, reducing Canadian exports. In brief, a rise in the Canadian price level will increase our imports and reduce our exports, reducing the amount of net export (export minus import) spending on Canadian-produced products.

More generally, the **foreign-trade effect** is this: A relative increase in a nation's price level reduces its net exports, resulting in a decline in the aggregate amount of domestic output demanded. Conversely, a relative decline in a nation's price level increases its net exports, thereby increasing the amount of domestic output demanded.

Derivation of the Aggregate Demand Curve from the Aggregate Expenditures Model[1]

We can derive the downsloping aggregate demand curve of Figure 11-1 directly from the aggregate

---

[1] This section presumes knowledge of the aggregate expenditures model discussed in Chapters 9 and 10 and can be skipped by readers who are not assigned those chapters.

expenditures model of Chapters 9 and 10. To do so, we simply need to relate the various possible price levels to corresponding equilibrium GDPs. Note first that in Figure 11-2 we have stacked the aggregate expenditures model (Figure 11-2a) and the aggregate demand curve (Figure 11-2b) vertically. We can do this because real GDP is measured on the horizontal axes of both models. Now suppose that the economy's price level is P_2 and its aggregate expenditures schedule is ($C_a + I_g + X_n +$

FIGURE 11-2 Deriving the aggregate demand curve from the expenditures-output model

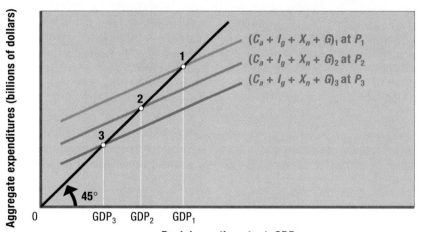

(a) Aggregate expenditures model

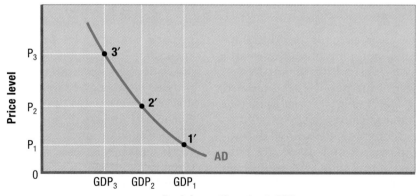

(b) Aggregate demand–aggregate supply model

Through the wealth, interest-rate, and foreign-trade effects, the consumption, investment, and net export schedules and therefore the aggregate expenditures schedule will rise when the price level declines and fall when the price level increases. If the aggregate expenditures schedule is ($C_a + I_g + X_n + G$)$_2$ when the price level is P_2, the equilibrium output is GDP$_2$; then P_2 and GDP$_2$ determine one point (2′) on the aggregate demand curve. A lower price level such as P_1 increases aggregate expenditures to ($C_a + I_g + X_n + G$)$_1$, providing point 1′ on the aggregate demand curve. Similarly, a high price level at P_3 shifts aggregate expenditures down to ($C_a + I_g + X_n + G$)$_3$, so P_3 and GDP$_3$ yield another point on the aggregate demand curve at 3′.

$G)_2$, the middle schedule in Figure 11-2a. The equilibrium GDP is then GDP_2. So in Figure 11-2b we can plot the equilibrium real output GDP_2 and the corresponding price level P_2. This gives us one point—namely, 2'—in Figure 11-2b.

Now assume the price level drops to P_1. Other things equal, this lower price level will (1) increase the value of wealth, boosting consumption expenditures; (2) reduce the interest rate, promoting investment expenditures; and (3) reduce imports and increase exports, increasing net export expenditures. The aggregate expenditures schedule will rise from $(C_a + I_g + X_n + G)_2$ to, say, $(C_a + I_g + X_n + G)_1$ in Figure 11-2a, giving us equilibrium at GDP_1. In Figure 11-2b we plot this new price-level–real-output combination, P_1 and GDP_1, as point 1'.

Now suppose the price level increases from the original P_2 to P_3. The real value of wealth falls, the interest rate rises, exports fall, and imports rise. Consequently, the consumption, investment, and net export schedules fall, shifting the aggregate expenditures schedule downward from $(C_a + I_g + X_n + G)_2$ to, say, $(C_a + I_g + X_n + G)_3$, which gives us equilibrium at GDP_3. This lets us locate a third point in Figure 11-2b, namely, point 3', where the price level is P_3 and real output is GDP_3.

In summary, a decrease in the economy's price level shifts its aggregate expenditures schedule upward and increases real GDP. An increase in the price level shifts its aggregate expenditures schedule downward, reducing real GDP. The resulting price-level–real-GDP combinations yield various points such as 1', 2', and 3' in Figure 11-2b. Together, such points locate the downsloping aggregate demand curve for the economy.

Determinants of Aggregate Demand

Changes in the price level change the level of aggregate spending (Figure 11-2a); this, in turn, changes the amount of real GDP demanded by the economy. More specifically, an increase in the price level, *other things equal*, will decrease the quantity of real GDP demanded; a decrease in the price level will increase the amount of real GDP demanded. These changes are represented graphically as movements along a fixed aggregate demand curve. However, if one or more of those "other things" change, the entire aggregate demand curve shifts. We refer to those "other things" as **determinants of aggregate demand**; they "determine" the *location* of the aggregate demand curve.

We must then distinguish between *changes in the quantity of real output demanded* (caused by changes in the price level) and *changes in aggregate demand* (caused by changes in one or more of the determinants of aggregate demand). A similar distinction was made in Chapter 4 in discussing demand curves for single products.

In Figure 11-3, an increase in aggregate demand is depicted by the rightward movement of the curve from AD_0 to AD_1. This shift indicates that, at each price level, the desired amount of real goods and services is larger than before.

A decrease in aggregate demand is shown as the leftward shift of the curve from AD_0 to AD_2, indicating that people desire to buy less real output at each price level.

To reemphasize: The changes in aggregate demand shown in Figure 11-3 occur when changes happen in any of the factors we have assumed to be constant under the phrase "other things equal." These determinants of aggregate demand, or *aggregate demand shifters*, are listed in Figure 11-3. Let's examine each of them in some detail.

Consumer Spending

Even if the price level is constant, domestic consumers collectively may alter their purchases of Canadian-produced real output. When this happens, the entire aggregate demand curve shifts. It shifts leftward, as from AD_0 to AD_2 in Figure 11-3, when consumers buy less output than before at each possible price level; it moves rightward, as from AD_0 to AD_1, when they buy more at each possible price level.

Several factors other than the price level may change consumer spending, thus shifting the aggregate demand curve. As indicated in Figure 11-3, these factors are real consumer wealth, consumer expectations, household indebtedness, and taxes.

CONSUMER WEALTH Consumer wealth includes all consumer assets, both financial assets such as stocks and bonds and physical assets such as houses and land. A sharp decline in the real value of consumer assets encourages people to save more (buy fewer products) to restore their wealth. The resulting decline in consumer spending will decrease aggregate demand—that is, shift the aggregate demand curve leftward. In contrast, an increase in the real value of consumer wealth will increase consumption spending at each price level; the aggregate demand curve will shift rightward.

Warning: We are *not* referring here to the previously discussed "wealth effect." That assumes a

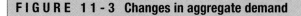

FIGURE 11-3 Changes in aggregate demand

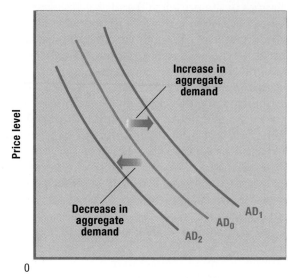

Increase in
aggregate
demand

Decrease in
aggregate
demand

Price level

Real domestic output, GDP

0

AD$_2$ AD$_0$ AD$_1$

**Determinants of aggregate demand:
factors that shift the aggregate demand curve**

1. Change in consumer spending
   a. Consumer wealth
   b. Consumer expectations
   c. Household indebtedness
   d. Taxes
2. Change in investment spending
   a. Interest rates
   b. Profit expectations on investment projects
   c. Business taxes
   d. Technology
   e. Degree of excess capacity
3. Change in government spending
4. Change in net export spending
   a. National income abroad
   b. Exchange rates

A change in one or more of the listed determinants of aggregate demand will change aggregate demand. An increase in aggregate demand is shown as a rightward shift of the AD curve, here from AD$_0$ to AD$_1$; a decrease in aggregate demand, as a leftward shift, here from AD$_0$ to AD$_2$.

fixed aggregate demand curve and results from a change in the price level. In contrast, the change in real wealth addressed here is independent of a change in the price level; it is a *non-price-level factor* that shifts the entire aggregate demand curve. An example would be a sharp increase in stock prices that increases consumer wealth, even though the price level has not changed. Similarly, a sharp decline in the real value of houses and land reduces consumer wealth, independent of changes in the general price level.

CONSUMER EXPECTATIONS Changes in expectations about the future may alter consumer spending. When people expect their future real incomes to rise, they spend more of their current incomes. Thus present consumption spending increases (present saving falls), and the aggregate demand curve shifts rightward. An expectation that real income will decline in the future reduces present consumption spending and therefore shifts the aggregate demand curve leftward.

Similarly, a widely held expectation of surging future inflation increases aggregate demand today because consumers want to buy products before prices escalate. Conversely, expectations of lower prices in the near future may reduce present consumption. People may postpone some of their present consumption to take advantage of the future lower prices.

HOUSEHOLD INDEBTEDNESS Households with high levels of indebtedness from past buying financed by borrowing may be forced to cut present spending to pay off their existing debt. The result is a decline in consumption spending and a leftward shift of the aggregate demand curve. When household indebtedness is low, borrowing and present consumption spending tend to increase. The aggregate demand curve shifts to the right.

TAXES A reduction in personal income tax rates raises take-home income and increases consumer purchases at each possible price level. So tax cuts shift the aggregate demand curve rightward. Tax increases reduce consumption spending and shift the aggregate demand curve to the left.

Investment Spending Investment spending—the purchase of capital goods—is a second major determinant of aggregate demand. A decline in the amount of new capital goods desired by businesses at each price level will shift the aggregate demand curve leftward. An increase in the desired amount of investment goods will increase aggregate demand. Let's consider the individual factors that can alter the level of investment spending, as listed in Figure 11-3.

INTEREST RATES All else equal, an increase in interest rates caused by a factor other than a change in the price level will lower investment spending and reduce aggregate demand. We are *not* referring here to the so-called "interest-rate effect" due to a change in the price level. Instead, we are identifying a change in the interest rate resulting from, say, a change in the nation's money supply. An increase in the money supply reduces the interest rate, increasing investment and aggregate demand. A decrease in the supply of money increases the interest rate, reducing investment and aggregate demand.

EXPECTED RETURNS ON INVESTMENT PROJECTS Higher expected returns on investment projects will increase the demand for capital goods and shift the aggregate demand curve rightward. For example, an anticipated rise in consumer spending can improve the expected returns of possible investment projects. Alternatively, if the profit outlook on possible investment projects dims because of an expected decline in consumer spending, investment spending will decline. Consequently, aggregate demand will also decline.

BUSINESS TAXES An increase in business taxes reduces after-tax profits from corporate investment and reduces investment spending and aggregate demand. Conversely, a tax reduction increases after-tax profits from corporate investment, boosts investment spending, and pushes the aggregate demand curve rightward.

TECHNOLOGY New and improved technologies stimulate investment spending and increase aggregate demand. Example: Recent advances in microbiology and electronics have spawned new labs and production facilities to exploit the new technologies.

DEGREE OF EXCESS CAPACITY A rise in excess capacity—unused existing capital—will retard the demand for new capital goods and reduce aggregate demand. Other things equal, firms operating factories at well below capacity have little incen-

tive to build new factories. But when firms collectively discover their excess capacity is dwindling, they build new factories and buy more equipment. Thus, investment spending rises and the aggregate demand curve shifts to the right.

Government Spending Government's desire to buy goods and services is a third determinant of aggregate demand. An increase in government purchases of real output at each price level will increase aggregate demand as long as tax collections and interest rates do not change as a result. An example would be a decision by government to expand the interstate highway system. In contrast, a reduction in government spending, such as a cutback in highway construction, will reduce aggregate demand.

Net Export Spending The final determinant of aggregate demand is net export spending. When foreign consumers change their purchases of Canadian goods independently of changes in the Canadian price level, the aggregate demand curve in Canada shifts. We specify "independently of changes in price level" to distinguish these changes from spending changes arising from the foreign trade effect. That effect helps explain why a change in the Canadian price level moves the economy *along* its existing AD curve.

In discussing aggregate demand shifters, we instead address changes in net exports caused by factors other than changes in the price level. Increases in net exports caused by these other factors push the Canadian aggregate demand curve rightward. The logic is as follows: First, a higher level of Canadian exports constitutes an increased *foreign demand* for Canadian goods. Second, a reduction of Canadian imports implies an increased *domestic demand* for Canadian-produced products.

The non-price-level factors that alter net exports are primarily national income abroad and exchange rates.

NATIONAL INCOME ABROAD Rising real GDP in a foreign nation increases the foreign demand for Canadian goods, increasing aggregate demand in Canada. As income levels rise in a foreign nation, its citizens can afford to buy both more products made at home *and* made in Canada. Canadian exports therefore rise in step with increases in the national income of our trading partners. Declines in GDP abroad have the opposite effect: Canadian net exports decline, shifting the aggregate demand curve in Canada leftward.

EXCHANGE RATES A change in the exchange rate (Chapter 6) between the dollar and other currencies also affects net exports and hence aggregate demand. Suppose the dollar price of yen rises, meaning the *dollar depreciates* in terms of the yen. This is the same as saying the yen price of dollars falls—the *yen appreciates*. The new relative values of dollars and yen means consumers in Japan can obtain *more* dollars with any particular number of yen. Consumers in Canada can obtain *fewer* yen for each dollar. Japanese consumers therefore discover that Canadian goods are cheaper in terms of yen. They buy more Canadian goods. Canadian consumers find that fewer Japanese products can be purchased with a set number of dollars. They buy fewer Japanese goods.

With respect to Canadian *exports*, a $40 pair of Canadian-made blue jeans now might be bought for 2,880 yen compared to 3,600 yen. And in terms our *imports*, a Japanese watch might now cost $225 rather than $180. In these circumstances Canadian exports will rise and imports will fall. This increase in net exports translates into a rightward shift of the Canadian aggregate demand curve.

You are urged to think through the opposite scenario in which the dollar appreciates (the yen depreciates).

11-1

QUICK REVIEW

- Aggregate demand reflects an inverse relationship between the price level and the amount of real domestic output demanded.

- Changes in the price level produce wealth, interest-rate, and foreign-trade effects that explain the downward slope of the aggregate demand curve.

- Changes in one or more of the determinants of aggregate demand (Figure 11-3) alter the amounts of real GDP demanded at each price level; they shift the aggregate demand curve.

- An increase in aggregate demand is shown as a rightward shift of the aggregate demand curve; a decrease, as a leftward shift of the curve.

Aggregate Demand Shifts and the Aggregate Expenditures Model[2]

The determinants of aggregate demand listed in Figure 11-3 are the components of Chapter 10's aggregate expenditures model. When one of these determinants changes, so does the location of the aggregate expenditures schedule. We can easily link shifts in the aggregate expenditures schedule to shifts of the aggregate demand curve.

Let's suppose that the price level is constant. In Figure 11-4 we begin with the aggregate expenditures schedule at $(C_a + I_g + X_n + G)_1$ in the top diagram, yielding real output of GDP_1. Assume now that more optimistic business expectations increase investment spending, so the aggregate expenditures schedule rises from $(C_a + I_g + X_n + G)_1$ to $(C_a + I_g + X_n + G)_2$. (The notation "at P_1" reminds us that the price level is assumed to be constant.) The result will be a multiplied increase in real output from GDP_1 to GDP_2.

In the lower graph the increase in investment spending is reflected in the horizontal distance between AD_1 and the broken curve to its right. The immediate effect of the increase in investment is an increase in aggregate demand by the exact amount of this new spending. But then the multiplier process magnifies the initial increase in investment into successive rounds of consumption spending and an ultimate multiplied increase in aggregate demand from AD_1 to AD_2. Equilibrium real output rises from GDP_1 to GDP_2, the same multiplied increase in real GDP as that in the top graph. *The initial increase in investment in the top graph has shifted the AD curve in the lower graph by a horizontal distance equal to the change in investment times the multiplier.* The change in real GDP is still associated with the constant price level P_1. To generalize,

$$\text{Shift of AD curve} = \text{initial change in spending} \times \text{multiplier}$$

AGGREGATE SUPPLY: THE SHORT RUN

The **short-run aggregate supply** *is a schedule or a curve showing the level of real domestic output that*

[2] This section presumes knowledge of the aggregate expenditures model (Chapters 9 ad 10). It may be skipped by instructors who wish to rely exclusively on the aggregate supply framework.

FIGURE 11-4 Shifts in the aggregate expenditures schedule and in the aggregate demand curve

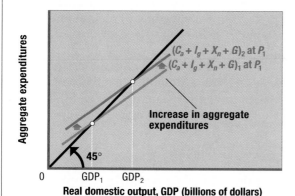

(a) Aggregate expenditures model

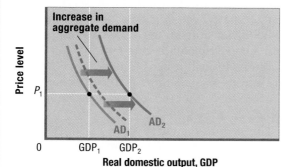

(b) Aggregate demand–aggregate supply model

(a) A change in some determinant of consumption, investment, or net exports (other than the price level) shifts the aggregate expenditures schedule upward from $(C_a + I_g + X_n + G)_1$ to $(C_a + I_g + X_n + G)_2$. The multiplier increases real output from GDP_1 to GDP_2. (b) The counterpart of this change is an initial rightward shift of the aggregate demand curve by the amount of initial new spending (from AD_1 to the broken curve). This leads to a multiplied rightward shift of the curve to AD_2, which is just sufficient to show the same increase in GDP as in the aggregate expenditures model.

will be produced at each price level. Higher price levels create an incentive for enterprises to produce and sell more output, while lower price levels reduce output. As a result, the relationship between the price level and the amount of real output businesses offer for sale is direct or positive.

The Shape of the Short-Run Aggregate Supply Curve

Figure 11-5 is a portrayal of the short-run aggregate supply curve. It shows a positive relationship between the price level and output. We define the short run as a period in which input prices—particularly nominal wages—remain fixed. The short-run aggregate supply curve is thus upward sloping because input prices are fixed in the short run, and as the price level rises, there is an incentive for producers to increase the quantity each supplies. We emphasize that in macroeconomic terms the duration of the short run may be several *years*. More will be said about why the short-run aggregate supply curve is upward sloping later in this chapter. Also later in this chapter, we will distinguish between the short run and the long run—a period long enough for all input prices to become fully responsive to the price level. You will see this implies that in the long run the aggregate supply curve is vertical at the natural rate of unemployment. For now we will concentrate on the short run, as we do in many parts of our macroeconomic analysis. To emphasize the importance of the short run we have purposely designated the short run aggregate supply curve simply AS. When we refer

FIGURE 11-5 The short-run aggregate supply curve

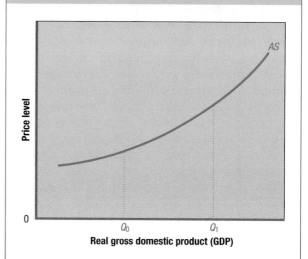

The short-run aggregate supply curve shows the level of real domestic output that will be produced at various price levels. The flatter it is, the more slack there is in the economy. The steeper it is, the closer the economy is to capacity utilization.

to the "aggregate supply," we implicitly mean the short run, unless stated otherwise.

The steepness of the aggregate supply in the short run will depend on current *capacity utilization*, which measures how much of existing productive capacity is being used. If all resources are used close to their maximum, the aggregate supply curve will be steep, since a small increase in output would require a relatively large increase in the price level. The more slack in the economy, the flatter the aggregate supply curve.

Unless specified otherwise, we assume the aggregate supply curve itself does not shift when the price level changes. You already know that the shape of the aggregate supply curve reflects what happens to per unit production costs as GDP expands or contracts. You also know from Chapter 8 that per unit production cost in found by dividing the total cost of all the resources used in production by the total quantity of output. That is, the per unit production cost of a particular level of output is the average cost of that output. And the average cost of a particular output will establish that output's price level, since the price level must be high enough to cover all the costs of production, including profit "costs."

If the short run aggregate supply curve is completely flat, there is slack in the economy. Large amounts of unused machinery and equipment and unemployed workers are available for production. These idle resources can be put back to work with no upward pressure on the price level. As output expands, no shortages or production bottlenecks will appear that would raise prices. Workers unemployed for a number of months will hardly expect wage increases when recalled to their jobs. Because producers can acquire labour and other inputs at stable prices, production costs do not rise as output is expanded per unit. There is no reason to raise product prices. Also, if the short run aggregate supply curve is completely flat, it implies that if real output falls, product and resource prices will not move downward. That means real output and employment may fall, but product prices and employment will decline because prices and wages are inflexible.

At the other extreme, the short run aggregate supply curve is almost completely vertical. The economy reaches its short-run full capacity level of real output. Any increase in the price level will not produce additional real output because the economy is operating at its full capacity. Individ-

ual firms may try to expand production by bidding resources away from other firms. But the resources and the additional production one firm gains will be lost by some other firm. This will raise resources prices (costs) and ultimately product prices, but real output will remain unchanged.

In most instances, the short run aggregate supply curve will be upward sloping; an expansion of real output is accompanied by a rising price level. The economy is neither in a severe recession, nor at full-capacity level. Since this is the range of the short-run aggregate supply curve in which the economy functions most of the time, it will be the range on which we will focus.

Determinants of Aggregate Supply in the Short Run

Changes in output resulting from *movements along* the aggregate supply curve need to be distinguished from shifts in the aggregate supply curve itself. An existing aggregate supply curve identifies the relationship between the price level and real output, *other things equal*. But when one or more of these "other things" change, the aggregate supply curve itself shifts.

The shift of the curve from AS_0 to AS_2 in Figure 11-6 represents an *increase* in aggregate supply. This shift is rightward, indicating that businesses collectively will produce more output at each price level. A leftward shift of the curve from AS_0 to AS_1 indicates a *decrease* in aggregate supply. Businesses now will produce less output at each price level than before (or charge higher prices at each level of output).

Figure 11-6 lists the "other things" that shift the aggregate supply curve when they change. Called the **determinants of aggregate supply**, they collectively determine the *location* of the aggregate supply curve. These determinants have one thing in common: When they change, per-unit production costs also change *at each price level*. This changes profits and causes producers to change their collective output *at each price level*. Hence, when one of the determinants listed in Figure 11-6 changes, the aggregate supply curve shifts. Changes that decrease per-unit production costs shift the aggregate supply curve to the right; changes that increase per-unit production costs shift it to the left. *When per-unit production costs change for reasons other than changes in real output, firms collectively alter the amount of output they produce at each price level.*

FIGURE 11-6 Changes in the short run aggregate supply

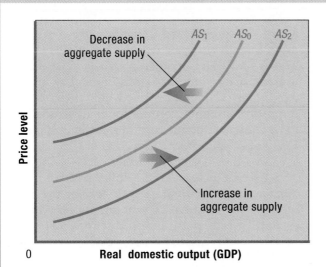

Determinants of the short run aggregate supply: factors that shift the aggregate supply curve

1. Change in input prices
   a. Domestic resource availability of:
      land
      labour
      capital
      entrepreneurial ability
   b. Price of imported resources
   c. Market power
2. Change in productivity
3. Change in legal-institutional environment
   a. Business taxes and subsidies
   b. Government regulation

A change in one or more of the determinants of aggregate supply listed will cause a change in aggregate supply. An increase in aggregate supply is shown as a "rightward" shift of the AS curve from AS_0 to AS_2; a decrease in aggregate supply, as a "leftward" shift from AS_0 to AS_1.

Let's examine the aggregate supply shifters in Figure 11-6 in more detail.

Input Prices Input or resource prices—to be distinguished from the output prices making up the price level—are a major determinant of aggregate supply. All else equal, higher input prices increase per-unit production costs and reduce aggregate supply. Lower input prices do just the opposite. A number of factors influence input prices.

DOMESTIC RESOURCE AVAILABILITY Increases in the supply of domestic resources lower resource prices and thus decrease per-unit production costs; that shifts the aggregate supply curve to the right. At any specific price level, firms collectively will then produce and offer for sale more real output than before. In contrast, declines in resource supplies increase input prices and shift the aggregate supply curve to the left.

How might changes in the availability of land, labour, capital, and entrepreneurial resources work to shift the aggregate supply curve? We can look at several examples.

1. **LAND** Land resources might expand through discoveries of mineral deposits, irrigation of land, or technical innovations, permitting us to transform what were previously "nonre-

sources" into valuable factors of production. An increase in the supply of land resources lowers the price of land inputs, lowering per-unit production costs. For example, the recent discovery that widely available materials at low temperatures can act as superconductors of electricity is expected eventually to reduce per-unit production costs by reducing electricity loss during transmission. This lower price of electricity will increase aggregate supply.

Two examples of reductions in land-resource availability may also be cited: (1) the widespread depletion of the nation's underground water reserves through irrigation, and (2) the nation's loss of topsoil through intensive farming. Eventually, these problems may increase water and land prices and shift the aggregate supply curve leftward.

2. **LABOUR** About 75 percent of all business costs are wages or salaries. Other things equal, changes in wages have a significant impact on per-unit production costs and on the location of the aggregate supply curve. An increase in the availability of labour resources reduces the price of labour and increases aggregate supply; a decrease has the opposite effect. Examples: The influx of women into the labour force during the past two decades placed a downward

pressure on wages and expanded Canadian aggregate supply. Emigration of employable workers from abroad also has historically increased the availability of labour in Canada and reduced wages.

The great loss of life during World War II greatly diminished the postwar availability of labour in Canada, raising per-unit production costs. Currently, the AIDS epidemic has reduced the supply of labour and thus diminished the nation's aggregate supply of real output.

3. **CAPITAL** Aggregate supply usually increases when society adds to its stock of capital. Such an addition would happen if society saved more of its income and used the savings to purchase capital goods. In much the same way, an improvement in the quality of capital reduces production costs and increases aggregate supply. For example, businesses over the years have increased aggregate supply by replacing poor-quality equipment with new, superior equipment.

On the other hand, aggregate supply declines when the quantity and quality of the nation's stock of capital diminishes. Example: In the depths of the Great Depression of the 1930s, the Canadian capital stock deteriorated because new purchases of capital were insufficient to offset the normal wearing out and obsolescence of plant and equipment. Aggregate supply declined.

4. **ENTREPRENEURIAL ABILITY** Finally, the amount of entrepreneurial ability available to the economy may change, shifting the aggregate supply curve. Recent media focus on individuals, such as Bill Gates, who have amassed fortunes through entrepreneurial efforts, might conceivably increase the number of people who have entrepreneurial aspirations. If so, the aggregate supply curve might shift rightward.

PRICES OF IMPORTED RESOURCES Just as foreign demand for Canadian goods contributes to Canadian aggregate demand, resources imported from abroad add to Canadian aggregate supply. Whether domestic or imported, resources boost a nation's production capacity. Generally, a decrease in the prices of imported resources expands a nation's aggregate supply; an increase in the prices of these resources reduces a nation's aggregate supply.

Exchange-rate fluctuations are one factor that alters the price of imported resources. Suppose the dollar price of foreign currency falls—the dollar appreciates—enabling Canadian firms to obtain more foreign currency with each Canadian dollar. This means that Canadian producers face a lower dollar price of imported resources. Under these conditions, Canadian firms would expand their imports of foreign resources and realize reductions in per-unit production costs at each level of output. Falling per-unit production costs of this type shift the Canadian aggregate supply curve to the right.

Also, an increase in the dollar price of foreign currency—dollar depreciation—raises the prices of imported resources. Canadian imports of these resources fall, per-unit production costs jump upward, and Canada's aggregate supply curve moves leftward.

MARKET POWER A change in the degree of market power or monopoly power held by sellers of resources can also affect input prices and aggregate supply. *Market power* is the ability to set a price above the price that would occur in a competitive situation. The rise and fall of market power held by the Organization of Petroleum Exporting Countries (OPEC) during the past three decades is a good illustration. The tenfold increase in the price of oil that OPEC achieved during the 1970s permeated the economy, drove up per-unit production costs, and jolted the Canadian aggregate supply curve leftward. But then a steep reduction in OPEC's market power during the mid-1980s reduced the cost of manufacturing and transporting products and, as a direct result, increased Canadian aggregate supply.

A change in the market power of labour unions also can affect the location of the aggregate supply curve. Some observers believe that unions experienced growing market power in the 1970s, resulting in union wage increases that widened the gap between union and nonunion workers. This higher pay may have increased per-unit production costs and produced leftward shifts of aggregate supply. But union market power waned during the 1980s. The price of union labour fell in many industries, resulting in lower per-unit production costs. The outcome then was an increase in aggregate supply.

Productivity Productivity relates a nation's level of real output to the quantity of input used to produce that output. In other words, **productivity** is a measure of average real output, or of real output per unit of input:

$$\text{Productivity} = \frac{\text{total output}}{\text{total inputs}}$$

An increase in productivity means the economy can obtain more real output from its limited resources—its inputs.

How does an increase in productivity affect the aggregate supply curve? We first need to see how a change in productivity alters the per-unit production cost. Suppose real output is 10 units, 5 units of input are needed to produce that quantity, and the price of each input unit is $2. Then

$$\text{Productivity} = \frac{\text{total output}}{\text{total inputs}} = \frac{10}{5} = 2$$

and

$$\text{Per-unit production cost} = \frac{\text{total input cost}}{\text{total output}} = \frac{\$2 \times 5}{10} = \$1$$

Note that we obtain the total input cost by multiplying the unit input cost by the number of inputs used.

Now suppose productivity increases so that real output doubles to 20 units, while the input unit price and quantity remain constant at $2 and 5 units. You should use the above equations to confirm that productivity rises from 2 to 4 and that the per-unit production cost of the output falls from $1 to $.50. That is, the doubled productivity caused the per-unit production cost to decrease by half.

By reducing the per-unit production cost, an increase in productivity shifts the aggregate supply curve rightward; a decline in productivity increases the per-unit production cost and shifts the aggregate supply curve leftward.

You will see in Chapter 18 that productivity growth is a major factor explaining the long-term expansion of aggregate supply in Canada and the corresponding growth of real GDP. More machinery and equipment per worker, improved production technology, a better-educated and better-trained labour force, and improved forms of business enterprises have raised productivity and increased aggregate supply.

Legal-Institutional Environment   Changes in the legal-institutional setting in which businesses collectively operate may alter the per-unit costs of output and shift the aggregate supply curve. Two changes of this type are (1) changes in taxes and subsidies, and (2) changes in the extent of regulation.

BUSINESS TAXES AND SUBSIDIES   Higher business taxes, such as sales, excise, and social insurance taxes, increase per-unit costs and reduce aggregate supply in much the same way as a wage increase. Example: An increase in social insurance taxes paid by businesses will increase production costs and reduce aggregate supply. Similarly, a business subsidy—a payment or tax break by government to firms—reduces production costs and increases aggregate supply.

GOVERNMENT REGULATION   It is usually costly for businesses to comply with government regulations. Thus, regulation increases per-unit production costs and shifts the aggregate supply curve leftward. "Supply-side" proponents of deregulation of the economy have argued forcefully that, by increasing efficiency and reducing the paperwork associated with complex regulations, deregulation will reduce per-unit costs. In this way the aggregate supply curve purportedly will shift rightward. Conversely, increases in regulation raise production costs and reduce aggregate supply.

11-2
QUICK REVIEW

- The aggregate supply curve is upward sloping in the short run—a period defined as one during which input prices, particularly wages, do not change.

- The shape of the short-run aggregate supply curve is determined by the extent of resource utilization.

- By altering the production cost independent of changes in the level of output, changes in one or more of the determinants of aggregate supply (Figure 11-6) shift the location of the short run aggregate supply curve.

- An increase in the short run aggregate supply is shown as a rightward shift of the curve, a decrease as a leftward shift of the curve.

EQUILIBRIUM: REAL OUTPUT AND THE PRICE LEVEL

We found in Chapter 4 that the intersection of a product's demand curve and supply curve determines its equilibrium price and quantity. Similarly, as we see here in Figure 11-7, the intersection of the aggregate demand and aggregate supply curves determines the economy's **equilibrium price level** and **equilibrium real domestic output**.

In *Figure 11-7 (Key Graph)*, where aggregate demand crosses aggregate supply, the equilibrium

price level and level of real domestic output are P_e and Q_e, respectively. To illustrate why P_e is the equilibrium price level and Q_e is the equilibrium level of output, suppose the price level were P_1 rather than P_e. We observe from the aggregate supply curve that price level P_1 would entice businesses to produce (at most) real output level Q_1. How much real output would domestic consumers, businesses, government, and foreign buyers want to purchase at P_1? The aggregate demand curve tells us the answer is Q_2. Competition among buyers to purchase the available real output Q_1 will drive up the price level to P_e.

KEY GRAPH

FIGURE 11-7 Determination of equilibrium real GDP and the equilibrium price level

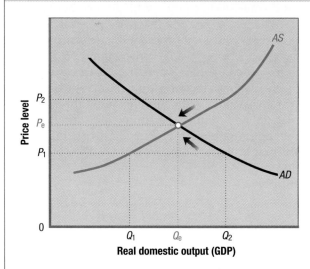

If the price level is below the equilibrium P_e, aggregate demand would be greater than aggregate supply (at P_1) and there would be upward pressure on the price level towards the equilibrium level P_e. The opposite would be the case at P_2.

11-7
QUICK QUIZ

1. The AD curve slopes downward because
   (a) per-unit production costs fall as real GDP increases.
   (b) the income and substitution effects are at work.
   (c) changes in the determinants of AD alter the amounts of real GDP demanded at each price level.

   (d) decreases in the price level give rise to wealth, interest-rate, and foreign-trade effects, which increase the amounts of real GDP demanded.

2. The AS curve slopes upward in the intermediate range because
   (a) per-unit production costs rise as real GDP expands towards and beyond its full-employment level.
   (b) the income and substitution effects are at work.
   (c) changes in the determinants of AS alter the amounts of real GDP supplied at each price level.
   (d) increases in the price level give rise to wealth, interest-rate, and foreign-purchases effects, which increase the amounts of real GDP supplied.

3. At price level P_1
   (a) a GDP surplus of Q_2 minus Q_1 occurs which drives the price level up to P_e.
   (b) a GDP shortage of Q_2 minus Q_1 occurs which drives the price level up to P_e.
   (c) the aggregate amount of real GDP demanded is less than the aggregate amount of GDP supplied.
   (d) the economy is in an "unemployment equilibrium."

4. At price level P_2, we would expect
   (a) the price level to fall below P_e.
   (b) the AD curve to shift to the right until it intersects AS at real GDP Q_2.
   (c) the price level to rise above P_e.
   (d) inventories to increase, compelling firms to reduce production to Q_e.

Answers: 1. (d); 2 (a); 3. (b); 4. (d).

As the arrows in Figure 11-7 indicate, the rise in the price level from P_1 to P_e encourages *producers* to increase their real output from Q_1 to Q_e and simultaneously causes *buyers* to scale back their purchases from Q_2 to Q_e. When equality occurs between the amount of real output produced and the amount purchased, as it does at P_e, the economy has achieved equilibrium.

At a price level above equilibrium, the story just told would be reversed. At P_2 aggregate supply would be greater than aggregate demand, creating forces that would lead to price level P_e and a GDP of Q_e.

Multiplier with Price Level Changes[3]

The assumption in the aggregate expenditures model is that prices are constant—a perfectly horizontal aggregate supply curve. Any change in aggregate demand leads to a change in real GDP and employment while the price level remains constant.

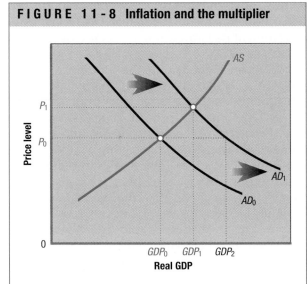

FIGURE 11-8 Inflation and the multiplier

The aggregate demand–aggregate supply model allows us to see how inflation reduces the size of the multiplier. The increase in aggregate demand from AD_0 to AD_1 is partly dissipated in inflation (P_0 to P_1) and real output increases only from GDP_0 to GDP_1.

---

[3] Instructors who do not assign Chapters 9 and 10 may want to use this section as a springboard for introducing MPC, MPS, and multiplier concepts.

But with an upward sloping supply curve, a part or all of any initial increase in aggregate demand will be dissipated in inflation and *not* be reflected in increased real output and employment. In Figure 11-8 the multiplier induced shift of aggregate demand from AD_0 to AD_1 is partly offset since a portion of the increase in aggregate demand is absorbed as inflation as the price level rises from P_0 to P_1. Real GDP rises to only GDP_1. If the aggregate supply curve were horizontal, the shift would have increased real domestic output to GDP_2. But inflation has reduced the multiplier so that the actual increase is to GDP_1, which is only about half as much.

Our conclusion is this: *for an increase in aggregate demand, the resulting increase in real GDP will be smaller the larger the increase in the price level.* Price level increases weaken the multiplier. You should sketch an increase in demand with a steeper aggregate supply curve to confirm that this increase in spending would be almost entirely absorbed as inflation; the steeper the aggregate supply curve the smaller the multiplier. (***Key Questions 5, 7, 9***)

11-3
QUICK REVIEW

- The equilibrium price level and amount of real output are determined at the intersection of the aggregate demand and aggregate supply curves.

- Decreases in aggregate supply cause cost-push inflation.

- Increases in aggregate supply expand real output.

SHORT-RUN AND LONG-RUN AGGREGATE SUPPLY

The story behind the shape of the aggregate supply curve becomes more complicated when long periods are considered. For instance, once workers fully recognize that the price level has increased, and thus that their real wages (their nominal wages divided by the price level) have declined, they will demand and obtain higher nominal wages to restore their real wages. This increase in nominal wages, other things equal, will shift the aggregate supply curve leftward. That is, nominal wages are one of the factors that determine the location of the aggregate supply curve itself.

To analyze longer time periods, then, we need to extend the analysis of aggregate supply to account for changes in nominal wages that *are in response to changes in the price level*. That is, we need to distinguish between short-run and long-run aggregate supply.

Definitions: Short Run and Long Run

Exactly what are the *short run* and the *long run* as they specifically relate to macroeconomics?

The Short Run   As already noted, the short run *is a period in which nominal wages (and other input prices) remain fixed as the price level changes*. There are at least two reasons why nominal wages may remain constant for a time even though the price level has changed:

1. Workers may not immediately be aware of the extent to which inflation (or deflation) has changed their real wages, and thus may not adjust their labour supply decisions and wage demands accordingly.
2. Many employees are hired under fixed-wage contracts. Unionized employees, for example, receive nominal wages spelled out in their collective bargaining agreements. Also, most managers and many professionals receive set salaries established in annual contracts. In these circumstances, nominal wages remain constant for the duration of the contracts, regardless of changes in the price level.

The upshot of these two factors is that price-level changes do not immediately give rise to changes in nominal wages. Instead, considerable amounts of time usually pass before these adjustments occur.

The Long Run   Once sufficient time has elapsed for contracts to expire and nominal wage adjustments to occur, the economy enters the long run—*a period in which nominal wages are fully responsive to changes in the price level*. With sufficient time, workers gain full information about price-level changes and thus determine how these changes have affected their real wages. For example, workers become aware that a price-level *increase* has reduced their real wages. If your *nominal* wage was $10 an hour when the price index was 100 (or,

in decimals, 1.0), your *real* wage was also $10 (=/$10 of nominal wage divided by 1.0). But when the price level has increased to, say, 120, your $10 real wage has declined to $8.33 (= $10/1.2). In such circumstances, you and other workers will demand and probably obtain increases in your nominal wages such that the purchasing power from an hour of work is restored. In our example, your nominal wage likely will rise from $10 to $12, returning your real wage to $10 (= $12/1.2).

Short-Run Aggregate Supply

With these definitions of short run and long run clearly in mind, we can extend our previous discussion of aggregate supply.

First, consider the short-run aggregate supply curve AS_1 in Figure 11-9a. Curve AS_1 is constructed on three assumptions: (1) the initial price level is P_1, (2) nominal wages have been established on the *expectation that this specific price level will persist*, and (3) the price level is flexible both upward and downward. Observe from point a_1 that at price level P_1 the economy is operating at its full-employment output Q_f. This output is the real production forthcoming when the economy is operating at its natural rate of unemployment, or potential GDP.

Now let's determine the short-run consequences of changes in the price level by first examining an *increase* in the price level from P_1 to P_2 in Figure 11-9a. The higher product prices associated with P_2 increase revenues to firms, and because the nominal wages they are paying are fixed, their profits rise. In response, firms collectively increase their output from Q_f to Q_2; the economy moves from a_1 to a_2 on curve AS_1. Observe that at Q_2 the economy is operating beyond its full-employment output. This is made possible by extending the work-hours of part-time and full-time workers, enticing new workers such as homemakers and retirees into the labour force, and hiring and training the structurally unemployed. Thus, the nation's unemployment rate declines below its natural rate.

How will producers respond when there is a *decrease* in the price level, say, from P_1 to P_3 in Figure 11-9a? Firms then discover their revenues and profits have diminished or disappeared. After all, the prices they receive for their products have dropped while the nominal wages they pay workers have not. Under these circumstances,

FIGURE 11-9 Short-run and long-run aggregate supply

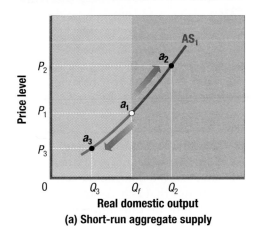

(a) Short-run aggregate supply

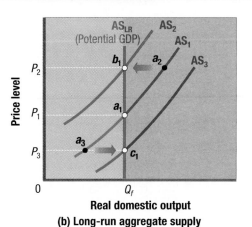

(b) Long-run aggregate supply

(a) In the short run, nominal wages are assumed to be fixed and based on price level P_1 and the expectation that it will continue. An increase in the price level from P_1 to P_2 increases profits and output, moving the economy from a_1 to a_2; a decrease in the price level from P_1 to P_3 reduces profits and real output, moving the economy from a_1 to a_3. The short-run aggregate supply curve therefore slopes upward. (b) In the long run, a price-level rise increases nominal wages and thus shifts the short-run aggregate supply curve leftward. Conversely, a decrease in the price level reduces nominal wages and shifts the short-run aggregate supply curve rightward. After such adjustments, the economy reaches equilibrium at points such as b_1 and c_1. Thus, the long-run aggregate supply curve is vertical.

firms reduce their employment and production, and, as shown by the move from a_1 to a_3, real output falls to Q_3. The decline in real output is accompanied by increased unemployment; at output Q_3 the unemployment rate is greater than the natural rate of unemployment associated with output Q_f.

Long-Run Aggregate Supply

By definition, nominal wages in the long run are fully responsive to changes in the price level. What are the implications of this responsiveness for aggregate supply?

For the answer, look at Figure 11-9b, again assuming the economy is initially at point a_1 (P_1 and Q_f). Our previous discussion indicated that an *increase* in the price level from P_1 to P_2 will move the economy from point a_1 to a_2 along the short-run aggregate supply curve AS_1. In the long run, however, workers discover their real wages have declined *because* of this increase in the price level. They demand and presumably obtain their previous level of real wages via hikes in their nominal wages. The short-run supply curve then shifts leftward from AS_1 to AS_2, which now reflects the higher price level P_2 *and the new expectation that P_2,*

not P_1, will continue. The leftward shift in the short-run aggregate supply curve to AS_2 moves the economy from a_2 to b_1. Real output returns to its full-employment level Q_f, and the unemployment rate returns to its natural rate.

And what is the result of a decrease in the price level? *Assuming downward wage flexibility*, a decline in the price level from P_1 to P_3 in Figure 11-9b works in the opposite way from a price-level increase. The economy initially moves from point a_1 to a_3 on AS_1. Profits are squeezed or eliminated because prices have fallen and nominal wages have not. But this movement along AS_1 is the short-run response. With enough time, the lower price level P_3—which has *increased* the real wage—results in a decline in nominal wages such that the original real wage is restored. Sufficiently lower nominal wages shift the short-run aggregate supply curve rightward from AS_1 to AS_3. Real output returns to its full-employment level of Q_f at point c_1.

By tracing a line between the long-run equilibrium points b_1, a_1, and c_1, we obtain a **long-run aggregate supply curve**. Observe that it is vertical at the full-employment level of real GDP. After long-run adjustments in nominal wages, real output is Q_f, regardless of the specific price level. (*Key Question 15*)

FIGURE 11-10 Equilibrium in the long-run AD-AS model

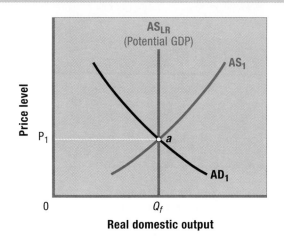

The equilibrium price level P_1 and level of real output Q_f occur at the intersection of the aggregate demand curve AD$_1$, the long-run aggregate supply curve AS$_{LR}$ (Potential GDP), and the short-run aggregate supply curve AS$_1$.

Equilibrium in the Long-Run AD-AS Model

Figure 11-10 shows the long-run equilibrium in the AD-AS model, now extended to include the distinction between short-run and long-run aggregate supply. Equilibrium in the figure occurs at point a, where the nation's aggregate demand curve AD$_1$ intersects the vertical long-run aggregate supply curve AS$_{LR}$. Observe at point a that the aggregate demand curve also intersects the short-run aggregate supply curve AS$_1$. In long-run equilibrium, the economy's price level and real output are P_1 and Q_f.

11-4
QUICK REVIEW

- The short-run aggregate supply curve has a positive slope because nominal wages remain constant as the price level changes.

- The long-run aggregate supply curve is vertical because nominal wages eventually change by the same amount as changes in the price level.

- The equilibrium GDP and price level occur at the intersection of the aggregate demand curve, the long-run aggregate supply curve, and the short-run aggregate supply curve.

EQUILIBRIUM VERSUS FULL-EMPLOYMENT GDP

We now turn from explaining to evaluating equilibrium GDP. A moment ago we distinguished between the short-run and long-run aggregate supply curves. The long-run aggregate supply curve represents the economy's potential GDP, or full employment, a concept you first encountered in Chapter 8. In the long run, an economy will return to its natural rate of unemployment. But in the short run, the economy can come to rest at an equilibrium that is accompanied by a higher than desired rate of unemployment or inflation. For example, in the early 1990s, the Canadian economy slowed down and actually contracted. The economy was in "equilibrium" in that at the lower rate of GDP aggregate demand equalled short-run aggregate supply. But the unemployment rate rose sharply from 7.5 percent in 1989 to over 11 percent in 1992. Clearly, the Canadian economy at that point was *below* its potential. Conversely, the economy can settle at a short-run equilibrium above potential GDP and generate inflationary pressures. To measure the divergence of the economy from its full employment potential, we use the notion of gaps, which you learned in Chapter 8.

Recessionary Gap

In *Figure 11-11a (Key Graph)* we have designated the full-employment non-inflationary level of output, or potential GDP, at $510 billion. Suppose aggregate demand falls from AD_0 to AD_1 because of a steep drop in net exports. AD_1 intersects the short-run aggregate supply AS at $490 billion, thus, the equilibrium level of GDP is $20 billion short of full-employment GDP. The **recessionary gap** is the amount by which equilibrium GDP falls short of full-employment GDP. A resolution of the recessionary gap requires a rightward shift of the aggregate demand curve, from AD_1 to AD_0, or a rightward shift of the short-run aggregate supply curve, from AS_0 to AS_1, or some combination of the two.

In Chapters 12 to 15 you will learn about policy tools at the disposal of governments that can shift aggregate demand to the right and close a recessionary gap. You will recall that a fall in the price level from P_0 to P_1 will shift the short-run aggregate supply curve from AS_0 to AS_1 so that in the long run the economy returns to full employment even without the help of a rightward shift of the aggregate demand

KEY GRAPH

FIGURE 11-11 Recessionary and inflationary gaps

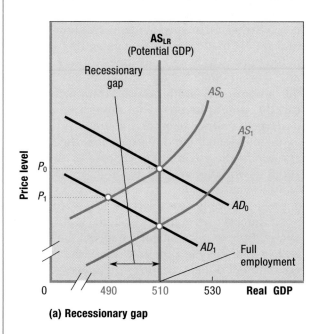

(a) Recessionary gap

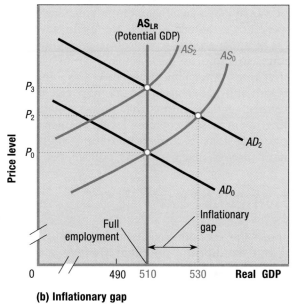

(b) Inflationary gap

The equilibrium and full-employment GDPs may not coincide. A recessionary gap, shown in (a), is the amount by which equilibrium GDP falls short of full-employment GDP. The inflationary gap in (b) is the amount by which equilibrium GDP exceeds full-employment GDP. The elimination of a recessionary gap requires either an increase of aggregate demand from AD_1 to AD_0 or a rightward shift of the short-run aggregate supply curve. The elimination of an inflationary gap requires either a decrease in aggregate demand or a decrease in the short-run aggregate supply.

11-11

QUICK QUIZ

1. A recessionary gap can be eliminated by
   (a) a contraction of consumption spending.
   (b) a fall in government expenditures.
   (c) an increase in investment spending.
   (d) a fall in net exports.

2. At a GDP of $510 billion
   (a) the economy is in recession.
   (b) there is an inflationary gap.
   (c) there is a recessionary gap.
   (d) the economy is at full employment.

3. An inflationary gap will close if
   (a) net exports rise sharply, *ceteris paribus*.
   (b) input prices fall, *ceteris paribus*.
   (c) productivity of the economy falls, *ceteris paribus*.
   (d) government spending rises sharply, *ceteris paribus*.

4. A recessionary gap will close if
   (a) input prices rise, *ceteris paribus*.
   (b) consumption spending rises sharply, *ceteris paribus*.
   (c) government regulation of business expands significantly, *ceteris paribus*.
   (d) government expenditures fall significantly, *ceteris paribus*.

Answers: 1. (c); 2 (d); 3. (c); 4. (b).

curve. We want to stress that such a supply response could take an unacceptably long period of time. Consider the length of time it has taken the Canadian economy to recover from the 1991–92 recession. The last time the Canadian economy was at full employment was in 1989 when the unemployment rate was 7.5 percent. At the end of 1998, the unemployment rate was still at around 8 percent despite numerous attempts to stimulate the economy through lower interest rates. After almost a decade the Canadian economy still had a recessionary gap. Such long adjustment periods means that unless a nation is willing to suffer unacceptable levels of unemployment, recessions require stimulating aggregate demand through macroeconomic policy tools.

INFLATIONARY GAP

Suppose the economy is at its full-employment long-run equilibrium and that there is a steep increase in net exports that shifts aggregate demand to the right. The amount by which equilibrium is above full employment GDP is an **inflationary gap**, created in Figure 11-11b by the shift of the aggregate demand curve from AD_0 to AD_2. As noted earlier, an unemployment rate above the natural rate is made possible by extending the work hours of part-time and full-time workers, enticing new workers such as homemakers and retirees into the labour force, and hiring and training the structurally unemployed. The government could undertake policies to quickly counteract the rise of aggregate demand and thereby close the inflationary gap. If the government chooses to do nothing about the inflationary gap, the higher price level P_2 would eventually lead to a shift of the short-run aggregate supply curve left to AS_2, which would push the price level higher still, to P_3. As with the elimination of recessionary gap, an inflationary gap will take some time to close without specific government policies to hurry the process along.

In The Media

Ice Storm Puts Big Chill on Quebec's Economy

Production losses could shrink 1998 growth, analysts say

BY KONRAD YAKABUSKI

MONTREAL—The economic freeze inflicted by Quebec's storm-induced blackouts continued yesterday as Montreal's office towers remained empty and factories in the province's industrial heartland were silent for another day.

With most business on ice until at least tomorrow in downtown Montreal—and possibly for another week on the city's blacked-out south shore—analysts say the province's economy may be affected for months to come.

"More and more, we're beginning to think that there could be a

drop in economic activity in Quebec for all of 1998," Yves St-Maurice, senior economist at Mouvement des caisses Desjardins, said yesterday.

"Much will depend on whether businesses are able to make up for the lost production in the past week. But that becomes more and more difficult to do as the days [without production] accumulate."

Mouvement Desjardins predicted last month that Quebec's economy would grow by 2.9 per cent this year, compared with 3.1 per cent for all of Canada. Mr. St-Maurice said Desjardins,

Quebec's largest financial institution, has not officially lowered its growth forecast yet. But he added that that may soon be unavoidable.

The blow to the provincial economy will be blunted slightly by the massive investment undertaken by Hydro-Québec to rebuild the parts of its transmission grid knocked out by the storms. But the utility's reconstruction effort—now pegged at "at least" $500-million by government sources cited yesterday in *La Presse*—will not fully offset the other costs inflicted on the economy, Mr. St-Maurice said.

At the peak of the blackouts last Friday, as much as a third of the province's economy was paralyzed. Mr. St-Maurice estimated production losses at about $125-million a day.

In the Montérégie region, south of Montreal, which accounts for around one-fifth of the Quebec economy, normal production levels may not resume for up to two weeks. And the effect of the storms may be felt long after that, he added.

Source: *Globe and Mail,* January 14, 1998, p. B1. Reprinted with permission from the *Globe and Mail.*

THE STORY IN BRIEF

A severe ice storm inflicts a heavy blow on the Quebec economy.

THE ECONOMICS BEHIND THE STORY

- A severe ice storm severs Quebec's hydro lines, leading to a massive disruption of electrical power in the province.

- Firms could not produce, thus much production was lost.
- Also, consumers could not go about making their usual purchases.
- Both a temporary shift to the left of the aggregate supply curve and a leftward shift of the aggregate demand curve contributed to put a (temporary) "big chill" on Quebec's economy.
- Using the aggregate demand–aggregate supply model, show what the impact was of the massive investment undertaken by Hydro-Québec. ■

The Last Word

WHY IS UNEMPLOYMENT IN EUROPE SO HIGH?

Are the high unemployment rates in Europe the result of structural problems or deficient aggregate demand?

SEVERAL EUROPEAN ECONOMIES HAVE HAD high rates of unemployment in the past several years. For example, in 1994 France had an unemployment rate of 12.3 percent; Great Britain, 10.0 percent; Italy, 11.2 percent; and Germany, 10.2 percent.

There is little dispute that recessions in Europe in the early 1990s contributed to these high rates. Declines in aggregate demand reduced real GDP and increased unemployment. Nevertheless, a mystery remains: Why were unemployment rates in many European nations so high even *before* their recessions? In 1990 the unemployment rate in France was 9.1 percent; in Great Britain, 6.9 percent; and in Italy, 7.0 percent. And why have European unemployment rates remained far higher than in other countries during economic recovery? There are two views on these questions:

1. High Natural Rates of Unemployment Many economists believe the high unemployment rates in Europe largely reflect high natural rates of unemployment. They envision a situation where aggregate demand and aggregate supply have produced the full-employment level of real output. But high levels of frictional and structural unemployment accompany this level of output. In this view, the recent extensive unemployment in Europe has resulted from a high natural rate of unemployment, not from deficient aggregate demand. An increase in aggregate demand would push these economies beyond their full-employment levels of output, causing demand-pull inflation.

The alleged sources of the high natural rates of unemployment are government policies and union contracts that have increased the costs of hiring workers and reduced the cost of being unemployed. Example: High minimum wages have discouraged employers from hiring low-skilled workers; generous welfare benefits have weakened incentives for people to take available jobs; restrictions against firings have discouraged firms from employing workers; 30 to 40 days per year of paid vacations and holidays have boosted the cost of hiring workers; high worker absenteeism has reduced productivity; and high employer costs of health, pension, disability, and other benefits have discouraged hiring.

2. Deficient Aggregate Demand   Not all economists agree that government and union policies have ratcheted up Europe's natural rate of unemployment. Instead, they point to insufficient aggregate demand as the culprit. They see the European economies in terms of Figure 11-11a, where real output is less than it would be if aggregate demand were stronger—Europe suffers from a recessionary gap. The argument is that the European governments have been so fearful of inflation that they have not undertaken appropriate fiscal and monetary policies (Chapters 12 and 15) to increase aggregate demand. In this view, increases in aggregate demand would not be inflationary, since these economies have considerable excess capacity. A rightward shift in aggregate demand curves would expand output and employment, even if it would create inflationary pressures.

Conclusion: The debate over high unemployment in Europe reflects disagreement on where European aggregate demand curves lie relative to full-employment levels of output. If these curves are *at* the full-employment real GDP, then the high levels of unemployment are "natural." Public policies should focus on lowering minimum wages, reducing vacation time, reducing welfare benefits, easing restrictions on layoffs, and so on. But if the aggregate demand curves in the European nations lie to the left of their full-employment levels of output, as in Figure 11-11a, then expansionary government policies such as reduced interest rates or tax cuts may be in order. The debate over the cause of high rates of unemployment in Europe extends to Canada. We have also experienced relatively high rates of unemployment compared with the United States, but much discussion still continues about the reason(s). ■

CHAPTER SUMMARY

1. For purposes of analysis we consolidate—or aggregate—the large number of individual product markets into a composite market in which there are two variables—the price level and the level of real output. This is accomplished through an aggregate demand–aggregate supply model.

2. The aggregate demand curve shows the level of real output that the economy will purchase at each price level.

3. The aggregate demand curve is downsloping because of the wealth effect, the interest-rate effect, and the foreign trade effect. The wealth effect indicates that inflation reduces the real value or purchasing power of fixed-value financial assets held by households, causing them to retrench on their consumer spending. The interest-rate effect means that, with a specific supply of money, a higher price level increases the demand for money, raising the interest rate and reducing consumption and investment purchases. The foreign trade effect suggests that an increase in one country's price level relative to other countries' reduces the net exports component of that nation's aggregate demand.

*4. A change in the price level alters the location of the aggregate expenditures schedule through the wealth, interest rate, and foreign trade effects. The aggregate demand curve is derived from the aggregate expenditures model by allowing the price level to change and observing the effect on the aggregate expenditures schedule and thus on equilibrium GDP.

5. The determinants of aggregate demand are spending by domestic consumers, businesses, government, and foreign buyers. Changes in the factors listed in Figure 11-3 cause changes in spending by these groups and shift the aggregate demand curve.

*This summary item presumes knowledge of the aggregate expenditures model presented in Chapters 9 and 10.

*6. With the price level held constant, increases in consumption, investment, and net export expenditures shift the aggregate expenditures schedule upward and the aggregate demand curve to the right.

7. The aggregate supply curve shows the levels of the real output that businesses produce at various possible price levels. The aggregate supply curve is upward sloping in the short run—a period during which input prices remain fixed.

8. The shape of the short-run aggregate supply curve depends on capacity utilization. The closer the economy is to current capacity utilization, the steeper the aggregate supply curve. The more slack in the economy the flatter the aggregate supply curve becomes.

9. Figure 11-6 lists the determinants of aggregate supply: input prices, productivity, and the legal-institutional environment. A change in any one of these factors will change per-unit production costs at each level of output and therefore alter the location of the aggregate supply curve.

10. The intersection of the aggregate demand and aggregate supply curves determines an economy's equilibrium price level and real GDP.

11. Given an upward-sloping aggregate supply, rightward shifts of aggregate demand will increase both real domestic output and the level of prices.

12. Leftward shifts of aggregate supply lead to real output declines and the price level rises; rightward shifts increase real output and lower the price level.

13. In macroeconomics, the short run is a period in which nominal wages are fixed; they do not change in response to changes in the price level. In contrast, the long run is a period in which nominal wages are fully responsive to changes in the price level.

14. The short-run aggregate supply curve is upsloping. Because nominal wages are fixed, increases in the price level (prices received by firms) increase profits and real output. Conversely, decreases in the price level reduce profits and real output. However, the long-run aggregate supply curve is vertical. With sufficient time for adjustment, nominal wages rise and fall with the price level, moving the economy along a vertical aggregate supply curve at the economy's full-employment output.

15. A recessionary gap is the amount by which equilibrium GDP falls short of full-employment GDP. An inflationary gap is the amount by which equilibrium GDP is above full-employment GDP.

TERMS AND CONCEPTS

aggregate demand
wealth effect
interest-rate effect
foreign-trade effect
determinants of aggregate demand
short-run aggregate supply

determinants of aggregate supply
productivity
equilibrium price level
equilibrium real domestic output
long-run aggregate supply curve
recessionary and inflationary gaps

STUDY QUESTIONS

1. Why is the aggregate demand curve downsloping? Specify how your explanation differs from that for the downsloping demand curve for a single product.

2. Explain the shape of the short-run aggregate supply curve, accounting for the horizontal, intermediate, and vertical ranges of the curve.

*3. Explain carefully: "A change in the price level shifts the aggregate expenditures curve but not the aggregate demand curve."

4. KEY QUESTION *Suppose that the aggregate demand and the short-run supply schedules for a hypothetical economy are as shown below:*

Amount of real domestic output demanded, billions	Price level (price index)	Amount of real domestic output supplied, billions
$100	300	$400
200	250	400
300	200	300
400	150	200
500	150	100

a. *Use these sets of data to graph the aggregate demand and supply curves. Find the equilibrium price level and level of real output in this hypothetical economy. Is the equilibrium real output also the full-capacity output? Explain.*
b. *Why will a price level of 150 not be an equilibrium price level in this economy? Why not 250?*
c. *Suppose that buyers desire to purchase $200 billion of extra real output at each price level. Sketch in the new aggregate demand curve as AD_1. What factors might cause this change in aggregate demand? What are the new equilibrium price level and level of real output?*

5. KEY QUESTION *Suppose that the hypothetical economy in question 4 has the following relationship between its real output and the input quantities necessary for producing that output:*

Input quantity	Real domestic output
150.0	400
112.5	300
75.0	200

a. *What is productivity in this economy?*
b. *What is the per-unit cost of production if the price of each input unit is $2?*
c. *Assume that the input price increases from $2 to $3 with no accompanying change in productivity. What is the new per-unit cost of production? In what direction would the $1 increase in input price push the aggregate supply curve? What effect would this shift in the short-run aggregate supply have on the price level and the level of real output?*
d. *Suppose that the increase in input price does not occur but instead that productivity increases by 100 percent. What would be the new per-unit cost of production? What effect would this change in per-unit production cost have on the short-run aggregate supply curve? What effect would this shift in the short-run aggregate supply have on the price level and the level of real output?*

6. Will an increase in the Canadian price level relative to price levels in other nations shift our aggregate demand curve? If so, in what direction? Explain. Will a decline in the Canadian dollar price of foreign currencies shift our aggregate supply curve rightward or simply move the economy along an existing aggregate supply curve? Explain.

7. KEY QUESTION *What effects would each of the following have on aggregate demand or short-run aggregate supply? In each case use a diagram to show the expected effects on the equilibrium price level and level of real output. Assume all other things remain constant.*
a. *A widespread fear of depression among consumers*
b. *A large purchase of wheat by Russia*
c. *A $1 increase in the excise tax on cigarettes*

---

*Questions designated with an asterisk presume knowledge of the aggregate expenditures model (Chapters 9 and 10).

    d. *A reduction in interest rates at each price level*
    e. *A cut in federal spending for higher education*
    f. *The expectation of a rapid rise in the price level*
    g. *The complete disintegration of OPEC, causing oil prices to fall by one-half*
    h. *A 10 percent reduction in personal income tax rates*
    i. *An increase in labour productivity*
    j. *A 12 percent increase in nominal wages*
    k. *Depreciation in the international value of the dollar*
    l. *A sharp decline in the national incomes of our main trading partners*
    m. *A decline in the percentage of the Canadian labour force that is unionized*

8. What is the relationship between the production possibilities curve discussed in Chapter 2 and the aggregate supply curve discussed in this chapter?

9. KEY QUESTION *Other things equal, what effect will each of the following have on the equilibrium price level and level of real output (assume an upward sloping AS curve):*
    a. *An increase in aggregate demand in an economy close to capacity utilization*
    b. *An increase in aggregate supply*
    c. *Equal increase in aggregate demand and aggregate supply*
    d. *A reduction in aggregate demand in an economy with much slack in it*
    e. *An increase in aggregate demand and a decrease in aggregate supply*
    f. *A decrease in aggregate demand*

*10. Suppose that the price level is constant and investment spending increases sharply. How would you show this increase in the aggregate expenditures model? What would be the outcome? How would you show this rise in investment in the aggregate demand–aggregate supply model?

*11. Explain how an upsloping aggregate supply curve weakens the multiplier.

12. "Unemployment can be caused by a leftward shift of aggregate demand or a leftward shift of aggregate supply." Do you agree? Explain. In each case, specify price level effects.

13. Distinguish between the short run and the long run as they relate to macroeconomics.

14. Which of the following statements are true? Which are false? Explain the false statements.
    a. Short-run aggregate supply curves reflect an inverse relationship between the price level and the level of real output.
    b. The long-run aggregate supply curve assumes that nominal wages are fixed.
    c. In the long run, an increase in the price level will result in an increase in nominal wages.

15. KEY QUESTION Suppose the full-employment level of real output (Q) for a hypothetical economy is \$250 and the price level (P) initially is 100. Use the short-run aggregate supply schedules below to answer the questions which follow:

AS (P_{100})		AS (P_{125})		AS (P_{75})	
P	**Q**	**P**	**Q**	**P**	**Q**
125	280	125	250	125	310
100	250	100	220	100	280
75	220	75	190	75	250

    a. What will be the level of real output in the *short run* if the price level unexpectedly rises from 100 to 125 because of an increase in aggregate demand? What if the price level falls unexpectedly from 100 to 75 because of a decrease in aggregate demand? Explain each situation, using numbers from the table.
    b. What will be the level of real output in the *long run* when the price level rises from 100 to 125? When it falls from 100 to 75? Explain each situation.

---

*Questions designated with an asterisk presume knowledge of the aggregate expenditures model (Chapters 9 and 10).

    c. Show the circumstances described in parts a and b on graph paper, and derive the long-run aggregate supply curve.

16. **(The Last Word)** State the alternative views on why unemployment in Europe has recently been so high. Discuss the policy implication of each view.

17. **WEB-BASED QUESTION** **The Interest-Rate Effect-Price Levels and Interest Rates** The interest-rate effect suggests that as the price level rises, so do interest rates, and rising interest rates reduce certain kinds of consumption and investment spending. Compare price levels (all items) www.statcan.ca/english/Pgdb/Economy/Economic/econ09a.htm and interest rates (prime business loan rate) www.statcan.ca/english/Pgdb/Economy/Economic/econ07.htm over the past five years. Do the data support the link between the price level and interest rates?

18. **WEB-BASED QUESTION** **Aggregate Demand and Supply—Equilibrium Prices and GDPs** Actual data showing aggregate demand and supply curves do not exist. However, data for prices (CPI) and GDP www.oecd.org/std/fas.htm do exist for several countries. Look at the data for Canada, the United States, Japan, and Germany. Assume that these CPI and GDP figures represent the equilibrium price and real GDPs for their respective years. Plot the price/GDP levels for the past three years for each country using a graph similar to Figure 11-7. Are there any similarities across countries? What changes in aggregate demand and supply are implied by the equilibrium points?

Fiscal Policy

FROM TIME TO TIME, NATIONAL GOVERNMENTS individually take purposeful budget action to "stimulate their economies" or to "rein in inflation." For example, in early 1998 the Japanese government cut income and corporate taxes in an effort to stimulate a low-growing economy. What is the logic of such fiscal action? Shouldn't government always match any increase in its spending with an increase in taxes, or match any tax cuts with cuts in government spending? Under what circumstances might government purposely manipulate its spending and taxation—engage in so-called *fiscal policy*—to stabilize the economy? Do such policies always work?

This chapter looks briefly at the legislative mandates that give the Canadian government authority to pursue its stabilization role in the economy. It then explores the tools of government fiscal policy in terms of the aggregate demand– aggregate supply model. Next, we examine some factors that automatically adjust government expenditures and tax revenues as GDP rises and falls. Finally, problems, criticisms, and complications of government fiscal policy are addressed.

IN THIS CHAPTER YOU WILL LEARN:

What fiscal policy is and what it is used for.

•

The distinction between discretionary and nondiscretionary fiscal policy.

•

What a cyclically adjusted budget is.

•

The shortcomings of fiscal policy.

The Big Picture

ONE OF THE MAJOR ISSUES IN MACROECONOMICS is how to avoid or to smooth out fluctuations in economic activity that cause recessions or inflation. Fluctuations can originate either on the aggregate demand or the aggregate supply side of the economy. For example, an economy can get "stuck" at an equilibrium GDP below full employment GDP (a recessionary gap), and possibly remain there for an unacceptably long period of time. Governments can influence the level of GDP through their spending and taxation—together referred to as fiscal policy. Fiscal policy will affect aggregate demand if it primarily has an impact on one of the expenditure categories, or affects aggregate supply if it primarily has an impact on the cost of production.

As you read this chapter, keep the following points in mind:

- **Key Concept 7** is discussed.
- A recessionary gap requires an increase in government spending and/or cut in taxes. Such policies

will help close the gap by shifting the demand curve to the right. An inflationary gap requires a decrease and/or an increase in taxes, which will shift the aggregate demand curve to the left.

- Discretionary fiscal policy is implemented by governments whenever there is a perceived need for stabilization; in contrast, fiscal stabilizers are automatically implemented according to the needs of the macroeconomy.
- The implementation of discretionary fiscal policy is subject to limitations, including difficulties encountered by governments in collecting up-to-date information about the economy, and problems associated with quickly implementing the right fiscal policy as soon as it is necessary.
- In recent years Canada has experienced large structural annual deficits and a mounting national debt, leaving the federal government little leeway for expansionary fiscal policy during recessions. ∎

LEGISLATIVE MANDATES

The idea that government fiscal actions can exert an important stabilizing influence on the economy emerged from the Great Depression of the 1930s. Macroeconomic employment theory played a major role in emphasizing the importance of remedial fiscal budgetary measures. The federal government brought in unemployment insurance during World War II, and in 1945 Mackenzie King won his last election on the promise of full employment and social security. Since then, no party running for office has promised less. Parties out of office have never failed to blame the government for whatever level of unemployment currently exists. And governments, while blaming current unemployment on economic conditions in the United States, have always insisted that their policies, either in place or to be unveiled in the next budget, will bring the country back to full—or at least "fuller"—employment.

Since 1945 one of the main tools used by governments in stabilization policy is fiscal policy. Fis-

cal policy can be one of two varieties: (1) discretionary and (2) nondiscretionary.

DISCRETIONARY FISCAL POLICY

Discretionary fiscal policy is the deliberate manipulation of taxes and government spending by Parliament to alter real GDP and employment, control inflation, and stimulate economic growth. "Discretionary" means that the changes in taxes and government spending are *at the option* of the federal government. These changes do not occur automatically, independent of specific parliamentary action.

For clarity, we assume government spending does not in any way affect planned private spending. Also, we assume for now that fiscal policy affects only the aggregate demand side of the macroeconomy; it has no intended or unintended effects on aggregate supply. Both assumptions will be dropped when we examine the real-world complications and shortcomings of discretionary fiscal policy—or more simply, *fiscal policy*.

First, we'll examine fiscal policy in two situations: (1) a recessionary gap and (2) an inflationary gap caused by demand-pull—a rightward shift of the aggregate demand curve beyond full employment GDP.

Expansionary Fiscal Policy

When recession occurs, an **expansionary fiscal policy** may be in order. Consider Figure 12-1 where we suppose a sharp decline in investment spending has shifted the economy's aggregate demand curve leftward from AD_1 to AD_0. Perhaps profit expectations on investment projects have dimmed, curtailing much investment spending and reducing aggregate demand. Consequently, real GDP has fallen to GDP_0 from its full-employment level of GDP_f. Accompanying this decline in real output is an increase in unemployment, since fewer workers are needed to produce the diminished output. This economy is experiencing recession and cyclical unemployment—the economy is not fully utilizing all its available resources.

What should the federal government do to rev up the economy? It has three main fiscal policy options: (1) increase government spending; (2) reduce taxes; or (3) some combination of the two. If the federal budget is balanced at the outset, fiscal policy during a recession or depression should create a government **budget deficit**—government spending in excess of tax revenues.

Increased Government Spending All else equal, an increase in government spending will shift an economy's aggregate demand curve to the right, as from AD_0 to AD_1 in Figure 12-1. To see why, suppose that the recession prompts government to initiate new spending on highways, satellite communications systems, and federal prisons. At *each* price level the amount of real output demanded is greater than before the increase in government spending. Real output increases to GDP_f, closing the recessionary gap, therefore unemployment will fall as firms call back workers laid off during the recession.

Tax Reductions Alternatively, government could reduce taxes to shift the aggregate demand curve rightward, as from AD_0 to AD_1. Suppose government cuts personal income taxes, which increases disposable income by the same amount. Consumption will rise by a fraction of the increase in disposable income—the other fraction goes to increased saving. The aggregate demand will shift rightward because of the increase in consumption produced by the tax cut. Real GDP will rise and employment will also increase accordingly.

Combined Government Spending Increases and Tax Reductions Government can combine spending increases and tax cuts to produce the desired initial increase in spending and eventual increase in aggregate demand and real GDP.

If the federal government chooses to do nothing about the recessionary gap, the lower price level P_0 will eventually lead to a shift of the short-run aggregate supply curve to the right until it meets AD_0 at full employment at a lower price level. (You should pencil in the new short-run aggregate supply curve.) As already pointed out in Chapter 11, such a supply response would take time, and a nation would endure an unacceptably high rate of unemployment for a longer period than necessary.

If you were assigned Chapters 9 and 10, you should think through these three fiscal policy options in terms of the aggregate expenditures model (Figure 10-7). Recall from Chapter 11 that rightward shifts of the aggregate demand curve relate directly to upshifts in the aggregate expenditures schedule.

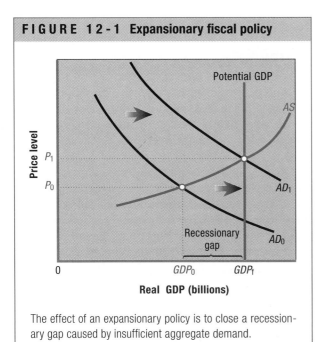

FIGURE 12-1 **Expansionary fiscal policy**

The effect of an expansionary policy is to close a recessionary gap caused by insufficient aggregate demand.

Contractionary Fiscal Policy

When the economy has an inflationary gap caused by excessive growth of aggregate demand, demand-pull inflation occurs, and a restrictive or **contractionary fiscal policy** may help control it. Look at Figure 12-2. Suppose that a shift of the aggregate demand curve from AD_2 to AD_3 above the full employment level increases the price level from P_2 to P_3. This increase in aggregate demand might have resulted from a sharp increase in, say, investment or net export spending. If government looks to fiscal policy to control this inflation, its options are opposite those used to combat recession. It can (1) decrease government spending, (2) raise taxes, or (3) use some combination of these two policies. When the economy faces demand-pull inflation, fiscal policy should move towards a government **budget surplus**—tax revenues in excess of government spending.

Decreased Government Spending Government can reduce its spending to eliminate the inflationary gap. This spending cut will shift the aggregate demand curve leftward from AD_3 to AD_2. Real output returns at its full employment level of GDP_f.

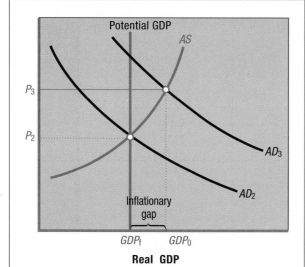

FIGURE 12-2 Contractionary fiscal policy

The effect of a contractionary policy is to close an inflationary gap caused by increases of aggregate demand beyond full employment GDP.

Increased Taxes Just as government can use tax cuts to increase consumption spending, it can use tax increases to reduce consumption spending. A tax increase reduces consumption (if it is borne by households) reducing aggregate demand from AD_3 to AD_2. The inflationary gap will have been closed and inflationary pressures alleviated.

Combined Government Spending Decreases and Tax Increases Government can combine spending decreases and tax increases to reduce aggregate demand from AD_3 to AD_2 and check inflation.

If the government does not embark on a contractionary fiscal policy, the higher price level P_3 will eventually lead to a shift of the short-run aggregate supply curve leftward until it meets AD_3 at potential GDP and thereby close the inflationary gap. (You should pencil in the new short-run aggregate supply curve.) Although such a supply response will be quicker than the case of a recessionary gap, the return to the economy's natural rate of unemployment will still require more time compared to pursuing an active anti-inflationary policy.

If you were assigned Chapters 9 and 10, you should be able to explain the three fiscal policy options for fighting inflation in terms of the aggregate expenditures model (Figure 10-8). Recall from Chapter 11 that leftward shifts of the aggregate demand curve are associated with downshifts of the aggregate expenditures schedule. *(Key Question 1)*

Financing Deficits and Disposing of Surpluses

The expansionary effect of a specific budget deficit on the economy depends on the method used to finance it. Similarly, the anti-inflationary impact of the creation of a budget surplus depends on what is done with the surplus.

Borrowing versus New Money There are two ways the federal government can finance a deficit: borrowing from (selling interest-bearing bonds to) the public, and issuing new money to its creditors. The impact of each method on aggregate demand is different:

1. **BORROWING** If the government enters the money market and borrows, it will compete with private business borrowers for funds. This added demand for funds may drive up the interest rate and may crowd out some private investment spending and interest-sensi-

tive consumer spending. Declines in private spending reduce the expansionary impact of the deficit spending.

2. **MONEY CREATION**   If the government finances its deficit spending by obtaining newly created money from its monetary authorities, the crowding-out of private spending can be avoided. Federal spending can increase without any adverse effect on investment or consumption. *The creation of new money is a more expansionary (but potentially more inflationary) way of financing deficit spending than is borrowing.*

Debt Retirement versus Idle Surplus   Demand-pull inflation calls for fiscal action that will result in a budget surplus. But the anti-inflationary effect of this surplus depends on what government does with it:

1. **DEBT REDUCTION**   Since the federal government had an outstanding net debt of some $465 billion by the end of 1997, it is logical that government should use a surplus to retire outstanding debt. Using it to pay off debt, however, may reduce the anti-inflationary impact of the creation of a surplus. To retire its debt, the government buys back some of its bonds; in doing so it transfers its surplus tax revenues back into the money market. This causes the interest rate to fall, and thus private borrowing and spending to rise. The increase in private spending somewhat offsets the contractionary fiscal policy that created the budget surplus.

2. **IMPOUNDING**   Government can realize a greater anti-inflationary impact from its budgetary surplus by impounding the surplus funds, that is, allowing them to stand idle. When a surplus is impounded, the government is extracting and withholding purchasing power from the economy. If surplus revenues are not put back into the economy, no portion of that surplus can be spent. There is no chance that the funds will create inflationary pressure to offset the anti-inflationary impact of the contractionary fiscal policy. We conclude that *the impounding of a budget surplus is more anti-inflationary than the use of the surplus to retire public debt.*

Policy Options: *G* or *T*?

Is it preferable to use government spending or taxes to eliminate recessionary and inflationary gaps? The answer depends on one's view as to whether the public sector is too large or too small.

"Liberal" economists, who think there are many unmet social needs, usually recommended that government spending be increased during recessions. In terms of demand-pull inflation, the trend is to recommend tax increases.

"Conservative" economists, who think the public sector is too large and inefficient, usually advocate tax cuts during recessions and cuts in government spending during times of demand-pull inflation. Both actions either restrain the growth of government or reduce its absolute size.

Discretionary fiscal policy designed to stabilize the economy can be associated with either an expanding or a contracting public sector.

12-1
QUICK REVIEW

- Discretionary fiscal policy is the purposeful manipulation of government expenditures and tax collections by government to promote full employment, price stability, and economic growth.

- Government uses expansionary fiscal policy to shift the aggregate demand curve rightward—that is, to stimulate spending and expand real output. This policy involves increases in government spending, reductions in taxes, or some combination of the two.

- Government uses contractionary fiscal policy to shift the aggregate demand curve leftward in an effort to halt demand-pull inflation. This policy entails reductions in government spending, tax increases, or some combination of the two.

- The expansionary effect of fiscal policy is greater when the budget deficit is financed through money creation rather than via borrowing; the contractionary effect of the creation of a budget surplus is greater when the budget surplus is impounded rather than used for debt reduction.

NONDISCRETIONARY FISCAL POLICY: BUILT-IN STABILIZERS

To some degree government tax revenues change automatically, and in a countercyclical direction, over the course of the business cycle. This automatic response or *built-in stability* results from the makeup of most tax systems. We did not include this built-in stability in our discussion of fiscal policy because we implicitly assumed that the same amount of tax revenue was collected at each level of GDP. That is not actually so. In reality, our net tax system is such that *net tax revenues vary directly with GDP*. (*Net taxes* are tax revenues less transfers and subsidies. From here on, we will use the simpler "taxes" to mean "net taxes.")

Virtually any tax will yield more tax revenue as GDP rises. In particular, personal income taxes have progressive rates and thus yield more than proportionate increases in tax revenues as GDP expands. Furthermore, as GDP increases and more goods and services are purchased, revenues from corporate income taxes and sales and excise taxes also increase. And, similarly, payroll tax payments increase as economic expansion creates more jobs. Conversely, when GDP declines, tax receipts from all these sources also decline.

Transfer payments (or "negative taxes") behave in the opposite way from tax revenues. Unemployment compensation payments, welfare payments, and subsidies to farmers all *decrease* during economic expansion and *increase* during a contraction.

Automatic or Built-In Stabilizers

Figure 12-3 shows how the Canadian tax system creates built-in stability. Government expenditures G are fixed and assumed to be independent of the level of GDP; a particular level of spending is decided on by Parliament. But Parliament does *not* determine the *level* of tax revenues; rather, it establishes tax *rates*. Tax revenues then vary directly with the level of GDP that the economy actually realizes. The direct relationship between tax revenues and GDP is shown by the upsloping line T.

Economic Importance   The economic importance of this direct relationship between tax receipts and GDP is revealed when we consider two things:

1. Taxes reduce spending and aggregate demand.
2. It is desirable from the standpoint of stability to reduce spending when the economy is moving towards inflation and to increase spending when the economy is slumping.

In other words, the tax system portrayed in Figure 12-3 builds some stability into the economy. It automatically brings about changes in tax revenues and therefore in the public budget which

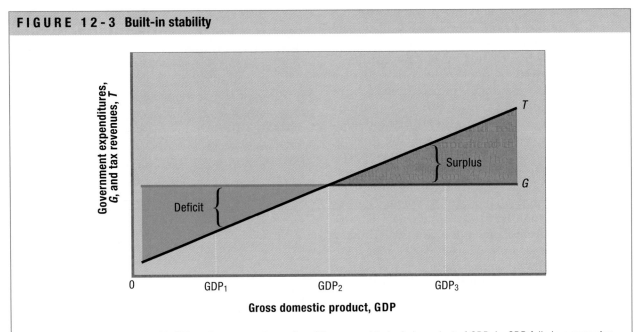

FIGURE 12-3 Built-in stability

Tax revenues *T* vary directly with GDP, and government spending *G* is assumed to be independent of GDP. As GDP falls in a recession, deficits will occur automatically and will help alleviate that recession. As GDP rises during expansion, surpluses will occur automatically and will off possible inflation.

counter both inflation and recession. A **built-in stabilizer** is *anything that increases the government's budget deficit (or reduces its budget surplus) during a recession and increases its budget surplus (or reduces its budget deficit) during inflation without requiring explicit action by policymakers.* As Figure 12-3 reveals, this is precisely what the Canadian tax system does.

As GDP rises during prosperity, tax revenues *automatically* increase and, because they reduce spending, they restrain the economic expansion. That is, as the economy moves towards a higher GDP, tax revenues automatically rise and move the budget from deficit towards surplus.

Conversely, as GDP falls during recession, tax revenues *automatically* decline, increasing spending and cushioning the economic contraction. With a falling GDP, tax receipts decline and move the government's budget from surplus towards deficit. In Figure 12-3, the low level of income GDP_1 will automatically yield an expansionary budget deficit; the high and perhaps inflationary income level GDP_3 will automatically generate a contractionary budget surplus.

Tax Progressivity   It is clear from Figure 12-3 that the size of the automatic budget deficits or surpluses—and therefore built-in stability—depends on how responsive tax revenues are to changes in GDP. If tax revenues change sharply as GDP changes, the slope of line T in the figure will be steep and the vertical distances between T and G—the deficits or surpluses—will be large. If tax revenues change very little when GDP changes, the slope will be gentle and built-in stability will be low.

The steepness of T in Figure 12-3 depends on the tax system itself. In a **progressive tax system**, the average tax rate (= tax revenue/GDP) rises with GDP. In a **proportional tax system**, the average tax rate remains constant as GDP rises. In a **regressive tax system**, the average tax rate falls as GDP rises. The progressive tax system has the steepest tax line T of the three. However, tax revenues will rise with GDP under both the progressive and proportional tax systems, and they may rise, fall, or remain the same under a regressive tax system. But what you should realize is this: *The more progressive the tax system, the greater the economy's built-in stability.*

Changes in public policies or laws that alter the progressivity of the tax system affect the degree of built-in stability. The federal government's "indexing" of the personal income tax and lowering of marginal tax rates has flattened the slope of T in Figure 12-3. Prior to the mid-1970s

inflation would push taxpayers into higher marginal tax brackets and thus increase government's tax revenues. Since then, income tax brackets have been "indexed," or widened, to adjust for inflation. As a result, changes in GDP do not produce as large automatic changes in tax revenue as previously and the economy's degree of built-in stability is less than it was.

The built-in stability provided by our tax system has reduced the severity of business fluctuation. But the built-in stabilizers can only diminish, *not* correct major changes in the equilibrium GDP. Discretionary fiscal policy—changes in tax rates and expenditures—may be needed to correct inflation or recession of any appreciable magnitude.

Actual versus the Cyclically Adjusted Budget

We have built-in stability because tax revenues vary directly with GDP. But those automatic increases or decreases in tax revenues means that the **actual budget** in any particular year does not tell us whether government's current discretionary fiscal policy is expansionary, neutral, or contractionary. Here's why: Suppose an economy is achieving full-employment output at GDP_f in Figure 12-4. But note from the government spending line G and the tax line T that there is an actual budget deficit shown by vertical distance ab. Now assume that investment spending plummets, swamping the expansionary effect of this budget deficit and causing a recession to GDP_r. Let's assume that government takes no new discretionary action, so lines G and T remain as shown in the figure. With the economy at GDP_r, tax revenues are lower than before, while government spending remains unaltered. The budget deficit therefore rises to ec, expanding from ab (= ed) by amount dc. The added deficit of dc is called a **cyclical deficit** because it relates to the business cycle. It is *not* the result of discretionary fiscal actions by government; rather, it is the by-product of the economy's slide into recession.

Note in Figure 12-4 that to find the actual deficit ec for year 2, we must know where lines G and T are located *and* the specific level of GDP. The same G and T lines give different deficits or surpluses with different GDPs. Thus, we cannot evaluate the government's fiscal policy—the extent to which it is expansionary, neutral, or contractionary—by looking only at the size of a current budget deficit or surplus. Because an actual bud-

FIGURE 12-4 Full-employment (structural) deficits and cyclical deficits

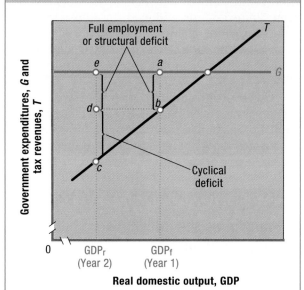

The actual budget deficit for any specific year is the amount by which government expenditures exceed its tax revenues. It consists of the structural deficit (or full-employment deficit) and the cyclical deficit. At full-employment output GDP$_f$ the actual deficit is *ab*, the structural deficit is *ab*, and the cyclical deficit is zero. At recessionary output GDP$_r$, the actual budget deficit is *ec*, the structural deficit is *ed* (= *ab*), and the cyclical deficit is *dc*.

get deficit or surplus is the result of more than fiscal decisions about spending and taxes (as shown by the locations of lines *G* and *T* in Figure 12-4), we must also consider the level of GDP (where the economy is operating on the horizontal axis of Figure 12-4). In the economy represented in Figure 12-4, the actual budget deficit in year 2 (GDP$_r$) differs from that in year 1 (GDP$_f$) only because GDP is lower in year 2 than in year 1.

Resolution of the Problem Economists resolve this problem by standardizing the budget deficits and surpluses for different years in the business cycle; they do this by using the **cyclically adjusted budget**, also called the *full-employment budget*. This budget *measures what the federal budget deficit or surplus would be with existing tax and government spending structures if the economy were at full employment throughout the year.* The idea is to compare actual government expenditures for each particular year with the tax revenues that would have occurred in that year if the economy had achieved full employment.

Consider Figure 12-4 once again. In full-employment year 1, the full-employment deficit is *ab*, the amount of the actual deficit. In year 2, however, the actual budget deficit of *ec* overstates the full-employment deficit. Specifically, the cyclical part of the deficit *dc* must be subtracted from the actual deficit *ec* to obtain the full-employment deficit, *ed*. We note, then, that the full-employment deficit for year 2 is the same as that for year 1 (*ed* = *ab*). By comparing these two full-employment deficits, we see that government did not change its fiscal policy between years 1 and 2.

A cyclically adjusted budget deficit is also called a **structural deficit** because it reflects the configuration of the *G* line and *T* line, *independent of any changes in GDP*. The structural deficits for years 1 and 2 in Figure 12-4 are the same (*ab* = *ed*). *Discretionary fiscal policy is reflected in deliberate changes in the full-employment deficit (structural deficit).* The actual budget deficit in any particular year is the sum of the structural and cyclical deficits. So changes in the *actual budget* deficit do not alone tell us whether fiscal policy has become more or less expansionary or contractionary. Changes in the *structural deficit* (or structural surplus) give us that information.

Historical Comparison Figure 12-5 compares the cyclically adjusted budget and the actual budget as percentages of GDP since 1961. In many years the sizes of the **actual budget** deficits or surpluses differ from the sizes of the deficits or surpluses of the cyclically adjusted budget. The key to assessing discretionary fiscal policy is to disregard the actual budget and instead observe the change in the *cyclically adjusted budget* in a particular year or period. For example, fiscal policy was restrictive between 1964 and 1970, reflected in the increase in cyclically adjusted deficit below the actual budget. Fiscal policy was also contractionary between 1972 and 1974.

Also observe in Figure 12-5 that cyclically adjusted or structural deficits have been particularly large since 1981. A large part of the actual deficits during the 1980s and early 1990s were not cyclical deficits resulting from automatic deficiencies in tax revenue brought forth from below-full employment GDP. Rather, much of the actual deficits reflected structural imbalances between government spending and tax collections. The year 1989 is an example. Although the economy had achieved full employment, a sizable cyclically adjusted deficit remained.

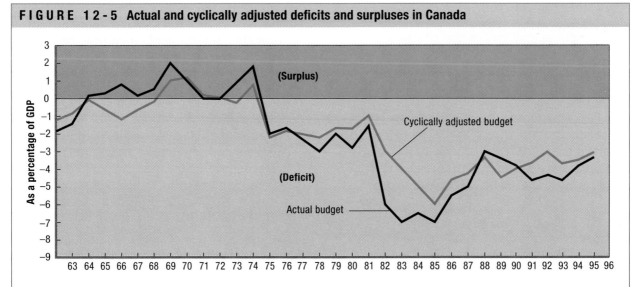

FIGURE 12-5 Actual and cyclically adjusted deficits and surpluses in Canada

The cyclically adjusted (or full-employment) budget deficits and surpluses often differ in size from actual budget deficits and surpluses. Changes in the full-employment budget deficit or surplus are better indicators of whether government's fiscal policy is expansionary, neutral, or contractionary than are changes in actual budget deficits or surpluses.

Source: Department of Finance, Economic and Fiscal Reference Tables, September, 1996.

Large cyclically adjusted budget deficits persisted into the mid-1990s. But deep government expenditure cuts along with an expanding economy resulted in a federal government budget surplus in 1997–98, the first surplus in almost 30 years. During the 1990s the Canadian government has largely abandoned countercyclical fiscal policy in its drive to reduce the large structural deficits. These deficits were so large that financing them increased real interest rates and crowded out much private investment, a scenario we will elaborate on shortly. Thus, in the 1990s the role of stabilizing the economy has fallen nearly exclusively to the nation's central bank, the Bank of Canada. This institution and its policies are the subject of Chapters 13 through 15. *(Key Question 5)*

Global Perspective 12-1 shows that budget deficits are not confined to Canada.

12-2

QUICK REVIEW

- Tax revenues automatically increase in economic expansions and decrease in recessions; transfers automatically decrease in expansions and increase in recessions.

- Automatic changes in taxes and transfers add a degree of built-in stability to the economy.

- The cyclically adjusted budget compares government spending to the tax revenues that would accrue if there were full employment; it is more useful than the actual budget in revealing the status of fiscal policy.

- Cyclically adjusted budget deficits are also called structural deficits.

PROBLEMS, CRITICISMS, AND COMPLICATIONS

Economists recognize that governments may encounter a number of significant problems in enacting and applying fiscal policy.

Problems of Timing

Several problems of timing may arise in connection with fiscal policy:

1. **RECOGNITION LAG** The recognition lag is the time between the beginning of a recession or an inflation and the certain awareness that it

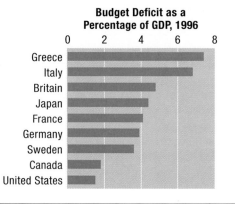

12-1

GLOBAL PERSPECTIVE

Budget deficits as a percentage of GDP, selected nations

In 1996 all the major industrial nations had budget deficits, but these deficits varied greatly as a percentage of GDP. In some cases the deficits were largely cyclical; in other instances they were mainly cyclically adjusted or structural deficits. In 1998 Canada recorded a budget surplus.

Budget Deficit as a Percentage of GDP, 1996

Source: Organization for Economic Cooperation and Development.

---

put, employment, or the price level. Although changes in tax rates can be put into effect quickly, government spending on public works—the construction of dams, highways, and so on—requires long planning periods and even longer periods of construction. Such spending is of questionable usefulness in offsetting short—for example, six- to eighteen-month—periods of recession. Because of such problems, discretionary fiscal policy has increasingly relied on tax changes rather than changes in spending as its main weapon.

Political Problems

Fiscal policy is created in the political arena, and this greatly complicates its use in stabilizing the economy.

Other Goals Economic stability is *not* the sole objective of government spending and taxing policies. Government is also concerned with providing public goods and services and redistributing income. During World War II, government spending for military goods rose dramatically, causing strong and persistent inflationary pressures in the early 1940s. The defeat of Nazi Germany and Japan was a higher priority goal than achieving price stability.

Provincial and Municipal Finance Fiscal policies of provincial and local governments are frequently pro-cyclical—they worsen rather than correct recession or inflation. Like households and private businesses, provincial and local governments increase expenditures during prosperity and cut them during recession. During the Great Depression of the 1930s, some of the increase in federal spending was offset by decreases in provincial and local spending.

Expansionary Bias? Rhetoric to the contrary, deficits may be politically attractive and surpluses politically painful. Fiscal policy may have an expansionary-inflationary bias. Tax reductions are politically popular. And so are increases in government spending, provided the constituents share in the benefits. But both can be inflationary. In contrast, higher taxes upset voters, while reducing government expenditures can be politically precarious.

Political Business Cycle? A few economists have suggested the notion of a **political business cycle**. They have argued that politicians might manipulate fiscal policy to maximize voter sup-

---

is actually happening. This lag arises because of the difficulty in predicting the future course of economic activity. Although forecasting tools such as the index of leading indicators (see this chapter's Last Word) provide clues to the direction of the economy, the economy may be four or six months into a recession or inflation before that fact appears in relevant statistics and is acknowledged. Meanwhile, the economic downslide or the inflation may become more serious than it would have if the situation had been identified and acted on sooner.

2. **ADMINISTRATIVE LAG** The wheels of democratic government turn slowly. There will typically be a significant lag between the time the need for fiscal action is recognized and the time action is actually taken. The Canadian Parliament has on occasion taken so much time in adjusting fiscal policy that the economic situation has changed in the interim, rendering the policy action inappropriate.

3. **OPERATIONAL LAG** There is also a lag between the time fiscal action is taken by Parliament and the time that action affects out-

port, even though their fiscal decisions *destabilize* the economy. In this view, fiscal policy as we have described it may be corrupted for political purposes and actually *cause* economic fluctuations.

The populace, it is assumed, takes economic conditions into account in voting. Incumbents are penalized at the polls if the economy is depressed; they are rewarded if it is prosperous. As an election approaches, the government cuts tax and increases spending. Not only are these actions popular, they push all the critical economic indicators in positive directions. Output and real incomes rise, and unemployment falls. As a result, the government enjoys a cordial economic environment in which to stand for re-election.

But after the election, continued expansion of the economy will be reflected increasingly in a rising price level and less in growing real incomes. Growing public concern over inflation prompts politicians to enact a contractionary fiscal policy. A "made-in-Ottawa" recession is engineered by trimming taxes to restrain inflation. A mild recession would not hurt the government because the next election is still three or four years away and the critical consideration for most voters is the performance of the economy in the year or so before the election. Indeed, the recession provides a new starting point from which fiscal policy can again be used to generate another expansion in time for the next election campaign.

Such a scenario is difficult to document and empirical tests of this theory are inconclusive. Nevertheless, there is some evidence in support of this political theory of the business cycle.

Crowding-Out Effect

We now move from practical problems in implementing fiscal policy to a basic criticism of fiscal policy itself. This criticism is based on an alleged **crowding-out effect:** *An expansionary fiscal policy (deficit spending) will increase the interest rate and reduce private spending, weakening or cancelling the stimulus of the fiscal policy.*

Suppose the economy is in recession and government enacts discretionary fiscal policy in the form of increased government spending. To finance its budget deficit, government borrows funds in the money market. The resulting increase in the demand for money raises the price paid for borrowing money: the interest rate. Because investment spending varies inversely with the interest rate, some investment will be choked off or

crowded out. (Some interest-sensitive consumption spending—for example, purchases of automobiles on credit—may also be crowded out.)

Graphical Presentation   An upsloping aggregate supply curve causes a part of the increase in aggregate demand, as in Figure 12-6, to be dissipated in higher prices with the result that the increase in real GDP is diminished. The price level rises from P_0 to P_1 and real domestic output increases to only \$$GDP_1$, rather than GDP_f.

Criticisms of the Crowding-Out Effect   While few would question the logic of the crowding-out effect, there is disagreement as to its existence under all circumstances. Some economists argue that little crowding out will occur when there is recession. They note that the increased government spending will likely improve business profit expectations, and these improved prospects may encourage private investment. Thus, private investment need not fall, even though interest rates rise.

Also, critics of the crowding-out view point out that policymakers can counteract the crowding-out effect. Specifically, the monetary authorities could increase the supply of money by just enough to offset the deficit-caused increase in the demand for money. Then the equilibrium interest rate would not change, and the crowding-out

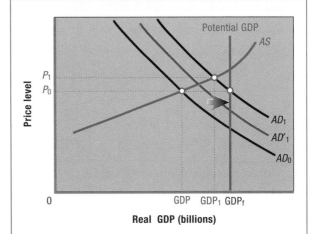

FIGURE 12-6 Fiscal policy: the effects of crowding out, inflation, and the net export effect

With an upward sloping aggregate supply curve, a part of the impact of an expansionary policy will be reflected in a rise in the price level rather than an increase in real output and employment.

effect would be zero. In the 1980s the monetary authorities did not increase the supply of money to "accommodate" the expansionary fiscal policy; consequently, the crowding-out effect of the large 1980s deficits may have been quite great. In comparison, in the 1960s the monetary authorities wanted to keep interest rates stable. Hence, they increased the money supply when government borrowing threatened to push up interest rates. As a result, crowding out was less significant.

Fiscal Policy, Aggregate Supply, and Inflation

Our discussion of the complications and criticisms of fiscal policy has thus far concentrated entirely on aggregate demand. We now consider a supply-side complication: *With an upsloping aggregate supply curve, some portion of the potential effect of an expansionary fiscal policy on real output and employment may be dissipated in the form of inflation.* As Figure 12-6 shows, with a rise in the price level, the increase in government expenditures that shifts the aggregate demand curved from AD_0 to AD_1, will be partially offset by declines in consumption, investment, and net exports expenditures, pushing equilibrium back from GDP_f to GDP_1. These declines result respectively from the wealth, interest-rate, and foreign-trade effects created by the higher domestic price level. Demand-side fiscal policy does not escape the realities imposed by the aggregate supply curve.

Fiscal Policy in the Open Economy

Additional complications arise from the fact that each national economy is a component of the world economy.

Shocks Originating from Abroad   Events and policies abroad that affect a nation's net exports affect its own economy. Economies are open to unforeseen international *aggregate demand shocks* that can alter domestic GDP and make current domestic fiscal policy inappropriate.

Suppose Canada is in a recession and has enacted an expansionary fiscal policy to increase aggregate demand and GDP without igniting inflation. Now suppose the economies of Canada's major trading partners unexpectedly expand rapidly. Greater employment and rising incomes in those nations mean more purchases of Canadian goods. Canadian net exports rise, Canadian aggre-

gate demand increases too rapidly; and Canada experiences demand-pull inflation. If it had known in advance that its net exports might rise significantly, Canada would have enacted a less expansionary fiscal policy. We see, then, that participation in the world economy brings with it the complications of mutual interdependence along with the gains from specialization and trade.

Net Export Effect   The **net export effect** may also work through international trade to reduce the effectiveness of fiscal policy. We concluded in our discussion of the crowding-out effect that an expansionary fiscal policy might boost interest rates, reducing *investment* and weakening fiscal policy. Now we want to know what effect an interest-rate increase might have on a nation's *net exports* (exports minus imports).

Suppose Canada undertakes an expansionary fiscal policy that causes a higher Canadian interest rate. The higher interest rate will attract financial capital from abroad, where interest rates are unchanged. But foreign financial investors must acquire Canadian dollars to invest in Canadian securities. We know that an increase in the demand for a commodity—in this case, dollars—will raise its price. So the price of the Canadian dollar rises in terms of foreign currencies; that is, the dollar appreciates.

What will be the impact of this dollar appreciation on Canadian net exports? Because more units of foreign currencies are needed to buy Canadian goods, the rest of the world will see Canadian exports as being more expensive. Hence, Canadian exports will decline. Canadians, who can now exchange their dollars for more units of foreign currencies, will buy more imports. Consequently, with Canadian exports falling and imports rising, net export expenditures in Canada will diminish; this is a contractionary change, so Canada's expansionary fiscal policy will be partially negated.[1]

A return to our aggregate demand and supply analysis in Figure 12-6 will clarify this point. An expansionary fiscal policy aimed at increasing aggregate demand from AD_0 to AD_1 may hike the domestic interest rate and ultimately reduce net exports through the process just described. The decline in the net export component of aggregate

---

[1] The appreciation of the dollar will also reduce the dollar price of foreign resources imported to Canada. As a result, aggregate supply will increase and part of the contractionary net export effect described here may be offset.

TABLE 12-1 Fiscal policy and the net export effect

(1) Expansionary fiscal policy	(2) Contractionary fiscal policy
Problem: Recession, slow growth	Problem: Inflation
↓	↓
Expansionary fiscal policy	Contractionary fiscal policy
↓	↓
Higher domestic interest rate	Lower domestic interest rate
↓	↓
Increased foreign demand for dollars	Decreased foreign demand for dollars
↓	↓
Dollar appreciates	Dollar depreciates
↓	↓
Net exports decline (aggregate demand decreases, partially offsetting the expansionary fiscal policy)	Net exports increase (aggregate demand increases, partially offsetting the contractionary fiscal policy)

demand will partially offset the expansionary fiscal policy. The aggregate demand curve will shift rightward from AD_0 to AD'_1 *not* to AD_1, and equilibrium GDP will not increase as much. Thus, the net export effect of fiscal policy joins the problems of timing, politics, crowding out, and inflation in complicating the "management" of aggregate demand.

Table 12-1 summarizes the net export effect resulting from fiscal policy. Column 1 reviews the analysis just discussed (Figure 12-6). But note that the net export effect works in both directions. By reducing the domestic interest rate, a *contractionary* fiscal policy *increases* net exports. In this regard, you should follow through the analysis in column 2 in Table 12-1 and relate it to the aggregate demand-aggregate supply model. *(Key Question 7)*

12-3
QUICK REVIEW

- Time lags and political problems complicate fiscal policy.

- The crowding-out effect indicates that an expansionary fiscal policy may increase the interest rate and reduce investment spending.

- The upsloping aggregate supply curve means that part of an expansionary fiscal policy may be dissipated in inflation.

- Fiscal policy may be weakened by the net export effect, that works through changes in **a** the interest rate, **b** the international value of the dollar, and **c** exports and imports.

In
The Media

Japan's Fiscal Moves Save the Day, Not the Economy

Package of tax cuts and aid to banks not enough, analysts say

BY DAVID HAMILTON
THE WALL STREET JOURNAL

TOKYO—A senior Japanese finance official declared that a new government package of tax cuts, public money for the banking system and other measures should alleviate concerns about Japan's weak economy.

But while stock of currency markets in Japan and elsewhere in Asia rose strongly on the announcement of the tax cut, economists said the plan won't solve

Japan's economic woes and that the nation's problems are far from over.

The Japanese government yesterday put the final touches on an economic plan that will cut income taxes by two trillion yen ($15.3-billion U.S.), cut corporate taxes by an additional 850 billion yen, halve a securities transaction tax and relax a land transaction tax. In addition, Tokyo plans to inject 10 trillion yen of public funds into the banking system to insure depositors and to rebuild confidence in a financial sector that has recently been rocked by a series of bank and securities firm failures, including that of Japan's oldest brokerage firm last month.

In Washington, the Japanese tax cut was greeted warmly as an overdue step to spur Japan's economy, which was hurt earlier in the year by a tax increase. "We welcome the policy actions," said U.S. Treasury Secretary Robert Rubin. "A strong economic recovery in Japan, led by domestic demand, is important for both our countries, for Asia and for the world economy."

Another Treasury official said Japan's intervention in currency markets to boost the yen's value was "appropriate and consistent with concerns we and Japan have shared in the past." There was no sign the United States was joining the Japanese to push up the yen, however.

A top Japanese finance official said the new measures should be enough to settle anxiety about Japan's financial system and its economy. "I expect no further bankruptcies are in sight," said Eisuke Sakakibara, vice-minister for international affairs at the ministry of finance. The economic measures, he said, "will stop this avalanche of low confidence in the Japanese financial system."

Mr. Sakakibara confirmed that the Bank of Japan had intervened in currency markets and said more intervention could follow. "I have always said that excess depreciation [of the yen] is not desirable and that we will take necessary action," he said. "We have taken decisive action and we will do so again."

A senior financial regulator said the bank had intervened because of worries that the yen was weakening so far that it might spark trade tensions with the United States. Japan's trade surplus has been rising sharply, and the government is eager to reverse the yen's weakness in order to counter the rise in the surplus, the regulator said. Absent such intervention, Japan could potentially face a far more disruptive rise in the yen's value if the United States grows more concerned about the trade balance.

Mr. Sakakibara said Japan will work to solve the current economic crisis in South Korea, although he didn't comment on recent reports that South Korea is seeking a bilateral bridge loan from Japan. "The Japan problem has been solved," he said. "The next problem to solve is the Korea problem."

However, economists said that while the package is a step in the right direction, it doesn't go anywhere near far enough. In part, that is because the income tax cut is a temporary measure that will be repealed after a year, which economists say is likely to encourage people to save the extra money instead of spending it.

David Wessel contributed to this article.

Source: *Globe and Mail*, December 18, 1997, p. B10. Reprinted with permission of the *Wall Street Journal* ©1997, Dow Jones & Company, Inc.

THE STORY IN BRIEF

Japan's central government cuts income and corporate taxes in an effort to revive a sluggish economy.

THE ECONOMICS BEHIND THE STORY

- It became evident during the course of 1997 that Japan was teetering on the verge of a recession.

Complicating the issue was that a number of banks were close to bankruptcy because of bad loans.

- The Japanese government cut both income and corporate taxes in the hope of reviving consumption and investment. The government had earlier raised taxes, slowing the economy more than intended.
- The Japanese yen had been depreciating against the American dollar, a good sign for much-needed net export growth that would complement an expansionary fiscal policy. Many analysts expressed pessimism that the tax cuts were sufficient for the intended goal.
- With the help of the AD-AS model, analyze the likely impact of Japan's expansionary policy. ■

The
Last Word

THE LEADING INDICATORS

One of the several tools policy makers use to forecast the future direction of real GDP is a monthly index of a group of variables that in the past have provided advanced notice of changes in GDP.

"INDEX OF LEADING INDICATORS FALLS FOR Third Month—Recession Feared"; "Index of Leading Indicators Surges Again"; "Decline in Stock Market Drags Down Index of Leading Indicators." Headlines such as these appear regularly in newspapers. The focus of the articles are Statistics Canada's weighted average—or composite index—of 10 economic variables that has historically reached its peak or trough in advance of the corresponding turns in the business cycle. Hence, changes in the index of leading indicators provide a clue to the future direction of the economy and thus may shorten the length of the recognition lag associated with the implementation of macroeconomic policy.

Let us examine the 10 components of the index of leading indicators in terms of a predicted *decline* in GDP, keeping in mind that the opposite changes forecast a rise in GDP.

1. Furniture and appliance sales   A slump in these retail trade sales portends reduced future production—that is, a decline in GDP.

2. Other durable goods sales   This part of retail trade is four times greater than the first. It includes sales of automobiles, which are more sensitive to interest rates than are purchases of other goods. A decline in sales here may be more a result of rising consumer loan rates than an impending downturn in the economy—though rising interest rates themselves often do precede a downturn.

3. House spending index   This is a composite index of housing starts (units) and house sales. Decreases in the number of housing starts and in house sales forecast declines in investment and therefore the distinct possibility that GDP will decline or at least grow more slowly.

4. New orders for durable goods   A decline in the number of orders received for durable goods indicates reduced future production—a decline in GDP.

5. Shipment to inventory ratio of finished goods   A decline in the ratio—a decline in shipments and/or an increase in inventory—indicates that sales are declining and, probably, that undesired investment in inventories is occurring. In either case, a decline in production is probable.

6. Average work week (hours)   Decreases in the length of the average work week in manufacturing foretell declines in future manufacturing output and GDP.

7. Business and personal service employment   A decline in employment, especially in view of the continuing growth of our labour force of some 250,000 a year, indicates a serious slowdown in the economy and therefore GDP.

8. United States composite leading index   With 70 percent of our trade with the United States—approximately 38 percent of our GDP—a slowdown in the United States is quickly transmitted to Canada. If the U.S. composite leading index is sharply down, Canada's GDP will almost certainly decline.

9. TSE 300 stock price index   The Toronto Stock Exchange (TSE) is the country's largest, and the price movements of the 300 stocks that make up its index are a good indication of market sentiment in Canada. If the index is dropping sharply, this is a strong indication that financial investors are pessimistic about the economy and expect GDP to decline. This can become a self-fulfilling prophecy, because lower stock market prices diminish consumer wealth, leading consumers to cut back on their spending. Lower stock market values also make it less attractive for firms to issue new shares of stock as a way to raise funds for investment. Hence, declines in the stock market can bring forth declines in aggregate demand and GDP.

10. Money supply   Decreases in the money supply are associated with falling GDP. The components of the money supply and its role in the macroeconomy are the subjects of Chapters 13 to 15.

None of these factors *alone* consistently predicts the future course of the economy. It is not unusual in any month, for example, for one or two of the indicators to be decreasing while the other is increasing. Rather, changes in the *weighted average*—or composite index—of the 10 components in the past have provided advance notice of a change in the direction of GDP. The rule of thumb is that three successive monthly declines or increases in the index indicate that the economy will soon turn in that same direction.

Although the composite index has correctly signalled business fluctuations on numerous occasions, it has not been infallible. At times the index has provided false warnings of recessions that have never occurred. In other instances, recessions have so closely followed the downturn in the index that policy makers have not had sufficient time to make use of the "early" warning. Moreover, changing structural features of the economy have on occasion rendered the existing index obsolete and necessitated its revision.

Given these caveats, the index of leading indicators can best be thought of as a useful but not totally reliable signalling device that authorities must employ with considerable caution in formulating macroeconomic policy. ■

CHAPTER SUMMARY

1. Increases in government spending expand, and decreases contract, aggregate demand and equilibrium GDP. Increases in taxes reduce, and decreases expand, aggregate demand and equilibrium GDP. Fiscal policy therefore calls for increases in government spending and decreases in taxes—a budget deficit—to correct for a recessionary gap. Decreases in government spending and increases in taxes—a budget surplus—are appropriate fiscal policy for correcting an inflationary gap.

2. Built-in stability arises from net tax revenues that vary directly with the level of GDP. During recession, the federal budget automatically moves towards a stabilizing deficit; during expansion, the budget automatically moves towards an anti-inflationary surplus. Built-in stability lessens, but does not fully correct, undesired changes in the GDP.

3. An actual budget deficit is made up of two elements: the structural deficit (if any) and the cyclical deficit (if any). The structural deficit—also known as the full-employment deficit—is that part of an actual deficit that would occur even if the economy were at its full-employment output. The cyclical deficit is that part of an actual deficit that arises when real GDP is less than full-employment GDP.

4. The full-employment budget or cyclically adjusted budget measures the federal budget deficit or surplus that would occur if the economy operated at full employment throughout the year. Changes in the full-employment deficit or surplus—also called the structural deficit or surplus—provide meaningful information as to whether government's fiscal policy is expansionary, neutral, or contractionary. Changes in the actual budget deficit or surplus do not, since such deficits or surpluses depend on the state of the economy.

5. The enactment and application of appropriate fiscal policy are subject to certain problems and questions. The most important ones are **a** Can the enactment and application of fiscal policy be better timed so as to maximize its effectiveness in heading off economic fluctuations? **b** Can the economy rely on Parliament to enact appropriate fiscal policy? **c** An expansionary fiscal policy may be weakened if it crowds out some private investment spending. **d** Some of the effect of an expansionary fiscal policy may be dissipated in inflation. **e** Fiscal policy may be rendered ineffective or inappropriate by unforeseen events occurring within the borders of international trading partners. Also, fiscal policy may precipitate changes in exchange rates that may weaken its effects.

TERMS AND CONCEPTS

discretionary fiscal policy

expansionary and contractionary fiscal policy

budget deficit

budget surplus

built-in stabilizers

progressive, proportional, and regressive tax systems

actual budget

cyclical deficit

cyclically adjusted budget

structural deficit

political business cycle

crowding-out effect

net export effect

STUDY QUESTIONS

1. **KEY QUESTION** *What are government's fiscal policy options for an inflationary gap caused by demand-pull inflation? Use the aggregate demand-aggregate supply model to show the impact of these policies on the price level. Which of these fiscal policy options do you think a "conservative" economist might favour? A "liberal" economist?*

2. (For students assigned Chapters 9 and 10) Use the aggregate expenditures model to show how government fiscal policy could eliminate either a recessionary gap or an inflationary gap (Figure 10-8). Use the concept of the balanced budget multiplier to explain how equal increases in G and T could eliminate a recessionary gap and how equal decreases in G and T could eliminate an inflationary gap.

3. Designate each statement true or false and justify your answer.
    a. Expansionary fiscal policy during a recession will have a greater positive effect on real GDP if government borrows the money to finance the budget deficit than if it creates new money to finance the deficit.
    b. Contractionary fiscal policy will be more effective if government impounds the budget surplus than using the surplus to pay off some of its past debt.

4. Explain how the built-in (or automatic) stabilizers work. What are the differences between a proportional, progressive, and regressive tax system as they relate to an economy's built-in stability?

5. **KEY QUESTION** *Define the "cyclically adjusted budget," explain its significance, and state how it differs from the "actual budget." What is the difference between a structural deficit and a cyclical deficit? Suppose the economy depicted in Figure 12-4 is operating at full-employment real output, GDP_f. What is the size of its structural deficit? Its cyclical deficit? Should government raise taxes or reduce government spending to eliminate this structural deficit? What are the risks of so doing?*

6. The actual budget deficit increased significantly in 1991 and 1992, but the cyclically adjusted budget deficit remained relatively constant. Can you think of a logical explanation?

7. **KEY QUESTION** *Briefly state and evaluate the problems in enacting and applying fiscal policy. Explain the notion of a political business cycle. What is the crowding-out effect and why is it relevant to fiscal policy? In what respect is the net export effect similar to the crowding-out effect?*

8. In view of your answers to question 7, explain the following statement: "While fiscal policy clearly is useful in combatting severe recession and demand-pull inflation, it is impossible to use fiscal policy to 'fine tune' the economy to the full-employment, noninflationary level of real GDP and keep the economy there indefinitely."

9. Suppose that government engages in deficit spending to push the economy from recession and that this spending is directed towards new "public capital" such as roads, bridges, dams, harbours, office parks, industrial sites, and the like. How might this spending increase the expected rate of return on some types of potential *private* investment projects? What are the implications for the crowding-out effect?

10. Use Figure 12-4 to explain why a deliberate increase in the structural deficit that causes the economy to expand from GDP_r to GDP_f might reduce the size of the actual deficit.

11. **Advanced Analysis** (Optional for students assigned Chapters 9 and 10) Assume that, without taxes, the consumption schedule for an economy is as shown below:

GDP, billions	Consumption, billions
$100	$120
200	200
300	280
400	360
500	440
600	520
700	600

a. Graph this consumption schedule and determine the size of the MPC.

b. Assume a lump-sum (regressive) tax is imposed such that the government collects $10 billion in taxes at all levels of GDP. Calculate the tax rate at each level of GDP. Graph the resulting consumption schedule and compare the MPC and the multiplier with that of the pretax consumption schedule.

c. Now suppose a proportional tax with a 10 percent tax rate is imposed instead of the regressive tax. Calculate the new consumption schedule, graph it, and note the MPC and the multiplier.

d. Finally, impose a progressive tax such that the tax rate is zero percent when GDP is $100, 5 percent at $200, 10 percent at $300, 15 percent at $400, and so forth. Determine and graph the new consumption schedule, noting the effect of this tax on the MPC and the multiplier.

e. Explain why the proportional and progressive taxes contribute to greater economic stability, while the regressive tax does not. Demonstrate using a graph similar to Figure 12-3.

12. (The Last Word) What is the composite index of leading economic indicators and how does it relate to discretionary fiscal policy?

13. WEB-BASED QUESTION **Latest Economic Indicators—How Goes the Economy?** The Conference Board www.tcb-indicators.org/lei/leilatest.htm. constantly tracks the latest economic indicators. Check the "3-month summary" to see how the Canadian economy is likely to fare in the near future.

14. WEB-BASED QUESTION **The Federal Budget Stance** Visit the Department of Finance site at www.fin.gc.ca/access/budinfoe.html and click on the latest budget. Now, access the budget overview. What are the main targets of the federal government?

Money, Banking, and Monetary Policy

PART 3

Money and Banking

"MONEY BEWITCHES PEOPLE. THEY FRET FOR IT, and they sweat for it. They devise most ingenious ways to get it, and most ingenuous ways to get rid of it. Money is the only commodity that is good for nothing but to be gotten rid of. It will not feed you, clothe you, shelter you, or amuse you unless you spend it or invest it. It imparts value only in parting. People will do almost anything for money, and money will do almost anything for people. Money is a captivating, circulating, masquerading puzzle."[1]

Money. A fascinating aspect of the economy. And a crucial element of economics. Money is more than a tool for facilitating the economy's operation. When it is working properly, the monetary system is the lifeblood of the circular flows of income and expenditure that typify all economies. A well-operating monetary system helps achieve both full employment and efficient resource use. A malfunctioning monetary system can contribute to severe fluctuations in the economy's levels of output, employment, and prices and can distort the allocation of resources.

In this chapter we are concerned with the nature and functions of money and the basic institutions of the Canadian banking system. In the next chapter we examine the ways individual chartered banks and the banking system as a whole can vary the money supply. In Chapter 15 we discuss how the Bank of Canada regulates the supply of money to promote full employment and price-level stability.

We begin here with a review of the functions of money. Next, we shift to the supply of money and pose the question: What constitutes money in Canada? Third, we consider what "backs" the supply of money and what is meant by the

> ## IN THIS CHAPTER
> ## YOU WILL LEARN:
>
> The definition and
> function of money.
>
> •
>
> What backs Canada's
> money supply.
>
> •
>
> About the structure of the
> Canadian financial system.
>
> •
>
> How the development of electronic
> money and smart cards are
> changing the financial system.

demand for money. Then we combine the supply of money and the demand for money to portray and explain the market for money. Finally, the institutional structure of the Canadian financial system is discussed, and recent developments relating to the banking industry are examined.

---

[1] Federal Reserve Bank of Philadelphia, "Creeping Inflation," *Business Review*, August 1957, p. 3.

The Big Picture

WE NOW LEAVE THE TOPIC OF HOW EQUILIBRIUM GDP and the price level are determined to focus on the often misunderstood concept of money and the role of the financial system in a market economy. While most people maintain that they desire more money, you should note that what they really want is more of what money can buy. Consider a world in which everyone could have whatever his or her heart desired; money in such a world would be literally worthless!

A market economy could function without money or a financial system, but it would certainly function much, much less efficiently. Money makes exchange and saving infinitely easier. You will better understand the role and importance of money and a financial system in the efficient functioning of a modern market economy if you imagine an economy without them. The cost of buying and selling goods and services, and borrowing and lending funds, would go way up. Thus, understanding what money is and how the financial system functions in Canada is important to comprehend the monetary side of this macroeconomy.

As you read this chapter, keep the following points in mind:

- **Key Concept 9** is discussed.
- Money makes exchange in any economy much easier compared to barter. Money is desired for the goods and services it can purchase. Money also makes it easier to save and put a value on goods and services.
- While money comes in many different forms, its functions are always the same.
- An economy can function, albeit with some difficulties, with only the use of cheque money.
- Chartered banks are profit-maximizing firms. The Bank of Canada is the "bankers' bank" and is responsible for the supply of money. ■

THE FUNCTIONS OF MONEY

Just what is money? There is an appropriate saying that "money *is* what money *does*." Anything that performs the functions of money is money. So what are these functions?

1. **MEDIUM OF EXCHANGE**   First, and foremost, money is a **medium of exchange**; it is usable for buying and selling goods and services. A worker in a bakery does not want to be paid 200 bagels per week. Nor does the bakery wish to receive, say, tuna fish for its bagels. Money, however, is readily acceptable as payment. It is a social invention with which resource suppliers and producers can be paid and that can be used to buy any of the full range of items available in the marketplace. As such a medium of exchange, money allows society to escape the complications of barter. And because it provides a convenient way of exchanging goods, money allows society to gain the advantages of geographic and human specialization.

2. **UNIT OF ACCOUNT**   Money is also a **unit of account**. Society uses the monetary unit as a yardstick for measuring the relative worth of a wide variety of goods, services, and resources. Just as we measure distance in kilometres, we gauge the value of goods in dollars. With a money system, we need not state the price of each product in terms of all other products for which it can be exchanged; we need not specify the price of cows in terms of corn, crayons, cigars, Chevrolets, and croissants.

This use of money as a common denominator means that the price of each product need be stated *only* in terms of the monetary unit. It permits buyers and sellers to readily compare the prices of various commodities and resources. Such comparisons aid rational decision making. In Chapter 7 we used money as a unit of account in calculating the size of the GDP. Money is also used as a unit of account for transactions involving future payments. Debt obligations of all kinds are measured in the monetary unit.

3. **STORE OF VALUE**   Finally, money serves as a **store of value**. Because money is the most liquid—meaning the most spendable—of all assets, it is a very convenient way to store

wealth. The money you place in a safe or chequing account will still be available to you months or years later when you wish to use it. Most methods of holding money do not yield monetary returns such as one gets by storing wealth in the form of real assets (property) or paper assets (stocks, bonds, and so forth). However, money does have the advantage of being *immediately* usable by a firm or a household in meeting all financial obligations.

THE SUPPLY OF MONEY

Conceptually, anything generally acceptable as a medium of exchange *is* money. Historically, whales' teeth, elephant tail bristles, circular stones, nails, slaves (yes, human beings), cattle, cigarettes, and pieces of metal have been used as media of exchange. In Canada the debts of governments and of chartered banks and other financial institutions are used as money, as you will see.

Defining Money: M1

There is no agreement on how broadly or narrowly the economy's money supply should be defined. In the most narrow useful definition, the money supply is designated **M1** and is composed of two items:

1. Currency (coins and paper money) outside chartered banks.
2. All **demand deposits,** meaning chequing account deposits in the chartered banks.

Coins and paper money are issued by the Bank of Canada, and demand deposits—personal chequing accounts—are a debt of the chartered banks. Table 13-1 shows the amount of each in the M1 money supply.

Currency: Coins + Paper Money From copper pennies to "two-nies," coins are the "small change" of our money supply. Coins, however, are a small portion of M1. They are "convenience money" that permits people to make very small purchases.

All coins in circulation in Canada are **token money**. This means the **intrinsic value**—the value of the bullion (metal) contained in the coin itself—is less than the face value of the coin. This is so to avoid the melting down of token money for profitable sale as a "commodity," in this case, bullion. If our 25¢ pieces each contained 50¢ worth of silver bullion, it would be profitable to melt them and sell the metal. Although it is illegal to do this,

TABLE 13-1 Money in Canada, March, 1998[†]

Money	Millions of dollars	Percent of M1	Percent of M2	Percent of M2+
Currency outside banks	$ 29.2	36.9	7.3	4.6
+ Demand deposits (current and personal chequing)	50.0	63.1	5.0	8.0
= M1	79.2	100.0	12.3	
+ Personal savings deposits and nonpersonal notice deposits	321.0		87.7	51.5
= M2	400.2		100.0	
+ Deposits at trust and mortgage companies, credit unions, and *caisses populaires*	222.9			35.9
+ Money market mutual funds and deposits at other institutions				
= M2+	$623.1			100.0

[†]Seasonally adjusted average monthly data

Source: *Bank of Canada Review,* Statistical supplement, August, 1998. Updates can be found at the Bank of Canada website at www.bank-banque-canada.ca

25¢ pieces would disappear from circulation. This is one of the potential defects of commodity money: its worth as a commodity may come to exceed its worth as money, ending its function as a medium of exchange. This happened with our *then* silver coins in the late 1960s and early 1970s. An 80 percent silver pre-1967 quarter is now worth several dollars.

Paper money constitutes about a third of the economy's narrowly defined (M1) money supply. Paper currency is in the form of **Bank of Canada notes**—the paper notes you carry in your wallet—issued by our government-owned central bank. A glance at any bill in your wallet will reveal "Bank of Canada" printed at the top of the face of the bill.

Together coins and paper money amounted to $29.2 million in March of 1998, almost 37 percent of M1.

Demand Deposits The safety and convenience of using cheques, or bank money, have made chequing accounts the largest component of the Canadian money supply. You would not think of stuffing $4,896.47 in bills and coins in an envelope and dropping it in a mailbox to pay a debt. But to write and mail a cheque for a large sum is commonplace. A cheque must be endorsed (signed on the reverse) by the person cashing it. Similarly, because the writing of a cheque requires endorsement by the person cashing the cheque, the theft or loss of a chequebook is not nearly so bad as losing an identical amount of currency. Finally, it is more convenient to write a cheque than it is to transport and count out a large sum of currency. For all these reasons, *chequebook money*, or demand deposit, is the dominant form of money in the Canadian economy. About 60 percent of M1 is in the form of demand deposits, on which cheques can be drawn.

It might seem strange that chequing accounts are part of the money supply. But it's clear why: Cheques, which are nothing more than a way to transfer the ownership of deposits in chartered banks and other financial institutions, are generally acceptable as a medium of exchange. True, as a stop at most gas stations will verify, cheques are less generally accepted than currency for small purchases. But, for major purchases, sellers willingly accept cheques as payment. Moreover, people can convert these deposits immediately into paper money and coins on demand; cheques drawn on these deposits are thus the equivalent of currency.

To summarize:

Money, M1 = currency + demand deposits

Institutions Offering Demand Deposits In Canada, several types of financial institutions allow customers to write cheques on funds they have deposited:

1. **CHARTERED BANKS**   These are the primary depository institutions. They accept the deposits of households and businesses; keep the money safe until it is demanded via cheques; and in the meantime use it to make available a wide variety of loans. Chartered bank loans provide short-term working capital to businesses and farmers, finance consumer purchases of automobiles and other durable goods.
2. **OTHER DEPOSITORY INSTITUTIONS**   The chartered banks are supplemented by other financial institutions—trust companies, *caisses populaires*, and credit unions. They gather the savings of households and businesses that are then used to finance housing mortgages and provide other loans. **Credit unions** accept the deposits of "members"—usually a group of individuals who work for the same company—and lend these funds to finance instalment purchases.

Qualification We must qualify our definition of money: Currency owned by the chartered banks, other depository institutions, and Government of Canada deposits are excluded.

A five-dollar bill in the hands of Jane Doe constitutes just $5 of the money supply. But, if we count dollars held by banks as a part of the money supply, that same $5 would count for $10 when deposited in a chartered bank. It would count for a $5 demand deposit owned by Doe and also for $5 worth of currency resting in the bank's till or vault. This problem of double-counting is avoided by excluding currency resting in the chartered banks in determining the total money supply.

Excluding deposits owned by the Government of Canada is more arbitrary. This exclusion permits economists to better gauge the money supply and rate of spending in the private sector of the economy, apart from spending initiated by government policy.

Near-Monies: M2 and M2+

There are two broader definitions of money that we will look at. These include M1 plus several near monies. **Near-monies** are highly liquid financial assets that do not directly function as a medium of exchange but can be readily converted into currency or chequable deposits. On demand you may withdraw currency from a **nonchequable savings account** at a chartered bank or trust and mortgage loan company, credit union, or *caisse populaire*. Or you may request that funds be transferred from a nonchequable savings account to a chequable account.

You cannot withdraw funds quickly from **term deposits**, which become available to a depositor only at maturity. For example, a 90-day or six-month term deposit is available without penalty when the designated period expires. Although term deposits are less liquid (spendable) than nonchequable savings accounts, they can be taken as currency or shifted into chequable accounts when they mature.

If these "near monies" are added to M1, we arrive at two more broad definitions of money. These are also set out in Table 13-1.

Money Definition M2
Adding personal savings deposits and nonpersonal (business) notice deposits to M1 gives us **M2.**

M2+
The broadest monetary aggregate is **M2+**, which is M2 plus deposits at trust and mortgage loan companies, and deposits at *caisses populaires* and credit unions, plus money market mutual funds, and deposits at other institutions.

Which definition of money shall we use? The simple M1 includes only items *directly* and *immediately* usable as a medium of exchange. For this reason it is an oft-cited statistic in discussions of the money supply. However, for some purposes economists prefer the broader M2 definition. And what of M2+? These definitions are so inclusive that many economists question their usefulness.

We will use the narrow M1 definition of money in our discussion and analysis, unless stated otherwise. The important principles that apply to M1 are also applicable to M2 and M2+ because M1 is a base component in these broader measures.

Near-Monies: Implications

Near-monies are important for several related reasons.

Spending Habits
These highly liquid assets affect people's consuming and saving habits. Usually, the greater the amount of financial wealth people hold as near-monies, the greater is their willingness to spend out of their money incomes.

Stability
Conversion of near-monies into money or vice versa can affect the economy's stability. For example, during the recovery and peak phases of the business cycle, nonchequable deposits converted into chequable deposits or currency adds to the money supply and could cause inflation. Such conversions can complicate the task of the monetary authorities in controlling the money supply and the level of economic activity.

Policy
The specific definition of money used is important for monetary policy. For example, the money supply as measured by M1 might be constant, while money defined as M2 might be increasing. If the monetary authorities believe it is appropriate to have an expanding supply of money, and if they measure the supply with the narrow M1 definition, they would likely call for specific actions to increase currency and chequable deposits. But if they used the broader M2 definition they would see that the desired expansion of the money supply is already taking place and that no specific policy action is needed. *(Key Question 4)*

Credit Cards

You may wonder why we have ignored credit cards—VISA, MasterCard, American Express, Discover, and so forth—in our discussion of how money is defined. After all, credit cards are a convenient way to make purchases. The answer is that a credit card is *not* really money, but rather a means of obtaining a short-term loan from the chartered bank or other financial institution that has issued the card.

When you purchase a sweatshirt with a credit card, the issuing bank will reimburse the store. Later, you reimburse the bank. You will pay an annual fee for the services provided, and if you choose to repay the bank in instalments, you will pay a sizable interest charge on the loan. Credit cards are merely a means of deferring or postponing payment for a short period.

However, credit cards and other forms of credit allow individuals and businesses to "economize" in the use of money. Credit cards permit you to have less currency and chequable deposits on hand for transactions. Credit cards help you synchronize your expenditures and your receipt of income, reducing the cash and chequable deposits you must hold.

13-1
QUICK REVIEW

- Money serves as a medium of exchange, a unit of account, and a store of value.

- The narrow M1 definition of money includes currency held by the public and demand (chequable) deposits in chartered banks.

- The M2 definition of money includes M1 plus personal savings deposits and nonpersonal notice deposits at chartered banks; M2+ is made up of M2 plus deposits at trust and mortgage loan companies, *caisses populaires*, and credit unions, plus money market mutual funds and deposits at other institutions.

WHAT "BACKS" THE MONEY SUPPLY?

This heading asks a slippery question. Our answer is at odds with most preconceptions. Essentially, what backs money is the government's ability to keep the value of money relatively stable.

Money as Debt

The major components of the money supply— paper money and demand deposits—are debts, or promises to pay. *In Canada, paper money is the circulating debt of the Bank of Canada. Demand deposits are the debts of the chartered banks.*

Paper currency and demand deposits have no intrinsic value. A $5 bill is just a piece of paper. A demand deposit is merely a bookkeeping entry. And coins, we know, have less intrinsic value than their face value. Nor will the Bank of Canada redeem that paper money you hold for anything tangible, such as gold. In effect, the government

has chosen to "manage" the nation's money supply. The Bank of Canada attempts to provide the amount of money needed for a particular volume of business activity that will promote full employment, price level stability, and a healthy rate of economic growth.

Most economists agree that managing the money supply is more sensible than linking it to gold or any other commodity, whose supply might arbitrarily and capriciously change. A large increase in the nation's gold stock as the result of a new gold discovery might increase the money supply far beyond the amount needed for a full-employment level of business activity and cause rapid inflation. Or a long-lasting decline in domestic gold production could reduce the domestic money supply to the point where economic activity is choked off and unemployment and a retarded growth rate results.

The point is that paper money cannot be converted into a fixed amount of gold or any other precious commodity. The Bank of Canada will swap one paper $5 bill for another bearing a different serial number. That is all you can get should you ask the Bank of Canada to redeem some of your paper money. Similarly, cheque money cannot be redeemed for gold but only for paper money, which will not be redeemed by the government for anything tangible.

Value of Money

If currency and chequable deposits have no intrinsic characteristics giving them value *and* they are not backed by gold or other precious materials, what gives a $20 bill or a $100 chequing account entry its value? The answer to these questions involves three points.

Acceptability   Currency and demand deposits are money because they are accepted as money. By virtue of long-standing business practice, currency and demand deposits perform the basic function of money: they are acceptable as a medium of exchange. Suppose that you swap a $20 bill for a shirt or blouse at a clothing store. Why does the merchant accept this piece of paper in exchange for that product? The merchant accepts paper money because he or she is confident that others will in turn accept it in exchange for goods, services, and resources. The merchant knows that paper money can purchase the services of clerks, acquire products from wholesalers, and pay the rent on the store. We accept paper money in exchange because we are confident it will be exchangeable for real goods, services, and resources when we spend it.

Legal Tender

Our confidence in the acceptability of paper money is partly a matter of law; currency has been designated as **legal tender** by government. This means paper currency *must* be accepted in payment of a debt, or else the creditor forfeits the privilege of charging interest and the right to sue the debtor for nonpayment. Thus, paper dollars are accepted partly because the government says they are money. The paper money in our economy is **fiat money**; it is money because the government has declared it so, not because it can be redeemed as precious metal. The general acceptability of currency is also enhanced because government accepts it in payment of taxes and other obligations due the government.

Relative Scarcity

The value of money, like the economic value of anything else, depends on supply and demand. Money derives its value from its scarcity relative to its utility (want-satisfying power). The utility of money lies in its capacity to be exchanged for goods and services, now or in the future. The economy's demand for money thus depends on the total dollar volume of transactions in any period, plus the amount of money individuals and businesses want to hold for possible future transactions. With a reasonably constant demand for money, the supply of money will determine the value or "purchasing power" of the monetary unit (dollar, pound, peso, or whatever).

Money and Prices

The purchasing power of money is the amount of goods and services a unit of money will buy. When money rapidly loses its purchasing power, it quickly loses its role as money.

Value of the Dollar

The amount a dollar will buy varies inversely with the price level; *a reciprocal relationship exists between the general price level and the value of the dollar.* Figure 13-1 shows this inverse relationship graphically. When the consumer price index or "cost-of-living" index goes up, the purchasing power of the dollar goes down, and vice versa. Higher prices lower the value of the dollar because more dollars will be needed to buy a particular amount of goods, services, or resources.

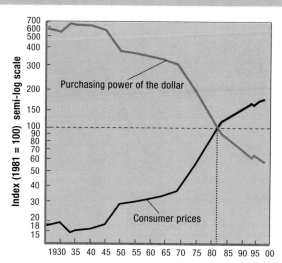

FIGURE 13-1 The price level and the value of money

A reciprocal or inverse relationship exists between the general price level and the purchasing power of the dollar. (This figure is called a "ratio" or "semi-log" chart, because equal vertical distances measure equal percentage changes rather than equal absolute changes.)

For example, if the price level doubles, the value of the dollar declines by one-half, or 50 percent.

Conversely, lower prices increase the purchasing power of the dollar because fewer dollars are needed to obtain a specific quantity of goods and services. If the price level falls by, say, one-half, or 50 percent, the purchasing power of the dollar doubles.

In equation form, the relationship looks like this:

$$D = \frac{1}{P}$$

To find the value of the dollar D, divide 1 by the price level P expressed as an index number (in hundredths). If the price level is 1.0, then the value of the dollar is 1. If the price level rises to, say, 1.20, D falls to .833; a 20 percent increase in the price level reduces the value of the dollar by 16.67 percent. Check your understanding of this reciprocal relationship by determining the value of D and its percentage rise when P falls by 20 percent to 0.80. *(Key Question 6)*

Inflation and Acceptability

In Chapter 8 we noted situations in which a nation's currency became worthless and unacceptable in exchange. These were circumstances in which government issued so many pieces of paper currency that the value of each of these units of money was almost totally undermined. The infamous post-World War I inflation in Germany is an example. In December 1919 there were about 50 billion marks in circulation. Four years later this figure had expanded to 496,585,345,900 billion marks! The result? The German mark in 1923 was worth an infinitesimal fraction of its 1919 value.[2]

How might inflation and the accompanying decreases in the value of a nation's currency affect the acceptability of paper currency as money? Households and businesses will accept paper currency as a medium of exchange as long as they know they can spend it without any noticeable loss in its purchasing power. But this is not the case when there is spiralling inflation. Runaway inflation, such as in Germany in the early 1920s and in several Latin American nations in the 1980s, may significantly depreciate the value of money between the time it is received and the time it is spent. It is as if the government were constantly taxing away the purchasing power of its currency. Rapid declines in the value of a currency may cause it to cease being used as a medium of exchange. Businesses and households may refuse to accept paper money in exchange because they do not want to bear the loss in its value that will occur while it is in their possession. (All this despite the fact that government says the paper currency is legal tender!) Without an acceptable domestic medium of exchange, the economy may try to substitute a more stable currency from another nation. Example: Many transactions in Russia and South America now occur in American dollars rather than less stable rubles or pesos. At the extreme, the economy may simply revert to inefficient barter.

Similarly, people will use a particular unit of money as a store of value only as long as there is no sizable deterioration in the value of that money because of inflation. And an economy can effectively employ money as a unit of account only when its purchasing power is relatively stable. A measure of value that is subject to drastic shrinkage does not permit buyers and sellers to establish the terms of trade clearly. When the value of the dollar is declining rapidly, sellers will not know what to charge, and buyers will not know what to pay, for goods and services.

Stabilization of Money's Value

Stability of the value of money entails (1) appropriate fiscal policy, as explained in Chapter 12, and (2) intelligent management or regulation of the money supply. Businesses and households accept paper money in exchange for goods, services, and resources only when they expect it to command a roughly equivalent amount of these items when it is spent. In Canada a blending of legislation, government policy, and social practice inhibits imprudent expansion of the money supply that might seriously jeopardize money's value in exchange.

That which is true for paper currency also applies to chequing account money—the debt of chartered banks and other depository institutions. Your chequing account of $200 means your bank is indebted to you for that number of dollars. You can collect this debt in one of two ways. You can go to the bank and demand paper currency for your chequable deposit; this amounts to changing the debts you hold from the debts of a bank to government-issued debts. Or, and this is more likely, you can "collect" the debt the bank or savings institution owes you by transferring this claim by cheque to someone else.

For example, if you buy a $200 coat from a store, you can pay for it by writing a cheque, which transfers your bank's indebtedness from you to the store. Your bank now owes the store the $200 it previously owed you. The store accepts this transfer of indebtedness (the cheque) as a medium of exchange because it can convert it into currency on demand or can transfer the debt to others in making purchases of its choice. Thus, cheques, as means of transferring the debts of banks, are acceptable as money because banks will honour these claims.

The ability of chartered banks to honour claims against them depends on their not creating too many of these claims. We will see that a decentralized system of private, profit-seeking banks may not contain sufficient safeguards against the creation of too much cheque money. Thus, the Canadian banking and financial system has substantial centralization and governmental control to guard against the imprudent creation of chequable deposits.

---

[2] Frank G. Graham, *Exchange, Prices and Production in Hyperinflation Germany, 1920–1923* (Princeton, N.J.: Princeton University Press, 1930), p. 13.

Caution: This does not mean that in practice the monetary authorities have always judiciously controlled the supplies of currency and demand deposits. Indeed, many economists allege that most of the inflationary woes Canada and other nations have experienced are the consequence of imprudent increases in the money supply by central banks. But that gets us ahead of our story; all you need to know for now is that a nation's monetary authorities control its supply of money.

13-2
QUICK REVIEW

- In Canada, all money is essentially the debts of government or chartered banks.

- These instruments efficiently perform the functions of money so long as their value, or purchasing power, is relatively stable.

- The value of money does not come from carefully defined quantities of precious metals, but rather in the amount of goods and services money will purchase.

- Government's responsibility in stabilizing the value of the monetary unit involves (1) appropriate fiscal policies, and (2) effective control over the supply of money.

THE CANADIAN BANKING SYSTEM

The main component of the money supply—demand deposits—is created by chartered banks, and the Bank of Canada-created money—coins and paper currency—comes into circulation through the chartered banks. We now take a look at the framework of the Canadian banking system.

Under the Constitution Act, money and banking are federal responsibilities. Under the Bank Act, each bank is incorporated under a separate Act of Parliament and granted a charter. Thus our commercial banks are called **chartered banks**.

In 1867, there were twenty-eight chartered banks; this number grew in the following years to forty-one, before failures and mergers brought the number to eight in the 1960s. The late 1960s and 1970s brought the formation of new banks, and after six more amalgamations and two failures, there were eight domestically owned banks by

1997. With the 1980 Bank Act revisions, foreign banks were allowed to establish Canadian subsidiaries. By 1997 there were forty-four foreign banks in Canada.

The size of the Canadian-owned banks varies widely, from the large Royal Bank of Canada to the relatively small Canadian Western Bank.

All the foreign-owned banks are destined to remain small: non-U.S. foreign bank loans *in total* may not exceed 12 percent of the total domestic assets of the Canadian-owned banks. Thus entry of the foreign banks has not had a large effect on competition.

The largest of the Canadian chartered banks control the lion's share of banking activity. About 90 percent of total banking assets and deposits and more than 75 percent of payments volume are accounted for by the big six chartered banks: the Royal Bank, the Bank of Montreal, the Bank of Nova Scotia, the Toronto-Dominion Bank, the Canadian Imperial Bank of Commerce, and National Bank of Canada. This constitutes a concentrated banking system compared to the United States, where there are some 9,500 commercial banks and 14,000 thrift institutions. In early 1998, the Royal Bank and the Bank of Montreal, and the Canadian Imperial Bank of Commerce and the Toronto-Dominion Bank announced plans to merge. If the proposed mergers had materialized, only three chartered banks would have been left, leading to an even more concentrated banking system. The Last Word in this chapter outlines the evolution of our banking system and the degree of concentration compared to other countries.

Global Perspective 13-1 lists the world's largest commercial banks. The Royal Bank of Canada ranks as the forty-seventh largest bank in the world, as measured by the amount of financial capital. If the proposed bank mergers had gone through, Canadian banks would certainly have moved up the ranks.

Table 13-2 sets out the balance sheet of the Canadian chartered banks. Its reserves are only a small percentage of deposits. As will be discussed in the next chapter, our banking system is a *fractional reserve system*—chartered banks loan out most of their deposit, keeping only a small percentage to meet everyday cash withdrawals. If depositors in the chartered banks were to come all at once to withdraw their money, there would not be enough cash reserves to meet their requests. In such an unlikely event, chartered banks borrow from the Bank of Canada, the bankers' bank.

13-1

GLOBAL PERSPECTIVE

The world's largest commercial banks

Japanese firms dominate the list of the world's largest commercial banks, as measured by the size of financial assets (1996 data). The Royal Bank, the largest Canadian bank, is only the 47th largest bank in the world.

Assets (billions of U.S. dollars)

Bank of Tokyo-Mitsubishi (Japan)	$752.3
Deutsche Bank (Germany)	575.7
Sumitomo Bank (Japan)	513.8
Dai-Ichi Kangyo (Japan)	476.7
Fuji Bank (Japan)	474.4
Sanwa Bank (Japan)	470.3
ABN Amro Holdings (Netherlands)	444.4
Sakura Bank (Japan)	436.9
Industrial and Commercial Bank (China)	435.7
HSBC Holdings (United Kingdom)	405.0
Norinchukin Bank (Japan)	400.0
Industrial Bank (Japan)	399.5
Dresdner Bank (Germany)	389.6
Banque Nationale de Paris (France)	358.2
Royal Bank (Canada)	184.0

Source: *Wall Street Journal*, Sept. 18, 1997, p. R27.

Profit Maximizing

Chartered banks have shareholders who seek a competitive return on their investments. Thus, the primary goal of chartered banks is to try to maximize profits. They loan out as much of their deposits as is prudently possible in order to increase profits. Those funds that cannot be safely loaned out are used to buy Government of Canada securities. The rate charged by banks on loans to their best corporate customers is referred to as the **prime rate**.

Financial Intermediaries

Although the present analysis focuses on chartered banks, the banking system is supplemented by other **financial intermediaries**. These include trust companies, loan companies, credit unions, and *caisses populaires*—savings institutions—that accept the funds of small savers and make them available to investors, by extending mortgage loans or by purchasing marketable securities. Insurance companies accept huge volumes of savings in the form of premiums on insurance policies and annuities and use these funds to buy a variety of private, corporate, and government securities.

The Canadian financial system is presently undergoing restructuring aimed at permitting more competition between the former "Four Pillars": the banking, insurance, trust, and securities industries.

Chartered banks and savings institutions have two basic functions: they hold the money deposits of businesses and households; and they make loans to the public in an effort to make profits. We will see in Chapter 15 that in doing so the intermediaries increase the economy's supply of money.

TABLE 13-2 The balance sheet of Canadian chartered banks, May 1998 (billions of dollars)

Assets		Liabilities	
Reserves (currency and deposits with Bank of Canada)	3.3	Demand deposits	52.7
Loans (determined in Canadian dollars)	550.0	Savings deposits	286.9
Government of Canada securities	11.9	Time deposits	141.1
Foreign-currency assets	562.4	Foreign-currency liabilities	594.9
Other assets	216.0	Other liabilities	268.0
Total	1,343.6	Total	1,343.6

Source: *Bank of Canada Review*, Statistical supplement, August 1998.

Cheque Clearing

As previously noted, a cheque is a written order the drawer may use to make a purchase or pay a debt. A cheque is collected, or "cleared," when one or more banks or near-banks negotiates a transfer of part of the drawer's chequing account to the chequing account of the recipient of the cheque. If Jones and Smith have chequing accounts in the same bank and Jones gives Smith a $10 cheque, Smith can collect this cheque by taking it to the bank, where his account will be increased by $10 and Jones's reduced by $10. In many cases, however, the drawer and the receiver of a cheque will be located in different towns or provinces and more likely than not, in different banks. Under federal law the **Canadian Payments Association** was set up in 1982 to take over the inter-bank cheque clearing system, which had been run by the Canadian Bankers' Association. The mechanics of cheque collecting, and its effect on the financial position of chartered banks, will be outlined in the next chapter.

RECENT DEVELOPMENTS IN MONEY AND BANKING

The banking industry is undergoing a series of sweeping changes, spurred by competition from other financial institutions, globalization of banking, and advances in information technology.

Expansion of Services   Chartered banks and trust companies have begun offering a variety of new services. For example, chartered banks in Canada have increased their lending for commercial real estate projects such as housing developments, apartments, and office buildings. Banks and trust companies have developed new loan "products" such as home equity loans (loans based on the value of one's house) and low- or zero-down-payment mortgages. They also now offer a variety of interest-bearing accounts such as money market deposit accounts.

Banks have made banking more convenient by opening up full-service branch banks in suburbs and "minibanks" in shopping malls and grocery stores. Supplementing these branches has been an explosion in the number of bank-owned automatic teller machines (ATMs) that allow customers to withdraw cash, deposit cheques, move money between accounts, and make other banking transactions. They have also introduced "bank-by-telephone" and, more recently, "bank by Internet" services.

Globalization of Financial Markets

Another significant banking development is the increased integration of world financial markets. Major foreign financial institutions have operations in Canada, and Canadian financial institutions do business abroad. For example, VISA and MasterCard offer worldwide credit card services. Moreover, Canadian mutual fund companies now offer a variety of international stock and bond funds. Globally, financial capital increasingly flows in search of the highest risk-adjusted returns. As a result, Canadian chartered banks must increasingly compete with foreign banks for both deposits and loan customers.

Recent advances in computer and communications technology mean the trend towards international financial integration is likely to accelerate. Nevertheless, we must not overstate the extent of this globalization. Studies indicate that the bulk of investment in the major nations is still financed through domestic saving within each nation.

Electronic Money

Technological progress has also led to a new form of money: electronic cash and "smart cards." Although still in their infancies, these innovations potentially are of great significance to chartered banks, trust companies, and central banks.

Electronic money, dubbed **E-cash**, is simply an entry in an electronic file stored in a computer. The Internet and the widespread availability of personal computers have made it possible for individuals to use E-cash instead of cheques or currency in making transactions. E-cash is deposited, or "loaded," into the account through Internet payments such as a paycheque, retirement benefit, or stock dividend. It is withdrawn, or "unloaded," from the account through Internet payments to others for a wide variety of goods and services.

In the future, account holders will be able to load sums from their E-cash accounts onto so-called *stored-value cards*. These **smart cards** are plastic cards containing computer chips which store information, including the amount the consumer has loaded. The amount of each purchase or other payment is then automatically deducted from the balance in the card's memory. Consumers will be able to transfer traditional money to their smart cards through their computers or telephones or at automatic teller machines. Thus, nearly all payments could be made with a personal computer or a smart card.

In The Media

Angola's Real Currency Is Beer

LUANDA, ANGOLA—Forget about the gold standard and welcome to Angola, where everyone has a little something going on the side and where monetary stability, such as it is, comes packed under pressure in a can—a beer can.

"Beer is the national currency here," said a Portuguese teacher working in Luanda.

As they earnestly seek a more solid footing for the world's wobbly monetary system, economists could perhaps do worse than to take a careful look at the sturdy Angolan model, where the black-market price of a case of 24 cans of imported European beer stands unshaken at 28,000 Angolan kwanzas.

At the official rate of exchange, this works out to $931—equivalent to a monthly salary for a mid-level government official—suggesting that beer is an unaffordable luxury for all but the most affluent Angolans.

In fact, however, almost nobody in Angola could survive by relying exclusively on his or her salary. Besides, the official rate of exchange carries very little weight in Angola. What carries weight is imported beer.

"Everything is more or less related to that," said an Argentine technician employed by the Angolan government. "For the past year, beer has stayed at about the same price."

Imported beer enters the economy by several means. European and U.S. petroleum companies with operations in Angola, for example, all run company stores where their employees can buy imported goods—including beer—for hard currency. And the Angolan government itself runs a huge duty-free retail emporium for diplomats and others with foreign currency.

Known as the Jumbo, the store sprawls near the inland edge of Luanda, filled with imported foods and consumer goods, including 10 brands of Scotch whiskey and seven kinds of imported beer.

It's the beer that catches the eye—the stacked cases of West German, Danish, and Belgian ales and lagers seem to stretch forever.

Sold at the official exchange rate, a case of 24 cans of beer here costs 395 kwanzas, or about $13. The lines at the Jumbo's 15 cash registers are dotted with people pushing shopping carts piled high with seven or eight cases.

Outside, the beer is promptly resold on the black market—called the "candongua"—for 28,000 kwanzas a case. It is then broken up and bartered or resold at 1,500 kwanzas a can.

Typically, foreign residents in Luanda pay their household staff in beer. An Angolan family can live, albeit frugally, on two cases a month, bartering or reselling the beer one can at a time.

This eccentric monetary system has developed largely because of the almost complete collapse of Angola's centrally planned official economy.

That collapse is immediately apparent from a visit to almost any state-run store in Luanda—places where ordinary Angolans theoretically buy their monthly rations. The shelves are almost utterly bare—always.

In fact, of 10 basic rationed commodities provided by one such store in central Luanda, only two—beans and sugar—were ever in stock last month.

War and the remarkable inefficiencies of the Angolan productive apparatus are to blame for these shortages. But even when basic goods are produced, they are liable to be purloined and sold on the black market long before they reach the official retailer's shelves.

The reason is simple. Official prices in Angola are tied to the official exchange rate and reflect a wholly artificial world that has not existed in Angola since the early 1970s, when the Portuguese were in power and the official monetary unit was the escudo.

Black market prices, on the other hand, are tied to the value of beer, which means they are between 60 and 70 times higher than official prices. They represent the world in which most urban Angolans dwell, or at least those with access to money or beer.

At the Roque Santeró, the largest of Luanda's sprawling, circuslike black markets, they may pay 10,000 kwanzas—or about six cans of beer—for a liter of vegetable oil prominently stamped with the information that it was "furnished by the people of the United States of America," who presumably did not expect it to be sold for profit.

Products shipped as international aid often end up being sold in this manner. In fact, most of the goods for sale at the condonguas probably have been pilfered from somewhere.

Angolans refer to such theft as *"fazer desvio"*—making detours—and it is the most common means by which people supplement their low official incomes, enabling them to live on the beer economy.

This heady economic activity—quietly tolerated by the government—may explain why the government-run Jumbo is never out of stock.

"They run out of milk," the Argentine technician said. "But beer? They never run out of beer."

Oakland Ross, "Angolan Economy Tied to Beer," *Lincoln Sunday Journal-Star*, December 13, 1987.

THE STORY IN BRIEF

In the mid-1980s, beer became one of the main mediums of exchange in Angola. Official prices were tied to the official exchange rate, which did not reflect the international market value of the kwanza, Angola's currency. Black market prices were unofficially tied to the value of beer, between 60 and 70 times higher than official prices.

THE ECONOMICS BEHIND THE STORY

- In the mid-1980s, Angola's economy was centralized and highly regulated. Prices were set by government authorities, as was the official exchange rate. The centrally planned economy collapsed, leading to severe shortages.
- A sizable black market arose, in which prices better reflected supply and demand conditions. Moreover, the dominant medium of exchange became beer since prices and wages in kwanzas, the official currency, were completely divorced from free market realities. For example, a mid-level government official earned enough to buy one case of beer in a month, but a family needed at least two cases of beer per month to live frugally!
- Market participants turned to a medium of exchange—beer—that better reflected relative scarcities of goods and services in the economy.
- What difficulties can a country expect to encounter using beer as money? ■

The
Last Word

BANK MERGERS FIRE UP DEBATE*

Some analysts see better, cheaper services; others wary sector becoming a closed club

BY SUSANNE CRAIG
Financial Services Reporter

CANADA'S HIGHLY CONCENTRATED BANKING system—built through decades of mergers and acquisi-

tions—appears poised to slip into the control of even fewer hands.

This latest wave of consolidation, financial industry officials say, shouldn't raise concerns, as cost savings from the proposed mergers will result in lower bank charges and better service. Other analysts, however, counter that the recent round of mergers threatens to turn the country's banking system into virtually a closed club.

*In December 1998 the federal government announced it would not allow the mergers.

"It begins to look more and more like an oligopoly and that has to mean less competition domestically, and less competition in the areas where the Canadian banks have done well," said Michael Mackenzie, who retired in 1994 after seven years as the well-respected head of the Office of the Superintendent of Financial Institutions, the Ottawa-based financial watchdog.

On Friday, just 12 weeks after Bank of Montreal and the Royal Bank of Canada unveiled their merger plans, Toronto Dominion Bank and Canadian Imperial Bank of Commerce got engaged—two unions that would put almost 50 per cent of Canada's total domestic banking assets and 70 per cent of total banking assets (domestic and foreign) under the control of just two banks.

The mergers' approval is in the hands of the federal Competition Bureau, OSFI and Finance Minister Paul Martin, who will have the final say on whether they can go ahead.

The two announcements may have surprised millions of Canadians, who were accustomed to a relatively stable banking industry. The Big Six banks, as a group, have remained largely unchanged for a generation.

But a global wave of banking consolidation, experts say, is being caused largely by the need to be big enough to finance purchases of technology that offer significant cost savings. Canada's banks argue they need to merge to compete on a world scale. Still, it also is true that the country's financial services industry always has been more consolidated than most.

This was the case, Mr. Mackenzie said in an interview, largely because of the country's large size and small population. Canada has relied on transportation and communication networks to prosper, and it has required large amounts of capital to fund them.

Larry Wyant, a professor at the Richard Ivey School of Business at the University of Western Ontario, said that shortly after Confederation, the federal government decided to foster a national banking system—a course not followed in the United States, which has a community banking system with state regulation.

Despite recent merger announcements in the United States, the country still has about 9,000 banks. Canada has just nine domestic banks. In addition, there are 44 foreign banks with subsidiaries in Canada, ranging from the largest, Hongkong Bank of Canada, to smaller players, such as Hanil Bank Canada. Even after taking into account credit union and trust companies, the number of financial players are comparatively few.

Concentration in banking
Share of total assets, domestic activity, 1995

Canada	%
Royal Bank	15.1
CIBC	13.6
Bank of Montreal	10.5
Bank of Nova Scotia	9.6
Toronto Dominion Bank	9.3

United States	
Bank of America	2.9
Chemical Bank Corp.	2.1
Citibank	1.9
Chase Manhattan	1.5
Wells Fargo Bank	1.3

Japan	
Sakura Bank	4.7
Mitsubishi	4.7
Sanwa Bank	4.4
Sumitomo Bank	3.9
Fuji Bank	3.8

Britain	
Barclays	10.2
Abbey Nationale	7.8
National Westminster	7.5
HSBC	7.1
Halifax Building Society	6.5

France	
Crédit Agricole	10.6
Crédit Lyonnais	5.4
Banque Nationale de Paris	4.9
Société Générale	4.4
Cie Financiére de Paribas	4.0

Germany	
Westdeutsche Landesbank Girozentrale	5.3
Deutsche Bank	4.3
Bayerische Vereinsbank	4.3
Commerzbank	3.8
Bayerische Landesbank Girozentrale	3.7

The Netherlands	
ABM-Amro	23.9
Rabobank Nederlanden	19.5
Internationale Nederlanden Bank	17.8
Bank Nederlandse Gemeenten	7.9
Credit Lyonnais Nederland	2.8

Source: Bank of Montreal

Source: *Globe and Mail*, April 20, 1998, pp B1 and B4. Reprinted with permission from the *Globe and Mail*.

While concentration levels in Canada are at historically high levels, the Canadian banking system is no stranger to mergers.

Bank of Montreal, Canada's first bank, was involved in a string of acquisitions and mergers 50 years after it was incorporated in 1817, beginning with the Commercial Bank of Canada in 1868 and ending in 1925 with Molsons Bank. Royal Bank and Bank of Nova Scotia snapped up a number of banks during the same period.

In 1961, CIBC was formed out of a merger between the Canadian Bank of Commerce and the Imperial Bank. Prior to that, the Canadian Bank of Commerce boasted an impressive string of acquisitions that started in the 1870s.

TD, a name that will disappear if the merger with CIBC is approved, was itself the result of a merger—one in 1955 between Bank of Toronto and Dominion Bank. (The smallest of the Big Six, National Bank of Canada, was formed in 1979 by the merger of Banque Canadienne Nationale and Bank Provinciale.)

While bank mergers stopped after that, at least until this year, the financial services industry continued to consolidate in other ways. In 1987, Ottawa allowed Canadian banks to buy investment dealers. The deals included Royal Bank buying Dominion Securities, Bank of Montreal swallowed Nesbitt Thomson and Scotiabank bought McLeod Young Weir. There are only a handful of independent investment dealers left on Bay Street.

Banks also have snapped up trust companies. In 1993, Royal picked up the trust operations of Royal Trustco and Scotiabank bought Montreal Trust. Scotiabank bought National Trust last year. ∎

CHAPTER SUMMARY

1. Anything that is accepted as **a** a medium of exchange, **b** a unit of monetary account, and **c** a store of value can be used as money.

2. Money is generally defined as demand deposits plus currency (coins and paper money) in circulation (M1). Demand deposits, the largest component of the money supply, are money because they can be spent by writing cheques against them. Savings, term, and notice deposits—some chequable and some not—are also money and are added to more broadly defined monetary aggregates (M2 and M2+). In our analysis we concentrate on M1 since its components are immediately spendable.

3. Money is the debts of government and depository institutions (chartered banks, trust companies, and credit unions) and has value because of goods, services, and resources it will command in the market. Maintaining the purchasing power of money depends largely on the government's effectiveness in managing the money supply.

4. The Canadian banking system is composed of **a** the Bank of Canada and **b** eight Canadian-owned and forty-four foreign-owned chartered banks. The chartered banks of the economy accept money deposits and make loans. The Canadian banking system is concentrated compared to other nations, particularly the United States.

5. Three recent developments in the Canadian banking system are the proposed bank mergers, the internationalization of banking, and the emergence of E-cash and smart cards.

TERMS AND CONCEPTS

medium of exchange
unit of account
store of value
M1, M2, and M2+
demand deposits
token money
intrinsic value

Bank of Canada notes
credit unions
near-monies
nonchequable savings account
term deposits
legal tender
fiat money

chartered banks
prime rate
financial intermediaries

Canadian Payments Association
E-cash
smart cards

STUDY QUESTIONS

1. Describe how rapid inflation can undermine money's ability to perform each of its three basic functions.

2. What are the disadvantages of commodity money (for example, money made from precious metals)? What are the advantages of paper money and cheque money compared with commodity money?

3. Explain and evaluate the following statements:
   a. The invention of money is one of the great achievements of humankind, for without it the enrichment which comes from broadening trade would have been impossible.
   b. Money is whatever society says it is.
   c. In most economies of the world, the debts of government and chartered banks are used as money.
   d. People often say they would like to have more money, but what they usually mean is that they would like to have more goods and services.
   e. When the prices of everything go up, it is not because everything is worth more but because the currency is worth less.
   f. Any central bank can create money; the trick is to create enough of it, but not too much of it.

4. **KEY QUESTION** *What are the components of the M1 money supply? What is the larges component? Why is the face value of a coin greater than its intrinsic value? Distinguish between M2 and M2+. What are near-monies? Of what significance are they? What arguments can you make for including term and notice deposits in a definition of money?*

5. What "backs" the money supply in Canada? What determines the value of money? Who is responsible for maintaining the value of money? Why is it important to be able to alter the money supply? What is meant by **a** "sound money" and **b** a "52¢ dollar"?

6. **KEY QUESTION** *Suppose the price level and the value of the dollar in year 1 are 1.0 and $1.00, respectively. If the price level rises to 1.25 in year 2, what is the new value of the dollar? If instead the price level had fallen to .50, what would have been the value of the dollar? What generalization can you draw from your answers?*

7. What are the two basic functions of our chartered banks? How do chartered banks differ from other financial intermediaries?

8. **(The Last Word)** What is the rationale for the proposed bank mergers in recent years? Are Canadian banking sector assets concentrated compared to the other countries mentioned in the article?

9. **WEB-BASED QUESTION** **Monetary Aggregates** Visit the Bank of Canada www.bank-banque-canada.ca/ and click on "Weekly Financial Statistics." Find the seasonally adjusted data for M1, M2, and M2+ for the most recent month.

10. **WEB-BASED QUESTION** **Everything You Wanted to Know About Canadian Currency but Were Afraid to Ask** Visit the Bank of Canada www.bank-banque-canada.ca/ and click "Currency Museum" on the SchoolNet. Search for Canada's First Coinage and Canada's First Notes. What denomination were they?

How Banks Create Money

THE BANK OF CANADA PRINTS SOME $3 MILLION in notes each day. Yet, for most transactions we use the demand (or chequable) deposits of chartered banks, trust companies, and credit unions, *not* currency. The amount of these deposits far exceeds the amount of currency banks hold. Who creates these extra demand deposits? The answer is loan officers at chartered banks! Although this may sound like something "The Fifth Estate" or a Parliamentary committee should investigate, banking authorities are well aware that banks create demand deposit money. In fact, the Bank of Canada *relies* on banks to create a large part of the nation's money supply.

Because the bulk of demand deposits are deposits of chartered banks, this chapter will explain how they can *create* demand deposit money. Specifically, you will see how money can be created by (1) a *single* chartered bank that is part of a multi-bank system, and (2) the chartered banking *system* as a whole. Keep in mind that near-banks also provide demand deposits. Therefore, when we say "chartered bank" we also mean the other "depository institutions."

IN THIS CHAPTER YOU WILL LEARN:

How chartered banks create (or destroy) money through loans to the public.

•

How new money can be created (or destroyed) by the chartered banks or the public buying (or selling) government bonds.

•

The maximum lending potential of the banking system.

•

What the monetary multiplier is and how to calculate it.

The Big Picture

AFTER READING CHAPTER 13, YOU NOW know more about the nature of money and the financial system, particularly the banking system, in Canada. The main question addressed in this chapter is: How does the Bank of Canada "create" new money to accommodate the need of a growing economy? You may have thought that "creating" money is the simple act of printing paper money and stamping coins. The printing of money and stamping coins actually comes after the chartered banking system creates money out of "thin air." If money creation began by printing money, how would the authorities know to whom to distribute it?

As you read this chapter, keep the following points in mind:

- The creation of money begins through the chartered banking system's ability to lend out more than it has on deposit—fractionally backed reserves.

Households and firms borrow money from the banking system as their need arises. To pay these loans back to chartered banks, households and firms work at producing goods and services and earn the "money" to pay back the loans.

- For every new deposit received, a chartered bank will keep part of it as vault cash and lend out the rest. It is through lending (or borrowing by households and firms) that money is created.
- The process of money creation works in reverse: if the banking system loses deposits (reserves), money is "destroyed."
- Chartered banks are profit-maximizing firms. It is the pursuit of profit that leads them to lend out money; they charge a higher interest rate on loans than they pay out on their deposits.
- Distinguish between a single chartered bank and the chartered banks as a group. ■

THE BALANCE SHEET OF A CHARTERED BANK

An understanding of the basic items on a bank's balance sheet, and how various transactions change these items, will provide the tools for analyzing the workings of the Canadian monetary systems.

A **balance sheet** is a statement of assets and claims that summarizes the financial position of a firm—in this case a chartered bank—at a specific point in time. Every balance sheet must balance because every known *asset*, being something of economic value, will be claimed by someone. Can you think of an asset—something of monetary value—that no one claims? A balance sheet balances when the value of assets equals the amount of claims against those assets. The claims shown on a balance sheet are divided into two groups: the claims of the owners of the firm against the firm's assets, called *net worth*, and the claims of nonowners, called *liabilities*. Thus, a balance sheet balances because:

Assets = liabilities + net worth

A balance-sheet approach to our study of the money-creating ability of chartered banks is invaluable in two respects.

1. A bank's balance sheet provides us with a convenient point of reference from which we can introduce new terms and concepts in an orderly way.
2. The use of balance sheets allows us to quantify certain concepts and relationships that are difficult to comprehend if discussed in words alone.

PROLOGUE: THE GOLDSMITHS

Let's now see how a *fractional reserve system of banking* operates. The characteristics and working of such a system can be understood by first considering a bit of economic history.

When early traders began to use gold in making transactions, they soon realized that it was both unsafe and inconvenient for consumers and merchants to carry gold and have it weighed and assessed for purity every time a transaction was negotiated. It therefore became commonplace by the sixteenth century to deposit one's gold with goldsmiths whose vaults or strong-rooms could be used for a fee. On receiving a gold deposit, a goldsmith issued a receipt to the depositor. Soon goods were traded for the goldsmith's receipts, and the receipts became the first kind of paper money.

At this point the goldsmiths—embryonic bankers—used a 100 percent reserve system; their circulating paper money receipts were fully backed by gold, which was "in reserve" in their vaults. But because of the public's acceptance of the goldsmiths' receipts as paper money, the goldsmiths became aware that the gold they stored was rarely redeemed. In fact, they found themselves in charge of enterprises where the amount of gold deposited with them in any week or month was likely to exceed the amount withdrawn.

Then some astute goldsmith hit on the idea that paper money could be issued *in excess of* the amount of gold held. Goldsmiths would put these additional "receipts" redeemable in gold—their paper money—into circulation by making interest-earning loans to merchants, producers, and consumers. Borrowers were willing to accept loans in the form of gold receipts because the receipts were accepted as a medium of exchange.

This was the beginning of the **fractional reserve system** of banking, in which only a fraction of the money supply is backed by currency (here, gold) held in reserve in bank vaults. If, for example, our ingenious goldsmith made loans equal to the amount of gold stored, then the total value of paper money in circulation would be twice the value of the gold. Gold reserves would be 50 percent of outstanding paper money.

Fractional reserve banking—the system in Canada and most other countries today—has two significant characteristics:

1. **MONEY CREATION AND RESERVES**   Banks in such a system can *create money*. When a goldsmith made loans by giving borrowers paper money not fully backed by gold reserves, money was being created. The quantity of such money the goldsmith could create would depend on the amount of reserves deemed prudent to keep on hand. The smaller the amount of reserves thought necessary, the larger the amount of paper money the goldsmith could create. Although gold is no longer used to "back" the Canadian money supply, bank lending (money creation) today is constrained by the amount of currency reserves banks feel obligated, or are required by law, to keep.

2. **BANK PANICS AND REGULATION**   Banks that operate on the basis of fractional reserves are vulnerable to bank "panics" or "runs." A goldsmith who issued paper money equal to twice the value of gold reserves could not convert all that paper money into gold in the event all holders of that paper money appeared simultaneously demanding gold. In fact, many European, U.S., and Canadian banks were once ruined by this unfortunate circumstance. However, a bank panic is highly unlikely *if* the banker's reserve and lending policies are prudent. Indeed, a basic reason why banking systems are highly regulated industries is to prevent bank runs. This is also the reason why Canada has in place a system of deposit insurance.

A SINGLE CHARTERED BANK

We need to explore how money can be created by a single bank that is part of a multibank banking system. Here are some questions we will consider: What items make up a chartered bank's balance sheet? How does a single chartered bank create money? If it can create money, can it destroy money too? What factors govern how a bank creates money?

Formation of a Chartered Bank

To answer these questions we must understand what's on a chartered bank's balance sheet, and how certain transactions affect it. Let's begin with the organization of a local chartered bank.

Transaction 1: The Birth of a Bank   Suppose some citizens of Vancouver decide Canada in general, and their province in particular, is in need of a new chartered bank. Once they get the Parliament of Canada to pass an Act granting a charter for their bank, they then sell, say, $250,000 worth of capital stock (equity shares) to buyers, both in and out of the province. The Bank of Vancouver now exists. How does the bank's balance statement appear at its birth?

The bank now has $250,000 in cash on hand and $250,000 worth of capital stock outstanding. The cash is an asset to the bank. Cash held by a bank is sometimes dubbed **vault cash** or *till money*. The outstanding shares of stock constitute an equal amount of claims the owners of the stock have against the bank's assets. The shares of stock are the net worth of the bank. The bank's balance sheet reads:

CREATING A BANK

BALANCE SHEET 1: BANK OF VANCOUVER

Assets		Liabilities and net worth	
Cash	$250,000	Capital stock	$250,000

Each item listed in a balance sheet such as this is called an *account*.

Transaction 2: Acquiring Property and Equipment
The first step for the new bank will be to acquire property and equipment. The bank purchases buildings for $220,000 and buys $20,000 worth of office equipment. This transaction changes the composition of the bank's assets. The bank now has $240,000 less in cash and $240,000 of new property assets. Using colour type to denote those accounts affected by each transaction, we find that the bank's balance sheet at the conclusion of Transaction 2 appears as follows:

ACQUIRING PROPERTY AND EQUIPMENT

BALANCE SHEET 2: BANK OF VANCOUVER

Assets		Liabilities and net worth	
Cash	$10,000	Capital stock	$250,000
Property	240,000		

Note that the balance sheet still balances, as it must.

Transaction 3: Accepting Deposits
Chartered banks have two basic functions: to accept deposits of money and to make loans. Now that our bank is in operation, suppose that the citizens and businesses of Vancouver decide to deposit $100,000 in the Bank of Vancouver. What happens to the bank's balance sheet?

The bank receives cash, an asset to the bank. Suppose this money is placed in the bank as demand deposits (chequing accounts), rather than savings accounts. These newly created demand deposits are claims that depositors have against the assets of the Bank of Vancouver. Thus the depositing of money in the bank creates a new liability account—demand deposits. The bank's balance sheet now looks like this:

ACCEPTING DEPOSITS

BALANCE SHEET 3: BANK OF VANCOUVER

Assets		Liabilities and net worth	
Cash	$110,000	Demand deposits	$100,000
Property	240,000	Capital stock	250,000

There has been no change in the economy's total supply of money, but a change has occurred in the composition of the money supply as a result of Transaction 3. Demand deposits have *increased* by $100,000 and currency in circulation has *decreased* by $100,000. Currency held by a bank is *not* part of the economy's money supply.

It is apparent that a withdrawal of cash will reduce the bank's demand-deposit liabilities and its holdings of cash by the amount of the withdrawal. This, too, changes the composition, but not the total supply, of money in the economy.

Deposits in the Bank of Canada The Bank of Vancouver has to have sufficient **cash reserves** to keep a minimum ratio between those assets and its deposit liabilities. These reserves are partly vault cash to serve the daily cash needs of the chartered bank's customers, and partly deposits in the Bank of Canada. Prior to 1995 chartered banks were required by law to keep a specified percentage of their deposit liabilities as reserves—referred to as *required reserves*. In 1991 changes to the Bank Act did away with required reserves so that chartered banks keep their reserves mostly as vault cash, with just enough deposited in the Bank of Canada for cheque clearing (see Transaction 4).[1] For simplicity, from now on we will refer only to vault cash.

Since banks still need to keep vault (till) cash to meet withdrawals in excess of deposits from day to day, this chapter's analysis will remain relevant even if reserves are no longer *required*. We refer to the "specified percentage" of deposit liabilities the chartered bank chooses to keep as vault cash as the **desired reserve ratio**. The ratio is calculated as follows:

$$\frac{\text{Reserve}}{\text{ratio}} = \frac{\text{chartered bank's desired reserves}}{\begin{array}{c}\text{chartered bank's} \\ \text{demand-deposit liabilities}\end{array}}$$

---

[1] The Bank Act was changed in 1991, but the elimination of required reserves was spread over four years, to the end of 1994. One of the main reasons the Bank of Canada did away with required reserves was the chartered banks' complaint that these reserves paid no interest while the chartered banks had to pay interest to their depositors.

If the desired reserve ratio were 10 percent, our bank, having accepted $100,000 in deposits from the public, would keep $10,000 as reserves to meet its daily cash needs.

There are two additional points to be made about reserves:

1. **EXCESS RESERVES** Some terminology: The amount by which the bank's **actual reserves** exceed its **desired reserves** is the bank's **excess reserves**:

$$\frac{\text{Actual}}{\text{reserves}} - \frac{\text{desired}}{\text{reserves}} = \text{excess reserves}$$

In this case,

Actual reserves	$110,000
Desired reserves	−10,000
Excess reserves	$100,000

The only reliable way of computing excess reserves is to multiply the bank's demand-deposit liabilities by the reserve ratio to obtain desired reserves ($100,000 × 10 percent = $10,000) and then to subtract required reserves from the actual reserves listed on the asset side of the bank's balance sheet.

To make sure you understand this, you should compute the bank's excess reserves from balance sheet 3, assuming that the desired reserve ratio is (a) 5 percent, (b) 20 percent, and (c) 50 percent.

We will soon demonstrate that the ability of a chartered bank to make loans depends on the existence of excess reserves. So, understanding this concept is essential in seeing how the banking system creates money.

2. **INFLUENCE** Excess reserves are a means by which the Bank of Canada can influence the lending ability of chartered banks. The next chapter will explain in detail how the Bank of Canada can implement certain policies that either increase or decrease chartered bank reserves and affect the ability of banks to grant credit. To the degree that these policies are successful in influencing the volume of chartered bank credit, the Bank of Canada can help the economy smooth out business fluctuations. Another function of reserves is to facilitate the collection or "clearing" of cheques. *(Key Question 2)*

Transaction 4: Clearing a Cheque Drawn Against the Bank Suppose that James Bradshaw, a Van-

couver lumberyard owner, deposited a substantial portion of the $100,000 in demand deposits that the Bank of Vancouver received in Transaction 3. Suppose Bradshaw buys $10,000 worth of lumber from the Ajax Forest Products Company of Chilliwack. Bradshaw pays for this lumber by writing a $10,000 cheque against his deposit in the Bank of Vancouver. We need to know (1) how this cheque is collected or cleared, and (2) the effect that the collection of the cheque has on the balance sheets of the banks involved in the transaction.

To learn this, we must consider the Bank of Vancouver, the Chilliwack bank (a branch, say, of the Bank of Manitoba), the Vancouver clearing house of the Canadian Payments Association, and, finally, the Bank of Canada office in Vancouver. To keep our illustration simple, we deal only with the changes that occur in the specific accounts affected by this transaction.

(a) Mr. Bradshaw gives his $10,000 cheque, drawn against the Bank of Vancouver, to the Ajax Company. Ajax deposits the cheque in its account with the Bank of Manitoba branch in Chilliwack. The Bank of Manitoba increases the Ajax Company's demand deposits by $10,000 when the cheque is deposited. The Ajax Company is now paid in full. Bradshaw receives his lumber.

(b) Now the Bank of Manitoba in Chilliwack has Bradshaw's cheque. This cheque is a claim against the assets of the Bank of Vancouver. The Bank of Manitoba collects this claim by sending the cheque to its main Vancouver branch (there being as yet no branch of the Bank of Vancouver in Chilliwack). The Vancouver branch of the Bank of Manitoba takes the cheque to the Vancouver clearing house of the Canadian Payments Association (CPA), which is operated by the chartered banks and the near-banks. At the clearing house, representatives of the financial institution meet every banking day. They bring with them all the cheques drawn on each other that have been presented to them for payment. Assuming, for simplicity, that on this day the only transaction involving the Banks of Vancouver and Manitoba is Mr. Bradshaw's cheque, the Bank of Canada will, on being informed by the clearing house, *reduce* the Bank of Vancouver's cash deposit by $10,000 and *increase* that of the Bank of Manitoba by the same amount.

(c) Finally, the cleared cheque is sent back to the Bank of Vancouver's main branch, which learns for the first time that one of its depositors has drawn a cheque for $10,000 against his deposit. Accordingly, the Bank of Vancouver reduces Mr.

Bradshaw's deposit by $10,000 and recognizes that the collection of this cheque has reduced its cash deposit at the Bank of Canada by $10,000.

Note that the balance statements of all three banks will balance. The Bank of Vancouver will have reduced both its assets and its liabilities by $10,000. The Bank of Manitoba will have $10,000 more in cash and in deposits. The ownership of deposits at the Bank of Canada will have changed, but total deposits will stay the same.

Whenever a cheque is drawn against one bank and deposited in another bank, collection of that cheque will reduce both reserves and demand deposits by the bank on which the cheque is drawn. In our example, the Bank of Vancouver loses $10,000 in both reserves and deposits to the Bank of Manitoba. Conversely, if a bank receives a cheque drawn on another bank, the bank receiving the cheque will, in the process of collecting it, have its reserves and deposits *increased* by the amount of the cheque. But there is no loss of reserves or deposits for the banking system as a whole. What one bank loses, another bank gains.

If we bring all the other assets and liabilities back into the picture, the Bank of Vancouver's balance sheet looks like this at the end of Transaction 4:

CLEARING A CHEQUE

BALANCE SHEET 4: BANK OF VANCOUVER

Assets		Liabilities and net worth	
Reserves	$100,000	Demand deposits	$90,000
Property	240,000	Capital stock	250,000

You should verify that with a 10 percent desired reserve ratio, the bank's *excess* reserves now stand at $91,000. We arrive at $91,000 by subtracting desired reserves of $9,000 (= .10 × 90,000) from the $100,000 the Bank of Vancouver has in reserves.

Transaction 4 is reversible. If a cheque drawn against another bank is deposited in the Bank of Vancouver, the Bank of Vancouver will receive both reserves and deposits equal to the amount of the cheque when it is collected.

14-1

QUICK REVIEW

- When a bank accepts deposits of cash, the composition of the money supply is changed, but the total supply of money is not directly altered.

- Chartered banks keep reserves (cash) equal to a desired percentage of their own deposit liabilities.

- The amount by which a bank's actual cash reserves exceeds its desired reserves is called excess reserves.

- A bank that has a cheque drawn and collected against it will lose to the recipient bank both cash and deposits equal to the value of the cheque.

Money-Creating Transactions of a Chartered Bank

The next two transactions are crucial, because they explain (1) how a chartered bank can literally create money by making loans, (2) how money is destroyed when loans are repaid, and (3) how banks create money by purchasing government bonds from the public.

Transaction 5: Granting a Loan Suppose the Grisley Meat Packing Company of Vancouver decides to expand. Suppose, too, that the company needs exactly $91,000—which, by coincidence, just happens to be equal to the Bank of Vancouver's excess reserves—to finance this project.

Grisley requests a loan for this amount from the Bank of Vancouver. Convinced of Grisley's ability to repay, the bank grants the loan. Grisley hands a promissory note—a fancy IOU—to the bank. Grisley wants the convenience and safety of paying its obligations by cheque. So, instead of receiving a bushel basket full of currency from the bank, Grisley gets a $91,000 increase in its demand deposit account in the Bank of Vancouver. The bank has acquired an interest-earning asset (the promissory note) and has created a deposit (a liability) to pay for this asset.

At the moment the loan is completed, the bank's position is shown by balance sheet 5A:

WHEN A LOAN IS NEGOTIATED

BALANCE SHEET 5A: BANK OF VANCOUVER

Assets		Liabilities and net worth	
Reserves	$100,000	Demand deposits	$181,000
Loans	91,000	Capital stock	250,000
Property	240,000		

A close examination of the bank's balance statement will reveal a startling fact: *When a bank makes loans, it creates money.* The president of Grisley went to the bank with something that is not money—her IOU—and walked out with something that *is* money—a demand deposit.

When banks lend, they create demand deposits (chequing accounts) that *are* money. By extending credit, the Bank of Vancouver has "monetized" an IOU. Grisley and the bank have created and then swapped claims. The claim created by the bank and given to the Grisley Company is money; cheques drawn against a deposit are acceptable as a medium of exchange. It is through the extension of credit by chartered banks that the bulk of the money used in our economy is created.

Assume that Grisley awards a $91,000 building contract to the Quickbuck Construction Company of Kamloops. Quickbuck completes the expansion job and is paid with a cheque for $91,000 drawn by Grisley against its demand deposit in the Bank of Vancouver. Quickbuck, with headquarters in Kamloops, does *not* deposit this cheque back in the Bank of Vancouver but instead deposits it in a Kamloops branch of the Bank of Manitoba. The Bank of Manitoba now has a $91,000 claim against the Bank of Vancouver. This cheque is collected in the manner described in Transaction 4. As a result, the Bank of Vancouver *loses* both reserves and deposits equal to the amount of the cheque; the Bank of Manitoba *acquires* $91,000 of reserves and deposits.

In summary, assuming a cheque is drawn by the borrower for the entire amount of the loan ($91,000) and given to a firm that deposits it in another bank, the Bank of Vancouver's balance sheet will read as follows *after the cheque has been cleared against it:*

AFTER A CHEQUE IS DRAWN ON THE LOAN

BALANCE SHEET 5B: BANK OF VANCOUVER

Assets		Liabilities and net worth	
Reserves	$9,000	Demand deposits	$90,000
Loans	91,000	Capital stock	250,000
Property	240,000		

After the cheque has been collected, the Bank of Vancouver is just barely meeting its desired reserve ratio of 10 percent. The bank has *no excess reserves;* it is "fully loaned up."

Transaction 6: Repaying a Loan   If chartered banks create demand deposits—money—when they make loans, is money destroyed when the loans are repaid? Yes. We see this by noting what happens when the Grisley Company repays the $91,000 it borrowed.

To simplify, we will (1) suppose that the loan is repaid not in instalments but in one lump sum two years after it is made, and (2) ignore interest charges on the loan. Grisley will simply write a cheque for $91,000 against its deposit. As a result, the Bank of Vancouver's deposit liabilities decline by $91,000; Grisley has given up $91,000 worth of its claim against the bank's assets. In turn, the bank will surrender Grisley's IOU. The bank and the company have reswapped claims.

But the claim given up by Grisley is money; the claim it is repurchasing—its IOU—is not. The supply of money has therefore been reduced by $91,000; that amount of deposits has been destroyed, unaccompanied by any increase in the money supply elsewhere in the economy.

This fact is shown in Balance Sheet 6. The Bank of Vancouver's loans return to zero and its demand deposits have increased by $91,000. In short, the bank has reverted to Balance Sheet 4, the situation that existed before the Grisley loan was negotiated.

REPAYING A LOAN

BALANCE SHEET 6: BANK OF VANCOUVER

Assets		Liabilities and net worth	
Reserves	$100,000	Demand deposits	$90,000
Loans	0	Capital stock	250,000
Property	240,000		

The decline in demand deposits increases the bank's holdings of excess reserves; this provides the basis for new loans to be made. (*Key Questions 4 and 8*)

Transaction 7: Buying Government Securities
When a chartered bank buys government bonds from the public, the effect is substantially the same as lending. New money is created.

Assume that the Bank of Vancouver's balance sheet initially stands as it did at the end of Transaction 6. Now suppose that instead of making a $91,000 loan, the bank buys $91,000 of government securities from a securities dealer. The bank receives the interest-bearing bonds, which appear on its balance statement as the asset "Securities" and give the dealer an increase in its deposit account. The bank's balance sheet appears as follows:

BUYING GOVERNMENT SECURITIES
BALANCE SHEET 7: BANK OF VANCOUVER

Assets		Liabilities and net worth	
Reserves	$100,000	Demand deposits	$181,000
Securities	91,000	Capital stock	250,000
Property	240,000		

Demand deposits, that is, the supply of money, have been increased by $91,000, as in Transaction 5. *Bond purchases from the public by chartered banks increase the supply of money in the same way as does lending to the public.*

Finally, the selling of government bonds to the public by a chartered bank—like the repayment of a loan—reduces the supply of money. The securities buyer pays by cheque and both "Securities" and "Demand deposits" (the latter being money) decline by the amount of the sale.

Profit and Liquidity

The asset items on a chartered bank's balance sheet reflect the banker's pursuit of two conflicting goals.

1. **PROFIT** One goal is profit. Chartered banks, like any other business, seek profits. This is why the bank makes loans and buys securities—the two major earning assets of chartered banks.

2. **LIQUIDITY** The other goal is safety. For a chartered bank, safety lies in liquidity—specifically, such liquid assets as cash. A bank must be on guard for depositors wanting to transform their demand deposits into cash. Similarly, it must guard against more cheques clearing against it than are cleared in its favour, causing a net outflow of cash. Bankers seek a proper balance between prudence and profit. The compromise is between assets that earn high returns and highly liquid assets.

14-2
QUICK REVIEW

- Banks create money when they make loans; money vanishes when bank loans are repaid.

- New money is created when banks buy government bonds from the public; money disappears when banks sell government bonds to the public.

- Banks balance profitability and safety in determining their mix of earning assets and highly liquid assets.

THE BANKING SYSTEM: MULTIPLE-DEPOSIT EXPANSION

Thus far we have seen that a single bank in a banking system can lend one dollar for each dollar of its excess reserves. The situation is different for chartered banks taken as a group. We will find that *the chartered banking system can lend, that is, can create money, by a multiple of its excess reserves. This multiple lending is accomplished despite the fact that each bank in the system can only lend "dollar for dollar" with its excess reserves.* How do these seemingly paradoxical conclusions come about?

To do this we must keep our analysis uncluttered. Therefore, we will rely on three simplifying assumptions.

1. The desired reserve ratio for all chartered banks is 5 percent.
2. Initially all banks are meeting this 5 percent desired reserve ratio. No excess reserves exist; all banks are "loaned up" (or "loaned out").
3. If any bank can increase its loans as a result of acquiring excess reserves, an amount equal to these excess reserves will be loaned to one borrower, who will write a cheque for the entire amount of the loan and give it to someone else who deposits the cheque in another bank.

The Banking System's Lending Potential

Suppose a junkyard owner finds a $100 bill while dismantling a car that has been on the lot for years. He deposits the $100 in Bank A, which adds the $100 to its reserves. We will record only *changes* in the balance sheets of the various chartered banks. The deposit changes Bank A's balance sheet as shown by entries (a_1):

MULTIPLE DEPOSIT EXPANSION PROCESS

BALANCE SHEET: CHARTERED BANK A

Assets		Liabilities and net worth	
Reserves	$+100 ($a_1$)	Demand deposits	$+100 ($a_1$)
	−95 (a_3)		+95 (a_2)
Loans	+95 (a_2)		−95 (a_3)

Bank A has acquired *excess reserves* of $95. Of the newly acquired $100 in reserves, 5 percent, or $5, is earmarked for desired reserves on the new $100 deposit and the remaining $95 is excess reserves that can be lent out. When a loan for this amount is made, Bank A's loans increase by $95, and the borrower gets a $95 deposit. We add these figures—entries (a_2)—to Bank A's balance sheet.

But now we use our third assumption: the borrower draws a cheque for $95—the entire amount of the loan—and gives it to someone who deposits it in another bank, Bank B. As we saw in Transaction 5, Bank A *loses* both reserves and deposits equal to the amount of the loan, as indicated in entries (a_3). The net result of the transaction is that Bank A's reserves now stand at +$5 (= $100 − $95), loans at +$95, and deposits at +$100 (= $100 + $95 − $95). When the dust has settled, Bank A is just meeting its 5 percent desired reserve ratio.

Recalling Transaction 4, we know Bank B *acquires* both the reserves and the deposits that Bank A has lost. Bank B's balance sheet is changed as in entries (b_1):

MULTIPLE DEPOSIT EXPANSION PROCESS

BALANCE SHEET: CHARTERED BANK B

Assets		Liabilities and net worth	
Reserves	$+95 ($b_1$)	Demand deposits	$+95 ($b_1$)
	−90.25 (b_3)		+90.25 (b_2)
Loans	+90.25 (b_2)		−90.25 (b_3)

When the borrower's cheque is drawn and cleared, Bank A *loses* $95 in reserves and deposits and Bank B *gains* $95 in reserves and deposits. But 5 percent, or $4.75, of Bank B's new reserves is kept as reserves against the new $95 in deposits. This means that Bank B has $90.25 (= $95 − $4.75) excess reserves. It can therefore lend $90.25 [entries ($b_2$)]. When the new borrower draws a cheque for the entire amount and deposits it in Bank C, the

reserves and deposits of Bank B each fall by the $90.25 [entries ($b_3$)]. As a result of these transactions, Bank B's reserves will now stand at +$4.75 (= $95 − $90.25), loans at +$90.25, and deposits at +$95 (= $95 + $90.25 − $90.25). After all this, Bank B is just meeting its 5 percent desired reserve ratio.

We are off and running again. Bank C acquires the $90.25 in reserves and deposits lost by Bank B. Its balance statement sheet changes as in entries (c_1):

MULTIPLE DEPOSIT EXPANSION PROCESS

BALANCE SHEET: CHARTERED BANK C

Assets		Liabilities and net worth	
Reserves	$+90.25 ($c_1$)	Demand deposits	$+90.25 ($c_1$)
	−85.74 (c_3)		+85.74 (c_2)
Loans	+85.74 (c_2)		−85.74 (c_3)

Exactly 5 percent, or $4.51, of these new reserves will be set aside, the remaining $85.74 being excess reserves. Thus, Bank C can lend a maximum of $85.74. Suppose it does [entries (c_2)]. And suppose the borrower draws a cheque for the entire amount and gives it to someone who deposits it in another bank [entries (c_3)].

Bank D—the bank receiving the $85.74 in reserves and deposits—now notes these changes on its balance sheet [entries (d_1)]:

MULTIPLE DEPOSIT EXPANSION PROCESS

BALANCE SHEET: CHARTERED BANK D

Assets		Liabilities and net worth	
Reserves	$+85.74 ($d_1$)	Demand deposits	$+85.74 ($d_1$)
	−81.45 (d_3)		+81.45 (d_2)
Loans	+81.45 (d_2)		−81.45 (d_3)

It can now lend $81.45 [entries ($d_2$)]. The newest borrower draws a cheque for the full amount and deposits it in still another bank [entries (d_3)].

Now, if we wanted to be particularly obnoxious, we could go ahead with this procedure by bringing banks E, F, G, H … N into the picture. Instead, we suggest that you work through the computations for banks E, F, and G, to ensure that you understand the procedure.

The entire analysis is summarized in Table 14-1. Data for banks E through N are supplied, so you can check your computations. Our con-

TABLE 14-1 Expansion of the money supply by the chartered banking system

Bank	(1) Acquired reserves and deposits	(2) Desired reserves (reserve ratio = .05)	(3) Excess reserves, (1) – (2)	(4) Amount that the bank can lend; new money created = (3)
Bank A	$ 100.00 (a_1)	$ 5.00	$ **95.00**	$ 95.00 (a_2)
Bank B	95.00 (a_3, b_1)	4.75	90.25	90.25 (b_2)
Bank C	90.25 (b_3, c_1)	4.51	85.74	85.74 (c_2)
Bank D	85.74 (c_3, d_1)	4.29	81.45	81.45 (d_2)
Bank E	81.45	4.07	77.38	77.38
Bank F	77.38	3.87	73.51	73.51
Bank G	73.51	3.68	69.83	69.83
Bank H	69.83	3.49	66.34	66.34
Bank I	66.34	3.32	63.02	63.02
Bank J	63.02	3.15	59.87	59.87
Bank K	59.87	2.99	56.88	56.88
Bank L	56.88	2.84	54.04	54.04
Bank M	54.04	2.71	51.33	51.33
Bank N	51.33	2.56	48.77	48.77
Other banks	975.36	48.77	926.59	926.59
Totals	$2,000.00	$100.00	$1,900.00	**$1,900.00**

clusion is that on the basis of only $95 in excess reserves (acquired by the banking system when someone deposited the $100 of currency in Bank A), the entire *chartered banking system* is able to lend $1,900, the sum of the amounts in column (4). The banking system can lend by a multiple of 20 of excess reserves when the desired reserve ratio is 5 percent. Yet each single bank in the banking system is lending an amount equal only to its own excess reserves. How do we explain this?

The answer is that reserves lost by a single bank are not lost to the banking system as a whole. The reserves lost by Bank A are acquired by Bank B. Those lost by B are gained by C. Bank C loses to D, D to E, E to F, and so forth. Although reserves can be, and are, lost by *individual* banks in the banking system, there is no loss of reserves for the banking *system* as a whole.

An individual bank can safely lend only an amount equal to its excess reserves, but the chartered banking system can lend by a multiple of its excess reserves. This contrast, incidentally, is an illustration of why it is imperative that we keep the fallacy of composition (Chapter 1) firmly in mind. Chartered banks *as a group* can create money by lending in a manner much different from that of the *individual banks* in that group.

The Monetary Multiplier

The banking system magnifies any original excess reserves into a larger amount of newly created demand-deposit money. The *demand-deposit multiplier*, or **monetary multiplier**, is similar in concept to the spending-income multiplier in Chapter 10. That multiplier exists because the expenditures of one household are received as income by another; it magnifies a change in initial spending into a larger change in GDP. The spending-income multiplier is the reciprocal of the MPS (the leakage into saving that occurs at each round of spending).

In contrast, the monetary multiplier exists because the reserves and deposits lost by one bank are received by another bank. It magnifies excess reserves into a larger creation of demand-deposit money. The monetary multiplier m is the reciprocal of the desired reserve ratio R (the leakage into desired reserves that occurs at each step in the lending process). In short,

$$\text{Monetary multiplier} = \frac{1}{\text{desired reserve ratio}}$$

or, using symbols,

$$m = \frac{1}{R}$$

In this formula, m represents the maximum amount of new demand-deposit money which can be created by a *single dollar* of excess reserves, given the value of R. By multiplying the excess reserves E by m, we can find the maximum amount of new demand-deposit money, D, which can be created by the banking system. That is,

$$\begin{array}{l} \text{Maximum demand-} \\ \text{deposit creation} \end{array} = \begin{array}{c} \text{initial} \\ \text{excess} \\ \text{reserves} \end{array} \times \begin{array}{c} \text{monetary} \\ \text{multiplier} \end{array}$$

or, more simply,

$$D = E \times m$$

In our example of Table 14-1, R is .05 so m is 20 (= 1/.05). Then

$$D = \$1,900 = \$95 \times 20$$

Higher desired reserve ratios mean lower monetary multipliers and therefore less creation of new deposit money via loans; smaller desired reserve ratios mean higher monetary multipliers and thus more creation of new deposit money via loans. With a high reserve ratio, say, 50 percent, the monetary multiplier would be 2 (= 1/.5), and in our example the banking system could create only \$160 (= \$80 of excess reserves × 2) of new deposit money. With a low desired reserve ratio, say, 2 percent, the monetary multiplier would be 50 (= 1/.02), and the banking system could create \$4,000 (= \$80 of excess reserves × 50) of new deposit money. Again you should note similarities with the spending-income multiplier, in which higher MPSs mean lower multipliers and lower

MPSs mean higher multipliers. Also, like the spending-income multiplier, the monetary multiplier works in both directions. *The monetary multiplier applies to money destruction as well as to money creation.*

But keep in mind that, despite the similar rationales underlying the spending, income and monetary multipliers, the former has to do with changes in income and output and the latter with changes in the supply of money.

Figure 14-1 depicts the final outcome of our example of a multiple-deposit expansion of the money supply. The initial deposit of \$100 of currency into the bank (lower right box) creates an initial demand deposit of an equal amount (upper box). With a 5 percent desired reserve ratio, however, only \$5 reserves are need to "back up" this \$100 demand deposit. The excess reserves of \$95 permit the creation of \$1,900 of new demand deposits via the making of loans, confirming a monetary multiplier of 20. The \$100 of new reserves thus supports a total supply of money of \$2,000, made up of the \$100 of initial demand

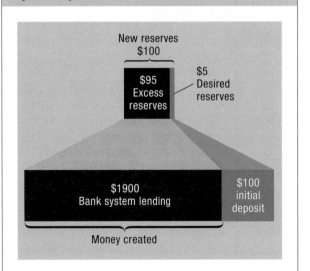

FIGURE 14-1 The outcome of the money expansion process

A deposit of \$100 of currency into a chequing account creates an initial demand deposit of \$100. If the desired reserve ratio is 5 percent, only \$5 of reserves are needed to support the \$100 demand deposit. The \$5 of excess reserves allows the banking system to create \$95 of demand deposits through making loans. The \$100 of reserves supports a total of \$2,000 of money (\$100 + \$1,900).

deposit plus $1,900 of demand deposits created through lending.

You might experiment with the following two brain teasers to test your understanding of multiple credit expansion by the banking system:

1. Rework the analysis of Table 14-1 (at least three or four steps of it) on the assumption that the desired reserve ratio is 10 percent. What is the maximum amount of money the banking system can create on acquiring $100 in new reserves and deposits? (No, the answer is not $950!)
2. Suppose a banking system is loaned up and with a 5 percent desired reserve ratio. Explain how the banking system might have to *reduce* its outstanding loans by $1,900 when a $100 cash withdrawal from a demand deposit account forces one bank to draw down its reserves by $100. *(Key Question 13)*

Some Modifications

There are complications that might modify the preciseness of our analysis.

Other Leakages
Aside from the leakage of desired reserves, two other leakages of money from the chartered banks might dampen the money-creating potential of the banking system.

1. **CURRENCY DRAINS**   A borrower might request that a part of his or her loan be paid in currency. Or the recipient of a cheque drawn by a borrower might ask the bank to redeem it partially or wholly in cash rather than add it to the recipient's account. If the person who borrowed the $95 from Bank A in our illustration asked for $15 of it in cash and the remaining $80 as a deposit, Bank B would later receive only $80 in new reserves (of which only $76 would be excess) rather than $95 (of which $90.25 was excess). This decline in excess reserves would reduce the lending potential of the banking system accordingly. In fact, if the first borrower had taken the entire $95 in cash and if this currency remained in circulation, the multiple expansion process would have stopped then and there. But the convenience and safety of deposits make this unlikely.
2. **EXCESS RESERVES**   Our analysis is based on the assumption that chartered banks are willing to hold a specific desired reserve ratio. To

the extent that bankers hold excess reserves, the overall credit expansion potential of the banking system will be reduced. For example, suppose Bank A, on receiving $100 in new cash, decided to add $10, rather than $5, to its reserves. Then it would lend only $90, rather than $95, and the monetary multiplier would be diminished accordingly.

In fact, the amount of excess reserves that banks have held in recent years has been very minimal. The explanation is simple: Excess reserves earn no interest income for a bank; loans and investments do. Thus, our assumption that a bank will lend an amount equal to its excess reserves is reasonable and generally accurate.

14-3
QUICK REVIEW

- Whereas a single bank in a multibank system can lend (create money) by an amount equal to its excess reserves, the banking system can lend (create money) by a multiple of its excess reserves.
- The monetary multiplier is the reciprocal of the desired reserve ratio. It is the multiple by which the banking system can expand the money supply for each dollar of excess reserves.
- Currency drains and a desire by banks to hold excess reserves may reduce the size of the monetary multiplier.

Need for Monetary Control

Our illustration of the banking system's ability to create money rests on the assumption that chartered banks are willing to create money by lending and that households and businesses are willing to borrow. In reality the willingness of banks to lend on the basis of excess reserves varies cyclically, and here lies the rationale for governmental control of the money supply to promote economic stability.

When prosperity reigns, banks will expand credit to the maximum of their ability. Loans are interest-earning assets, and in good economic times there is little fear of borrowers' defaulting. But, as you will find in Chapter 15, the money supply has an effect on aggregate demand. By lending and thereby creating money to the maximum of their ability during prosperity, chartered banks may contribute to excessive aggregate demand and therefore to inflation.

If a recession appears on the economic horizon, bankers may withdraw their invitations to borrow, seeking the safety of liquidity (excess reserves) even if it means sacrificing potential interest income.

We thus conclude that profit-motivated bankers can be expected to vary the money supply in a way that reinforces cyclical fluctuations. For this reason the Bank of Canada has at its disposal certain monetary tools to alter the money supply in a countercyclical rather than pro-cyclical fashion. We turn to these tools in Chapter 15.

In The Media

Face of Banking Changing*

Foolish for Martin to try to stop forces reshaping North American industry, players say

By John Heinzl
The Globe and Mail

An unprecedented and perhaps unstoppable wave of consolidation is about to change the face of Canada's banking sector forever, observers said yesterday in the wake of news

*In December 1998 the federal government announced it would not allow the bank mergers.

that two more of Canada's Big Six banks plan to merge.

Canadian Imperial Bank of Commerce and Toronto-Dominion Bank, Canada's first and fifth-largest banks by assets, respectively, are planning to combine forces in a deal valued at $47 billion. The proposed marriage comes less than three months after Royal Bank of Canada and Bank of Montreal announced their intention to merge.

Both deals require the approval of Finance Minister Paul Martin. But, given the powerful forces reshaping the North American banking industry, it would be foolish for him to try stand in the way, industry players said.

"For the industry, I think it's inevitable that consolidation is going to happen," said Larry Pollock, president and chief executive officer of Edmonton-based Canadian

The Big Six Banks in Canada

All figures for 1997 financial year ended Oct. 31, 1997, unless otherwise indicated.

All dollars are $billion	CIBC	TD	CIBC plus TD	Royal Bank	Bank of Montreal	Royal plus B of M	Bank of Nova Scotia	National Bank	All 6 banks
Assets (Jan. 31, 1998)	$282.7	177.0	**559.7**	257.4	218.5	**475.9**	210.7	68.6	**1,215.0**
Net interest revenue	$4.5	2.8	**7.3**	5.0	4.1	**9.1**	3.7	1.3	**21.5**
Other revenue	$4.0	2.7	**6.6**	4.3	3.0	**7.3**	2.7	1.1	**17.6**
Profit	$1.6	1.1	**2.7**	1.7	1.3	**3.0**	1.5	0.3	**7.5**
Return on equity	17.9%	16.7%		19.3%	17.0%		20.5%	14.1%	**18.1%**
Market cap, yesterday	$24.0	21.7	**45.7**	27.9	22.2	**50.1**	21.1	5.3	**122.2**
Employees	42,446	28,001	**70,447**	50,719	34,286	**85,005**	38,648	13,327	**207,427**
Branches	1,386	**919	**2,305**	1,558	1,246	**2,804**	1,658	*637	**7,404**
ATMs	3,169	2,038	**5,207**	4,248	2,035	**6,283**	1,801	738	**14,029**

Note: Branches are as reported by the banks in Canada
**excludes 187 brokerage offices
Source: Canadian Bankers Association, bank 1997 annual reports

Western Bank, which operates 22 branches in western Canada.

"It's happened in Europe, it's happening in the U.S. and for us to say we're going to close our market off and live in a cocoon and not allow our banks to merge, the [stock market] values of those banks are just going to plummet."

At least one more major deal will shake the banking industry before the dust settles, Mr. Pollock and others predicted. The betting is that Bank of Nova Scotia will go to the altar with CT Financial Services Inc. of London, Ont., best known for its Canada Trust operating unit.

Scotiabank, which acquired National Trustco Inc. last year, will be left far behind its rivals unless it finds a significant partner. For its part, Canada Trust is known to be open to a possible merger: It came close to cutting a deal with CIBC last year but it was blocked by the federal government. It's also possible Scotiabank could team up with a foreign bank.

"There are other shoes to drop in this exercise," concurred Tom Caldwell, president of Caldwell Securities Inc. in Toronto. "Everybody feels they're going to be left behind without a dancing partner."

Source: *Globe and Mail*, April 17, 1998, p. B1. Reprinted with permission from the *Globe and Mail*.

THE STORY IN BRIEF

Merger mania sweeps Canadian chartered banks in response to financial mergers in the United States.

THE ECONOMICS BEHIND THE STORY

- Chartered banks, like all private companies, try to maximize profits. The deregulation of financial services led to foreign banks establishing in Canada. With mergers between banks in the United States, Canadian banks seem to believe the best way to keep pace with the potential foreign competition is to merge to capture economies of scale.
- Bank mergers have to be approved by the federal government. While many analysts expect the proposed mergers of the Bank of Montreal with the Royal Bank, and the Canadian Imperial Bank of Commerce with the Toronto-Dominion Bank to be approved, only time will tell if these analysts are correct.
- What is the total assets of Canadian banks reported by the article, and which bank will have the most ATM machines? ■

The Last Word

THE BANK PANICS OF 1930–1933

A series of bank panics in 1930–33 in the United States resulted in a multiple contraction of the money supply.

IN THE EARLY MONTHS OF THE GREAT Depression, before there was deposit insurance, several financially weak U.S. banks became insolvent. As word spread that customers of these banks had lost their deposits, a general concern arose that something similar could happen at other banks. Depositors became frightened that their banks did not, in fact, still have all the money they had deposited. And, of course, in a fractional reserve banking system, that is precisely the reality. Acting on their fears, people *en masse* tried to withdraw currency—that is, "cash out" their accounts—from their banks. They wanted to get their money before it was all gone. This "run on the banks" caused many previously financially sound banks to declare bankruptcy. More than 9,000 banks failed within three years.

The massive conversion of chequable deposits to currency during 1930–33 reduced the nation's money supply. This might seem strange since a cheque written for "cash" reduces demand-deposit money and increases currency in the hands of the public by the same amount. So how does the money supply decline? Our discussion of the money *creation* process provides the answer—but now the story becomes one of money *destruction*.

Suppose that people collectively cash out $10 billion from their chequing accounts. As an immediate result, demand deposit money declines by $10 billion, while currency held by the public increases by $10 billion. But here is the catch: Assuming a reserve ratio of 20 percent, the $10 billion of currency in the banks had been supporting $50 billion of deposit money, the $10 billion of deposits plus $40 billion created through loans. The $10 billion withdrawal of currency forces banks to reduce loans (and thus demand-deposit money) by $40 billion to continue to meet their reserve requirement. In short, a $40 billion destruction of deposit money occurs. This is the scenario that occurred in the early years of the 1930s.

Accompanying this multiple contraction of demand deposits was the banks' "scramble for liquidity" to try to meet further withdrawals of currency. To obtain more currency, they sold many of their holdings of government securities to the public. You know from this chapter that a bank's sale of government securities to the public, like a reduction in loans, reduces the money supply. The public writes cheques for the securities, reducing their demand deposits, and the bank uses the currency it obtains to meet the ongoing bank run. In short, the loss of reserves from the banking system, in conjunction with the scramble for security, reduced the amount of demand-deposit money by far more than the increase in currency in the hands of the public. Thus, the money supply collapsed.

In 1933, President Franklin Roosevelt ended the bank panics by declaring a "national bank holiday," which closed all national banks for one week and resulted in the federally insured deposit program, later also adopted in Canada. Meanwhile, the nation's money supply had plummeted by 25 percent, the largest such drop in U.S. history. This decline in the money supply contributed to the nation's worst and longest depression. A steep decline in the Canadian money supply also contributed to a severe depression in Canada.

Today, a multiple contraction of the money supply on the 1930–33 magnitude is unthinkable. Deposit insurance has kept individual bank failures from becoming general panics. For example, the failure of two Canadian chartered banks in 1985 had no repercussion on the Canadian banking system. Also, while the Federal Reserve stood idly by during the bank panics of 1930–33, today it would take immediate and dramatic actions (as would the Bank of Canada) to maintain the banking system's reserves and the nation's money supply. These actions are the subject matter of Chapter 15. ■

CHAPTER SUMMARY

1. The operation of a chartered bank can be understood through its balance sheet, where assets equal liabilities plus net worth.

2. Modern banking systems are fractional reserve systems: only a fraction of deposits are backed by currency.

3. Chartered banks keep reserves as vault cash and a small amount in the Bank of Canada for cheque-clearing purposes. This reserve is equal to a desired percentage of the chartered bank's deposit liabilities. Excess reserves are equal to actual reserves minus desired reserves.

4. Banks lose both reserves and deposits when cheques are drawn against them.

5. Chartered banks create money—create demand deposits, or deposit money—when they make loans. The creation of demand deposits by bank lending is the most important source of money in the Canadian economy. Money is destroyed when bank loans are repaid.

6. The ability of a single chartered bank to create money by lending depends on the size of its *excess* reserves. Generally speaking, a chartered bank lends only an amount equal to the amount of its excess reserves.

7. Rather than making loans, chartered banks may decide to use excess reserves to buy bonds from the public. In doing so, banks merely credit the demand-deposit accounts of the bond sellers, thus creating demand-deposit money.

Money vanishes when banks sell bonds to the public because bond buyers must draw down their demand-deposit balances to pay for the bonds.

8. The chartered banking system as a whole can lend by a multiple of its excess reserves because the banking *system* cannot lose reserves, although individual banks can lose reserves to other banks in the system.

9. The multiple by which the banking system could lend on the basis of each dollar of excess reserves is the reciprocal of the desired reserve ratio. This multiple credit expansion process is reversible.

10. The fact that profit-seeking banks would tend to alter the money supply in a pro-cyclical direction underlies the need for the Bank of Canada to control the money supply.

TERMS AND CONCEPTS

balance sheet
fractional reserve system of banking
vault cash
cash reserves

desired reserve ratio
actual, desired and excess cash reserves
money multiplier

STUDY QUESTIONS

1. Why must a balance sheet always balance? What are the major assets and claims on a chartered bank's balance sheet?

2. KEY QUESTION *Why do chartered banks have reserves? Explain why reserves are an asset to chartered banks but a liability to the Bank of Canada. What are excess reserves? How do you calculate the amount of excess reserves held by a bank? What is the significance of excess reserves?*

3. "Whenever currency is deposited in a chartered bank, cash goes out of circulation and, as a result, the supply of money is reduced." Do you agree? Explain why or why not.

4. KEY QUESTION *"When a chartered bank makes loans, it creates money; when loans are repaid, money is destroyed." Explain.*

5. Explain why a single chartered bank could lend an amount equal only to its excess reserves, but the chartered banking system could lend by a multiple of its excess reserves. What is the monetary multiplier and how does it relate to the desired reserve ratio?

6. Assume that Jones deposits $500 in currency in the Bank of Vancouver. A half-hour later, Smith obtains a loan for $750 at this bank. By how much and in what direction has the money supply changed? Explain.

7. Suppose the Bank of Newfoundland has excess reserves of $8,000 and outstanding deposits of $150,000. If the desired reserve ratio is 10 percent, what is the size of the bank's actual reserves?

8. KEY QUESTION *Suppose the Yukon Bank has the following simplified balance sheet and that the desired reserve ratio is 6.25 percent.*

ASSETS		(1)	(2)	LIABILITIES AND NET WORTH		(1)	(2)
Reserves	$22,000	_____	_____	Deposits	$100,000	_____	_____
Securities	38,000	_____	_____				
Loans	40,000	_____	_____				

a. What is the maximum amount of new loans this bank can make? Show in column 1 how the bank's balance sheet will appear after the bank has loaned this additional amount.
b. By how much has the supply of money changed? Explain.
c. How will the bank's balance sheet appear after cheques drawn for the entire amount of the new loans have been cleared against this bank? Show this new balance sheet in column 2.
d. Answer questions a, b, and c on the assumption that the desired reserve ratio is 10 percent.

9. The Bank of Manitoba has reserves of $10,000 and deposits of $100,000. The desired reserve ratio is 10 percent. Households deposit $5,000 in currency in the bank, which is added to reserves. How much excess reserves does the bank now have?

10. Suppose again that the Bank of Manitoba has reserves of $10,000 and deposits of $100,000. The desired reserve ratio is 10 percent. The bank now sells $5,000 in securities to the Bank of Canada, receiving a $5,000 increase in its deposit there in return. How much excess reserves does the bank now have? Why does your answer differ (yes, it does!) from the answer to question 9?

11. Suppose a chartered bank discovers its reserves will temporarily fall slightly short of those it desires to hold. How might it remedy this situation? Now, assume the bank finds that its reserves will be substantially and permanently deficient. What remedy is available to this bank? (Hint: Recall your answer to question 4.)

12. Suppose that Bob withdraws $100 of cash from his chequing account at Calgary Chartered Bank and uses it to buy a camera from Joe, who deposits the $100 in his chequing account in Annapolis Valley Chartered Bank. Assuming a desired reserve ratio of 10 percent and no initial excess reserves, determine the extent to which **a** Calgary Chartered Bank must reduce its loans and demand deposits because of the cash withdrawal and **b** Annapolis Valley Chartered Bank can safely increase its loans and demand deposits because of the cash deposit. Have the cash withdrawal and deposit changed the money supply?

13. **KEY QUESTION** Suppose the following is a simplified consolidated balance sheet for the entire chartered banking system. All figures are in billions. The desired reserve ratio is 4 percent.

ASSETS		(1)	LIABILITIES AND NET WORTH		(1)
Reserves	$ 6.1	___	Deposits	$150	___
Securities	20	___			
Loans	123.9	___			

a. How much excess reserves does the chartered banking system have? What is the maximum amount the banking system might lend? Show in column 1 how the consolidated balance sheet would look after this amount has been lent. What is the money multiplier?
b. Answer the questions in 13a assuming that the desired reserve ratio is 5 percent. Explain the resulting difference in the lending ability of the chartered banking system.

14. What are banking "leakages"? How might they affect the money-creating potential of the banking system?

15. Explain why there is a need for the Bank of Canada to control the money supply.

16. **(The Last Word)** Can bank panics produce a decline in a nation's money supply? Why are such panics unlikely today?

17. WEB-BASED QUESTION **How To Spot a Counterfeit Bank Note** Counterfeit bank notes have always been a concern for the Bank of Canada. Visit the Bank of Canada www.bank-banque-canada.ca/english/bknote.htm to find out how to detect counterfeit Canadian bank notes.

18. WEB-BASED QUESTION **The Balance Sheet of Canadian Chartered Banks** Statistics Canada provides the balance sheet of chartered banks at www.statcan.ca/english/Pgdb/Economy/Finance/fin25.htm. What has the trend been in the last five years for bank assets and liabilities?

The Bank of Canada and Monetary Policy

IN CHAPTER 14 YOU LEARNED THAT THE BANKING system can create deposit money, thus greatly affecting the supply of money. In this chapter you will see how the Bank of Canada can change the supply of money and thus change the equilibrium interest rate. You will also explore the circumstances under which and reasons why it would want to do so.

In this chapter, we first discuss the objectives of *monetary policy* and the roles of participating institutions. Next, we look at the combined balance sheet of the Bank of Canada; it is through these central banks that monetary policy is implemented. Third, we analyze in detail the techniques of monetary control, asking what the key instruments of monetary control are and how they work. Fourth, we combine the supply of money and the demand for money to portray and explain the market for money. Fifth, we examine the cause-and-effect chain of monetary policy and evaluate the effectiveness of monetary policy. We end the chapter with a brief recapitulation of mainstream macroeconomic theory and policy.

IN THIS CHAPTER YOU WILL LEARN:

The main functions of the Bank of Canada.

•

How the Bank of Canada can expand or contract the money supply.

•

The components of money demand.

•

How the equilibrium interest rate is determined.

•

The mechanism by which the interest rate affects GDP.

The Big Picture

IN THE LAST TWO CHAPTERS YOU HAVE become acquainted with the function of money in a market economy and how money is created (and destroyed). But what is the connection between the total money supply and the output performance and price level in a macroeconomy?

Recall from Chapter 8 that market economies are subject to instability, often experiencing substantial unemployment and sometimes inflationary pressures. In this chapter you will learn that a change in money supply affects interest rates, which influence the level of investment and real GDP. Thus the Bank of Canada, within limits, can help smooth out the fluctuation in the Canadian economy by influencing interest rates through its control of the money supply. The main aim of the Bank of Canada policies is price stability, but it would also like to achieve full employment. Price stability facilitates the ultimate aim of ensuring a nation is employing all its resources—particularly its labour force—to their fullest extent. Note that monetary policy is in broad measure a substitute for fiscal policy, but there are situations where they both need to be used in unison.

As you read through this chapter, keep the following points in mind:

- **Key Concepts 9** and **10** are discussed.
- The Bank of Canada is the "bankers' bank," overseeing the operation of Canada's banking system and its money supply. The Bank of Canada is not motivated by profits, as is the case with the chartered banks.
- Given that a market economy is prone to instability, one of the main roles of the Bank of Canada is to pursue policies that smooth out the fluctuation of the Canadian economy. The transmission mechanism between the monetary side of the economy and the "real" side of the economy is through interest rates, which affect investments, thereby influencing aggregate demand.
- If the economy is experiencing a recessionary gap, the Bank of Canada embarks on policies to lower interest rates, thereby stimulating investments and increasing aggregate demand. If the economy is experiencing an inflationary gap, the Bank of Canada embarks on policies to increase interest rates, thereby dampening investments and lowering aggregate demand. ■

GOALS OF MONETARY POLICY

Recall from Chapter 13 that the Bank of Canada is responsible for supervising and controlling the operation of the Canadian banking system. (For the names of central banks in various nations, see Global Perspective 15-1.) The bank formulates the basic policies that the banking system follows. Because it is a public body, its decisions are made in what it perceives to be the public interest.

The *objective* of **monetary policy** *is to help assist the economy to attain a full-employment, noninflationary level of total output.* Monetary policy consists of altering the economy's money supply for the purpose of stabilizing aggregate output, employment, and the price level. It entails increasing the money supply during a recession to stimulate spending and restricting it during inflation to constrain spending.

The Bank of Canada alters the amount of the nation's money supply by manipulating the amount of excess reserves held by chartered banks. Excess reserves, you will recall, are critical to the money-creating ability of the banking system. Once we see how the Bank of Canada controls excess reserves and the money supply, we will explain how changes in the stock of money affect interest rates, aggregate demand, and the economy.

FUNCTIONS OF THE BANK OF CANADA

The functions of the Bank of Canada—the bankers' bank—can be divided into five categories. The most important will be discussed last.

1. **THE "BANKERS' BANK"** You head for the nearest chartered bank if you either want to deposit, withdraw, or borrow money; the char-

15-1

GLOBAL PERSPECTIVE

Central banks, selected nations

The monetary policies of the central banks in the world's major nations are often in the international news. Here are some of their official names, along with a few of their popular nicknames.

- Australia: Reserve Bank of Australia
- Canada: Bank of Canada
- France: Banque de France
- Germany: Deutsche Bundesbank (the "Bubba")
- Italy: La Banca d'Italia
- Japan: The Bank of Japan ("BOJ")
- Russia: Central Bank of Russia
- United Kingdom: Bank of England
- United States: Federal Reserve System (the "Fed") (12 regional Federal Reserve Banks)

5. REGULATING THE SUPPLY OF MONEY Finally, and most important of all, the Bank of Canada has ultimate responsibility for regulating the supply of money, and this in turn enables it to affect interest rates. The major task of the central bank is to manage the money supply (and thus interest rates) on the basis of the needs of the economy. This involves making an amount of money available that is consistent with high and steadily rising levels of output and employment and a relatively constant price level. While all the other functions of the bank are of a more or less routine or service nature, correctly managing the money supply requires making basic but unique policy decisions.

Bank of Canada Independence

The independence of the Bank of Canada is a matter of continuing controversy. Opponents of an independent central bank say that it is undemocratic to have a powerful economic agency whose members are not elected and thus not directly subject to the will of the people. They also point out that the government bears ultimate responsibility for maintaining economic stability and promoting economic growth, thus they should have available *all* the policy tools essential to the economy's health, including monetary policy. Voters tend to hold Parliament responsible for the consequences of Bank of Canada policies over which they have no control. Critics cite instances of the Bank of Canada using monetary policy to counter the effects of the federal government's fiscal policy.

Defenders of Bank of Canada independence, including most economists, contend that the Bank of Canada must be protected from political pressures so that it can effectively control the money supply and maintain price stability. They point out that countries with less central bank independence, on average, have higher rates of inflation than countries with more central bank independence (see Global Perspective 15-2). It is often politically useful for Parliament to enact inflationary fiscal policies, including tax cuts and special-interest spending. Citizens would likely pressure the Bank of Canada to keep interest rates low, via expansions in the money supply, even though at times high interest rates are necessary to reduce aggregate demand and thus to control inflation. Bank of Canada defenders argue that an independent monetary authority is needed to control the consequent inflation.

tered banks turn to the Bank of Canada as their "bank." There are times when the chartered banks need to borrow from the central bank. As well, chartered banks keep minimal reserves with the Bank of Canada to settle bilateral payment balances among themselves.

2. ISSUING CURRENCY It is the responsibility of the Bank of Canada to supply the economy with needed paper currency—Bank of Canada notes.

3. ACTING AS FISCAL AGENT The Bank of Canada acts as the fiscal agent (provider of financial services) for the federal government. The federal government collects funds through taxation, spends these funds on a variety of goods and services, and sells and redeems bonds. The federal government uses the Bank of Canada's facilities in carrying out these activities.

4. SUPERVISING THE CHARTERED BANKS The Department of Finance and the Bank of Canada supervise the operations of chartered banks. Periodic examination of bank profitability ascertains that the chartered banks perform in accordance with myriad regulations to which they are subjected.

15-2

GLOBAL PERSPECTIVE

Central bank independence and inflation, 1960–1992

Nations with the most independent central banks had the lowest average annual rates of inflation between 1960 and 1992. Note the inflation rates for Germany, Switzerland, and Canada compared with the rates for Portugal, New Zealand, and Greece.

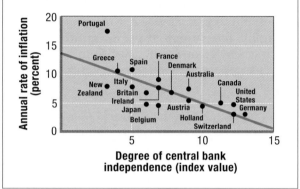

STATEMENT OF ASSETS AND LIABILITIES OF THE BANK OF CANADA

Because Canadian monetary policy is implemented by the Bank of Canada, we need to consider its balance sheet. Some of the Bank of Canada's assets and liabilities differ from those found on the balance sheet of a chartered bank. Table 15-1 is a simplified balance sheet showing all the pertinent assets and liabilities of the Bank of Canada.

Assets

The two Bank of Canada assets we need to consider are:

1. **SECURITIES** The securities shown in the table are Government of Canada bonds and Treasury bills (government bonds with terms of three months to a year) issued by the Government of Canada to finance past and present budget deficits. These securities are part of the public debt—money borrowed and owed by the federal government. Some were bought directly from the government, most from the public (through investment dealers) and the chartered banks. Although the interest on these bonds represents the Bank of Canada's income, they are not bought and sold purposely to make a profit. Rather, they are bought and sold primarily to influence the amount of chartered bank reserves, and therefore the banks' ability to create money by lending.

2. **ADVANCES TO CHARTERED BANKS** For reasons we will soon discuss, chartered banks occasionally borrow from the Bank of Canada. The IOUs the chartered banks give to the Bank of Canada in negotiating advances are listed as advances to chartered banks. From the Bank of Canada's point of view, these IOUs are assets—they are claims against the chartered banks that have borrowed from it. To the chartered banks, these IOUs are liabilities. By borrowing, the chartered banks obtain increases in their reserves in exchange for IOUs.

Liabilities

On the liability side we find three items.

TABLE 15-1 Bank of Canada statement of assets and liabilities, December 31, 1997 (in millions)

Assets		Liabilities	
Treasury bills of Canada	$14,065	Notes in circulation	$30,542
Other securities issued or guaranteed by Canada	12,965	Government of Canada deposits	41
		Chartered bank deposits	539
Foreign currency deposits	386	Other deposits	157
Other assets	4,333	Other liabilities	470
Total	$31,749	Total	$31,749

Source: Bank of Canada, *Bank of Canada Review,* Summer, 1998.

1. **CHARTERED BANK DEPOSITS**   These deposits are assets from the viewpoint of the chartered banks but a liability to the Bank of Canada.

    With the abolition of required reserves, these deposits have been considerably reduced, since their only function will be to permit cheque-clearing.

2. **GOVERNMENT OF CANADA DEPOSITS**   Just as businesses and private individuals find it convenient and desirable to pay their obligations by cheque, so does the Government of Canada. By far, the major part of the government's funds—mostly tax receipts—are transferred by the Bank of Canada to government deposit accounts with the various chartered banks. To the government, all such deposits are assets, while to the banks, including the central bank, they are liabilities.

3. **NOTES IN CIRCULATION**   The paper money supply in Canada consists of bank notes issued by the Bank of Canada. When it is in circulation, this paper money constitutes claims against the assets of the Bank of Canada and is thus treated by them as a liability. These notes, which come into circulation through chartered banks, are not a part of the money supply until they are in the hands of the public.

15-1
QUICK REVIEW

- The functions of the Bank of Canada are: **a** to hold deposits of the chartered banks; **b** to supply the economy's needs for paper currency; **c** to act as fiscal agent for the federal government; **d** to supervise the operations of chartered banks; and **e** to regulate the money supply.

- The Bank of Canada's two major assets are Government of Canada securities and advances to chartered banks. Its three major liabilities are chartered bank deposits, Government of Canada deposits, and notes in circulation.

TOOLS OF MONETARY POLICY

There are two main instruments of monetary control at the disposal of the Bank of Canada to influence chartered bank reserves: (1) open-market operations and (2) switching Government of Canada deposits.

Open-Market Operations

The term **open-market operations** refers to the *buying and selling of government bonds and Treasury bills (securities) by the Bank of Canada in the open market*—that is, the buying and selling of bonds from or to chartered banks and the public (through investment dealers).

Buying Securities   Suppose the Bank of Canada decides to buy government bonds in the open market, that is, from chartered banks or the public. In both cases, the overall effect is the same—chartered bank reserves are increased.

FROM CHARTERED BANKS   When the Bank of Canada buys government bonds *from chartered banks*,

(a) The chartered banks give up a part of their holdings of securities to the Bank of Canada.

(b) The Bank of Canada pays for these securities by increasing the deposits of the chartered banks by the amount of the purchase.

A chartered bank may pay for a bond bought from a private individual by increasing the seller's demand deposit; similarly, the bankers' bank may pay for bonds bought from chartered banks by increasing the banks' reserves. The transaction would change the consolidated balance sheets of the chartered banks and the Bank of Canada as follows:

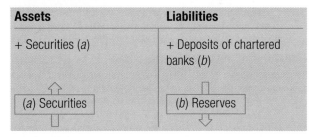

BANK OF CANADA BUYS BONDS FROM CHARTERED BANKS

BANK OF CANADA

Assets	Liabilities
+ Securities (*a*)	+ Deposits of chartered banks (*b*)
(*a*) Securities ⬆	(*b*) Reserves ⬇

CHARTERED BANKS

Assets	Liabilities
– Securities (*a*)	
+ Reserves (*b*)	

The upward arrow shows that securities have moved from the chartered banks to the Bank of Canada. Therefore, we write "–Securities" (minus securities) in the asset column of the balance sheet of the chartered banks. For the same reason, we write "+ Securities" in the asset column of the balance sheet of the Bank of Canada.

The downward arrow indicates that the Bank of Canada has provided reserves to the chartered banks. Therefore we write "+Reserves" in the asset column of the balance sheet of the chartered banks. The plus sign in the liability column of the balance sheet of the Bank of Canada indicates that chartered bank deposits have increased; they are a liability to the Bank of Canada.

The important aspect of this transaction is that when the Bank of Canada purchases securities from chartered banks, the reserves—and therefore the lending ability—of the chartered banks are increased.

FROM THE PUBLIC If the Bank of Canada purchases securities *from the public* (through investment dealers), the effect on chartered bank deposits in the central bank would be much the same. Suppose Mariposa Investments Limited (a large Toronto dealer representing the public) possesses Government of Canada bonds that it sells in the open market to the Bank of Canada. The transaction goes like this:

(a) Mariposa Investments gives up securities to the Bank of Canada and gets in payment a cheque drawn by the Bank of Canada on itself.

(b) Mariposa Investments promptly deposits this cheque in its account with the Bank of York.

(c) The Bank of York collects against the Bank of Canada by sending the cheque to the Toronto clearing house for collection. As a result, the Bank of York receives an increase in its reserves.

Balance sheet changes will appear as shown at top of next column.

We need to understand two aspects of this transaction.

1. As with Bank of Canada purchases of securities directly from chartered banks, the reserves and lending ability of the chartered banking system have been increased. This is indicated by the "+Reserves," showing an increase in assets of the Bank of York.

2. The supply of money is directly increased by the central bank's purchase of government bonds (aside from any expansion of the money supply that may occur from the increase in chartered bank reserves). This direct increase in the money supply has taken the form of an increased amount of chequing account money in the economy, as a result

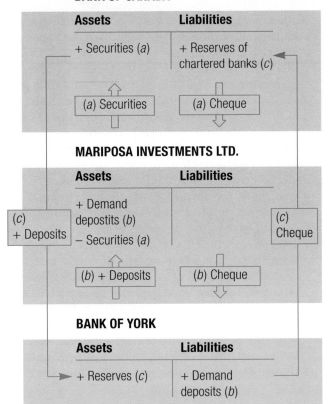

BANK OF CANADA BUYS BONDS FROM THE PUBLIC

of Mariposa's deposit, thus the "+Demand deposit" in the Bank of York balance sheet. Because these demand deposits are an asset as viewed by Mariposa Investments, demand deposits have increased (plus sign) on Mariposa Investments' balance sheet.

There is a slight difference between the Bank of Canada's purchases of securities from the chartered banks and from the public. If we assume all chartered banks are "loaned up" initially, the Bank of Canada bond purchases *from chartered banks* increase actual reserves and excess reserves of chartered banks by the entire amount of the bond purchases. As shown in the left panel of Figure 15-1, a $1,000 bond purchase from a chartered bank would increase both the actual and excess reserves of the chartered bank by $1,000.

In contrast, Bank of Canada purchases of bonds *from the public* increase actual reserves but also increase demand deposits. Thus, a $1,000 bond purchase from the public would increase demand deposits and hence actual reserves of the "loaned up" banking system by $1,000. But with

FIGURE 15-1 The Bank of Canada's purchase of bonds and the expansion of the money supply

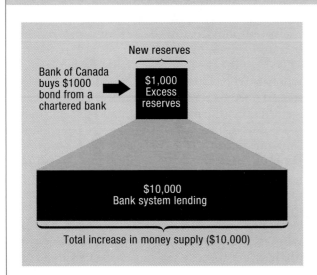
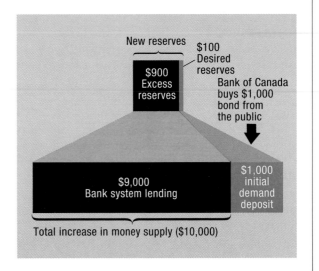

Assuming all chartered banks are "loaned up" initially, a Bank of Canada purchase of a $1,000 bond from either a chartered bank or the public can increase the money supply by $10,000 when the desired reserve ratio is 10 percent. In the left portion of the diagram, the purchase of a $1,000 bond from a chartered bank creates $1,000 of excess reserves that support an expansion of demand deposits of $10,000 through making loans. In the right portion, the purchase of a $1,000 bond from the public creates only $900 of excess reserves, because $100 of reserves are needed to "back up" the $1,000 new demand deposit in the banking system. The chartered banks can therefore expand the money supply by $9,000 by making loans. This $9,000 of chequing account money plus the initial new demand deposit of $1,000 together equal $10,000 of new money.

a 10 percent desired reserve ratio applied to demand deposits, the excess reserves of the banking system would only be $900.

However, in both transactions, the result is the same: *When the Bank of Canada buys securities (bonds) in the open market, chartered banks' reserves are increased.* When the chartered banks lend out their excess reserves, the nation's money supply will rise. Observe in Figure 15-1 that a $1,000 purchase of bonds by the Bank of Canada results in $10,000 of additional money, regardless of whether the purchase was made from the banks or the general public.

Selling Securities You should now suspect that Bank of Canada sales of government bonds reduce chartered bank reserves. Let's see why.

TO CHARTERED BANKS Suppose the Bank of Canada sells securities in the open market to *chartered banks*:

(a) The Bank of Canada gives up securities, which the chartered banks acquire.

(b) Chartered banks pay for these securities by drawing cheques against their deposits—

that is, against their reserves—in the Bank of Canada. The Bank of Canada collects these cheques by reducing the chartered banks' reserves accordingly.

The balance sheet changes appear as follows:

BANK OF CANADA SELLS BONDS TO CHARTERED BANKS

BANK OF CANADA

Assets	Liabilities
− Securities (a)	− Reserves of chartered banks (b)
(a) Securities ⬇	(b) Reserves ⬆

CHARTERED BANKS

Assets	Liabilities
− Reserves (b)	
+ Securities (a)	

The reduction in chartered bank deposits in the Bank of Canada is indicated by the minus signs before these entries.

TO THE PUBLIC If the Bank of Canada sells securities *to the public* (which goes through investment dealers) the final outcome is the same. Let's put Mariposa Investments Ltd. on the buying end of government bonds that the Bank of Canada is selling:

(a) The Bank of Canada sells Government of Canada bonds to Mariposa Investments, who pays for these securities by a cheque drawn on the Bank of York.

(b) The Bank of Canada clears this cheque against the Bank of York by reducing York's reserves.

(c) The Bank of York returns the cancelled cheque to Mariposa Investment, reducing the company's demand deposit accordingly.

The balance sheets change as shown below:

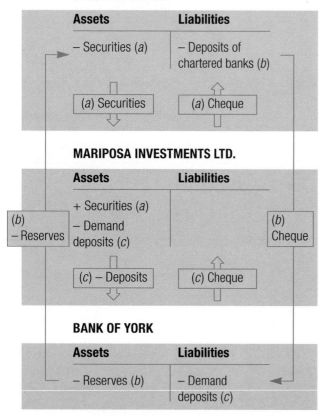

BANK OF CANADA SELLS BONDS TO THE PUBLIC

The Bank of Canada bond sales of $1,000 to the chartered banking system reduce the system's actual and excess reserves by $1,000. But a $1,000 bond sale to the public reduces excess reserves by $900, because demand deposit money is also reduced by $1,000 in the sale. Since the chartered banking system has reduced its outstanding deposits by $1,000 it need only keep $100 less in reserves.

Whether the Bank of Canada sells securities to the public or to chartered banks, the conclusion is the same: *When the Bank of Canada sells securities in the open market, chartered bank reserves are reduced.*

If all excess reserves are already lent out, this decline in chartered bank reserves will translate into a decline in the nation's money supply. In our example, a $1,000 sale of government securities will result in a $10,000 decline in the money supply whether the sale was made to chartered banks or the public. You can verify this by re-examining Figure 15-1 and tracing the effects of *a sale* of a $1,000 bond by the Bank of Canada either to chartered banks or the public.

Switching Government of Canada Deposits

The chartered banks' lending power (and thus money-creating power) is restricted by their demand deposits and reserves. The Bank of Canada can affect the chartered banks' demand deposit and reserves by either depositing or withdrawing funds from the banking system. You will recall that the Bank of Canada is the federal government's bank, and thus has billions of dollars of government deposits in its possession at any given time. By **switching government deposits** from chartered banks to itself, the Bank of Canada immediately *reduces* the deposits and the reserves of the chartered banks by the amount of the switched deposits. The effect on the money supply is similar to the open-market operation of selling government bonds.

Alternatively, by switching government deposits from itself to the chartered banks, the Bank of Canada *increases* the deposits and the reserves of the chartered banks, making it possible to increase the nation's money supply. The effect of switching government deposits to the chartered banks will be the same as the Bank of Canada buying bonds on the open market.

In the last decade, switching of government deposits has become the *main* method by which the Bank of Canada has tried to control the money supply.

The Bank Rate and the Overnight Loans Rate

One of the functions of a central bank is to be a "lender of last resort." Just as chartered banks may lend to the public, so the bankers' bank may lend to the chartered banks [and to a select group of money market (investment) dealers]. The rate of interest charged by the Bank of Canada on these loans is called the **bank rate**.

Since February 1996 the bank rate has been set at half a percentage point above the **overnight loans rate**, the interest rate at which chartered banks, investment dealers, and other financial market participants borrow and lend funds for one day. The Bank of Canada has a publicized target on the overnight loans rate, and maintains it within a range of one-half of a percentage point (50 basis points) of the target range through its two main monetary policy tools. By lending and borrowing in the overnight market, the Bank of Canada affects the liquidity position of the chartered banks. *(Key Question 3)*

15-2
QUICK REVIEW

- The objective of monetary policy is to help the economy achieve a full-employment, noninflationary level of output.
- The Bank of Canada has two main instruments of monetary control, each of which works by changing the amount of reserves in the banking system. The two mechanisms are: **a** open-market operations and **b** switching Government of Canada deposits.

THE DEMAND FOR MONEY

Now that we know what constitutes the supply of money and how the supply of money is "backed," let's turn to the demand for money. The public wants to hold some of its wealth as *money* for two basic reasons: to make purchases with it, and to hold it as an asset.

Transactions Demand, D_t

People want money—it is a medium of exchange; it is convenient for purchasing goods and services. Households must have enough money on hand to buy groceries and pay mortgage and utility bills until the next paycheque. Businesses need money to pay for labour, materials, power, and other inputs. Money demanded for all such purposes is called the **transactions demand** for money.

The basic determinant of the amount of money demanded for transactions is the level of nominal GDP. The larger the total money value of all goods and services exchanged in the economy, the larger will be the amount of money needed to negotiate these transactions. *The transactions demand for money varies directly with nominal GDP.* We specify *nominal* GDP because households and firms will want more money for transactions if either prices rise *or* real output increases. In both instances, there will be a larger dollar volume of transactions to accomplish.

In *Figure 15-2a (Key Graph)* we graph the quantity of money demanded for transactions against the interest rate. Because the amount demanded depends on the level of nominal GDP and is independent of the interest rate, the transactions demand, D_t, graphs as a vertical line. That is, we assume changes in the interest rate do not affect the amount of money demanded for transactions.

The transactions demand curve is placed at $30 billion on the assumption that each dollar held for transactions purposes is spent on the average 15 times per year *and* that nominal GDP is $460 billion. Thus the public needs $30 billion (= $450 billion ÷ 15) of money to purchase that GDP.

Asset Demand, D_a

The second reason for holding money derives from money's function as a store of value. People may hold their financial assets in many forms—for example, as corporate stocks, private or government bonds, or as M1 money. Thus, there is an **asset demand** for money.

What determines the kind of demand for money? First, we must recognize that each of the various ways to hold financial assets has advantages and disadvantages. To simplify, let's compare money as an asset with holding bonds. The advantages of holding money are its liquidity and

KEY GRAPH

FIGURE 15-2 **The demand for money and the money market**

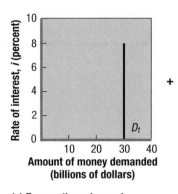

**(a) Transactions demand
for money, D_t**

+

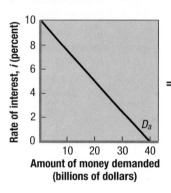

**(b) Asset demand for
money, D_a**

=

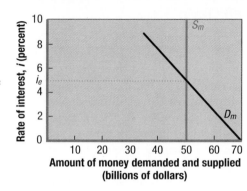

**(c) Total demand for money,
$D_m = D_t + D_a$, and supply**

The total demand for money D_m is determined by horizontally adding the asset demand for money D_a to the transactions demand D_t. The transactions demand is vertical because it is assumed to depend on nominal GDP rather than on the real interest rate. The asset demand varies inversely with the real interest rate because of the opportunity cost involved in holding currency and chequable deposits that pay no interest or very low interest. Combining the money supply (stock) S_m with total money demand D_m portrays the money market and determines the equilibrium real interest rate i_e.

15-2

QUICK QUIZ

1. In this graph, at the interest rate i_e,
    (a) the amount of money demanded as an asset is $50 billion.
    (b) the amount of money demanded for transactions is $200 billion.
    (c) bond prices will decline.
    (d) $30 billion is demanded for transactions, $20 billion is demanded as an asset, and the money supply is $50 billion.

2. In this graph, at an interest rate of 10 percent,
    (a) no money will be demanded as an asset.
    (b) total money demanded will be $50 billion.
    (c) the Bank of Canada will supply $100 billion of money.

(d) there will be a $100 billion shortage of money.

3. Curve D_a slopes downward because
    (a) lower interest rates increase the opportunity cost of holding money.
    (b) lower interest rates reduce the opportunity cost of holding money.
    (c) the asset demand for money varies directly (positively) with the interest rate.
    (d) the transactions-demand-for-money curve is perfectly vertical.

4. Suppose the supply of money declined to $25 billion. The equilibrium interest rate would
    (a) fall, the amount of money demanded for transactions would rise, and the amount of money demanded as an asset would decline.
    (b) rise and the amounts of money demanded for transactions and as an asset would both fall.
    (c) fall and the amounts of money demanded for transactions and as an asset would both increase.
    (d) rise, the amount of money demanded for transactions would be unchanged, and the amount of money demanded as an asset would decline.

Answers: 1. d; 2. a; 3. b; 4. d

lack of risk. Money is the most liquid of all assets; it is immediately usable in the making of purchases. Money is an attractive asset to be holding when the prices of goods, services, and other financial assets are expected to decline. When the price of a bond falls, the bondholder will suffer a loss if the bond is sold before maturity. There is no such risk with holding money.

The disadvantage of holding money as an asset is that in comparison with holding bonds, it does *not* earn interest, or, if it is an interest-bearing chequing account, earn as much interest as bonds or nonchequable deposits. Idle currency, of course, earns no interest at all.

Knowing this, the problem is deciding how much of your financial assets to hold as, say, bonds (i.e., all interest-bearing financial assets) and how much as money. The solution depends primarily on the interest rate. A household or business incurs an opportunity cost when holding money; interest income is forgone or sacrificed. If a bond pays 9 percent interest, then it costs $9 per year of forgone income to hold $100 as cash or in a noninterest chequable account.

It is no surprise, then, that *the asset demand for money varies inversely with the rate of interest.* When the interest rate or opportunity cost of holding money as an asset is low, the public will choose to hold a large amount of money as assets. When the interest rate is high, it is costly to "be liquid," and the amount of assets held as money will be small. This inverse relationship between the interest rate and the amount of money people will want to hold as an asset is shown by D_a in Figure 15-2b.

Total Money Demand, D_m

As shown in Figure 15-2, the **total demand for money**, D_m, is found by horizontally adding the asset demand to the transactions demand. The resulting downsloping line in Figure 15-2c represents the total amount of money the public wants to hold—for transactions *and* as an asset—at each possible interest rate.

Recall that the transactions demand for money depends mainly on the nominal GDP. A change in the nominal GDP—working through the transactions demand for money—will shift the total money demand curve. Specifically, an increase in nominal GDP means the public wants to hold a larger amount of money for transactions, and this will shift the total money demand curve

to the right. A decline in the nominal GDP will shift the total money demand curve to the left. As an example, suppose nominal GDP increases from $450 to $600 billion and the average dollar held for transactions is still spent 15 times per year. Then the transactions demand curve will shift from $30 billion (= $450 billion ÷ 15) to $40 billion (= $600 billion ÷ 15). The total money demand curve will then lie $10 billion farther to the right at each possible interest rate.

THE MONEY MARKET

We can combine the demand for money with the supply of money to portray the **money market** and determine the equilibrium real rate of interest. In Figure 15-2c the vertical line, S_m, represents the money supply. It is shown as a vertical line because we assume that the monetary authorities and financial institutions have provided the economy with some particular *stock* of money, such as the M1 total shown in Table 13-1.

Just as in a product or resource market, the intersection of demand and supply determines equilibrium price. Here, the "price" is the equilibrium interest rate (i_e), that is, the price paid for the use of money.

If disequilibrium existed in the money market, how would the money market achieve equilibrium? Consider Figure 15-3, which repeats Figure 15-2c and adds two alternative supply-of-money curves.

Response to a Shortage of Money

Suppose the supply of money is reduced from $50 billion, S_{m0}, to $38 billion, S_{m1}. At the previous interest rate of 5 percent, the quantity of money demanded exceeds the quantity supplied by $12 billion. People will attempt to make up for this shortage of money by selling some of the financial assets they own (we assume for simplicity that these assets are bonds). But one person's receipt of money through the sale of a bond is another person's loss of money through the purchase of that bond. Overall, there is only $38 billion of money available. The collective attempt to get more money by selling bonds will increase the supply of bonds relative to demand in the bond market, but will not increase the amount of money available as a whole. The outcome is that the price of bonds will fall.

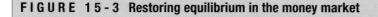

FIGURE 15-3 Restoring equilibrium in the money market

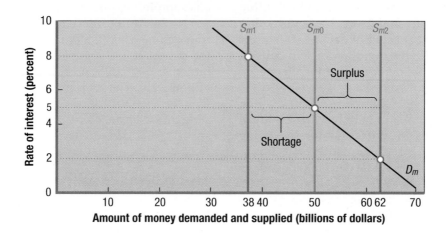

A decrease in the supply of money creates a temporary shortage of money in the money market. People and institutions attempt to gain more money by selling bonds. The supply of bonds therefore increases, which reduces bond prices and raises interest rates. At higher interest rates, people reduce the amount of money they wish to hold. As a result, the amount of money supplied and demanded once again are equal at the higher interest rate. An increase in the supply of money creates a temporary surplus of money, resulting in an increase in the demand for bonds and higher bond prices. Interest rates fall and equilibrium is re-established in the money market.

Generalization: *Lower bond prices increase interest rates.* To clarify this, suppose a bond with no expiration date pays a fixed $50 annual interest and is selling for its face value of $1,000. The interest yield on this bond is 5 percent:

$$\frac{\$50}{\$1,000} = 5\%$$

Now suppose that the price of this bond drops to $625 because of the increased supply of bonds. The $50 fixed annual interest payment will now yield 8 percent to whoever buys the bond:

$$\frac{\$50}{\$625} = 8\%$$

Because all borrowers must compete by offering to pay lenders interest rates similar to those available on bonds, a higher general interest rate thus emerges. In Figure 15-3 the interest rate rises from 5 percent at the money supply $50 billion to 8 percent when the money supply is $38 billion. This higher interest rate raises the opportunity cost of holding money and reduces the amount of money firms and households want to hold. Specifically,

the amount of money demanded declines from $50 billion at the 5 percent interest rate to $38 billion at the 8 percent interest rate. The money market is back in equilibrium, now with the quantity of money demanded and supplied equalling $38 billion at the new 8 percent interest rate.

Response to a Surplus of Money

An increase in the supply of money from $50 billion, S_{m0}, to $62 billion, S_{m2}, results in a surplus of $12 billion at the initial 5 percent interest rate. People will now try to rid themselves of money by purchasing more bonds. The collective attempt to buy more bonds therefore will increase the demand for bonds and pull bond prices upward.

Corollary: *Higher bond prices reduce interest rates.* In our example, the $50 interest payment on a bond now priced at, say, $2,500, will yield a bond buyer only a 2 percent interest rate:

$$\frac{\$50}{\$2500} = 2\%$$

The point is that interest rates in general will fall as people unsuccessfully attempt to reduce their money holding below $62 billion by buying bonds. In this case, the interest rate will fall to a new equilibrium at 2 percent. Because the opportunity cost of holding money now is lower—being liquid is less expensive—consumers and businesses will increase the amount of currency and chequable deposits they are willing to hold from $50 billion to $62 billion. Eventually equilibrium in the money market will be restored: the quantity of money demanded and supplied will each be $62 billion at an interest rate of 2 percent. *(Key Question 4)*

15-3

QUICK REVIEW

- People hold money for transaction and asset purposes.

- The total demand for money is the sum of the transaction and asset demands; it is drawn as an inverse relationship (downsloping line) between the interest rate and the quantity of money demanded.

- The equilibrium interest rate is determined by money demand and supply; it occurs when people are willing to hold the exact amount of money being supplied by the monetary authorities.

- Bond prices and interest rates are inversely related.

MONETARY POLICY, REAL GDP, AND THE PRICE LEVEL

Cause-Effect Chain: The Transmission Mechanism

How does monetary policy work towards the goal of full employment with price-level stability? The central factors and relationships are illustrated in *Figure 15-4 (Key Graph)*.

Money Market Figure 15-4a represents the money market, in which the demand curve for money and the supply curve of money are brought together. Recall that the total demand for money is made up of the transactions and asset demands. The transactions demand is directly related to the nominal GDP. The asset demand is inversely related to the interest rate. The interest rate is the opportunity cost of holding money as

an asset; the higher the cost, the smaller the amount of money the public wants to hold. The total demand for money D_m is thus inversely related to the interest rate, as indicated in Figure 15-4a. Also, recall that an increase in nominal GDP will shift D_m to the right and a decline in nominal GDP will shift D_m to the left.

We complete our graphical portrayal of the money market by showing three potential money supply curves, S_{m0}, S_{m1}, and S_{m2}. In each case the money supply is shown as a vertical line representing some fixed amount of money determined by the Bank of Canada. While monetary policy (specifically, the supply of money) helps determine the interest rate, the interest rate does *not* determine the location of the money supply curve.

The equilibrium interest rate is the interest rate at which the amount of money demanded and supplied are equal. With money demand D_m in Figure 15-4a, if the supply of money is $50 billion ($S_{m0}$), the equilibrium interest rate is 10 percent. With a money supply of $75 billion ($S_{m1}$), the interest rate is 8 percent; with a money supply of $100 billion ($S_{m2}$), it is 6 percent.

We know from Chapter 10 that the real, not the nominal, rate of interest is critical for investment decisions. So here we assume Figure 15-4a portrays real interest rates.

Investment These 10, 8, and 6 percent real interest rates are carried rightward to the investment demand curve of Figure 15-4b. This curve shows the inverse relationship between the interest rate—the cost of borrowing to invest—and the amount of investment spending. At the 10 percent interest rate it will be profitable for the nation's businesses to invest $15 billion; at 8 percent, $20 billion; at 6 percent, $25 billion.

The investment component of total spending is more likely to be affected by changes in the interest rate than is the consumer spending component. Of course, consumer purchases of automobiles, which depend heavily on instalment credit, are sensitive to interest rates. But overall the interest rate is *not* a very crucial factor in determining how households divide their disposable income between consumption and saving.

The impact of changing interest rates on investment spending is great because of the large cost and long-term nature of capital purchases. Capital equipment, factory buildings, and warehouses are tremendously expensive. In absolute

KEY GRAPH

FIGURE 15-4 **Monetary policy and equilibrium GDP**

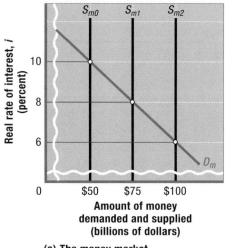

(a) The money market

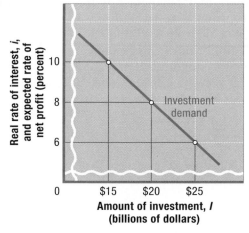

(b) Investment demand

An expansionary monetary policy will lower the interest rate, increase the investment component of aggregate demand, and increase the equilibrium level of GDP. Conversely, a contractionary monetary policy will raise the rate of interest, reduce the investment component of aggregate demand, and restrain demand-pull inflation.

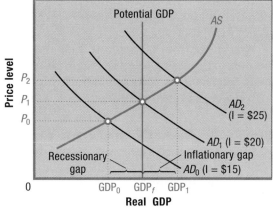

(c) Equilibrium real GDP and the price level

15-4

QUICK QUIZ

1. The ultimate objective of an easy money policy is depicted by
   (a) a decrease in the money supply from S_{m2} to S_{m1}.
   (b) a reduction of the interest rate from 8 to 6 percent.
   (c) an increase in investment from $20 billion to $25 billion.
   (d) an increase in real GDP from GDP_0 to GDP_f.

2. A successful tight money policy is shown as a shift in the money supply curve from

   (a) S_{m2} to S_{m1}, an increase in investment from $20 billion to $25 billion, and a decline in aggregate demand from AD_3 to AD_2.
   (b) S_{m0} to S_{m1}, an increase in investment from $20 billion to $25 billion, and an increase in real GDP from GDP_0 to GDP_f.
   (c) S_{m2} to S_{m1}, a decrease in investment from $25 billion to $20 billion, and a decline in the price level from P_2 to P_1.
   (d) S_{m2} to S_{m1}, a decrease in investment from $25 billion to $20 billion, and an increase in aggregate demand from AD_1 to AD_2.

3. The Bank of Canada could increase the money supply from S_{m0} to S_{m1} by
   (a) increasing the bank rate.
   (b) reducing taxes.
   (c) buying government securities in the open market.
   (d) selling government securities in the open market.

4. If the spending-income multiplier is 4 in the economy depicted, an increase in the money supply from $75 billion to $100 billion will
   (a) shift the aggregate demand curve rightward by $20 billion.
   (b) increase real GDP by $25 billion.
   (c) increase real GDP by $100 billion.
   (d) shift the aggregate demand curve leftward by $5 billion.

Answers: 1. d; 2. c; 3. c; 4. a.

terms, interest charges on funds borrowed for these purchases are considerable.

Similarly, the interest cost on a house purchased on a long-term contract will be very large: A one-half percentage point change in the interest rate could amount to thousands of dollars on the total cost of a home.

Also, changes in the interest rate may affect investment spending by changing the relative attractiveness of purchases of capital equipment versus purchases of bonds. In purchasing capital goods, the interest rate is the *cost* of borrowing the funds to make the investment. In purchasing bonds, the interest rate is the *return* on the financial investment. If the interest rate increases, the cost of buying capital goods increases while the return on bonds increases. Businesses are then more inclined to use business saving to buy securities than to buy equipment. Conversely, a drop in the interest rate makes purchases of capital goods relatively more attractive than bond ownership.

In brief, the impact of changing interest rates is mainly on investment (and, through that, on aggregate demand, output, employment, and the price level). Moreover, as Figure 15-4b shows, investment spending varies inversely with the interest rate.

Equilibrium GDP

Figure 15-4c shows the impact of our three interest rates and corresponding levels of investment spending on aggregate demand. As noted, aggregate demand curve AD_0 is associated with the $15 billion level of investment, AD_1 with investment of $20 billion, and AD_2 with investment of $25 billion. That is, investment spending is one of the determinants of aggregate demand. Other things equal, the greater this investment spending, the farther to the right lies the aggregate demand curve.

Suppose the money supply in Figure 15-4a is $50 billion ($S_{m0}$), producing an equilibrium interest rate of 10 percent. In Figure 15-4b we see this 10 percent interest rate will bring forth $15 billion of investment spending. This $15 billion of investment spending joins with consumption spending, net exports, and government spending to yield aggregate demand curve AD_0 in Figure 15-4c. The equilibrium levels of real output and prices are GDP_0 and P_0, as determined by the intersection of AD_0 and the aggregate supply curve AS.

To test your understanding of these relationships, you should explain why each of the other two levels of money supply in Figure 15-4a results in a different interest rate, level of investment, aggregate demand curve, and equilibrium real output and price level.

Effects of an Expansionary Monetary Policy

We have assumed the money supply is $50 billion ($S_m$) in Figure 15-4a. Because the resulting real output GDP_0 in Figure 15-4c is far below the full-employment output, GDP_f, the economy must be experiencing substantial unemployment, or a recessionary gap. The Bank of Canada therefore should institute an **expansionary monetary policy** (Column 1 of Table 15-2).

To increase the money supply the Bank of Canada will take one or both of the following actions: (1) buy government securities from chartered banks and the public in the open market; (2) switch government deposits to the chartered banks. The result will be an increase in excess reserves in the chartered banking system. Because excess reserves are the basis on which chartered banks can earn profit by lending and thereby expand the money supply, the nation's money supply likely will rise. An increase in the money supply will lower the interest rate, increasing investment, aggregate demand, and equilibrium GDP.

For example, an increase in the money supply from $50 to $75 billion ($S_{m0}$ to S_{m1}) will reduce the interest rate from 10 to 8 percent, as indicated in Figure 15-4a, and increase investment from $15 billion to $20 billion, as shown in Figure 15-4b. This $5 billion increase in investment spending will shift the aggregate demand curve rightward by more than the increase in investment because of the multiplier effect. If the open economy multiplier is 2, the $5 billion increase in investment will shift the AD curve rightward by $10 billion (= $2 \times \$5$) at each price level. Specifically, aggregate demand will shift from AD_0 to AD_1, as shown in Figure 15-4c. This rightward shift in the aggregate demand curve will increase from GDP_0 to the desired full-employment output at GDP_f, thereby closing the recessionary gap.

You should note that if the Bank of Canada chooses not to pursue an expansionary monetary policy to close a recessionary gap, the lower price level P_0, brought about by a drop in aggregate demand, will eventually lead the short-run aggregate supply curve to shift right until the gap has been closed (you should pencil in the new short-run aggregate supply curve). Recall that such a

---

TABLE 15-2 Monetary policy: the transmission mechanism

(1) Expansionary monetary policy	(2) Contractionary monetary policy
Problem: Recessionary gap	*Problem:* Inflationary gap
Bank of Canada buys bonds, switches government deposits into the chartered banks, or both	Bank of Canada sells bonds, switches government deposits out of the chartered banks, or both
↓	↓
Money supply rises	Money supply falls
↓	↓
Excess reserves increase	Excess reserves decrease
↓	↓
Interest rate falls	Interest rate rises
↓	↓
Investment spending increases	Investment spending decreases
↓	↓
Aggregate demand increases	Aggregate demand decreases
↓	↓
Real GDP rises by a multiple of the increase in investment	Inflation declines

---

supply response could take many years, needlessly prolonging a recession.

Column (1) in Table 15-2 summarizes the chain of events associated with an expansionary monetary policy.

Effects of a Contractionary Monetary Policy

Now let's assume the money supply and interest rate are $100 billion ($S_{m2}$) in Figure 15-4a. This results in an interest rate of 6 percent, investment spending of $25 billion, and aggregate demand of AD_2. As you can see in Figure 15-4c, we have depicted an inflationary gap. Aggregate demand AD_2 is excessive relative to the economy's full-employment level of real output GDP$_f$. To rein in spending, the Bank of Canada will institute a **contractionary monetary policy**.

The Bank of Canada will undertake one or both of the following actions: (1) sell government bonds to chartered banks and to the public in the open market; (2) switch government deposits out of the chartered banks. Banks then will discover their reserves are too low to meet possible cash withdrawals and therefore will need to reduce

their demand deposits by refraining from issuing new loans as old loans are paid back. This will shrink the money supply and increase the interest rate. The higher interest rate will discourage investment, decreasing aggregate demand, and closing the inflationary gap.

If the Bank of Canada reduces the money supply from $100 billion to $75 billion ($S_{m2}$ to S_{m1} in Figure 15-4a), the interest rate will increase from 6 to 8 percent and investment will decline from $25 to $20 billion (Figure 15-4b). This $5 billion decrease in investment, bolstered by the multiplier process, will shift the aggregate demand curve leftward from AD_2 to AD_1. For example, with an open economy multiplier of 2, the aggregate demand curve will shift leftward by $10 billion (= 2 × $5 billion of investment) at each price level. This leftward shift of the aggregate demand curve will eliminate the excessive spending and thus the inflationary gap.

If the Bank of Canada chooses not to embark on a contractionary policy to close the inflationary gap, the new price level P_2 will eventually lead the short-run aggregate supply curve to shift left until the economy is back to its natural rate of unemployment (you should pencil in the new short-run aggregate supply curve). As noted previously, such a supply response takes time, even if an inflationary gap will tend to resolve itself faster than a recessionary gap.

Column (2) of Table 15-2 summarizes the cause-effect chain of contractionary monetary policy. *(Key Question 8)*

Refinements and Feedback

The components of Figure 15-4 allow us to (1) see some of the factors that determine the effectiveness of monetary policy and (2) note the existence of a "feedback" or "circularity" problem that complicates monetary policy.

Policy Effectiveness   Figure 15-4 reveals the magnitudes by which an expansionary or contractionary monetary policy will change the interest rate, investment, and aggregate demand. These magnitudes are determined by the particular shapes of the money-demand and investment-demand curves. Pencil in other curves to see that *the steeper the D_m curve is, the larger will be the effect of any change in the money supply on the equilibrium rate of interest. Furthermore, any change in the interest rate will have a larger impact on investment—and hence on aggregate demand and GDP—the flatter the investment-demand curve.* A specific change in money supply will be most effective when the demand curve for money is relatively steep and the investment-demand curve is relatively flat.

A particular change in the quantity of money will be relatively ineffective when the money-demand curve is flat and the investment-demand curve is steep. As you will see in Chapter 17, there is controversy as to the precise shapes of these curves.

Feedback Effects   You may have sensed in Figure 15-4 a feedback problem that complicates monetary policy. The problem is this: By reading Figure 15-4a to 15-4c, we discover that the interest rate, working through the investment-demand curve, is a determinant of the equilibrium GDP. Now we must recognize that causation also runs the other way. The level of GDP is a determinant of the equilibrium interest rate. This link comes about because the transactions component of the money-demand curve is directly related to the level of nominal GDP.

How does this feedback from Figure 15-4c to 15-4a affect monetary policy? It means that the increase in the GDP that an expansionary monetary policy brings about will *increase* the demand for money, partially offsetting the interest rate-reducing effect of the expansionary policy. A contractionary monetary policy will reduce the nominal GDP. But this will *decrease* the demand for money and dampen the initial interest-increasing effect of the contractionary monetary policy. *(Key Question 9)*

Monetary Policy and Aggregate Supply

As is true of fiscal policy, the effect of a specific monetary policy depends on where the initial and subsequent equilibrium points are located on the aggregate supply curve. The cause-effect chain represented in Figure 15-3 and Table 15-2 indicates that monetary policy primarily affects investment spending and, therefore, aggregate demand, real output, and the price level. The aggregate supply curve explains how the change in investment and aggregate demand *is divided* between changes in real output and changes in the price level.

As we noted in Chapter 11, in the short run the more slack there is in an economy the flatter (more horizontal) the aggregate supply curve will be. In such a situation, a rightward shift of the aggregate demand curve will have a large impact on real GDP, but little or no impact on the price level.

Similarly, if in the short run the economy is close to its capacity utilization, the aggregate supply curve will be very steep (vertical). In such a situation, a rightward shift of the aggregate demand curve will have little effect on real GDP but will greatly increase the price level.

EFFECTIVENESS OF MONETARY POLICY

In this section we discuss some of the strengths and weaknesses of monetary policy as a stabilization tool and see how it has worked in the real world.

Strengths of Monetary Policy

Most economists regard monetary policy as an essential component of Canadian national stabilization policy, especially in view of the following features and evidence.

Speed and Flexibility   Compared with fiscal policy, monetary policy can be quickly altered. Recall that the application of fiscal policy may be delayed by parliamentary deliberations. In contrast, the Bank of Canada can buy or sell securities on a daily basis and affect the money supply and interest rates almost immediately.

Isolation from Political Pressure   Since the governor and deputy governor of the Bank of Canada are appointed for seven-year terms and may be removed from office only by an Act of Parliament, they are not often subject to lobbying and need not concern themselves about their popularity with voters. Thus, the Bank of Canada can engage in politically unpopular policies that it thinks might be necessary for the long-term health of the economy.

But while the governor can be removed only by Parliament, the Bank Act allows the Minister of Finance to issue an instruction to the governor to undertake policy changes. It is understood by convention that any such instruction would cause the governor of the Bank of Canada to resign because his or her judgement has been questioned.

Monetary policy is a more subtle and more politically conservative measure than is fiscal policy. Changes in government spending directly affect the allocation of resources, and changes in taxes can have extensive political ramifications. By contrast, monetary policy works more subtly and therefore is more politically palatable.

Success During the 1980s and 1990s   The case for monetary policy has been greatly bolstered by its successful use during the 1980s and 1990s. A contractionary monetary policy helped bring the inflation rate down from 12.5 percent in 1981 to 4.4 percent three years later.

In the early 1990s, the Bank of Canada successfully used monetary policy to help move the economy out of the 1990–91 recession. This success is noteworthy because the huge budget deficits of the 1980s and early 1990s had put fiscal policy "on the shelf." The federal government budgeting was mainly aimed at reducing the budget deficit, not at stimulating the economy. From a fiscal policy perspective, the tax hikes and government spending reductions during this period were mildly contractionary. But the Bank of Canada's expansionary monetary policy reduced the prime rate on chartered banks' loans from 13 percent in 1990 to 8 per-

cent in 1993. Eventually, these low interest rates had their intended effects: investment spending and interest-sensitive consumer spending rose rapidly, increasing the economy's real GDP.

The expansion of GDP that began in 1992 has continued, but the unemployment rate has remained stubbornly high, dropping to below 9 percent for the first time in many years in 1998. In an effort to stimulate the economy further, the Bank of Canada continued to increase reserves in the banking system in 1996 and 1997 to put downward pressure on short-term interest rates. Interest rates reached their lowest levels in a generation as the prime rate fell below 5 percent. At the same time, the lowering of interest rates has not rekindled inflation in Canada. The inflation rate continues to hover in the 1 to 2 percent range.

In view of Canada balancing its budget and these successes in controlling inflation and promoting growth, for the time being *monetary policy has assumed the role of primary stabilization tool in Canada.*

Shortcomings and Problems

Despite its recent successes, monetary policy has certain limitations and encounters real-world complications.

Less Control?   Some economists fear that changes in banking practices may reduce the Bank of Canada's control of the money supply. Financial innovations have allowed people quickly to move near-monies from mutual funds and other investment accounts to chequing accounts, and vice versa. A particular monetary policy aimed at changing chartered bank reserves might then be rendered less effective by movements of funds within the financial system. For example, people might respond to a contractionary monetary policy by quickly converting near-monies in their mutual funds accounts or other liquid financial investments to money in their chequing accounts. Thus, bank reserves may not fall as intended, the interest rate might not rise, and aggregate demand might not change. Also, banking and finance are increasingly global. Flows of funds to or from Canada might undermine or render inappropriate a particular domestic monetary policy. Finally, the prospects of E-cash and smart cards might complicate the measurement of money and make its issuance more difficult to control.

How legitimate are these concerns? These financial developments could make the Bank of Canada's task of monetary policy more difficult. But recent studies and Bank of Canada experience confirm that the traditional central bank tools of monetary policy remain effective in changing the money supply and interest rates.

Cyclical Asymmetry

If pursued vigorously enough, tight or contractionary monetary policy can deplete chartered bank reserves to the point where banks are forced to reduce the volume of loans. This means a contraction of the money supply. But an easy or expansionary monetary policy suffers from a "You can lead a horse to water, but you can't make it drink" kind of problem. An easy monetary policy can ensure only that chartered banks have the excess reserves needed to make loans. It cannot guarantee that the bank will actually make the loans and thus that the supply of money will increase. If chartered banks, seeking liquidity, are unwilling to lend, the efforts of the Bank of Canada will be of little avail. The public can frustrate the intentions of the Bank of Canada by deciding not to borrow excess reserves. Or the money the central bank injects into the system by the open market buying of bonds from the public could be used by the public to pay off existing loans.

In short, a potential *cyclical asymmetry* is at work. Monetary policy may be highly effective in slowing expansions and controlling inflation, but largely ineffective in moving the economy from a recession towards its full-employment output. This potential cyclical asymmetry, however, has *not* created major difficulties for monetary policy in recent eras. Since the Great Depression, higher excess reserves have generally translated into added lending and therefore into an increase in the money supply.

Changes in Velocity

Total expenditures may be regarded as the money supply *multiplied* by the **velocity of money**—the number of times per year the average dollar is spent on goods and services. If the money supply is $50 billion, total spending will be $600 billion if velocity is 12, but only $450 billion if velocity is 9.

Some economists believe that velocity changes in the opposite direction from the money supply, offsetting or frustrating policy-related changes in the money supply. During inflation, when the money supply is restrained by policy, velocity may increase. Conversely, when measures are taken to increase the money supply during recession, velocity may well fall.

Velocity might behave this way because of the asset demand for money. An expansionary monetary policy, for example, means an increase in the supply of money relative to the demand for it and therefore a reduction in the interest rate (Figure 15-4a). But when the interest rate—the opportunity cost of holding money as an asset—is lower, the public will hold larger money balances. This means dollars will move from hand to hand—from households to businesses and back again—less rapidly. That is, the velocity of money will decline. A reverse sequence of events may cause a contractionary monetary policy to induce an increase in velocity.

The Investment Impact

Some economists doubt that monetary policy has as much impact on investment as Figure 15-4 implies. A combination of a relatively flat money-demand curve and a relatively steep investment-demand curve will mean that a particular change in the money supply will not cause a very large change in investment and, thus, not a large change in the equilibrium GDP.

Furthermore, the operation of monetary policy as portrayed in Figure 15-4 may be complicated, or temporarily offset, by unfavourable changes in the location of the investment-demand curve. For example, a contractionary monetary policy designed to drive up interest rates may have little impact on investment spending if the investment demand curve in Figure 15-4b at the same time shifts to the right because of business optimism, technological progress, or expectations of higher future prices of capital. Monetary policy would have to raise interest rates extraordinarily high under these circumstances to be effective in reducing aggregate demand. Conversely, a severe recession may undermine business confidence, push the investment-demand curve to the left, and frustrate an easy money policy.

Interest as Income

Monetary policy is based on the idea that expenditures on capital goods and interest-sensitive consumer goods are *inversely* related to interest rates. We must now acknowledge that businesses and households are also *recipients* of interest income. The size of such income and the spending that flows from it vary *directly* with the level of interest rates.

Suppose inflation is intensifying and the Bank of Canada raises interest rates to increase the cost of capital goods, housing, and automobiles. The complication is that higher interest rates on a wide range of financial instruments (for example, bonds, certificates of deposits, chequing accounts) will increase the incomes and spending of the households and businesses who own them. Such added spending is obviously at odds with the Bank of Canada's effort to restrict aggregate demand. Here is an opposite example: In 1991 and 1992 the Bank of Canada repeatedly lowered interest rates to stimulate a sluggish economy. One possible reason this strategy took so long to become effective was that households who were receiving 8 or 10 percent on their bonds and GICs in the late 1980s received only 4 or 5 percent in the early 1990s. This diminished interest income undoubtedly lowered their spending.

The point is this: For those who pay interest as an *expense*, a rise in the interest rate reduces spending, while a decline in the interest rate increases spending. But for those who view interest as *income*, a rise in the interest rate increases spend-

ing, while a decline in the interest rate reduces spending. The change in spending by interest-income receivers *partly* offsets and weakens the change in spending by purchasers of capital goods, homes, and autos.

Recent Focus: The Overnight Loans Rate

Up to February 1996 the bank rate was set at 1/4 of a percentage point above the yield on the government three-month Treasury bill, set after the weekly auction. Since then the Bank of Canada has set the bank rate based on the upper limit of its operating band for the overnight loans rate. The operating band is set from time to time by the Bank of Canada, depending on the expected future performance of the Canadian economy. An increase in the upper limit of the operating band would signal "tighter" monetary policy is coming, while statements that it intends to reduce the upper limit of the operating band foretells an "easier" monetary policy. Such changes would be reflected in the bank rate, which in turn would affect interest rates in general. For example, in Figure 15-5 observe that changes in the **prime interest rate**—the interest rate banks charge their most

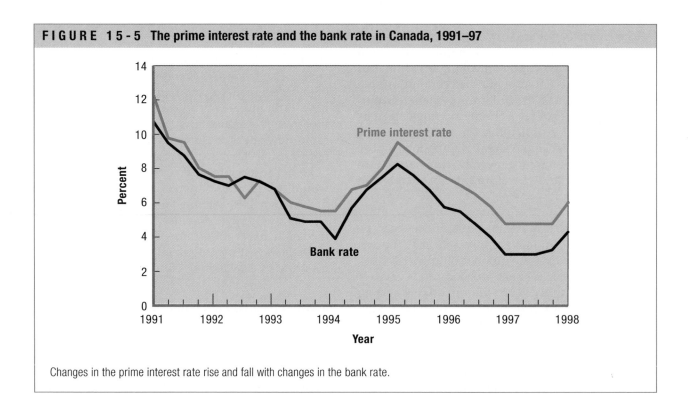

FIGURE 15-5 The prime interest rate and the bank rate in Canada, 1991–97

Changes in the prime interest rate rise and fall with changes in the bank rate.

creditworthy customers—generally track changes in the bank rate.

The Bank of Canada does not *set* either the overnight loans rate or the prime rate; each is established by the interaction of lenders and borrowers. But because the Bank of Canada can change the supply of excess reserves in the banking system and then the money supply, it normally can obtain the short-term interest rate it desires. To increase the rate on overnight loans, the Bank of Canada *sells* bonds in the open market or switches government deposits *out* of the banking system. Both the sale of bonds and switching government deposits out of the banking system reduce excess reserves, lessening the excess reserves available for overnight loans in the overnight market. This decreased supply of excess reserves in the market increases the interest rate on overnight financing. In addition, reduced excess reserves decrease the amount of bank lending and hence the amount of deposit money. We know that declines in the supply of money lead to increases in interest rates in general, including the prime interest rate.

In contrast, when the Bank of Canada wants to reduce the interest rate on overnight loans, it *buys* bonds from the chartered banks and the public, or switches government deposits *into* the banking system. As a result, the supply of reserves in the overnight market increases and the overnight interest rate declines. The money supply rises because the increased supply of excess reserves leads to greater lending and creation of deposit money. As a result, interest rates in general fall, including the prime interest rate.

15-4
QUICK REVIEW

- The Bank of Canada is engaging in an expansionary monetary policy when it increases the money supply to reduce interest rates and increase investment spending and real GDP; it is engaging in a contractionary monetary policy when it reduces the money supply to increase interest rates and reduce investment spending and inflation.

- The steeper the money demand curve and the flatter the investment demand curve, the larger the impact of a change in the money supply on the economy.

- The main strengths of monetary policy are **a** speed and flexibility and **b** political acceptability; its main weaknesses are **a** potential reduced effectiveness during recession and **b** the possibility that changes in velocity will offset it.

- The Bank of Canada communicates changes in monetary policy by announcing changes in the bank rate. The bank rate is set at the upper limit of the Bank of Canada's operating band for the overnight loans rate.

- In the past two decades, the Bank of Canada has quite successfully used alternate tight and loose money policies to stabilize the economy.

Monetary Policy and the International Economy

In Chapter 12 we noted that linkages among the economies of the world complicate domestic fiscal policy. These linkages also extend to monetary policy.

Net Export Effect   You saw in Chapter 12 that an expansionary Canadian fiscal policy (a budget deficit) increases the demand for money and boosts the domestic interest rate. The higher interest rate increases foreign financial investment in Canada, strengthening the demand for dollars in the foreign exchange market and boosting the international price of dollars. This dollar appreciation produces lower net exports and thus weakens the stimulus of the expansionary fiscal policy.

Will an easy money policy have a similar effect? The answer is no. As outlined in column 1, Table 15-3, an easy money or expansionary monetary policy does indeed produce a net export effect, but its direction is opposite that of an expansionary fiscal policy. An easy money policy in, say, Canada, reduces the domestic interest rate. The lower interest rate discourages the inflow of financial capital to Canada. The demand for dollars in foreign exchange markets falls, causing the dollar to depreciate in value. It takes more dollars to buy, say, a Japanese yen or a French franc. All foreign goods become more expensive to Canadian residents, and Canadian goods become cheaper to foreigners. Canadian imports thus fall, and Canadian exports rise; so Canada's net exports

TABLE 15-3 Monetary policy and the net export effect

(1) Expansionary monetary policy	(2) Contractionary monetary policy
Problem: recession, slow growth	Problem: inflation
↓	↓
Expansionary monetary policy (lower interest rate)	Contractionary monetary policy (higher interest rate)
↓	↓
Decreased foreign demand for dollars	Increased foreign demand for dollars
↓	↓
Dollar depreciates	Dollar appreciates
↓	
Increased demand for imports	
↓	↓
Net exports increase (aggregate demand increases, strengthening the expansionary monetary policy)	Net exports decrease (aggregate demand decreases, strengthening the contractionary monetary policy)

increase. As a result, aggregate expenditures and equilibrium GDP expand in Canada.

Conclusion: Unlike an expansionary fiscal policy that reduces net exports, an expansionary monetary policy increases net exports. *Exchange-rate changes that occur in response to interest-rate changes strengthen domestic monetary policy.* This conclusion holds equally for a tight money policy, which we know increases the domestic interest rate. To see how this happens, follow through the analysis in column 2, Table 15-3.

Macro Stability and the Trade Balance Assume that, in addition to domestic macroeconomic stability, a widely held economic goal is that Canada should balance its exports and imports. That is, Canadian net exports should be zero. In simple terms, Canada wants to "pay its own way" in international trade by earning from its exports an amount of money sufficient to finance its imports.

Consider column 1 in Table 15-3 once again, but now suppose Canada initially has a very large balance-of-international-trade *deficit*, which means its imports substantially exceed its exports and so

it is *not* paying its way in world trade. By following through the cause-effect chain in column 1, we find that an expansionary monetary policy lowers the international value of the dollar and so that Canadian exports increase and Canadian imports decline. This increase in net exports works to correct the assumed initial balance-of-trade deficit.

Conclusion: *The easy money policy that is appropriate for the alleviation of unemployment and sluggish growth is compatible with the goal of correcting a balance-of-trade deficit.* Similarly, if the initial problem was a Canadian trade surplus, a *tight* money policy would tend to resolve that surplus.

Now consider column 2 in Table 15-3 and assume again that Canada has a large balance-of-trade deficit. In using a tight money policy to restrain inflation the Bank of Canada would cause net exports to decrease—Canadian exports would fall and imports would rise. This means a larger trade deficit.

Conclusion: *A tight money policy used to alleviate inflation conflicts with the goal of correcting a balance-of-trade deficit.* However, if the initial problem were a trade surplus, a tight money policy would help to resolve it.

Overall we find that an easy money policy alleviates a trade deficit and aggravates a trade surplus; a tight money policy alleviates a trade surplus and aggravates a trade deficit. The point is that certain combinations of circumstances create conflicts or tradeoffs between the use of monetary policy to achieve domestic stability and the realization of a balance in the nation's international trade. *(Key Question 9)*

THE "BIG PICTURE"

Figure 15-6 (Key Graph on pages 342–43*)* brings together the analytical and policy aspects of macroeconomics discussed in this and the eight preceding chapters. This "big picture" shows how the many concepts and principles discussed relate to one another and how they constitute a coherent theory of what determines the level of resource use in a market economy.

Study this diagram and you will see that the levels of output, employment, income, and prices all result from the interaction of aggregate supply and aggregate demand. In particular, note those items—shown in green—that constitute, or are strongly influenced by, public policy.

In
The Media

Central Bank Raises Interest Rates at Last

By David Thomas
Economics Reporter
The Financial Post

The central bank capped a week of heated debate in the economic community by raising interest rates Friday in an attempt to halt the slide in the C$.

The Bank of Canada increased rates 50 basis points and succeeded in turning the ailing C$ around—helped by aggressive buying with its foreign reserves.

But critics predicted the reprieve will be short-lived and warned the trend to higher rates will take an unnecessary toll on economic growth.

The C$ traded as low as US68.19¢ but rallied in the afternoon to close at US68.70¢, up US0.45¢.

Some economists were confused by the bank's apparent policy flip-flop after its top brass hinted a week earlier that rates would remain steady or even decline. Others said the bank did the

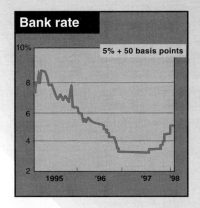

Bank rate

5% + 50 basis points

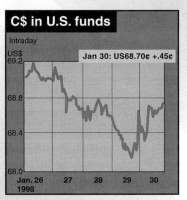

C$ in U.S. funds

Intraday

Jan 30: US68.70¢ +.45¢

right thing, but it would have to go up another 50 basis points or more before the C$ bounces back.

Friday's increase lifted the bank's key lending rate to 5% and brought total increases since the end of September to 175 basis points.

There was not much debate at the chartered banks about how to react—the increase was passed on to their customers. The prime lending rate rose half a percentage point to 6.5% and mortgage rates for terms less than one year increased by 40 basis points.

The central bank's move was designed to support the C$ and remove some of the stimulus the weak currency had injected into the economy, the bank said in a statement.

"Downward pressure on the exchange rate for the C$ has intensified in recent days, leaving the dollar at levels inconsistent with the underlying trends of the Canadian economy."

Source: By David Thomas, *The Financial Post*, January 31, 1998, p. 1.

THE STORY IN BRIEF

The Bank of Canada raises the bank rate by one-half of one percent.

THE ECONOMICS BEHIND THE STORY

- In late 1997 and early 1998 the Canadian dollar came under heavy selling pressure, falling to an all-time low against the U.S. dollar of U.S. $0.6819 (later in 1998, it fell below U.S. $0.64). One way to defend the currency is to raise domestic interest rates, to make the Canadian dollar more attractive to investors.
- The Bank of Canada announced an increase in the bank rate—the rate it lends to chartered banks.

Behind the scenes the Bank of Canada was either buying bonds on the open market, switching government deposits out of the chartered banks, or both. It is the two tools, open market operations and switching of government deposits, that actually raise interest rates by reducing excess reserves. The bank rate is a signal of the level the Bank of Canada wants short-term interest rates to be.

- Note that while in many instances the monetary policy of the Bank of Canada affects the Canadian exchange rate, in this instance it was the international value of the Canadian dollar that affected central bank's interest rate policy.
- Use Figure 15-6 to explain how a higher real interest rate affects aggregate demand. ■

KEY GRAPH

FIGURE 15-6 **The theory of employment and stabilization policies**

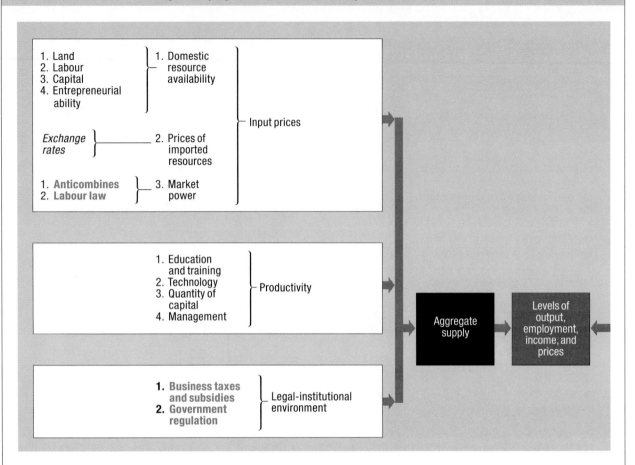

This figure integrates the various components of macroeconomic theory and stabilization policy. Determinants that either constitute public policy or are strongly influenced by public policy are shown in bold green.

15-6
QUICK QUIZ

1. All else equal, an increase in domestic resource availability will
   (a) increase input prices, reduce aggregate supply, and increase real output.
   (b) raise labour productivity, reduce interest rates, and lower the international value of the dollar.
   (c) increase net exports, increase investment, and reduce aggregate demand.
   (d) reduce input prices, increase aggregate supply, and increase real output.

2. All else equal, an expansionary monetary policy during a recession will
   (a) lower the interest rate, increase investment, and reduce net exports.
   (b) lower the interest rate, increase investment, and increase aggregate demand.
   (c) increase the interest rate, increase investment, and reduce net exports.
   (d) reduce productivity, aggregate supply, and real output.

3. A personal income tax cut, combined with a reduction in corporate income and excise taxes, would
   (a) increase consumption, investment, aggregate demand, and aggregate supply.
   (b) reduce productivity, raise input prices, and reduce aggregate supply.
   (c) increase government spending, reduce net exports, and increase aggregate demand.

KEY GRAPH

FIGURE 15-6 *(continued)*

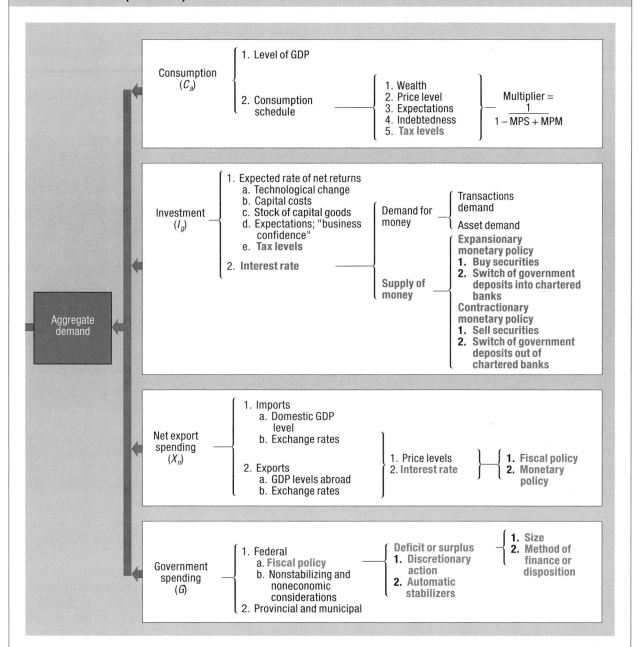

(d) increase the supply of money, reduce interest rates, increase investment, and expand real output.

4. An appreciation of the dollar would
  (a) reduce the price of imported resources, lower input prices, and increase aggregate supply.
  (b) increase net exports and aggregate demand.

(c) increase aggregate supply and aggregate demand.
(d) reduce consumption, investment, net export spending, and government spending.

Answers: 1.d; 2.b; 3.a; 4.a.

The
Last Word

BANK OF CANADA CONFOUNDS CRITICS

As this piece makes clear, it is difficult for the Bank of Canada to please everyone with its policies.

BY BRUCE LITTLE
Economics Reporter

THE BANK OF CANADA IS HAVING TROUBLE finding friends and admirers these days.

On the surface, its decision 10 days ago to rescue the sagging Canadian dollar with higher interest rates has been a splendid success. The dollar bounced back from a record low of 68.25 cents (U.S.) the day before the rate hike to close at 69.86 cents Friday, an increase of 2.4 per cent.

But even economists who supported the rate increase think the bank's credibility has suffered this month because it said—or appeared to say—one thing, and did another.

"They definitely gave mixed signals," said Sherry Cooper, chief economist at Nesbitt Burns Inc. and a vocal supporter of the bank's decision to raise rates.

She said the "biggest mistake" came from the central bank's senior deputy governor, Bernard Bonin. His January statement that the bank was "not uncomfortable" with monetary conditions at a time when the dollar had been sliding for two weeks greased the dollar's decline, she said, because investors thought he meant the bank would not raise rates.

The bank's critics are harsher. As they see it, the bank not only dithered, but in the end did the wrong thing, and its actions have now put the brakes on an economy that is still a long way from robust health.

"Unless quickly reversed, this move is an error that could have very serious consequences," said economists Peter Dungan and Steve Murphy of the University of Toronto's Institute for Policy Analysis in a blistering memo to its members.

Economist William Robson of the C.D. Howe Institute said the Bank of Canada has "shown an inability to steer a steady course." It has wavered from accepting some weakness in the dollar to making a strong move when there was more currency weakness than it liked; "there's no coherent philosophy evident there."

Last week, as arguments over the bank's latest move rattled around the financial community, the majority view was that the Bank of Canada had blundered. The dollar's decline was what many economists call an external shock—the Asian financial crisis has sent commodity prices tumbling—and the bank should have let it go, so its decline could cushion the economy from the worst of the Asian flu, the critics said.

On the other side was a smaller bank of supporters for a defence of the dollar.

Ms. Cooper, the most prominent member of the latter group, reflected her position in a written commentary that she titled "All alone and feeling blue."

She said a country's currency is like the stock price of a company. If management were silly enough to say it was unconcerned that its stock price was hitting record lows, the price decline would continue and the company would become a takeover target, she said.

"The same is true for Canada. When our central bank appeared to be sanguine about the currency hitting record lows—even suggesting that monetary conditions should ease further—the speculative forces of short sellers were massively unleashed."

Ms. Cooper took issue with economists who have cheered the dollar's long-term decline as a boon for jobs and exports. "We cannot devalue our way to prosperity. Beggar-thy-neighbour policies do not work." ∎

Source: *Globe and Mail*, February 9, 1998, p. B1. Reprinted with permission from the *Globe and Mail*.

CHAPTER SUMMARY

1. The major functions of the Bank of Canada are to **a** hold deposits of the chartered banks, **b** to supply the economy with paper currency, **c** act as fiscal agent for the federal government, **d** supervise the operations of chartered banks (together with the Department of Finance), and **e** regulate the supply of money in the best interest of the economy.

2. The Bank of Canada's two major assets are Government of Canada securities and advances to chartered banks. Its three major liabilities are chartered bank reserves, Government of Canada deposits, and notes in circulation.

3. The goal of monetary policy is to assist the economy in achieving price stability, full-employment, and economic growth.

4. As regards to monetary policy, the most important assets of the Bank of Canada are Government of Canada bonds and Treasury bills.

5. The two instruments of monetary policy are **a** open-market operations; and **b** switching of government deposits.

6. The total demand for money is made up of the transactions and asset demands for money. The transactions demand varies directly with nominal GDP; the asset demand varies inversely with the interest rate. The money market combines the demand for money with the money supply to determine the equilibrium interest rate.

7. Disequilibriums in the money market are corrected through changes in bond prices. As bond prices change, interest rates move in the opposite direction. At the equilibrium interest rate, bond prices tend to stabilize and the amounts of money demanded and supplied are equal.

8. Monetary policy operates through a complex cause-effect chain: **a** policy decisions affect chartered bank reserves; **b** changes in reserves affect the supply of money; **c** changes in the money supply alter the interest rate; **d** changes in the interest rate affect investment; **e** changes in investment affect aggregate demand; **f** changes in aggregate demand affect equilibrium real GDP and the price level. Table 15-3 draws together all the basic notions relevant to the use of monetary policy.

9. The advantages of monetary policy include its flexibility and political acceptability. In the past two decades monetary policy has been used successfully both to reduce rapid inflation and to push the economy away from recession. Today, almost all economists view monetary policy as a significant stabilization tool.

10. Monetary policy has some limitations and potential problems: **a** Financial innovations and global considerations have made monetary policy more difficult to administer and its impact less certain. **b** Policy-instigated changes in the supply of money may be partially offset by changes in the velocity of money. **c** The impact of monetary policy will be lessened if the money-demand curve is flat and the investment-demand curve is steep. The investment-demand curve may also shift, negating monetary policy. **d** Changes in interest rates resulting from monetary policy change the amount of interest income received by lenders, altering some people's spending in a way that is opposite to the intent of the monetary policy.

11. The bank rate is the interest rate the Bank of Canada charges chartered banks when it makes loans to them. Since February 1996 the Bank of Canada has set the bank rate on the upper limit of its operating band for overnight financing.

12. The effect of an expansionary monetary policy on domestic GDP is strengthened by the increase in net exports that results from a lower domestic interest rate. Likewise, contractionary, or a tight, money policy is strengthened by a decline in net exports. In some situations, there may be a tradeoff between the effect of monetary policy on the international value of a nation's currency (and thus on its trade balance) and the use of monetary policy to achieve domestic stability.

TERMS AND CONCEPTS

monetary policy
open-market operations
switching government deposits
bank rate

overnight loans rate
transactions demand
asset demand
total demand for money

money market
expansionary (easy)
contractionary (tight) monetary policy

velocity of money
prime interest rate

STUDY QUESTIONS

1. Use chartered bank and Bank of Canada balance sheets to demonstrate the impact of the following transactions on chartered bank reserves: **a** The Bank of Canada purchases securities from dealers. **b** The Bank of Canada makes an advance to a chartered bank.

2. In what way are E-cash accounts and smart cards potentially related? Do you think E-cash and smart cards will dominate transactions sometime within the next 20 years?

3. **KEY QUESTION** *In the table below you will find simplified consolidated balance sheets for the chartered banking system and the Bank of Canada. Use columns 1 and 2 to indicate how the balance sheets would read after each transaction in (a) and (b) is completed. Do not accumulate your answers; analyze each transaction separately, starting in each case from the figures provided. All accounts are in billions of dollars.*

CONSOLIDATED BALANCE SHEET: ALL CHARTERED BANKS (BILLIONS OF DOLLARS)		(1)	(2)
Assets:			
Reserves . . . .$ 4.8		_____	_____
Securities 20.0		_____	_____
Loans 71.2		_____	_____
Liabilities:			
Demand deposits $96.0		_____	_____
Advances from Bank of Canada 0.0		_____	_____

BALANCE SHEET: BANK OF CANADA (BILLIONS OF DOLLARS)		(1)	(2)
Assets:			
Securities $15.8		_____	_____
Advances to chartered banks 0.0		_____	_____
Liabilities:			
Reserves of chartered banks . . . .$ 4.8		_____	_____
Government of Canada deposits 0.1		_____	_____
Notes in circulation 10.9		_____	_____

a.   *The Bank of Canada sells $100 million in securities to the public, who pay for the bonds with cheques. Show the new balance sheet figures in column 1.*

b. ⸱ *The Bank of Canada buys $200 million of securities from chartered banks. Show the new balance sheet figures in column 2.*

c.   *Now review both of these transactions, asking yourself these three questions: (1) What change, if any, took place in the money supply as a direct and immediate result of each transaction? (2) What increase or decrease in chartered banks' reserves took place in each transaction? (3) Assuming a desired reserve ratio of 5 percent, what change in the money-creating potential of the chartered banking system occurred as a result of each transaction?*

4. **KEY QUESTION** *What is the basic determinant of **a** the transactions demand and **b** the asset demand for money? Explain how these two demands might be combined graphically to determine total money demand. How is the equilibrium interest rate determined in the money market? How might **a** the expanded use of credit cards; **b** a shortening of worker pay periods; and **c** an increase in nominal GDP affect the transactions demand for money and the equilibrium interest rate?*

5. Suppose the following data characterize a hypothetical economy: money supply = $200 billion; quantity of money demanded for transactions = $150 billion; quantity of money demanded as an asset = $10 billion at 12 percent interest, increasing by $10 billion for each 2-percentage-point rise in the interest rate.
   a. What is the equilibrium interest rate? Explain.
   b. At the equilibrium interest rate, what are the quantity of money supplied, the total quantity of money demanded, the amount of money demanded for transactions, and the amount of money demanded as an asset?

6. Suppose that a bond has a face value of $10,000 and annually pays a fixed amount of interest of $800. Compute and enter in the space provided either the interest rate that a bond buyer could secure at each of the bond prices listed or the bond price at each of the interest rates shown. State the generalization that can be drawn from the completed table.

Bond price	Interest rate(s)
$ 8,000	_____
_____	8.9
$10,000	_____
$11,000	_____
_____	6.2

7. Assume the money market is initially in equilibrium and that the money supply is now increased. Explain the adjustments towards a new equilibrium interest rate. What effects would you expect this interest rate change to have on the levels of output, employment, and prices? Answer the same questions for a decrease in the money supply.

8. **KEY QUESTION** *Suppose you are the governor of the Bank of Canada. The economy is experiencing a sharp and prolonged inflationary trend. What changes in **a** open-market operations and **b** switching government deposits would you consider? Explain in each case how the change you advocate would affect chartered bank cash reserves and influence the money supply.*

9. **KEY QUESTION** *What is the basic objective of monetary policy? State the cause-effect chain through which monetary policy is made effective. Discuss how **a** the shapes of the demand-for-money and investment-demand curves, and **b** the size of the MPS and MPM influence the effectiveness of monetary policy. How do feedback effects influence the effectiveness of monetary policy?*

10. **KEY QUESTION** *Suppose the Bank of Canada decides to engage in a contractionary monetary policy as a way to close an inflationary gap. Use the aggregate demand-aggregate supply model to show what this policy is intended to accomplish in a closed economy. Now introduce the open economy and explain how changes in the international value of the dollar might affect the location of the aggregate demand curve.*

11. **(The Last Word)** What is the risk to the Canadian economy when the Bank of Canada raises interest rates to defend the Canadian dollar?

12. **WEB-BASED QUESTION** **Principles of Monetary Policy** The Bank of Canada is responsible for monetary policy. Visit its site at www.bank-banque-canada.ca/english/monpol.htm to discover its overriding goal for monetary policy.

13. **WEB-BASED QUESTION** **The Bank of Canada's Monetary Policy Report** The Bank of Canada's Monetary Policy Report www.bank-banque-canada.ca/english/mprsum.htm provides an overview of the performance of the Canadian economy, and the Bank of Canada's monetary policy goals given the economy's performance. What is (are) the current monetary policy goal(s)?

The Long Run and Problems and Controversies in Macroeconomics

Long-Run Macroeconomic Adjustments

MACROECONOMIC THEORY AND STABILIZATION policy as represented in Figure 15-4 has dominated the thinking of most economists in market-oriented industrial economies since the early 1960s, including Canada. Presently, the stabilization policies of nearly all the major industrial nations can be understood through Figure 15-4.

But it would be misleading to suggest there is agreement on all aspects of macroeconomic theory and policy. In particular, there has been new thinking about aggregate supply in the short run and the long run. The result has been renewed debates on whether the economy is "self-correcting" and the desirability and effectiveness of fiscal and monetary policy.

This chapter deals with this new analysis of aggregate supply along with related topics. We apply the *long-run AD-AS model* to demand-pull inflation, cost-push inflation, and recession, gleaning new insights on each. Next, we examine the relationships between inflation and unemployment and look at how expectations can affect the economy. Finally, we state and evaluate the tenets of so-called supply-side economics.

IN THIS CHAPTER YOU WILL LEARN:

That there is a tradeoff between inflation and unemployment in the short run, but not in the long run.

•

To distinguish between adaptive and rational expectation.

•

The tenets of supply-side economists.

The Big Picture

UP TO THIS CHAPTER WE HAVE STRESSED THE short- to medium-term dynamics of the economy. We have stressed the pivotal role aggregate demand plays in achieving and maintaining full employment and price stability. But the pivotal role of aggregate demand in achieving full employment ceases when the economy is at a long-run full-employment GDP. At such a point, further aggregate demand increases (shifts to the right) will only put upward pressure on the price level since all the economy's resources are being utilized.

As you read this chapter, keep the following points in mind:

- **Key Concept 10** is discussed.
- The incorporation of expectations in the macro model has led to the conclusions that some trade-off may exist between inflation and unemployment in the short run, but not in the long run. In particular, in the long run nominal wages are fully responsive to changes in the price level.
- The discussion of the tradeoff between unemployment and inflation (the Phillips curve) is meant to shed light on the evolution of macroeconomic theory with regard to long-run adjustment in the last three decades. ■

APPLYING THE LONG-RUN AD-AS MODEL

The long-run AD-AS model introduced in Chapter 11 helps us better understand the economy and the controversies occasionally swirling around macroeconomics. We will defer discussion of most of these controversies until the next chapter. For now, our intention is simply to apply the long-run AD-AS model to three situations: demand-pull inflation, cost-push inflation, and recession.

Demand-Pull Inflation in the Long-Run AD-AS Model

Recall that *demand-pull inflation* occurs when an increase in aggregate demand pulls up the price level. In our more complex version of aggregate supply, however, an increase in the price level will eventually produce an increase in nominal wages and thus a leftward shift of the short-run aggregate supply curve. This is shown in Figure 16-1, where we initially suppose the price level is P_1 at the intersection of aggregate demand curve AD_1, short-run supply curve AS_1, and long-run aggregate supply curve AS_{LR}. Observe that at point a the economy is achieving its full-employment real output Q_f.

Now consider the effects of an increase in aggregate demand as represented by the right-

ward shift from AD_1 to AD_2. This shift can result from any one of a number of factors, including an increase in investment spending and a rise in net exports. Whatever its cause, the increase in aggre-

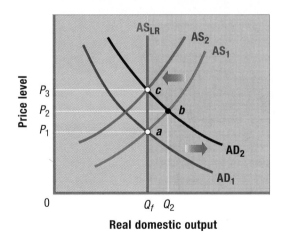

FIGURE 16-1 Demand-pull inflation in the long-run AD-AS model

An increase in aggregate demand from AD_1 to AD_2 drives up the price level and increases real output in the short run. But in the long run, nominal wages rise and the short-run aggregate supply curve shifts leftward, as from AS_1 to AS_2. Real output then returns to its prior level, and the price level rises even more. In this scenario, the economy moves from a to b and then eventually to c.

gate demand boosts the price level from P_1 to P_2 and expands real output from Q_f to Q_2 at point b.

So far, none of this is new to you. But now we want to emphasize the distinction between short-run and long-run aggregate supply. Once workers have realized that their real wages have declined, and when their existing contracts have expired, nominal wages will rise. As they do, the short-run aggregate supply curve will ultimately shift leftward such that it intersects long-run aggregate supply at point c.[1] There, the economy has reestablished long-run equilibrium, with the price level and real output now P_3 and Q_f, respectively. Only at point c does the new aggregate demand curve AD_2 intersect both the short-run aggregate supply curve AS_2 and the long-run aggregate supply curve AS_{LR}.

In the short run, demand-pull inflation drives up the price level and increases real output; in the long run, only the price level rises. In the long run, the initial increase in aggregate demand has moved the economy *along* its vertical aggregate supply curve AS_{LR}. For a while, an economy can operate beyond its full-employment level of output. But the demand-pull inflation eventually causes adjustments of nominal wages that move the economy back to its full-employment output Q_f.

Cost-Push Inflation in the Long-Run AD-AS Model

Cost-push inflation arises from factors that increase the cost of production at each price level—that is, factors that shift the aggregate supply curve leftward—and therefore increase the price level. But in our previous analysis we considered only short-run aggregate supply. We now want to examine cost-push inflation in its long-run context.

Analysis   Look at Figure 16-2, in which we again assume the economy is initially operating at price level P_1 and output level Q_f (point a). Suppose that international oil producers get together and boost the price of oil by, say, 50 percent. What is the effect

---

[1] We say "ultimately" because the initial leftward shift in short-run aggregate supply will intersect the long-run aggregate supply curve AS_{LR} at price level P_2. But the intersection of AD_2 and this new short-run aggregate supply curve (not shown) will produce a price level above P_2. (You may want to pencil this in to make sure that you understand this point.) Again nominal wages will rise, shifting the short-run aggregate supply curve farther leftward. The process will continue until the economy moves to point c, where the short-run aggregate supply curve is AS_2, the price level is P_3, and real output is Q_f.

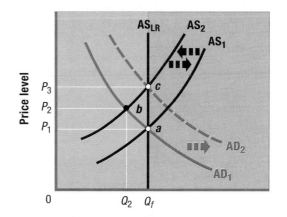

FIGURE 16-2 Cost-push inflation in the long-run AD-AS model

Cost-push inflation occurs when the short-run aggregate supply curve shifts leftward, as from AS_1 to AS_2. If government counters the decline in real output by increasing aggregate demand to the broken line, the price level rises even more. That is, the economy moves in steps from a to b to c. In contrast, if government allows a recession to occur, nominal wages eventually fall and the aggregate supply curve shifts back rightward to its original location. The economy moves from a to b and then eventually back to a.

on the short-run aggregate supply curve of a major oil-consuming economy? The answer is that the hike in the oil price increases the per-unit production cost of producing and transporting goods and services. This shifts the short-run aggregate supply curve to the left, as from AS_1 to AS_2. The price level rises from P_1 to P_2, as seen by comparing points a and b. In this case, the increase in the price of a key resource—namely, oil—shifts the short-run aggregate supply curve to the left. This shift is not a *response* to a price-level increase, as it was in our previous discussions of demand-pull inflation; it is the initiating *cause* of the price-level increase.

Policy Dilemma   Cost-push inflation creates a dilemma for policymakers. Without expansionary stabilization policy, aggregate demand in Figure 16-2 remains at AD_1—the curve does not shift—and real output declines from Q_f to Q_2. Government can counter this recession and the attendant rise in unemployment by using fiscal policy and monetary policy to increase aggregate demand to AD_2. But there is a potential policy trap here: An increase in aggregate demand to AD_2 will further increase inflation by increasing the price level from P_2 to P_3 (a move from point b to c).

Also, the P_2 to P_3 increase in the price level is not likely to be the end of the story because wage earners eventually respond to their decline in real wages by seeking and presumably receiving increases in nominal wages. The higher nominal wages cause another increase in per-unit production costs, which in turn shifts the short-run aggregate supply curve to a position to the left of AS_2. This (not shown) leftward shift of the aggregate supply curve is in *response* to the higher price level P_3, which was caused by the policy-created rightward shift of aggregate demand to AD_2. The new leftward shift of short-run aggregate supply will regenerate recession. In brief, government will have to increase aggregate demand once again to restore the Q_f level of real output. But if it does so, the scenario may simply repeat itself.

Suppose government recognizes this policy trap and decides *not* to increase aggregate demand from AD_1 to AD_2 (so you can now disregard the dashed AD_2 curve). Instead, it implicitly decides to allow a cost-push-created recession to run its course. How will that happen? Widespread layoffs, plant shutdowns, and business failures eventually occur. At some point the demands for oil, labour, and other inputs fall such that oil prices and nominal wages decline. When that happens, the initial leftward shift of the short-run aggregate supply curve is undone. In time the recession will shift the short-run aggregate supply curve rightward from AS_2 to AS_1. The price level will return to P_1, and the full-employment level of output will be restored at Q_f (point a on the long-run aggregate supply curve AS_{LR}).

This analysis yields two generalizations:

1. If government attempts to maintain full employment when there is cost-push inflation, an inflationary spiral may occur.
2. If government takes a hands-off approach to cost-push inflation, a recession will occur. Although the recession eventually may undo the initial rise in per-unit production costs, the economy in the meantime will experience high unemployment and a loss of real output.

Recession and the Long-Run AD-AS Model

By far the most controversial application of the long-run AD-AS model is to recession (or depres-

sion). This controversy will be looked at in some detail in Chapter 17; here we simply want to present the model and identify the key point of contention.

Suppose in Figure 16-3 that aggregate demand initially is AD_1 and that short-run and long-run aggregate supply curves are AS_1 and AS_{LR}, respectively. Therefore, as shown by point a, the price level is P_1 and output is Q_f. Now suppose that investment spending dramatically declines, reducing aggregate demand to AD_2. Real output declines from Q_f to Q_1, meaning a recession has occurred. But if we make the assumption that prices and wages are flexible downward, the price level falls from P_1 to P_2. This lower price level increases *real* wages for people still working since each dollar of nominal wage has greater purchasing power. Eventually, nominal wages themselves fall to restore the previous real wage; when this happens, the short-run aggregate supply curve shifts rightward from AS_1 to AS_2. The recession ends—without expansionary fiscal or monetary policy—since real output expands from Q_1 (point b) back to Q_f (point c). The economy is again located on its long-run aggregate supply curve AS_{LR}, but now at lower price level P_3.

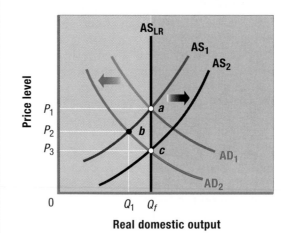

FIGURE 16-3 Recession in the long-run AD-AS model

A recession occurs when aggregate demand shifts leftward, as from AD_1 to AD_2. If prices and wages are downwardly flexible, the price level falls from P_1 to P_2. This decline in the price level reduces nominal wages, which in turn eventually shift the aggregate supply curve from AS_1 to AS_2. The price level declines to P_3, and output increases back to Q_f. The economy moves from a to b and then eventually to c.

There is disagreement about this scenario. The key point of dispute is how long it would take in the real world for the necessary price and wage adjustments to occur to achieve the indicated outcome. For now, suffice it to say that most economists believe that *if* such adjustments are forthcoming, they will only occur after the economy has experienced a long-lasting recession with its accompanying high unemployment and great loss of output. (*Key Question 1*)

16-1
QUICK REVIEW

- In the short run, demand-pull inflation increases both the price level and real output; in the long run, nominal wages rise, the short-run aggregate supply curve shifts to the left, and only the price level increases.

- Cost-push inflation creates a policy dilemma for government: If it engages in an expansionary policy to increase output, an inflationary spiral may occur; if it does nothing, a recession will occur.

- In the short run, a decline in aggregate demand reduces real output (creates a recession); in the long run, prices and nominal wages fall, the short-run aggregate supply curve shifts to the right, and real output returns to its full-employment level.

THE PHILLIPS CURVE

Cost-push inflation and the macroeconomic distinction between the short run and the long run shed light on a relationship called the *Phillips Curve*, named after A. W. Phillips, who developed the idea in Great Britain.

The Basic Idea

To convey the concept of the Phillips Curve, let's look at the short-run aggregate supply curve in Figure 16-4 and perform a simple mental experiment. Suppose that in a specific period aggregate demand expands from AD_0 to AD_2. This shift could result from a change in any one of the determinants of aggregate demand. Businesses may decide to buy more investment goods, or government may decide to increase its expenditures. Whatever the cause of the increase in aggregate

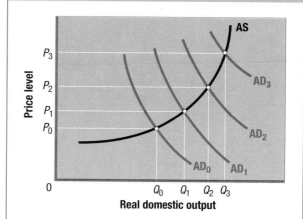

FIGURE 16-4 The effect of changes in aggregate demand on real output and the price level

Comparing the effects of various possible increases in aggregate demand yields the conclusion that the larger the increase in aggregate demand, the higher the rate of inflation and the greater the increase in real output. Because real output and the unemployment rate are inversely related, we can generalize that, given short-run aggregate supply, high rates of inflation should be accompanied by low rates of unemployment.

demand, in the short run the price level rises from P_0 to P_2 and real output expands from Q_0 to Q_2. We know that this increase in real output is accompanied by a decrease in the unemployment rate.

Now let's compare what would have happened if the increase in aggregate demand had been larger, say, from AD_0 to AD_3. The new equilibrium tells us that the amount of inflation and the growth of real output would both have been greater (and that the unemployment rate would have been lower). Similarly, suppose aggregate demand in our specific year had increased only modestly, from AD_0 to AD_1. Compared with our shift from AD_0 to AD_2, the amount of inflation and the growth of real output would have been smaller (and the unemployment rate higher).

The generalization from this mental experiment is this: Assuming a constant short-run aggregate supply curve, high rates of inflation are accompanied by low rates of unemployment, and low rates of inflation are accompanied by high rates of unemployment. Figure 16-5a generalizes how the expected relationship should look.

Do the facts fit the theory? Empirical work by economists in the late 1950s and 1960s verified this inverse relationship for various countries, includ-

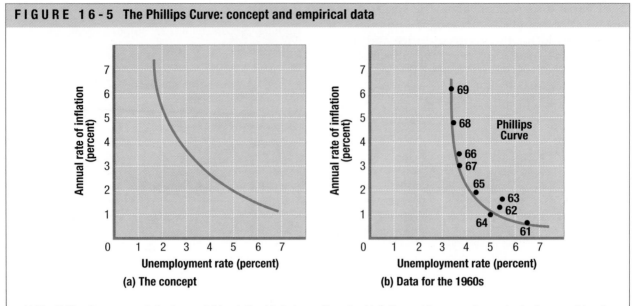

FIGURE 16-5 The Phillips Curve: concept and empirical data

(a) The concept

(b) Data for the 1960s

(a) The Phillips Curve purports to show a stable relationship between the rate of inflation and the unemployment rate. Because this relationship is inverse, there is presumably a tradeoff between unemployment and inflation. (b) Data points for the 1960s seemed to confirm the Phillips Curve concept.

ing Great Britain, the United States, and Canada. As we have noted, it came to be known as the **Phillips Curve**. Figure 16-5b shows the relationship between the unemployment rate and the rate of inflation in Canada for 1961–69.

Tradeoffs

On the basis of the kind of evidence shown in Figure 16-5b, economists came to believe that a stable, predictable tradeoff existed between unemployment and inflation. Moreover, national economic policy was built on this supposed tradeoff. According to this thinking, it was impossible to achieve "full employment without inflation": Manipulation of aggregate demand through fiscal and monetary measures would simply move the economy along the Phillips Curve. An expansionary fiscal and monetary policy that boosts aggregate demand and lowers the unemployment rate would simultaneously cause a higher rate of inflation. A restrictive fiscal and monetary policy could be used to reduce the rate of inflation, but only at the cost of a higher unemployment rate and more forgone production. Society had to choose between incompatible goals of price stability and full employment; it had to decide where to *locate* on its Phillips Curve.

Stagflation: A Shifting Phillips Curve?

The stable Phillips Curve of the 1960s gave way to great instability of the curve in the 1970s and 1980s. Events during those years were clearly at odds with the notion of a stable inflation-unemployment tradeoff. Figure 16-6 enlarges Figure 16-5b by adding data for 1970 through 1997. The obvious inverse relationship of 1961–69 has now become obscure and highly questionable.

Note in Figure 16-6 that in many years of the 1970s the economy experienced increasing inflation and rising unemployment—in a word, **stagflation**—a term combining the words "stagnation" and "inflation." Trace, for example, the data points for 1972–74 and 1977–81. At best, the data in the figure suggest the Phillips Curve shifted to less desirable positions where each level of unemployment is accompanied by more inflation or where each level of inflation is accompanied by more unemployment. At worst, the data imply *no* dependable tradeoff between unemployment and inflation.

Adverse Aggregate Supply Shocks

What caused the stagflation of the 1970s and early 1980s? One answer is that a series of adverse

FIGURE 16-6 Inflation rates and unemployment rates, 1959–1997

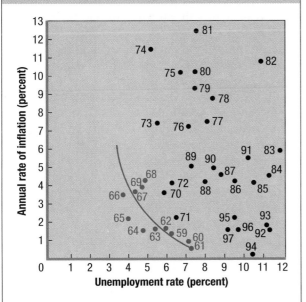

Data points for 1959–1997 suggest no clear relationship between unemployment rates and rates of inflation. This raises questions as to the stability or existence of the Phillips Curve. Some economists think the curve shifted to the right in the 1970s and early 1980s, and then collapsed back inward during the later 1980s.

aggregate supply shocks occurred. Such shocks are rapid and significant increases in resource costs, which jolt an economy's short-run aggregate supply curve leftward. The most significant of these supply shocks was a quadrupling of oil prices by the Organization of Petroleum Exporting Countries (OPEC). The cost of producing and distributing virtually every product and service rose rapidly. (Other factors working to increase Canadian costs during this period included agricultural shortfalls, a greatly depreciated dollar, catch-up of wages held down by earlier wage-price controls, and declining productivity.)

Leftward shifts of the short-run aggregate supply curve make a difference. Remember that we derived the inverse relationship between the rate of inflation and the unemployment rate shown in Figure 16-5a by shifting the aggregate demand curve along a stable short-run aggregate supply curve in Figure 16-4. But review the cost-push inflation model shown in Figure 16-2. There, a leftward shift of the short-run aggregate supply

curve causes the price level to rise and the level of output to fall (unemployment to rise). This, say most economists, is what happened in two periods in the 1970s. The Canadian unemployment rate shot up from 5.3 percent in 1974 to 8.1 percent in 1977. In the same period, the Canadian price level rose by 28 percent. The stagflation scenario recurred in 1978, when OPEC increased oil prices by more than 100 percent. The Canadian price level increased by 50 percent over the 1978–82 period, while unemployment increased from 8.4 to 11.0 percent.

The "Great Stagflation" of the 1970s and early 1980s made it clear that the Phillips Curve did not represent a stable inflation-unemployment relationship. Declines in short-run aggregate supply were at work, which explain those occasions when the inflation rate and the unemployment rate increased simultaneously. To most economists, the experience of the 1970s and early 1980s suggests that the Phillips Curve was shifting to the right and confronting the economy with higher rates of inflation and unemployment.

Stagflation's Demise

Another look at Figure 16-6 reveals a generally inward movement of the inflation-unemployment points between 1983 and 1989. By 1989 the lingering effects of the early period had subsided. One precursor to this favourable trend was the deep recession of 1981–83, largely caused by a tight money policy aimed at reducing double-digit inflation. The recession upped the unemployment rate to 11.9 percent in 1983. With so many workers unemployed, those who were working accepted smaller increases in their nominal wages—or in some cases wage reductions—to preserve their jobs. Firms, in turn, restrained their price increases to try to retain their relative shares of a greatly diminished market.

Other factors were also at work. Foreign competition throughout this period held down wage and price hikes in several basic industries such as automobile and steel. Deregulation of the airline and trucking industries also resulted in wage reductions or so-called wage givebacks. A significant decline in OPEC's monopoly power produced a stunning fall in the price of oil and its derivative products, such as gasoline.

All these factors combined to reduce per-unit production costs and to shift the short-run aggre-

16-1

GLOBAL PERSPECTIVE

The misery index, selected nations, 1987–1997

The so-called misery index adds together a nation's unemployment rate and its inflation rate to get a measure of national economic discomfort. For example, a nation with a 5 percent rate of unemployment and 5 percent inflation rate would have a misery index number of 10, as would a nation with an 8 percent unemployment rate and 2 percent inflation.

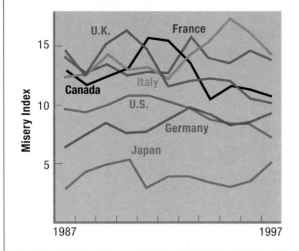

Source: *Economic Report of the President*, 1998.

gate supply curve rightward (as from AS$_2$ to AS$_1$ in Figure 16-2). Employment and output expanded and the unemployment rate fell from 11 percent in 1983 to 7.5 percent in 1989. Figure 16-6 reveals that the inflation-unemployment points for recent years are concentrated in the lower right quadrant, with low inflation accompanied by relatively high unemployment.

NATURAL-RATE HYPOTHESIS

The standard explanation for the scattering of inflation rate-unemployment points to the right of the 1960s Phillips Curve is that a series of supply shocks shifted the short-run aggregate supply curve leftward, moving the Phillips Curve right-ward and upward as in Figure 16-6. The inward movement of inflation rate-unemployment points in the 1980s was caused by rightward shifts of short-run aggregate supply curves. In this view, there is still a tradeoff between the inflation rate and the unemployment rate, but changes in short-run aggregate supply may alter the menu of inflation and unemployment choices—that is, shift the Phillips Curve itself—during abnormal periods.

A second explanation of simultaneously higher rates of unemployment and inflation, the **natural-rate hypothesis**, questions the very existence of an inverse relationship between the rate of inflation and the rate of unemployment. This view is that the economy is generally stable at its natural rate of unemployment (or full-employment rate of output). We know from Chapter 8 that the natural rate of unemployment is the rate of unemployment existing when cyclical unemployment is zero; it is the full-employment rate of unemployment.

According to the natural-rate hypothesis, the incorrect assumption of a stable Phillips Curve resulted in misguided attempts by government to push the unemployment rate below the economy's natural rate. The end result was accelerating inflation. The natural-rate hypothesis has its empirical roots in Figure 16-6, where you can argue that a vertical line located at a presumed 6 percent natural rate of unemployment for the full period represents the inflation-unemployment "relationship" better than the traditional down-sloping Phillips Curve. In the natural-rate hypothesis, any rate of inflation is compatible with the economy's natural rate of unemployment.

There are two variations of this natural-rate perspective: the adaptive expectations theory and the rational expectations theory.

Adaptive Expectations Theory

The **adaptive expectations theory** assumes people form their expectations of future inflation on the basis of previous and present rates of inflation and only gradually change their expectations as experience unfolds.

In this theory, there is a short-run tradeoff between inflation and unemployment but not a long-run tradeoff. Any attempt to reduce the unemployment rate below the natural rate sets in motion forces that destabilize the Phillips Curve and shift it rightward. Thus, the adaptive expectations view distinguishes between a "short-run" and "long-run" Phillips Curve.

Short-Run Phillips Curve

Consider Phillips Curve PC_1 in Figure 16-7. Suppose the economy initially is experiencing a 3 percent rate of inflation and a 6 percent natural rate of unemployment. In the adaptive expectations theory, such short-term curves as PC_1, PC_2, and PC_3 (drawn as straight lines for simplicity) exist because the actual rate of inflation is not always the same as the expected rate.

Establishing an additional point on Phillips Curve PC_1 will clarify this for you. We begin at a_1, where we assume nominal wages are set on the assumption that the 3 percent rate of inflation will

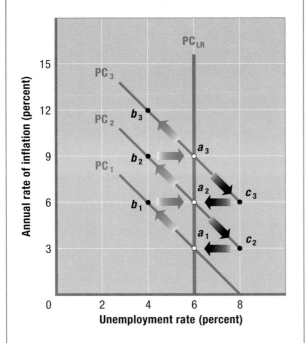

FIGURE 16-7 The adaptive expectations theory

Expansionary monetary policy and fiscal policy may temporarily boost profits, output, and employment (as from a_1 to b_1). But nominal wages will soon rise, reducing profits and thereby negating the short-run stimulus to production and employment (the economy moves from b_1 to a_2). Consequently, there is no tradeoff between the rates of inflation and unemployment in the long run; that is, the long-run Phillips Curve is vertical.

continue. But suppose government mistakenly judges the full-employment unemployment rate to be 4 percent instead of 6 percent. This misjudgement might occur because the economy achieved a 4 percent rate of unemployment in some earlier, inflationary period. To achieve the targeted 4 percent rate of unemployment, government undertakes expansionary fiscal and monetary policies.

The increase in aggregate demand that results causes the rate of inflation to rise to 6 percent. With a specific level of nominal wages set on the expectation that the 3 percent rate of inflation will continue, the higher product prices raise business profits. Firms respond to these expanded profits by hiring more workers and increasing output. In the short run, the economy moves to b_1, which, in contrast to a_1, involves a lower rate of unemployment (4 percent) and higher rate of inflation (6 percent). The movement from a_1 to b_1 is consistent both with an upsloping aggregate supply curve and with our previous interpretation of the Phillips Curve. Presumably, the economy has accepted some additional inflation as the "cost" of achieving a reduced level of unemployment. But the natural-rate theory interprets the movement from a_1 to b_1 differently. In this view, it is simply a manifestation of the following principle: *When the actual rate of inflation is higher than expected, profits temporarily rise and the unemployment rate temporarily falls.*

Long-Run Vertical Phillips Curve

Point b_1 is not a stable equilibrium position in this theory. Workers will recognize their nominal wages have not increased as fast as inflation and will therefore obtain nominal wage increases to restore their lost purchasing power. But as nominal wages rise to restore the level of real wages that existed at a_1, business profits will fall to their earlier level. The reduction in profits means the original motivation to employ more workers and increase output has disappeared.

Unemployment then returns to its natural level at point a_2. Note, however, that the economy now faces a higher actual *and* expected rate of inflation—6 percent rather than 3 percent. The higher level of aggregate demand that originally moved the economy from a_1 to b_1 still exists, so the inflation it created still persists.

In view of the higher 6 percent expected rate of inflation, the short-run Phillips Curve shifts upward from PC$_1$ to PC$_2$ in Figure 16-7. An "along-the-Phillips-Curve" kind of movement from a_1 to b_1 on PC$_1$ is merely a short-run or transient occurrence. In the long run, after nominal wages catch up with price-level increases, unemployment returns to the natural rate at a_2, and there is a new short-run Phillips Curve PC$_2$ at the higher expected rate of inflation.

The process may now be repeated. Government may reason that certain extraneous events like oil price increases have frustrated its expansionary policies and it will try again. Fiscal policy and monetary policy are then used to increase aggregate demand, and the scenario repeats. Prices rise momentarily ahead of nominal wages, profits expand, and employment and output increase (as implied by the move from a_2 to b_2). But, in time, nominal wages increase so as to restore real wages. Profits then fall to their original level, pushing employment back to the normal rate at a_3. Government's "reward" for forcing the actual rate of unemployment below the natural rate is the perverse one of a still higher (9 percent) rate of inflation.

If we conceive of a_1b_1, a_2b_2, and a_3b_3 as a series of short-run Phillips Curves, the adaptive expectations theory says that government attempts to move the economy along the short-run Phillips curve (a_1 to b_1 on PC$_1$) *cause* the curve to shift to a less favourable position (PC$_2$, then PC$_3$, and so on). A stable Phillips Curve with the dependable series of unemployment rate-inflation rate tradeoffs does not exist in the long run.

The vertical line through a_1, a_2, and a_3 shows the *long-run relationship* between unemployment and inflation. Any rate of inflation is consistent with the 6 percent natural rate of unemployment. So society ought to choose a low rate of inflation rather than a high one.

Disinflation   We can also employ the adaptive expectations theory to explain **disinflation**—reductions in the rate of inflation. Suppose that in Figure 16-7 the economy is at a_3, where the inflation rate is 9 percent. Next assume that a decline in aggregate demand such as that occurring in the 1981–82 recession reduces inflation below the 9 percent expected rate, say, to 6 percent. Business profits fall because product prices are rising less rapidly than wages. The nominal wage increases, remember, were set on the assumption that the 9 percent rate of inflation would continue. In

response to the profit decline, firms reduce their employment and consequently the unemployment rate rises. The economy temporarily slides downward from point a_3 to c_3 along the short-run Phillips Curve PC$_3$. In the natural-rate theory, *when the actual rate of inflation is lower than the expected rate, profits temporarily fall and the unemployment rate temporarily rises.*

Firms and workers eventually adjust their expectations to the new 6 percent rate of inflation, and thus newly negotiated wage increases decline. Profits are restored, employment rises, and the unemployment rate returns to its natural rate of 6 percent at a_2. Because the expected rate of inflation is now 6 percent, the short-run Phillips Curve PC$_3$ shifts leftward to PC$_2$.

If aggregate demand falls farther, the scenario will continue. Inflation declines from 6 percent to, say, 3 percent, moving the economy from a_2 to c_2 along PC$_2$. The lower-than-expected rate of inflation (lower prices) squeezes profits and reduces employment. But, in the long run, firms respond to the lower profits by reducing their nominal wage increases. Profits are restored and unemployment returns to its natural rate at a_1 as the short-run Phillips Curve moves from PC$_2$ to PC$_1$. Once again, the long-run Phillips Curve is vertical at the natural rate of unemployment.

Rational Expectations Theory

The adaptive expectations theory assumes that increases in nominal wages lag behind increases in the price level because the increases in the price level are not anticipated. This lag gives rise to *temporary* increases in profits that *temporarily* stimulate employment.

The **rational expectations theory** is the second version of the natural-rate hypothesis. It contends that businesses, consumers, and workers understand how government policies will affect the economy and *anticipate* the impacts in their own decision making.

Suppose, when government undertakes expansionary policies, workers anticipate that the result will be higher inflation and thus a decline in their real wages. They thus immediately incorporate this expected inflation into their nominal wage demands. If workers correctly and fully anticipate the amount of inflation and adjust their current nominal wage demands accordingly, then even the temporary increases in profit, output, and employment will *not* occur. Instead of the temporary decline in unemployment from a_1 to b_1 in Figure 16-7, the movement is directly from a_1 to a_2. Fully anticipated inflation by labour means that the price level and nominal wages rise simultaneously and by the same percent. Inflation, fully anticipated in the nominal wage demands of workers, therefore generates a vertical "Phillips Curve" through a_1, a_2, and a_3.

The policy implication is this: Fiscal and monetary policy designed to push unemployment below its natural rate will quickly (if not instantaneously) increase the rate of inflation, not reduce unemployment. Note that the adaptive and rational expectations theories are consistent with the conservative philosophy that government's attempts to do good deeds typically fail, and at a considerable cost to society. In this instance the "cost" is accelerating inflation. *(Key Question 3)*

Changing Interpretations

Interpretations of the Phillips Curve have changed dramatically over the past three decades. The original idea of a stable tradeoff between inflation and unemployment has given way to the adaptive expectations view that while there is a short-run tradeoff, there is no such tradeoff in the long run. The much more controversial rational expectations theory stresses that macroeconomic policy is completely ineffective when its outcomes are fully anticipated by workers and other participants in the economy. Not even a short-run tradeoff between inflation and unemployment exists. This conclusion is clearly contrary to the idea of the original Phillips Curve.

Which perspective is correct? Does an inverse relationship exist between the inflation rate and unemployment rate as the original Phillips Curve implies? Or is there no long-run tradeoff as the natural-rate theory contends? Perhaps the safest answer is that most economists accept the idea of a short-run tradeoff—where the short run may last several years—while now recognizing that in the long run such a tradeoff is much less likely. Also, most economists agree that adverse aggregate supply shocks, such as those of the 1970s, can cause periods of rising unemployment rates and rising inflation, particularly when government undertakes policies to limit the rise in the unemployment rate. That is, most economists contend that the episodes of stagflation during the 1970s

and early 1980s were *not* exclusively the results of misguided government stabilization policies, as some natural-rate theorists suggest.

16-2

QUICK REVIEW

- The original Phillips Curve for the 1960s showed an apparent stable, inverse relationship between annual inflation rates and unemployment rates over a period of years.

- Stagflation occurred from 1973 to 1975 and 1978 to 1982, producing Phillips Curve data points above and to the right of the Phillips Curve for the 1960s.

- The central cause of the stagflation in the 1970s and early 1980s was a series of large increases in oil prices that reduced short-run aggregate supply.

- In the natural-rate theory, the economy automatically gravitates to its natural rate of unemployment; therefore, the Phillips Curve is vertical at that rate in the long run.

SUPPLY-SIDE ECONOMICS

Our final aggregate supply topic is **supply-side economics**. "Supply-siders" contend that changes in aggregate supply must be recognized as active forces in determining the levels of both inflation and unemployment. Economic disturbances can be generated on the supply side, as well as on the demand side, of the economy. Moreover, certain government policies allegedly have reduced the growth of aggregate supply over time. By reversing these policies, say the supply-siders, the Canadian economy can achieve low levels of unemployment without producing rapid inflation.

Tax-Transfer Disincentives

Supply-side economists argue that the spectacular growth of the Canadian tax-transfer system has negatively affected incentives to work, invest, innovate, and assume entrepreneurial risks. The tax-transfer system allegedly has eroded the economy's productivity, and this decline in efficiency has slowed the expansion of long-run aggregate supply. The argument is that high taxes reduce the after-tax rewards of workers and producers, making work, innovation, investing, and risk bearing less financially attractive. According to supply-side economists, *marginal tax rates* are most relevant to decisions to undertake *additional* work and *additional* saving and investing.

Taxes and Incentives to Work

Supply-siders believe that how long and how hard individuals work depends on how much additional *after-tax* earnings they derive from work. To induce more work—to increase aggregate inputs of labour—government should reduce marginal tax rates on earned incomes. Lower marginal tax rates make work more attractive by increasing the opportunity cost of leisure. Thus, individuals choose to substitute work for leisure. This increase in productive effort can occur in many ways: by increasing the number of hours worked per day or week, by encouraging workers to postpone retirement, by inducing more people to enter the labour force, by making people willing to work harder, and by discouraging long periods of unemployment.

Transfer Disincentives

Supply-side economists also believe the existence of a wide variety of public transfer programs has eroded incentives to work. Employment insurance and welfare programs have made job loss less of an economic crisis for some people. The fear of being unemployed, and therefore the need to be a disciplined, productive worker, is simply less acute than it once was. Many transfer programs are structured to discourage work. Our social insurance program and welfare system encourage recipients *not* to be productive by imposing a "tax" in the form of a loss of transfer benefits on those who work. Only very recently have changes in eligibility and time limits been introduced to these programs to provide incentives to return to work.

Incentives to Save and Invest

The rewards for saving and investing have also been reduced by high marginal tax rates. Assume you save $1,000 at 10 percent, so you earn $100 interest per year. If your marginal tax rate is 40 percent, your after-tax-interest earnings will be $60 and the after-tax interest rate you receive is only 6 percent. While you might be willing to save (forgo current consumption) for a 10 percent return on your saving,

you might prefer to consume when the return is only 6 percent.

Saving, remember, is the prerequisite of investment. Thus supply-side economists recommend lower marginal tax rates on saving. They also call for lower taxes on investment income to ensure there are ready investment outlets for the economy's enhanced pool of saving. A critical determinant of investment spending is the expected *after-tax* return of that spending.

To summarize: Lower marginal tax rates encourage saving and investing. Workers therefore find themselves equipped with more and technologically superior machinery and equipment. Labour productivity rises, and this expands aggregate supply, which in turn keeps unemployment rates and inflation low.

Laffer Curve

In the supply-side view, reductions in marginal tax rates increase the nation's aggregate supply. Moreover, according to supply-side economist Arthur Laffer, lower tax *rates* are compatible with constant or even enlarged tax *revenues*. Thus, supply-side tax cuts need not produce federal budget deficits.

This idea is based on the **Laffer Curve**, which, as shown in Figure 16-8, depicts the relationship between tax rates and tax revenues. As tax rates

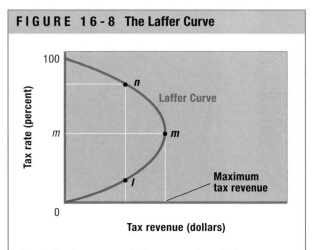

FIGURE 16-8 The Laffer Curve

The Laffer Curve suggests that up to point *m* higher tax rates will result in larger tax revenues. But still higher tax rates will adversely affect incentives to work and produce, reducing the size of the tax base (output and income) to the extent that tax revenues will decline. It follows that if tax rates are above *m*, reductions in tax rates may produce increases in tax revenues.

increase from 0 to 100 percent, tax revenues increase from zero to some maximum level (at *m*) and then decline to zero. Tax revenues decline beyond some point because higher tax rates discourage economic activity, diminishing the tax base (domestic output and income). This is easiest to see at the extreme, where tax rates are 100 percent. Tax revenues here are, in theory, reduced to zero because the 100 percent confiscatory tax rate has halted production. A 100 percent tax rate applied to a tax base of zero yields no revenue.

In the early 1980s, Laffer suggested that at a point such as *n* on the curve in Figure 16-8, tax rates are so high that production is discouraged to the extent that tax revenues are below the maximum at *m*. If the economy is at *n*, then lower tax rates are quite compatible with constant tax revenues. Lowering tax rates moves the economy from point *n* to point *l*, and government brings in the same total amount of tax revenue as before. Laffer's reasoning is that lower tax rates stimulate incentives to work, save and invest, innovate, and accept business risks, thus triggering an expansion of real output and income. This enlarged tax base sustains tax revenues even though tax rates are lowered. Indeed, between *n* and *m*, lower tax rates result in increased tax revenue.

Supply-side economists think tax rates can be lowered without producing budget deficits for two additional reasons:

1. **LESS TAX EVASION** Tax avoidance (which is legal) and tax evasion (which is not) decline when taxes are reduced. High marginal tax rates prompt taxpayers to avoid taxes through various tax shelters. They also encourage some taxpayers to conceal income from Revenue Canada. Lower tax rates reduce the inclination to engage in tax avoidance and tax evasion.
2. **REDUCED TRANSFERS** The stimulus to production and employment that a tax cut provides reduces government transfer payments. For example, having more job opportunities reduces transfer payments and decreases a budget deficit. *(Key Question 5)*

Criticisms of the Laffer Curve

The Laffer Curve and its supply-side implications have been subject to severe criticism.

Taxes, Incentives, and Time A fundamental criticism has to do with the sensitivity of economic incentives to changes in tax rates. Skeptics say there is ample empirical evidence showing that the impact of a tax cut on incentives is small, of uncertain direction, and relatively slow to emerge. For example, with respect to work incentives, studies indicate that decreases in tax rates lead some people to work more but others to work less. Those who work more are enticed by the higher after-tax pay; they substitute work for leisure because the opportunity cost of leisure has increased. Those who work less do so because the higher after-tax pay increases their ability to "buy leisure." They can meet their after-tax income goals by working fewer hours.

Reinforcing Inflation Most economists think that the demand-side effects of a tax cut exceed the supply-side effects. Thus, tax cuts undertaken when the economy is at or near its full-employment level of output may produce increases in aggregate demand that overwhelm any increase in aggregate supply. Demand-pull inflation is the likely result.

Position on the Curve Skeptics say the Laffer Curve is merely a logical proposition, asserting that there must be some level of tax rates between 0 and 100 percent at which tax revenues will be at their maximum. Economists of all persuasions can agree with this. But the issue of where a particular economy is located on its Laffer Curve is an empirical question. If we assume—as Laffer did in the early 1980s—that we are at point *n* in Figure 16-8, then tax cuts will increase tax revenues. But critics say that the economy's location on the Laffer Curve is undocumented and unknown. If the economy is at any point below *m* on the curve, then tax *reductions* will reduce tax revenues and create budget deficits.

Overregulation Supply-siders also claim that government's regulatory involvement in the economy has adversely affected productivity and long-run aggregate supply. Two points should be noted here:

1. "Industrial regulation"—government regulation of specific industries such as transportation or communications—frequently provides regulated firms with a legal monopoly or cartel. Government regulation protects such firms from competition, the result being that

these firms are less efficient and incur higher costs of production.

2. The "social regulation" of industry has increased substantially in the past decades. New government regulations have been imposed on industry in response to problems of pollution, product safety, worker health and safety, and equal access to job opportunities. Supply-side economists point out that social regulation has greatly increased the costs of doing business. The overall impact of both types of regulation is that costs and prices are higher and economic growth is slower.

16-3
QUICK REVIEW

- Supply-side economists say that the tax-transfer system reduces work effort, saving and investing, innovation, and risk bearing.

- The Laffer Curve suggests that when tax rates are higher than optimal from a revenue standpoint, reductions in tax rates can expand real output and income (the tax base) and simultaneously increase tax revenue.

In The Media

Turkey Can't Kick Addiction to Inflation

Economy's 'most disruptive force' hurts business, politics, equality

By Hugh Pope
The Wall Street Journal

ANKARA, TURKEY—Inflation is rising toward an annual 100 per cent. Another Turkish treasury chief has resigned in apparent disgust. The government is wobbling, and a botched austerity program lies in pieces ahead of key meetings next week with the International Monetary Fund.

If inflation were to go up to 500 per cent, outgoing undersecretary of the treasury, Mahfi Egilmez, told a Turkish magazine before he quit last week, "another kind of regime will tackle the problem."

In today's Turkey, beset by militarists, separatists and fundamentalists, alternative regimes range from early parliamentary elections to a full takeover by the armed forces. But whatever the political outcome, the latest resignation shows there is still no solution to what Turkey's bureau-

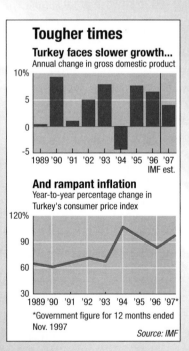

Tougher times

Turkey faces slower growth...
Annual change in gross domestic product

1989 '90 '91 '92 '93 '94 '95 '96 '97
IMF est.

And rampant inflation
Year-to-year percentage change in Turkey's consumer price index

1989 '90 '91 '92 '93 '94 '95 '96 '97*

*Government figure for 12 months ended Nov. 1997

Source: IMF

cratic elite now says is the country's No. 1 problem: a national addiction to inflation.

"I've never seen such a degree of policy disarray," says analyst Mina Toksoz of London-based Caspian Securities. "They had a chance to fight inflation. Now they are probably going to do very little about it."

A new study by Turkey's central bank says inflation robbed Turks of 30 per cent of their real purchasing power over the past five years, shrank corporate profits, caused unemployment and placed an unfair tax on the poor and middle classes. Central bank governor Gazi Ercel calls it "the most disruptive force in the economy."

Despite this, Turkey remains the biggest and most dynamic commercial power between southeastern Europe and the Middle East. International bankers are lining up to arrange big loans, arguing that Turkey is used to inflation and is immune to the spread of the financial turmoil plaguing Southeast Asia.

Some bankers say Turkey's lax approach to state finances could end in disaster. The costs of inflation are rising. The rate was 95.8 per cent in the year to November, and the state is now servicing its debts at compound interest rates that hit 123 per cent on Tuesday. It now has virtually no money left for new investment and is short-changing government functions.

The Turkish treasury, the central bank, and the ministry of finance have produced a three-year plan and a 1998 budget that aims to bring inflation down to 50 per cent next year, 15 per cent in 1999 and 3 per cent in 2000. A plausible plan was developed to broaden and improve tax collection.

But hopes of reform have been dashed by politicians' fear that austerity loses elections. Prime Minister Mesut Yilmaz announced a six-month state-sector price freeze, then back-tracked. There have been flip-flops by the minister in charge of the economy, Gunes Taner, on whether the plan should last one or three years.

Source: *Globe and Mail*, December 11, 1997, B6. Reprinted by permission by the *Wall Street Journal* © 1997, Dow Jones & Company, Inc.

THE STORY IN BRIEF

At the end of 1997, inflation in Turkey was approaching 100 percent per annum.

THE ECONOMICS BEHIND THE STORY

- As the inflation rate approaches 100 percent per year, Turkey faces a short-term dilemma. If the central bank were to slow down the expansion of the money supply, inflation would certainly ease, but economic growth would also slow. Such a situation is always unappealing to politicians who have to be re-elected.
- Inflation is primarily a monetary phenomenon. If the central bank slowed monetary growth, inflation would also slow. But in the short term, real interest rates would be driven up, slowing the economy via lower investment spending, which would then spread to consumption spending. Higher interest rates would appreciate the currency, possibly leading to lower net exports. Thus, Turkey could suffer a recession before inflation slowed.
- How do expectations about inflation lead to possibly even higher inflation? Would the central bank need to accommodate the rising price level? ∎

The Last Word

PRICE AND WAGE CONTROLS

If inflation is a problem for a society, why not simply outlaw inflationary price and wage increases? That is, why not enact price and wage controls?

DURING INFLATIONARY TIMES, IT IS NATURAL for people to look for culprits. Who exactly is causing prices and wages to rise and how can government alter their actions? Casual observation leads many to conclude that firms are the *cause* of rising prices and unions are the *cause* of rising wages. After all, firms and unions are the ones directly announcing price increases and negotiating wage increases.

If firms and unions are viewed as the causes of inflation, then one solution is to limit price and wage increases by law so that inflation would be held to, say, 2 percent annually. Such kinds of *price and wage controls* have a long history. For example, the Roman emperor Diocletian attempted them in 301. So did the Mongol, Kublai Khan, in the thirteenth century; the city leaders of Antwerp in 1584; the United States in 1971;

Canada in 1975; and several South American countries in the 1980s. In each case, inflation eventually won and controls lost. The reasons why are as follows:

1. Controls for Symptoms, Not Causes.   In most circumstances, increases in prices and wages are the *symptoms*, not the underlying *cause*, of inflation. Inflation is caused by excessive growth of the money supply, excessive investment spending, inappropriate fiscal policy, or oil price "shocks." Wage and price controls leave the root cause of inflation untreated.

2. Circumvention and Compliance Problems. Wage and price controls have the force of law; therefore, government can use fines and imprisonment to coerce labour and management to obey them. Nevertheless, enforcement and compliance problems can be severe. Because the controls produce below-equilibrium prices and wages, they also produce shortages of products and workers. *Black markets*—illegal markets in which prices and wages exceed legal maximums— become common. Buyers willing to pay more than the controlled price seek out sellers willing to sell the product for more than the controlled price. Thus, price increases show up "off the books."

Businesses and workers also respond in other ways to circumvent controls. For example, firms can reduce product quality instead of raising product price. If the price of a candy bar is frozen at 60 cents, reducing its size by one-half can effectively double its price. Workers can sidestep wage controls by moving to newly created job classifications that firms set up to circumvent the wage controls. The firm, in a sense, converts *illegal* wage increases into *legal* promotions.

3. Inability to Maintain Long-Term Public Support. The same public that called for wage and price controls often turns against them once it realizes their impacts. Wage and price controls interfere with accepted, well-established rights and expectations. They interfere with the right of workers to freely bargain for wages with employers through union representation. They interfere with the right of firms to freely set prices and adjust them rapidly to changing supply and demand circumstances. And the shortages they create do not fit with consumer expectations of products being available in shops and stores. As a result, the public often quickly tires of wage and price controls.

4. Allocative Inefficiency and Rationing.   Where effective, wage and price controls prohibit the market system from making necessary price and wage adjustments. If the demand for one product, say, retirement housing, should rise sharply (independent of inflation), its price could not rise to signal society's wish for more of this output and therefore more resources to produce it. The same problem occurs in the labour market. A large increase in the demand for, say, software designers could not produce the salary increase needed to attract workers from other occupations. Nor would there be proper incentives for college and university students to take up this field of study.

Also, price controls strip the market mechanism of the rationing function—its ability to equate quantity demanded and quantity supplied. Which buyers are to obtain the product when there are shortages? The product can be rationed on a first-come, first-served basis or by favouritism. But both are highly arbitrary and inequitable; those first in line or those able to cultivate a friendship with the seller get as much of the product as they want, while others get none at all. Government may therefore decide to impartially ration the product to all consumers by issuing ration coupons to prospective buyers on a fair basis. But this means adding another costly government bureaucracy to that already required to police compliance with the controls.

In view of the distortions caused by price and wage controls and their overall poor results, most contemporary economists reject this approach to trying to reduce inflation. ■

CHAPTER SUMMARY

1. In the short run, demand-pull inflation increases the price level and real output. Once nominal wages have increased, the temporary increase in real output is reversed.

2. In the short run, cost-push inflation increases the price level *and* reduces real output. Unless government expands aggregate demand, nominal wages eventually will decline under conditions of recession and the short-run aggregate supply curve will shift back to its initial location. Prices and real output will eventually return to their original levels.

3. If prices and wages are flexible downward, a decline in aggregate demand will reduce output *and* the price level. The decline in the price level will eventually reduce nominal wages and shift the short-run aggregate supply curve rightward. Full-employment output will thus be restored.

4. Assuming a stable upsloping aggregate supply curve, rightward shifts of the aggregate demand curve of various sizes yield the generalization that high rates of inflation are associated with low rates of unemployment, and vice versa. This inverse relationship is known as the Phillips Curve, and empirical data for the 1960s seemed to be consistent with it.

5. In the 1970s and early 1980s, the Phillips Curve apparently shifted rightward, reflecting stagflation—simultaneously rising inflation rates and unemployment rates. The standard interpretation is that the stagflation mainly resulted from huge oil price increases that caused large leftward shifts in the short-run aggregate supply curve (so-called supply shocks). The Phillips Curve shifted inward towards its original position in the 1980s. By 1989 stagflation had subsided.

6. The adaptive expectations version of the natural-rate hypothesis says that while there is a short-run tradeoff between inflation and unemployment, there is no such long-run tradeoff. Workers will adapt their expectations to new inflation realities, and when they do, the unemployment rate will return to the natural rate. The long-run Phillips Curve is therefore vertical at the natural rate, meaning that higher rates of inflation do not "buy" the economy less unemployment.

7. The rational expectations version of the natural-rate hypothesis contends that workers will anticipate the inflationary effects of monetary policy and fiscal policy and will build these expectations into their wage demands. As a result, not even a short-run Phillips Curve will exist; the economy will simply move along its vertical long-run Phillips Curve when the government undertakes expansionary policies.

8. Supply-side economists trace slow economic growth to expansion of government and, specifically, to the negative effects of the tax-transfer system on incentives. They say that excessive government regulation of business has contributed to slow growth. The Laffer Curve relates tax rates to levels of tax revenue and suggests that, under some circumstances, cuts in tax rates can expand the tax base (output and income) and increase tax revenues.

TERMS AND CONCEPTS

Phillips Curve
stagflation
aggregate supply shocks
natural-rate hypothesis
adaptive expectations theory

disinflation
rational expectations theory
supply-side economics
Laffer Curve

STUDY QUESTIONS

1. **KEY QUESTION** *Use graphical analysis to show how each of the following would affect the economy first in the short run and then in the long run. Assume that Canada is initially operating at its full-employment level of output, that prices and wages are eventually flexible both upward and downward, and that there is no counteracting fiscal or monetary policy.*
   a. *Because of a war abroad, the oil supply to Canada is disrupted, sending oil prices rocketing upward.*
   b. *Construction spending on new homes rises dramatically, greatly increasing total Canadian investment spending.*
   c. *Economic recession occurs abroad, significantly reducing foreign purchases of Canadian exports.*

2. Assume that a particular short-run aggregate supply curve exists for an economy and that the curve is relevant for several years. Use the AD-AS analysis to show graphically why higher rates of inflation over this period would be associated with lower rates of unemployment, and vice versa. What is this inverse relationship called?

3. **KEY QUESTION** *Distinguish between adaptive expectations and rational expectations. Why are adaptive expectations consistent with a short-run Phillips Curve while rational expectations are not? Explain why both types of expectations result in a vertical long-run Phillips Curve.*

4. Explain: "If expectations are rational and fully correct, the unemployment rate will never diverge from the natural rate."

5. **KEY QUESTION** *What are the two broad tenets of supply-side economics? What is the Laffer Curve, and how does it relate to one of these tenets?*

6. Why might one person work more, earn more, and pay more income tax when his or her tax rate is cut, while another person will work less, earn less, and pay less income tax under the same circumstance?

7. **(The Last Word)** Relate this statement to price and wage controls: "Controlling prices to halt inflation is like breaking a thermometer to control the heat."

8. **WEB-BASED QUESTION** **The Phillips Curve—Do Real Data Confirm?** The Phillips Curve purports to show a stable relationship between the rate of inflation and the unemployment rate. Plot the data points between inflation and unemployment over the past five years. For inflation data, use the Consumer Price Index (all items), which can be retrieved from www.statcan.ca/english/Pgdb/Economy/Economic/econ09a.htm. For unemployment data, click on www.statcan.ca/english/Pgdb/Economy/Economic/econ10.htm. Do any of your data point plots confirm the Phillips Curve concept?

Disputes in Macro Theory and Policy

ONE OF THE GREAT TRADITIONS IN SCHOLARSHIP is the challenging of mainstream thinking. Many such challenges to the "conventional wisdom" fail; either the new theories are not logical or they do not conform to facts. At the opposite extreme, some new theories gain full support and replace the existing theories. More often, the new ideas modify the existing body of mainstream thinking, which thereafter is improved or extended. This certainly is true in economics.

As any academic discipline evolves, it draws criticism and disagreement. In this chapter we examine some of the major disputes in macro theory and policy. We initially provide historical background by contrasting classical and Keynesian macroeconomic theories. Then we turn to contemporary disagreements on three interrelated questions: (1) What causes instability in the economy? (2) Is the economy self-correcting? (3) Should government adhere to *rules* or use *discretion* in setting economic policy? Finally, we summarize the alternative perspectives discussed in this chapter and the previous chapter.

IN THIS CHAPTER YOU WILL LEARN:

The main difference between classical and Keynesian theories of the causes of macroeconomic instability.

•

The various current explanations of the causes of macroeconomic instability.

•

About the debate of whether the economy has self-correcting powers.

•

About different policy recommendations stemming from different views about the causes of macroeconomic instability.

The Big Picture

WHILE IN MANY AREAS OF MACROECONOMICS something resembling a consensus has emerged in the last 25 years, many disagreements remain. This chapter serves two purposes. The first is to look at the evolution of macroeconomics; the second, to make you aware of the main controversies that still rage and those that have been at least partially resolved.

At the heart of all controversies in macroeconomics has been the issue of how quickly markets clear—the elimination of any excess supply or excess demand, particularly labour markets. In order for markets to clear you need flexible prices. Many economists do not believe prices are fully flexible, particularly the price of labour—wages. If markets do not clear quickly, the economy can get "stuck" in a recession for a considerable period of time.

As you read this chapter, keep the following points in mind:

• Economists of the nineteenth and early twentieth centuries believed the economy had self-correcting powers and that recessions and inflationary periods would work themselves out and the economy would return to full employment.

• Keynes argued in the 1930s that although economics would eventually return to full employment, the adjustment mechanism worked much too slowly, particularly in the case of a recession. The stimulation of aggregate demand through government spending could quicken the resolution of a recession. Keynesian economics enlarged the scope of government initiatives in stabilizing the economy.

• The monetarist school emphasized the important role of money and argued that markets cleared more rapidly than the Keynesian school proposed.

• The rational expectation school proposed nearly instant market clearing, making government macroeconomic policy unnecessary.

• The mainstream has adopted some of the monetarist and rational expectation schools' arguments. ∎

SOME HISTORY: CLASSICS AND KEYNES

Classical economics, which dominated economic thought in the 1800s, suggested that full employment is the norm in a market economy and that a *laissez-faire* ("let it be") policy by government is best. In contrast, Keynes contended in the 1930s that laissez-faire capitalism is subject to recurring recessions or depressions with widespread unemployment. In the Keynesian view, active government stabilization policy is required to avoid the waste of idle resources.

Because the classical and Keynesian views of the macroeconomic world provide great insight on modern debates, it is worthwhile to compare their basic forms through modern aggregate demand and aggregate supply analysis.

Classical View

In the classical view, the aggregate supply curve is vertical and exclusively determines the level of real output. The downsloping aggregate demand curve is stable and solely establishes the price level.

Vertical Aggregate Supply Curve

In the classical perspective, the aggregate supply curve is a vertical line as shown in Figure 17-1a. This line is located at the full-employment level of real output, which in this designation is also the full-capacity real output. According to the classical economists, the economy will operate at its full-employment level of output, Q_f, because of (1) Say's law (Chapter 9) and (2) responsive, flexible prices and wages.

We stress that classical economists believed that Q_f does *not* change in response to changes in the price level. Observe that as the price level falls from P_1 to P_2 in Figure 17-1a, real output remains anchored at Q_f.

But this stability of output might seem at odds with Chapter 4's upsloping supply curves for individual products. There we found that lower prices would make production less profitable and cause producers to offer *less* output and employ

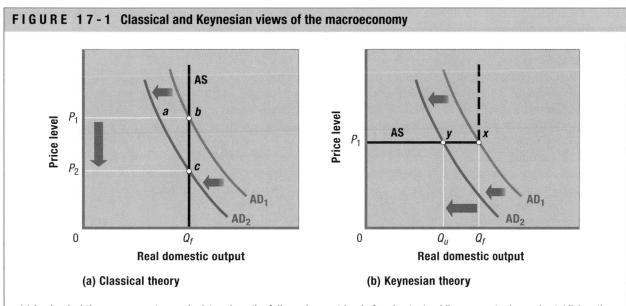

FIGURE 17-1 Classical and Keynesian views of the macroeconomy

(a) In classical theory, aggregate supply determines the full-employment level of real output, while aggregate demand establishes the price level. Aggregate demand normally is stable, but if it should decline, say, from AD_1 to AD_2, the price level will quickly fall from P_1 to P_2 to eliminate the temporary excess supply of *ab* and to restore full employment at *c*. (b) The Keynesian view is that aggregate demand is unstable and that prices and wages are downwardly inflexible. An AD_1 to AD_2 decline in aggregate demand has no effect on the price level. Instead, the economy moves from point *x* to *y* and real output falls to Q_u, where it can remain indefinitely.

fewer workers. The classical response to this view is that input costs would fall along with product prices to leave *real* profits and output unchanged.

Consider a one-firm economy in which the firm's owner must receive a *real* profit of $20 to produce the full-employment output of 100 units. You know from Chapter 8 that what ultimately counts is the *real* reward one receives and not the level of prices. Assume the owner's only input (aside from personal entrepreneurial talent) is 10 units of labour hired at $8 per worker for a total wage cost of $80 (= $10 \times \$8$). Also suppose the 100 units of output sell for $1 per unit, so total revenue is $100 (= $100 \times \$1$). This firm's *nominal* profit is $20 (= $\$100 - \$80$), and, using the $1 price to designate the base price index of 100 percent, its *real* profit is also $20 (= $\$20 \div 1.00$). Well and good; full employment is achieved. But suppose the price level declines by one-half. Would our producer still earn the $20 of real profits needed to support production of a 100-unit full-employment output?

The classical answer is "yes." Now that product price is only 50¢, total revenue will be only $50 (= $100 \times 50¢$). But the cost of 10 units of labour will be reduced to $40 (= $10 \times \$4$) because the wage rate will be halved. Although *nominal* profits fall to $10 (= $\$50 - \$40$), *real* profits remain at $20. By divid-

ing money profits of $10 by the new price index (expressed as a decimal), we obtain *real* profits of $20 (= $\$10 \div .50$).

With perfectly flexible wages there would be no change in the real rewards and therefore in the production behaviour of businesses. With perfect wage flexibility, a change in the price level will not cause the economy to stray from full employment.

Stable Aggregate Demand Classical economists theorize that money underlies aggregate demand. The amount of real output that can be purchased depends on (1) the quantity of money households and businesses possess and (2) the purchasing power of that money as determined by the price level. The purchasing power of the dollar refers to the real quantity of goods and services a dollar will buy. Thus, as we move down the vertical axis of Figure 17-1a, the price level is falling. This means that the purchasing power of each dollar is rising. If the price level declined by one-half, a particular quantity of money would now purchase a real output twice as large. With a fixed money supply, the price level and real output are inversely related.

And what of the *location* of the aggregate demand curve? According to the classical economists, aggregate demand will be stable as long as the nation's monetary authorities maintain a constant supply of money. With a fixed aggregate supply of output, increases in the supply of money will shift the aggregate demand curve rightward and spark demand-pull inflation. Reductions in the supply of money will shift the curve leftward and trigger deflation. The key to price-level stability, then, is to control the nation's money supply to prevent unwarranted shifts in aggregate demand.

A final observation: Even if there are declines in the money supply and therefore in aggregate demand, the economy depicted in Figure 17-1a will *not* experience unemployment. Admittedly, the immediate effect of a decline in aggregate demand from AD_1 to AD_2 is an excess supply of output since the aggregate output of goods and services exceeds aggregate spending by the amount *ab*. But, with the presumed downward flexibility of product and resource prices, this excess supply will reduce product prices along with workers' wages and the prices of other inputs. As a result, the price level will quickly decline from P_1 to P_2 until the amounts of output demanded and supplied are brought once again into equilibrium, this time at *c*. While the price level has fallen from P_1 to P_2, real output remains at the full-employment level.

Keynesian View

The core of crude, or extreme, **Keynesianism** is that product prices and wages are downwardly inflexible over very long time periods. The result is graphically represented as a horizontal aggregate supply curve. Also, aggregate demand is subject to periodic changes caused by changes in the determinants of aggregate demand.

Horizontal Aggregate Supply Curve (to Full-Employment Output)
The presumed downward inflexibility of prices and wages translates to a horizontal aggregate supply curve as shown in Figure 17-1b. Here, a decline in real output from Q_f to Q_u will have no impact on the price level. Conversely, an increase in real output from Q_u to Q_f will also leave the price level unchanged. The aggregate supply curve therefore extends from zero real output rightward to point *x*, where real output is at its full-employment level, Q_f. Once full employment is reached, the aggregate supply curve is vertical. This is shown by the dashed line

extending upward from the horizontal aggregate supply curve at *x*.

Unstable Aggregate Demand Keynesian economists view aggregate demand as unstable from one period to the next, even without changes in the money supply. In particular, the investment component of aggregate demand fluctuates, altering the location of the aggregate demand curve. Suppose aggregate demand in Figure 17-1b declines from AD_1 to AD_2. The sole impact is on output and employment. Real output falls from Q_f to Q_u, while the price level is unchanged at P_1. Moreover, Keynesians believe that unless there is a fortuitous offsetting increase in aggregate demand, real output may remain at Q_u, which is below the full-employment level Q_f. Active government policies to increase aggregate demand are essential to move the economy from point *y* to point *x*. Otherwise, the economy will suffer the wastes of recession and depression. *(Key Question 1)*

> ### 17-1
> ### QUICK REVIEW
>
> **In classical macroeconomics:**
> - The aggregate supply curve is vertical at the full-employment level of real output.
> - The aggregate demand curve is stable as long as the money supply is constant.
>
> **In Keynesian macroeconomics:**
> - The aggregate supply curve is horizontal up to the full-employment level of output; then it becomes vertical.
> - The aggregate demand curve is unstable largely because of the volatility of investment spending; such shifts cause either recession or demand-pull inflation.

WHAT CAUSES MACRO INSTABILITY?

You are aware from previous chapters that the capitalist economies have, in fact, experienced considerable instability during this century. Canada, for example, has experienced the Great Depression, numerous recessions, and periods of inflation. Contemporary economists have different perspectives on why this instability occurs.

Mainstream View

The mainstream view is Keynesian-based. It holds that instability in the economy arises from two sources: (1) significant changes in investment spending that change aggregate demand, and, occasionally, (2) adverse aggregate supply shocks that change aggregate supply. These factors are not new to you, so let's just briefly review them here.

Changes in Investment Spending Mainstream macroeconomics focuses on aggregate spending and its components. Recall that the basic equation underlying aggregate expenditures is

$$C_a + I_g + X_n + G = \text{GDP}$$

That is, the aggregate amount of after-tax consumption, gross investment, net exports, and government spending determines the total amount of the goods and services produced and sold. In equilibrium, $C_a + I_g + X_n + G$ (aggregate expenditures) is equal to GDP (real output). A decrease in the price level increases equilibrium GDP and thus allows us to trace out a downsloping aggregate demand curve for the economy. Any change in one of the spending components in the aggregate expenditures equation shifts the aggregate demand curve. This, in turn, changes equilibrium real output, the price level, or both.

Investment spending, in particular, is subject to wide "booms" and "busts." Significant increases in investment spending get multiplied into even greater increases in aggregate demand and thus can produce demand-pull inflation. In contrast, major declines in investment spending get multiplied into even greater decreases in aggregate demand and thus can cause recessions.

Adverse Aggregate Supply Shocks In the mainstream view, the second source of macroeconomic instability arises on the supply side. Occasionally, such external events as wars or artificial supply restrictions boost prices of key imported resources and significantly raise per-unit production costs. The result is a sizable decline in a nation's aggregate supply, which destabilizes the economy by simultaneously causing cost-push inflation *and* recession.

Monetarist View

Classical economics has emerged in several modern forms. One is **monetarism**, which (1) focuses on the money supply, (2) holds that markets are highly competitive, and (3) says that a competitive market system gives the economy a high degree of macroeconomic stability. Like classical economics, monetarists argue that the price and wage flexibility provided by competitive markets would cause fluctuations in aggregate demand to alter product and resource prices rather than output and employment. Thus the market system would provide substantial macroeconomic stability *were it not for government interference in the economy*.

The problem, as monetarists see it, is that government has promoted downward wage inflexibility through the minimum-wage law, pro-union legislation, guaranteed prices for some farm products, pro-business monopoly legislation, and so forth. The free-market system could provide macroeconomic stability, but, despite good intentions, government interference has undermined this capability. Moreover, monetarists say that government has contributed to the economy's business cycles through its clumsy and mistaken attempts to achieve greater stability through monetary policies.

Equation of Exchange The fundamental equation of monetarism is the **equation of exchange:**

$$MV = PQ$$

where M is the supply of money; V is the **velocity** of money, that is, *the number of times per year the average dollar is spent on final goods and services*; P is the price level or, more specifically, the average price at which each unit of physical output is sold; and Q is the physical volume of all goods and services produced.

The label "equation of exchange" is easily understood. The left side, MV, represents the total amount *spent* by purchasers of output, while the right side, PQ, represents the total amount *received* by sellers of that output. The nation's money supply (M) multiplied by the number of times it is spent each year (V) *must* equal the nation's nominal GDP ($= P \times Q$). The dollar value of total spending has to equal the dollar value of total output.

Stable Velocity Monetarists say that velocity, V, in the equation of exchange is stable. As used here, "stable" is not synonymous with "constant." Monetarists are aware that velocity is higher today than it was several decades ago. Shorter pay periods, greater use of credit cards, and faster means of making payments enable people to hold less money and turn it over more rapidly than was possible in earlier times. These factors have enabled people to reduce their holdings of cash and demand deposit money relative to the size of the nation's nominal GDP.

When monetarists say velocity is stable they mean that the factors altering velocity change gradually and predictably. Changes in velocity from one year to the next can be easily anticipated. Moreover, velocity does not change in response to changes in the money supply itself. In this view, people have a stable desire to hold money relative to holding other financial assets, holding real assets, and buying current output. The factors which determine the amount of money the public wants to hold depend mainly on the level of nominal GDP.

Example: Suppose that when the level of nominal GDP is $400 billion, the public desires $100 billion of money to purchase this output. That means V is 4 (= $400 billion of nominal GDP/$100 billion of money). If we further assume that the actual supply of money is $100 billion, the economy is in equilibrium with respect to money; the *actual* amount of money supplied equals the *desired* amount the public wants to hold.

If velocity is stable, the equation of exchange suggests there is a predictable relationship between the money supply and nominal GDP (= PQ). An increase in the money supply of, say, $10 billion upsets equilibrium in our example since the public finds itself holding more money or liquidity than it wants. That is, the actual amount of money held ($110 billion) exceeds the amount of holdings desired ($100 billion). The reaction of the public (households and businesses) is to restore its desired balance of money relative to other items, such as stocks and bonds, factories and equipment, houses and automobiles, and clothing and toys. But the spending of money by individual households and businesses leaves more cash in others' demand deposits or billfolds. Households and firms also try to "spend down" their excess cash balances, but, overall, *the $110 billion supply of money cannot be spent down.*

Instead, the collective attempt to reduce cash balances increases aggregate demand, boosting the *nominal* GDP. Because velocity in our example is 4—that is, the typical dollar is spent four times per year—nominal GDP rises from $400 to $440

billion. At that higher nominal GDP, the money supply of $110 billion equals the amount of money desired ($440 billion/4 = $110 billion), and equilibrium is reestablished.

The $10 billion increase in the money supply thus eventually increases nominal GDP by $40 billion. Spending on goods, services, and assets expands until nominal GDP has gone up enough to restore the original 4-to-1 equilibrium relationship between nominal GDP and the money supply.

Note that the relationship GDP/M defines V. A stable relationship between nominal GDP and M means a stable V. And a change in M causes a proportionate change in nominal GDP. Thus, changes in the money supply allegedly have a predictable effect on nominal GDP (= $P \times Q$). An increase in M increases P or Q, or some combination of both; a decrease in M reduces P or Q, or some combination of both. *(Key Question 4)*

Monetary Causes of Instability *Monetarists say that inappropriate monetary policy is the single most important cause of macroeconomic instability.* An increase in the money supply directly increases aggregate demand. Under conditions of full employment, this increase in aggregate demand increases the price level. For a time, higher prices cause firms to increase their real output, and the rate of unemployment falls below its natural rate. But once nominal wages rise to reflect the higher prices and thus to restore real wages, real output moves back to its full-employment level and the unemployment rate returns to its natural rate. The inappropriate increase in the money supply leads to inflation, together with instability of real output and employment.

Conversely, a decrease in the money supply reduces aggregate demand. Real output temporarily falls, and the unemployment rate rises above its natural rate. Eventually, nominal wages fall and real output returns to its full-employment level. The inappropriate decline in the money supply leads to deflation, together with instability of real GDP and employment.

The contrast between mainstream macroeconomics and monetarism on the causes of instability thus comes into sharp focus. Mainstream economists view instability of investment as the main cause of the economy's instability. They see monetary policy as a stabilizing factor. Changes in the money supply raise or lower interest rates as needed, smooth out swings in investment, and thus reduce macroeconomic instability. In contrast, monetarists view changes in the money supply as the main cause of the instability in the economy. For example, they say that the Great Depression largely occurred because central banks allowed the money supply to fall. According to Milton Friedman, a prominent monetarist, the case of the United States was typical:

> And [the money supply] fell not because there were no willing borrowers—not because the horse would not drink. It fell because the Federal Reserve System forced or permitted a sharp reduction in the [money supply], because it failed to exercise the responsibilities assigned to it in the Federal Reserve Act to provide liquidity to the banking system. The Great Contraction is tragic testimony to the power of monetary policy—not as Keynes and so many of his contemporaries believed, evidence of its impotence.[1]

Real-Business-Cycle View

A third modern view of the cause of macroeconomic instability is that business cycles are caused by *real* factors affecting aggregate supply rather than by *monetary*, or spending, factors causing fluctuations in aggregate demand. In the **real-business-cycle theory,** business fluctuations result from significant changes in technology and resource availability. Those changes affect productivity and thus the long-run growth trend of aggregate supply.

An example focusing on recession will clarify this thinking. Suppose productivity (output per worker) sharply declines because of a large increase in oil prices, which makes it prohibitively expensive to operate certain types of machinery. This decline in productivity implies a reduction in the economy's ability to produce real output. The result would be a decrease in the economy's long-run aggregate supply curve, as represented by the leftward shift from AS_{LR1} to AS_{LR2} in Figure 17-2.

As real output falls from Q_1 to Q_2, the public does not need as much money to buy the reduced volume of goods and services. So the demand for money falls. Moreover, the slowdown in business activity lessens business borrowing from banks,

[1] Milton Friedman, *The Optimum Quantity of Money and Other Essays* (Chicago: Aldine, 1969), p. 97.

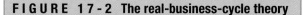

FIGURE 17-2 The real-business-cycle theory

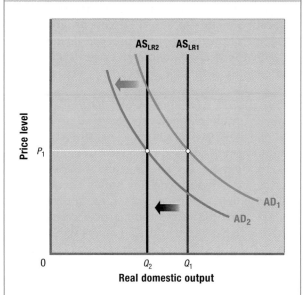

In the real-business-cycle theory, a decline in resource availability shifts the nation's long-run aggregate supply curve to the left from AS_{LR1} to AS_{LR2}. The decline in real output from Q_1 to Q_2, in turn, reduces money demand (less is needed) and money supply (fewer loans are taken out) such that aggregate demand shifts leftward from AD_1 to AD_2. The result is a recession in which the price level remains constant.

reducing demand deposits. Thus, the supply of money also falls. In this controversial scenario, changes in the supply of money respond to changes in the demand for money. The decline in the money supply then reduces aggregate demand, as from AD_1 to AD_2 in Figure 17-2. The overall outcome is a decline in real output from Q_1 to Q_2, with no change in the price level.

Conversely, a large increase in aggregate supply (not shown) caused by, say, major new innovations in the production process would shift the long-run aggregate supply curve rightward. Real output would increase, and money demand and money supply would both increase. Aggregate demand would shift rightward by an amount equal to the rightward shift of long-run aggregate supply. Real output would increase, without driving up the price level.

Conclusion: In the real-business-cycle theory, macro instability arises on the aggregate supply side of the economy, not on the aggregate demand side as mainstream economists and monetarists generally say.

Coordination Failures

A fourth and final modern view of macroeconomic instability relates to so-called **coordination failures**. Such failures occur *when people do not reach a mutually beneficial equilibrium because they lack some way to jointly coordinate their actions.*

Noneconomic Example   Consider first a noneconomic example. Suppose you learn of an impending volleyball party at a nearby lake, but it looks like it might rain. If you expect others to be there, you will decide to go. If you expect that others will not attend, you will decide to stay home. There are several possible equilibrium outcomes, depending on the mix of people's expectations. Let's consider just two. If each person assumes all others will be at the party, all will go. The party and volleyball game will occur and presumably everyone will have a good time. But if each person assumes that everyone else will stay home, each person will stay home and there will be no party. When the volleyball party does *not* take place, *even though all would be better off if it did happen,* a coordination failure has occurred.

Macroeconomic Example   Now let's apply this idea to macroeconomic instability, specifically recession. Suppose individual firms and households expect other firms and consumers to cut back their investment and consumption spending. As a result, each firm and household will anticipate a reduction of aggregate demand. Firms therefore will cut back their own investment spending since they will anticipate future excess production capacity. Households will also reduce their own spending (increase their saving) because they anticipate reduced work-hours, possible layoffs, and falling income. Aggregate demand will indeed decline and the economy will experience a recession *due to a self-fulfilling prophecy.* Moreover, the economy will *stay* at a below-full-employment level of output because, once there, producers and households have no individual incentive to increase spending. If *all* producers and households would agree to simultaneously increase their investment and consumption spending, then aggregate demand would rise, and real output and real income would expand. Each producer and consumer would be better off. However, this outcome does not occur because there is no mechanism for firms and households to agree on such a joint spending increase.

In this case, the economy is stuck in an *unemployment equilibrium* because of a coordination fail-

ure. With a different set of expectations, a coordination failure might leave the economy in an *inflation equilibrium*. In this view, there are a number of such potential equilibrium positions in the economy, some good and some bad, depending on people's mix of expectations. Macroeconomic instability, then, reflects the movement of the economy from one such equilibrium position to another as expectations change.

> ## 17-2
> ### QUICK REVIEW
>
> • Mainstream economists say that macroeconomic instability usually stems from swings in investment spending and, occasionally, from adverse aggregate supply shocks.
>
> • Monetarists view the economy through the equation of exchange ($MV = PQ$). If velocity V is stable, changes in the money supply M directly lead to changes in nominal GDP ($= P \times Q$). For monetarists, changes in M via inappropriate monetary policy are the single most important cause of macroeconomic instability.
>
> • In the real-business-cycle theory, significant changes in "real" factors such as technology, resource availability, and productivity change the economy's long-run aggregate supply, causing macroeconomic instability.
>
> • Macroeconomic instability can result from coordination failures—less-than-optimal equilibrium positions that occur because businesses and households lack some way to jointly coordinate their actions.

DOES THE ECONOMY "SELF-CORRECT"?

Just as there are disputes over the causes of macroeconomic instability, there are debates on whether the economy corrects itself when instability does occur. Also, economists disagree as to the length of time it will take for any such self-correction to happen.

New Classical View of Self-Correction

Monetarist and rational expectations economists (Chapter 16) take the view of **new classical eco-**

nomics, which is that when the economy occasionally diverges from its full-employment output, internal mechanisms within the economy automatically move it back to that output. This perspective is associated with the adaptive and rational expectations theories (the natural-rate theories) discussed in Chapter 16.

Graphical Analysis   Figure 17-3a is useful for relating the new classical analysis to the issue of self-correction. Specifically, an increase in aggregate demand, say, from AD_1 to AD_2, moves the economy upward along its short-run aggregate supply curve AS_1 from a to b. The price level rises and real output increases. In the long run, however, nominal wages rise to restore real wages. Per-unit production costs then increase, and the short-run aggregate supply curve shifts leftward, eventually from AS_1 to AS_2. The economy moves from b to c and real output returns to its full-employment level, Q_1. This level of output is dictated by the economy's vertical long-run aggregate supply curve, here AS_{LR}.

Conversely, a decrease in aggregate demand from AD_1 to AD_3 in Figure 17-3b first moves the economy downward along its short-run aggregate supply curve AS_1 from point a to d. The price level *and* the level of real output fall. But in the

long run, nominal wages decline such that real wages fall to their previous levels. When that happens, per-unit production costs decline and the short-run aggregate supply curve shifts to the right, eventually from AS_1 to AS_3. The economy moves back to e, where it again achieves its full-employment level, Q_1. As in Figure 17-3a, the economy in Figure 17-3b has automatically self-corrected to its full-employment output and natural rate of unemployment.

Speed of Adjustment   There is some disagreement among new classical economists on how long it will take for self-correction to occur. Monetarists usually hold the *adaptive expectations* view that people form their expectations on present realities and only gradually change their expectations as experience unfolds. This means that the shifts in the short-run aggregate supply curves shown in Figure 17-3 may not occur for two or three years, or even longer. Other new classical economists, however, accept the *rational expectations* assumption that workers *anticipate* some future outcomes before they occur. When price-level changes are fully anticipated, adjustments of nominal wages are very quick, or even instantaneous. Let's see why.

Although several new theories incorporate rational expectations, including Keynesian ones,

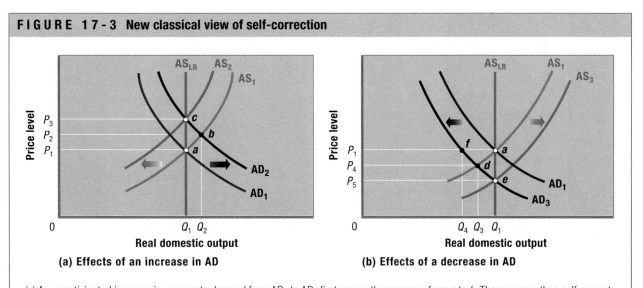

FIGURE 17-3   New classical view of self-correction

(a) Effects of an increase in AD

(b) Effects of a decrease in AD

(a) An unanticipated increase in aggregate demand from AD_1 to AD_2 first moves the economy from a to b. The economy then self-corrects to c. An anticipated increase in aggregate demand moves the economy directly from a to c. (b) An unanticipated decrease in aggregate demand from AD_1 to AD_3 moves the economy from a to d. The economy then self-corrects to e. An anticipated decrease in aggregate demand moves the economy directly from a to e. (Mainstream economists, however, say that if the price level remains at P_1, the economy will move from a to f, and even if the price level falls to P_2, the economy may remain at d because of downward wage inflexibility.)

our interest here is the new classical version of the rational expectations theory (hereafter, RET). RET is based on two assumptions:

1. People behave rationally, gathering and intelligently processing information to form expectations about things that are economically important to them. These expectations are adjusted quickly as new developments affecting future economic outcomes occur. Where there is adequate information, people's beliefs about future economic outcomes *accurately reflect the likelihood that those outcomes will occur*. For example, if it is clear that some policy will cause inflation, people will recognize that fact and adjust their economic behaviour in anticipation of inflation.

2. Like classical economists, RET economists assume that all product and resource markets are highly competitive and that prices and wages are flexible both upward and downward. RET goes further, assuming that new information is quickly (in some cases instantaneously) taken into account in the demand and supply curves of such markets. The upshot is that equilibrium prices and quantities adjust rapidly to unforeseen events, say, technological change or aggregate supply shocks. They adjust instantaneously to events with known outcomes, for example, changes in fiscal or monetary policy.

Unanticipated Price-Level Changes

The implication of RET is not only that the economy is self-correcting but that self-correction occurs quickly. In this thinking, *unanticipated* changes in the price level—so called **price-level surprises**—do cause temporary changes in real output. Suppose, for example, an unanticipated increase in foreign demand for goods increases Canada's aggregate demand from AD_1 to AD_2 in Figure 17-3a. The immediate result is an unexpected increase in the price level from P_1 to P_2.

But now an interesting question arises. If wages and prices are flexible as assumed in RET, why doesn't the higher price level immediately cause nominal wages to rise, such that there is no increase in real output at all? Why does the economy temporarily move from point a to b along AS_1? In RET, firms increase output from Q_1 to Q_2 because of *misperceptions* about rising prices of their own products relative to prices of other products (and to prices of labour). They mistakenly

think the higher prices of their own products have resulted from increased demand for those products relative to the demands for other products. Expecting higher profits, they increase their own production. But in fact *all* prices, including the price of labour (nominal wages), are rising because of the general increase in aggregate demand. Once firms see that *all* prices and wages are rising, they decrease their production to previous levels.

In terms of Figure 17-3a, the increase in nominal wages shifts the short-run aggregate supply curve leftward, ultimately from AS_1 to AS_2, and the economy moves from b to c. Thus, the increase in real output caused by the *price-level surprise* corrects itself.

The same analysis applies in reverse for an *unanticipated* price-level decrease. In the economy represented by Figure 17-3b, firms misperceive that the prices for their own products are falling due to decreases in the demands for those products relative to other products. They respond to anticipated profit declines by cutting production. As a result of their collective actions, real output in the economy falls. But seeing that *all* prices and wages are dropping, firms increase their output to prior levels. The short-run aggregate supply curve in Figure 17-3b shifts rightward from AS_1 to AS_3, and the economy "self-corrects" by moving from d to e.

Fully Anticipated Price-Level Changes

In RET, fully *anticipated* price-level changes do *not* change real output, even for short periods. In Figure 17-3a, again consider the increase in aggregate demand from AD_1 to AD_2. Businesses immediately recognize that the higher prices being paid for their products are part of the inflation they had anticipated. They understand that the same forces that are causing the inflation result in higher nominal wages, leaving their profits unchanged. The economy therefore moves *directly* from a to c. The price level rises as expected, and output remains at its full-employment level Q_1.

Similarly, a fully *anticipated* price-level decrease will leave real output unchanged. Firms conclude that nominal wages are declining by the same percentage amount as the declining price level, leaving profits unchanged. The economy represented by Figure 17-3b therefore moves *directly* from a to e. Deflation occurs, but the economy continues to produce its full-employment output Q_1. The anticipated decline in aggregate demand causes no change in real output.

Mainstream View of Self-Correction

Almost all economists acknowledge that new classical economists have made significant contributions to the theory of aggregate supply. In fact, mainstream economists have incorporated some aspects of RET into their own more detailed models. However, most economists strongly disagree with RET on the question of *downward* price and wage flexibility. While the stock market, foreign exchange market, and certain commodity markets experience day-to-day or minute-to-minute price changes, including price declines, this is not true in many product markets and in most labour markets. There is ample evidence, say mainstream economists, that *many prices and wages are inflexible downward for long periods*. As a result, it may take years for the economy to move from recession back to full-employment output, unless it gets help from fiscal and monetary policy.

Graphical Analysis To understand this mainstream view, again examine Figure 17-3b. Suppose aggregate demand declines from AD_1 to AD_3 because of a significant decline in investment spending. If the price level remains at P_1, the economy will *not* move from a to d to e, as suggested by RET. Instead, the economy will move from a to f, as if it were moving along a *horizontal aggregate supply curve* between these two points. Real output will decline from its full-employment level, Q_1, to the recessionary level, Q_4.

But let's assume that surpluses in product markets eventually cause the price level to fall to P_4. Will this lead to the decline in nominal wages needed to shift aggregate supply from AS_1 to AS_2, as suggested by new classical economists? "Highly unlikely," say mainstream economists. Even more so than prices, nominal wages tend to be inflexible downward. If nominal wages do not decline in response to the decline in the price level, then the short-run aggregate supply curve will not shift rightward. The self-correction mechanism assumed by RET and new classical economists will break down. Instead, the economy will remain at d, experiencing less-than-full-employment output and a high rate of unemployment.

Downward Wage Inflexibility In Chapter 11 we listed and discussed several reasons firms may not be able to, or may not want to, reduce nominal wages. Firms *may not be able to* cut wages because of wage contracts and the minimum wage. And

firms *may not want to* reduce wages if they fear potential problems with morale, effort, and efficiency. Businesses also may not want to cut wages if doing so will mean losing skilled workers to other firms—workers in whom the current firms have heavy training investments.

While contracts are thought to be the main cause of wage rigidity, so-called *efficiency wages* and *insider-outsider relationships* may also play a role. Let's explore these aspects of **new Keynesian economics**.

Efficiency Wage Theory Recall from Chapter 11 that an **efficiency wage** is one that minimizes the firm's labour cost per unit of output. Normally, we would think that the market wage is the efficiency wage since it is the lowest wage at which a firm can obtain a particular type of labour. But where the cost of supervising workers is high, or where worker turnover is great, firms may discover that paying a wage that is higher than the market wage will lower their wage cost per unit of output. Example: Suppose a firm's workers, on average, produce 8 units of output at a $9 market wage but 10 units of output at a $10 above-market wage. The efficiency wage is $10, not the $9 market wage. At the $10 wage, the per-unit cost of output is only $1 (= $10 wage/10 units of output), compared with $1.12 (= $9 wage/8 units of output) at the $9 wage.

How can a higher wage result in greater efficiency?

1. **GREATER WORK EFFORT** The above-market wage, in effect, raises the cost to workers of losing their jobs because of poor performance. Because workers have a strong incentive to retain their relatively high-paying jobs, they are more apt to provide greater work effort. Looked at differently, workers are more reluctant to *shirk* (neglect or avoid work) because the higher wage makes job loss more costly to them. Consequently, the above-market wage can be the efficient wage; it can enhance worker productivity so much that the higher wage more than pays for itself.

2. **LOWER SUPERVISION COSTS** With less worker incentive to shirk, the firm needs fewer supervisory personnel to monitor work performance. This, too, can lower the firm's overall wage cost per unit of output.

3. **REDUCED JOB TURNOVER** The above-market pay discourages workers from voluntarily leaving their jobs. The lower *job turnover*

reduces the firm's cost of hiring and training workers. It also gives the firm a more experienced, more productive workforce.

The key implication for macroeconomic instability is that efficiency wages add to downward wage inflexibility. Firms paying efficiency wages will be reluctant to cut wages when aggregate demand declines since such cuts may encourage shirking, require more supervisory personnel, and increase turnover. In other words, wage cuts that reduce productivity and raise per-unit labour costs are self-defeating.

Insider-Outsider Relationships

Other new Keynesian economists theorize that downward wage inflexibility may relate to relationships between "insiders" and "outsiders." *Insiders* are workers who retain employment even during recession. *Outsiders* are workers laid off from a particular firm and other unemployed workers who would like to work at that firm.

When recession produces layoffs and widespread unemployment, we might expect outsiders to offer to work for less than the current wage rate, in effect, bidding down wage rates. We might also expect firms to accept such wage offers to reduce their costs. But, according to the **insider-outsider theory**, outsiders may not be able to underbid existing wages because employers may view the cost of hiring them to be prohibitive. Employers might conclude that insiders would view this underbidding as undermining years of efforts to increase wages or, worse, as "stealing" jobs. Insiders therefore may refuse to cooperate with the new workers who have undercut their pay. Where teamwork is critical for production, such lack of cooperation will reduce overall productivity and thereby lower the firms' profits.

Even if firms were willing to employ outsiders at less than the present wage, these unemployed workers might not choose to work for less than the existing wage. To do so would risk harassment from the insiders whose pay they have undercut. Thus, outsiders may remain unemployed, relying on past saving, unemployment compensation, and other social programs to makes ends meet.

As in the efficiency wage theory, the insider-outsider theory implies that wages will be inflexible downward when aggregate demand declines. Self-correction may *eventually* occur, but not nearly as rapidly as the new classical economists contend. *(Key Question 7)*

17-3 QUICK REVIEW

- New classical economists believe that the economy "self-corrects" when unanticipated events divert it from its full-employment level of real output.
- In RET unanticipated price-level changes cause changes in real output in the short run but not in the long run.
- According to RET, market participants immediately change their actions in response to anticipated price-level changes such that no change in real output occurs.
- Mainstream economists believe that downward price and wage inflexibility means that the economy can get mired in recession for long periods.
- Sources of downward wage inflexibility include contracts, efficiency wages, and insider-outsider relationships.

RULES OR DISCRETION?

The different views on the causes of instability and the speed of self-correction lead to vigorous debate on macro policy. Should government adhere to *policy rules* that prohibit it from causing instability in an economy that otherwise is stable? Or should it use *discretionary fiscal and monetary policy*, when needed, to stabilize a sometimes unstable economy?

In Support of Policy Rules

Monetarists and other new classical economists believe policy rules would reduce instability in the economy. The rules would prevent government from trying to "manage" aggregate demand. In this view, such management is misguided and thus likely to *cause* more instability than it cures.

Monetary Rule Since inappropriate monetary policy is the major source of macroeconomic instability, say monetarists, then enactment of a **monetary rule** would make sense. Such a rule would direct the Bank of Canada to expand the money supply each year at the same annual rate as the typical growth of the economy's production capacity. The Bank of Canada's sole monetary role would then be to use its tools (open-market operations, bank-rate changes, and shifting of government deposits) to ensure that the nation's money supply grows steadily by, say, 3 to 5 percent a year. According to Milton Friedman,

> Such a rule ... would eliminate ... the major cause of instability in the economy—the capricious and unpredictable impact of countercyclical monetary policy. As long as the money supply grows at a constant rate each year, be it 3, 4, or 5 percent, any decline into recession will be temporary. The liquidity provided by a constantly growing money supply will cause aggregate demand to expand. Similarly, if the supply of money does not rise at a more than average rate, any inflationary increase in spending will burn itself out for lack of fuel.[2]

Figure 17-4 helps illustrate the rationale for a monetary rule. Suppose the economy represented there is operating at its full-employment real output, Q_1. Also suppose the nation's long-run aggregate supply curve shifts rightward, as from AS_{LR1} to AS_{LR2}, each year, depicting the average annual potential increase in real output. You know from earlier chapters that these annual increases in "potential GDP" result from added resources, improved resources, and improved technology.

Monetarists argue that a monetary rule would tie increases in the money supply to the typical rightward shift of long-run aggregate supply. In view of the direct link between changes in the money supply and aggregate demand, this would ensure that the AD curve will shift rightward, as from AD_1 to AD_2, each year. As a result, real GDP would rise from Q_1 to Q_2 and the price level would remain constant at P_1. A monetary rule, then, would promote steady growth of real output along with price stability.

Generally, RET economists also support a monetary rule. They conclude that an easy or tight money policy will alter the rate of inflation but not real output. Suppose, for example, the Bank of Canada implements an easy money policy to reduce interest rates, expand investment spending, and boost real GDP. On the basis of past experience and economic knowledge, the public anticipates that this policy is inflationary and takes

[2] As quoted in Lawrence S. Ritter and William L. Silber, *Money*, 5th ed. (New York: Basic Books, 1984), pp. 141-142.

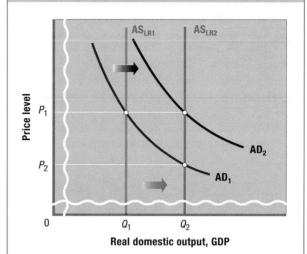

FIGURE 17-4 Rationale for a monetary rule

A monetary rule that fixed the annual increase in the money supply to the increase in potential GDP would shift aggregate demand rightward, as from AD_1 to AD_2, at the same pace as the shift in long-run aggregate supply, here AS_{LR1} to AS_{LR2}. Thus the economy would experience growth without inflation or deflation.

self-protective actions. Workers press for higher nominal wages; firms increase their product prices; and lenders raise their nominal interest rates on loans.

All these responses are designed to prevent inflation from having adverse effects on the real incomes of workers, businesses, and lenders. But collectively this behaviour immediately raises wage and price levels. So the increase in aggregate demand brought about by the easy money policy is completely dissipated in higher prices and wages. Real output and employment do not expand.

In this view, the combination of rational expectations and instantaneous market adjustments dooms monetary policy to ineffectiveness. If monetary policy produces only inflation (or deflation), say the RET economists, then it makes sense to limit the Bank of Canada's discretion. Specifically, Parliament ought to enact a monetary rule consistent with achieving zero or low inflation at all times.

Balanced Budget Monetarists and new classical economists question the effectiveness of fiscal policy. At the extreme, a few of these economists favour a constitutional amendment to require the federal government to balance its budget annually. Others simply suggest that government be "passive" in its fiscal policy, not *intentionally* creating budget deficits or surpluses. Deficits and surpluses caused by recession or inflationary expansion will eventually correct themselves as the economy self-corrects to its full-employment output.

Monetarists particularly oppose expansionary fiscal policy. They believe that the deficit spending accompanying such a policy has a strong tendency to crowd out private investment. Suppose government runs a budget deficit by printing and selling Canadian securities, which means borrowing from the public. Through this borrowing, government competes with private businesses for funds. The added government borrowing increases the demand for money, which then raises the interest rate and crowds out a substantial amount of private investment that would otherwise have been profitable. The net effect of a budget deficit on aggregate demand therefore is unpredictable and, at best, modest.

If a deficit was financed through printing new money instead of borrowing, the crowding out could be avoided and the deficit would be followed by expansion of real GDP. The monetarists point out, however, that such an expansion would *not* be the result of the deficit *per se* but, rather, of the expansion of the money supply. Moreover, this expansion of real output would be only temporary. A boost in nominal wages would soon follow the inflation, returning real output to its previous level.

RET economists reject discretionary fiscal policy for the same reason they reject active monetary policy: they do not think it works. Business and labour will immediately adjust their behaviour in anticipation of the price-level effects of a change in fiscal policy. The economy will move directly to the anticipated new price level. Like monetary policy, say the RET theorists, fiscal policy can move the economy along its vertical long-run aggregate supply curve. But because its effects on inflation are fully anticipated, fiscal policy cannot alter real GDP even in the short run. The best course of action for government is to balance its budget.

In Defence of Discretionary Stabilization Policy

Mainstream economists oppose a monetary rule and a balanced-budget requirement. They believe that monetary policy and fiscal policy are impor-

tant tools for achieving and maintaining full employment, price stability, and economic growth.

Discretionary Monetary Policy In supporting discretionary monetary policy, mainstream economists argue that the rationale for a monetary rule is flawed. While there is indeed a close relationship between the money supply and nominal GDP over long periods, in shorter periods this relationship breaks down. The reason is that the velocity of money has proved to be more variable and unpredictable than monetarists contend. Arguing that velocity is variable both cyclically and over time, mainstream economists contend that a constant annual rate of increase in the money supply need not eliminate fluctuations in aggregate demand. In terms of the equation of exchange, a steady rise of M does not guarantee a steady expansion of aggregate demand because V—the rate at which money is spent—can change.

Again reconsider Figure 17-4, in which we demonstrated the monetary rule. During the period in question, optimistic business expectations might create a boom in investment spending and thus shift the aggregate demand curve to some location to the right of AD_2. (You may want to pencil in a new AD curve, labelling it AD_3.) The price level would then rise above P_1; that is, demand-pull inflation would occur. In this case, the monetary rule will not accomplish its goal of maintaining price stability. Mainstream economists say that the Bank of Canada can use a tight money policy to reduce the excessive investment spending and thereby hold the rightward shift of aggregate demand to AD_2, thus avoiding inflation.

Similarly, suppose that investment instead declines because of pessimistic business expectations. Aggregate demand will then increase by some amount less than the increase from AD_1 to AD_2 in Figure 17-4. Again, the monetary rule fails the stability test: the price level sinks below P_1 (deflation occurs). Or if the price level is inflexible downward at P_1, the economy does not achieve its full-employment output (unemployment rises). An easy money policy can help avoid either outcome.

Mainstream economists quip that the trouble with the monetary rule is that it tells the policy-maker: "Don't do something, just stand there."

Discretionary Fiscal Policy Mainstream economists support the use of fiscal policy to keep recessions from deepening or to keep mild inflation from becoming severe inflation. They recognize the possibility of crowding out but do not think it is a serious problem when business borrowing is depressed, as is usually the case in recession. Because politicians can abuse fiscal policy, most economists feel that it should be held in reserve for situations where monetary policy appears to be ineffective or working too slowly.

As indicated earlier, mainstream economists oppose requirements to balance the budget annually. Tax revenues fall sharply during recessions and rise briskly during periods of demand-pull inflation. Therefore, a law or constitutional amendment mandating an annually balanced budget would require government to *increase* tax rates and *reduce* government spending during recession and *reduce*

tax rates and *increase* government spending during economic booms. The first set of actions would worsen recession, and the second set would fuel inflation.

Increased Macro Stability

Finally, mainstream economists point out that the Canadian economy has been more stable since 1946 than in earlier periods. It is not a coincidence, they say, that use of discretionary fiscal and monetary policy characterized the latter period but not the former. These policies have helped tame the business cycle. Moreover, mainstream economists point out several specific policy successes in the past two decades:

TABLE 17-1 Alternative macroeconomic theories and policies

| Issue | Mainstream macroeconomics (Keynesian based) | NEW CLASSICAL ECONOMICS (NATURAL-RATE HYPOTHESIS) | | |
		Monetarism	Rational expectations	Supply-side economics
View of the economy	Potentially unstable	Stable in long run at natural rate of unemployment	Stable in long run at natural rate of unemployment	May stagnate without proper work, saving, and investment incentives
Cause of the observed instability of the economy	Investment plans unequal to saving plans (changes in AD); AS shocks	Inappropriate monetary policy	Unanticipated AD and AS shocks in the short run	Changes in AS
Appropriate macro policies	Active fiscal and monetary policy	Monetary rule	Monetary rule	Policies to increase AS
How changes in the money supply affect the economy	By changing the interest rate, which changes investment and real GDP	By directly changing AD, which changes GDP	No effect on output because price-level changes are anticipated	By influencing investment and thus AS
View of the velocity of money	Unstable	Stable	No consensus	No consensus
How fiscal policy affects the economy	Changes AD and GDP via the multiplier process	No effect unless money supply changes	No effect on output because price-level changes are anticipated	Affects GDP and price level via changes in AS
View of cost-push inflation	Possible (wage-push, AS shock)	Impossible in the long run in the absence of excessive money supply growth	Impossible in the long run in the absence of excessive money supply growth	Possible (tax-transfer disincentives, higher costs due to regulation)

1. A tight money policy dropped inflation from 12.4 percent in 1981 to 4.4 percent in 1985.
2. An expansionary fiscal policy reduced the unemployment rate from 11 percent in 1982 to 7.5 percent in 1989.
3. An easy money policy helped the economy recover from the 1990–91 recession. *(Key Question 13)*

SUMMARY OF ALTERNATIVE VIEWS

Here and in Chapter 16 we presented the central ideas and policy implications of a number of macroeconomic theories. In Table 17-1 we summarize four of them: mainstream macroeconomics, monetarism, rational expectations theory, and supply-side economics. You will observe that we broadly defined new classical economics to include both monetarism and the rational expectations theory since both adhere to the natural-rate hypothesis that the economy tends automatically to achieve equilibrium at its full-employment output. Also note that "mainstream macroeconomics" remains based on Keynesian ideas.

These different perspectives have forced mainstream economists to rethink some of their fundamental principles. And as is true of many debates, much compromise and revision of positions have occurred. Although considerable disagreement remains, mainstream macro economists agree with monetarists that "money matters" and that excessive growth of the money supply is the major cause of long-lasting, rapid inflation. They also agree with RET proponents and theorists of coordination failures that expectations are important. If government can create expectations of price stability, full employment, and economic growth, households and firms will tend to act in ways to make that happen. Finally, mainstream economists concur with supply-side economists and real-business-cycle theorists that government needs to focus on policies to increase economic growth. In short, thanks to ongoing challenges to the conventional wisdom, macroeconomics continues to evolve.

The Last Word

PROFIT SHARING: MAKING WAGES FLEXIBLE

Are there any ways that downward wage flexibility can be increased so that declines in aggregate demand do not have such a negative effect on output and employment?

OUR COMPARISON OF MAINSTREAM AND NEW classical views on the macroeconomy suggests that if wages are inflexible downward, output and employment will decline when aggregate demand falls. Most economists recognize that labour contracts, among other considerations, make wages inflexible downward, at least in the short run. The declines in labour demand accompanying recessions therefore primarily affect real output and employment. This problem has led some economists to propose profit sharing as a way to increase the flexibility of wage rates. The idea is to make labour markets operate more like the new classical model, with its vertical aggregate supply curve, by creating greater employment stability.

The essence of these profit-sharing proposals is to tie some portion of wages directly to the firm's profitability, making profit-sharing payments a part of workers' pay. Instead of paying workers a guaranteed wage rate of, say, $10 per hour, workers might be guaranteed $5 per hour (the base wage) and additional compensation equal to some predetermined percentage of the firm's profits (the profit-share wage). Total compensation (base wage + profit-share wage) may exceed or fall short of $10 per hour, depending on the firm's economic fortunes.

How would such a plan affect employment? Initially assume workers are receiving $10 per hour—$5 as a guaranteed wage and another $5 as profit—sharing compensation. Now suppose a recession occurs and the employer's sales and profits plummet. The $5 of profit-sharing income will fall and might decline to zero, so the actual wages paid by the firm fall from $10 to $5 an hour. With the new, depressed demand for labour, the firm would clearly choose to employ more workers under this wage system than the standard system. Hourly wages will have automatically fallen from $10 to $5.

There are a number of criticisms of such profit-sharing wage plans. The plans might jeopardize the wage uniformity and wage gains achieved by organized labour. A further criticism is that employers might respond to the low base wage by adopting production techniques that use relatively more labour and less capital. Because the amount of capital equipment per worker is critical to productivity and economic growth, this pay scheme might impair the long-run expansion of

real GDP. At the pragmatic level, critics point out that wage plans linked to profits eliminate the present certainty that workers have as to whether their employers have properly fulfilled the labour contract. With profit sharing, employers might use accounting and other techniques to hide profits and therefore evade paying share wages.

Finally, there is the fundamental question of whether workers will accept more jobs and greater employment stability in exchange for a reduced hourly wage guarantee and higher variability of earnings. But it should be noted that in the past decade a growing number of union and nonunion contracts have contained profit-sharing arrangements. Although a full-blown profit-sharing economy seems improbable, limited profit sharing appears to be spreading. ■

CHAPTER SUMMARY

1. In classical economics the aggregate supply curve is vertical and establishes the level of real output, while the aggregate demand curve is generally stable and establishes the price level. In this view the economy is highly stable.

2. In Keynesian economics the aggregate supply curve is horizontal at less-than-full-employment levels of real output, while the aggregate demand curve is inherently unstable. In this view the economy is highly unstable.

3. The mainstream view is that macro instability is caused by volatility of investment spending, which shifts the aggregate demand curve. If aggregate demand increases too rapidly, demand-pull inflation can occur; if aggregate demand decreases, recession can occur. Occasionally, adverse supply shocks also cause instability.

4. Monetarism focuses on the equation of exchange: $MV = PQ$. Because velocity is thought to be stable, changes in M create changes in nominal GDP ($= PQ$). Monetarists believe that the most significant cause of macroeconomic instability has been inappropriate monetary policy. Too rapid increases in M cause inflation; insufficient growth of M causes recession. In this view, a major cause of the Great Depression was inappropriate monetary policy that allowed the money supply to decline.

5. Real-business-cycle theory views changes in resource availability and technology (real factors), which alter productivity, as the main causes of macroeconomic instability. In this theory, shifts in the economy's long-run aggregate supply curve change real output. In turn, money demand and money supply change, shifting the aggregate demand curve in the same direction as the initial change in long-run aggregate supply. Real output thus can change without a change in the price level.

6. A coordination failure is said to occur when people do not reach a mutually beneficial equilibrium because they lack some way to jointly coordinate their actions to achieve it. Depending on people's expectations, the economy can come to rest at a good equilibrium (noninflationary full-employment output) or bad equilibriums (less-than-full-employment output or demand-pull inflation). These bad equilibriums are coordination failures.

7. The rational expectations theory (RET) rests on two assumptions: (1) With sufficient information, people's beliefs about future economic outcomes accurately reflect the likelihood that those outcomes will occur; and (2) markets are highly competitive, meaning that prices and wages are flexible both upward and downward.

8. New classical economists (monetarists and rational expectations theorists) see the economy as automatically correcting itself when disturbed from its full-employment level of real output. In RET, unanticipated changes in aggregate demand change the price level, which in the short run leads firms to change output. But once the firms

realize that all prices are changing (including nominal wages) as part of general inflation or deflation, they change their output to the previous level. Anticipated changes in aggregate demand produce only changes in the price level, not changes in real output.

9. Mainstream economists reject the new classical view that all prices and wages are flexible downward. Nominal wages, in particular, are inflexible downward because of several factors including labour contracts, efficiency wages, and insider-outsider relationships. This means that declines in aggregate demand decrease real output, not simply wages and prices.

10. Monetarist and RET economists recommend a monetary rule in which the money supply is increased at a rate equal to the long-run growth of potential GDP. They also support maintaining a "neutral" fiscal policy, as opposed to using discretionary fiscal policy to create budget deficits or budget surpluses. A few monetarists and RET economists favour a constitutional amendment that would require the federal government to balance its budget annually.

11. Mainstream economists oppose a monetary rule and a balanced-budget requirement, vigorously defending discretionary monetary and fiscal policy. They say that theory and evidence suggest that these policies are helpful in achieving full employment, price stability, and economic growth.

TERMS AND CONCEPTS

classical economics
Keynesianism
monetarism
equation of exchange
velocity
real-business-cycle theory
coordination failures

new classical economics
price-level surprises
new Keynesian economics
efficiency wage
insider-outsider theory
monetary rule

STUDY QUESTIONS

1. **KEY QUESTION** *Use the aggregate demand-aggregate supply model to compare the "old" classical and Keynesian interpretations of* **a** *the aggregate supply curve and* **b** *the stability of the aggregate demand curve. Which of these interpretations seems most consistent with the realities of the Great Depression?*

2. What is the usual cause of macroeconomic instability, according to mainstream economists? What role does the spending-income multiplier play in creating instability? How might adverse aggregate supply factors cause instability, according to mainstream economists?

3. State and explain the basic equation of monetarism. What is the major cause of macroeconomic instability, as viewed by monetarists?

4. **KEY QUESTION** *Suppose that the money supply and the nominal GDP for a hypothetical economy are $96 billion and $336 billion, respectively. What is the velocity of money? How will households and businesses react if the central bank reduces the money supply by $20 billion? By how much will nominal GDP have to fall to restore equilibrium, according to the monetarist perspective?*

5. Briefly describe the difference between a so-called real business cycle and a more traditional "spending" business cycle.

6. Andrew and Craig were walking directly towards each other in a congested store aisle. Andrew moved to his left to avoid Craig, and at the same time Craig moved to his right to avoid Andrew. They bumped into each other. What concept does this example illustrate? How does this idea relate to macroeconomic instability?

7. **KEY QUESTION** *Use an AD-AS graph to demonstrate and explain the price-level and real-output outcome of an anticipated decline in aggregate demand, as viewed by RET economists. (Assume that the economy initially is operating at its full-employment level of output.) Then, demonstrate and explain on the same graph the outcome, as viewed by mainstream economists.*

8. What is an efficiency wage? How might payment of an above-market wage reduce shirking by employees and reduce worker turnover? How might efficiency wages contribute to downward wage inflexibility, at least for a time, when aggregate demand declines?

9. How might relationships between so-called insiders and outsiders contribute to downward wage inflexibility?

10. Use the equation of exchange to explain the rationale for a monetary rule. Why does the rule run into trouble if V unexpectedly falls because of, say, a drop in investment spending by businesses?

11. Answer questions (a) and (b) on the basis of the following information for a hypothetical economy in year 1: money supply = $400 billion; long-term annual growth of potential GDP = 3 percent; velocity = 4. Assume that the banking system initially has no excess reserves and the desired reserves are 10 percent. Also assume that velocity is constant and the economy initially is operating at its full-employment real output.
    a. What is the level of nominal GDP in year 1?
    b. Suppose the Bank of Canada adheres to a monetary rule through open-market operations. What amount of Canadian bonds will it have to sell to, or buy from, banks or the public between years 1 and 2 to meet its monetary rule?

12. Explain the difference between "active" discretionary fiscal policy advocated by mainstream economists and "passive" fiscal policy advocated by new classical economists. Explain: "The problem with a balanced-budget amendment is that it would, in a sense, require active fiscal policy—but in the *wrong* direction—as the economy slides into recession."

13. **KEY QUESTION** *Place MON, RET, or MAIN besides statements that most closely reflect monetarist, rational expectations, or mainstream views, respectively.*
    a. *Anticipated changes in aggregate demand affect only the price level; they have no effect on real output.*
    b. *Downward wage inflexibility means that declines in aggregate demand can cause long-lasting recession.*
    c. *Changes in the money supply M increase PQ; at first only Q rises because nominal wages are fixed, but once workers adapt their expectations to new realities, P rises and Q returns to its former level.*
    d. *Fiscal and monetary policy smooth out the business cycle.*
    e. *The Bank of Canada should increase the money supply at a fixed annual rate.*

14. You have just been elected Prime Minister of Canada and the present governor of the Bank of Canada has resigned. You need to appoint a new person to this position, as well as a person for minister of finance. Using Table 17-1 and your knowledge of macroeconomics, identify the perspectives on macro theory and policy you would want your appointees to hold. Remember, the economic health of the entire nation—and your party's chances for reelection—may depend on these selections.

15. **(The Last Word)** How would profit sharing by labour increase downward "wage" flexibility? Why is greater downward wage flexibility desirable?

16. **WEB-BASED QUESTION The Equation of Exchange—What Is the Current Velocity of Money?** The fundamental equation of monetarism is the equation of exchange: $MV = PQ = GDP$. The velocity of money, V, can be found by dividing GDP by M, the money supply. Calculate the velocity of money for the past few years. Which GDP data should be used: real or nominal GDP? Why? How stable is V during this time? Is V increasing or decreasing? Get GDP data from Statistics Canada www.statcan.ca/english/Pgdb/Economy/Economic/econ04.htm. Money supply data can also be found at Statistics Canada www.statcan.ca/english/Pgdb/Economy/Economic/econ07.htm.

17. **WEB-BASED QUESTION Canadian Real GDP—Is It Really More Stable Than Other Countries'?** Since 1946, quarterly changes in Canadian real GDP have been less volatile than in earlier decades. How does recent Canadian GDP volitility compare to other countries? Would you expect it to be more or less stable? Why or why not? Is there a pattern (e.g., is lower volatility associated with higher GDP countries)? Would the comparison be valid if nominal GDP data was used rather than real GDP data? Visit the Quarterly Growth Rates in GDP at Constant Prices section at the OECD www.oecd.org/std/nahome.htm.

Economic Growth

DESPITE PERIODS OF MACROECONOMIC INSTABILITY, the market economies have experienced impressive economic growth during this century. In Canada, real output has increased twenty fold since 1900, while population has only tripled. This means that seven times more goods and services are available to the average Canadian resident than were available in 1900. Moreover, today's goods and services are of much higher quality than those of 1900. This expansion and improvement of output has created greater material abundance, lifted the standard of living, and eased the unlimited-wants-scarce-resources problem.

But the Canadian growth story is not totally upbeat. Since 1970 Canadian economic growth has slowed considerably relative to that in earlier periods and other nations. Twenty-one advanced industrial nations, not to mention many developing nations, grew more rapidly than Canada over the past three decades.

We begin our analysis of economic growth by clearly defining it. Next, we show how economic growth can be depicted within our graphical models. Then, we examine the long-term growth record of Canada paying particular attention to the contributing factors. Since productivity is one of these factors, we examine the post-1970 slowdown of productivity growth in Canada. Next, we explore whether Canada is achieving a "new economy," which might deliver a stronger future rate of growth. Finally, we ask what government can do, if anything, to boost the rate of economic growth.

IN THIS CHAPTER YOU WILL LEARN:

The definition of economic growth and how to measure it.

•

The factors that make economic growth possible.

•

About Canada's productivity slowdown and its causes.

•

That there are signs that Canada's productivity has started to pick up again.

The Big Picture

IN CHAPTER 7 WE POINTED OUT THAT THERE are two main themes in macroeconomics: In the short to medium term, to attempt to keep an economy on its production possibility curve with stable prices through the appropriate policies; and to bring about economic growth in the long run to very long run (an outward shift of the production possibility curve). This chapter is concerned with the second of these objectives.

As you read this chapter, keep the following points in mind:

- **Key Concept 8** is discussed.

- Both aggregate demand and aggregate supply factors can affect long-term economic growth, but aggregate supply factors are more important.
- There are two ways to achieve economic growth: **a** by increasing the amounts of factor inputs, and **b** getting more output from available factor inputs—an increase in productivity.
- There are those who believe economic growth cannot be sustained forever; natural resources are fixed, and there is a limit to the pollutants that the environment can absorb. Others disagree, claiming that technological advancement will save us. ■

GROWTH ECONOMICS

The subset of economics called *growth economics* examines the factors that expand an economy's production capacity over time. It also analyzes public policies designed to increase economic growth.

Two Definitions

Economic growth is defined and measured in two ways:

1. An increase in real GDP occurring over some time period.
2. An increase in real GDP *per capita* occurring over some time period.

In measuring military potential or political preeminence, the first definition is more relevant. The second definition, however, is superior for comparing living standards. While China's GDP is $744 billion compared with Denmark's $155 billion, Denmark's GDP per capita is $29,890 compared with only $620 in China.

In either definition, economic growth is calculated as an annual percentage rate of growth. For example, if real GDP was $200 billion in some country last year and $210 billion this year, the rate of growth would be 5 percent {= ($210 – $200)/$200] × 100}.

Growth as a Goal

Growth is a widely held economic goal. The expansion of total output relative to population means rising real wages and incomes and thus higher standards of living. *An economy experiencing economic growth is better able to meet people's wants and resolve socioeconomic problems.* Rising real wages and incomes provide new opportunities to individuals and families—a vacation trip, a home computer, higher education—*without* sacrificing other opportunities and enjoyments. A growing economy can take on new programs to alleviate poverty and clean up the environment *without* impairing existing levels of consumption, investment, and public goods production.

In short, *growth lessens the burden of scarcity*. A growing economy, unlike a static economy, can consume more today while increasing its capacity to produce more in the future. By easing the burden of scarcity—by relaxing society's production constraints—economic growth allows a nation to attain economic goals more fully and to undertake new endeavours that require goods and services.

Arithmetic of Growth

Why do economists make such a big deal about small changes in the rate of growth? Because it really matters! For Canada, with a current real GDP of about $850 billion, the difference between a 3 percent and a 4 percent rate of growth is about $1 billion of output per year. For a very poor country, a 0.5-percentage-point change in the growth rate may mean the difference between starvation and mere hunger.

When viewed over many years, an apparently small difference in the rate of growth becomes highly significant because of compounding. Suppose Alta and Zorn have identical GDPs, but Alta grows at a 4 percent yearly rate, while Zorn grows at 2 percent. Based on the rule of 70, Alta's GDP would double in about 18 years (= 70/4); Zorn's would double in 35 years (= 70/2).

Some economists argue that growth is more important to a nation's future than is economic stability. Eliminating a gap between actual GDP and potential GDP might increase the national income by, say, 3 percent on a one-time basis. In contrast, a 3 percent annual growth rate will increase the national income by more than 6 percent in 2 years, more than 9 percent in 3 years, and so on.

INGREDIENTS OF GROWTH

There are six ingredients in the growth of any economy. They can be grouped as supply, demand, and efficiency factors.

Supply Factors

Four ingredients of growth relate to the physical ability of the economy to expand. They are (1) increases in the quantity and quality of natural resources, (2) increases in the quantity and quality of human resources, (3) increases in the supply (or stock) of capital goods, and (4) improvements in technology. These **supply factors**—physical and technical agents of greater production—permit an economy to increase its real output.

Demand Factor

The fifth ingredient of economic growth is the **demand factor**. To realize its growing production potential, a nation must fully employ its expanding supplies of resources. This requires a growing level of aggregate demand.

Efficiency Factor

The sixth ingredient of economic growth is the **efficiency factor**. To reach its production potential, a nation must achieve not only full employment but also economic efficiency. The country must use its existing and added resources in the least costly way (*productive efficiency*) in producing the specific mix of goods and services that maximizes society's well-being (*allocative efficiency*). The ability to expand production, together with the full use of available resources, is *not* sufficient for achieving maximum possible growth. Also required is the efficient use of those resources.

The supply, demand, and efficiency factors in growth are related. Unemployment caused by insufficient aggregate demand (the demand factor) can retard the rate of new capital accumulation (a supply factor) and slow expenditures on research (also a supply factor). Conversely, low spending on innovation and investment (supply factors) can cause insufficient aggregate demand (the demand factor) and unemployment. Widespread inefficiency in the use of resources (the efficiency factor) may translate into higher costs of goods and services and thus lower profits. This may slow the accumulation of capital (a supply factor).

GRAPHICAL ANALYSIS

We can place the six factors underlying economic growth in proper perspective through Chapter 2's production possibilities curves and Chapter 16's long-run AD-AS analysis.

Growth and Production Possibilities

Recall that a curve such as *AB* in Figure 18-1 is a production possibilities curve. It indicates the various *maximum* combinations of products the economy can produce with its fixed quantity and quality of natural, human, and capital resources and its stock of technological knowledge. An improvement in any of the supply factors will push the production possibilities curve outward, as from *AB* to *CD*.

But the demand and efficiency factors remind us the economy need not attain its maximum production potential. The curve may shift outward but leave the economy behind at some level of operation such as *a* on *AB*. Because *a* is inside the new production possibilities curve *CD*, the economy has not achieved its growth potential. This enhanced production potential won't be realized unless (1) aggregate demand increases sufficiently to sustain full employment, and (2) the additional resources

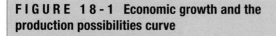

FIGURE 18-1 Economic growth and the production possibilities curve

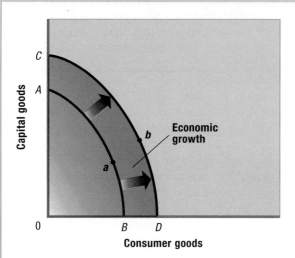

Economic growth is made possible by the four supply factors that shift the production possibilities curve outward, as from *AD* to *CD*. Economic growth is realized when the demand factor and efficiency factor move the economy from point *a* to *b*.

are employed efficiently such that they make the maximum possible dollar contribution to output.

An increase in aggregate demand is needed to move the economy from *a* to a point on *CD*. And to realize the greatest increase in the monetary value of its output—its greatest real GDP growth—this location on *CD* must be optimal. You know from Chapter 2 that this "best allocation" is determined by expanding production of each good until its marginal benefit equals its marginal cost. Here, we assume this optimal combination of capital and consumer goods is *b*.

Example: The net increase in the labour force of Canada is roughly 200,000 workers per year. This increment raises the production capacity of the economy. But obtaining the extra output these added workers can produce presumes they can find jobs. It also presumes these jobs are in firms and industries where their talents are fully and optimally used. Society does not want new labour-force entrants to be unemployed. Nor does it want pediatricians working as plumbers or workers producing goods that have higher marginal costs than marginal benefits. *(Key Question 2)*

Labour and Productivity
Although demand and efficiency considerations are important, discus-

sions of growth focus primarily on the supply side. Figure 18-2 provides a framework for discussing the supply factors in growth. It indicates two fundamental ways society can increase its real output and income: (1) by increasing its inputs of resources, and (2) by increasing the productivity of those inputs. Let's focus on inputs of labour. We can say *that a nation's real GDP in any year depends on the input of labour (measured in worker-hours) multiplied by* **labour productivity** *(measured as real output per worker per hour).*

$$\frac{\text{Total}}{\text{output}} = \text{worker-hours} \times \text{labour productivity}$$

Illustration: Assume an economy has 10 workers, each working 2,000 hours per year (50 weeks at 40 hours per week). The total input of worker-hours therefore is 20,000 hours. If productivity—average real output per worker-hour—is $5, then total output or real GDP will be $100,000 (= 20,000 × $5).

What determines the number of hours worked each year? And what determines labour productivity? Figure 18-2 provides some answers. The hours of labour input depend on the size of the employed labour force and the length of the average workweek. Labour-force size depends on the size of the working-age population and the **labour-force participation rate**—*the percentage of the working-age population actually in the labour*

FIGURE 18-2 The determinants of real output

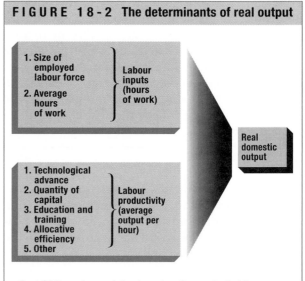

Real GDP can be usefully viewed as the product of the quantity of labour inputs multiplied by labour productivity.

force. The average workweek is governed by legal and institutional considerations and by collective bargaining.

Productivity is determined by technological progress, the quantity of capital goods available to workers, the quality of labour itself, and the efficiency with which inputs are allocated, combined, and managed. Productivity rises when the health, training, education, and motivation of workers are improved; when workers have more and better machinery and natural resources with which to work; when production is better organized and managed; and when labour is reallocated from less efficient industries to more efficient industries.

Long-Run AD-AS Model

We can also view economic growth through the long-run AD-AS model developed in Chapter 16.

Suppose an economy's aggregate demand curve, long-run aggregate supply curve, and short-run aggregate supply curve are AD_1, AS_{LR1}, and AS_1, as shown in Figure 18-3. The equilibrium price level and level of real output are P_1 and Q_1.

At price level P_1, the short-run aggregate supply is AS_1; it slopes upward because, in the short run, changes in the price level change the level of real output. However, in the long run, nominal wages change in the same direction and by the same percentage as the price level. Real output then returns to its prior level, making the long-run aggregate supply curve vertical at the economy's full-employment level of output, here Q_1. As with the location of the production possibilities curve, real supply factors—the quantity and quality of resources and technology—determine the full-employment level of real output. Price-level changes do not shift a nation's production possibilities curve; neither do they shift the nation's long-run aggregate supply curve.

Increase in Short- and Long-Run Aggregate Supply Let's now assume that changes in the supply factors shift the long-run aggregate supply curve rightward from AS_{LR1} to AS_{LR2}. This means the production possibilities curve in Figure 18-2 has moved outward. The economy's *potential* output has increased.

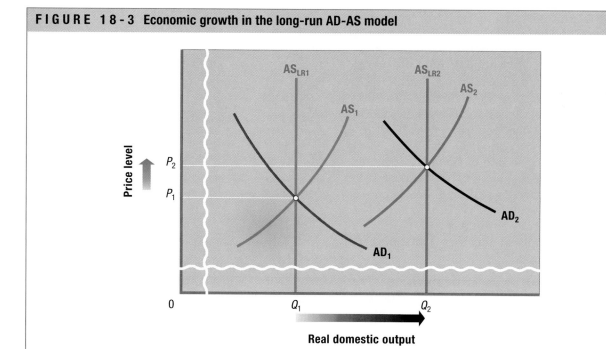

FIGURE 18-3 Economic growth in the long-run AD-AS model

Long-run and short-run aggregate supply have increased over time, as from AS_{LR1} to AS_{LR2} and AS_1 to AS_2. Simultaneously, aggregate demand has shifted rightward, as from AD_1 to AD_2. The outcome of these combined shifts has been economic growth, shown as the increase in real output from Q_1 to Q_2, accompanied by inflation, shown as the rise in the price level from P_1 to P_2.

Increase in Aggregate Demand Assuming downward price and wage inflexibility, the economy can *realize* its greater production potential only through an increase in aggregate demand. In Figure 18-3, suppose that increases in consumption, investment, government, and net export spending shift the aggregate demand curve from AD_1 to AD_2. Also suppose the economy continues to use its resources efficiently.

Economic Outcomes The increases of aggregate supply and aggregate demand in our figure have increased real output from Q_1 to Q_2 and boosted the price level from P_1 to P_2. At the higher price level P_2, the economy confronts a new short-run aggregate supply curve AS_2. The result of the dynamics described in Figure 18-3 is economic growth, accompanied by mild inflation. These outcomes are consistent with the actual secular trend of real GDP and the price level in Canada. (You can confirm this by examining the national accounts at the end of this book.) **(Key Question 3)**

GROWTH IN CANADA

Table 18-1 provides an overview of economic growth in Canada over past decades. Column 2 shows the economy's growth as measured by increases in real GDP. Although not steady, the growth of real GDP has been strong. *Real GDP has increased over tenfold since 1946.* But the Canadian population has also increased. Nevertheless, in column 4 we find that *real per capita GDP has increased almost fivefold since 1946.*

What has been the rate of Canada's growth? Global Perspective 18-1 shows that the post-1948 growth rate of Canada's real GDP has been 4.1 percent per year, while real GDP per capita has grown at more than 2 percent per year.

However, we must qualify these bare numbers in four ways:

1. **IMPROVED PRODUCTS AND SERVICES** The numbers in Table 18-1 and Global Perspective 18-1 don't fully account for improvements in the quality of products and services; they thus understate the growth of economic well-being. Purely quantitative data do not accurately compare an era of iceboxes and LPs and one of refrigerators and CDs.
2. **ADDED LEISURE** The increases in real GDP and per capita GDP identified in Table 18-1

(1) Year	(2) GDP (billions of 1992 dollars)	(3) Population (millions)	(4) Per capita GDP (1992 dollars) (2) ÷ (3)
1900	$ 20.2	5.3	3,811
1910	33.9	7.0	4,843
1920	42.1	8.6	4,895
1926	48.3	9.5	5,084
1929	58.2	10.0	5,820
1933	42.1	10.6	3,972
1939	61.8	11.0	5,618
1942	93.3	11.5	8,113
1946	95.8	12.3	7,789
1951	120.3	14.0	8,592
1956	174.3	16.1	10,826
1961	201.3	18.2	11,060
1966	289.0	20.0	14,450
1971	359.0	21.6	16,620
1976	464.8	23.0	20,208
1981	550.4	24.3	22,650
1986	632.1	25.4	24,886
1991	695.2	27.0	25,748
1997	798.2	30.2	26,430

TABLE 18-1 Real GDP and per capita GDP, 1900-1997

Sources: (1) 1900-1920: Derived from O.J. Firestone, *Canada's Economic Development, 1867-1953* (London: Bowes and Bowes, 1958), p. 66; (b) 1926-1983: Statistics Canada, *National Income and Expenditure Accounts, 1926-1986* (1988); (c) 1984-1997; ibid., various years. For years prior to 1997, GDP and per capita GDP have been changed from 1986 to 1992 dollars by a coefficient of 1.281.

were accomplished despite large increases in leisure. The standard workweek, once 70 hours, is now about 40 hours. Again the raw growth numbers understate the gain in economic well-being.
3. **ENVIRONMENTAL EFFECTS** In contrast, these measures of growth do *not* take into account adverse effects growth may have on the environment and the quality of life. If growth debases the physical environment, and creates a stressful work environment, the

18-1
GLOBAL PERSPECTIVE

Average annual growth rates since 1948, selected nations

Real GDP in Canada has grown at a respectable rate compared to several other advanced industrial countries since 1948. Japan and Germany have had the highest average annual growth rates in this period.

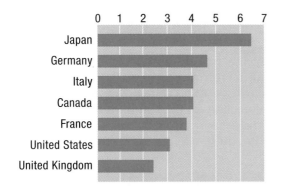

Average Annual Growth of Real GDP, 1948–1997

Source: Organization for Economic Cooperation and Development.

bare growth numbers will overstate the gains from growth.

4. **INTERNATIONAL COMPARISONS** Over the past half century, the growth record of Canada is less impressive than that of several other nations. Observe in Global Perspective 18-1, that Japan's growth rate has averaged more than 50 percent of Canada's growth during this period. In recent years, however, the growth rate in Japan and Germany has slowed. Also, in recent decades there has been a tendency for countries with smaller GDPs per capita to grow more rapidly than countries with already high GDPs per capita.

18-1
QUICK REVIEW

• Economic growth can be measured as **a** an increase in real GDP over time or **b** an increase in real GDP per capita over time.

• Graphically, economic growth is shown as **a** an outward shifts of a nation's production possibilities curve (accompanied by the movement from some point on the old curve to a point on the new curve), or **b** combined rightward shifts of the long-run aggregate supply curve, the short-run aggregate supply curve, and the aggregate demand curve.

• Annual growth of real GDP in Canada has averaged more than 4 percent since World War II.

ACCOUNTING FOR GROWTH

Postwar output growth has been considerably greater than that which can be attributed solely to increase in the inputs of labour and capital. There are two other factors involved. The first is inter-industry shifts from lower to higher productivity occupations. The best-known example is the shift of workers out of relatively low-productivity farming to higher-productivity urban industry. The second factor is **total factor productivity (TFP)**, the efficiency with which factors are used together in the production process. It includes technological progress, organizational structure, economies of scale, regulation, entrepreneurship and risk-taking, labour-management relations, capacity utilization, and the efficiency with which resources are allocated. TFP is output growth less input growth.

Table 18-2 shows the sources of the growth of real GDP from 1961 to 1997.

Inputs Versus Productivity

There are two ways a society can increase its real income: (1) by increasing its inputs of resources and (2) by increasing the productivity of those inputs. In Canada about 75 percent of our growth between 1961 and 1996 was due to the use of more inputs and about 25 percent was the consequence of rising productivity—getting more output per unit of labour and capital input. These data emphasize that *productivity growth has been a significant force underlying the growth of our real GDP*. However, the rate of growth of productivity has greatly diminished since 1975, as will be discussed below.

Quantity of Labour

Figure 18-4 indicates that our population and labour force have both increased. Until recently, a

TABLE 18-2 Sources of growth of real GDP, 1961–1996

Growth in	AVERAGE ANNUAL RATES OF GROWTH (AS PERCENT)				CONTRIBUTION TO TOTAL GROWTH (AS PERCENT)		
	1961-75	1975-82	1982-91	1961-96	1961-75	1975-82	1961-96
GDP	5.2	2.5	2.8	3.7			
Labour productivity*	3.3	1.5	1.3	2.0			
Capital/labour ratio	2.9	4.5	1.8	2.4			
Input of labour**	2.3	1.2	1.6	1.1	28.0	33.9	29
Input of capital	5.3	5.7	3.4	4.2	38.4	63.0	44.5
Aggregate TFP†	1.7	−0.4	0.5	1.0	33.5	3.2	26.7

Source: Statistics Canada, Cansim, 7898.
*Real GDP per person hour. **Measured in person hours. †Also referred to as Multifactor Productivity (MFP).

high birth rate, a declining death rate, and continuous (and at times heavy) immigration have combined to provide Canada with substantial population growth throughout much of its history. From New France's 65,000 in 1759, the population of Canada grew to almost 2.5 million by 1851.

By the middle of 1998, the population and civilian labour force were 30.2 million and 15.5 million respectively; they continue to grow. Historical declines in the length of the average workweek have reduced labour inputs, but the workweek has declined very modestly since World War

FIGURE 18-4 Population and civilian labour force growth, 1900–1996

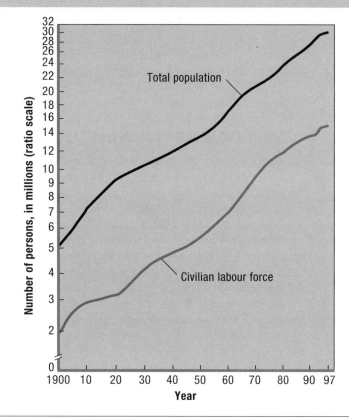

The Canadian civilian labour force as a percentage of the total population has averaged about 40 percent since 1900, but has been rising in the 1970s and 1980s to reach almost 50 percent in 1994. *Source: Historical Statistics of Canada and Statistics Canada.*

II. Declining birth rates in the past 30 years have brought about a decline in the rate of population growth. However, largely because of immigration and increased participation of women in labour markets, our civilian labour force continues to grow by about 200,000 workers a year. As Table 18-2 shows, the input of labour, measured in person hours, has grown at about 1.1 percent per annum in the last 35 years.

Technological Advance

Technological advance is broadly defined so as to include not only new production techniques and product innovation but also new managerial techniques and new forms of business organization. Generally, technological advance is linked with *the discovery of new knowledge* that permits firms to combine a specific amount of resources in ways to achieve a greater output.

Technological advance and capital formation (investment) are closely related; technological advance often, but not always, requires investment in new machinery and equipment. The sense there was a more efficient way to catch a rabbit than by running it down led to investment in the bow and arrow. The purchase of new computers not only means more of these computers, but quicker, more powerful computers embodying new technology. In contrast, modern crop-rotation practices and contour ploughing are ideas that contribute to expanded output, although they do not necessarily use new kinds of, or increased amounts of, capital equipment.

Technological advance has been both rapid and profound. Gas and diesel engines, conveyor belts, and assembly lines are examples of significant developments of the past. More recently, technology has produced automation and the push-button factory. Bigger, faster, and more fuel-efficient commercial aircraft; integrated microcircuits, computers, xerography, containerized shipping, and the Internet—not to mention biotechnology, lasers, and superconductivity—are technological achievements that were in the realm of fantasy a generation or two ago.

Quantity of Capital

Almost 45 percent of the annual growth of real output since 1961 is attributable to increases in the quantity of capital. A worker will be more productive when equipped with a larger amount of capital goods. And how does a nation acquire more capital? Capital accumulation results from saving and the investment in plant and equipment that these savings make possible. A recent estimate suggests that total output will increase by about one-fourth of a percentage point for each extra percentage of GDP invested in machinery and equipment.

The critical consideration for labour productivity is the amount of capital goods *per worker*. The aggregate stock of capital might expand in a specific period, but if the labour force also increases rapidly, labour productivity need not rise because each worker will not necessarily be better equipped. This happened in Canada in the 1970s and 1980s when the labour force surged, contributing to a slowing of Canadian productivity growth.

Education and Training

Education and training improve a worker's productivity and result in higher earnings. Like investment in physical capital, investment in human capital is an important means of increasing labour productivity. Perhaps the simplest measure of labour quality is the level of educational attainment. Figure 18-5 reflects the educational gains in the past two decades. University is now being attended by almost 20 percent of those aged 18 to 24 years, as opposed to about 12 percent in the early 1970s; those attending community colleges have increased during the same period from 12 percent to almost 24 percent in the 1995–96 school year. It is clear from Figure 18-5 that education has become accessible to more people in Canada.

But there are concerns about the quality of Canadian education. Scores on standardized achievement tests have declined relative to scores of a few decades ago. Furthermore, Canadian students in science and mathematics do not do as well as students in many other industrialized nations. Japanese children have a longer school day and attend school 240 days per year compared to 180 in Canada. Also, we have been producing fewer engineers and scientists, a problem that may be a result of inadequate training in math and science in elementary and high schools. And it is argued that on-the-job training (apprenticeship programs) in Japan and Germany—nations with fast rates of productivity growth—are more available and far superior to those in Canada.

FIGURE 18-5 Full-time post-secondary enrolment by level, relevant population, 1973–1974 to 1992–1993

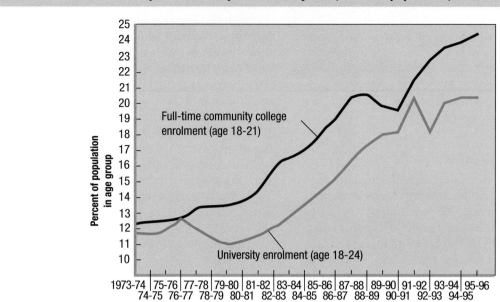

The percentage of young Canadians attending colleges and universities has been rising in the last 25 years, although university enrolment has recently dropped.

Source: Statistics Canada, *Education in Canada, 1997* (Ottawa, 1998), cat. no. 81-229, Table 23.

Resource Allocation and Scale Economies

Labour productivity in Canada has increased in part because of economies of scale and improved resource allocation. Let's consider resource allocation first.

Improved Resource Allocation

Improved resource allocation means that workers over time have reallocated themselves from low-productivity employment to high-productivity employment. Historically, much labour has been shifted from agriculture—where labour productivity is low—to manufacturing, where it is quite high. More recently, labour has shifted away from some manufacturing industries to even higher productivity industries such as legal, health, consulting, and financial services. As a result of such shifts, the average productivity of Canadian workers in the aggregate has increased.

Also, labour market discrimination has historically denied women and minorities access to high-productivity jobs. The decline of such discrimination over time has shifted these groups from low-productivity jobs to higher-productivity jobs, increasing overall labour productivity and raising real GDP.

Tariffs, import quotas, and other barriers to international trade often keep resources in relatively unproductive employments. The long-run movement towards freer international trade has therefore improved the allocation of resources and expanded real output in Canada.

Economies of Scale

Economies of scale are production advantages deriving from increased market and firm size. A large corporation often can select more efficient production techniques than can a small-scale firm. A large manufacturer of autos can use elaborate assembly lines, with computerization and robotics, while smaller producers must settle for less advanced technologies. Markets have increased in scope over time and firms have increased in size, allowing more efficient production methods to be used. Accordingly, Canadian labour productivity has increased and economic growth has occurred.

Detriments to Growth

Some developments *detract* from the growth of real output and income. There have been several changes in the regulation of industry, environmental pollution, and worker health and safety since World War II that have negatively affected growth. The expansion of government regulation in such areas as pollution control, worker health and safety, and access for the disabled has diverted investment spending away from growth-increasing capital goods and towards expenditures providing cleaner air and water, greater worker protection, and improved access for disabled workers and consumers.

A firm required to spend $1 million on a new scrubber to meet government standards for air pollution or to make its stores accessible to the disabled will not have that $1 million to spend on machinery and equipment that would expand real output. The diversion of resources to deal with dishonesty and crime, the effects of work stoppages because of labour disputes, and the impact of bad weather on agricultural output are also factors that impede economic growth.

While worker safety, clean air and water, equal access for the disabled, and the overall quality of life may come at the expense of economic growth, the reverse is also true. Economic growth does not automatically enhance society's welfare. Growth of real output may involve opportunity costs of other things (a clean environment, a fair society) we value more highly. *Productivity measures output per hour of work, not overall well-being per hour of work.* Increases in real GDP are not necessarily matched with equal increases in well-being. Thus, society may rationally decide to "trade off" some economic growth to achieve other desirable ends. *(Key Question 5)*

Other Contributing Factors

There are other difficult-to-quantify characteristics that affect an economy's growth rate. For example, Canada's large and varied supplies of natural resources have been an important contributor to its economic growth. Canada enjoys an abundance of fertile soil, desirable climatic and weather conditions, large quantities of most mineral resources, and generous sources of power. Canada has a larger variety and greater quantity of natural resources than the vast majority of other nations.

While an abundant natural resource base is helpful to growth, a meagre resource base does not doom a nation to slow growth. Although Japan's natural resources are severely constrained, its post-World War II growth has been remarkable. In contrast, some of the lower income countries of Africa and South America have substantial amounts of natural resources.

There are additional unmeasurable factors affecting a nation's growth rate. In particular, the overall social-cultural-political environment of Canada generally has promoted economic growth. Several factors contribute to this favourable environment:

1. Unlike many other nations, there are virtually no social or moral taboos on production and material progress. Canadian social philosophy has embraced material advance as an attainable and desirable economic goal. The inventor, the innovator, and the business executive are accorded high degrees of prestige and respect in Canadian society.

2. Canadians have traditionally possessed positive attitudes towards work and risk taking; Canada has benefited from a willing labour force and an ample supply of entrepreneurs.

3. The market system has many personal and corporate incentives encouraging growth; the Canadian economy rewards actions that increase output.

4. The Canadian economy is founded on a stable political system characterized by democratic principles, internal order, the right of property ownership, the legal status of enterprise, and the enforcement of contracts. Recent studies show that politically open societies grow much more rapidly on average than those where freedom is limited.

Though difficult to quantify, these characteristics have provided an excellent foundation for Canadian economic growth.

Macroeconomic Instability and Growth

The information in Table 18-2 reflects the actual growth experience of Canada, not potential or full-employment, real national income. Our annual growth rate would have been approximately 0.4 to 0.5 percentage points higher over this period if the economy's full-employment output had been achieved year after year.

The Great Depression of the 1930s in particular was a serious blow to Canada's long-run growth record. Between 1929 and 1933 our real GDP (measured in 1986 prices) actually *declined* from $53 to $38 billion. In 1939 the real GDP was only slightly higher than in 1929. More recently, the severe 1980–82 recessions cost Canada more than $60 billion in lost output and income.

But that is only part of the picture. Recession and unemployment can have harmful "carryover" effects on the growth rate in subsequent years of full employment though negative effects on other growth factors. Recession and unemployment may depress investment and capital accumulation. Moreover, firms may cut back on research and development efforts during recession so that technological advance diminishes; union resistance to technological change may stiffen; skills of idle workers deteriorate; and so forth. While it is difficult to quantify the effect of these considerations on the growth rate, they undoubtedly are important.

18-2
QUICK REVIEW

- Increases in total factor productivity have accounted for about one-quarter of increases in Canadian real GDP; the use of more labour and capital inputs accounts for the remainder.

- Improved technology, more capital, more education and training, economies of scale, and improved resource allocation have been the main contributors to Canadian economic growth.

- The average annual growth rate in Canada has been diminished by periods of depression and

---

THE PRODUCTIVITY SLOWDOWN IN CANADA

As shown in Table 18-2, total factor productivity growth has slowed down considerably since 1975. Labour productivity growth has also markedly diminished since 1975, particularly during the 1980s when it grew at just 1.3 percent per annum, almost a third of the growth rate in the 1961–75 period. While both total factor productivity and labour productivity growth improved during the

1990s, both are still well below the growth rates achieved during the 1961–75 period.

Although labour productivity growth has been slowing worldwide, Canadian productivity growth has been slower than most other major industrialized nations. Canada still enjoys one of the highest absolute levels of output per worker, but the productivity advantage is diminishing.

Significance

The Canadian productivity slowdown has many implications.

1. **STANDARD OF LIVING** Productivity growth is the basic source of improvements in real wage rates and the standard of living. Over long periods, real income per worker-hour can increase only at the same rate as real output per worker-hour. More output per hour means more real income to distribute for each hour worked. The simplest case is of Robinson Crusoe on his deserted island. The number of fish he can catch or coconuts he can pick per hour *is* his real income or wage per hour.

   The broadest measure of living standards —the growth of real per-capita GDP—follows the path of labour productivity.

2. **INFLATION** Productivity increases partly or fully offset increases in nominal-wage rates, lessening cost-push inflationary pressures. Other things equal, a decline in the rate of productivity growth contributes to rising unit labour costs and a higher rate of inflation. Many economists believe that productivity stagnation contributed to the unusually high inflation rates of the 1970s.

3. **WORLD MARKETS** Other things equal, the slow rate of productivity growth in Canada compared to some of our major international trading partners increases relative prices of Canadian goods in world markets. The result is a decline in Canadian competitiveness and a loss of international markets for Canadian producers.

Causes of the Slowdown

There is no consensus among experts as to why Canadian productivity growth has slowed and fallen behind the rate of other industrialized nations. Because so many factors affect a country's productivity performance, there may be no simple explanation. Nevertheless, let's survey some of the possible causes.

Investment   Other things equal, the greater the percentage of a nation's GDP devoted to investment goods, the larger are its productivity gains. A worker using a bulldozer can move more landfill per hour than can that same worker using a hand shovel. Canada has had lower productivity increases than other industrial countries despite investing approximately the same percentage of GDP. Moreover, our productivity performance has been relatively poor over several decades. Let's survey some of the possible causes.

1. LOW SAVING RATE   Canada has seen its saving rate fall, which, coupled with strong private and public demands for credit, has resulted in high real interest rates relative to historical standards. High real interest rates discourage investment spending.

2. IMPORT COMPETITION   Growing import competition may have made some Canadian producers reluctant to invest in new capital equipment. They may have shifted more investment overseas towards nations with low-wage workers.

3. REGULATION   The expansion of government regulations in the areas of pollution control, worker health and safety, and access for the disabled diverted some investment spending away from output-increasing capital goods. This investment spending surely increased total utility to society, but did not directly increase output itself. The composition of investment may have shifted towards uses that do not increase productivity.

Energy Prices   The sharp increases in energy prices in the 1970s made energy-intensive capital stock uncompetitive.

The *direct* impact of higher oil prices was to increase the cost of operating capital equipment, in effect raising the "price" of capital relative to labour. Producers were more inclined to use less productive labour-intensive techniques.

The *indirect* macroeconomic effects of rising energy prices may have been even more important in reducing productivity growth. The two episodes of soaring energy prices precipitated stagflation—simultaneous inflation and rising unemployment. Government's use of restrictive macroeconomic policies to control inflation worsened and prolonged the periods of recession and slow economic growth. Recessions diminish productivity—output per worker—in that output tends to decline more rapidly than employment. The long periods of underuse of production capacity in many industries contributed to the productivity slowdown.

Technological Progress   Technological advance—usually reflected in improvements in the quality of capital goods and the efficiency with which inputs are combined—may also have faltered. Technological progress is fuelled by expenditures for formal research and development (R&D) programs. R&D spending in Canada declined as a percent of GDP from a peak of 3 percent of GDP in the mid-1960s to about 1 percent by the late 1970s, before rising once again in the early 1990s to about 1.5 percent of GDP.

However, some economists discount the importance of the R&D decline in explaining the productivity slowdown. R&D *spending* alone tells us little about R&D *accomplishments*. There is clear evidence of continuing technological advance during the past two decades.

Labour Quality   One possibility is that slower improvements in labour quality may have dampened productivity growth. The following factors may have been at work.

1. DECLINE IN EXPERIENCE LEVEL   The experience level of the labour force may have declined. The large number of baby-boom workers who entered the labour force had little experience and training and were therefore less productive. The labour force participation of women increased significantly over the past two decades. Many were married women with little or no prior labour force experience who therefore had low productivity.

2. LESS ABLE WORKERS   The declining test scores of sample students on international standardized examinations during the 1970s and 1980s may indicate a decline in worker capabilities. If so, this decline may have contributed to the productivity slowdown.

Dismal Growth of Service Productivity   Finally, it is important to note that the slowdown in Canada's productivity growth has been greater in the service sector than in the manufacturing (goods-producing) sector. Since 1973 productivity in manufacturing has increased by about 3.0 percent annually compared with over 4 percent between 1960 and 1972. But productivity in the service sector has increased by only 1 percent annually since 1973, compared to almost 3 percent between 1960 and 1972. This slow growth of service-sector productivity has been a drag on the overall productivity rate.

There are several possible reasons for the slower productivity growth in services:

1. It may be more difficult for service companies to increase their productivity by substituting capital for workers. How do you substitute machinery for a barber, dentist, cook, day-care worker, or retail clerk?

2. The competitive pressures to increase productivity may be weaker in services. Customers may be more loyal to service providers than to brands of manufactured products. Moreover, the Canadian service sector has been relatively immune from stiff foreign competition.

3. As they become wealthier, consumers usually demand higher-quality services that often require more, not fewer, service workers. Service firms may need to employ more retail clerks, security personnel, pizza deliverers, maintenance workers, or stock market analysts to stay competitive.

Some economists contend that the slow growth of productivity in services is at least partly illusory. Unlike the case in manufacturing, there are no "product quantities" to count in determining service productivity. Many increases in productivity show up as improvements in services, and such improvements are not always reflected in higher product prices (and thus greater output). Because present measurement methods do not adequately "pick up" increases in service productivity, say some economists, the overall increase of productivity growth is greatly understated.

A "NEW ECONOMY"?

Since 1981 there has been a modest improvement in productivity growth. Observe in Table 18-2 that the 2 percent annual productivity decline for 1975 to 1982 improved to a 0.5 percent annual increase between 1982 and 1991. The recession of 1990–91 halted this upward trend, but productivity growth eventually picked up during the recovery and averaged just over 1 percent over the 1990–1996 period. In 1996 real GDP grew by a healthy 4 percent.

Is Canada experiencing a resurgence of productivity growth? Is it, as a few economists claim, establishing a "new economy," based on innovations in computers and communications, coupled with global capitalism? Can it now grow at a 3 to 4 percent annual rate, rather than the previous 2 to 2.5 percent annual rate, without igniting inflation?

Indeed, many of the factors that were depressing productivity growth have eased or been reversed. Energy prices are stable, and the stagflation problem has been overcome. Research and development spending has generally increased as a percentage of GDP. Innovations in computers, telecommunications, genetic engineering, and medicine are providing a stimulus to productivity. Also, real interest rates are now low, promoting purchases of new plant and equipment. Downsizing of workforces has boosted productivity in many firms. Wages of college and university graduates have risen relative to wages of high school graduates, and this wage premium is attracting more students to universities. The inexperienced baby boomers who flooded labour markets in previous decades are now more mature, more experienced, and thus more productive workers. International markets are opening up, expanding Canada's exports. Meanwhile, global competition is spreading, holding down Canada's rate of inflation.

Nevertheless, whether these factors will produce a long period of high Canadian productivity and real GDP growth remains to be seen; one or two years does not constitute a trend. The current higher rates of productivity and real GDP growth *are* consistent with that possibility. Unfortunately, they are also consistent with the possibility that Canada is simply experiencing a rapid short-run economic expansion fuelled by high levels of investment and consumption spending. Such "booms" raise productivity by increasing real output faster than employment (labour inputs), but they are unsustainable over longer periods. History tells us that demand-pull inflation, restrictive government stabilization policy, and economic recession often follow short-run surges in productivity and GDP growth. Hence, only time will tell whether the very recent increases in productivity are permanent or transitory. The jury is still out on the notion of a "new economy." **(Key Question 8)**

GROWTH POLICIES

If we accept the view that economic growth is desirable and sustainable, then a question arises as to what public policies might stimulate growth. Several policies either are in use or have been suggested. They fit within two broad categories: demand-side policies and supply-side policies.

Demand-Side Policies

Low growth is often the consequence of inadequate aggregate demand and the GDP gap to which it gives rise. The purpose of demand-side policies is to eliminate or reduce the severity of recessions through discretionary fiscal and monetary policies. The idea is to use these tools to ensure that aggregate demand increases at an appropriate, noninflationary pace. Adequate aggregate demand not only keeps present resources fully employed, it also creates an incentive for firms to expand their operations.

In particular, monetary policy that provides low real interest rates helps promote high levels of investment spending. This spending not only sustains full employment of existing resources but also expands capital resources and thus the economy's production capacity. Government can achieve low real interest rates through a combination of a relatively easy money policy and a fiscal policy that eliminates budget deficits. Recall that the government borrowing required for financing large budget deficits drives up real interest rates, particularly when the economy is near or at full employment.

Supply-Side Policies

These policies emphasize factors that directly increase the potential output of the economy over time. Regarding Figure 18-3, the goal is to shift the economy's long-run aggregate supply curve rightward. Policies fitting this category include *education and training policies* designed to increase the nation's stock of human capital. Recent examples are (1) programs that provide retraining for workers who lose jobs because of international trade, and (2) tuition tax credits designed to increase college and university enrolment.

Other programs fitting the supply-side category include *tax policies* designed to increase saving, investment, and R&D. An example is tax deductions for those who save money in a special retirement account. Some economists favour a national consumption tax (like the federal goods and services tax, or GST) as a full or partial replacement for the personal income tax. The idea is to make consumption more expensive and thereby encourage saving. Similarly, some economists propose eliminating the corporate income tax or allowing more generous tax credits for investment and research spending. Such spending often "pays off" in rightward shifts of the nation's long-run aggregate supply curve.

Government might also promote growth via other pro-growth initiatives. Specifically, it might redirect some of its current expenditures away from transfer payments and towards expansion of public infrastructure and funding of research, basic education, and skill training. It might promote growth by further deregulating industries where sufficient competition exists to ensure improved efficiency. And it might negotiate further international trade agreements, which increase specialization, boost output, and expand trade.

While the litany of potential growth-enhancing policies is long and involved, most economists agree that it is not easy to increase a nation's growth rate through public policy. Nevertheless, they also agree there is ample international evidence to suggest that government policies *can make a difference*; they can affect an economy's long-term growth rate for better or worse.

18-3
QUICK REVIEW

- Economists have cited the following reasons for the slowdown in Canada's productivity over the past 25 years: **a** declines in labour quality, **b** a slowing of technological progress, **c** decreasing investment spending as a percentage of GDP, **d** high energy prices during the 1970s and early 1980s, and **e** lagging growth of service productivity.

- Some observers see the recent upsurge in productivity as evidence of a "new economy" that can achieve higher rates of GDP growth than those in the past two decades. This new economy is based on innovation in computers and communications coupled with the globalization of markets.

- Skeptics of the new-economy view say that it is far too early to tell whether the recent upsurge of productivity growth is transient or permanent.

In The Media

Shortage of science grads stunts growth of high-tech industries

Education policies should address the needs of the new economy, says Nortel report

NEVILLE NANKIVELL

With a post-deficit era looming, governments in Canada are readying for new education policy thrusts that include more money, tax breaks and other measures to help offset the rising costs of post-secondary tuition.

None of this will pay off properly, however, unless the culture of advanced education in Canada changes to meet the new economy's needs.

Finance Minister Paul Martin is expected to make "investment in education" a priority in his coming budget. Details should be out soon on Prime Minister Jean Chrétien's millennium megafund for post-secondary scholarships. Some provincial governments are considering a freeze on university tuition fees, which last year were up 10% on average across Canada.

In an increasingly knowledge-based economy, higher education must be a policy priority. However, just throwing more taxpayers' money at post-secondary institutions isn't the answer. Tax-relief assistance, and more innovative loan and scholarship programs will help. But it's also critically important to get resource allocations right and give more focus to real-world needs.

As a brief just presented to the Ontario government by Northern Telecom Ltd. points out, today's job requirements are different. Demand for science and technology graduates is far outstripping sup-ply. The shortage is especially true for software and computing specialists. This is holding back the potential growth of Canada's high-tech industries.

Compared with other major economies, Canada has the highest university and college enrolment rate of 18- to 21-year-olds. It also has the highest proportion of people with university and college degrees. But these trends don't hold true for the sciences. The number of our science graduates as a proportion of the labour force in the 25 to 34 age range is at the lower end of the scale internationally. Most of our major trade competitors rank higher, including the U.S.

Something has to be done about the mix of post-secondary graduates. Nortel, Canada's flagship high-tech company, says more emphasis should be placed on information technology disciplines. These include computer sciences, computer engineering, electrical engineering, applied physics and maths. Graduates in these fields play an increasingly key role in industry and commerce. In the 1980s, 45 percent of Nortel's employees in Canada were knowledge professionals. That's now nearly 80 percent.

Yet the company says our universities and colleges are struggling to meet industry's requirements. "These institutions do not have the capability or capacity to be aligned with the needs of the new economy nor the career choices of high school students," its brief says bluntly. "The system needs to be fixed. This is a problem of fundamental importance."

Significant changes are required, or we'll quickly lose the benefits of Canadian industry's improved competitiveness in recent years. Employment in the information technology sector has been growing at 20 percent annually. Old-line manufacturing jobs have been declining. Canada's fastest growing industries are knowledge-based ones. But growth will be blunted if the right skills are in short supply. Nortel estimates its Canadian hiring needs over the next five years as 4,000 new graduates and 12,000 experienced technology professionals.

Our firms also have to compete for high-tech skills with aggressive recruiters from other countries. Every year we lose good graduates to the higher paying and lower taxed U.S. The problem with this kind of brain drain is that most will never return.

At the same time, universities are turning away qualified applicants—even honour roll students, says Nortel—because they don't have the capacity for them. The solution isn't necessarily a whole lot more government funding. Giving universities more flexibility on fee-setting for high-tech professional programs can help finance their expansion. So can removing disincentives in present funding formulas that work against increasing enrolments in technology oriented courses.

To offset higher fees, assistance for needy students is required, such as loan programs that link repayment schedules more directly to income. The private sector can do more to support loan programs for high-tech graduates, increase scholarship activity and contribute equipment to university labs.

Nortel suggests other priority areas for business and universities include expanding highly successful co-op work and education programs, internship programs, and programs such as distance learning and video conferencing—virtual classroom concepts. These can lower costs and increase student access. Companies could encourage university professors to spend sabbaticals in private-sector labs.

"Collaboration with the academic community is vital for industry," the Nortel brief concludes. This is essential to take advantage of leading edge research expertise and ensure a strong flow of skills and talent for the workforce of the future.

Neville Nankivell is The Financial Post's editor-at-large, based in Ottawa.

Source: By Neville Nankivell, *The Financial Post*, February 14, 1998, p. 12.

THE STORY IN BRIEF

There is a shortage of science and technology graduates in Canada that is impeding the growth of Canada's high-tech industries.

THE ECONOMICS BEHIND THE STORY

- Canada's long-term economic growth prospects are being held back by a shortage of science and technology graduates. To shift Canada's production possibility curve outward—or to shift Canada's long-run aggregate supply curve to the right—requires the growth of an adequately trained labour force that can feed one of the most rapidly growing sectors of the Canadian economy, the software and computer industry.
- Northern Telecom makes a proposal in a brief to the Ontario government that will help increase the supply of science and technology college and university graduates. Nortel suggests providing incentives to students choosing computer sciences, computer engineering, electrical engineering, and applied physics and math. It also suggests increasing the capacity of college and universities to take in more students.
- Should governments lower tuition fees for all students to achieve their goals of more college and university graduates? ■

The
Last Word

IS GROWTH DESIRABLE?

Economists usually take for granted that growth is desirable. Is It?

The Antigrowth View   Critics of growth say industrialization and growth result in pollution, global warming, ozone depletion, and other environmental problems. These adverse spillover costs occur because inputs in the production process reenter the environment as some form of waste. The more rapid our growth and the higher our standard of living, the more waste the environment must absorb—or attempt to absorb. In an already wealthy society, further growth usually means satisfying increasingly trivial wants at the cost of mounting threats to our ecological system.

Critics of growth also argue there is little compelling evidence that economic growth has solved sociological problems such as poverty, homelessness, and discrimination. Consider poverty. In the antigrowth view, American poverty is a problem of distribution, not production. The requisite for solving the problem is commitment and political courage to redistribute wealth and income, not further increases in output.

Antigrowth sentiment also says that while growth may permit us to "make a better living," it does not give us "the good life." We may be producing more and enjoying it less. Growth means assembly-line jobs, worker burnout, and alienated employees who have little or no control over decisions affecting their lives. The changing technology at the core of growth poses new anxieties and new sources of insecurity for workers. Both high-level and low-level workers face the prospect of having their hard-earned skills and experience rendered obsolete by an onrushing technology. High-growth economies are high-stress economies, which may impair our physical and mental health.

In Defence of Growth   The primary defence of growth is that it is the path to greater material abundance and rising living standards. Rising output and incomes allow us to buy:

> more education, recreation, and travel, more medical care, closer communications, more skilled personal and professional services, and better-designed as well as more numerous products. It also means more art, music, and poetry, theater, and drama. It can even mean more time and resources devoted to spiritual growth and human development.*

Growth also enables us to improve the nation's infrastructure, enhance the care of the sick and elderly, provide greater access for the disabled, and provide more police and fire protection. Economic growth may be the only realistic way to reduce poverty, since there is little political support for greater redistribution of income. The way to improve the economic position of the poor is to increase household incomes through higher produc-

tivity and economic growth. Also, a no-growth policy among industrial nations might severely limit growth in poor nations. Foreign investment and development assistance in these nations would fall, keeping the world's poor in poverty longer.

Economic growth has not made labour more unpleasant or hazardous, as critics suggest. New machinery is usually less taxing and less dangerous than the machinery it replaces. Air-conditioned workplaces are more pleasant than steamy workshops. Furthermore, why would an end to economic growth reduce materialism or alienation? The loudest protests against materialism are heard in those nations and groups who now enjoy the highest levels of material abundance! The high standard of living that growth provides has increased our leisure and given us more time for reflection and self-fulfilment.

Does growth threaten the environment? The connection between growth and environment is tenuous, say growth proponents. Increases in economic growth need not mean increases in pollution. Pollution is not so much a by-product of growth as it is a "problem of the commons." Much of the environment—streams, lakes, oceans, and the air—is treated as "common property," with no restrictions on its use. The commons have become our dumping grounds; we have overused and debased them. Environmental pollution is a case of spillover or external costs, and correcting this problem involves regulatory legislation or specific taxes ("effluent charges") to remedy misuse of the environment.

There *are* serious pollution problems. But limiting growth is the wrong solution. Growth has allowed economies to reduce pollution, be more sensitive to environmental considerations, set aside wilderness, and clean up hazardous waste, while still enabling rising household incomes. ■

*Alice M. Rivlin, *Reviving the American Dream* (Washington: Brookings Institution, 1992), p. 36.

CHAPTER SUMMARY

1. Economic growth may be defined either in terms of **a** an expanding real domestic output (income) or **b** an expanding per-capita real output (income). Growth lessens the burden of scarcity and provides increases in real output that can be used to resolve domestic and international socioeconomic problems.

2. The supply factors in economic growth are **a** the quantity and quality of a country's natural resources, **b** the quantity and quality of its human resources, **c** its stock of capital facilities, and **d** its technology. Two other factors—a sufficient level of aggregate demand and economic efficiency—are essential for the economy to realize its growth potential.

3. Economic growth can be shown graphically as an outward shift of a nation's production possibility curve or as a rightward shift of its long-run aggregate supply curve.

4. The post-World War II growth rate of real GDP for Canada has been around 4 percent; real GDP per capita has grown at slightly more than 2 percent.

5. Real GDP of Canada has grown partly because of increased inputs of labour, but primarily because of increases in the productivity of labour. Technological progress, increases in the quantity of capital per worker, improvements in the quality of labour, and improved allocation of labour are among the more important factors that increase labour productivity.

6. The rate of productivity growth declined in the 1970s and early 1980s, causing a slowdown in the rise of our living standards and contributing to inflation. Although productivity growth increased in the 1980s and early 1990s, it remains substantially below the rates attained in the three decades following World War II.

7. Suspected causes of the decline in productivity growth include decreases in labour quality; slowing of technological progress; declining investment spending as a percentage of GDP; higher energy prices; and dismal growth in service productivity.

8. Many of the trends that are thought to have slowed productivity growth in the 1970s and 1980s have slowed or reversed themselves. Also, the Canadian economy has recently had a surge of innovation in computers and communications. This technological progress, coupled with the opening of global markets, has led a few economists to speak of a "new economy" characterized by high growth of productivity and real GDP.

9. Skeptics of the new-economy notion urge a wait-and-see approach. They point out that surges in productivity and real GDP growth are common during vigorous economic expansions but are not necessarily permanent.

10. Government can promote economic growth through demand-side policies (fiscal policy, monetary policy) that ensure that present production capacity is fully used and that the capital stock enlarges. It can also promote growth through supply-side policies (education and training policies, tax policies, and other pro-growth initiatives) that directly increase the economy's potential output over time.

TERMS AND CONCEPTS

economic growth

supply factors

demand factor

efficiency factor

labour productivity

labour-force participation rate

total factor productivity (TFP)

STUDY QUESTIONS

1. Why is economic growth important? Explain why the difference between a 2.5 percent and a 3.0 percent annual growth rate might be of great significance over many years.

2. **KEY QUESTION** *What are the major causes of economic growth? "There is both a demand and a supply side to economic growth." Explain. Illustrate the operation of both sets of factors in terms of the production possibilities curve.*

3. **KEY QUESTION** *Suppose an economy's real GDP is $30,000 in year 1 and $31,200 in year 2. What is the growth rate of its real GDP? Assume that population was 100 in year 1 and 102 in year 2. What is the growth rate of GDP per capita? Between 1949 and 1997, Canada's price level rose by 606 percent, while its real output has increased by 515 percent. Use the aggregate demand–aggregate supply model to show these outcomes graphically.*

4. Briefly describe the growth record of Canada in this century. Compare the rates of growth in real GDP and real GDP per capita, explaining any differences. How does Canada's growth rate compare to the rates of Japan and Germany since World War II? To what extent might growth rates understate or overstate economic well-being?

5. **KEY QUESTION** *To what extent have increases in Canada's real GDP been the result of more capital and labour inputs? Of increasing productivity? Discuss the factors that contribute to productivity growth in order of their quantitative importance.*

6. Using examples, explain how changes in the allocation of labour can affect labour productivity.

7. How do you explain the close correlation between changes in the rate of productivity growth and changes in real wage rates? Discuss the relationship between productivity growth and inflation.

8. **KEY QUESTION** *Account for the slowdown in Canada's rate of productivity growth. What are the consequences of this slowdown? What is the nature of a low-productivity trap? "Most of the factors that have contributed to poor productivity in the past two decades are now behind us and are unlikely to recur in future." Do you agree?*

9. "If you want economic growth in a free society, we may have to accept a measure of instability." Evaluate. The philosopher Alfred North Whitehead once remarked that "the art of progress is to preserve order amid change and to preserve change amid order." What did he mean? Is this contention relevant for economic growth? What implications might this have for public policy? Explain.

10. True or false? If false, explain why.
    a. Technological advance, which thus far has played only a small role in Canada's economic growth, is destined to play a more important role in the future.
    b. Nations lacking political freedom on average have faster growth rates than democratic nations.
    c. Many public capital goods are complementary to private capital goods.
    d. The rate of productivity growth in the manufacturing sector severely lags such advances in the service sector.

11. Suppose you are the chief economic adviser to the federal government and have been asked to prepare a set of proposals for increasing the productivity of Canada's workers as a way to raise the rate of economic growth. What would you put on your list? What impediments do you see to accomplishing your policies?

12. Evaluate: "Major innovations in computer and communication technologies in Canada, together with the globalization of markets, is creating a 'new economy' capable of achieving much faster rates of productivity and real GDP growth than those in the 1970s and 1980s."

13. Productivity often rises during economic expansions and falls during economic recessions. Can you think of reasons why? Briefly explain. (Hint: Remember that the level of productivity involves both levels of output and levels of labour input.)

14. **(The Last Word)** Do you think economic growth is desirable? Explain your position on this issue.

15. **WEB-BASED QUESTION Current GDP Growth Rates and Per Capita Incomes—Is There a Relationship?** The OECD (Organization for Economic Cooperation and Development) www.oecd.org/std/nahome.htm provides both quarterly growth rates of real gross domestic product (GDP) for OECD member countries and an annual comparison of levels of GDP per capita based on exchange rates and purchasing power parities (PPPs). Which countries have the highest and lowest current GDP growth rates? Which have the highest and lowest per capita incomes? Does there seem to be a relationship? In your comparison, does it matter if you use per-capita income based on exchange rates or PPPs? Which is more reliable?

16. **WEB-BASED QUESTION Increased Productivity Through Technology—Find Examples of Innovations in Computers and Communications** Recent innovations in computers and communications technologies are increasing productivity. Lucent Technologies (formerly Bell Labs) www.lucent.com/ideas2/ideas.html provides a timeline of innovations over the past 70 years. During this period, which increased the fastest: technological "home runs" (e.g., the transistor in 1947) or technological "singles" (e.g., free space optical switching in 1990)? Which innovation do you think has increased productivity the most? What are some current innovations that could increase productivity and in what way?

Budget Deficits and the Public Debt

UP TO 1997 FEDERAL DEFICITS AND THE EXPANDING public debt received much attention from the media and the public. Both debts expanded particularly quickly between 1990 and 1996. Indeed, the public debt reached almost $500 billion by 1997, up from a mere $30 billion in 1973. Then in early 1998 came the good news that the federal government was going to record a budget surplus for the first time in nearly 30 years! Whether we have seen the end of large federal budget deficits and a rising public debt remains to be seen.

In this chapter, we examine past federal budget deficits and the public debt that arose from these deficits. We first present relevant definitions and then compare different public philosophies. Next, we explore the quantitative dimensions of the public debt. How large is the debt relative to the Canadian GDP? We then consider the alleged problems associated with the public debt, explaining why some are bogus, while others are real. Next, we look at the budget deficits during the past two decades and explain why these past deficits may have negatively affected Canadian investments and international trade.

IN THIS CHAPTER YOU WILL LEARN:

What a budget deficit is, and its connection to the public debt.

•

About the recent history of Canada's budget deficits and public debt.

•

The misconceptions about budget deficits and the national debt and the real economic consequences of deficits and debt.

•

The effect of the recent budgetary surplus.

The
Big Picture

GOVERNMENTS RAISE REVENUES THROUGH taxes and spend the revenues on all sorts of goods, services, and capital projects. In the last 20 years the federal government has consistently spent more than it has taken in. Just as a family's debt rises if every week it spends more than it takes in, so the federal government's debt level has soared. However, the federal government has eliminated its deficits and appears on the road to surpluses.

The analogy with a family is slightly misleading; governments live on indefinitely and can increase their revenues by raising taxes. Still, the federal government's debt load—and that of a few provinces—has become worrisome to some economists because of its potential effects on interest rates and the value of our dollar.

As you read this chapter, keep the following points in mind:

- Government debt must be measured against the government's—and indirectly, the nation's—ability to repay it.
- If the growth of the public debt outpaces the economy's growth rate over long periods, there will be significant implications.
- The primary implication of very large public debt in relation to a nation's ability to pay it is through higher interest rates, which lead to other implications. Among the most important ones in Canada are cutbacks in social programs and the inability to embark on expansionary fiscal policy to avert recession. ■

DEFICITS AND DEBT: DEFINITIONS

A **budget deficit** is the amount by which a government's expenditures exceed its revenues during a particular year. For example, during 1996–97 the federal government spent $167 billion and its receipts were only $154 billion, producing a $13 billion deficit.

The national or **public debt** is the total accumulation of the federal government's total deficits and surpluses that have occurred through time. At the end of 1997 the net public debt was about $465 billion.

Note that "public debt" does *not* include the entire public sector; provincial and local finance is omitted.

BUDGET PHILOSOPHIES

Is it good or bad to incur deficits and let the public debt grow? Should the budget be balanced annually, if necessary or constitutional amendment? We saw in Chapter 12 that counter-cyclical fiscal policy should move the federal budget towards a deficit during recession and towards a surplus

during inflation. This means discretionary fiscal policy is unlikely to result in a balanced budget in any particular year. Is this a matter for concern?

Let's approach this question by examining the economic implications of several contrasting budget philosophies.

Annually Balanced Budget

Until the Great Depression of the 1930s, the **annually balanced budget** was viewed as the desirable goal of public finance. However, an annually balanced budget largely is not compatible with government fiscal activity as a counter-cyclical, stabilizing force. Indeed, an annually balanced budget intensifies the business cycle.

Illustration: Suppose the economy encounters an onset of unemployment and falling incomes. As Figure 12-3 shows, in such circumstances tax receipts automatically decline. To balance its budget, government must either (1) increase tax rates, (2) reduce government expenditures, or (3) do both. All these policies are contractionary; each further dampens, rather than expands, aggregate demand.

Similarly, an annually balanced budget will intensify inflation. Again, Figure 12-3 tells us that as nominal incomes rise during the course of inflation, tax collections automatically increase. To avoid the impending surplus, government must either (1) cut tax rates, (2) increase government expenditures, or (3) do both. But any of these policies adds to inflationary pressures.

An annually balanced budget is not neutral; the pursuit of such a policy is pro-cyclical, not counter-cyclical.

Some economists have advocated an annually balanced budget, not because of a fear of deficits and a mounting public debt, but because they believe an annually balanced budget is essential in constraining an undesirable expansion of the public sector. Budget deficits, they argue, are a manifestation of political irresponsibility. Deficits allow politicians to give the public the benefits of government spending programs while *currently* avoiding raising taxes to pay for them.

These economists believe government has a tendency to grow larger than it should because there is less popular opposition to this growth when it is financed by deficits rather than taxes. Wasteful governmental expenditures are likely to creep into the federal budget when deficit financing is readily available. Deficits are viewed as a symptom of a more fundamental problem—government encroachment on the vitality of the private sector.

Cyclically Balanced Budget

The idea of a **cyclically balanced budget** is that government exerts a counter-cyclical influence and at the same time balances its budget. However, this budget would not be balanced annually—there is nothing sacred about 12 months as an accounting period—but rather over the course of the business cycle.

The rationale is simple, plausible, and appealing. To offset recession, government should lower taxes and increase spending, purposely incurring a deficit. During the ensuing inflationary upswing, taxes would be raised and government spending slashed. The resulting surplus could be used to retire the federal debt incurred in offsetting the recession. Government fiscal operations would therefore exert a positive, counter-cyclical force, and the government could still balance its budget—not annually, but over a period of years.

The problem with this budget philosophy is that the upswings and downswings of the business cycle may not be of equal magnitude and duration. The goal of stabilization may therefore conflict with balancing the budget over the cycle.

A long and severe slump followed by a modest and short period of prosperity would mean a large deficit during the slump, little or no surplus during prosperity, and a cyclical deficit in the budget.

Functional Finance

With **functional finance**, a balanced budget—annually or cyclically—is secondary. The primary purpose of federal finance is to provide for noninflationary full employment to balance the economy, not the budget. If this objective causes either persistent surpluses or a large and growing public debt, so be it. In this philosophy, the problems of government deficits or surpluses are minor compared with the undesirable alternatives of prolonged recession or persistent inflation. The federal budget is first and foremost an instrument for achieving and maintaining macroeconomic stability. How best to finance government spending—through taxation or borrowing—depends on existing economic conditions. Government should not hesitate to incur any deficits and surpluses required to achieve macroeconomic stability and growth.

To those who express concern about the large federal debt that might result from the pursuit of functional finance, advocates of this budget philosophy offer three arguments.

1. The Canadian tax system is such that tax revenues automatically increase as the economy expands. Assuming constant government expenditures, a deficit that is successful in increasing GDP will be partially self-liquidating.
2. Because of its taxing powers and the ability to create money, the government has a remarkable capacity to finance deficits.
3. A large federal debt is less burdensome than most people think. *(Key Question 1)*

THE PUBLIC DEBT: FACTS AND FIGURES

Because modern fiscal policy endorses unbalanced budgets to stabilize the economy, its application may lead to a growing public debt. Let's consider the public debt—its causes, characteristics, size, and its burdens and benefits.

The public debt, as column 5 in Table 19-1 shows, has grown considerably in nominal terms

TABLE 19-1 The Government of Canada public debt and interest payments in relation to GDP, selected years, 1926–1997*

(1) End of year	(2) Public debt held by Bank of Canada (billions)	(3) Public debt held by Canadian banks and general public (billions)	(4) Public debt held by non-residents (billions)	(5) Total federal public debt (billions) (2)+(3)+(4)	(6) Gross domestic product (billions)	(7) Interest payments (billions)	(8) Public debt as per cent of GDP (5)÷(6)	(9) Interest payments as per cent of GDP (7)÷(6)	(10) Per capita public debt
1926	—	—	—	$ 2.481	$ 5.354	$ 0.130	46.3%	2.4%	$ 263
1929	—	—	—	2.284	6.400	0.122	35.6	1.9	228
1940	$ 0.572	$ 3.302	$ 1.276	5.150	6.987	0.137	73.7	2.0	453
1946	1.909	12.999	1.091	15.998	12.167	0.444	131.4	3.6	1,301
1954	2.267	11.203	0.792	14.262	26.531	0.482	55.7	1.8	933
1958	2.670	11.857	0.632	15.159	35.689	0.568	42.5	1.6	888
1960	2.744	13.329	0.808	16.881	39.448	0.753	42.8	1.9	945
1966	3.473	15.980	0.810	20.263	64.388	1.151	31.5	1.8	1,012
1969	4.112	17.798	0.959	22.869	83.026	1.589	27.5	1.9	1,089
1973	6.025	22.971	0.741	29.737	127.372	2.518	23.3	2.0	1,349
1975	7.880	29.073	0.967	37.920	171.540	3.705	22.1	2.2	1,671
1979	13.754	49.861	6.985	70.600	276.096	8.080	25.6	2.9	2,973
1983	17.184	109.254	12.256	138.694	405.717	17.420	34.2	4.3	5,571
1988	20.653	201.049	52.778	273.856	605.906	31.882	45.2	5.3	10,574
1991	22.404	246.610	78.877	347.820	676,477	41.815	51.6	6.2	12,770
1994	30.317	298.212	106.856	435.385	750.053	40.142	58.0	5.4	14,886
1997	27.004	325.945	112.108	465.057	855.103	44.289	54.3	5.2	15,399

*In current dollars.
Sources: Columns (2) to (7): Bank of Canada Review, Summer, 1998, data previous to 1983 from Statistics Canada, National Income and Expenditure Accounts, 1926-1986.

since 1926. (Although the table does not show it, the public debt has also increased rapidly in real terms.) As we have noted, the public debt is the accumulation of all past deficits, minus surpluses, of the federal budget.

Causes

Why has Canada's public debt increased? What has caused us to incur these large and persistent deficits? The answer is threefold: wars, recessions, and the lack of political will.

Wars Some of the public debt has resulted from the deficit financing of wars. The public debt

increased substantially during World War I and grew almost fourfold during World War II.

Consider World War II and the options it posed. The task was to reallocate a substantial portion of the economy's resources from civilian to war goods production. Government expenditures for armaments and military personnel soared. There were three financing options: increase taxes, print the needed money, or use deficit financing. Government feared that tax financing would require tax rates so high that they would diminish incentives to work. The national interest required attracting more people into the labour force and encouraging those already participating to work longer hours. Very high tax rates would interfere with these goals. Printing and spending additional money would be inflationary. Thus, much of World War II was financed by selling bonds to the public, draining off spendable income and freeing resources from civilian production so they would be available for defence industries.

Recessions   Another cause of the public debt is recessions, and, more specifically, the built-in stability characterizing Canada's fiscal system. In periods when the income declines, tax collections automatically fall and deficits arise. Thus the public debt rose during the Great Depression of the 1930s and, more recently, during the recessions of 1981–82 and 1991–92.

Lack of Political Will   Without being too cynical, one might also assert that deficits and a growing public debt are the result of lack of political will and determination: spending tends to gain votes; tax increases precipitate political disfavour. While opposition to deficits is widely expressed both by politicians and by their constituencies, *specific* proposals to raise taxes or cut programs typically encounter more opposition than support. University students may favour smaller deficits so long as funds for student loans are not eliminated in the process.

Similarly, new taxes or tax increases to reduce budget deficits may be acceptable in the abstract, but far less popular when specific tax changes are proposed. The popular view of taxation seems to be "Don't tax me, don't tax thee, tax the person behind the tree." The problem is there are not a sufficient number of taxpayers "behind the tree" to raise the amounts of new revenue needed to close the budget deficit.

Quantitative Aspects

The public debt was approximately $465 billion at the beginning of 1998. That's more than twice what it was a mere eight years ago. *But we must not fear large numbers.* You'll see why when we put the size of Canada's public debt into better perspective.

Debt and GDP   A statement of the absolute size of the debt ignores the fact that the wealth and productive ability of our economy have also increased tremendously. A wealthy nation can more easily incur and carry a large public debt than can a poor nation. It is more meaningful to measure changes in the public debt *in relation* to the economy's GDP,

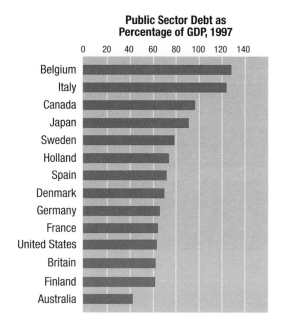

19-1
GLOBAL PERSPECTIVE

Public debt: International comparisons

Canada has the third largest public debt as a percentage of GDP. Only Belgium and Italy have larger debts as a percentage of their GDPs.

Public Sector Debt as Percentage of GDP, 1997

Source: Organization for Economic Cooperation and Development.

as shown in column 8 in Table 19-1. Instead of the large increase in the debt between 1940 and 1997 shown in column 5, we now find that the *relative* size of the debt has *declined* since 1946. However, our data do show that the relative size of the debt and the resulting interest payments have increased significantly since 1975.

International Comparisons   As shown in Global Perspectives 19-1, in the last 15 years Canada's public debt compared with other industrial nations has grown rapidly. From having the lowest net debt (as a percentage of GDP) in 1980, it had the third highest by the mid-1990s.

Interest Charges   Many economists conclude that the primary burden of the debt is the annual interest charge accruing as a result. The absolute size of these interest payments is shown in column

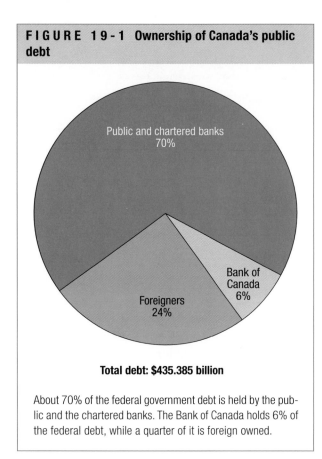

FIGURE 19-1 Ownership of Canada's public debt

Total debt: $435.385 billion

About 70% of the federal government debt is held by the public and the chartered banks. The Bank of Canada holds 6% of the federal debt, while a quarter of it is foreign owned.

7 of Table 19-1. Interest payments have increased sharply beginning in the mid-1970s. Interest charges as a percentage of the GDP are shown in column 9 of Table 19-1. Interest payments as a proportion of GDP beginning in the early 1980s increased significantly, but have recently started to decline. This ratio reflects the level of taxation (the average tax rate) required to service the public debt. In 1997 government had to collect taxes equal to 5.2 percent of GDP to pay interest on its debt.

Ownership Figure 19-1 reveals that about 6 percent of the total public debt is held by the Bank of Canada, the remaining 94 percent by private individuals, chartered banks, insurance companies, and corporations. About 25 percent of the total debt is held by foreigners. This is significant because, as we will see shortly, there are different implications of internally and externally held debt.

Accounting and Inflation The data on budget deficits and public debt may not be as straightforward as they appear. Governmental accounting procedures may not reflect the government's actual financial position. Private firms have a sep-

arate *capital budget* because, in contrast to current expenses on labour and raw materials, expenditures for capital equipment represent tangible money-making assets. In calculating its budget deficits, the federal government treats expenditures for highways, harbours, and public buildings in the same fashion as it does welfare payments. But in fact, the former outlays are investments in physical assets. The federal government holds more than $100 billion in such tangible assets.

Also, inflation works to the benefit of debtors. A rising price level reduces the real value or purchasing power of the dollars paid back by borrowers. Taking this "inflationary tax" into account further reduces the sizes of deficits and public debt.

The point is that there are different ways of measuring the public debt and government's overall financial position. Some of these alternative measures differ greatly from the data presented in Table 19-1.

19-1

QUICK REVIEW

- A budget deficit is an excess of government expenditures above tax revenues in a particular year; the public debt is the total accumulation of budget deficits minus surpluses through time.

- The three major budget philosophies are: **a** an annually balanced budget; **b** a budget balanced over the business cycle; and **c** functional finance.

- The $465 billion public debt in Canada has resulted mainly from wartime financing, recessions, and lack of political will.

- Canada's public debt as a percent of GDP has been growing rapidly in the last 20 years but has recently begun to decline.

ECONOMIC IMPLICATIONS: FALSE ISSUES

How does the public debt and its growth affect the economy? Can a rising public debt bankrupt the nation? Does the debt place a burden on our children and grandchildren?

Fortunately, these are false issues. The debt is not about to bankrupt the government or the nation. Nor, except under certain specific circumstances that we will explore, does the debt place a burden on future generations.

Going Bankrupt?

Can a large public debt bankrupt the federal government, leaving it unable to meet its financial obligations? No, for the following three points.

1. **REFINANCING** There is no reason why the public debt need be reduced, much less eliminated. As portions of the debt come due each month, government does not cut expenditures or raise taxes to provide funds to *retire* the maturing bonds. Rather, the government *refinances* the debt by selling new bonds and using the proceeds to pay off holders of the maturing bonds.

2. **TAXATION** Government has the constitutional authority to levy and collect taxes. A tax increase is an option for gaining sufficient revenue to pay interest and principal on the public debt. Financially distressed private households and corporations *cannot* raise revenue via taxes, but governments *can*. Private households and corporations *can* go bankrupt; the federal government *cannot*.

3. **CREATING MONEY** Bankruptcy is also difficult to imagine because the federal government (via the Bank of Canada) can print money to pay both the principal and interest on the debt. A government bond obligates the government to redeem that bond for some specific amount of money on its maturity date. Government can use the proceeds from the sale of other bonds *or* it can borrow newly created money from the Bank of Canada to retire the maturing bonds. The creation of new money to pay interest on or to retire debt, however, will be inflationary. But it is difficult to conceive of governmental bankruptcy when government has the power to create new money by running the printing presses. However, it *is* possible for lower-level governments to bankrupt themselves; they do not have the federal government's unlimited power of taxation, nor do they have a central bank ready to buy their bonds.

Shifting Burdens

Does the public debt impose a burden upon future generations? Recall that per-capita public debt at the beginning of 1998 was $15,399. Did each child born in 1998 enter the world with a $15,399 bill from Ottawa? Not really!

To whom does Canada owe the public debt? For the most part, it owes it to itself. About 75 per-cent of Government of Canada bonds are held by citizens and institutions—banks, businesses, insurance companies, government agencies, and pensions and trust funds—within Canada. Thus the *federal public debt is also a public credit*. While the public debt is a liability to Canadians (as taxpayers), part of the same debt is simultaneously an asset to Canadians (as bondholders).

To retire the public debt would call for a gigantic transfer payment from Canadians to Canadians. Taxpayers would pay higher taxes and the government, in turn, would pay out those tax revenues to those same taxpaying individuals in the aggregate, to redeem the Canadian bonds they hold. Although a redistribution of wealth would result from this huge financial transfer, it need not result in any immediate decline in the economy's aggregate wealth or standard of living. Repayment of an internally held public debt entails no leakage of purchasing power from the economy as a whole.

We noted earlier that the public debt increased sharply during World War II. Was some of the economic burden of World War II, for example, shifted to future generations by the decision to finance military purchases through the sale of government bonds? The answer is no. The burden of the war was borne almost entirely by the people who lived during the war; they were the ones who did without a multitude of consumer goods to permit Canada to arm itself and help arm its allies.

Also, wartime production may cause a nation's stock of capital to cease to grow or to dwindle as precious resources are shifted from the production of capital goods to the production of war goods. As a result, future generations inherit a smaller stock of capital goods. This occurred in Canada during World War II. But, again, this shifting of costs is independent of how a war is financed.

19-2
QUICK REVIEW

- There is no danger of the federal government going bankrupt because it need only refinance (not retire) the public debt and can raise revenues, if needed, through higher taxes or, in the short run, printing money.

- Usually, the public debt is not a means of shifting economic burdens to future generations.

IMPLICATIONS AND ISSUES

We must be careful not to leave the impression that the public debt is of no concern to economists. The large debt *does* pose some real and potential problems, although economists attach varying degrees of importance to them.

Income Distribution

The distribution of government bond ownership is uneven. Some people own much more than their per-capita share of government securities; others less or none at all. Although our knowledge of the owners of the public debt by income class is limited, we presume that ownership is concentrated among wealthier groups. Because the tax system is mildly progressive, payment of interest on the public debt probably increases income inequality. If greater income equality is one of our social goals, then this redistributive effect is clearly undesirable.

Incentives

Table 19-1 indicates that the 1997 federal public debt necessitated an annual interest payment of over $40 billion. Adding in the lower-level governments, interest charges on the total public debt amounted to over $50 billion. With no increase in the size of the debt, this annual interest charge must be paid out of tax revenues. These added taxes dampen incentives to bear risk, to innovate, to invest, and to work. Indirectly, the existence of a large debt can impair economic growth. As noted earlier, the ratio of interest payments to the GDP indicates the level of taxation needed to pay interest on the debt. Thus, many economists are concerned by the fact that this ratio has increased sharply in recent years (column 9 of Table 19-1).

External Debt

A part of the public debt—**external debt**—is *not* "owed to ourselves," and in real terms the payment of interest and principal requires the transfer of some of Canada's real output to other nations. Our federal public debt held by foreigners has risen rapidly since 1973, rising from about 2 percent to 24 percent in 1997. Starting in 1975, the provinces, local governments, and provincial Crown corporations reacted to the Bank of Canada's high-interest-rate policy by borrowing abroad, thus increasing the burden of the total public debt on Canadians. *(Key Question 3)*

Curb on Fiscal Policy

A large and growing public debt makes it politically difficult to use fiscal policy during a recession. For example, in 1991 and 1992 the Bank of Canada substantially reduced interest rates to stimulate a sluggish economy. But this expansionary monetary policy was slow to expand output and reduce unemployment. Had the public debt not been at an historic high and increasing due to the aforementioned structural deficit, it would have been politically feasible to reduce taxes or increase government spending to generate the stimulus of a deficit. But the growing "debt problem" ruled out this stimulus on political grounds. In general, a large and growing public debt creates political impediments to the use of antirecessionary fiscal policy.

Crowding Out and the Stock of Capital

There is a potentially more serious problem. One way the public debt can transfer a real economic burden to future generations is by causing future generations to inherit a smaller stock of capital goods—a smaller "national factory"—than otherwise. This possibility involves the *crowding-out effect*, which you will recall is the idea that deficit financing will increase interest rates and reduce private investment spending. If this happens, future generations would inherit an economy with a smaller productive capacity and, other things equal, the standard of living would be lower than otherwise.

Suppose the economy is operating at its full-employment level of output and the federal budget is initially in balance. Then assume that for some reason government increases its spending. The impact of this increase on government spending will fall on those living at the time it occurs. Think of a nation's production possibilities curve with "government goods" on one axis and "private goods" on the other. In a full-employment economy an increase in government spending will move the economy *along* the curve in the direction of the government-goods axis, meaning fewer private goods.

But private goods may be consumer or investment goods. If the increased government goods are provided at the expense of *consumer goods*, then the present generation bears the entire burden as a lower current standard of living. The current investment level is *not* affected and therefore neither is the size of the national factory inherited by future generations. But if the increase in government goods entails a reduction in production of *capital goods*, then the present generation's level of consumption (standard of living) will be unimpaired. In the future our children and grandchildren will inherit a smaller stock of capital goods and will have lower income levels than otherwise.

Two Scenarios
Let's sketch two scenarios yielding these different results.

FIRST SCENARIO Suppose the presumed increase in government spending is financed by an increase in personal income taxes. We know that most income is consumed. Therefore, consumer spending falls by almost as much as the increase in taxes. Here, the burden of the increase in government spending falls primarily on today's generation; it has fewer consumer goods.

SECOND SCENARIO Assume the increase in government spending is financed by increasing the public debt, meaning the government enters the money market and competes with private borrowers for funds. With the supply of money fixed, this increase in money demand will increase the interest rate—the "price" paid for the use of money.

In Figure 19-2, the curve I_{d1} reproduces the investment-demand curve of Figure 9-5. (Ignore curve I_{d1} for now.) The investment-demand curve is downsloping, indicating investment spending varies inversely with the interest rate. Here, government deficit financing drives up the interest rate, reducing private investment. If government borrowing increases the interest rate from 6 percent to 10 percent, investment spending would fall from $25 billion to $15 billion; thus, $10 billion of private investment would be crowded out.

Conclusion: An assumed increase in public goods production is more likely to come at the expense of private investment goods when financed by deficits. In comparison with tax financing, the future generation inherits a smaller national factory and therefore has a lower standard of living with deficit financing.

Two Qualifications
But there are two loose ends to our discussion that might mitigate or even eliminate the size of the economic burden shifted to future generations.

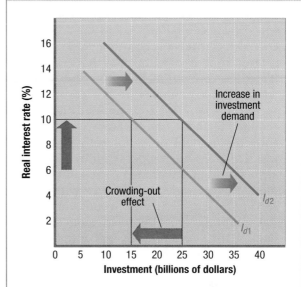

FIGURE 19-2 The investment-demand curve and the crowding-out effect

The crowding-out effect suggests that, with a fixed investment-demand curve (I_{d1}), an increase in the interest rate caused by a government deficit will reduce private investment spending and thereby decrease the size of the "national factory" inherited by future generations. In this case an increase in the interest rate from 6 percent to 10 percent crowds out $10 billion of private investment. However, if the economy is initially in a recession, the government deficit may improve business profit expectations and shift the investment-demand curve rightward as from I_{d1} to I_{d2}. This shift may offset the crowding-out effect wholly or in part.

1. **PUBLIC INVESTMENT** Our discussion has neglected the character of the increase in government spending. Just as private goods may involve consumption or investment, so it is with public goods. If the increase in government spending consists of consumption-type outlays—purchases of recreational equipment for prisons or the provision of limousines for government officials—then our second scenario's conclusion that the debt increase has shifted a burden to future generations is correct. But what if the government spending is investment-type outlays, for example, for construction of highways, harbours, and flood-control projects? Similarly, what if they are "human capital" investments in education, job training, and health?

   Like private expenditures on machine and equipment, **public investments** increase the economy's future production capacity. The capital stock of future generations need not be diminished, but rather its composition is changed so there is more public capital and less private capital.

2. **UNEMPLOYMENT** The other qualification relates to our assumption that the initial increase in government expenditures occurs when the economy is at full employment. Again the production possibilities curve reminds us that, *if* the economy is at less than full employment or, graphically, at a point inside the production possibilities curve, then an increase in government expenditures can move the economy *to* the curve without any sacrifice of either current consumption or capital accumulation. If unemployment exists initially, deficit spending by government need *not* mean a burden for future generations in the form of a smaller national factory.

Look at Figure 19-2 again. If deficit financing increases the interest rate from 6 percent to 10 percent, a crowding-out effect of $10 billion will occur. But suppose the increase in government spending stimulates a recession economy via the multiplier effect, improving profit expectations and shifting investment demand rightward to I_{d2}. Then, investment spending remains at $25 billion despite the higher 10 percent interest rate. Of course, the increase in investment demand might be smaller or larger than that in Figure 19-2. In the former case, the crowding-out effect would not be fully offset; in the latter, it would be more than offset. The point? An increase in investment demand may counter the crowding-out effect. *(Key Question 7)*

RECENT FEDERAL DEFICITS

Federal deficits and the growing public debt have been in the economic spotlight in the last two decades.

Enormous Size

As Figure 19-3 makes clear, the absolute size of the annual federal deficits increased enormously in the 1980s and 1990s. The average annual deficit for the 1970s was under $10 billion. In the 1980s annual deficits averaged between $20 and $30 bil-

lion. Consequently the public debt increased more than fourfold during the 1980s.

The federal deficit jumped to $30 billion in 1991 mainly because of the 1991–92 recession and a weak recovery, which slowed the inflow of tax revenues. The deficit peaked at $40 billion in 1993, but began to come down in 1994 as the economy's expansion quickened and Parliament's efforts to reduce the deficit took hold. By 1998 the federal deficit was eliminated, actually recording a small surplus.

Rising Interest Costs

Interest costs on the debt rose sharply in the 1980s and early 1990s. By 1989, the annual interest costs exceeded the *total* federal debt that existed in 1973 (Table 19-1, columns 7 and 5). The massive federal budget deficits up to the mid-1990s were entirely caused by the interest costs of past deficits. If it were not for the interest payments, the federal budget would have been in surplus. Because interest payments are part of government expenditures, the debt can feed on itself through interest charges.

Inappropriate Policy

A further point of concern is that some large annual deficits in Canada occurred in an economy operating at or close to full employment, such as those in the late 1980s.

Large deficits during times of economic prosperity raise the concern of fuelling demand-pull inflation. To counteract potentially rising prices, the Bank of Canada is forced to employ a tighter monetary policy. Along with the strong demand for money in the private sector, the tight money policy raises real interest rates and reduces investment spending. The greatest potential for budget deficits to produce a crowding-out effect occurs when the economy is near or at full employment.

Balance of Trade Problems

Large budget deficits can make it difficult for the nation to achieve a balance in its international trade. Large annual budget deficits promote imports and stifle exports.

Graphic Portrayal

Let's trace out graphically the manifold effects of large budget deficits. The cause-effect chain is quite lengthy, but it yields important insights.

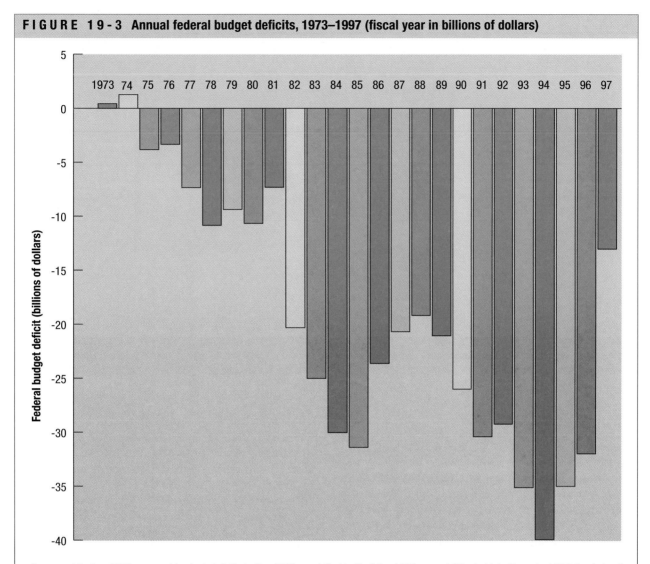

FIGURE 19-3 Annual federal budget deficits, 1973–1997 (fiscal year in billions of dollars)

Compared to the 1970s, annual budget deficits in the 1980s and first half of the 1990s are strikingly high. By early 1998 the federal deficit was eliminated.

Source: Statistics Canada. Updates can be retrieved from Statistics Canada Web site at www.statcan.ca/english/Pgdb/State/Government/govt02b.ht.

Higher Interest Rates

Beginning with boxes 1 and 2 in Figure 19-4, we note that in financing its deficits government must go into the money market to compete with the private sector funds. This drives up real interest rates, which has two important effects. First, as shown in box 3, they discourage private investment spending; this is the crowding-out effect. When the economy is closer to full employment, the crowding-out effect is likely to be large. Therefore, although they are willing to admit that the short-run impact of deficits is expansionary, some economists express concern that the long-run effect of structural deficits will retard the economy's growth rate. They envision deficits being used to finance consumption-type government goods at the expense of investment in modernized factories and equipment. Deficits, it is contended, force the economy on to a slower long-run growth path.

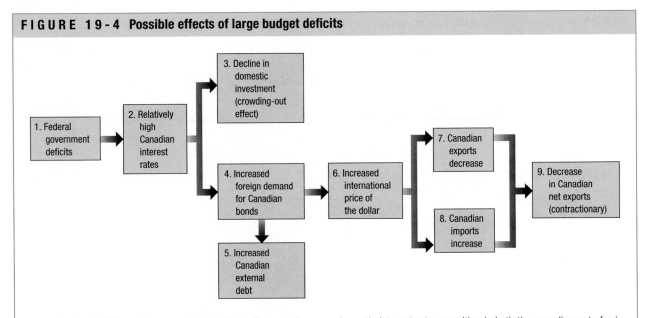

FIGURE 19-4 Possible effects of large budget deficits

Large budget deficits can have a variety of effects. They can increase domestic interest rates, resulting in both the crowding out of private investment and an increase in the demand for Canadian bonds. The latter increases Canada's external debt and increases the demand for dollars. The strong demand for dollars raises the international value of the dollar, making our exports more expensive to foreigners and imports less costly to Canadians. The consequent decline in our net exports has a contractionary effect on the Canadian economy.

Dollar Appreciation

The second effect, shown by box 4, is that high real interest rates on both Canadian government and corporation bonds make financial investment in Canada more attractive for foreigners. While the resulting inflow of foreign funds is helpful in financing both the deficit and private investment, box 5 reminds us that this inflow represents an increase in Canada's external debt. Paying interest on and retiring debts to the rest of the world means a reduction in future real output available to the Canadian domestic economy.

Box 6 indicates that, to purchase high-yielding Canadian bonds, foreigners must first buy Canadian dollars with their own currencies. This increases the worldwide demand for dollars and increases the international price or exchange value of the dollar.

Decreased Net Exports

The appreciation of the dollar eventually depresses our exports (box 7) and increases our imports (box 8), giving rise to an "unfavourable" balance of trade. Net exports are a component of aggregate demand. When net exports decline, this has a contractionary effect on the economy, as

shown in box 9. As our exports fall, unemployment will rise in Canadian exporting industries such as agriculture, wood, and paper. Canadian import-competing industries such as automobiles and textiles will also be adversely affected. The increase in the value of the dollar makes foreign exports of these products less expensive and the Canadian auto and textile industries find themselves with excess productive capacity and redundant labour. *(Key Question 8)*

19-3
QUICK REVIEW

- The borrowing and interest payments associated with the public debt may **a** increase income inequality, **b** require higher taxes, which dampen incentives, **c** curb the use of antirecessionary fiscal policy, and **d** impede the growth of the nation's capital stock through crowding out of private investment.

- Past federal deficits were of concern because of **a** their enormous size, **b** rising total interest costs, and **c** their inappropriateness when the economy was near, or at, full-employment output.

- Budget deficits can be linked to trade deficits as follows: budget deficits increase domestic real interest rates; the dollar appreciates; Canadian exports fall; and Canadian imports rise, and a trade deficit emerges.

Positive Role of Debt

Having completed this survey of imagined and real problems of deficits and the public debt, we conclude our discussion on a more positive note. We must not forget that debt—both public and private—plays a positive role in a prosperous and growing economy. As income expands, so does

saving. Macroeconomic theory and fiscal policy tell us that if aggregate demand is to be sustained at the full-employment level, this expanding volume of saving or its equivalent must be obtained and spent by consumers, businesses, or government. The process by which saving is transferred to spenders is *debt creation*. Consumers and businesses do borrow and spend a great amount of saving.

But, at times, consumers and firms are unwilling to borrow, and thereby to increase private debt sufficiently fast to absorb the growing volume of saving. On these occasions, it is appropriate for government to increase its debt to absorb the remainder. If this doesn't happen, the economy might falter from full employment and not realize its growth potential.

In The Media

Ottawa's sounds of surplus: silence

BRUCE LITTLE

Let's take a moment to savour what might qualify as the statistic of the decade. It emerged ever so quietly last week from the federal Finance Department. The government didn't even mention it, although it has been the Holy Grail for a generation of finance ministers.

It's this: Over a full 12-month period, Ottawa had a surplus. Not a deficit, but a surplus.

Put that in historical context. Ottawa last ran a surplus over an entire fiscal year in 1969-70. No Canadian under the age of 28 has lived with the experience of seeing a federal surplus. No voter under the age of 46 has cast a ballot for a government that ran one.

The finance minister responsible for the previous surplus was Edgar Benson, in Pierre Trudeau's first full term in office. Between

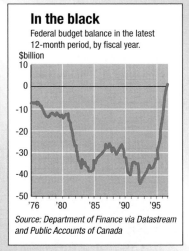

In the black

Federal budget balance in the latest 12-month period, by fiscal year.
$billion

Source: Department of Finance via Datastream and Public Accounts of Canada

him and Paul Martin, the current minister, have come nine others who didn't manage to post a single surplus. (Students of Canadian politics can test their knowledge by naming the nine. The answer is at the end of the column.)

The actual report from the Finance Department was simple enough. It said the government had a small surplus in November—$579-million. These monthly figures bounce around a lot so, in itself, these few hundred million dollars don't look impressive.

What made the November figure special was its cumulative effect. A rolling tally of the deficit for the most recent 12-month period shows that Ottawa had a surplus of $596-million over that span. It took in $146.3-billion in revenues and spent $145.7-billion ($102-billion on programs and 43.7-billion on interest payments on the public debt). The surplus may be small, but our figures on these monthly deficits go back to 1975 and it's the first one recorded over that whole period. (We even keep track of the annual year-end adjustment, the so-called 13th month of each fiscal year.)

The biggest deficit by this measure occurred in the year from June, 1992, to May, 1993, when the government spent $44.5-billion more than it took in.

Why, you might ask, didn't Mr. Martin shout last week's news from the Peace Tower on Parliament Hill?

Possible answers, alas, lead us into cynical territory that seems unfitting for the moment, but they are necessary nonetheless.

One is that Mr. Martin prefers to muffle his good news because he doesn't want a public debate on how to handle a surplus. His latest annual mid-year fiscal update—rolled out before the Commons finance committee and the television cameras last fall in Vancouver—was notable for not containing a fiscal update. In other words, he didn't revise the estimate of the 1997-98 deficit he had put forward in his February budget. Officially, Mr. Martin is still tied to a ludicrous forecast that this year's deficit will be $17-billion, even though the deficit for 1996-97 was only $8.9-billion.

Many economists think the government is heading for a surplus in the current fiscal year, which ends March 31. In the first eight months of the year alone (April to November), the surplus amounted to almost $1.4-billion. If Mr. Martin were to acknowledge this possibility, of course, he might find it harder to resist the hordes who want him either to raise spending substantially or cut taxes substantially in his next budget. Obfuscation aids his cause.

The other possibility is that he wants to leave the door wide open to accounting fiddles at the end of the year. He could, for example, announce a big spending program (like the government's proposed millennium scholarship fund, which could amount to $3-billion) in the budget and count it as having been spent—or committed, at least—in the 1997-98 fiscal year. He could easily turn a cash surplus into an accounting deficit.

Such tricks are not unusual. Mr. Martin did one just last year when $800-million of seed money for an innovation foundation to encourage scientific research was counted as money owed (but effectively spent) at the end of the 1996-97 fiscal year, even though nary a penny had rolled out of the treasury.

Auditor-General Denis Desautels didn't much like this little deception. He complained that the money was owed to an organization that didn't exist on March 31, the last day of the fiscal year, and a formal financing deal wasn't signed until July, 1997. In his view, last year's books should not have included the $800-million liability, so the recorded deficit should have been $8.1-billion, not $8.9-billion.

Still, he passed the books and his reservation amounted to little more than a slap on the wrist, which doesn't even bother opposition politicians. In crude political terms, governments can safely ignore the negative fallout from such accounting fiddles.

Since he's done it once, are there any bets that Mr. Martin might do it again?

◆ To answer the puzzler posed above, here's the list of finance ministers (with their prime ministers in brackets): John Turner, Donald Macdonald and Jean Chrétien (all under Mr. Trudeau); John Crosbie (Joe Clark); Allan MacEachen and Marc Lalonde (Mr. Trudeau again); Michael Wilson and Don Mazankowski (Brian Mulroney) and Gilles Loiselle (Kim Campbell).

Source: *Globe and Mail*, January 28, 1998, p. A10. Reprinted with permission from the *Globe and Mail*.

THE STORY IN BRIEF

In January 1998 the federal government recorded its first budget surplus in almost 30 years.

THE ECONOMICS BEHIND THE STORY

- A budget deficit or surplus is the difference between what a government receives in tax revenues and what it spends. In November 1997 the federal government accrued a budget surplus of over $500 million in its operations during the previous 12 months.

- The budget surplus for the fiscal year 1997–98 would actually come in at over $1 billion. This represents a stunning turnaround in a relatively short period. Only five years earlier, the federal government reported its largest deficit ever: $44.5 billion.

- Why do you think the finance minister was hesitant to draw attention to this public finance milestone? ■

The
Last Word

LOTTERIES: FACTS AND CONTROVERSIES AS A WAY OF RAISING GOVERNMENT REVENUES

Lotteries, which began in the 1970s, are a potentially important source of public revenue. What are the characteristics of lotteries? And what are the arguments for and against this means of enhancing provincial government revenues?

THE AVERAGE LOTTERY RETURNS ABOUT 46 percent of its gross revenues to ticket purchasers as prizes and 36 percent goes to the provincial treasury. The remaining 18 percent is for designing and promoting the lottery and for commissions to retail outlets that sell tickets. Although provinces sponsoring lotteries currently obtain only a small share of their total revenues in this way, per-capita sales of lottery tickets increased substantially in the 1975-96 period.

Lotteries have been controversial. Critics make the following arguments. First, the 40 percent of gross revenues from lotteries that goes to the provincial governments is in effect a 40 percent tax on ticket purchases. This tax is higher than the taxes on cigarettes and liquor. Furthermore, research indicates that the "lottery tax" is highly regressive in that there is little relationship between ticket purchases and household incomes. This means that low-income families spend a larger proportion of their incomes on lotteries than do high-income families. The 10 percent of the adults who patronize lotteries most heavily account for one-half of total ticket sales. Second, critics argue that it is ethically wrong for the government to sponsor gambling. Gambling is generally regarded as immoral and, in other forms, is illegal in most provinces. It is also held that lotteries may whet the appetite for gambling and generate compulsive gamblers who will impoverish themselves and their families. Third, lotteries may be sending the message that luck and fate—rather than education, hard work, and saving

and investing—are the route to success and wealth in Canada.

But there are counterarguments. It is contended, in the first place, that lottery revenue should not be regarded as a tax. Tax collections are compulsory and involve coercion; the purchase of a lottery ticket is voluntary and a free consumer choice. A second and related argument is that within wide limits it is not appropriate to make moral judgements about how people should spend their incomes. Individuals allegedly achieve the maximum satisfaction from their incomes by spending without interference. If some people derive satisfaction from participating in lotteries, they should be free to do so. Third, faced with tax revenue shortfalls and intense pressure not to raise taxes, lotteries are a relatively painless source of revenue to finance important services such as education and welfare programs. Finally, lotteries are competitive with illegal gambling and thereby may be socially beneficial in curtailing the power of organized crime.

Two observations seem certain at the moment. One is that total lottery revenue will continue to increase. More and more provinces are establishing lotteries and people seem to enjoy gambling, particularly when they feel their losses are being used for "good causes." The other point is that this source of revenue will remain controversial. ■

Source: Adapted from Charles T. Clotfelter and Philip J. Cook, "On the Economics of State Lotteries," *Journal of Economic Perspectives*, Fall, 1990, pp. 105-119.

CHAPTER SUMMARY

1. A budget deficit is the excess of government expenditures over its receipts; the public debt is the total accumulation of its deficits and surpluses over time.

2. Budget philosophies include the annually balanced budget, the cyclically balanced budget, and functional finance. The basic problem with an annually balanced budget is that it is pro-cyclical rather than counter-cyclical. Similarly, it may be difficult to balance the budget over the course of the business cycle if upswings and downswings are not of roughly comparable magnitude. Functional finance is the view that the primary purpose of federal finance is to stabilize the economy, and the problems associated with consequent deficits or surpluses are of secondary importance.

3. Historically, growth of the public debt has been caused by the deficit financing of wars, recessions, and lack of political will. The large structural deficits up to the mid-1990s were primarily the result of recession and increased transfer payments. The federal government recorded a small surplus in 1998, the first time in almost 30 years.

4. The federal public debt was about $465 billion at the end of 1997. Since the 1970s the debt and associated interest charges both rose as a percentage of the GDP up to the mid-1990s.

5. The contention that a large public debt may bankrupt the government is false because **a** the debt need only be refinanced rather than refunded and **b** the federal government has the power to levy taxes and create money.

6. The crowding-out effect aside, the public debt is not a vehicle for shifting economic burdens to future generations.

7. More substantive problems associated with the public debt include the following: **a** Payment of interest on the debt may increase income inequality. **b** Interest payments on the debt require higher taxes that may impair incentives. **c** A large and growing public debt creates political impediments to the use of antirecessionary fiscal policy. **d** Paying interest or principal on the portion of the debt held by foreigners means a transfer of real output abroad. **e** Government borrowing to refinance or pay interest on a debt may increase interest rates and crowd out private investment spending.

8. Federal budget deficits were much larger from 1980 to the mid-1990s. Some economists think these large deficits increased real interest rates in Canada that have then **a** crowded out private investment and **b** increased foreign demand for Canadian bonds. Increased demand for Canadian bonds, some economists argue, increased the international price of the dollar, causing Canadian exports to fall and Canadian imports to rise. Declining net exports had a contractionary effect on our domestic economy.

TERMS AND CONCEPTS

budget deficit
public debt
annually balanced budget
cyclically balanced budget

functional finance
external debt
public investments

STUDY QUESTIONS

1. **KEY QUESTION** *Assess the potential for using fiscal policy as a stabilization tool under* **a** *an annually balanced budget,* **b** *a cyclically balanced budget, and* **c** *functional finance.*

2. What have been the major sources of the public debt historically? Why have deficits been so large since the mid-1970s? Why did the deficits rise sharply in 1991 and 1992?

3. **KEY QUESTION** *Discuss the two ways of measuring the size of the public debt. How does an internally held public debt differ from an externally held public debt? What would be the effects of retiring an internally held public debt? Distinguish between refinancing and retiring the debt.*

4. Explain or evaluate each of the following statements:
   a. "A public debt is like a debt of the left hand to the right hand."
   b. "The least likely problem arising from a large public debt is that the federal government will go bankrupt."
   c. "The basic cause of the federal debt was a lack of political courage."

5. Is the crowding-out effect likely to be larger during recession or when the economy is near or at full employment? Explain.

6. Some economists argue that the quantitative importance of the public debt can best be measured by interest payments on the debt as a percentage of the GDP. Explain why.

7. KEY QUESTION *Is our $465 billion public debt (at the end of 1997) a burden to future generations? If so, in what sense? Why might deficit financing be more likely to reduce the future size of Canada's "national factory" than financing government expenditures through taxes?*

8. KEY QUESTION *Trace the cause-and-effect chain through which large deficits might affect domestic real interest rates, domestic investment, the international price of the dollar, and our international trade. Comment: "There is too little recognition that the deterioration of Canada's position in world trade is more the result of our own policies than the harm wrought by foreigners."*

9. Explain how a significant decline in the federal budget deficit could be expected to reduce **a** the size of a trade deficit, **b** the total debt Canadians owe to foreigners, and **c** foreign purchases of Canadian assets such as factories and real estate.

10. Do you favour a constitutional amendment requiring the federal budget to be balanced annually? Why or why not?

11. **(The Last Word)** What are the pros and cons of raising government revenues through lotteries?

12. WEB-BASED QUESTION **The Debt** Go to the Web site of Statistics Canada www.statcan.ca/english/Pgdb/State/Government/govt03.htm and find the amount of the gross federal debt in the most recent year. How does it compare to the gross federal debt five years earlier?

13. WEB-BASED QUESTION **Federal Government Deficits and Surpluses** Visit Statistics Canada's Web site at www.statcan.ca/english/Pgdb/State/Government/govt02b.htm and answer the following questions. What has the trend been in the federal government's deficit/surplus in the last five years? What is the largest expenditure category?

International Economics and the World Economy

International Trade

THE WTO, TRADE DEFICITS AND SURPLUSES, dumping. Exchange rates, the EU, the G-7 nations. The IMF, official reserves, currency interventions. Capital flight, brain drains, the ruble. This is the language of international economics, and people across the globe are speaking it in newspapers, corporate offices, retail outlets, and union halls.

This chapter builds on Chapter 6, providing deeper analysis of international trade and protectionism. We begin by reviewing key facts about world trade, and then we look more closely at how international specialization based on comparative advantage can mutually benefit the participating nations. After using supply and demand analysis to examine equilibrium prices and quantities of imports and exports, we examine the economic impact of trade barriers such as tariffs and import quotas and evaluate the arguments for protectionism. Finally, we discuss the costs of protectionism and look at continuing controversies in international trade.

IN THIS CHAPTER YOU WILL LEARN:

The facts about Canada's international trade.

•

The distinction between absolute and comparative advantage.

•

That trading on the basis of comparative advantage results in gains to trading nations.

•

About trade barriers and their negative effects on nations' economic well-being.

The
Big Picture

THE ECONOMIZING PROBLEM CONSISTS OF limited resources, unlimited wants, and thus the need for choices. In a world of limited resources, if we can somehow get more output of goods and services from those resources, the constraints an individual or a society faces are less severe. One of the ways to get more output from the limited resources available is specialization. Adam Smith, the so-called father of economics, noticed the beneficial effect of specialization in the celebrated pin factory he talks about in *The Wealth of Nations*. Just as a factory can greatly increase its output if each person specializes, the world output of goods and services would increase if each nation specialized in those pursuits to which it is best suited. In technical terms, it should specialize in the line of production in which it enjoys a comparative advantage. Each nation would then import goods to satisfy its other needs. In this manner, each nation would be materially better off than if each tried to produce all the goods and services it consumes. These beneficial effects are the driving force behind the globalization of trade, such as manifested by the Canada–U.S. Free Trade Agreement

(FTA), and the North American Free Trade Agreement (NAFTA).

As you read this chapter, keep the following points in mind:

- **Key Concepts 3** and **5** are discussed.
- It may be helpful for you to think of trading between two nations as similar to trading between two individuals. Each specializes in what he or she does best and then trades.
- The purpose of tariffs is to protect domestic industries from international competition. Tariff protection implies an inability to successfully compete with imports. Firms in the protected industries enjoy a level of profit higher than would be the case if they had to compete. Consumers lose because they have to pay higher prices for goods produced by the protected industries.
- Protecting domestic industry has an intuitive appeal, particularly in regards to "saving jobs." But ultimately, consumers and society at large will pay for the tariff protection through higher prices. Each of the jobs saved will be very costly. ■

FACTS OF INTERNATIONAL TRADE

In Chapter 6 we presented a number of facts about international trade. Let's briefly review those facts and add a few others.

1. Exports of goods and services are 38 percent of Canadian GDP. The percentage is high by world standards; only the Netherlands, at 56 percent, is higher among the industrialized nations.
2. Canadian exports and imports have increased in volume and risen by more than a third as a percentage of GDP since 1965 (Figure 6-2).
3. In 1997 Canada had a $27 billion trade surplus, meaning that the export of goods exceeded the import of goods by this amount. But in that year Canada's imports of services exceeded its exports of services by $8 billion. Thus, the goods and services surplus was $19 billion.

4. Canada's principal commodity exports are automotive products, machinery and equipment, and forestry products. Its main imports are machinery and equipment and automotive products.
5. Like other advanced industrial nations, Canada imports some of the same categories of goods that it exports (Figure 6-3).
6. The bulk of Canadian export and import trade is with other industrially advanced nations, specifically the United States, nations of western Europe, and Japan (Figure 6-4).
7. Improved transportation and communications technologies, declines in tariffs, and peaceful relations among major industrial nations have all helped expand world trade since World War II.
8. Although trade is still dominated by industrially advanced nations, several new "players" have greatly increased their roles (Global Perspective 20-1). The four "Asian tigers" of

20-1
GLOBAL PERSPECTIVE

Shares of world exports, selected nations

The United States has the largest share of world exports, followed closely by Germany and Japan. Canada, a much smaller economy, represents over 4 percent of the world's exports. The seven largest export nations account for nearly 50 percent of world exports.

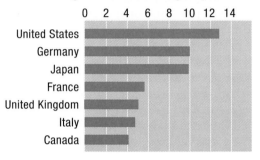

Percentage share of world exports, 1997

Source: Organization for Economic Cooperation and Development.

Hong Kong, Singapore, South Korea, and Taiwan have expanded their share of world trade from 3 percent in 1972 to nearly 10 percent today. China has emerged as a major new international trader, and the collapse of communism has led Eastern European nations and Russia to look globally for new trade partners.

9. International trade (and finance) link economies. Through trade, changes in economic conditions in one spot on the globe can quickly affect other places. Example: In early 1998, economists scaled back forecasts for economic growth in Canada and Europe because of economic problems in the Southeast Asian countries of Japan, South Korea, Indonesia, Malaysia, and the Philippines. Reduced purchases of Canadian and European imports mean lower Canadian and European exports and thus slower Canadian and European output growth.

10. International trade is often at the centre of international policy. Examples: The North American Free Trade Agreement (NAFTA), the conclusion of negotiations on the General Agreement on Tariffs and Trade (GATT).

With these facts in mind, let's look more closely at the economics of international trade.

THE ECONOMIC BASIS FOR TRADE

In Chapter 6 we found that international trade is a way nations can specialize, increase the productivity of their resources, and realize a larger total output than otherwise. Sovereign nations, like individuals and regions of a nation, can gain by specializing in products they can produce with the greatest relative efficiency and by trading for goods they cannot produce efficiently.

This rationale for trade is correct, but a more detailed understanding is needed. The more complete answer to the question "Why do nations trade?" hinges on two points.

1. The distribution of economic resources—natural, human, and capital goods—among nations is uneven; nations are different in their endowments of economic resources.
2. Efficient production of various goods requires different technologies or combinations of resources.

The character and interaction of these two facts can be readily illustrated. Japan, for example, has a large, well-educated labour force; skilled labour is abundant and therefore inexpensive. Japan can produce efficiently (at low cost) a variety of goods whose design and production require much skilled labour: Cameras, transistor radios, and video recorders are examples of such **labour-intensive goods**.

In contrast, Australia has vast amounts of land compared with its human and capital resources and can inexpensively produce goods requiring much land; it produces such **land-intensive goods** as wheat, wool, and meat. Brazil has the soil, tropical climate, rainfall, and lots of unskilled labour needed for efficient, low-cost production of coffee.

Industrially advanced economies with relatively large amounts of capital can produce inexpensively those goods whose production requires much capital. Automobiles, agricultural equipment, machinery, and chemicals are such **capital-intensive goods**.

The distribution of both resources and technology among nations, however, is not forever fixed. When the distribution changes, the relative efficiency with which nations produce goods also changes. For example, in the past few decades South Korea has upgraded the quality of its labour force and has greatly expanded its stock of capital. Although South Korea was primarily an exporter of agricultural products and raw materials a half-century ago, it now exports large quantities of manufactured goods. Similarly, the new technologies that gave us synthetic fibres and synthetic rubber drastically altered the resource mix needed to produce these goods and changed the relative efficiency of nations in manufacturing them.

As national economies evolve, the size and quality of their labour forces may change, the volume and composition of their capital stocks may shift, new technologies will develop, and even the quality of land and quantity of natural resources may be altered. As these changes occur, the relative efficiency with which a nation can produce specific goods will also change.

SPECIALIZATION AND COMPARATIVE ADVANTAGE

Let's now use the concept of comparative advantage to analyze the basis for international specialization and trade.

The Basic Principle   The central concept underlying comparative advantage can be illustrated by posing a problem. Consider the case of a chartered accountant (CA) who, we will assume, is also a skilled house painter. Suppose the CA can paint her house in less time than the professional painter she is thinking of hiring. Also suppose the CA can earn $50 per hour doing her accounting and must pay the painter $15 per hour. It will take the accountant 30 hours to paint her house; the painter, 40 hours. Finally, assume the CA receives no special pleasure from painting.

Should the CA take time off from her accounting to paint her own house or should she hire the painter? The CA should hire the painter. Her opportunity cost of painting her house is $1,500 (= 30 hours × $50 per hour of sacrificed income). The cost of hiring the painter is only $600 (= 40 hours × $15 per hour paid to the painter). Although the CA is better at both accounting and painting, the CA's relative or comparative advantage lies in accounting. She will *lower her cost of getting her house painted* by specializing in accounting and using some of the proceeds to hire the house painter.

Note that the CA has **absolute advantage** in both accounting and painting; she can do accounting and paint more efficiently than our hypothetical house painter. Despite this, the CA should hire the house painter to paint her house because of her "comparative advantage."

Similarly, the house painter perhaps can reduce his cost of obtaining accounting services by specializing in painting and using some of his income to hire the CA. Suppose it would take the painter 10 hours to prepare his income tax, while the CA could handle this task in 2 hours. The house painter would sacrifice $150 of income (= 10 hours × $15 per hour of sacrificed time) to get a task done that he could hire out for $100 (= 2 hours × $50 per hour of the CA's time). By using the CA to prepare his tax return, the painter *lowers his cost of getting the tax return completed*.

What is true for our hypothetical CA and house painter is also true for two nations. Countries can reduce their cost of obtaining desirable goods by specializing where they have comparative advantages.

With this simple example in mind, let's turn to an international trade model to acquire an understanding of the gains from international specialization and trade.

Two Isolated Nations

Suppose the world economy has just two nations, Canada and Brazil. Each can produce both steel and soybeans, but at differing levels of economic efficiency. Suppose Canadian and Brazilian domestic production possibilities curves for soybeans and steel are as shown in Figure 20-1a and b. Two characteristics of these production possibilities curves should be noted:

1. **CONSTANT COSTS**   The "curves" are drawn as straight lines, in contrast to the concave-from-the-origin production possibilities frontiers introduced in Chapter 2. This means the law of increasing costs has been replaced with the assumption of constant costs. This simplifies our discussion and will not impair the validity of our analysis and conclusions. We later will consider the effect of the more realistic increasing costs.

2. **DIFFERENT COSTS**   The production possibilities curves of Canada and Brazil are different, reflecting different resource mixes and differing levels of technological progress. Specifi-

FIGURE 20-1   Production possibilities for Canada and Brazil

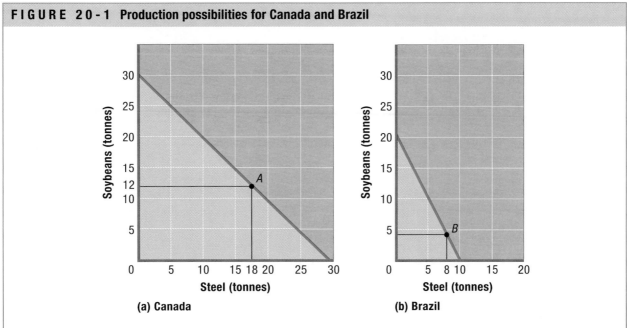

(a) Canada

(b) Brazil

The two production possibilities lines show the amounts of soybeans and steel (a) Canada and (b) Brazil can produce domestically. The curves for both countries are straight lines because we are assuming constant costs. The different cost ratios, 1 steel = 1 soybean for Canada, and 1 steel = 2 soybeans for Brazil are reflected in the different slopes of the two lines.

cally, the opportunity costs of producing steel and soybeans differ between the two nations.

Canada   In Figure 20-1a, with full employment, Canada will operate on its production possibilities curve. On that curve, it can increase its output of steel 30 tonnes by forgoing an output of 30 tonnes of soybeans. This means the slope of the production possibilities curve is –1 (= –30 soybeans/ +30 steel), implying that 1 tonne of steel can be obtained for every tonne of soybeans sacrificed. In Canada the domestic exchange ratio or **cost ratio** for the two products is 1 tonne of steel for 1 tonne of soybean, or

$$1\ S_t = 1\ S_{oy}$$

Canada can "exchange" a tonne of steel for a tonne of soybeans. Our constant-cost assumption means this exchange or opportunity cost equation prevails for all possible moves from one point to another along Canada's production possibilities curve.

Brazil   Brazil's production possibilities curve in Figure 20-1b represents a different opportunity cost ratio. In Brazil 20 tonnes of soybeans must be given up to get 10 tonnes of steel. The slope of the production possibilities curve is –2 (= –20 soy-

beans/ +10 steel). This means that in Brazil the domestic cost ratio for the two goods is 1 tonne of steel for 2 tonnes of soybeans, or

$$1\ S_t = 2\ S_{oy}$$

3. **SELF-SUFFICIENCY**   If Canada and Brazil are isolated and are to be self-sufficient, each must choose some output mix on its production possibilities curve. Assume point A in Figure 20-1a is the optimal output mix in Canada. The choice of this combination of 18 tonnes of steel and 12 tonnes of soybeans equates the marginal benefit and marginal cost of both goods. Suppose Brazil's optimal product mix is 8 tonnes of steel and 4 tonnes of soybeans, indicated by point *B* in Figure 20-1b. These choices are also reflected in column 1, Table 20-1.

Specialization According to Comparative Advantage

With these different cost ratios, determining the product in which Canada and Brazil should specialize is as follows: The **principle of comparative advantage** says that *total output will be greatest when each good is produced by that nation that has the*

TABLE 20-1 International specialization according to comparative advantage and the gains from trade (*in tonnes*)

Country	(1) Outputs before specialization	(2) Outputs after specialization	(3) Amounts exported (−) and imported (+)	(4) Outputs available after trade	(5) = (4) − (1) Gains from specialization and trade
Canada	18 steel 12 soybeans	30 steel 0 soybeans	−10 steel +15 soybeans	20 steel 15 soybeans	2 steel 3 soybeans
Brazil	8 steel 4 soybeans	0 steel 20 soybeans	+10 steel −15 soybeans	10 steel 5 soybeans	2 steel 1 soybeans

lowest domestic opportunity cost. In our two-nation illustration, Canada's domestic opportunity cost is lower for steel. Canada need only forgo 1 tonne of soybeans to produce 1 tonne of steel, whereas Brazil must forgo 2 tonnes of soybeans for 1 tonne of steel. *Canada has a comparative (cost) advantage in steel and should specialize in steel production.* The "world" (Canada and Brazil) is *not* economizing in the use of its resources if a specific product (steel) is produced by a high-cost producer (Brazil) when it could have been produced by a low-cost producer (Canada). To have Brazil produce steel would mean that the world economy would have to give up more soybeans than is necessary to obtain a tonne of steel.

Brazil has the lower domestic opportunity cost for soybeans; it must sacrifice only $\frac{1}{2}$ tonne of steel in producing 1 tonne of soybeans, while Canada must forgo 1 tonne of steel in producing a tonne of soybeans. *Brazil has a comparative advantage in soybeans and should specialize in soybean production.*

Economizing—using fixed quantities of scarce resources so as to obtain the greatest total output—requires that any particular good be produced by that nation having the lower domestic opportunity cost, or a comparative advantage. Canada should produce steel and Brazil soybeans. Note that this conclusion holds even though Canada has an absolute advantage in both steel and soybeans.

In column 2 of Table 20-1 we can verify that specialized production in accordance with the principle of comparative advantage allows the world to get more output from given amounts of resources. By specializing completely in steel, Canada can produce 30 tonnes of steel and no soybeans: Brazil, by specializing completely in soybeans, produces 20 tonnes of soybeans and no

steel. The world ends up with more steel—30 tonnes, compared with 26 (= 18 + 8) tonnes—*and* more soybeans—20 tonnes, compared with 16 (= 12 + 4) tonnes—than where there is self-sufficiency or unspecialized production.

Terms of Trade

But consumers of each nation want *both* steel and soybeans. They can have both if the two nations trade or exchange the two products. But what will be the **terms of trade**? At what exchange ratio will Canada and Brazil trade steel and soybeans?

Because $1\ S_t = 1\ S_{oy}$ in Canada, Canada must get *more than* 1 tonne of soybeans for each tonne of steel exported or it will not pay Canada to export steel in exchange for Brazilian soybeans. Canada must get a better "price" (more soybeans) for its steel in the world market than it can get domestically, or there is no gain from trade and it will not occur.

Similarly, because $1\ S_t = 2\ S_{oy}$ in Brazil, Brazil must get 1 tonne of steel by exporting some amount *less than* 2 tonnes of soybeans. Brazil must pay a lower "price" for steel in the world market than it must pay domestically, or it will not want to trade. The international exchange ratio or *terms of trade* must lie somewhere between

$$1\ S_t = 1\ S_{oy}\ \text{(Canada's cost conditions)}$$

and

$$1\ S_t = 2\ S_{oy}\ \text{(Brazil's cost conditions)}$$

But where between these limits will the world exchange ratio fall? Canada will prefer a ratio close to $1\ S_t = 2\ S_{oy}$, say, $1\ S_t = 1\frac{3}{4}\ S_{oy}$. Canadians want to get a great deal of soybeans for each tonne of steel they export. Similarly, Brazil wants a rate near 1 S_t = 1 S_{oy}, say 1 S_t = $1\frac{1}{4}$ S_{oy}. Brazil wants to export as little soybeans as possible for each tonne of steel it receives in exchange. The exchange ratio or terms of trade determines how the gains from international specialization and trade are divided between the two nations.

The final exchange ratio depends on world supply and demand for the two products. If overall world demand for soybeans is weak relative to its supply and the demand for steel is strong relative to its supply, the price of soybeans will be lower and the price of steel higher. The exchange ratio will settle near the 1 S_t = 2 S_{oy} figure Canada prefers. Under the opposite world supply and demand conditions, the ratio will settle near the 1 S_t = 1 S_{oy} level favourable to Brazil. (We will take up the topic of equilibrium world prices later in this chapter.)

Gains from Trade

Suppose the international exchange ratio or terms of trade is 1 S_t = $1\frac{1}{2}$ S_{oy}. The possibility of trading on these terms permits each nation to supplement its domestic production possibilities line with a **trading possibilities line**. This can be seen in *Figure 20-2 (Key Graph)*. A trading possibilities line shows the options that a nation has by specializing in one product and trading (exporting) its specialty to obtain the other product. The trading possibilities lines in Figure 20-2 are drawn on the assumption that both nations specialize based on comparative advantage—Canada specializes completely in steel (point *S* in Figure 20-2a) and Brazil completely in soybeans (at point *c* in Figure 20-2b).

Improved Options Now Canada is not constrained by its domestic production possibilities line, which requires it to give up 1 tonne of steel for every tonne of soybeans it wants as it moves up its domestic production possibilities line, say, from point *S*. Instead, Canada, through trade with Brazil, can get $1\frac{1}{2}$ tonnes of soybeans for every tonne of steel it exports to Brazil, so long as Brazil has soybeans to export. Trading possibility line *SC'* thus represents the 1 S_t = $1\frac{1}{2}$ S_{oy} trading ratio.

Similarly, Brazil, starting at, say, point *c*, no longer has to move down its domestic production possibilities curve, giving up 2 tonnes of soybeans for each tonne of steel it wants. It can now export just $1\frac{1}{2}$ tonnes of soybeans for each tonne of steel it wants by moving down its trading possibilities line *cs'*.

Specialization and trade create a new exchange ratio between steel and soybeans, reflected in a nation's trading possibilities line. This exchange ratio is superior for both nations to the self-sufficiency exchange ratio embodied in the production possibilities line of each. By specializing in steel and trading for Brazil's soybeans, Canada can obtain *more than* 1 tonne of soybeans for 1 tonne of steel. By specializing in soybeans and trading for Canada's steel, Brazil can get 1 tonne of steel for *less than* 2 tonnes of soybeans.

Added Output By specializing according to comparative advantage and trading for those goods produced in other nations with greater domestic efficiency, Canada and Brazil can realize combinations of steel and soybeans beyond their production possibilities boundaries. *Specialization according to comparative advantage results in a more efficient allocation of world resources, and larger outputs of both steel and soybeans are therefore available to both nations.*

Suppose that at the 1 S_t = $1\frac{1}{2}$ S_{oy} terms of trade, Canada exports 10 tonnes of steel to Brazil and in return Brazil exports 15 tonnes of soybeans to Canada. How do the new quantities of steel and soybeans available to the two nations compare with the optimal product mixes that existed before specialization and trade? Point *A* in Figure 20-2a reminds us that Canada chose 18 tonnes of steel and 12 tonnes of soybeans originally. But, by producing 30 tonnes of steel and no soybeans, and by trading 10 tonnes of steel for 15 tonnes of soybeans, Canada can obtain 20 tonnes of steel and 15 tonnes of soybeans. This new, superior combination of steel and soybeans is shown by point *A'* in Figure 20-2a. Compared with the nontrading figures of 18 tonnes of steel and 12 tonnes of soybeans, Canada's **gains from trade** are 2 tonnes of steel and 3 tonnes of soybeans.

Similarly, recall that Brazil's optimal product mix was 4 tonnes of soybeans and 8 tonnes of steel (point *B*) before specialization and trade. Now, by specializing in soybeans and trading—producing 20 tonnes of soybeans and no steel and exporting 15 tonnes of its soybeans in exchange for 10 tonnes of Canadian steel—Brazil can have 5 tonnes of soybeans and 10 tonnes of steel. This new position is indicated by point *B'* in Figure 20-2b. Brazil's gains from trade are 1 tonne of soybeans and 2 tonnes of steel.

As a result of specialization and trade, both countries have more of both products. Table 20-1 summarizes the transaction and outcomes. You should study it very carefully.

KEY GRAPH

FIGURE 20-2 Trading possibilities lines and the gains from trade

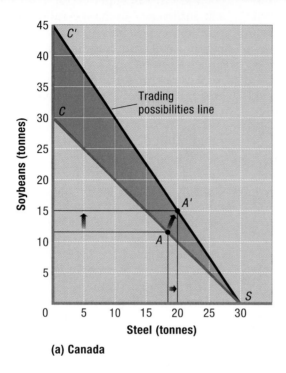

(a) Canada

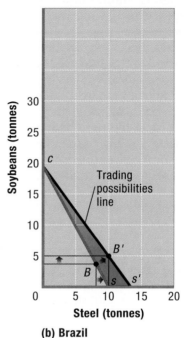

(b) Brazil

As a result of international specialization and trade, Canada and Brazil both can have levels of output higher than those attainable on their domestic production possibilities curves. (a) Canada can move from point A on its domestic production possibilities curve to, say, A′ on its trading possibilities line. (b) Brazil can move from B to B′.

20-2

QUICK QUIZ

1. The production possibilities curves in graphs (a) and (b) imply:
   (a) increasing domestic opportunity costs.
   (b) decreasing domestic opportunity costs.
   (c) constant domestic opportunity costs.
   (d) first decreasing, then increasing, domestic opportunity costs.

2. Before specialization, the domestic opportunity cost of producing 1 unit of steel is:
   (a) 1 unit of soybeans in both Canada and Brazil.
   (b) 1 unit of soybeans in Canada and 2 units of soybeans in Brazil.

   (c) 2 units of soybeans in Canada and 1 unit of soybeans in Brazil.
   (d) 1 unit of soybeans in Canada and $\frac{1}{2}$ unit of soybeans in Brazil.

3. After specialization and trade, the world output of steel and soybeans is:
   (a) 20 tons of steel and 20 tons of soybeans.
   (b) 45 tons of steel and 15 tons of soybeans.
   (c) 30 tons of steel and 20 tons of soybeans.
   (d) 10 tons of steel and 30 tons of soybeans.

4. After specialization and international trade:
   (a) Canada can obtain units of soybeans at less cost than before trade.
   (b) Brazil can obtain more than 20 tons of soybeans, if it so chooses.
   (c) Canada no longer has a comparative advantage in producing steel.
   (d) Brazil can benefit by prohibiting soybean imports from Canada.

Answers: 1. (c) 2. (b) 3. (c) 4. (a)

The fact that points A' and B' are economic positions superior to A and B is extremely important. Recall, from Chapter 2, that a nation can expand beyond its production possibilities boundary by (1) expanding the quantity and improving the quality of its resources or (2) realizing technological progress. We have now explained another way—international trade—for a nation to circumvent the output constraint imposed by its production possibilities curve. The effects of international specialization and trade are the equivalent of having more and better resources or discovering improved production techniques.

Trade with Increasing Costs

To explain the basic principles underlying international trade, we simplified our analysis in several ways. For example, we limited discussion to two products and two nations. But multiproduct/multinational analysis yields the same conclusions. We also assumed constant opportunity costs (linear) production possibilities curves, which is a more substantive simplification. Let's consider the effect of allowing increasing opportunity costs (concave-from-the-origin production possibilities curves) to enter the picture.

Suppose that Canada and Brazil are initially at positions on their concave production possibilities curves where their domestic cost ratios are $1 \, S_t = 1 \, S_{oy}$ and $1 \, S_t = 2 \, S_{oy}$ as they were in our constant-cost analysis. As before, comparative advantage indicates that Canada should specialize in steel and Brazil in soybeans. But now, as Canada begins to expand steel production, its $1 \, S_t = 1 \, S_{oy}$ cost ratio will *fall*, it will have to sacrifice *more than* 1 tonne of soybeans to get 1 additional tonne of steel. Resources are no longer perfectly shiftable between alternative uses, as the constant-cost assumption implied. Resources less and less suited to steel production must be allocated to the Canadian steel industry in expanding steel output, and this means increasing costs—the sacrifice of larger and larger amounts of soybeans for each additional tonne of steel.

Similarly, Brazil, starting from its $1 \, S_t = 2 \, S_{oy}$ cost ratio position, expands soybean production. But as it does, it will find that its $1 \, S_t = 2 \, S_{oy}$ cost ratio begins to *rise*. Sacrificing a tonne of steel will free resources that can be used to produce something *less than* 2 tonnes of soybeans, because these transferred resources are less suitable to soybean production.

As the Canadian cost ratio falls from $1 \, S_t = 1 \, S_{oy}$ and Brazil's rises from $1 \, S_t = 2 \, S_{oy}$, a point will

be reached where the cost ratios are equal in the two nations, perhaps at $1 \, S_t = 1\frac{3}{4} \, S_{oy}$. At this point, the underlying basis for further specialization and trade—differing cost ratios—has disappeared. Most important, this point of equal cost ratios may be reached where Canada is still producing *some* soybeans along with its steel and Brazil is producing some steel along with its soybeans. *The primary effect of increasing costs is to make specialization less than complete.* For this reason we often find domestically produced products competing directly against identical or similar imported products within a particular economy. **(Key Question 4)**

The Case for Free Trade Restated

The case for free trade reduces to this one potent argument. *Through free trade based on the principle of comparative advantage, the world economy can achieve a more efficient allocation of resources and a higher level of material well-being than without free trade.* The resource mixes and technological knowledge of each country are somewhat different. Therefore each nation can produce particular commodities at different real costs. Each nation should produce goods for which its domestic opportunity costs are lower than the domestic opportunity cost of other nations, and exchange these specialties for products for which its domestic opportunity costs are high relative to those of other nations. If each nation does this, the world can realize the advantages of geographic and human specialization. The world— and each free-trading nation— can obtain a larger real income from the fixed supplies of resources available to it. Protection—barriers to free trade—lessens or eliminates gains from specialization. If nations cannot freely trade, they must shift resources from efficient (low-cost) to inefficient (high-cost) uses to satisfy their diverse wants.

One side benefit of free trade is that it promotes competition and deters monopoly. The increased competition from foreign firms forces domestic firms to adopt the lowest-cost production techniques. It also compels them to be innovative and progressive with respect to both product quality and production methods, thereby contributing to economic growth. And free trade provides consumers with a wider range of product choices. The reasons to favour free trade are essentially the same reasons that endorse competition.

A second side-benefit of free trade is that it links national interest and breaks down national animosities. Confronted with political disagreements, trading partners tend to negotiate rather than make war.

20-1

QUICK REVIEW

- International trade has always been important to Canada, and it is becoming increasingly so.

- International trade enables nations to specialize, enhance the productivity of their resources, and obtain a larger output.

- Comparative advantage means total world output will be greatest when each good is produced by that nation having the lowest domestic opportunity cost.

- Specialization is less than complete among nations because opportunity costs normally rise as any particular nation produces more of a particular good.

SUPPLY AND DEMAND ANALYSIS OF EXPORTS AND IMPORTS

Supply and demand analysis helps us see how equilibrium prices and quantities of exports and imports are determined. The amount of a good or service that a nation will export or import depends on differences between equilibrium world and domestic prices. The equilibrium **world price** derives from the interaction of *world* supply and demand; it is the price at which the quantities supplied and demanded are equal globally. The equilibrium **domestic price** is determined by *domestic* supply and demand; it is the price that would prevail in a closed economy—one having no international trade. It is the price at which domestic supply and demand are equal.

Because of comparative advantages and disadvantages, no-trade domestic prices *may* or *may not* equal world equilibrium prices. When economies are opened for international trade, differences between world and domestic prices motivate exports or imports. To see how, let's now look at the international effects of such price differences in a simple two-nation world.

Supply and Demand in Canada

Suppose the world consists of just Canada and the United States, each producing aluminum. There are no trade barriers such as tariffs and quotas. Also, to keep things simple, let's ignore international transportation costs.

Figure 20-3a shows the domestic supply curve S_d and domestic demand curve D_d for aluminum in Canada. The intersection of S_d and D_d determines the equilibrium domestic price is $1.25 per kilogram and the equilibrium domestic quantity of 100 million kilograms. The market clears at $1.25—there are no domestic surpluses nor shortages of aluminum.

But what if the Canadian economy is opened to world trade and the *world price* of aluminum is above or below this $1.25 domestic price?

Canadian Export Supply If the world aluminum price exceeds $1.25, Canadian firms will produce more than 100 million kilograms and export the excess domestic output to the rest of the world (United States). First, consider a world price of $1.50. We see from the supply curve S_d that Canadian aluminum firms will produce 125 million kilograms of aluminum at that price. The demand curve D_d tells us that Canadians will purchase only 75 million kilograms at $1.50. A domestic surplus of 50 million kilograms of aluminum will result. Canadian producers will export these 50 million kilograms at the $1.50 world price.

What if the world price is $1.75? The supply curve shows that Canadian firms will produce 150 million kilograms of aluminum, while the demand curve tells us that Canadian consumers will buy only 50 million kilograms. The domestic surplus of 100 million kilograms will be exported.

Towards the top of Figure 20-3b we plot on the horizontal scale the domestic surpluses—the Canadian exports—occurring at world prices above the $1.25 domestic equilibrium price. When the world and domestic prices are equal (= $1.25), the quantity of exports supplied is zero (point *a*). There is *no* surplus of domestic output to export. But when the world price is $1.50, Canadian firms export 50 million kilograms of surplus aluminum (point *b*). At a $1.75 world price, the domestic surplus of 100 million kilograms is exported (point *c*).

The Canadian **export supply curve**, found by connecting points such as *a*, *b*, and *c*, shows the amount of aluminum that Canadian producers will export at each world price above $1.25. This curve *slopes upward*, revealing a direct or positive relationship between the world price and amount of Canadian exports. *As world prices rise relative to domestic prices, Canadian exports increase.*

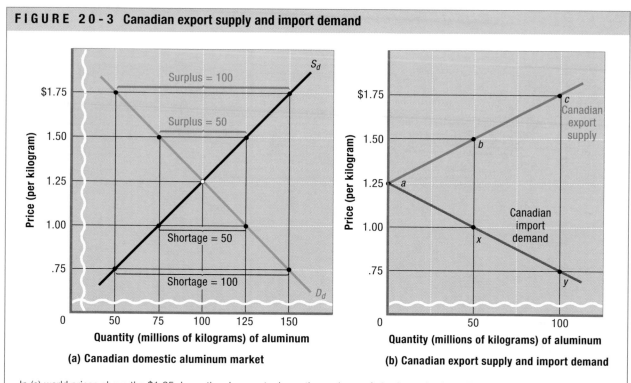

FIGURE 20-3 Canadian export supply and import demand

(a) Canadian domestic aluminum market

(b) Canadian export supply and import demand

In (a) world prices above the $1.25 domestic price create domestic surpluses of aluminum. As shown by the export supply curve in (b), these surpluses are exported. Domestic shortages occur when the world price is below $1.25 (a). These shortages are met by importing aluminum (b). The export supply curve shows the direct relationship between world prices and Canadian exports; the import supply curve portrays the inverse relationship between world prices and Canadian imports.

Canadian Import Demand

If the world price is below $1.25 Canada will end up importing aluminum. Consider a $1.00 world price. The supply curve in Figure 20-3a reveals at that price Canadian firms will produce only 75 million kilograms of aluminum. But the demand curve shows that Canadians want to buy 125 million kilograms at that price. The result is a domestic shortage of 50 million kilograms. To satisfy this shortage, 50 million kilograms of aluminum will be imported into Canada.

At an even lower $.75 world price, Canadian producers supply only 50 million kilograms. Because Canadian consumers want to buy 150 million kilograms, there is a domestic shortage of 100 million kilograms. Imports will flow to Canada to make up the difference. That is, at a $.75 world price Canadian firms supply 50 million kilograms and foreign firms supply 100 million kilograms.

In Figure 20-3b we plot the Canadian **import demand curve**. This *downsloping curve* shows the amounts of aluminum that will be imported at world prices below the $1.25 Canadian domestic price. The relationship between world prices and

imports is inverse or negative. At a world price of $1.25, domestic output will satisfy Canadian demand; imports will be zero (point *a*). But at $1.00 Canadians will import 50 million kilograms of aluminum (point *x*); at $.75, they will import 100 million kilograms (point *y*). Connecting points *a*, *x*, and *y* yields a *downsloping* Canadian import demand curve. *It reveals that as world prices fall relative to domestic prices, Canadian imports increase.*

Supply and Demand in the United States

We repeat our analysis in Figure 20-4, this time for the United States. (We have converted American dollar prices to Canadian dollar prices via the exchange rate.) Note that the domestic supply curve S_d and demand curve D_d for aluminum in the United States yield a domestic price of $1.00, which is $.25 lower than the $1.25 Canadian domestic price.

The analysis proceeds exactly as for Canada. If the world price is $1.00, Americans will neither export nor import aluminum (which gives us

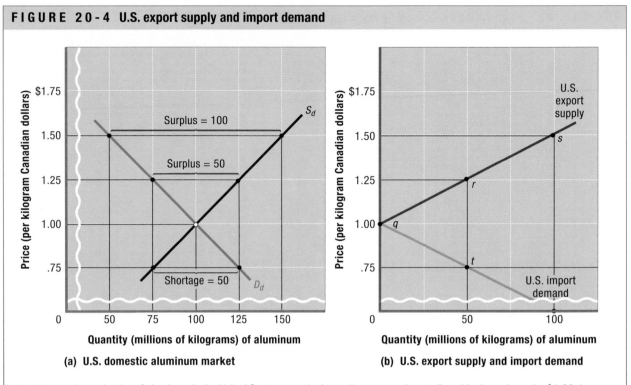

FIGURE 20-4 U.S. export supply and import demand

(a) U.S. domestic aluminum market

(b) U.S. export supply and import demand

In (a) domestic production of aluminum in the United States exceeds domestic consumption at all world prices above the $1.00 domestic price. These domestic surpluses result in U.S. exports (b). When the domestic price falls below $1.00, domestic shortages occur (a) and imports flow to the United States (b). The U.S. export supply curve and import demand curve depict these relationships.

point *q* in Figure 20-4b). At world prices above $1.00, American firms will produce more aluminum than American consumers will buy. The surplus will be exported. At a $1.25 world price, Figure 20-4a tells us that the United States will have and export a domestic surplus of 50 million kilograms (yielding point *r*). At $1.50 it will have and export a domestic surplus of 100 million kilograms (point *s*). Connecting these points yields the upsloping American *export supply curve* that reflects the domestic surpluses (and thus exports) occurring when the world price exceeds the $1.00 American domestic price.

Domestic shortages occur in the United States at world prices below $1.00. At a $.75 world price, Figure 20-4a shows that American consumers want to buy 125 million kilograms of aluminum but American firms will produce only 75 million kilograms. The shortage will bring 50 million kilograms of imports to Canada (point *t* in Figure 20-4b). The American *import demand curve* in that figure shows American imports at world aluminum prices below the $1.00 American domestic price.

Equilibrium World Price, Exports, and Imports

We now have the tools to determine the equilibrium world price of aluminum and the equilibrium world levels of exports and imports. Figure 20-5 combines the Canadian export supply curve and import demand curve in Figure 20-3b and the American export supply curve and import demand curve in Figure 20-4b. The two Canadian curves proceed rightward from the $1.25 domestic price; the two American curves proceed rightward from the $1.00 American domestic price. *International equilibrium occurs in this two-nation model where one nation's import demand curve intersects another nation's export supply curve.* In this case Canada's import demand curve intersects America's export supply curve at *e*. There, the world price of aluminum is $1.12. The American export supply curve indicates that the United States will export 25 million kilograms of aluminum at this price. Also at this price Canada will import 25 million kilograms from the United States, indicated

FIGURE 20-5 Equilibrium world price and quantity of exports and imports

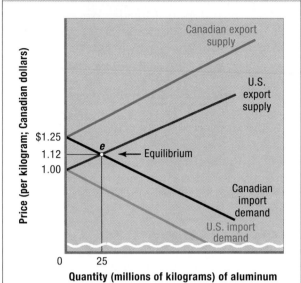

In a two-nation world, the equilibrium world price (= $1.12) is determined at the intersection of one nation's export supply curve and another nation's import demand curve. This intersection also decides the equilibrium volume of exports and imports. Here, the United States exports 25 million kilograms of aluminum to Canada.

by the Canadian import demand curve. The $1.12 world price equates the quantity of imports demanded and the quantity of exports supplied (= 25 million kilograms). Thus there will be world trade of 25 million kilograms of aluminum at $1.12 per kilogram.

Note that after trade, the single $1.12 world price will prevail in both Canada and the United States. *Only one price for a standardized commodity can persist in a highly competitive market.* With trade, all consumers can buy a kilogram of aluminum for $1.12 and all producers can sell it for that price. This world price means that Americans will pay more for aluminum with trade (= $1.12) than without it (= $1.00). The increased American output caused by trade raises American production costs and therefore the price of aluminum in the United States. Canadians, however, pay less for aluminum with trade (= $1.12) than without it (= $1.25). The Canadian gain comes from America's comparative cost advantage in producing aluminum.

Why would the United States willingly send 50 million kilograms of its aluminum output to Canada for consumption? Producing this output uses up scarce American resources and drives up the price of aluminum for Americans. Americans are willing to export aluminum to Canada because Americans can gain the means—the earnings of Canadian dollars—to import other goods, say, automobile parts, from Canada. American exports enable Americans to acquire imports that have greater value to Americans than the exported aluminum. American exports to Canada finance American imports from Canada. *(Key Question 6)*

TRADE BARRIERS

No matter how compelling the case for free trade, barriers to free trade *do* exist. Let's examine Chapter 6's list of trade impediments more closely.

1. **Tariffs** are excise taxes on imported goods; they may be imposed for purposes of revenue or to protect domestic firms.

    A **revenue tariff** is usually applied to a product not produced domestically, for example, coffee and bananas. Rates on revenue tariffs are modest; their purpose is to provide the federal government with revenues.

    A **protective tariff** is designed to shield domestic producers from foreign competition. Although protective tariffs are usually not high enough to stop importation of foreign goods, they put foreign producers at a competitive disadvantage in selling in domestic markets.

2. An **import quota** specifies the maximum amount of a commodity that may be imported in any period. Import quotas can more effectively retard international commerce than tariffs. A product might be imported in large quantities despite high tariffs; low import quotas completely prohibit imports once the quotas are filled.

3. A **nontariff barrier** (NTBs) is a licensing requirement, unreasonable standards pertaining to product quality and safety, or unnecessary red tape used to restrict imports. Japan and the European countries frequently require their domestic importers of foreign goods to obtain licences. By restricting the issuance of licences, imports can be restricted. Great Britain uses this barrier to bar the importation of coal.

4. A **voluntary export restriction** (VER) is a trade barrier by which foreign firms "volun-

tarily" limit the amount of their exports to a particular country. VERs, which have the effect of import quotas, are agreed to by exporters in the hope of avoiding more stringent trade barriers. Japanese auto manufacturers agreed to a VER on exports to Canada under the threat of the imposition of low import quotas.

Later in this chapter we will consider the specific arguments and appeals made to justify protection.

Economic Impact of Tariffs

Once again we use supply and demand analysis—now to examine the economic effects of protective tariffs. Curves D_d and S_d in Figure 20-6 show domestic demand and supply for a product in which Canada has a comparative *dis*advantage, for example, video cassette recorders (VCRs). (Disregard $S_d + Q$ for now.) Without world trade, the domestic price and output would be P_d and q respectively.

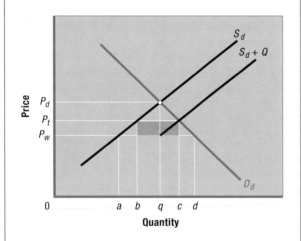

FIGURE 20-6 The economic effects of a protective tariff or an import quota

A tariff of P_wP_t will reduce domestic consumption from d to c. Domestic producers will be able to sell more output (b rather than a) at a higher price (P_t rather than P_w). Foreign exporters are injured because they are able to sell less output (bc rather than ad) in Canada. The shaded area represents the amount of tariffs paid by Canadian consumers. An import quota of bc units will have the same effects as the tariff, with one exception: the shaded area will go to foreign producers rather than to the Canadian government.

Assume now that the domestic economy is opened to world trade and that the Japanese, who have a comparative advantage in VCRs, begin to sell their recorders in Canada. We assume that with free trade the domestic price cannot differ from the world price, which here is P_w. At P_w domestic consumption is d and domestic production is a. The horizontal distance between the domestic supply and demand curves at P_w represents imports of ad. Thus far, our analysis is similar to the analysis of world prices in Figure 20-3.

Direct Effects Suppose now that Canada imposes a tariff on each imported VCR. This will raise the domestic price from P_w to P_t and has four effects.

1. **DECLINE IN CONSUMPTION** Consumption of video recorders in Canada will decline from d to c as the higher price moves buyers up and to the left along their demand curve. The tariff prompts consumers to buy fewer recorders and to reallocate a portion of their expenditures to less-desired substitute products. Canadian consumers are injured by the tariff, since they pay P_wP_t more for each of the c units they now buy at price P_t.

2. **INCREASED DOMESTIC PRODUCTION** Canadian producers—who are *not* subject to the tariff—receive higher price P_t per unit. Because this new price is higher than the pre-tariff or world price of P_w, the domestic VCR industry moves up and to the right along its supply curve S_d, increasing domestic output from a to b. Domestic producers thus enjoy both a higher price and expanded sales, which explains why domestic producers lobby for protective tariffs. But from a social point of view, the expanded domestic production of ab means that the tariff permits domestic producers of recorders to bid resources away from other, more efficient, Canadian industries.

3. **DECLINE IN IMPORTS** Japanese producers are hurt. Although the sale price of recorders is higher by P_wP_t, that amount accrues to the Canadian government, not to Japanese producers. The after-tariff world price, and thus the per-unit revenue to Japanese producers, remains at P_w, while the volume of Canadian imports (Japanese exports) falls from ad to bc.

4. **TARIFF REVENUE** The shaded rectangle indicates the amount of revenue that the tariff yields. Total revenue from the tariff is deter-

mined by multiplying the tariff, P_wP_t per unit, by the number of imported recorders, bc. This tariff revenue is a transfer of income from consumers to government and does *not* represent any net change in the nation's economic well-being. The result is that government gains a portion of what consumers lose by paying more for VCRs.

Indirect Effects Tariffs have a subtle effect beyond what our supply and demand diagram can show. Because of diminished sales of VCRs in Canada, Japan will earn fewer dollars with which to buy Canadian exports. Canadian export industries—industries in which Canada has a comparative advantage—will cut production and release resources. These are highly efficient industries, as evidenced by their comparative advantage and ability to sell goods in world markets.

Tariffs directly promote the expansion of inefficient industries that do not have a comparative advantage; they also indirectly cause contraction of relatively efficient industries that do have a comparative advantage. This means tariffs cause resources to be shifted in the wrong direction. We know that specialization and world trade lead to more efficient use of world resources and greater world output. But protective tariffs reduce world trade. Therefore, tariffs also reduce efficiency and the world's real output.

Economic Impact of Quotas

We noted previously that an import quota is a legal limit placed on the amount of some product that can be imported each year. The economic impact of quotas is similar to that of a tariff with one salient difference: While tariffs generate revenue for the Canadian government, a quota transfers that revenue to foreign producers.

Suppose in Figure 20-6 that, instead of imposing a tariff of P_wP_t per unit, Canada prohibits any Japanese imports of VCRs in excess of bc units. In other words, an import quota of bc VCRs is imposed on Japan. We have deliberately chosen the size of this quota to be the same amount as imports would be under a P_wP_t tariff so we are comparing "equivalent" situations. As a consequence of the quota, the supply of recorders is $S_d + Q$ in Canada. This consists of the domestic supply plus the constant amount bc ($= Q$), that importers will provide at each domestic price. The $S_d + Q$ supply curve does not exist below price P_w because Japanese producers would not export

VCRs to Canada at any price *below* P_w when they can sell them to other countries at the world market price of P_w.

Most of the economic results are the same as with a tariff. VCR prices are higher (P_t instead of P_w) because imports have been reduced from ad to bc. Domestic consumption of VCRs is down from ad to bc. Canadian producers enjoy both a higher price (P_t rather than P_w) and increased sales (b rather than a).

The difference is that the price increase of P_wP_t paid by Canadian consumers on imports of bc—the shaded area—no longer goes to Revenue Canada as tariff (tax) revenue, but flows to those Japanese firms that have acquired the rights to sell VCRs in Canada. Other things being the same, the economic effects of a tariff are better for Canadians than are those of a quota. A tariff generates government revenue, which can be used to cut other taxes or to finance public goods and services that benefit Canadians. In contrast, the higher price created by quotas results in additional revenue for foreign producers. **(Key Question 7)**

THE CASE FOR PROTECTION: A CRITICAL REVIEW

Despite the logic of specialization and trade, there are still protectionists in some union halls, corporate boardrooms, and Parliament. What arguments do protectionists make to justify trade barriers? How valid are these arguments?

Military Self-Sufficiency Argument

The argument here is not economic but political-military: Protective tariffs are needed to preserve or strengthen industries that produce the materials essential for national defence. In an uncertain world, the political-military objectives (self-sufficiency) sometimes must take precedence over economic goals (efficiency in the use of world resources).

Unfortunately, it is difficult to measure and compare the benefit of increased national security against the cost of economic inefficiency when protective tariffs are imposed. The economist can only point out that there are economic costs when a nation levies tariffs to increase military self-sufficiency.

The self-sufficiency argument is open to serious abuse. Nearly every industry can claim that it makes direct or indirect contributions to national security and hence deserves protection from imports.

Are there not better ways than tariffs to provide needed strength in strategic industries? When it is achieved through tariffs, this self-sufficiency increases the domestic prices of the products of the protected industry. Thus only those consumers who buy the industry's products shoulder the cost of greater military security. A direct subsidy to strategic industries, financed out of general tax revenues, would distribute these costs more equitably.

Increased Domestic Employment Argument

Arguing for a tariff to "save Canadian jobs" becomes fashionable as an economy encounters a recession. In an economy that engages in international trade, exports involve spending on domestic output and imports reflect spending to obtain part of another nation's output. So, in this argument, reducing imports will divert spending on another nation's output to spending on domestic output. Thus domestic output and employment will rise. But this argument has several shortcomings:

1. **JOB CREATION FROM IMPORTS** While imports may eliminate some Canadian jobs, they create others. Imports may have eliminated the jobs of some Canadian steel and textile workers in recent years, but other workers have gained jobs unloading ships and selling imported cars and imported electronic equipment. Import restrictions alter the composition of employment, but they may have little or no effect on the volume of employment.

2. **FALLACY OF COMPOSITION** All nations cannot simultaneously succeed in restricting imports while maintaining their exports; what is true for *one* nation is not true for *all* nations. The exports of one nation must be the imports of another nation. To the extent that one country is able to expand its economy through an excess of exports over imports, the resulting excess of imports over exports worsens another economy's unemployment problem. It is no wonder that tariffs and import quotas meant to achieve domestic full employment are called "beggar my neighbour" policies:

They achieve short-run domestic goals by making trading partners poorer.

3. **POSSIBILITY OF RETALIATION** Nations adversely affected by tariffs and quotas are likely to retaliate, causing a "trade-barrier war" that will choke off trade and make all nations worse off. For example, when the United States, under the Smoot-Hawley Tariff Act of 1930, imposed the highest tariffs ever enacted, the action backfired miserably. Rather than increasing U.S. output, this tariff act only led to retaliatory restrictions by affected nations, including Canada. This trade war caused a further contraction of international trade and lowered the income and employment levels of all nations. As stated by an international trade expert:

> A trade war in which countries restrict each other's exports in pursuit of some illusory advantage is not much like a real war. On the one hand, nobody gets killed. On the other, unlike real wars, it is almost impossible for anyone to win, since the main losers when a country imposes barriers to trade are not foreign exporters but domestic residents. In effect, a trade war is a conflict in which each country uses most of its ammunition to shoot itself in the foot.[1]

4. **LONG-RUN FEEDBACKS** In the long run, forcing an excess of exports over imports cannot exceed in raising domestic employment. It is through Canadian imports that foreign nations earn dollars for buying Canadian exports. In the long run a nation must import to export. The long-run impact of tariffs is not to increase domestic employment but at best to reallocate workers away from export industries and to protected domestic industries. This shift implies a less efficient allocation of resources.

Diversification for Stability Argument

Highly specialized economies such as Saudi Arabia's (based on oil) and Cuba's (based on sugar) are very dependent on international markets for their incomes. In these economies, wars, international political developments, recessions abroad, and random fluctuations in world supply and

[1] Paul Krugman, *Peddling Prosperity* (New York: W. W. Norton & Co., 1994), p. 287.

demand for one or two particular goods can cause deep declines in export revenues and therefore in domestic income. Tariff and quota protection are allegedly needed in such nations to enable greater industrial diversification. That way, these economies will not be so dependent on exporting one or two products to obtain the other goods they need. Such goods will be available domestically, thereby providing greater domestic stability.

There is some truth in this diversification for stability argument. There are also two serious shortcomings:

1. The argument has little or no relevance to Canada and other advanced economies.
2. The economic costs of diversification may be great; for example, one-crop economies may be highly inefficient at manufacturing.

Infant Industry Argument

The infant industry argument contends that protective tariffs are needed to allow new domestic industries to establish themselves. Temporarily shielding young domestic firms from the severe competition of more mature and more efficient foreign firms will give infant industries a chance to develop and become efficient producers.

This argument for protection rests on an alleged exception to the case for free trade. The exception is that young industries have not had, and if they face mature foreign competition will never have, the chance to make the long-run adjustments needed for larger scale and greater efficiency in production. In this view, tariff protection for such infant industries will correct a misallocation of world resources perpetuated by historically different levels of economic development between domestic and foreign industries.

Counterarguments There are some logical problems with this infant industry argument:

1. In the developing nations it is difficult to determine which industries are the infants that are capable of achieving economic maturity and therefore deserving protection.
2. Protective tariffs may persist even after industrial maturity has been realized.
3. Most economists believe that if infant industries are to be subsidized, there are better means than tariffs for doing it. Direct subsidies, for example, have the advantage of mak-

ing explicit which industries are being aided and to what degree.

Strategic Trade Policy In recent years the infant industry argument has taken a modified form in advanced economies. Now proponents contend that government should use trade barriers to reduce the risk of investing in product development by domestic firms, particularly where advanced technology is involved. Firms protected from foreign competition can grow more rapidly and achieve greater economies of scale than unprotected foreign competitors. The protected firms can eventually dominate world markets because of their lower costs. Supposedly, dominance of world markets will enable the domestic firms to return high profits to the home nation. These profits will exceed the domestic sacrifices caused by trade barriers. Also, advances in high-technology industries are deemed beneficial because the advances achieved in one domestic industry often can be transferred to other domestic industries.

Japan and South Korea, in particular, have been accused of using this form of **strategic trade policy**. The problem with this strategy, and therefore this argument for tariffs, is that the nations put at a disadvantage by strategic trade policies tend to retaliate with tariffs of their own. The outcome may be higher tariffs worldwide, reductions of world trade, and the loss of potential gains from technological advances.

Protection Against Dumping Argument

This argument contends that tariffs are needed to protect domestic firms from "dumping" by foreign producers. **Dumping** is the selling of excess goods in a foreign market at a price below cost. Economists cite two plausible reasons for this behaviour:

1. Firms may use dumping abroad to drive out domestic competitors there, thus obtaining monopoly power and monopoly prices and profits for the importing firm. The long-term economic profits resulting from this strategy may more than offset the earlier losses that accompany the below-cost sales.
2. Dumping may be a form of *price discrimination*, which is charging different prices to different customers even though costs are the same. The foreign seller may find it can maximize its profit by charging a high price in its monopolized domestic market while unloading its sur-

plus output at a lower price in Canada. The surplus output may be needed so the firm can obtain the overall per-unit cost saving associated with large-scale production. The higher profit in the home market more than makes up for the losses incurred on sales abroad.

Because dumping is a legitimate concern, many nations prohibit it. For example, where dumping is shown to injure Canadian firms, the federal government imposes tariffs called "antidumping duties" on the specific goods (see this chapter's In the Media). But there are relatively few documented cases of dumping each year, and those few cases do *not* justify widespread, permanent tariffs.

In fact, foreign producers argue that Canada uses dumping allegations and antidumping duties to restrict legitimate trade. Some foreign firms clearly can produce certain goods at substantially less per-unit cost than Canadian competitors. So, what may seem to be dumping actually is comparative advantage at work. If antidumping laws are abused, they can increase the price of imports and restrict competition in the Canadian market. This reduced competition can allow Canadian firms to raise prices at consumers' expense. And even where true dumping does occur, Canadian consumers gain from the lower-priced product, at least in the short run, much as they gain from a price war among Canadian producers.

Cheap Foreign Labour Argument

The cheap foreign labour argument says that domestic firms and workers must be shielded from the ruinous competition of countries where wages are low. If protection is not provided, cheap imports will flood Canadian markets and the prices of Canadian goods—along with the wages of Canadian workers—will be pulled down. That is, the domestic living standards in Canada will be reduced.

This argument can be rebutted at several levels. The logic of the argument suggests that it is *not* mutually beneficial for rich and poor persons to trade with one another. However, that is not the case. A low-income farm worker may pick lettuce or tomatoes for a rich landowner, and both may benefit from the transaction. And Canadian consumers gain when they buy a Taiwanese-made pocket radio for $12 as opposed to a similar Canadian-made radio selling for $20.

Also, recall that gains from trade are based on comparative advantage, not on absolute advantage. Looking back at Figure 20-1, suppose Canada and Brazil have labour forces of exactly the same size. Noting the positions of the production possibilities curves, we observe that Canadian labour can produce more of *either* good. Thus, it is more productive. Because of this greater productivity, we can expect wages and living standards to be higher for Canadian labour. Brazil's less productive labour will receive lower wages.

The cheap foreign labour argument suggests that, to maintain our standard of living, Canada should not trade with low-wage Brazil. Suppose it does not. Will wages and living standards rise in Canada as a result? No. To obtain soybeans, Canada will have to reallocate a portion of its labour from its efficient steel industry to its inefficient soybean industry. As a result, the average productivity of Canadian labour will fall, as will real wages and living standards. The labour forces of *both* countries will have diminished standards of living because without specialization and trade they will have less output available to them. Compare column 4 with column 1 in Table 20-1 or points A' and B' with A and B in Figure 20-2 to confirm this point.

A Summing Up

These many arguments for protection are not weighty. Under proper conditions, the infant-industry argument stands as a valid exception, justifiable on economic grounds. And on political-military grounds, the self-sufficiency argument can be used to validate some protection. But both arguments are open to severe overuse, and both neglect other ways of promoting industrial development and military self-sufficiency. Most other arguments are emotional appeals—half-truths and fallacies. These arguments see only the immediate and direct consequences of protective tariffs. They ignore the fact that in the long run a nation must import to export.

There is also compelling historical evidence suggesting that free trade has led to prosperity and growth and that protectionism has had the opposite effects. Here are several examples:

1. The Canadian Constitution forbids individual provinces from levying tariffs, and that makes Canada a huge free-trade area. Economic his-

torians cite this as a positive factor in the economic development of Canada.

2. Great Britain's shift towards freer international trade in the mid-nineteenth century was instrumental in its industrialization and growth at that time.

3. The creation of the Common Market in Europe after World War II eliminated tariffs among member nations. Economists agree that creation of this free-trade area, now the European Union, was a major ingredient in Western European prosperity.

4. The trend towards tariff reduction since the mid-1930s stimulated post-World War II expansion of the world economy.

5. The high tariffs imposed by the Smoot-Hawley Act of 1930 in the United States and the retaliation by most of the industrialized world worsened the Great Depression of the 1930s.

6. Studies of developing countries strongly suggest that those that have relied on import restrictions to protect their domestic industries have had slow growth compared to those pursuing more open economic policies (see Global Perspective 20-2).

20-2
QUICK REVIEW

- A nation will export a particular product if the world price exceeds the domestic price; it will import the product if the world price is less than the domestic price.

- In a two-country model, equilibrium world prices and equilibrium quantities of exports and imports occur where one nation's export supply curve intersects the other nation's import demand curve.

- Trade barriers include tariffs, import quotas, non-tariff barriers, and voluntary export restrictions.

- A tariff on a product increases price, reduces consumption, increases domestic production, reduces imports, and generates tariff revenue for government; an import quota does the same, except a quota generates revenue for foreign producers rather than for the government imposing the quota.

- Most arguments for trade protection are special-interest pleas that, if followed, would create gains for protected industries and their workers at the expense of greater losses for the economy.

20-2
GLOBAL PERSPECTIVE

Growth per capita and level of trade protection

Higher levels of trade protection in less developed nations are generally associated with lower levels of economic growth, as measured by average annual increases in output per person.

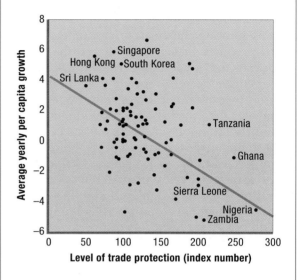

Source: David M. Gould, Graeme L. Woodbridge, and Roy J. Ruffin, "The Theory and Practice of International Trade," *Economic Review*, Federal Reserve Bank of Dallas, 4th Quarter, 1993, p. 3. Data are for 1976–1985.

COSTS OF PROTECTION

In spite of the weakness of most arguments for trade protection, Canada and most other countries continue to impose some protective measures. (These tariffs and quotas, however, are falling under terms of the recent world trade agreements.) How costly are trade protections to Canada?

Cost to Society

Figure 20-6 shows that tariffs and quotas impose costs on domestic consumers, but provide gains to domestic producers, and in the case of tariffs, revenue to the federal government. The consumer cost of trade restrictions can be calculated by determining the effect they have on prices of protected goods. Protection will raise the price of a product in three ways.

1. The price of the imported product goes up.
2. The higher price of imports causes some consumers to shift their purchases to higher-priced domestically produced goods.
3. The prices of domestically produced goods rise because import competition has declined.

Studies indicate the costs to consumers of protected products substantially exceed the gains to producers and government. There is a sizable net cost or efficiency loss to society from trade protection. Furthermore, net losses from trade barriers are greater than the losses reported in most studies. Tariffs and quotas produce myriad costly, difficult-to-quantify secondary effects. For example, the import restraints on steel in the 1980s drove up the price of steel to all Canadian buyers of steel—including the Canadian automobile industry. Therefore Canadian automakers had higher costs than otherwise and were less competitive in world markets.

Finally, industries employ large amounts of economic resources to influence Parliament to pass and retain protectionist laws. Because these rent-seeking efforts divert resources away from more socially desirable purposes, trade restrictions impose that cost on society.

Conclusion: The gains that Canada's trade barriers create for protected industries and their workers come at the expense of much greater losses for the entire economy. The result is economic inefficiency.

Impact on Income Distribution

Studies also show that import restrictions affect low-income families proportionately more than high-income families. Because tariffs and quotas act much like sales or excise taxes, these trade restrictions are highly regressive. That is, the "overcharge" associated with trade protection falls *as a percentage of income* as income increases. Example: Households pay more per year for clothing because of trade restrictions. Relative to their incomes, the burden of this protectionism is heavier for poorer households than for wealthier ones. *(Key Question 11)*

CANADIAN INTERNATIONAL TRADE POLICY

We now turn to Canadian trade policy, the results of these policies, and proposed alternatives.

The National Policy

The general policy on which the present tariff structure of Canada was built was adopted shortly after Confederation. The **National Policy**, introduced in 1879, imposed high tariffs to protect Canada's manufacturing sector. Canada's manufacturing remained highly protected up to 1945. Tariffs on our manufactured goods have been falling ever since, but until very recently our manufacturing sector was highly protected.

If tariffs are economically undesirable, why has Parliament been willing to employ them? The answer lies in the political realities of tariff making and the special-interest effect. A small group of domestic producers who will receive large economic gains from tariffs and quotas will press vigorously for protection through well-financed political lobbyists. The large number of consumers who individually will have small losses imposed on them will be generally uninformed, and unorganized.

The public may be won over, not only by the vigour, but also by the apparent plausibility ("Cut imports and prevent domestic unemployment") and the patriotic ring ("Buy Canadian!") of the protectionists. Alleged tariff benefits are immediate and clear-cut to the public. The costs are obscure and widely dispersed over the economy. Moreover, the public is likely to stumble on the fallacy of composition: "If a quota on Japanese automobiles will preserve profits and employment in the Canadian automobile industry, how can it be detrimental to the economy as a whole?"

GENERAL TRADE LIBERALIZATION

The across-the-board reduction of tariffs has come about because of various bilateral agreements Canada signed. By incorporating **most-favoured-nation clauses** in these agreements, the resulting tariff reductions not only apply to the specific nation negotiating with Canada, but would apply to all nations.

But bilateral (two-nation) negotiations were slow and cumbersome. This approach was broadened in 1947 when 23 nations, including Canada, signed the **General Agreement on Tariffs and Trade (GATT)**. GATT is based on three principles: (1) equal, nondiscriminatory treatment for all member nations; (2) the reduction of tariffs by *multilateral* negotiations; and (3) the elimination of import quotas. GATT is a forum for the negotiation of reductions in tariff barriers on a multilateral basis. There is little doubt that GATT has been an important force in the trend towards liberalized trade. Under its sponsorship, seven "rounds" of negotiations to reduce trade barriers have been completed in the post-World War II period.

In 1994 more than 120 of the world's nations successfully completed the eighth "round" of negotiation, of the Uruguay Round of the GATT. Provisions to be implemented between 1995 and 2005 included:

1. reduction of tariffs worldwide;
2. liberalization of rules that have impeded trade in services;
3. reduction of agricultural subsidies that have distorted the global pattern of trade in agricultural goods;
4. new protections for intellectual property (copyrights, patents, trademarks);
5. a phasing out of quotas on textiles and apparel, replacing them with gradually declining tariffs;
6. establishment of the World Trade Organization to oversee the provisions of the agreement and to resolve any disputes under the new rules.

When completed in 2005, GATT will boost the world's GDP by an estimated $6 trillion, or 8 percent.

Economic Integration

Another development in trade liberalization has taken the form of **economic integration**—the joining of the markets of two or more nations into a free-trade zone. Three illustrations of economic integration are the European Union (EU)—also called the Common Market—the Canada–United States Free Trade Agreement (FTA), and the North American Free-Trade Agreement (NAFTA).

The Common Market   The best example is the **European Union (EU)**—formerly called the European Economic Community. Begun in 1958 with six nations, the EU is now made up of 15 Western European nations—France, Germany, Italy, Belgium, the Netherlands, Luxembourg, Denmark, Ireland, United Kingdom, Greece, Spain, Portugal, Austria, Finland, and Sweden.

Goals   The original Common Market calls for (1) the gradual abolition of tariffs and import quotas on all products traded among the participating nations, (2) establishment of a common system of tariffs applicable to all goods received from nations outside the EU, (3) free movement of capital and labour within the Common Market, (4) the creation of common policies with respect to other economic matters of joint concern, such as agriculture, transportation, and restrictive business practices. The EU has achieved most of these goals and is now a strong **trade bloc**.

Results   Motives for creating the European Union were both political and economic. The economic motive was to gain the advantages of freer trade for members. While it is difficult to determine how much EU prosperity and growth have resulted from integration, integration has created mass markets essential to EU industries. The economies of large-scale production have permitted European industries to achieve the lower costs that small, localized markets have historically denied them.

Effects on nonmember nations such as Canada are less certain. A peaceful and increasingly prosperous EU makes member nations better potential customers for Canadian exports. But Canadian firms encounter tariffs that make it difficult to compete in EU markets. For example, before the establishment of the EU, Canadian, German, and French manufacturers all faced the same tariff in selling their products to, say, Belgium. However, with the establishment of internal free trade among EU members, Belgian tariffs on German Volkswagens and French Renaults fell to zero, but an external tariff still applies to all nonmember nations such as Canada. This puts Canadian firms and those of other nonmember nations at a competitive disadvantage.

By giving preferences to other countries within their free-trade zone, trade blocs such as the EU may reduce their trade with nonbloc members. Thus, the world loses some of the benefits of a completely open global trading system. Eliminating this disadvantage has been one of the motivations for promoting freer global trade through GATT.

THE CANADA–U.S. FREE TRADE AGREEMENT

Other examples of economic integration are the **Canada–U.S. Free Trade Agreement (FTA)** enacted in 1989 and the North American Free Trade Agreement (NAFTA), which came into effect in 1995. More will be said about NAFTA below.

Although three-fourths of the trade between Canada and the United States was already free in 1988, the FTA accord was highly significant: It created the largest free-trade area in the world. Under terms of the agreement, all trade restrictions such as tariffs, quotas, and nontariff barriers would be eliminated by 1999. Canadian producers gained increased access to a market ten times the size of Canada, while U.S. consumers gained the advantage of lower-priced Canadian goods. In return, Canada cut its tariffs by more than the United States because Canadian tariffs were higher.

The North American Free-Trade Zone

In 1993 Canada, Mexico, and the United States formed a trade bloc. The **North American Free Trade Agreement (NAFTA)** established a free-trade zone having about the same combined output as the EU, but a much larger geographical area. The agreement went into effect January 1, 1995. When fully implemented in 1999, the agreement is expected to generate $1 billion to $3 billion of annual gains for each nation.

Free trade with Mexico is even more controversial in Canada than is free trade with the United States. Critics fear a loss of Canadian jobs as firms move to Mexico to take advantage of lower wages and less stringent pollution and workplace safety regulations. Critics also are concerned that Japan and South Korea will build plants in Mexico to ship goods tariff-free through the United States and into Canada, further hurting domestic firms and workers.

Defenders of NAFTA reject these concerns and cite several strong arguments in its favour.

1. Specialization according to comparative advantage will enable Canada to obtain more total output from its scarce resources.
2. The reduction of high Mexican tariffs will increase Canadian exports to Mexico.

3. This free-trade zone will encourage worldwide investment in Mexico, enhancing Mexican productivity and national income. Mexican consumers will use some of that increased income to buy Canadian exports.
4. The resulting higher standard of living in Mexico will enable Mexico to afford more pollution-control equipment and to provide safer workplaces.
5. The loss of specific Canadian jobs to Mexico may have occurred anyway to low-wage countries such as South Korea, Taiwan, and Hong Kong. NAFTA will enable and encourage Canadian firms to be more efficient, enhancing their long-term competitiveness with firms in Japan and the European Union.

Reasons for Joining NAFTA

It may appear that the world's nations are combining into potentially hostile trade blocs. But NAFTA constitutes a vehicle to negotiate reductions in trade barriers with the EU, Japan, and other trading countries. Access to the vast North American market is as important to the EU and Japan as is access to their markets by Canada, the United States, and Mexico. NAFTA gives Canada a lever in future trade negotiations with the EU and Japan. Conceivably, direct negotiations between NAFTA and the EU could eventually link the two free-trade zones. Japan and other major trading nations, not wishing to be left out of the world's wealthiest trade markets, would be forced to eliminate their high trade barriers—to open their domestic markets to additional imports. Nor do other nations and trade blocs want to be excluded from North America. Examples:

1. **APEC** In 1989 Canada and 16 other members of the Asia-Pacific Economic Cooperation (APEC) nations agreed to establish freer trade and more open investment over the next few decades. APEC nations are Australia, Brunei, Canada, Chile, Hong Kong, Indonesia, Japan, Malaysia, Mexico, New Zealand, the Philippines, Papua New Guinea, Singapore, South Korea, Taiwan, Thailand, and the United States.
2. **ADMISSION OF CHILE INTO NAFTA** At the invitation of Canada, Mexico, and the United States, Chile has agreed to become the fourth partner in NAFTA.

3. **MERCOSUR**   The free-trade area encompassing Brazil, Argentina, Uruguay, and Paraguay—called Mercosur—is interested in linking up with NAFTA. So are other South American countries. The Canadian prime minister and 33 other prime ministers and presidents of Western hemisphere nations have agreed to begin negotiations on a free-trade area from "Alaska to Argentina."

Canada had defensive reasons to join in NAFTA. If it had chosen to exclude itself from the agreement, it would have been excluded from bilateral agreements between the United States and Mexico, to the detriment of Canadian exporters seeking access to the Mexican market. Even in the U.S. market, Canada could have ended up at a competitive disadvantage vis à vis Mexico in the American market.

Subsequent events to the signing of NAFTA have also pointed to another reason for joining NAFTA—trade liberalization that may eventually include the Western hemisphere. If, as it is likely, Chile officially joins NAFTA, there will undoubtedly be demands from other nations in the Western hemisphere to join in; many of these claims will probably be defensive actions in a bid not to be excluded.

NAFTA's Strengthening of the Rules of Origin

NAFTA has strengthened the rules of origin to ensure a certain amount of North American content in goods produced and traded among Canada, United States, and Mexico. For example, a car built by Toyota in Ontario must have a specified minimum percentage of its parts produced in North America. This will in effect protect some producers against foreign competition.

Already disputes have arisen between the Canadian and U.S. governments over whether the Honda plant in Canada was meeting the content requirements on its automobiles shipped to the United States. While the rules of origin are clearer in NAFTA compared to the FTA, they will likely continue to be a source of dispute.

NAFTA and Concerns About Environmental and Labour Laws

Critics of NAFTA were particularly vocal against Canada joining because of concern over the perceived less stringent regulations of Mexico's environmental and workplace safety regulations, which would put producers there at a huge competitive advantage when added to the lower wages in Mexico. These concerns were expressed equally strongly in both Canada and the United States over the course of negotiations.

Proponents of NAFTA pointed out that Mexico has adequate laws to protect the environment and workplace safety but these laws are not strongly enforced. Provisions in the agreement make it possible for Canada and the United States to demand Mexico enforce its own environmental and labour laws. Thus NAFTA ensures a higher compliance by its three members to laws that protect the environment and make the workplace safer for workers than in its absence.

Both critics and defenders of NAFTA agree on one point: It constitutes a powerful trade bloc to counter the European Union. Access to the vast North American market is as important to European Union nations as is access to the European market by Canada, the United States, and Mexico. Observers believe negotiations between the North American trade bloc and the European Union will follow, eventually resulting in a free-trade agreement between the two blocs.

Economists agree that the ideal free-trade area would be the world.

20-3
QUICK REVIEW

- The various "rounds" of the General Agreement on Tariffs and Trade (GATT) have established multinational reductions in tariffs and import quotas among the more than 120 member nations.

- The Uruguay Round of GATT that went into effect in 1995: **a** reduced tariffs worldwide; **b** liberalized rules impeding barriers to trade in services; **c** reduced agricultural subsidies; **d** created new protections for intellectual property; **e** phased out quotas on textiles and apparel; and **f** set up the World Trade Organization.

- The European Union (EU), the Canada-U.S. Free Trade Agreement (FTA), and the North American Free Trade Agreement (NAFTA) have reduced trade barriers by establishing large free-trade zones.

In
The Media

Gerber Faces Duty on Baby Food Imports

Revenue Canada sides with Heinz

BY HEATHER SCOFFIELD
PARLIAMENTARY BUREAU

OTTAWA—Revenue Canada has decided to impose a provisional duty that averages 69 per cent on Gerber jarred baby food, saying the U.S. company is dumping its product in Canada.

The department said it agreed with a complaint from H.J. Heinz Co. of Canada Ltd., the only Canada-based producer of jarred baby food, that Gerber Products Co. of Michigan was selling its product at unfairly low prices, cutting into Heinz's profit and causing layoffs at its plant in Leamington, Ont.

"We want to stop the unfair trade practices. That's the main objective," said Ana Relyea, spokeswoman for Heinz in Toronto.

Food for tots is worth big bucks in Canada. Heinz estimates that the country's jarred baby food market is worth $60-million to $70-million a year. Heinz has a 78-per-cent market share, and

Gerber has the other 22 per cent, Ms. Relyea said.

Gerber officials could not be reached for comment.

Revenue Canada began an investigation into Heinz's dumping claims in October, and found that jarred baby food from the United States was being sold in Canada at prices well below prices in the United States.

"There is a reasonable indication that the dumping has caused injury [to the Canadian industry]," the department said in its statement of reasons for the duty decision.

The department said it will continue its investigation to see if the duty should be permanent, and issue a final decision by the end of March. At the same time, the Canadian International Trade Tribunal will investigate to see if the dumped exports are harming Canadian production. The tribunal is to decide by April 29 if the duty should stick.

Gerber shut its Canadian baby food plant in Niagara Falls, Ont.,

in 1992. Since then, Heinz said, Gerber's imports have forced Heinz to lose sales and market share, to cut production and to lay off 57 out of 200 employees making baby food in Leamington.

In Ontario, where sales were hit the hardest, the price of Heinz jars of baby food has dropped to 43 cents from 49 cents four years ago, Ms. Relyea said.

"In order for us to compete, we've had to lower our prices too," she said.

She would not say whether Heinz planned to raise its prices because of the ruling.

H.J. Heinz Co. of Canada Ltd. is a private, wholly owned subsidiary of H.J. Heinz Co. of Pittsburgh.

The duty applies to all U.S. jarred baby food exports to Canada, but Gerber is the only U.S. company involved in the Canadian market for now, Revenue Canada said.

Source: Globe and Mail, December 31, 1997, p. B5. Reprinted with permission from the *Globe and Mail*.

THE STORY IN BRIEF

Revenue Canada imposed an import duty on the U.S. firm Gerber Product Company after it found that Gerber was dumping its jarred baby food in Canada.

THE ECONOMICS BEHIND THE STORY

- H.J Heinz Company of Canada came under intense price pressure from Gerber as the U.S. firm aggres-

sively cut the price of its jarred baby food. Heinz's profit declined, leading to layoffs. Heinz accused Gerber of dumping its jarred baby food.

- Revenue Canada found Gerber guilty of dumping; it sold its products at prices below those it charged in the United States. Such tactics are illegal under international law.

- Who benefited and who lost from the dumping of jarred baby food in Canada? How does an economist decide whether the dumping was on balance beneficial or detrimental to Canada's economic well-being? ■

The
Last Word

PETITION OF THE CANDLEMAKERS, 1845

The French economist Frédéric Bastiat (1801–1850) devastated the proponents of protectionism by satirically extending their reasoning to its logical and absurd conclusions.

PETITION OF THE MANUFACTURERS OF CANDLES, Wax-lights, Lamps, Candlesticks, Street Lamps, Snuffers, Extinguishers, and of the Producers of Oil Tallow, Rosin, Alcohol, and, Generally, of Everything Connected with Lighting.

TO MESSIEURS THE MEMBERS
OF THE CHAMBER OF DEPUTIES.

Gentlemen—You are on the right road. You reject abstract theories, and have little consideration for cheapness and plenty. Your chief care is the interest of the producer. You desire to emancipate him from external competition, and reserve the *national market for national industry*.

We are about to offer you an admirable opportunity of applying your—what shall we call it? your theory? No; nothing is more deceptive than theory; your doctrine? your system? your principle? but you dislike doctrines, you abhor systems, and as for principles, you deny that there are any in social economy: we shall say, then, your practice, your practice without theory and without principle.

We are suffering from the intolerable competition of a foreign rival, placed, it would seem, in a condition so far superior to ours for the production of light, that he absolutely inundates our national market with it at a price fabulously reduced. The moment he shows himself, our trade leaves us—all consumers apply to him; and a branch of native industry, having countless ramifications, is all at once rendered completely stagnant. This rival ... is no other than the Sun.

What we pray for is, that it may please you to pass a law ordering the shutting up of all windows, skylights, dormerwindows, outside and inside shutters, curtains, blinds, bull's-eyes; in a word, of all openings, holes, chinks, clefts, and fissures, by or through which the light of the sun has been in use to enter houses, to the prejudice of the meritorious manufactures with which we flatter ourselves we have accommodated our country,— a country which, in gratitude, ought not to abandon us now to a strife so unequal.

If you shut up as much as possible all access to natural light, and create a demand for artificial light, which of our French manufactures will not be encouraged by it?

If more tallow is consumed, then there must be more oxen and sheep; and, consequently, we shall behold the multiplication of artificial meadows, meat, wool, hides, and, above all, manure, which is the basis and foundation of all agricultural wealth.

The same remark applies to navigation. Thousands of vessels will proceed to the whale fishery; and, in a short time, we shall possess a navy capable of maintaining the honour of France, and gratifying the patriotic aspirations of your petitioners, the undersigned candlemakers and others.

Only have the goodness to reflect, Gentlemen, and you will be convinced that there is, perhaps, no Frenchman, from the wealthy coalmaster to the humblest vendor of lucifer matches, whose lot will not be ameliorated by the success of this our petition. ∎

Source: Frédéric Bastiat, *Economic Sophisms* (Edinburgh: Oliver and Boyd, Tweeddale Court, 1873) pp.49–53, abridged.

CHAPTER SUMMARY

1. International trade is important to most nations, including Canada. Since 1965 our exports and imports have more than doubled as a percentage of GDP. Our major trading partner is the United States. Other major trading nations

are Germany, Japan, the Western European nations, and the newly industrialized Asia tigers (Hong Kong, Singapore, South Korea, and Taiwan).

2. World trade is based on two considerations: the uneven distribution of economic resources among nations, and the fact that efficient production of various goods requires particular techniques or combinations of resources.

3. Mutually advantageous specification and trade are possible between any two nations if they have different opportunity cost ratios for any two products. By specializing based on comparative advantage, nations can obtain larger real incomes with fixed amounts of resources. The terms of trade determine how this increase in world output is shared by the trading nations. Increasing (rather than constant) costs limits specialization and trade.

4. A nation's export supply curve shows the quantity of product it will export at world prices that exceed the domestic price—the price in a closed, no-international-trade economy. Its import demand curve reveals the quantity of a product it will import at world prices below the domestic price. In a two-nation model, the equilibrium world price and the equilibrium quantities of exports and imports occur where one nation's import supply curve intersects the other nation's export demand curve.

5. Trade barriers take the form of protective tariffs, quotas, nontariff barriers, and "voluntary" export restrictions. Supply and demand analysis reveals that protective tariffs and quotas increase the prices and reduce the quantities demanded of affected goods. Sales by foreign exporters diminish; domestic producers, however, enjoy higher prices and enlarged sales. Tariffs and quotas promote a less efficient allocation of domestic and world resources.

6. The strongest arguments for protection are the infant-industry and military self-sufficiency arguments. Most of the other arguments for protection are half-truths, emotional appeals, or fallacies that emphasize the immediate effects of trade barriers while ignoring long-run consequences. Numerous historical examples suggest that free trade promotes economic growth; protectionism does not.

7. Protectionism costs Canadian consumers substantial amounts annually. The cost to consumers for each job saved is far greater than the average salary paid. Consumer losses from trade restrictions greatly exceed producer and government gains, creating an efficiency loss to society.

8. Recent Canadian international trade policy entails **a** general liberalization of trade through NAFTA and GATT; **b** aggressive export promotion by government; and **c** bilateral negotiations over specific trade disputes.

9. The Uruguay Round of GATT negotiations, completed in 1993: **a** reduced tariffs; **b** liberalized trade in services; **c** reduced agricultural subsidies; **d** reduced pirating of intellectual property; **e** phased out import quotas on textiles and apparel; and **f** established the World Trade Organization, which replaces GATT.

10. Free-trade zones (trade blocs) may liberalize trade within regions but may also impede trade with nonbloc members. Three examples of free-trade arrangements are **a** the European Union (EU), formerly the European Community or "Common Market"; **b** the Canada-U.S. Free Trade Agreement (FTA); and **c** the North American Free Trade Agreement (NAFTA), comprising Canada, Mexico, and the United States, and later, Chile.

TERMS AND CONCEPTS

labour-intensive goods
land-intensive goods
capital-intensive goods
absolute advantage
cost ratio
comparative advantage
terms of trade
trading possibilities line
gains from trade
world price
domestic price
export supply curve
import demand curve
revenue and protective tariffs

import quotas
nontariff barriers (NTBs)
voluntary export restrictions (VERs)
strategic trade policy
dumping
National Policy
most-favoured-nation clause
General Agreement on Tariffs and Trade (GATT)
economic integration
European Union (EU or Common Market)
trade bloc
Canada-U.S. Free Trade Agreement (FTA)
North American Free Trade Agreement (NAFTA)

STUDY QUESTIONS

1. Quantitatively, how important is international trade to Canada relative to other nations?

2. Distinguish among land-, labour- and capital-intensive commodities, citing an example of each. What role do these distinctions play in explaining international trade?

3. Suppose nation A can produce 80 units of X by using all its resources to produce X and 60 units of Y by devoting all its resources to Y. Comparative figures for nation B are 60 of X and 60 of Y. Assuming constant costs, in which product should each nation specialize? Why? What are the limits of the terms of trade?

4. **KEY QUESTION** *The following are hypothetical production possibilities tables for New Zealand and Spain.*

New Zealand's production possibilities table (millions of bushels)

PRODUCT	PRODUCTION ALTERNATIVES			
	A	**B**	**C**	**D**
Apples	0	20	40	60
Plums	15	10	5	0

Spain's production possibilities table (millions of bushels)

PRODUCT	PRODUCTION ALTERNATIVES			
	R	**S**	**T**	**U**
Apples	0	20	40	60
Plums	60	40	20	0

Plot the production possibilities data for each of the two countries separately. Referring to your graphs, determine:
   a. *Each country's cost ratio of producing plums and apples;*
   b. *Which nation should specialize in which product;*
   c. *The trading possibilities lines for each nation if the actual terms of trade are 1 plum for 2 apples. (Plot these lines on your graph.)*
   d. *Suppose the optimum product mixes before specialization and trade were B in New Zealand and S in Spain. What are the gains from specialization and trade?*

5. "Canada can produce product X more efficiently than can Great Britain. Yet we import X from Great Britain." Explain.

6. **KEY QUESTION** *Refer to Figure 4-5. Assume the graph depicts Canada's domestic market for oats. How many bushels of corn, if any, will Canada export or import at a world price of $1, $2, $3, $4, and $5? Use this information to construct Canada's export supply curve and import demand curve for corn. Suppose the only other corn-producing nation is France, where the domestic price is $4. Why will the equilibrium world price be between $3 and $4? Who will export corn at this world price; who will import it?*

7. **KEY QUESTION** *Draw a domestic supply and demand diagram for a product in which Canada does not have a comparative advantage. Indicate the impact of foreign imports on domestic price and quantity. Now show a protective tariff that eliminates approximately one-half the assumed imports. Indicate the price-quantity effects of this tariff to **a** domestic consumers, **b** domestic producers, and **c** foreign exporters. How would the effects of a quota that creates the same amount of imports differ?*

8. "The most valid arguments for tariff protection are also the most easily abused." What are these particular arguments? Why are they susceptible to abuse? Evaluate the use of artificial trade barriers, such as tariffs and import quotas, as a means of achieving and maintaining full employment.

9. Evaluate the following statements:
   a. "Protective tariffs limit both the imports and the exports of the nation levying tariffs."

b. "The extensive application of protective tariffs destroys the ability of the international market system to allocate resources efficiently."

c. "Unemployment can often be reduced through tariff protection, but by the same token inefficiency typically increases."

d. "Foreign firms that 'dump' their products onto the Canadian market are in effect presenting the Canadian people with gifts."

e. "In view of the rapidity with which technological advance is dispersed around the world, free trade will inevitably yield structural maladjustments, unemployment and balance of payments problems for industrially advanced nations."

f. "Free trade can improve the composition and efficiency of domestic output. Only the Volkswagen forced Detroit to make a compact car, and only foreign success with the oxygen process forced Canadian steel firms to modernize."

g. "In the long run foreign trade is neutral with respect to total employment."

10. From 1981 to 1985 the Japanese agreed to a voluntary export restriction that reduced Canadian imports of Japanese automobiles by about 10 percent. What would you expect the short-run effects to have been on the Canadian and Japanese automobile industries? If this restriction were permanent, what would be its long-run effects in the two nations on **a** the allocation of resources, **b** the volume of employment, **c** the price level, and **d** the standard of living?

11. KEY QUESTION *What are the benefits and the costs of protectionist policies? Which are larger?*

12. What are NAFTA and GATT and how do they relate to international trade? What policies has the Canadian government recently used to promote our exports?

13. **(The Last Word)** What point is Bastiat trying to make with his petition of the candlemakers?

14. WEB-BASED QUESTION **Multilateral Trade Liberation—GATT and WTO** GATT (General Agreement on Tariffs and Trade) was founded in 1947 to reduce world trade barriers on a multilateral basis. GATT partners have to grant each other the best conditions they grant any of the other nations that have most favoured nation status. GATT was subsumed by the World Trade Organization (WTO) www.wto.org/ on January 1, 1995. Review how the WTO is trying to reduce trade barriers in two disparate industries: information technology and textiles; visit www.wto.org/wto/goods/goods.htm. What types of trade barriers are present in each industry? What timetable has been set for barrier reductions? Why is it more difficult to negotiate trade barrier reductions in textiles rather than information technology?

15. WEB-BASED QUESTION **Canada's Main Trading Partners** Statistics Canada www.statcan.ca/english/Pgdb/Economy/International/gblec02a.htm sets out Canada's main trading partners. Which country is our largest trading partner? Now visit www.statcan.ca/english/Pgdb/Economy/International/gblec04.htm to determine Canada's biggest export sector. What sector is a close second?

Exchange Rates and the Balance of Payments

IF YOU TAKE A CANADIAN DOLLAR TO THE BANK and ask to exchange it for Canadian currency, you will get a puzzled look. If you persist, you may get a dollar's worth of change: One Canadian dollar can buy exactly one Canadian dollar. But as of mid-October 1998, one Canadian dollar could buy 179,858 Turkish lira, 1.05 Australian dollars, .38 British pounds, 1.54 American dollars, 3.55 French francs, 1.05 German marks, 75.50 Japanese yen, or 5.12 Swedish krona. What explains this seemingly haphazard array of exchange rates?

In Chapter 20 we examined comparative advantage as the underlying economic basis of world trade and discussed the effects of barriers to free trade. Here we first introduce the monetary or financial aspects of international trade: How are currencies of different nations exchanged when import and export transactions occur? Next, we analyze and interpret the international balance of payments: What is meant by a "favourable" or "unfavourable" balance of payments? Then we look at the two "pure" types of exchange-rate systems— flexible and fixed—which could be used to determine the worth of one currency in terms of another. After that, we examine the systems of exchange rates which major trading nations have actually used.

IN THIS CHAPTER YOU WILL LEARN:

What determines the supply of and demand for a nation's currency.

•

To distinguish between a nation's current account, capital account, and international reserves.

•

How a balance of payment deficit and surplus affect the international value of a nation's currency (foreign exchange).

•

The difference between a flexible and fixed exchange-rate regime.

•

About the history of the world's exchange-rate regimes.

The
Big Picture

NATIONS TRADE WITH ONE ANOTHER, BUT EACH has a different currency. Moreover, as they trade with one another, in any given year some nations import more than they export, or export more than they import. To complicate matters, financial capital moves across international markets seeking the highest returns. This chapter looks at how nations keep a record of these international transactions and how the value of the Canadian dollar against other currencies is determined.

As you read this chapter, keep the following points in mind:

- If nations did not trade and there were no capital movements across national boundaries, there would be no need for a balance of payment account or an exchange-rate market.

- Think of transactions between nations as roughly similar to exchange between individuals. It will help you to better understand trade and financial transactions between nations.
- The value of any currency is determined by the demand and supply for that currency.
- In order for Canada to purchase goods and services from other nations, it needs to earn foreign exchange by exporting goods or services, otherwise it will have to either borrow foreign exchange or draw down its reserves (savings) of foreign exchange.
- There is a tradeoff between rate stability and the desire for autonomy in domestic macroeconomic policy making. Exchange-rate volatility is an ongoing political issue. ■

FINANCING INTERNATIONAL TRADE

One factor that international trade different from domestic trade is the involvement of different national currencies. When a Canadian firm exports goods to a South Korean firm, the Canadian exporter wants to be paid in dollars. But South Korean importers deal in won; they must exchange their wons for dollars to enable the Canadian export transaction to occur.

This problem is resolved in foreign exchange markets in which dollars can purchase South Korean wons, British pounds, Japanese yen, German marks, or any other currency, and vice versa. Sponsored by major banks in Toronto, New York, London, Zurich, Tokyo, and elsewhere, foreign exchange markets facilitate exports and imports.

Canadian Export Transaction

Suppose a Canadian exporter agrees to sell $30,000 of lumber to a British firm. Assume also that the rate of exchange—the rate at which pounds can be exchanged for, or converted into, dollars, and vice versa—is $2 for £1. This means the British importer must pay the equivalent of £15,000 to the Canadian exporter. Let's track what occurs in

terms of the simple bank balance sheets in Figure 21-1. (A *balance sheet* is a statement showing a firm's *assets* and its *liabilities plus net worth*; the latter are claims on the assets by creditors and owners, respectively. Assets must always equal liabilities plus net worth because every asset of a firm is claimed by someone; those assets not claimed by creditors are claimed by owners.)

(a) To pay for the lumber, the British buyer draws a cheque for £15,000 on its chequing account in a London bank. This is shown by the – £15,000 chequing account entry on the right side of the London bank's balance sheet.

(b) The British firm sends this £15,000 cheque to the Canadian exporter. But the Canadian exporting firm must pay its bills in dollars, not pounds. Thus the exporter sells the £15,000 cheque on the London bank to its bank in, say, Vancouver, which is a dealer in foreign exchange. The bank adds $30,000 to the Canadian firm's chequing account for the £15,000 cheque. Note the new chequing account entry of +$30,000 in the Vancouver bank.

(c) The Vancouver bank deposits the £15,000 in a correspondent London bank for future sale. Thus, +£15,000 of deposits appear in the liabilities column for the London bank. To simplify, we assume that the correspondent bank in London is the same bank from which the British importer

FIGURE 21-1 **Financing a Canadian export transaction**

LONDON BANK: BALANCE SHEET 1		VANCOUVER BANK: BALANCE SHEET 2	
Assets	Liabilities and net worth	Assets	Liabilities and net worth
	(a) Chequing account of British importer − £15,000	(c) Deposit in London bank + £15,000 ($30,000)	(b) Chequing account of Canadian exporter + $30,000
	(c) Deposit of Vancouver bank + £15,000		

In transaction (a) a British importer writes a cheque for £15,000 on its London bank account and uses it to pay for a Canadian import. In transaction (b) the Canadian exporter sells the £15,000 British cheque to its Vancouver bank at the $1 = £2 exchange rate and deposits $30,000 in its Vancouver chequing account. In transaction (c) the Vancouver bank deposits the £15,000 British cheque in its correspondent British bank for future use.

obtained the £15,000 draft. This +£15,000 ($30,000) is an asset as viewed by the Vancouver bank, and it appears as such on that bank's balance sheet.

Note this important point: *Canadian exports create a foreign demand for dollars, and the fulfilment of this demand increases the supply of foreign currencies (pounds in this case) owned by Canadian banks and available to Canadian buyers.*

Canadian Import Transaction

Why would the Vancouver bank be willing to buy pounds for dollars? As just indicated, the Vancouver bank is a dealer in foreign exchange; it is in the business of buying (for a fee) and selling (also for a fee) one currency for another.

Let's now examine how the Vancouver bank would sell pounds for dollars in financing a Canadian import (British export) transaction. Suppose a Canadian retail firm wants to import £15,000 of compact disks produced in Britain by a hot new rock group. Again, bank balance sheets, as shown in Figure 21-2, track what happens.

(a) Because the British exporting firm wants to be paid in pounds rather than dollars, the Canadian importer must exchange dollars for pounds, which it does by going to the Vancouver bank and purchasing £15,000 for $30,000. (Perhaps the

FIGURE 21-2 **Financing a Canadian import transaction**

LONDON BANK		VANCOUVER BANK	
Assets	Liabilities and net worth	Assets	Liabilities and net worth
	(b) Chequing account of British exporter + £15,000	(a) Deposit in London bank − £15,000 ($30,000)	(a) Chequing account of Canadian importer − $30,000
	(a) Deposit of Vancouver bank − £15,000		

In transaction (a) a Canadian importer purchases £15,000 at the $1 = £2 exchange rate by writing a cheque for $30,000 on its Vancouver bank. This reduces the importer's Vancouver chequing account by $30,000 and reduces the Vancouver bank's £15,000 deposit in its correspondent London bank. In transaction (b) the £15,000 payment goes to the British exporter, who deposits it in its chequing account in its London bank.

Canadian importer purchases the same £15,000 which the Vancouver bank acquired from the Canadian exporter.) In Figure 21-2, this purchase reduces the Canadian importer's chequing account in the Vancouver bank by $30,000, and the Vancouver bank gives up its £15,000 deposit in the London bank.

(b) The Canadian importer sends its newly purchased cheque for £15,000 to the British firm, which deposits it in the London bank; there, it is recorded as a +£15,000 deposit in the London bank.

Here you see that Canadian *imports create a domestic demand for foreign currencies (pounds, in this case), and the fulfilment of this demand reduces the supplies of foreign currencies held by Canadian banks and available for Canadian consumers.*

The combined export and import transactions bring one more point into focus. Canadian exports (lumber) make available, or "earn," a supply of foreign currencies for Canadian banks, and Canadian imports (the compact disks) create a demand for these currencies. In a broad sense, any nation's exports finance or "pay for" its imports. Exports provide the foreign currencies needed to pay for imports.

Postscript: Although our examples are confined to exporting and importing goods, demand for and supplies of pounds also arise from transactions involving services and the payment of interest and dividends on foreign investments. Canadians demands pounds not only to buy imports but also to buy insurance and transportation services from the British, to vacation in London, to pay dividends and interest on British investments in Canada, and to make new financial and real investments in Britain. *(Key Question 2)*

THE BALANCE OF PAYMENTS

A nation's **balance of payments** is the sum of all transactions that take place between its residents and the residents of all foreign nations. These transactions include merchandise exports and imports, imports of goods and services, tourist expenditures, interest and dividends received or paid abroad, and purchases and sales of financial or real assets abroad. *The balance of payments statement shows all the payments a nation receives from foreign countries and all the payments it makes to them.* Table 21-1 is a simplified balance of payments statement for Canada in 1997. Let's take a close

TABLE 21-1 Canada's balance of payments, 1997 (in billions)

Current account:
(1) Merchandise exports	. . . . $+301.1	
(2) Merchandise imports	. . . . −276.8	
(3) *Balance of trade*	+24.3	
(4) Exports of services	+41.6	
(5) Imports of services	−50.3	
(6) *Balance on goods and services* . .	−8.7	
(7) Net investment income	−28.9	
(8) Net transfers	+0.5	
(9) **Current account balance**	**−12.8**	

Capital account:
(10) Net change in foreign investment in Canada (capital inflow)	+67.5*	
(11) Net change in foreign investment abroad (capital outflow)	−51.3*	
(12) **Capital account balance**	**+16.2**	

Official settlements account:
(13) **Official international reserves**	**−3.4**	
Balance of payments	**0**	

*Includes one-half of a $7 billion statistical discrepancy that shows up in the balance of payments account.
Source: *Bank of Canada Review, Summer, 1998.* For updates visit Statistics Canada's Web site at www.statcan.ca/english/Pgdb/Economy/Economic/econ01a.htm.

look at this accounting statement to see what it reveals about Canadian international trade and finance. To help our explanation, we divide the single balance of payments account into three components: the current account, the capital account, and the official reserves account.

Current Account

The top portion of Table 21-1 summarizes Canada's trade in currently produced goods and services and is called the **current account**. Items 1 and 2 show exports and imports of goods (merchandise) in 1997. Exports have a *plus* (+) sign because they are a *credit*; they earn and make available foreign exchange in Canada. As you saw in the previous section, any export-type transaction that obligates foreigners to make "inpayments" to Canada generates supplies of foreign currencies in the Canadian banks.

Imports have a *minus* (−) sign because they are a *debit*; they reduce the stock of foreign currencies in Canada. Our earlier discussion of trade financing indicated that Canadian imports obligate Canadians to make "outpayments" to the rest of the world that reduce available supplies of foreign currencies held by Canadian banks.

Trade Balance   Items 1 and 2 in Table 21-1 reveal that in 1997 Canada's goods exports of $301.1 billion earned enough foreign currencies to more than finance Canada's goods imports of $276.8 billion. A country's goods balance of trade, or simply, its **trade balance**, is the difference between its exports and imports of goods. If exports exceed imports, the result is a trade surplus or "favourable balance of trade." If imports exceed exports, there is a trade deficit or "unfavourable balance of trade." We note in item 3 that in 1997 Canada incurred a trade surplus (of goods) of $24.3 billion. (Global Perspective 21-1 shows Canadian trade deficits and surpluses for selected nations or groups of nations.)

Balance on Goods and Services   Item 4 reveals that Canada not only exports goods, such as airplanes and computer software, but also services, such as insurance, consulting, travel, and brokerage services, to residents of foreign nations. These service "exports" totalled $41.6 billion in 1997 and are a credit (thus the + sign). Item 5 indicates that Canadians "imports" similar services from foreigners; these service imports were $50.3 billion in 1997 and are a debit (thus the – sign).

The **balance on goods and services**, shown as item 6, is the difference between Canadian exports of goods and services (items 1 and 4) and Canadian imports of goods and services (items 2 and 5). In 1997, Canadian imports of goods and services exceeded Canadian exports of goods and services by $12.8 billion.

Balance on Current Account   Item 7, *net investment income*, represents the difference between interest and dividend payments people abroad have paid Canadians for the services of exported Canadian capital and what Canadians paid in interest and dividends for the use of foreign capital invested in Canada. It shows that in 1997 Canadian net investment income was $–28.9 billion; we paid more in interest and dividends to people abroad than they paid us.

Item 8 shows net transfers, both public and private, between Canada and the rest of the world. Included here are foreign aid, pensions paid to citizens living abroad, and remittances by immigrants to relatives abroad. These $0.5 billion of transfers are net Canadian outpayments that decrease available supplies of foreign exchange. They are, in a sense, the exporting of good will and the importing of "thank-you notes."

By adding all transactions in the current account, we obtain the **current account balance** shown in item 9. In 1997 Canada had a current account deficit of $12.8 billion. This means that Canada's current account transactions (items 2, 5, and 8) created a greater outpayment of foreign currencies from Canada than an inpayment of foreign currencies to Canada.

Capital Account

The second account within the overall balance of trade account is the **capital account**, which summarizes the flows of payments (money "capital") from the purchase or sale of real or financial assets. For example, a foreign firm may buy a *real* asset, say, an office tower in Canada or a financial asset, for instance, a Canadian government bond. Both kinds of transactions involve the "export" of the ownership of Canadian assets from Canada in return for inpayments of foreign currency (money "capital"

21-1

GLOBAL PERSPECTIVE

Canada's trade balance with selected nations, 1997

Canada has a net export surplus with the United States and Japan, but a net export deficit with the European Union, and other countries.

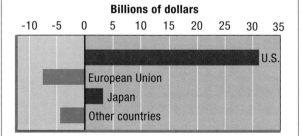

Billions of dollars

Source: Statistics Canada. For updates visit Statistics Canada's Web site at www.statcan.ca/english/Pgdb/Economy/International/gbleco2a.htm.

inflows). As indicated in line 10, these "exports" of ownership of assets are designated *net change in Canadian investment in Canada*. It has a *plus* sign, since like exports of Canadian goods and services, it represents an inpayment of foreign currencies.

Conversely, a Canadian firm may buy, say, a hotel chain (real asset) in a foreign country or common stock (financial asset) of a foreign firm. Both transactions involve "imports" of the ownership of real or financial assets to Canada and are paid for by outpayments of Canadian currency (money "capital" outflows). These "imports" are designated Canadian *net change in foreign investment abroad* and, as shown in line 11, has a – sign; like Canadian imports of goods and services, it represents an outpayment of foreign currencies from Canada.

Items 10 and 11 combined yield a **capital account balance** of $16.2 billion in 1997 (line 12). In 1997 Canada "exported" $67.5 billion of ownership of its real and financial assets and "imported" $51.3 billion. This capital account surplus brought in $16.2 billion of foreign currencies to Canada.

Official Settlement Account

The third account in the overall balance of payments is the official settlement account. The central banks of nations hold quantities of foreign curren-

cies called **official international reserves**. These reserves can be drawn on to make up any net deficit in the combined current and capital accounts (much as you would draw on your savings to pay for a special purchase). In 1997 Canada had a $3.4 billion surplus in the combined current and capital accounts (line 9 minus line 12). Balance in the Canadian international payments led the Canadian government to increase its official international reserves of foreign currencies by $3.4 billion (item 13). The *negative* sign indicates that this increase of reserves is a debit—the inpayment to official international reserves that was needed to balance the overall balance of payments account.

In some years, the current and capital accounts balances may be negative, meaning that Canada earned fewer foreign currencies than it needed. The deficit would create an inpayment, not from other countries, but from the stock of official international reserves. As such, item 14 would have a plus sign since it is a credit.

The three components of the balance of payments—the current account, the capital account, and the official settlement reserves account—must together equal zero. Every unit of foreign exchange used (as reflected in a *minus* outpayment or debit transaction) must have a source (a *plus* inpayment or credit transaction).

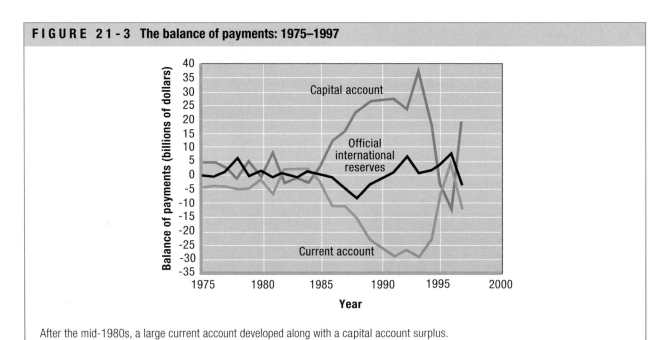

FIGURE 21-3   The balance of payments: 1975–1997

After the mid-1980s, a large current account developed along with a capital account surplus.

Source: *Bank of Canada Review*, Summer 1998.

Payments Deficits and Surpluses

Although the balance of payments *must always sum to zero*, economists and political officials speak of **balance of payment deficits and surpluses**; they are referring to imbalances between the current and capital accounts (line 9 minus line 12) which cause a drawing down or building up of foreign currencies. *A drawing down of official international reserves (to create a positive official reserves entry in Table 21-1) measures a nation's balance of payments deficit; a building up of official international reserves (which is shown as a negative official international reserves entry) measures its balance of payments surplus.*

Figure 21-3 shows the trend in Canada's current, capital, and the official international reserves since 1975. What stands out is that after 1985 Canada's current account has been in a persistent and growing deficit, while the capital account has been in a surplus. The cause of the current account deficit is not a deficit on the merchandise balance but the persistent deficit in services and investment income. We have been net borrowers of capital, and our usual surplus in our merchandise balance is not enough to cover the capital outflows to repay Canada's debts to nonresidents.

A balance of payments deficit is not necessarily bad, nor is a balance of payments surplus necessarily good. Both simply are realities. However, any nation's official international reserves are limited. Persistent payments deficits, which must be financed by drawing down those reserves, would ultimately deplete the reserves. That nation would have to make policies to correct its balance of payments. These policies might require painful macroeconomic adjustments, trade barriers and similar restrictions, or a major depreciation of its currency. For this reason, nations seek to achieve payments balance, at least over several-year periods. *(Key Question 3)*

21-1

QUICK REVIEW

- Canadian exports create a foreign demand for dollars, and fulfilment of that demand increases the domestic supply of foreign currencies; Canadian imports create a domestic demand for foreign currencies, and fulfilment of that demand reduces the supplies of foreign currency held by Canadian banks.

- The current account balance is a nation's exports of goods and services less its imports of goods and services plus its net investment income and net transfers.

- The capital account balance is a nation's sale of real and financial assets to people living abroad less its purchases of real and financial assets from foreigners.

- A balance of payments deficit occurs when the sum of the balances on current and capital accounts is negative; a balance of payments surplus arises when the sum of the balances on current and capital accounts is positive.

FLEXIBLE EXCHANGE RATES

Both the size and persistence of a nation's balance of payments deficits and surpluses and the adjustments it must make to correct these imbalances depend on the system of exchange rates being used. There are two "pure" types of exchange-rate systems:

1. A **flexible** or **floating exchange-rate system** by which the rates that national currencies are exchanged for one another are determined by demand and supply. In such a system no government intervention occurs.

2. A **fixed exchange-rate system** by which governments determine the rates at which currencies are exchanged and make necessary adjustments in their economies to ensure that these rates continue.

We begin by looking at flexible exchange rates. Let's examine the rate, or price, at which Canadian dollars might be exchanged for British pounds. *Figure 21-4 (Key Graph)* shows demand D_1 and supply S_1 of pounds in the currency market.

The *demand for pounds curve* is downsloping because, if pounds become less expensive to Canadians, then all British goods and services will be cheaper to Canadians. That is, at lower dollar prices for pounds, Canadians can get more pounds and therefore more British goods and services per dollar. To buy these cheaper British goods, Canadian consumers will increase the quantity of pounds they demand.

The *supply of pounds curve* is upsloping because, as the dollar price of pounds rises (that is, the

KEY GRAPH

FIGURE 21-4 The market for foreign currency (pounds)

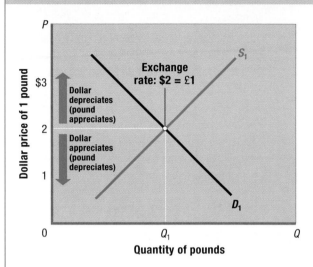

The intersection of the demand for pounds D_1 and the supply of pounds S_1 determines the equilibrium dollar price of pounds, here, $2. That means that the exchange rate is $2 = £1. The upward green arrow is a reminder that a higher dollar price of pounds (say, $3 = £1) means that the dollar has depreciated (pound has appreciated). The downward green arrow tells us that a lower dollar price of pounds (say, $1 = £1) means that the dollar has appreciated (pound has depreciated). Such changes in equilibrium exchange rates would result from shifts of the supply and demand curves.

21-4

QUICK QUIZ

1. Which of the following is a true statement?
   (a) The quantity of pounds demanded falls when the dollar appreciates.
   (b) The quantity of pounds supplied declines as the dollar price of pounds rises.
   (c) At the equilibrium exchange rate, the pound price of $1 is 1/2 pound.
   (d) The dollar would appreciate if the demand for pounds increased.

2. At the price of $2 for 1 pound in this figure,
   (a) the dollar-pound exchange rate is unstable.
   (b) the quantity of pounds supplied equals the quantity demanded.
   (c) the dollar price of 1 pound equals the pound price of $1.
   (d) Canadian merchandise exports to Britain must equal Canadian merchandise imports from Britain.

3. All else equal, a leftward shift of the demand curve in this figure
   (a) would depreciate the dollar.
   (b) creates a shortage of pounds at the previous price of $2 for 1 pound.
   (c) might be caused by a major recession in Canada.
   (d) might be caused by a significant rise of real interest rates in Britain.

4. All else equal, a rightward shift of the supply curve in this figure would
   (a) depreciate the dollar and might be caused by a significant rise of real interest rates in Britain.
   (b) depreciate the dollar and might be caused by a significant fall of real interest rates in Britain.
   (c) appreciate the dollar and might be caused by a significant rise of real interest rates in Canada.
   (d) appreciate the dollar and might be caused by a significant fall of interest rates in Canada.

Answers: 1. (c); 2. (b); 3. (c); 4. (c).

---

pound price of dollars falls), the British will purchase more Canadian goods. When the British buy more Canadian goods, they supply a greater quantity of pounds to the foreign exchange market. In other words, they must exchange pounds for dollars to purchase Canadian goods.

The intersection of the supply curve and demand curve will determine the dollar price of pounds. Here, that price (exchange rate) is $2 for £1.

Depreciation and Appreciation

An exchange rate determined by market forces can, and often does, change daily, just as do stock and bond prices. When the dollar price of pounds increases, for example, from $2 for £1 to $3 for £1, the value of the dollar has depreciated relative to the pound. When a nation's currency depreciates, it takes more units of that nation's currency (dollars) to buy a single unit of some foreign currency (a pound).

When the dollar price of pounds decreases, say, from $2 for £1 to $1 for £1, the dollar has appreciated relative to the pound. When a nation's currency appreciates, it takes fewer units of that nation's currency (dollars) to buy a single unit of some foreign currency (pounds).

In our Canada-Britain illustrations, depreciation of the dollar means an appreciation of the pound, and vice versa. A change in the exchange rate from $2 = £1 to $3 = £1 means that it takes more dollars to buy £1; the dollar has depreciated. But it now takes fewer pounds to buy $1. At the initial rate it took £$\frac{1}{2}$ to buy $1; at the new rate it takes only £$\frac{1}{3}$ to buy $1. The pound has appreciated relative to the dollar. If the dollar depreciates relative to the pound, the pound appreciates relative to the dollar. If the dollar appreciates relative to the pound, the pound depreciates relative to the dollar.

Determinants of Exchange Rates

So what factors would cause a nation's currency to appreciate or depreciate in the market for foreign exchange? Here are three generalizations:

1. If the demand for a nation's currency increases (all else equal), that currency will appreciate; if the demand declines, that currency will depreciate.
2. If the supply of a nation's currency increases, that currency will depreciate; if the supply decreases, that currency will appreciate.
3. If a nation's currency appreciates, some foreign currency depreciates relative to it.

With these generalizations in mind, let's examine the determinants of exchange rates, which are the factors that change either the demand for or supply of a nation's currency.

Changes in Tastes Any change in consumer tastes or preferences for the products of a foreign country may alter the demand for that nation's currency and change its exchange rate. If technological advances in lumber make it more attractive to British consumers and businesses, then the British will supply more pounds in the exchange market in order to purchase more Canadian lumber. The supply-of-pounds curve will shift rightward, the pound will depreciate, and the dollar will appreciate.

In contrast, if British woollen apparel becomes more fashionable in Canada, the Canadian demand for pounds will increase, the pound will appreciate, and the dollar will depreciate.

Relative Income Changes If the growth of a nation's income is more rapid than that of other countries', its currency is likely to depreciate. Here's why. A country's imports vary directly with its level of income. As total income rises in Canada, Canadians buy both more domestically produced goods *and* more foreign goods. If the Canadian economy is expanding rapidly and the British economy is stagnant, Canadian imports of British goods, and therefore Canadian demands for pounds, will increase. The dollar price of pounds will rise, so the dollar will depreciate.

Relative Price-Level Changes Changes in the relative price levels of two nations can change the demand and supply of currencies and alter the exchange rate between the two nations' currencies.

At the extreme, the **purchasing power parity theory** holds that exchange rates *equate* the purchasing power of various currencies. That is, the exchange rates among national currencies adjust to match the ratios of the nations' price levels: If a certain market basket of goods costs $100 in Canada and £50 in Great Britain, the exchange rate will be $2 = £1. In this theory, a dollar spent on goods sold in Britain, Japan, Turkey, and other nations will have equal purchasing power.

In practice, however, exchange rates depart from purchasing power parity, even over long periods. Nevertheless, changes in relative price levels are a determinant of exchange rates. If, for example, the domestic price level rises rapidly in Canada and remains constant in Great Britain, Canadian consumers will seek out low-priced British goods, increasing the demand for pounds. The British will purchase fewer Canadian goods, reducing the supply of pounds. This combination of demand and supply changes will cause the pound to appreciate and the dollar to depreciate.

Relative Interest Rates Changes in relative interest rates between two countries can alter their exchange rate. Suppose that real interest rates rise in Canada but stay constant in Great Britain. British citizens will then find Canada an attractive place in which to make financial investments. To undertake these investments, they will have to supply pounds in the foreign-exchange market to obtain dollars. The increase in the supply of pounds results in depreciation of the pound and appreciation of the dollar.

Speculation *Currency speculators* are people who buy and sell currencies with an eye to reselling or repurchasing them at a profit. Suppose speculators expect the Canadian economy to (1) grow more rapidly than the British economy and (2) experience a more rapid rise in its price level than Britain. These expectations translate to an anticipation that the pound will appreciate and the dollar will depreciate. Speculators who are holding dollars will therefore try to convert them into pounds. This effort will increase the demand for pounds and cause the dollar price of pounds to rise (that is, the dollar to depreciate). A self-fulfilling prophecy occurs: The pound appreciates and the dollar depreciates because speculators act on the belief that these changes will in fact take place. In this way, speculation can cause changes in exchange rates. (We deal with currency speculation in more detail in this chapter's Last Word.)

Table 21-2 has more illustrations of the determinants of exchange rates; we urge you to give the table a good look.

Flexible Rates and the Balance of Payments

Proponents argue that flexible exchange rates have an important feature: *They automatically adjust to eventually eliminate balance of payment deficits or surpluses.* We can explain this concept with S_1 and D_1 in Figure 21-5; they are the supply and demand curves for pounds from Figure 21-4.

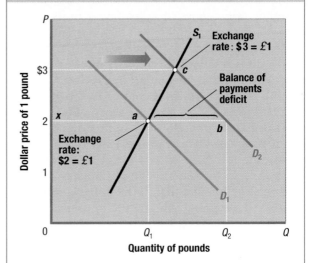

FIGURE 21-5 Adjustments under flexible exchange rates and fixed exchange rates

Under flexible exchange rates, a shift in the demand for pounds from D_1 to D_2, other things equal, would cause a Canadian balance of payments deficit *ab*; it would be corrected by a change in the exchange rate from $2 = £1 to $3 = £1. Under fixed exchange rates, Canada would cover the shortage of pounds *ab* by using international monetary reserves, restricting trade, implementing exchange controls, or enacting a contractionary stabilization policy.

The equilibrium exchange rate of $2 = £1 means there is no balance of payments deficit or surplus between Canada and Britain. At the $2 = £1 exchange rate, the quantity of pounds demanded by Canadian consumers to import British goods, buy British transportation and insurance services,

---

TABLE 21-2 Determinants of exchange rates: factors that change the demand or supply of a particular currency and thus alter the exchange rate

1. **Changes in tastes** Examples: Japanese autos decline in popularity in Canada (Japanese yen depreciates, Canadian dollar appreciates); German tourists flock to Canada for vacations (Canadian dollar appreciates, German mark depreciates).

2. **Changes in relative incomes** Example: England encounters a recession, reducing its imports, while Canadian real output and real income surge, increasing Canadian imports (British pound appreciates, Canadian dollar depreciates).

3. **Changes in relative prices** Example: Germany experiences a 3% inflation rate compared to the United States' 10% rate (German mark appreciates, American dollar depreciates).

4. **Changes in relative real interest rates** Example: The Bank of Canada drives up interest rates in Canada, while the Bank of England takes no such action (Canadian dollar appreciates, British pound depreciates).

5. **Speculation** Examples: Currency traders believe France will have much more rapid inflation than Sweden (French franc depreciates; Swedish krona appreciates); currency traders think German interest rates will plummet relative to Canadian rates (German mark depreciates, Canadian dollar appreciates).

and pay interest and dividends on British investments in Canada equals the amount of pounds supplied by the British in buying Canadian exports, purchasing services from the Canadians and making interest and dividend payments on Canadian investments in Britain. Canada would have no need to either draw down or build up its official reserves to balance its payments.

Suppose tastes change and Canadians buy more British automobiles; the Canadian price level increases relative to Britain's; or interest rates fall in Canada compared to those in Britain. Any or all of these changes will cause the Canadian demand for British pounds to increase from D_1 to, say, D_2 in Figure 21-5.

If the exchange rate remains at the initial $2 = £1$, a Canadian balance of payments deficit will be created in the amount of ab. That is, at the $2 = £1$ rate, Canadians consumers will demand the quantity of pounds represented by point b, but Britain will supply the amount represented by a; there will be a shortage of pounds. However, because this is a competitive market, the shortage will alter the exchange rate (the dollar price of pounds) from $2 = £1$ to, say, $3 = £1$; that is, the dollar will depreciate.

At this point we need to reemphasize that the exchange rate links all domestic (Canadian) prices with all foreign (British) prices. The dollar price of a foreign good is found by multiplying the foreign price by the exchange rate (in dollars per unit of the foreign currency). At an exchange rate of $2 = £1$, a British automobile priced at £9,000 will cost a Canadian consumer $18,000 (= 9,000 × \$2)$.

A change in the exchange rate alters the prices of all British goods to Canadian consumers and all Canadian goods to British buyers. The shift in the exchange rate (here from $2 = £1$ to $3 = £1$) changes the relative attractiveness of Canadian imports and exports and restores equilibrium in the Canadian (and British) balance of payments. From the Canadian point of view, as the dollar price of pounds changes from $2 to $3, the British auto priced at £9,000, which formerly cost a Canadian consumer $18,000, now costs $27,000 (= 9,000 × \$3)$. Other British goods will also cost Canadian consumers more, and Canadian imports of British goods will decline. A movement from point b towards point c in Figure 21-5 graphically illustrates this concept.

From Britain's standpoint, the exchange rate (the pound price of dollars) has fallen (from $£\frac{1}{2}$ to $£\frac{1}{3}$ for $1). The international value of the pound

has appreciated. The British previously got only $2 for £1; now they get $3 for £1. Canadian goods are therefore cheaper to the British, and Canadian exports to Britain will rise. In Figure 21-5, this is shown by a movement from point a towards point c.

The two adjustments—a decrease in Canadian imports from Britain and an increase in Canadian exports to Britain—are just what are needed to correct the Canadian balance of payments deficit. These changes end when, at point c, the quantities of British pounds demanded and supplied are equal. *(Key Questions 6 and 9)*

Disadvantages of Flexible Exchange Rates

Even though flexible exchange rates automatically work to eliminate payment imbalances, they may cause several significant problems.

Uncertainty and Diminished Trade The risks and uncertainties associated with flexible exchange rates may discourage the flow of trade. Suppose a Canadian automobile dealer contracts to purchase 10 British cars for £90,000. At the current exchange rate of, say, $2 for £1, the Canadian importer expects to pay $180,000 for these automobiles. But if in the three-month delivery period the rate of exchange shifts to $3 for £1, the £90,000 payment contracted by the Canadian importer will now be $270,000.

This increase in the dollar price of pounds may thus turn the Canadian importer's anticipated profit into substantial losses. Aware of the possibility of an adverse change in the exchange rate, the Canadian importer may not be willing to assume the risks involved. The Canadian firm may confine its operations to domestic automobiles, with the result that international trade in this item does not occur.

The same thing can happen with investments. Assume that, when the exchange rate is $3 to £1, a Canadian firm invests $30,000 (or £10,000) in a British enterprise. It estimates a return of 10 percent; that is, it anticipates annual earnings of $3,000 or £1,000. Suppose these expectations prove correct in that the British firm earns £1,000 in the first year on the £10,000 investment. But suppose that during the year, the value of the dollar appreciates to $2 = £1$. The absolute return is now only $2,000 (rather than $3,000), and the rate of return falls from the anticipated 10 percent to only $6\frac{2}{3}$

percent (= \$2,000/\$30,000). Investment is risky anyway. The added risk of changing exchange rates may persuade the Canadian investor to not venture overseas.[1]

Terms of Trade Changes

A nation's terms of trade will be worsened by a decline in the international value of its currency. For example, an increase in the dollar price of pounds will mean that Canada must export more goods and services to finance a specific level of imports from Britain.

Instability

Flexible exchange rates may have destabilizing effects on the domestic economy because wide fluctuations stimulate and then depress industries producing exported goods. If the Canadian economy is operating at full employment and its currency depreciates as in our illustration, the results will be inflationary, for two reasons. (1) Foreign demand for Canadian goods may increase, increasing total spending and pulling up Canadian prices. Also, the prices of all Canadian imports will increase. (2) Conversely, appreciation of the dollar will lower Canadian exports and increase imports, possibly causing unemployment.

Flexible or floating exchange rates may also complicate the use of domestic stabilization policies in seeking full employment and price stability. This is especially true for nations whose exports and imports are large relative to their total domestic output.

FIXED EXCHANGE RATES

To circumvent the disadvantages of flexible exchange rates, at times nations have fixed or "pegged" their exchange rates. For our analysis of fixed exchange rates, we assume Canada and Britain agree to maintain a \$2 = £1 exchange rate.

The problem is that such a governmental agreement cannot keep from changing the demand for and supply of pounds. With the rate fixed, a shift in demand or supply will put pressure on the exchange rate system, and government must intervene if the exchange rate is to be maintained.

---

[1] You will see in this chapter's Last Word, however, that a trader can circumvent part of the risk of unfavourable exchange rate fluctuations by "hedging" in the "futures market" or "forward market" for foreign exchange.

In Figure 21-5, suppose the Canadian demand for pounds increases from D_1 to D_2 and a Canadian payment deficit *ab* arises. This means that the Canadian government is committed to an exchange rate (\$2 = £1) which is below the new equilibrium rate (\$3 = £1). How can the Bank of Canada prevent the shortage of pounds from driving the exchange rate up to the new equilibrium level? The answer is to alter market demand or market supply or alter both so that they will intersect at the \$2 = £1 rate of exchange. There are several ways to do this.

Use of Reserves

One way to maintain a pegged exchange rate is to manipulate the market through the use of official international reserves. By selling part of its reserves of pounds, the Bank of Canada could increase the supply of pounds, shifting supply curve S_1 to the right so that it intersects D_2 at *b* in Figure 21-5 and thereby maintains the exchange rate at \$2 = £1.

How do official international reserves originate? Perhaps in the past the opposite market conditions prevailed, so there was a surplus, rather than a shortage, of pounds. The Bank of Canada would have acquired that surplus. That is, at some earlier time the Bank of Canada may have spent dollars to buy surplus pounds that were threatening to reduce the \$2 = £1 exchange rate to, say, \$1 = £1. That condition would have built up its official reserves of pounds.

Nations have also used gold as "international money" to obtain official international reserves. In our example, the Bank of Canada could sell some of the gold it owns to Britain for pounds. The pounds acquired could then be sold for dollars, as above, to shift the supply of pounds to the right so as to maintain the \$2 = £1 exchange rate.

It is critical that the amount of international reserves and gold be enough to accomplish the required increase in the supply of pounds. This is not a problem if deficits and surpluses occur more or less randomly and are about the same size. That is, last year's balance of payments surplus with Britain will increase Canada's reserve of pounds, and that reserve can be used to "finance" this year's deficit. But if Canada encounters persistent and sizable deficits for an extended period, its international reserves can become exhausted, forcing it to abandon fixed exchange rates. Or, at the least, a nation whose international reserves are inadequate must use less appealing options to maintain exchange rates. Let's consider some of these options.

Trade Policies

To maintain fixed exchange rates, a nation can try to control the flow of trade and finance directly. Canada could try to maintain the $2 = £1 exchange rate in the face of a shortage of pounds by discouraging imports (thereby reducing the demand for pounds) and encouraging exports (thus increasing the supply of pounds). Imports can be reduced with new tariffs or import quotas; special taxes can be levied on the interest and dividends Canadian financial investors receive from foreign investments. Also, the Canadian government could subsidize certain Canadian exports to increase the supply of pounds.

The fundamental problem is that these policies reduce the volume of world trade and change its makeup from what is economically desirable. When we impose tariffs and quotas, we lose some of the economic benefits of a free flow of world trade. This loss should not be underestimated: Trade barriers by one nation lead to retaliatory responses from other nations, multiplying the loss.

Exchange Controls and Rationing

Another option is exchange controls and rationing. Under exchange controls, Canada could handle the problem of a pound shortage by requiring that all pounds obtained by Canadian exporters be sold to the the Bank of Canada. Then the government would allocate or ration this short supply of pounds (represented by *xa* in Figure 21-5) among various Canadian importers, who actually demand the quantity *xb*. The effect of this policy is to restrict the value of Canadian imports to the amount of foreign exchange earned by Canadian exports. Assuming balance in the capital account, there is then no balance of payments deficit. Canadian demand for British imports with the value *ab* would simply not be fulfilled.

There are major objections to exchange controls:

1. **DISTORTED TRADE**   Like tariffs, quotas, and export subsidies (trade controls), exchange controls distort the pattern of international trade away from that suggested by comparative advantage.
2. **FAVOURITISM**   The process of rationing scarce foreign exchange can lead to govern-

ment favouritism towards selected importers (big contributors to reelection campaigns, for example).
3. **RESTRICTED CHOICE**   Controls limit freedom of consumer choice. The Canadian consumers who prefer Volkswagens may have to buy Chevrolets. The business opportunities for some Canadian importers may be impaired because government limits imports.
4. **BLACK MARKETS**   There are likely to be enforcement problems. Canadian importers might want foreign exchange badly enough to pay more than the $2 = £1 official rate, setting the stage for black-market dealings between importers and illegal sellers of foreign exchange.

Domestic Macroeconomic Adjustments

A final way to maintain a stable exchange rate is to use domestic stabilization policies (monetary policy and fiscal policy) to eliminate the shortage of foreign currency. Tax hikes, reductions in government spending, and a high-interest-rate policy would reduce total spending in the Canadian economy and thus domestic income. Because imports vary directly with domestic income, demand for British goods, and therefore for pounds, would be restrained.

If these "contractionary" policies reduce the domestic price level relative to Britain's, Canadian buyers of consumer and capital goods would divert their demands from British goods to Canadian goods, also reducing the demand for pounds. Moreover, the high-interest-rate policy would lift Canadian interest rates relative to those in Britain.

Lower prices on Canadian goods and higher Canadian interest rates would increase British imports of Canadian goods and increase British financial investment in Canada. Both developments would increase the supply of pounds. The combination of a decrease in the demand for and an increase in the supply of pounds would reduce or eliminate the original Canadian balance of payments deficit. In Figure 21-5 the new supply and demand curves would intersect at some new equilibrium point on line *ab*, where the exchange rate remains at $2 = £1.

This way to maintain pegged exchange rates is hardly appealing. The "price" of exchange-rate stability for Canada would be falling output, employment, and price levels—in other words, a recession. Eliminating a balance of payments deficit and realizing domestic stability are both important national economic goals, but to sacrifice stability for payments balance is to let the tail wag the dog.

21-2

QUICK REVIEW

- In a system in which exchange rates are flexible (meaning that they are free to float), the rates are determined by the demand for and supply of individual national currencies in the foreign exchange market.

- Determinants of flexible exchange rates—factors which shift currency supply and demand curves—include changes in **a** tastes, **b** relative national incomes, **c** relative price levels, **d** real interest rates, and **e** speculation.

- Under a system of fixed exchange rates, nations set their exchange rates and then maintain them by buying or selling reserves of currencies, establishing trade barriers, employing exchange controls, or incurring inflation or recession.

INTERNATIONAL EXCHANGE-RATE SYSTEMS

In recent times the world's nations have used three different exchange-rate systems: a fixed rate system, a modified fixed rate system, and a modified flexible-rate system.

The Gold Standard: Fixed Exchange Rates

Between 1879 and 1934 the major nations of the world adhered to a fixed-rate system called the **gold standard**. In this system, each nation must

1. Define its currency in terms of a quantity of gold
2. Maintain a fixed relationship between its stock of gold and its money supply
3. Allow gold to be freely exported and imported

If each nation defines its currency in terms of gold, the various national currencies will have fixed relationships to one another. For example, if Canada defines $1 as worth 25 grains of gold, and Britain defines its pound as worth 50 grains of gold, then a British pound is worth 2 × 25 grains,

or $2. This exchange rate would be fixed; it would not change in response to changes in currency demand and supply.

Gold Flows   If we ignore the costs of packing, insuring, and shipping gold between countries, under the gold standard the rate of exchange would not vary from this $2 = £1 rate. No one in Canada would pay more than $2 = £1 because 50 grains of gold could always be bought for $2 in Canada and sold for £1 in Britain. Nor would the British pay more than £1 for $2. Why should they when they could buy 50 grains of gold in Britain for £1 and sell it in Canada for $2?

Under the gold standard, the potential free flow of gold between nations would result in exchange rates that are fixed.

Domestic Macroeconomic Adjustments   When the demand for, or supply of, currencies changes, the gold standard requires domestic macroeconomic adjustments for the fixed exchange rate to be maintained. To see why, suppose that Canadians' tastes change such that they want to buy more British goods. The demand for pounds increases such that there is a shortage of pounds in Canada (recall Figure 21-5), implying a Canadian balance of payments deficit.

What will happen? Remember that the rules of the gold standard prohibit the exchange rate from moving from the fixed $2 = £1 rate; the rate cannot move to, say, a new equilibrium at $3 = £1 to correct the imbalance. Instead, gold will flow from Canada to Britain to remove the payments imbalance.

But recall that the gold standard required participants to maintain a fixed relationship between their domestic money supplies and their quantities of gold. The flow of gold from Canada to Britain will require a reduction of the money supply in Canada. Other things equal, this will reduce total spending in Canada and thereby lower Canadian real domestic output, employment, income, and perhaps, prices. Also, the decline in the money supply will boost Canadian interest rates.

The opposite will occur in Britain. The inflow of gold will increase the money supply, which will increase total spending in Britain. Domestic output, employment, income, and perhaps prices will rise. The British interest rate will fall.

Declining Canadian incomes and prices will reduce Canadian demand for British goods and therefore reduce the Canadian demand for pounds. Lower interest rates in Britain will make it less attractive for Canadians investors to make financial investments there, also lessening the demand for pounds. For all these reasons, the demand for pounds in Canada will decline. In Britain, higher incomes, prices, and interest rates will make Canadian imports and Canadian financial investments more attractive. In buying these imports and making these financial investments, British citizens will supply more pounds in the exchange market.

In short, domestic macroeconomic adjustments in Canada and Britain, triggered by the international flow of gold, will produce new demand and supply conditions for pounds such that the $2 = £1 exchange rate is maintained. After all the adjustments are made, Canada will not have a payments deficit, and Britain will not have a payments surplus.

The gold standard thus has the advantage of stable exchange rates and automatic correction of balance of payments deficits and surpluses. However, its critical drawback is that nations must accept domestic adjustments in such distasteful forms as unemployment and falling incomes, on the one hand, or inflation, on the other hand. Under this system, a nation's money supply is altered by changes in supply and demand in currency markets. Under the gold standard, nations cannot set their own money supply in their own national interest. If Canada, for example, was experiencing declining output and incomes, the loss of gold under the gold system would reduce the Canadian money supply, which might cause higher interest rates, lower borrowing and spending, and cause further declines in output and income.

Demise of the Gold Standard   The worldwide depression in the 1930s led to the collapse of the gold standard. As domestic outputs and employment fell worldwide, the restoration of prosperity became the primary goal of afflicted nations. These nations enacted protectionist measures to reduce imports. The idea was to expand consumption of domestically produced goods and get their economies moving again. To make their exports less expensive abroad, many nations redefined their currencies at lower levels in terms of gold. For example, a country previously defining the value of its currency at 1 unit = 25 ounces of gold might redefine it as 1 unit = 10 ounces of gold. Such redefining is an example of **devaluation**—a delib-

erate action by government to reduce the international value of its currency. A series of such devaluations in the 1930s meant that exchange rates were no longer fixed; a major tenet of the gold standard was violated, and the system broke down.

The Bretton Woods System

The Great Depression and World War II left world trade and the world monetary system in shambles. To lay the groundwork for a new international monetary system, an international conference of nations was held at Bretton Woods, New Hampshire, in 1944. The conference produced a commitment to a modified fixed exchange-rate system called an *adjustable-peg system*, or, simply, the **Bretton Woods system**. The new system sought to capture the advantages of the old gold standard (fixed exchange rate) while avoiding its disadvantages (painful domestic macroeconomic adjustments).

Furthermore, the conference created the **International Monetary Fund** (IMF) to make the new exchange-rate system feasible and workable. The new international monetary system managed through the IMF prevailed with modifications until 1971. (The IMF still plays a basic role in international finance; in recent years it has performed a major role in providing loans to developing countries and to economies making transitions to capitalism.)

IMF and Pegged Exchange Rates   How did the adjustable-peg system of exchange rates work? First, as with the gold standard, each IMF member had to define its currency in terms of gold (or dollars), thus establishing rates of exchange between its currency and the currencies of all other members. In addition, each nation was obligated to keep its exchange rate stable with respect to every other currency. To do so, nations would have to use their official currency reserves to intervene in foreign exchange markets.

Assume again that the Canadian dollar and the British pound were "pegged" to each other at $2 = £1. Now again suppose that the demand for pounds temporarily increases so that a shortage of pounds occurs in Canada (Canada has a balance of payments deficit). How can Canada keep its pledge to maintain a $2 = £1 exchange rate when the new equilibrium rate is, say, $3 = £1? Canada can supply additional pounds to the exchange market, increasing the supply of pounds such that the equilibrium exchange rate falls back to $2 = £1.

Under the Bretton Woods system there were three main sources of the needed pounds:

1. **OFFICIAL INTERNATIONAL RESERVES** Canada might currently possess pounds in its official international reserves, as the result of past actions against the opposite exchange-market condition (payments surplus).

2. **GOLD SALES** The Canadian government might sell some of its gold to Britain for pounds. The proceeds would then be offered in the exchange market to augment the supply of pounds.

3. **IMF BORROWING** The needed pounds might be borrowed from the IMF. Nations participating in the Bretton Woods system were required to make contributions to the IMF based on the size of their national income, population, and volume of trade. If necessary, Canada could borrow pounds on a short-term basis from the IMF by supplying its own currency as collateral.

Fundamental Imbalances: Adjusting the Peg

The Bretton Woods system recognized that from time to time a nation may be confronted with persistent and sizable balance of payments problems that cannot be corrected through the means listed above. In these cases, the nation would eventually run out of official reserves and be unable to maintain its fixed exchange-rate system. The Bretton Woods remedy was correction by devaluation, that is, by an "orderly" reduction of the nation's pegged exchange rate. Also, the IMF allowed each member nation to alter the value of its currency by 10 percent, on its own, to correct a so-called fundamental (persistent and continuing) balance of payments deficit. Larger exchange-rate changes required the permission of the Fund's board of directors. By requiring approval of significant rate changes, the Fund guarded against arbitrary and competitive currency devaluations by nations seeking only to boost output in their own countries at the expense of other countries. In our example, devaluation of the dollar would increase Canadian exports and lower Canadian imports, correcting its persistent payments deficit.

Demise of the Bretton Woods System
Under this adjustable-peg system, gold and the dollar came to be accepted as international reserves. The acceptability of gold as an international medium of exchange derived from its earlier use under the gold standard. The American dollar became accepted as international money because the United States had accumulated large quantities of gold and between 1934 and 1971 it maintained a policy of buying gold from, and selling gold to, foreign governments at a fixed price of $35 per ounce. The U.S. dollar was convertible into gold on demand; thus the dollar came to be regarded as a substitute for gold, or "as good as gold." And, since the discovery of new gold was limited, the growing volume of U.S. dollars helped provide a medium of exchange for the expanding world trade.

But a major problem arose. The United States experienced persistent payments deficits throughout the 1950s and 1960s. These deficits were financed in part by U.S. gold reserves, but mostly by payment of U.S. dollars. As the amount of dollars held by foreigners soared and the U.S. gold reserves dwindled, other nations began to question whether the dollar was really "as good as gold." The U.S. ability to continue to convert dollars into gold at $35 per ounce became increasingly doubtful, as did the role of U.S. dollars as international monetary reserves. Thus the dilemma was: To maintain the dollar as a reserve medium, the U.S. payment deficit had to be eliminated. But elimination of the payment deficit would remove the source of additional U.S. dollar reserves and thus limit the growth of international trade and finance.

The problem came to a head in 1971 when the United States ended its 37-year-old policy of exchanging gold for dollars at $35 per ounce. It severed the link between gold and the international value of the dollar, thereby "floating" the dollar and letting its value be determined by market forces. The floating of the dollar in effect withdrew U.S. support from the Bretton Woods system of fixed exchange rates and sounded the system's death knell.

The Current System: The Managed Float

The current international exchange-rate system (1971–present) is an "almost" flexible system called **managed floating exchange rates**. Exchange rates among major currencies are free to float to their equilibrium market levels, but nations occasionally intervene in the foreign exchange market to stabilize or alter market exchange rates.

Normally, the major trading nations allow their exchange rates to float up or down to equilibrium levels based on supply and demand in the foreign exchange market. They recognize that changing economic conditions among nations re-quire continuing changes in equilibrium exchange rates to avoid persistent payments deficits or sur-pluses. They rely on freely operating foreign exchange markets to accomplish the necessary adjustments. The result has been considerably more volatile exchange rates than during the Bret-ton Woods era (see Global Perspective 21-2).

But nations also recognize that some trends in the movement of equilibrium exchange rates may be at odds with national or international objec-tives. On occasion, nations therefore intervene in the foreign exchange market by buying or selling large amounts of specific currencies. This way, they can "manage" or stabilize exchange rates by influencing currency demand and supply.

For example, in 1987 the Group of Seven industrial nations (G-7 nations)—Canada, the United States, Germany, Japan, Britain, France, and

Italy—agreed to stabilize the values of the U.S. dol-lar. During the previous two years the U.S. dollar (as well as the Canadian dollar) had declined rapidly because of large U.S. trade deficits. Although the U.S. trade deficits remained sizable, the G-7 nations concluded that further dollar depreciation might disrupt economic growth in member nations (other than the United States). The G-7 nations therefore purchased large amounts of U.S. dollars to boost its value. Since 1987 the G-7 nations (now G-8 with the addition of Russia) have periodically intervened in foreign exchange mar-kets to stabilize currency values.

The current exchange-rate system is thus an "almost" flexible exchange-rate system. The "almost" mainly refers to the periodic currency interventions by governments; it also refers to the fact that the actual system is more complicated than described. While the major currencies—dol-

21-2
GLOBAL PERSPECTIVE

Changes in exchange rates relative to the dollar

The floating exchange rate system (managed float) introduced in 1971 has produced far more volatile exchange rates than those produced during the earlier Bretton Woods era. (Here, changes in the index show changes in each nation's U.S. dol-lar exchange rate relative to the U.S. dollar exchange rate that existed in 1948.)

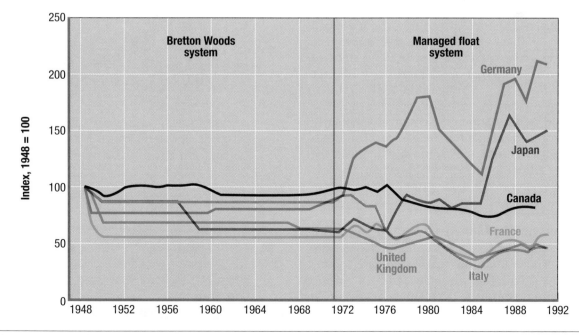

Source: *Economic Report of the President*, 1993, p. 287.

lars, marks, pounds, yen, and the like—fluctuate in response to changing supply and demand, some of the European nations have tried to peg their currencies to one another. Also, many developing nations peg their currencies to the U.S. dollar and allow their currencies to fluctuate with it against other currencies. Finally, some nations peg the value of their currencies to a "basket" or group of other currencies.

How well has the managed float worked? It has both proponents and critics.

In Support of the Managed Float Proponents argue that the managed float system has functioned well-far better than anticipated. Skeptics had predicted that fluctuating exchange rates would reduce world trade and finance. But in real terms world trade under the managed float has grown at about the same rate as during the 1960s under the Bretton Woods system of the fixed exchange rates. Moreover, as supporters are quick to point out, the currency crises in Mexico and Southeast Asia in the last half of the 1990s were not the result of the floating exchange-rate system itself. Rather, the abrupt currency devaluations and depreciations resulted from internal problems in those nations, in conjunction with the nations' tendency to peg their currencies to the dollar or to a basket of currencies. In some cases, flexible exchange rates would have made these adjustments far more gradual.

Proponents also point out that the managed float has weathered severe economic turbulence that might have caused a fixed-rate system to break down. Such events as extraordinary oil price increases in 1973–74 and again in 1981–83, inflationary recessions in several nations in the mid-1970s, and major national recessions in the early 1980s all caused substantial imbalances in international trade and finance. Flexible rates allowed the system to adjust to these developments, whereas the same events would have put unbearable pressures on a fixed-rate system.

Concerns with the Managed Float There is still much sentiment in favour of greater exchange-rate stability. Those favouring stable exchange rates see problems with the current system. They argue that exchange rates have been excessively volatile under the managed float; this volatility threatens the continued expansion of international investment and trade. Moreover, some volatility has occurred even when underlying economic and

financial conditions have been relatively stable, suggesting that speculation is playing too large a role in determining exchange rates. Perhaps more importantly, assert the critics, the managed float has not eliminated trade imbalances, as flexible rates are supposed to do. Thus, some countries run persistent trade deficits for many years, while others have had persistent surpluses. Changes in exchange rates have not yet corrected these imbalances, as is supposed to be the case under flexible exchange rates.

Skeptics say the managed float is basically a "nonsystem"; the guidelines concerning what each nation may or may not do with its exchange rates are not specific enough to keep the system working in the long run. Nations inevitably will be tempted to intervene in the foreign exchange market, not merely to smooth out short-term fluctuations in exchange rates but to prop up their currency if it is chronically weak or to manipulate the exchange rate to achieve domestic stabilization goals.

Flexible exchange rates have not worked perfectly, but they have not failed miserably. Thus far they have *survived*, and no doubt *eased*, several major shocks to the international trading system. Meanwhile, the "managed" part of the float has given nations some sense of control over their collective economic destinies. On balance, most economists favour continuation of the present system of "almost" flexible exchange rates.

21-3
QUICK REVIEW

- Under the gold standard (1879–1934), nations fixed exchange rates by valuing their currencies in terms of gold, by tying their stocks of money to gold, and by allowing gold to flow between nations when balance of payments deficits and surpluses occurred.

- The Bretton Woods exchange-rate system (1944–71) fixed or pegged short-run exchange rates but permitted orderly long-run adjustments of the pegs.

- The managed floating system of exchange rates (1971–present) relies on foreign exchange markets to establish equilibrium exchange rates. The system also permits nations to buy and sell foreign currency to stabilize short-term changes in exchange rates or to correct exchange-rate imbalances that are negatively affecting the world economy.

In
The Media

Trade surplus falls to lowest since late '93

October report worse than expected

BY HEATHER SCOFFIELD
PARLIAMENTARY BUREAU

OTTAWA—Canada's trade surplus has dropped to its lowest level since December, 1993, and economists say that's a sign of things to come.

"We're beginning to see the leading edge of the impact of the Asian slowdown," said Doug Porter, senior economist at Nesbitt Burns Inc. "The trend is definitely not Canada's friend. There's a distinct pattern there that probably won't change."

October's merchandise trade surplus was $581-million, down dramatically from surpluses of $1.37-billion in September and $1.19-billion in August, Statistics Canada reported yesterday. In October of last year, Canada had a trade surplus of $2.43-billion.

So far this year, the trade surplus adds up to $19.4-billion, compared with a surplus of $35.5-billion from January to October of 1996.

This October's drop was pushed by a significant decline in the exports of industrial goods—mainly precious metals—as well as in forestry products and energy products.

The trade report was worse than analysts had expected, and led to a slight weakening of the Canadian dollar, prompting the Bank of Canada to defend the currency. The dollar closed at 70.12 cents (U.S.) down from Wednesday's close of 70.30 cents.

Exports declined slightly in October to $25.1-billion (Canadian) from $25.2-billion in September, while imports rose 2.7 per cent to $24.5-billion from $23.8-billion, Statscan said.

Imports were up in all sectors except energy, it said. Purchases of machinery and equipment were particularly strong, as Canadian companies made major investments. And strong consumer demand pushed up imports of motor vehicles in October.

Economists say the rise in imports is an encouraging sign of the strength of the Canadian economy, as both consumers and businesses are ready to spend more.

Mr. Porter said he believes the falling trade balance "is still largely a story of booming imports and not falling exports."

But the fall in exports is worrisome, economists said.

"The narrowing of the trade surplus isn't good news for the Canadian economy," Lévesque Beaubien Geoffrion said in its daily commentary. "It implies that net exports will continue to act as a drag on economic activity, shaving roughly two percentage points to overall GDP growth."

Exports account for about 40 per cent of Canada's gross domestic product.

Nesbitt Burns said in its economic commentary: "Export prospects are hardly encouraging, given the hit to commodity-related shipments from the Asian flu, and the fact that Canadian manufacturers are already operating at around full capacity."

Resource-based goods make up about 30 per cent of Canadian exports and Asia is an important market for Canadian commodities, such as lumber and precious metals.

Source: *Globe and Mail*, December 19, 1997, p. B6. Reprinted with permission from the *Globe and Mail*.

THE STORY IN BRIEF

Canada's trade surplus falls to its lowest level in five years.

THE ECONOMICS BEHIND THE STORY

- A trade surplus means a country exports more than it imports. Canada's trade surplus fell sharply in late 1997. While exports fell slightly in October 1997, imports rose almost 3 percent. This implies that Canadian GDP was rising significantly; Canadian imports vary directly with Canadian GDP.
- In late 1997 the Pacific Rim economies were at or near recession. Some analysts worried that the "Asian flu" would lower Canadian exports, possibly leading to a lower trade surplus or a deficit.
- What is the likely impact on the Canadian dollar of a lower Canadian trade surplus, or a trade deficit? ■

The
Last Word

SPECULATION IN CURRENCY MARKETS

Contrary to popular belief, speculators often play a positive role in currency markets.

MOST PEOPLE BUY FOREIGN CURRENCY TO facilitate the purchase of goods or services produced in another country. A Canadian importer buys Japanese yen to purchase Japanese-made automobiles. A British investor purchases marks to buy shares in the German stock market. But there is another group of participants in the currency market—speculators—who buy foreign currencies solely to resell for profit. A British pound bought for $2.00 earns a 10 percent return when it is sold for $2.20.

Speculators sometimes contribute to exchange-rate volatility. The expectation of currency appreciation or depreciation can be self-fulfilling. If speculators expect the Japanese yen to appreciate, they sell other currencies to buy yen. The sharp increase in demand for yen boosts its value, which may attract other speculators—people expecting the yen to rise further. Eventually, the yen's value may soar too high relative to economic realities such as tastes, real interest rates, price levels, and trade balances. The "speculative bubble" bursts and the yen plummets.

But speculative bubbles are not the norm in currency markets. Changed economic realities, not speculation, usually are the cause of changing currency values. Anticipating changes in currency values, speculators simply hasten the adjustment process. Most major adjustments in currency values persist long *after* the speculators have sold their currency and made their profits.

Speculation, in fact, has two positive effects in foreign exchange markets.

1. Lessening Rate Fluctuations   Speculation smooths out fluctuations in currency prices. When temporarily low demand or excess supply reduces a currency's value, speculators quickly buy it, adding to the demand and strengthening its value. When temporarily strong demand or weak supply increases a currency's value, speculators sell the currency. This selling increases the supply of the currency and reduces its value. In this way speculators smooth out supply and demand—and

thus exchange rates—from period to period. And that exchange rate stability facilitates international trade.

2. Absorbing Risk   Speculators aid international trade in another way: *They absorb risk that others do not want to bear.* International transactions are riskier than domestic transactions because of potential adverse changes in exchange rates. Suppose AnyTime, a hypothetical Canadian retailer, signs a contract with a German manufacturer to buy 10,000 German clocks to be delivered in three months. The stipulated price is 75 marks per clock, which in dollars is $50 per clock at an exchange rate of $1 = 1.5 mark. AnyTime's total bill will be $500,000 (= 750,000 marks).

But if the German mark were to appreciate, say, to $1 = 1 mark, the dollar price per clock would rise from $50 to $75 and AnyTime would owe $750,000 for the clocks (= 750,000 marks). AnyTime may reduce the risk of such an unfavourable exchange-rate fluctuation by hedging in the futures market. *Hedging is an action by a buyer or a seller to protect against a change in future prices. The futures market is a market where items are bought and sold at prices fixed now, for delivery at a specified date in the future.*

AnyTime can arrange now to purchase the needed 750,000 marks at the current $1 = 1.5 mark exchange rate, but with delivery in three months when the German clocks are delivered. And here is where speculators arrive on the scene. For a price determined in the futures market, they agree to deliver the 750,000 marks to AnyTime in three months at the $1 = 1.5 mark exchange rate, regardless of the exchange rate then. The speculators need not own marks at the time the agreement is made. If the German mark *depreciates* to, say, $1 = 2 marks in this period, the speculators make a profit. They can buy the 750,000 marks stipulated in the contract for $375,000, pocketing the difference between that amount and the $500,000 AnyTime has agreed to pay for the 750,000 marks.

If the German mark *appreciates*, the speculators—but not AnyTime—suffer a loss.

The amount AnyTime will have to pay for this futures contract will depend on how the market views the likelihood of the mark depreciating, appreciating, or staying constant over the three-month period. As in all highly competitive markets, supply and demand determine the price of the futures contract.

The futures market thus eliminates much of the exchange-rate risk associated with buying foreign goods for future delivery. Without it AnyTime might have decided against importing German clocks. But the futures market and currency speculators greatly increase the likelihood the transaction will occur. Operating through the futures market, speculation promotes international trade. ∎

CHAPTER SUMMARY

1. Canadian exports create a foreign demand for dollars and make a supply of foreign exchange available to Canadians. Conversely, Canadian imports create a demand for foreign exchange and make a supply of dollars available to foreigners. Generally, a nation's exports earn the foreign currencies needed to pay for its imports.

2. The balance of payments records all international trade and financial transactions taking place between a given nation and the rest of the world. The trade balance compares exports and imports of goods. The balance on goods and services compares exports and imports of both goods and services. The current account balance includes not only goods and services transactions but also net investment income and net transfers.

3. A deficit in the current account may be offset by a surplus in the capital account. Conversely, a surplus in the current account may be offset by a deficit in the capital account. A balance of payments deficit occurs when the sum of the current and capital accounts is negative. Such a deficit is financed with official international reserves. A balance of payments surplus occurs when the sum of the current and capital accounts is positive. A payments surplus results in an increase in official reserves. The desirability of a balance of payments deficit or surplus depends on its size and its persistence.

4. Flexible or floating exchange rates between international currencies are determined by the demand for and supply of those currencies. Under floating rates a currency will depreciate or appreciate as a result of changes in tastes, relative income changes, relative price changes, relative changes in real interest rates, and speculation.

5. The maintenance of fixed exchange rates requires adequate international reserves to accommodate periodic payments deficits. If reserves are inadequate, nations must invoke protectionist trade policies, engage in exchange controls, or endure undesirable domestic macroeconomic adjustments.

6. The gold standard, a fixed rate system, provided exchange-rate stability until its disintegration during the 1930s. Under this system, gold flows between nations precipitated sometimes painful changes in price, income, and employment levels in bringing about international equilibrium.

7. Under the Bretton Woods system, exchange rates were pegged to one another and were stable. Participating nations were obligated to maintain these rates by using stabilization funds, gold, or loans from the IMF. Persistent or "fundamental" payments deficits could be resolved by IMF-sanctioned currency devaluations.

8. Since 1971 the world's major nations have used a system of managed floating exchange rates. Rates are generally set by market forces, although governments intervene with varying frequency to alter their exchange rates.

TERMS AND CONCEPTS

balance of payments

current account

trade balance

balance on goods and services

current account balance

capital account

capital account balance

official international (foreign exchange) reserves

balance of payments deficits and surpluses

flexible or floating exchange-rate system

fixed exchange-rate system

purchasing power parity theory

gold standard

devaluation

Bretton Woods system

International Monetary Fund

managed floating exchange rates

STUDY QUESTIONS

1. Explain how a Canadian automobile importer might finance a shipment of Toyotas from Japan. Demonstrate how a Canadian export of machinery to Italy might be financed. Explain: "Canadian exports earn supplies of foreign currencies that Canadians can use to finance imports."

2. **KEY QUESTION** *Indicate whether each of the following creates a demand for, or a supply of, French francs in foreign exchange markets:*
   a. *A Canadian importer purchases a shipload of Bordeaux wine.*
   b. *A French automobile firm decides to build an assembly plant in Halifax.*
   c. *A Canadian university student decides to spend a year studying at the Sorbonne.*
   d. *A French manufacturer ships machinery from one French port to another on a Canadian freighter.*
   e. *Canada incurs a balance of payments deficit in its transactions with France.*
   f. *A Canadian government bond held by a French citizen matures and the loan amount is paid back to that person.*
   g. *It is widely believed that the international value of the franc will fall in the near future.*

3. **KEY QUESTION** *Alpha's balance of payments data for 1999 are shown below. All figures are in billions of dollars. What are **a** the balance of trade, **b** the balance on goods and services, **c** the balance on current account, and **d** the balance on capital account? Does Alpha have a balance of payments deficit or surplus? Explain.*

Goods exports	+$40	Net transfers	+$10
Goods imports	− 30	Foreign investment in Canada	+ 10
Service exports	+ 15	Foreign investment abroad	− 40
Service imports	− 10	Official international reserves	+ 10
Net investment income	− 5		

4. "A rise in the dollar price of yen necessarily means a fall in the yen price of dollars." Do you agree? Illustrate and elaborate: "The critical thing about exchange rates is that they provide a direct link between the prices of goods and services produced in all trading nations of the world." Explain the purchasing power parity theory of exchange rates.

5. The Swedish auto company Saab imports car components from Germany and exports autos to Canada. In 1990 the dollar depreciated, and the German mark appreciated, relative to the Swedish krona. Speculate as to how this hurt Saab—twice.

6. **KEY QUESTION** *Explain why the Canadian demand for Mexican pesos is downsloping and the supply of pesos to Canadians is upsloping. Assuming a system of flexible exchange rates between Mexico and Canada, indicate whether each of the following would cause the Mexican peso to appreciate or depreciate:*
   a. *Canada unilaterally reduces tariffs on Mexican products.*
   b. *Mexico encounters severe inflation.*
   c. *Deteriorating political relations reduce Canadian tourism in Mexico.*
   d. *The Canadian economy moves into a severe recession.*
   e. *Canada engages in a high-interest rate monetary policy.*

    f.   *Mexican products become more fashionable to Canadians.*

    g.   *The Mexican government encourages Canadian firms to invest in Mexican oil fields.*

    h.   *The rate of productivity growth in Canada diminishes sharply.*

7. Explain why you agree or disagree with the following statements:

    a.   "A country that grows faster than its major trading partners can expect the international value of its currency to depreciate."

    b.   "A nation whose interest rate is rising more rapidly than in other nations can expect the international value of its currency to appreciate."

    c.   "A country's currency will appreciate if its inflation rate is less than that of the rest of the world."

8. "Exports pay for imports. Yet in 1993 the rest of the world exported about $3.2 billion more worth of goods and services to Canada than were imported from Canada." Resolve the apparent inconsistency of these two statements.

9. KEY QUESTION *Diagram a market in which the equilibrium dollar price of one unit of fictitious currency Zee is $5 (the exchange rate is $5 = Z1). Then show on your diagram a decline in the demand for Zee.*

    a.   *Referring to your diagram, discuss the adjustment options Canada would have in maintaining the exchange rate at $5 = Z1 under a fixed exchange-rate system.*

    b.   *How would the Canadian balance of payments surplus that is created (by the decline in demand) get resolved under a system of flexible exchange rates?*

10. Compare and contrast the Bretton Woods system of exchange rates with that of the gold standard. What caused the demise of the gold standard? What caused the demise of the Bretton Woods system?

11. Describe what is meant by the term "managed float." Did the managed float system precede or follow the adjustable-peg system? Explain.

12. **(The Last Word)** Suppose Winter Sports—a French retailer of snowboards—wants to order 5,000 snowboards made in Canada. The price per board is $200, the present exchange rate is 6 francs = $1, and payment is due in dollars when the boards are delivered in 3 months. Use a numerical example to explain why exchange-rate risk might make the French retailer hesitant to place the order. How might speculators absorb some of Winter Sports' risk?

13. WEB-BASED QUESTION **Canada's International Trade in Goods and Services** Statistics Canada www.statcan.ca/english/Pgdb/Economy/International/gblec02a.htm sets out Canada's merchandise trade balance for the last five years. Has Canada had a surplus or deficit on the merchandise trade balance in the last five years? With which country do we have a trade deficit? A trade surplus?

14. WEB-BASED QUESTION **Canada's Balance of International Payments** Statistics Canada provides a link to the International Monetary Fund (IMF) www.statcan.ca/english/econoind/imf/dsbbcan.htm External Sector that sets out Canada's balance of international payments for the latest quarter for which data are available. What did Canada hold in international reserves in the latest quarter? What is the exchange rate between the Canadian and U.S. dollar for the latest period? Has the Canadian dollar appreciated or depreciated against the U.S. dollar in the last year?

The Economics of Developing Countries

IT IS DIFFICULT FOR THOSE OF US IN CANADA WHERE per-capita (per person) GDP in 1995 was U.S.$19,380, to grasp the fact that some two-thirds of the world's population lives at, or perilously close to, the subsistence level. Hunger, squalour, and disease are common in many nations of the world. More than 1 billion people—about 20 percent of the world population—live on incomes of less than $2 per day.

Here we first identify the *developing countries* and discuss their characteristics. Then we discuss why these countries have such low standards of living: What obstacles have impeded their growth? Next, we examine the potentials and pitfalls of government's role in economic development. We also examine private money flows from the *advanced industrial countries* to the developing countries and assess the debt problem the developing countries face. Finally, we distill a list of possible policies that might help developing countries increase their growth rates.

IN THIS CHAPTER YOU WILL LEARN:

The extent of income inequality between rich and poor nations.

•

About the obstacles to growth in developing nations.

•

How governments of developing nations and industrially advanced nations can facilitate the economic development process.

The Big Picture

ONE OF THE MOST PERPLEXING QUESTIONS facing economists is why some nations are rich while others are desperately poor. The per-capita GDP in some of the richest nations is 4,000 times higher than that of the world's poorest nations. This chapter sets out to measure the economic discrepancy between rich and poor nations and to offer explanations for it.

As you read this chapter, keep the following points in mind:

- **Key Concepts 7** and **8** are discussed.

- We should always focus on the impediments to output growth. The impediments occur in one of the following factor categories: land, labour, capital, and entrepreneurial talent.
- More often than not the barriers to development are political, not "economic."
- In many developing nations it is in the best interest of the ruling elite to keep the country in a state of relative economic backwardness.
- Some developing nations have been experiencing rapid growth in the 1990s, while others are stagnating. ■

THE RICH AND THE POOR

Just as there is considerable income inequality among individual families within a nation, so too is there great income inequality among the family of nations. Table 22-1 shows the remarkable degree of income differences in the world. The richest 20 percent of the world's population receive almost 83 percent of the world's income; the poorest 20 percent obtain less than 1.5 percent. The poorest 60 percent get less than 6 percent of the world's income.

Figure 22-1 helps us sort out the rich and poor by grouping high-income, middle-income, and low-income nations.

1. **INDUSTRIALLY ADVANCED COUNTRIES** The 26 high-income nations are known as the **industrially advanced countries (IACs)**; they include Canada, the United States, Japan, Australia, New Zealand, and most of the nations of western Europe. These nations have well-developed market economies based on large stocks of capital goods, advanced production technologies, and well-educated workers. In 1995 these economies had a per-capita output (or income) of U.S. $24,930.
2. **DEVELOPING COUNTRIES** The remaining nations of the world, located mainly in Africa, Asia, and Latin America, are called **developing countries (DVCs)**. These 107 nations have

relatively low levels of industrialization. In general, literacy rates are low, unemployment is high, population growth is rapid, and exports consist largely of agricultural produce (such as cocoa, bananas, sugar, raw cotton) and raw materials (such as copper, iron ore, natural rubber). Capital equipment is minimal, production technologies are relatively simple, and labour productivity is very low. About three-fourths of the world's population live in these nations, all of which have widespread poverty.

Figure 22-1 breaks down these developing nations into *middle-income* and *low-income countries*. The first group of 58 middle-income DVCs had an average per-capita output of $2,390 in 1995. Per-

TABLE 22-1 Global income disparity

World population	Percentage of world income
Richest 20%	82.7
Second 20%	11.7
Third 20%	2.3
Fourth 20%	1.9
Poorest 20%	1.4

Source: United Nations Development Program, *Human Development Report 1992* (New York: Oxford University Press, 1992), p. 36.

F I G U R E   2 2 - 1   Groups of economies

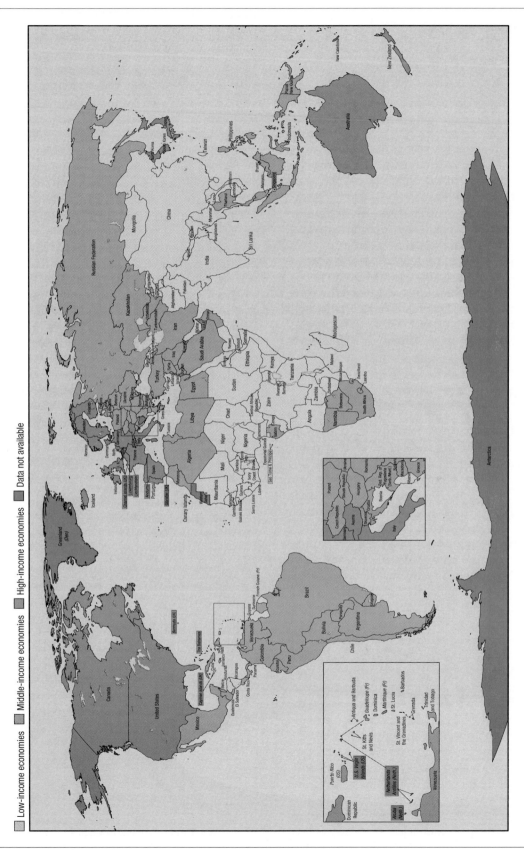

The world's nations are grouped into industrially advanced countries (IACs) and developing countries (DVCs). The IACs are high-income countries. The DVCs are middle-income and low-income countries. (Source: World Bank data.)

capita output for this diverse group ranged from $766 to $9,385. The other group is made up of 49 low-income DVCs with per-capita outputs of $765 or less in 1995 and averaging only $430 that year. India, China, and the sub-Saharan nations of Africa dominate this group.

Several comparisons will bring global income differences into sharper focus.

1. In 1995, total output in Canada and the United States was approximately $7.5 trillion; the combined GDPs of the 107 DVCs in that year were only $5.5 trillion.
2. Canada and the United States, with about 5 percent of the world's population, produce over one-fourth of the world's output.
3. The annual sales of the world's largest corporations exceed the GDPs of many of the DVCs. General Motors' annual world revenues are greater than the GDPs of all but 22 nations.
4. Per-capita GDP in Canada is 242 times greater than in Mozambique, the world's poorest nation.

Growth, Decline, and Income Gaps

Two other things concerning Figure 22-1 should be noted. First, the various nations have demonstrated considerable differences in ability to improve their circumstances over time. On the one hand, DVCs such as China, Malaysia, Chile, and Thailand achieved high annual growth rates in their GDPs in recent decades. Consequently, their real output per capita rose several fold. Several previous DVCs such as South Korea, Singapore, and Hong Kong (now part of China) have achieved IAC-status. In contrast, many DVCs, such as those in sub-Saharan Africa, have experienced declining GDPs per capita during the past decade.

Second, the *absolute income gap* between rich and poor nations has been widening. To understand this point, suppose the per-capita incomes of the advanced and developing countries were growing at about 2 percent per year. Because the income base in the advanced countries is initially much higher, the absolute income gap grows. If per-capita income is $400 a year in a DVC, a 2 percent growth rate means an $8 increase in income. Where per-capita income is $20,000 per year in an IAC, the same 2 percent growth rate translates into a $400 increase in income. Thus, the absolute income gap will have increased from $19,600 (=

$20,000 − $400) to $19,992 (= $20,400 − $408). The DVCs must grow faster than the IACs to narrow the gap. *(Key Question 3)*

Implications

Mere statistics conceal the human implications of the extreme poverty characterizing so much of our planet:

… let us examine a typical "extended" family in rural Asia. The Asian household is likely to comprise ten or more people, including parents, five to seven children, two grandparents, and some aunts and uncles. They have a combined annual income, both in money and in "kind" (i.e., they consume a share of the food they grow), of from $250 to $300. Together they live in a poorly constructed one-room house as tenant farmers on a large agricultural estate owned by an absentee landlord who lives in the nearby city. The father, mother, uncle, and the older children must work all day on the land. None of the adults can read or write; of the five school-age children, only one attends school regularly; and he cannot expect to proceed beyond three or four years of primary education. There is only one meal a day; it rarely changes and it is rarely sufficient to alleviate the children's constant hunger pains. The house has no electricity, sanitation, or fresh water supply. There is much sickness, but qualified doctors and medical practitioners are far away in the cities attending to the needs of wealthier families. The work is hard, the sun is hot and aspirations for a better life are constantly being snuffed out. In this part of the world the only relief from the daily struggle for physical survival lies in the spiritual traditions of the people.[1]

In Table 22-2 we contrast various socioeconomic indicators for selected DVCs with those for Canada, the United States, and Japan. You will see that these data confirm the major points stressed in the quotation from Todaro.

---

[1] Michael P. Todaro, *Economic Development in the Third World*, 5th ed. (New York: Longman, 1994), p. 4.

TABLE 22-2 Selected socioeconomic indicators of development

Country	(1) Per capita output, 1995**	(2) Life expectancy at birth, 1995	(3) Infant mortality per 1,000 live births, 1995	(4) Adult illiteracy rate, percent, 1995	(5) Percent of labour force in agriculture, 1990	(6) Per capita energy consumption, 1994*
Japan	$39,640	80 years	4	under 5	11	3,856
United States	26,980	77	8	under 5	3	7,819
Canada	19,380	78	6	under 5	3	7,854
Brazil	3,640	67	44	17	23	718
Mauritania	460	51	96	—	55	103
China	620	69	34	19	74	664
India	340	62	68	48	64	248
Bangladesh	240	58	79	62	64	64
Ethiopia	100	49	112	65	80	22
Mozambique	80	47	113	60	83	40

*Kilograms of oil equivalent.
**In U.S. dollars.
Source: *World Development Report*, 1997.

OBSTACLES TO ECONOMIC DEVELOPMENT

The paths of economic development (economic growth) are essentially the same for developing countries as for the industrially advanced economies.

1. The DVCs must use their existing supplies of resources more efficiently. This means they must eliminate unemployment and underemployment and also combine labour and capital resources efficiently to achieve lowest-cost production. The DVCs must also direct their scarce resources such that they achieve allocative efficiency.
2. The DVCs must expand their available supplies of resources. Through greater supplies of raw materials, capital equipment, and productive labour, together with improved technological knowledge, a DVC can push its production possibilities curve outward.

All DVCs are aware of these two paths. Why then have some nations successfully travelled these paths while others have lagged far behind? The difference is in the physical, human, and socioeconomic environments of the various nations.

Natural Resources

There is no simple generalization as to the role of natural resources in the economic development of DVCs because the distribution of natural resources among them is very uneven. Some DVCs have valuable deposits of bauxite, tin, copper, tungsten, nitrates, and petroleum and have been able to use their natural resource endowments to achieve rapid growth and a significant redistribution of income from the rich to the poor nations. The Organization of Petroleum Exporting Countries (OPEC) is a standard example. In other instances, natural resources are owned or controlled by the multinational corporations of industrially advanced countries, with the economic benefits from these resources largely diverted abroad. Furthermore, world markets for many of the farm products and raw materials that the DVCs export are subject to large price fluctuations that contribute to instability in their economies.

Other DVCs lack mineral deposits, have little arable land, and have few sources of power. Also, most of the poor countries are in Central and South America, Africa, the Indian subcontinent, and Southeast Asia, where tropical climates prevail. The hot, humid climate hinders productive labour; human, crop, and livestock diseases are widespread; and weed and insect infestations plague agriculture.

A weak resource base can be a serious obstacle to growth. Real capital can be accumulated and the quality of the labour force improved through education and training. But it is difficult to augment the natural resource base. It may be unrealistic for many of the DVCs to envision an economic destiny comparable with that of, say, Canada and the United States. But we must be careful in generalizing: Switzerland and Japan, for example, have achieved high levels of living *despite* small natural resource bases.

Human Resources

Three statements describe many of the DVCs' circumstances with respect to human resources:

1. They are overpopulated.
2. Unemployment and underemployment are widespread.
3. Labour productivity is low.

Overpopulation
Many of the DVCs with the most meagre natural and capital resources have the largest populations to support. Table 22-3 shows the high population densities and population growth rates of a few selected nations compared with those of the United States and the world.

Most important for the long run is the contrast in growth rates. The middle- and low-income DVCs in Figure 22-1 currently are experiencing a 1.6 percent annual increase in population compared with a 0.7 percent annual rate for IACs. Since such a large percentage of the world's present population already resides in DVCs, this percentage difference in population growth rates is highly significant: 9 out of every 10 people added to the world population during the next 15 years will live in developing nations. (See Global Perspective 22-1.)

Population statistics help explain why the per-capita income gap between the DVCs and IACs has widened. In some of the poorest DVCs, rapid population growth actually presses on the food supply so much that per-capita food consumption falls to or below the biological subsistence level. In

TABLE 22-3 Population statistics for selected countries

Country	Population per square mile, 1996	Annual rate of population increase, 1990-1995
Canada	8	1.1%
United States	75	1.0
Pakistan	430	2.9
Bangladesh	2,380	1.6
Venezuela	65	2.3
India	829	1.8
China	336	1.1
Kenya	128	2.7
Philippines	647	2.2
World	114	1.5

Sources: *Statistical Abstract of the United States*, 1996; *World Development Report*, 1997.

the worst instances, only malnutrition and disease, and the high death rate they cause, keep incomes near subsistence.

It would seem at first glance that, since

$$\frac{\text{Standard}}{\text{of living}} = \frac{\text{consumer goods (food) production}}{\text{population}}$$

the standard of living could be raised by boosting consumer goods—particularly food—production. But the problem is more complex because any increase in consumer goods production that initially raises the standard of living may induce a population increase. This increase, if sufficiently large, will dissipate the improvement in living standards, and subsistence living levels will again prevail.

But why might population growth in DVCs accompany increases in output? First, the nation's *death* or *mortality rate* will decline with initial increases in production. This decline is the result of (1) a higher level of per-capita food consumption and (2) the basic medical and sanitation programs that accompany the initial phases of economic development.

Second, the *birth rate* will remain high or may increase, particularly as medical and sanitation

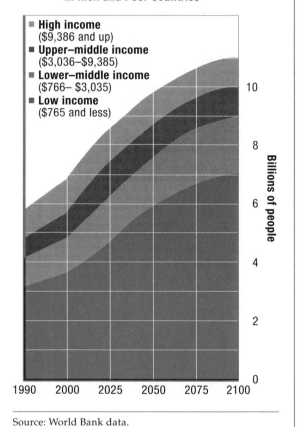

22-1
GLOBAL PERSPECTIVE

Population growth in rich and poor countries

World population is expected to double over the next century, with the poorest nations accounting for most of the increase.

Actual and Projected Population Growth in Rich and Poor Countries

■ **High income**
($9,386 and up)
■ **Upper–middle income**
($3,036–$9,385)
■ **Lower–middle income**
($766– $3,035)
■ **Low income**
($765 and less)

Billions of people

1990   2000   2025   2050   2075   2100

Source: World Bank data.

SAVING AND INVESTMENT   Large families reduce the capacity of households to save, restricting the economy's ability to accumulate capital.

PRODUCTIVITY   As population grows, more investment is required to maintain the amount of real capital per person. If investment fails to keep pace, each worker will have fewer tools and equipment, reducing worker productivity (output per worker). Declining productivity implies stagnating or declining per-capita incomes.

RESOURCE OVERUSE   Because most developing countries are heavily dependent on agriculture, rapid population growth may result in overuse of limited natural resources such as land. The much-publicized African famines are partially the result of past overgrazing and overplanting of land caused by the pressing need to feed a growing population. (This chapter's Last Word is relevant.)

URBAN PROBLEMS   Rapid population growth in the cities of the DVCs, accompanied by unprecedented flows of rural migrants, are generating massive urban problems. Substandard housing in impoverished slums, poor public services, congestion, pollution, and crime are all problems worsened by rapid population growth. The resolution or lessening of these difficulties necessitates a diversion of resources from growth-oriented uses.

Most authorities advocate birth control as the most effective means for breaking out of this dilemma. And breakthroughs in contraceptive technology in recent decades have made this solution increasingly relevant. But obstacles to population control are great. Low literacy rates make it difficult to disseminate information about contraceptive devices. In peasant agriculture, large families are a major source of labour. Adults may regard having many children as a kind of informal social security system: The more children, the greater the probability of having a relative to care for you during old age. Finally, many nations that stand to gain the most through birth control are often the least willing, for religious and sociocultural reasons, to embrace contraception programs. Population growth in Latin America, for example, is among the most rapid in the world.

China—with about one-fifth of the world's population—adopted a harsh "one-child" program in 1980. The government advocated late marriages and one child per family. Couples having more than one child are fined or lose various

programs cut infant mortality. The cliché that "the rich get richer and the poor get children" is uncomfortably accurate for many of the poorest DVCs. An increase in the per-capita standard of living may lead to a population upsurge that will cease only when the standard of living has again been reduced to the level of bare subsistence.

In addition to the fact that rapid population growth can convert an expanding GDP into a stagnant or slow-growing GDP per capita, there are four other reasons why population expansion is often an obstacle to development.

social benefits. Even though the rate of population growth has diminished under this program, China's population continues to expand at about 100 million per decade. India, the world's second most populous nation, had a 242 million or 35 percent population increase in the 1980–95 period. With a total population of 929 million, India has 16 percent of the world's population but less than 2.5 percent of its land mass.

Qualifications

But our focus on population growth as a major cause of low incomes needs to be qualified in several ways.

As with natural resources, the relationship between population and economic growth is less clear than one might expect. A high population density and rapid population growth do not necessarily mean poverty. China and India have immense populations and are poor, but Japan and Hong Kong are densely populated and wealthy.

Also, population growth rates for the DVCs as a group have declined somewhat in recent decades. In the 1960s the annual population growth rate was about 2.0 percent; for the 1990s, it looks like it will be about 1.4 percent. Experts predict that this percentage will fall to about 1.2 percent by 2010.

Finally, there is a view contrary to the traditional one that reducing population growth is the key to increasing GDP per capita in developing countries. The **demographic transition view** holds that rising income first must be achieved; only then will slower population growth follow. This view observes there are both marginal benefits and marginal costs of having another child. In DVCs the marginal benefits are relatively large because the extra child becomes an extra worker who can help support the family. Extra children can provide financial support and security for their parents in their old age, so people in poor countries have high birth rates. But in wealthy IACs the marginal cost of children is much greater than in the DVCs. Care of children may require that one of the parents sacrifice high earnings, or there may be the need to purchase expensive childcare. Also, children require extended and expensive education for the highly skilled jobs characteristic of the IAC economies. Finally, the wealth of the IACs results in "social safety nets" that protect adults from the insecurity associated with old age and the inability to work. In this view, people in the IACs recognize that high birth rates are not in the family's short-term or long-term interest, so they choose to have fewer children.

Note the differences in causation the two views imply. The traditional view says that reduced birth rates must come first and then higher per-capita income will follow; lower birth rates are the cause of per-capita income growth. The demographic transition view says that higher incomes must first be achieved and then lower rates of population growth will follow; higher incomes cause slower population growth. *(Key Question 6)*

Unemployment and Underemployment

Employment-related data for many DVCs either are nonexistent or highly unreliable. But observation suggests that *unemployment* is high; many people are unable to find jobs. There is also significant **underemployment**, which means that a large number of people are employed fewer hours per week than they want, work at jobs unrelated to their training, or spend much of the time on their jobs unproductively.

Many economists contend that unemployment may be as much as 15 to 20 percent in the rapidly growing urban areas of the DVCs. There has been substantial migration in most developing countries from rural to urban areas, motivated by the *expectation* of finding jobs with higher wage rates than are available in agricultural and other rural employments. But this huge migration reduces the chance of a migrant in fact obtaining a job. Migration to the cities has greatly exceeded the growth of urban job opportunities, resulting in very high urban unemployment rates. Thus, rapid rural-urban migration has given rise to urban unemployment rates that are two or three times as great as rural rates.

Underemployment is widespread and characteristic of most DVCs. In many of the poorer developing nations, rural agricultural labour may be so abundant relative to capital and natural resources that a significant percentage of this labour contributes little or nothing to agricultural output. Similarly, many DVC workers are self-employed as proprietors of small shops, in handicrafts, or as street vendors. A lack of demand means that small shop owners or vendors spend idle time in the shop or on the street. While they are not without jobs, these people are underemployed.

Low Labour Productivity

Labour productivity tends to be low in DVCs. As we will see, the developing nations have found it difficult to invest in *physical capital*. As a result, their workers are under-equipped with machinery and tools and hence are relatively unproductive. Keep in mind that rapid population growth tends to reduce the amount of physical capital available per worker, which decreases labour productivity and real incomes.

In addition, most poor countries have not been able to invest sufficiently in their *human capital* (see Table 22-2, columns 3 and 4); that is, expenditures on health and education have been meagre. Low levels of literacy, malnutrition, lack of proper medical care, and insufficient educational facilities all contribute to populations that are ill-equipped for industrialization and economic expansion. Attitudes may also play a role: In some countries, hard work is associated with slavery, servitude, and inferiority, so people try to avoid it.

Particularly vital is the absence of a vigorous entrepreneurial class willing to bear risks, accumulate capital, and provide the organizational requisites essential to economic growth. Closely related is the lack of labour trained to handle the routine supervisory functions basic to any program of development. Ironically, the higher education systems of some DVCs are oriented towards the humanities and offer little work in business, engineering, and the sciences. Some DVCs are characterized by an authoritarian view of human relations—often fostered by repressive governments—that generates an environment hostile to independent thinking, taking initiatives, and assuming economic risks. Authoritarianism discourages experimentation and change—the essence of entrepreneurship.

An additional irony is that, while migration from the DVCs has modestly offset rapid population growth, it has also deprived some DVCs of highly productive workers. Often the best-trained and most highly motivated workers—physicians, engineers, teachers, and nurses—leave the DVCs to seek their fortunes in the IACs. This so-called **brain drain** contributes to the deterioration in the overall skill level and productivity of the labour force.

Capital Accumulation

An important focal point of economic development is the accumulation of capital goods, for several reasons:

1. All DVCs suffer from shortages of capital goods such as factories, machinery and equipment, and public utilities. Better-equipped labour forces would greatly enhance their productivity and help boost the per-capita standard of living. There is a close relationship between output per worker (labour productivity) and real income per worker. A nation must produce more goods and services per worker to enjoy more goods and services per worker as income. One way of increasing labour productivity is to provide each worker with more tools and equipment. Indeed, studies for the DVCs confirm a positive relationship between investment and the growth of GDP. On the average, a 1 percentage point increase in the ratio of investment to GDP raises the overall growth rate by about one-tenth of 1 percentage point. Thus an increase in the investment-to-GDP ratio from 10 to 15 percent would increase the growth of real GDP by one-half of 1 percentage point.[2]

2. Increasing the stock of capital goods is crucial because of the very limited possibility of increasing the supply of arable land. If there is little likelihood of increasing agricultural output by increasing the supply of land, an alternative is to use more and better capital equipment with the available agricultural workforce.

3. Once initiated, the process of capital accumulation *may* be cumulative. If capital accumulation can increase output faster than population grows, a margin of saving may arise that permits further capital formation. In a sense, capital accumulation can feed on itself.

Let's first consider the prospects for developing nations to accumulate capital domestically. Then we will examine the possibility of foreign funds flowing into them to support expansion of capital.

Domestic Capital Formation   A developing nation, as does any nation, accumulates capital through saving and investing. A nation must save (refrain from consumption) in order to release resources from production of consumer goods. Investment spending must then absorb these released resources in the production of capital goods. But impediments to saving and investing

---

[2] International Monetary Fund, *World Economic Outlook* (Washington, 1988), p. 76.

are much greater in a low-income nation than in an advanced economy.

SAVINGS POTENTIAL   Consider first the savings side of the picture. The situation here is mixed and varies greatly between countries. Some of the very poor countries, such as Ethiopia, Bangladesh, Uganda, Haiti, and Madagascar, save only 2 to 5 percent of their GDPs. The people are simply too poor to save a significant portion of their incomes. Interestingly, however, other developing countries save as large a percentage of their domestic outputs as do advanced industrial countries. In 1995 India and China saved 22 and 42 percent of their domestic outputs, respectively, compared to 29 percent for Japan, 23 percent for Germany, and 21 percent for Canada. The problem is that the domestic outputs of the DVCs are so low that even when saving rates are comparable to advanced nations, the total absolute volume of saving is not large.

Capital Flight   Some of the developing countries have suffered **capital flight**, the transfer of private DVC savings to accounts held in the IACs. (In this usage, "capital" is simply "money," "money capital," or "financial capital.") Many wealthy citizens of DVCs have used their savings to invest in the more economically advanced nations, allowing them to avoid the high investment risks at home, such as loss of saving or real capital from government expropriation, abrupt changes in taxation, potential hyperinflation, or high volatility of exchange rates. If a DVC's political climate is unsettled, savers may shift their funds overseas to a "safe haven" in fear that a new government might confiscate their wealth. Likewise, rapid or skyrocketing inflation in a DVC would have similar detrimental effects. The transfer of saving overseas may also be a means of evading high domestic taxes on interest income or capital gains. Finally, money capital may flow to the IACs, where there are higher interest rates or a greater variety of investment opportunities.

Whatever the motivation, the amount of capital flight from some nations is significant. This outflow of money capital offsets a considerable portion of the IACs' lending and giving of money capital to the developing nations.

Investment Obstacles   There are as many obstacles on the investment side of capital formation in DVCs as on the saving side. These investment obstacles involve a lack of investors and a lack of incentives to invest.

In some developing nations, the major obstacle to investment is the lack of entrepreneurs who are willing to assume the risks associated with investment. This is a special case of the qualitative limitations of the labour force previously discussed.

But the incentive to invest may be weak even if substantial saving and a large number of willing entrepreneurs are present. Several factors may combine in a DVC to reduce investment incentives. In our discussion of capital flight we mentioned such factors as political instability and higher rates of inflation. Similarly, very low incomes in a DVC result in a limited domestic market, meaning a lack of buying power and thus weak demand for all but agricultural goods. This factor is crucial because the chances of successfully competing with mature industries in the IACs in the international market are slim. Then, too, lack of trained administrative personnel may be a factor in retarding DVC investment.

Finally, many DVCs simply do not have an adequate **infrastructure** (stock of public capital goods), which is necessary for achieving adequate returns on private investment. Poor roads and bridges, inadequate railways, little gas and electricity production, poor communications, unsatisfactory housing, and meagre educational and public health facilities create an inhospitable environment for private investment. Much of any new private investment would have to be for the infrastructure needed by all firms. Rarely can firms provide such infrastructure themselves and still earn a positive return on their overall investment.

For all these reasons, investment incentives in many DVCs are lacking. It is significant that for multinational firms, about four-fifths of their overseas investments goes to IACs.

How then can developing nations build up the infrastructure necessary to attract investment? The higher-income DVCs may be able to accomplish this through taxation and public spending. But there is little income to tax in the poorest DVCs. Nevertheless, with leadership and a willingness to cooperate, a poor DVC can accumulate capital by transferring surplus agricultural labour to the improvement of the infrastructure. If each agricultural village allocated its surplus labour to the construction of irrigation canals, wells, schools, sanitary facilities, and roads, significant amounts of capital might be accumulated at no significant sacrifice of consumer goods production. Such investment simply bypasses the problems inherent in the financial aspects of the capital accumulation process. It does not require consumers to save portions of their money income, nor does it presume the presence of an entrepreneurial class anxious to invest. When leadership and cooperative spirit are present, this "in-kind" investment is a promising avenue for accumulation of basic capital goods. *(Key Question 7)*

Technological Advance

Technological advance and capital formation are frequently part of the same process. Yet there are advantages in treating technological advance and capital formation as separate processes.

The rudimentary state of technology in the DVCs leaves them far from the frontiers of technological advance. But there is an enormous body of technological knowledge accumulated by the advanced nations that developing countries *might* adopt and apply without expensive research. Crop rotation and contour ploughing require no additional capital equipment and may contribute significantly to productivity. By raising grain storage bins a few inches aboveground, a large amount of grain spoilage can be avoided. Such changes may sound trivial to people of advanced nations. However, resulting gains in productivity can mean the difference between subsistence and starvation in some poverty-ridden nations.

In most instances application of either existing or new technological knowledge involves new and different capital goods. But, within limits, this capital can be obtained without an increase in the rate of capital formation. If the annual flow of replacement investment is rechannelled from technologically inferior to technologically superior capital equipment, productivity can be increased out of a constant level of investment spending. Actually, some technological advances may be **capital-saving technology** rather than **capital-using technology**. A new fertilizer, better adapted to a nation's topography and climate, might be cheaper than one currently employed. A seemingly high-priced metal plough that will last 10 years may be cheaper in the long run than an inexpensive but technologically inferior wooden plough that requires annual replacement.

To what extent have DVCs transferred and effectively used available IAC technological knowledge? The picture is mixed. There is no doubt that such technological borrowing has been instrumental in the rapid growth of such Pacific Rim countries as Japan, South Korea, Taiwan, and Singapore. Similarly, the OPEC nations benefited greatly from IAC knowledge of oil exploration, production, and refining. Recently Russia, the nations of eastern Europe, and China have been using western technology to hasten their conversions to market-based economies.

At the same time, we must be realistic about the transferability of advanced technologies to the poorest developing countries. In industrially advanced nations technologies are usually predicated on relatively scarce, highly skilled labour and relatively abundant capital. Such technologies tend to be capital-using or, alternatively stated, labour-saving. In contrast, developing economies require technologies appropriate to *their* resource endowments—abundant unskilled labour and very limited quantities of capital goods. Labour-using and capital-saving technologies are appropriate to DVCs. But much of the highly advanced technology of advanced nations is inappropriate in the developing countries; they must develop their own technologies. Recall, too, that many DVCs still have "traditional economies" and are not highly receptive to change. This is particularly true in peasant agriculture, which dominates the economies of most poorer DVCs. A potential technological advance that fails can mean hunger and malnutrition; therefore, there is a strong tendency to retain traditional production techniques.

Sociocultural and Institutional Factors

Economic considerations alone do not explain why an economy does or does not grow. Substantial social and institutional readjustments are usually an integral part of the growth process. Economic development means not only changes in a nation's physical environment (new transportation and communications facilities, new schools, new housing, new plants and equipment) but also changes in the way people think, behave, and associate with one another. Emancipation from custom and tradition is frequently a prerequisite of economic development. A critical but intangible ingredient in economic development is **the will to develop**. Economic growth may hinge on what individuals within DVCs want for themselves and their children. Do they want more material abundance? If so, do they want it badly enough to make the necessary changes in their institutions and old ways of doing things?

Sociocultural Obstacles
Sociocultural impediments to growth are numerous and varied:

1. Some of the very low income countries have failed to achieve the preconditions for a national economic unit. Tribal and ethnic allegiances take precedence over national identity. Warring tribes confine all economic activity to within the tribe, eliminating any possibility for production-increasing specialization and trade. The desperate economic circumstances in Somalia, Sudan, Liberia, Zaire, and other sub-Saharan nations of Africa are due in no small measure to martial and political conflicts among rival clans.

2. The existence of a formal or informal caste system causes labour to be allocated to occupations on the basis of status or tradition rather than on the basis of skill or merit. The result is a misallocation of human resources.

3. Religious beliefs and observances may seriously restrict the length of the workday and divert resources that might have been used for investment to ceremonial uses. Some religious and philosophical beliefs are dominated by the fatalistic **capricious universe view**, that is, the notion that there is little or no correlation between an individual's activities and endeavours and the outcomes or experiences that person encounters.

> If the universe is deemed capricious, the individual will learn to expect little or no correlation between actions and results. This will result in a fatalistic attitude...
>
> These attitudes impinge on all activities including saving, investment, long-range perspective, supply of effort, and family planning. If a higher standard of living and amassing of wealth is treated as the result of providence rather than springing from hard work and saving, there is little rationale for saving, hard work, innovations, and enterprise.[3]

Other attitudes and cultural factors may impede economic activity and growth: emphasis on the performance of duties rather than the exertion of individual initiative; the focus on group rather than individual achievement; the notion of a preordained and unalterable universe; and the belief in reincarnation, which reduces the importance of one's present life.

Institutional Obstacles
Political corruption and bribery are common in many DVCs. School systems and public service agencies are often ineptly administered and their functioning impaired by petty politics. Tax systems are frequently arbitrary, unjust, cumbersome, and detrimental to incentives to work and invest. Political decisions are often motivated by a desire to enhance the nation's international prestige rather than to foster development.

Because of the predominance of farming in DVCs, the problem of achieving an optimal institutional environment in agriculture is a vital consideration in any growth program. Specifically, the institutional problem of **land reform** demands attention in many DVCs. But needed reform may vary tremendously between specific nations. In some DVCs the problem is excessive concentration of land ownership in the hands of a few wealthy families. This situation is demoralizing for tenants, weakening their incentive to produce, and typically does not promote capital improvements. At the other extreme is the absurd arrangement whereby each family owns and farms a minute fragment of land far too small for the application of modern agricultural technology. An important complication to the problem of land reform is that political considerations sometimes push reform in that direction which is least defensible on economic grounds. For many nations, land reform may well be the most acute institutional problem to be resolved in initiating the process of economic development.

Examples: Land reform in South Korea undermined the political control of the landed aristocracy and made way for the development of strong commercial and industrial middle classes, all to the benefit of the country's economic development. In contrast, the prolonged dominance of the landed aristocracy in the Philippines has allegedly helped stifle the development of that economy.

[3] Inder P. Nijhawan, "Socio-Political Institutions, Cultural Values, and Attitudes: Their Impact on Indian Economic Development," in J. S. Uppal (ed.), *India's Economic Problems* (New Delhi: Tata McGraw-Hill Publishing Company, Ltd., 1975), p. 33.

22-1

QUICK REVIEW

- About three-fourths of the world's population lives in the DVCs of Africa, Asia, and Latin America.

- Natural resource scarcities and inhospitable climates restrict economic growth in many DVCs.

- Most of the poorest DVCs are characterized by overpopulation, high unemployment rates, underemployment, and low labour productivity.

- Low saving rates, capital flight, weak infrastructures, and lack of investors impair capital accumulation in many DVCs.

- Sociocultural and institutional factors are often serious impediments to growth in DVCs.

THE VICIOUS CIRCLE

Many of the characteristics of DVCs just described are simultaneously *causes* and *consequences* of their poverty. These countries are caught in a vicious **circle of poverty**. They *stay* poor because they *are* poor! Consider Figure 22-2. The fundamental feature of a DVC is low per-capita income. Being poor, a family has little ability or incentive to save. Furthermore, low incomes mean low levels of product demand. Thus, there are few available resources, on the one hand, and no strong incentives, on the other hand, for investment in physical or human capital, which means that labour productivity is low. And, since output per person is real income per person, it follows that per-capita income is low.

Many economists think that the key to breaking out of this vicious circle is to increase the rate of capital accumulation, to achieve a level of investment of, say, 10 percent of the national income. But Figure 22-2 reminds us that rapid population growth may partially or entirely undo the potentially beneficial effects of this higher rate of capital accumulation. Suppose that initially a DVC is realizing no growth in its real GDP. But now it somehow manages to increase its saving and investment to 10 percent of its GDP. As a result, its real GDP begins to grow at, say 2.5 per-

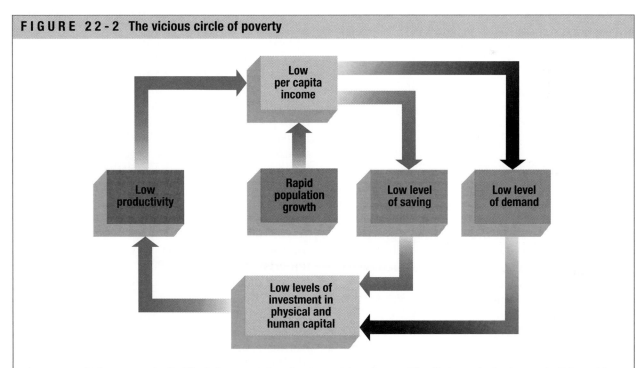

FIGURE 22-2 The vicious circle of poverty

Low per-capita incomes make it difficult for poor nations to save and invest, a condition that perpetuates low productivity and low incomes. Furthermore, rapid population growth may quickly absorb increases in per-capita real income and thereby may negate the possibility of breaking out of the poverty circle.

cent per year. With a stable population, real GDP per capita will also grow at 2.5 percent per year. If this growth persists, the standard of living will *double* in about 28 years. But what if population grows at the middle east and northern Africa rate of 2.5 percent per year? Then real income per person is unchanged and the vicious circle persists.

More optimistically, *if* population can be kept constant or constrained to some growth rate significantly below 2.5 percent, then real income per person will rise. This implies the possibility of still further enlargement in the flows of saving and investment, continued advances in productivity, and the continued growth of per-capita real income. If a process of self-sustaining expansion of income, saving, investment, and productivity can be achieved, the self-perpetuating vicious circle of poverty can be transformed into a self-regenerating, beneficent circle of economic progress. The challenge is to make effective those policies and strategies that will accomplish this transition. *(Key Question 13)*

ROLE OF GOVERNMENT

Economists do not agree on the appropriate role of government in fostering DVC growth.

A Positive Role

One view is that, at least during initial stages of development, government should play a major role because of the character of the obstacles facing DVCs.

Law and Order
Some of the poorest countries are plagued by banditry and intertribal warfare that divert both attention and resources from the task of development. A strong and stable national government is needed to establish domestic law and order and to achieve peace and unity. Research demonstrates that political instability (as measured by the number of revolutions and coups per decade) is associated with slow growth.

Lack of Entrepreneurship
The lack of a sizable and vigorous entrepreneurial class, ready and willing to accumulate capital and initiate production, indicates that in some DVCs, private enterprise is not capable of spearheading the growth process. Government may initially have to take the lead.

Infrastructure
Many obstacles to economic growth relate to an inadequate infrastructure. Sanitation and basic medical programs, education, irrigation and soil conservation projects, and construction of highways and transportation-communication facilities are all essentially nonmarketable goods and services yielding widespread spillover benefits. Government is the sole institution in a position to provide these public goods and services in required quantities.

Forced Saving and Investment
Government action may also be required to break through the saving-investment dilemma that impedes capital formation in DVCs.

It may be that only governmental fiscal action can provide a solution by forcing the economy to accumulate capital. There are two alternatives. One is to force the economy to save by increasing taxes. These tax revenues can then be channelled into priority investment projects. However, problems of honestly and efficiently administering the tax system and achieving a high degree of compliance with tax laws can be great.

The other alternative is to force the economy to save through inflation. Government can finance capital accumulation by creating and spending new money or by selling bonds to banks and spending the proceeds. The resulting inflation is the equivalent of an arbitrary tax on the economy.

There are serious arguments against public sector saving through inflation. First, inflation often distorts the composition of investment away from productive facilities to such items as luxury housing, precious metals and jewels, or foreign securities, which provide a better hedge against rising prices. Also, significant inflation may reduce voluntary private saving as potential savers become less willing to accumulate depreciating money or securities payable in money of declining value. Inflation also often induces capital flight. Internationally, inflation may boost the nation's imports and retard its flow of exports, creating balance of payments difficulties.

Social-Institutional Problems
Government is in the key position to deal effectively with the social-institutional obstacles to growth. Controlling population growth and land reform are problems that call for the broad approach only government can provide. And government is in a position to nurture the will to develop, to change a philosophy of

"Heaven and faith will determine the course of events" to one of "God helps those who help themselves."

Public Sector Problems

But serious problems and disadvantages may exist with a governmentally directed development program. If entrepreneurial talent is lacking in the private sector, can we expect quality leaders in the ranks of government? Is there not a real danger that government bureaucracy will impede, not stimulate, much-needed social and economic change? And what of the tendency of some political leaders to favour spectacular "showpiece" projects at the expense of less showy but more productive programs? Might not political objectives take precedence over the economic goals of a governmentally directed development program?

Development experts are less enthusiastic about the role of government in the growth process than they were 30 years ago. Government maladministration and corruption are common in many DVCs. Government officials often line their own pockets with foreign aid funds. Similarly, political leaders frequently confer monopoly privileges on relatives, friends, and political supporters. A political leader may grant exclusive rights to relatives or friends to produce, import, or export certain products. These monopoly privileges lead to higher domestic prices for the relevant products and diminish the DVC's ability to compete in world markets. Similarly, managers of state-owned enterprises are often appointed on the basis of cronyism rather than competence. Many DVC governments, particularly in Africa, have created "marketing boards" as the sole purchaser of agricultural products from local farmers. The boards buy farm products at artificially low prices and sell the output at higher world prices; the "profit" ends up in the pockets of government officials. In recent years the perception of government has shifted from that of catalyst and promoter of growth to that of a potential impediment to development.

A Mixed Bag

It is possible to muster causal evidence on both sides of this question. Positive government contributions to development are evident in Japan, South Korea, and Taiwan. In comparison, Mobutu's Zaire, Somoza's Nicaragua, Marcos's Philippines, and Haiti under the Duvaliers are recognized examples of corrupt and inept governments that functioned as impediments to economic progress. Certainly the revolutionary transformations of the former Soviet Union and other eastern European nations away from communism and towards market-oriented economies make clear that central planning is no longer recognized as an effective mechanism for development. Many DVCs are belatedly recognizing that capitalism, with its focus on individual economic incentives and on competition, is the surest, most sustainable, avenue to economic growth.

ROLE OF ADVANCED NATIONS

How can industrially advanced nations help developing countries in their quest for growth? To what degree have IACs pursued these avenues of assistance?

Generally, developing nations can benefit from (1) an expanding volume of trade with advanced nations, (2) foreign aid in the form of grants and loans from governments of advanced nations, and (3) flows of private capital from the more affluent nations.

Expanding Trade

Some authorities maintain that the simplest and most effective way Canada and other industrially advanced nations can aid developing nations is by lowering international trade barriers. Such actions enable DVCs to expand their national incomes through increased trade.

Although there is some truth in this view, lowered trade barriers are not a panacea. Some poor nations do need only large foreign markets for their raw materials to achieve growth. But the problem for many poor nations is not one of obtaining markets to use existing production capacity or to sell relatively abundant raw materials but the more fundamental problem of getting the capital and technical assistance needed to produce something for export.

Moreover, close trade ties with advanced nations have some disadvantages. Dependence on import demand from the IACs leaves DVCs vulnerable to temporary declines in the IACs' production. By reducing the demand for resources, recessions in the IACs can have disastrous consequences for the prices of raw materials and the export earnings of the DVCs. For example, during the recession in the IACs in the early 1990s, the world price of zinc fell from $.82 per pound to $.46 per pound and the world price of tin fell from $5.20 per pound to $3.50 per pound. Because mineral exports are a major source of DVC income, stability and growth in IACs are important to economic progress in the developing nations.

Foreign Aid: Public Loans and Grants

Foreign capital—both public and private—can supplement an emerging country's saving and investment and play a crucial role in breaking the circle of poverty.

As previously noted, many DVCs are lacking in the infrastructure prerequisites for attracting either domestic or foreign private capital. Foreign public aid that increases infrastructure can thus enhance the flow of private capital to the DVCs.

Direct Aid   Canada and other IACs have assisted DVCs directly through a variety of programs and through participating in international institutions designed to stimulate economic development. Over the past decade, Canadian aid to the DVCs in the forms of both loans and grants averaged about 2.5 billion per year. Other advanced nations also have substantial foreign aid programs. In recent years foreign aid from all IACs has been about $60 billion per year.

The IACs' aid programs merit several additional comments. First, aid is typically distributed on the basis of political and military rather than economic considerations. Israel, Turkey, Egypt, and Greece are major recipients of U.S. aid at the expense of Asian, Latin American, and African nations with much lower standards of living. Second, aid from the IACs amounts to only about one-third of 1 percent of the IAC's collective GDPs (see Global Perspective 22-2). Finally, the shift of Russia and eastern Europe towards more democratic, market-oriented systems has made these nations "new players" as foreign aid recipients. The DVCs worry that IAC aid that formerly flowed to Latin America, Asia, and Africa is now redirected to, say, Poland, Hungary, and Russia. Similarly, there is the prospect of a substantially larger aid flow to the Middle East if the PLO-Israeli peace accord is durable.

The World Bank Group   Canada is a participant in the **World Bank**, whose major objective is help-

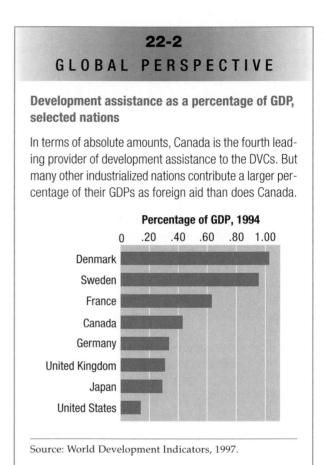

22-2

GLOBAL PERSPECTIVE

Development assistance as a percentage of GDP, selected nations

In terms of absolute amounts, Canada is the fourth leading provider of development assistance to the DVCs. But many other industrialized nations contribute a larger percentage of their GDPs as foreign aid than does Canada.

Source: World Development Indicators, 1997.

ing DVCs achieve growth. [The World Bank was established in 1945, along with the International Monetary Fund (IMF).] Supported by nearly 180 member nations, the World Bank not only lends out of its capital funds, it also (1) sells bonds and lends the proceeds and (2) guarantees and insures private loans.

Several characteristics of the World Bank are noteworthy:

1. The World Bank is a "last resort" lending agency; its loans are limited to economic projects for which private funds are not readily available.
2. Because many World Bank loans have been for basic development projects—dams, irrigation projects, health and sanitation programs, communications and transportation facilities—the Bank's activities help provide the infrastructure needed to encourage flows of private capital.
3. The Bank has provided technical assistance to the LDCs by helping them discover what avenues of growth seem appropriate for their economic development.

The World Bank affiliates function in areas where the World Bank has been weak. The *International Finance Corporation (IFC)* has the primary function of investing in *private* enterprises in the DVCs. The *International Development Association (IDA)* makes "soft loans" (which may not be self-liquidating) to the poorest DVCs on more liberal terms than does the World Bank.

Foreign Harm?

However, foreign aid to the DVCs has been subject to several criticisms:

DEPENDENCY AND INCENTIVES A basic criticism is that, like domestic welfare programs, foreign aid may generate dependency rather than self-sustaining growth. It is argued that transfers of wealth from the IACs allow the DVCs to avoid the painful economic decisions, the institutional and cultural changes, and the alterations in attitudes regarding thrift, industry, hard work, and self-reliance that are needed for growth. Critics say that, after some five decades of foreign aid, the DVCs' demand for foreign aid has increased; if aid programs had been successful in promoting sustainable growth, demand should have fallen.

BUREAUCRACY AND CENTRALIZED GOVERNMENT IAC aid is given, not directly to the residents and businesses of the DVCs, but to their governments. The consequence is that aid typically generates massive, relatively unproductive government bureaucracies and centralizes government power over the economy. The stagnation and collapse of the Soviet Union and eastern Europe is evidence that market-oriented economies are much more conducive to growth and development than are centrally planned economies. Furthermore, not only does the bureaucratization of the DVCs divert valuable human resources from the private to the public sector, it shifts the nation's focus from the *production* of output and income to its *redistribution*.

CORRUPTION AND MISUSE Critics also allege that foreign aid is ineffectively used. Corruption is rampant in many DVCs, and some estimates suggest 10 to 20 percent of aid is diverted to government officials. Some of the wealthiest individuals in the world are rulers of DVCs. Foreign aid may create an ironic and perverse incentive for DVCs leaders to keep their populations poor so they continue to qualify for aid.

Also, IAC-based aid consultants and multinational corporations are major beneficiaries of aid programs. Some economists contend that as much as one-fourth or more of each year's aid is spent on expert consultants. Furthermore, because IAC corporations carry out most aid projects, they are major beneficiaries of, and lobbyists for, foreign aid.

The Decline of Foreign Aid

Foreign aid to developing countries is on the decline. In 1990 IACs provided $58 billion of foreign aid; by 1996 that aid had dropped to $40 billion. The criticisms of foreign aid just discussed are undoubtedly one reason for this decline. Another reason is the end of the Cold War, in which the United States and the former Soviet Union vied for the political and military allegiance of developing nations. Nations such as Cuba, Ethiopia, and North Korea that adhered to communist principles received substantial foreign aid from the Soviet Union. The United States, in turn, lavished foreign aid on developing nations such as Egypt, Mexico, Thailand, Turkey, and Chile, which tended to support U.S. policies. But with the disintegration of the former Soviet Union, the political-military rationale for foreign aid lost much of its force.

Private Capital Flows

The DVCs have also received substantial flows of *private* capital from the IACs. These private investors are corporations, commercial banks, and, more recently, financial investment companies. General Motors or Chrysler might finance construction of plants in Mexico or Brazil to assemble autos or produce auto parts. ScotiaBank might make loans to private firms operating in Argentina or China or directly to the governments of Thailand and Malaysia. And financial investment companies might purchase stock of promising Hungarian and Chilean firms as part of their "emerging markets" mutual funds, which then could be purchased by individual investors in the IACs.

The DVCs' Debt Crisis of the 1980s

Private capital flows to the DVCs averaged $28 billion annually in the 1970s and increased throughout the period. Then in the 1980s several DVCs experienced a major *debt crisis*: They could not pay back their loans. This crisis was precipitated by a combination of factors:

1. Soaring prices of imported oil caused growing current account deficits in the DVCs, which financed these deficits largely through foreign borrowing.

2. In the early 1980s, tight money policies in many IACs had two detrimental effects on the DVCs. First, national income in many of the IACs fell, causing a decline in imports from the DVCs. This decline sharply reduced DVC export earnings—earnings needed to pay interest and principal on their debts. Second, the high interest rates in the IACs greatly increased the interest expense to the DVCs in refinancing loans from private banks.

3. An appreciating dollar meant that DVCs had to pay more for their imports of goods. And because much DVC debt is denominated in dollars, it also meant that DVCs had to export a larger amount of their output to acquire each dollar needed to pay interest and principal on their debts.

4. Because of political corruption and economic mismanagement, DVC investment of loan funds was frequently unproductive. Returns on such investments were not sufficient to cover interest and principal payments, thereby generating loan defaults.

Actual defaults or near-defaults on existing loans in Mexico and several other DVCs brought an end to most of the flow of new and private foreign capital to the DVCs. A period of "muddling through" followed, in which creditor nations in cooperation with the International Monetary Fund tried to cope with the crisis on a nation-by-nation basis. The debts of many DVCs were rescheduled (stretched out over a longer period) to reduce the burden of annual interest and principal payments. And in some cases, commercial banks in the IACs had to "write off" much DVC debt as uncollectible, and thus as losses.

Reform and Revival in the 1990s   Although private capital flows to the DVCs virtually ceased in the 1980s, they have increased briskly in the 1990s. Specifically, they jumped from $50 billion in 1990 to $250 billion in 1996. The major reason is that, as part of the debt renegotiations, heavily indebted DVCs agreed to reform their economies to promote growth and avert future debt crises. At the macro level, DVCs have made greater efforts to reduce budget deficits and control inflation. At the micro level, some governments have privatized state-owned businesses and deregulated industry. Some DVCs have reduced tariffs and adjusted unrealistically fixed exchange rates. In general, the DVCs have reduced the economic role of govern-ment and increased the role of free markets. These reforms have made the DVCs more attractive to foreign lenders.

The makeup of the revived private capital flows to the DVCs, however, is now different than before the debt crisis. First, private IAC firms and individuals, rather than commercial banks, are the primary lenders. Second, a greater proportion of the flows is now **direct foreign investment** in DVCs, rather than loans to DVC governments. Such direct investment includes the building of new factories by multinational firms in DVCs and the purchases of DVC firms (or parts of them). Whereas once DVCs viewed direct foreign investment as "exploitation," many of them now seek out direct foreign investment as a way to expand their capital stock and improve their citizens' job opportunities and wages. These wages are often very low by IAC standards but high by DVC standards. Another potential advantage of directly investing in DVCs is that management skills and technological knowledge often accompany such capital flows.

Two words of caution: The revived flow of capital is highly selective. Recently, most of the flow has been directed towards China, Mexico, Southeast Asian nations, and eastern European nations. Relatively little IAC capital is flowing towards extremely impoverished DVCs such as those in Africa.

Also, it is still premature to say that the DVC debt crisis has been totally resolved. Some developing nations still face staggering debt burdens, and there is no assurance that some combination of circumstances will not bring about future defaults. The DVC debt problem has been alleviated, not solved. For example, in 1995 Canada, other G-7 nations, and the IMF found it necessary to provide a $50 billion package of loan guarantees to offset the collapse of the Mexican peso. The immediate cause of the peso's dramatic fall was an expansion of Mexican debt in excess of export earnings. More recently, in late 1997 and early 1998 the currencies of Thailand, Malaysia, South Korea, and Indonesia suddenly nose-dived in international value. Because most of these nations' debts are dollar-denominated, the depreciation of their currencies increased their expense of making interest and principal payments on their loans from the IACs. As in the earlier Mexican situation, the IMF coordinated multibillion-dollar "financial rescue efforts" to help these countries cope with their domestic economic difficulties and to meet their financial obligations.

22-2

QUICK REVIEW

- Governments of the DVCs may encourage growth by **a** providing law and order, **b** taking the lead in establishing enterprises, **c** improving the infrastructure, **d** forcing higher levels of saving and investing, and **e** resolving social-institutional problems.

- The IACs can assist the DVCs through expanded trade, foreign aid, and private capital flows.

- Many DVCs have large external debts that have become an additional obstacle to growth.

- A decline in foreign aid to DVCs and an increase in private capital flows (particularly direct investment) have characterized the 1990s.

WHERE FROM HERE?

The developing nations face daunting tasks. There simply are no magic methods for quick economic development. Nevertheless, our discussion provided, or at least implied, several policies that DVCs and IACs might undertake to increase economic growth in the developing nations. We end this chapter by briefly summarizing these policies.

DVC Policies for Promoting Growth

Economists suggest that developing nations have several ways of enhancing their economic growth:

1. **ESTABLISHING THE RULE OF LAW**   Clearly defined and enforced property rights bolster economic growth by ensuring that individuals receive and retain the fruits of their labour. The rule of law also encourages direct foreign investments by firms from the IACs since legal protections reduce investment risk. Government itself must live by the law. The presence of government corruption in a sense sanctions criminality throughout the entire economic system. Such criminality undermines the growth of output because it diverts scarce resources towards activities that "transfer" income from others and away from activities that actually produce goods and services.

2. **OPENING ECONOMIES TO INTERNATIONAL TRADE**   Studies indicate that, other things equal, open economies grow as much as 1.2 percentage points per year faster than closed economies.

3. **CONTROLLING POPULATION GROWTH**   Slower population growth converts increases in real output and income to increases in real output and income *per capita*. Fewer children reduce family consumption and enable family saving; smaller families also free up time for women to participate in the labour market.

4. **ENCOURAGING FOREIGN DIRECT INVESTMENT**   DVCs that welcome and encourage direct foreign investment have had greater growth rates than nations that view such investment suspiciously and thus place severe obstacles in its way.

5. **BUILDING HUMAN CAPITAL**   Programs that increase basic literacy, education, and labour-market skills help enhance economic growth. Higher education loans and grants should contain strong incentives for recipients to remain in the home country (or return to the home country) after receiving their degrees.

6. **MAKING PEACE WITH NEIGHBOURS**   Countries at war or fear of war with neighbouring nations divert scarce resources to armaments, rather than to, say, private capital or public infrastructure. Peace among neighbouring nations can eventually lead to economic cooperation and integration, broadened markets, and enhanced growth.

7. **ESTABLISHING INDEPENDENT CENTRAL BANKS**   Hyperinflation is not conducive to economic investment and growth. DVCs can keep inflation in check by establishing independent central banks that maintain proper control over the nations' money supplies. Studies indicate that DVCs that control inflation have higher growth rates than those that do not.

8. **ESTABLISHING REALISTIC EXCHANGE-RATE POLICIES**   Exchange rates fixed at unrealistic levels invite balance of payments problems and speculative currency trading. Often, such trading forces a nation into abrupt revaluation of its currency, which shocks its economy. More flexible exchange rates enable more gradual adjustments and thus less susceptibility to major currency shocks and the domestic disruption they can cause.

9. **PRIVATIZING STATE INDUSTRIES**   Many DVCs could benefit by converting state enterprises into private firms. State enterprises often are inefficient; for example, they may be more concerned with appeasing labour

unions than using modern technology and delivering goods and services at minimum per-unit cost. Also, relative to private firms, state enterprises are poor "incubators" for the development of profit-focused, entrepreneurial persons who may leave the firm to set up their own businesses.

IAC Policies for Fostering DVC Growth

What can the IACs do to improve living conditions and promote growth in the developing nations? While there is no consensus view, development economists offer a variety of suggestions, some of which we have already discussed:

1. **DIRECTING FOREIGN AID TO THE POOREST DVCS** Much of the foreign aid from the IACs is strongly influenced by political and military considerations. Consequently, DVCs do not receive aid based on their economic needs or degree of destitution. Only one-fourth of foreign aid goes to those 10 countries whose population constitutes 70 percent of the world's poorest people. The most affluent 40 percent of the DVC population receives over twice as much aid as the poorest 40 percent. Many economists argue that the IACs should shift foreign aid away from the middle-income developing countries and towards the poorest group of DVCs.

2. **REDUCING TARIFFS AND IMPORT QUOTAS** Trade barriers in the IACs are often highest for labour-intensive manufactured goods such as textiles, clothing, footwear, and processed agricultural products. These are precisely the types of goods in which DVCs have a comparative advantage. Also, many tariffs increase with the degree of product processing; for example, tariffs on chocolates are higher than on cocoa. This effectively denies the DVCs the opportunity to develop processing industries. One estimate suggests that trade barriers reduce the DVCs' gross domestic products by 3 percent, causing an annual loss of $75 billion in income. Thus, reducing such tariffs could greatly benefit the DVCs.

3. **PROVIDING DEBT RELIEF TO DVCS** Development economists argue that, to the extent possible, the IACs should help the DVCs by stretching out payments of their debts. The present DVC debt is so large that it is a severe roadblock to DVC growth.

4. **ALLOWING IN TEMPORARY WORKERS WHILE DISCOURAGING BRAIN DRAINS** Economists recognize that the IACs could help the DVCs by accepting more temporary workers from the DVCs. Temporary migration is not only an outlet for surplus DVC labour but also a source of income in the form of migrant remittance to their families in the home country. Also, IACs could discourage "brain drains" from the DVCs, in which the brightest and best-educated workers in the DVCs are recruited to the IACs. As you might imagine, these proposals have more support in the DVCs than in the IACs.

5. **DISCOURAGING ARMS SALES TO THE DVCS** Finally, the IACs should discourage sale of military equipment to the DVCs. Such purchases by the DVCs divert public expenditures from infrastructure and education.

In

The Media

Trade barriers make comeback

Brazil, Argentina, Malaysia may be at head of protectionism wave

By ROBERT S. GREENBERGER
AND HELENE COOPER
THE WALL STREET JOURNAL

So far, the turmoil in Asian markets has produced only a few new trade barriers to protect vulnerable economies. But these early warnings could mean that the free-trade momentum that has characterized the decade may slow.

Brazil and Argentina, which lead South America's Merocosur trade bloc, recently raised tariffs on a number of products. In October, Malaysia increased tariffs on such items as construction equipment. And some experts warn that the U.S. Congress's rejection of fast-track trade authority sent a protectionist message that offers aid and comfort to other nations considering erecting trade barriers.

"There's no immediate evidence that countries (in the Asia-Pacific region) will begin to second-guess the enthusiasm for more open trade," says Jeffrey Garten, dean of the Yale School of Management and former senior trade official at the U.S. Commerce Department. "But it's a real stretch to think that the trajectory of trade growth will remain the same."

The first big test comes next week, when the world's trading nations try to complete work on a global financial services agreements. The United States and Europe, pushing to get big banks and insurance companies into Asia and Latin America, may be stalled by developing countries in currency turmoil.

Philippines secretary of trade and industry Cesar Bautista said recently: "Countries will still make the offers. But they will say they want to do it next year or the year after."

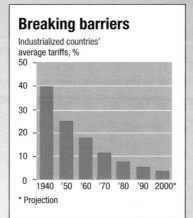

Breaking barriers

Industrialized countries' average tariffs, %

* Projection

This tension between expanding trade and protecting domestic economies was at play last week in Vancouver at the Asia-Pacific Economic Co-operation summit. Fred Bergsten, director of the Institute for International Economics, notes that the Asia-Pacific trading nations agreed to work in the next year to cut tariffs in nine sectors. But APEC didn't back the financial services pact as strongly because of the reluctance of such nations as Malaysia.

Which way will the Asian and Latin American economies go? After its peso devaluation crisis in 1994, Mexico didn't raise tariff

barriers or take other protectionist steps. But, said Yale's Mr. Garten, optimism based on the Mexico example may not be warranted, given its dependence on the United States for a rescue and its obligations under the North American free-trade agreement. Asian tigers will be under pressure to continue absorbing imports from Europe, whose main source of growth comes from exports, and Japan, which is using the cheaper yen to stimulate its economy. That may pressure the Asian tigers to raise tariffs.

And the leaders of Argentina and Brazil appeared to be moving backward when they met last month. Brazil, battered by the fallout from the turmoil in Asia, is using tariffs to help lower its trade and current-account deficits. To Argentina, the three-percentage-point increase in tariffs replaces a so-called statistical tax on imports that the World Trade Organization ordered it to eliminate.

Source: *Globe and Mail*, December 2, 1997, p. B14. Reprinted by permission of the *Wall Street Journal* © 1997, Dow Jones & Company, Inc.

THE STORY IN BRIEF

Some developing nations are adopting trade barriers to protect them from currency depreciation in some exporting countries.

THE ECONOMICS BEHIND THE STORY

- In late 1997 and early 1998 many nations in the Pacific Rim suffered financial turmoil and currency depreciations. Depreciation of a currency will make that nation's exports less expensive to nations whose currencies have remained stable.

- Argentina and Brazil raised tariffs to protect them from the Asian turmoil. Both these countries were vulnerable because of an already existing current account deficit.

- Is it always wrong to raise tariffs to protect an economy from currency turmoil? ■

The Last Word

FAMINE IN AFRICA

The roots of Africa's persistent famines include both natural and human causes.

THE EARLY 1990s FAMINE IN SOMALIA— documented by shocking photos of fly-tormented, emaciated children with bloated bellies—is not uncommon in sub-Saharan Africa. Before U.S. armed forces and U.N. aid arrived in Somalia in late 1992, severe famine had caused an estimated 2,000 deaths each day; 1 out of 4 Somali children under the age of 5—about 300,000— are believed to have died. Similarly, despite an outpouring of aid from the rich nations, the 1983–84 Ethiopian famine caused 1 million deaths. A number of other African nations—including Ethiopia, Sudan, Angola, Liberia, Zaire, Mozambique, and Malawi—are persistently threatened by famine. Estimates put 5 to 20 million Africans at risk. This tragedy is ironic because most African countries were self-sufficient in food at the time they became independent nations; they are now heavily dependent on imported foodstuffs for survival.

The immediate cause of this catastrophe is drought. But the ultimate causes of Africa's declining ability to feed itself are more complex, an interplay of natural and human conditions. Lack of rainfall, chronic civil strife, rapid population growth, widespread soil erosion, and counterproductive public policies, all contribute to Africa's famines.

1. Civil Strife   Regional rebellions and prolonged civil wars have devastated some African nations. Both Ethiopia and Sudan, for example, have been plagued by decades of civil strife. Not only do these conflicts divert precious resources from civilian uses, they also greatly complicate the ability of wealthy nations to provide famine and developmental aid. In the 1983–84 famine the Ethiopian government denied food aid to areas occupied by rebel forces. Donated food is frequently diverted to the army and denied to starving civilians. During Ethiopia's 1973–74 famine, Haile Selassie sold much of the donated food on world markets to enrich his regime! In Somalia, factional feuding destroyed most institutions—schools, factories, and government ministries— and reduced the country to anarchy. Armed gangs stole water pumps, tractors, and livestock from farms and looted ports of donated foodstuffs.

2. Population Growth   In Africa population is growing more rapidly than is food production. Population is increasing about 3 percent per year while food output is growing only 2 percent per year. This grim arithmetic suggests declining living standards, hunger, and malnutrition. The World Bank reports that during the 1980s per-capita incomes of the sub-Saharan nations fell to about three-quarters of the level reached by the end of the 1970s.

3. Ecological Degradation   But apart from the simple numbers involved, population growth has contributed to the ecological degradation of Africa. With population pressures and the increasing need for food, marginal land has been deforested and put into crop production. In many cases trees that have served as a barrier to the encroachment of the desert have been cut for fuel, allowing the fragile topsoil to be blown away by desert winds. The scarcity of wood that has accompanied deforestation has forced the use of animal dung for fuel, thereby denying its traditional use as fertilizer. Furthermore, traditional fallow periods have been shortened, resulting in overplanting and overgrazing and a wearing out of the soil. Deforestation and land overuse have reduced the capacity of the land to absorb moisture, diminishing its productivity and its ability to resist drought. Some authorities feel that the diminished ability of the land to absorb water reduces the amount of moisture that evaporates into the clouds to return ultimately as rainfall. All this is complicated by the fact that there are few facilities for crop storage. Even when crops are good, it is difficult to accumulate a surplus for future lean years. A large percentage of domestic farm output in some parts of Africa is lost to rats, insects, and spoilage.

4. Public Policies and Debt   Ill-advised public policies have contributed to Africa's famines. First, African governments generally have neglected investment in agriculture in favour of industrial development and military strength. It is estimated that African governments on the average spend four times as much on armaments as they do on agriculture. Second, many African governments have followed the policy of establishing the prices of agricultural commodities at low levels to provide cheap food for growing urban populations. This low-price policy has diminished farmers' incentives to increase productivity. While foreign aid has helped ease the effects of Africa's food-population problems, most experts reject aid as a long-term solution. Experience suggests that aid in the form of food can provide only temporary relief and may undermine the realization of long-run local self-sufficiency. Foreign food aid, it is contended, treats symptoms, not causes.

All this is made more complex by the fact that the sub-Saharan nations are burdened with large and growing external debts. The IMF reports that the aggregate debt of these nations rose from $84 billion in 1980 to $226 billion in 1995. As a condition of further aid, these nations have had to invoke austerity programs that have contributed to declines in their per-capita incomes. One tragic consequence is that many of these nations have cut back on social service programs for children. ∎

CHAPTER SUMMARY

1. The majority of the world's nations are developing countries (low- and middle-income nations) as opposed to high-income industrially advanced countries. While some DVCs have been realizing rapid growth rates in recent years, other have experienced little or no growth.

2. Initial scarcities of natural resources and the limited possibility of increasing existing supplies may limit a nation's ability to develop.

3. The large and rapidly growing populations in many DVCs contributes to low per-capita incomes. Increases in per capita incomes frequently induce greater population growth, again reducing per-capita incomes to near subsistence levels. The "demographic transition view," however, suggests that rising living standards must precede declining birth rates.

4. Most DVCs suffer from unemployment and underemployment. Labour productivity is low because of insufficient investment in physical and human capital.

5. In many DVCs, formidable obstacles impede both the saving and investment aspects of capital formation. In some of the poorest DVCs, the savings potential is very low. Many savers in DVCs transfer their funds to the IACs rather than invest domestically. The lack of a vigorous entrepreneurial class and the weakness of investment incentives also impede capital accumulation.

6. Appropriate social and institutional changes and, in particular, the presence of "the will to develop" are essential ingredients in economic development.

7. The vicious circle of poverty brings together many of the obstacles to growth, saying in effect that "poor countries stay poor because of their poverty." Low incomes inhibit saving and accumulation of physical and human capital, making it difficult to increase productivity and incomes. Rapid population growth can offset otherwise promising attempts to break the vicious circle.

8. The nature of the obstacles to growth—the absence of an entrepreneurial class, the dearth of infrastructure, the saving-investment dilemma, and the presence of social-institutional obstacles to growth—suggests a major role for government in initiating growth. However, the corruption and maladministration that are quite common to the public sectors of many DVCs suggest that government may not be very effective in instigating growth.

9. Advanced nations can assist in DVC development by reducing IAC trade barriers and by providing both public and private capital. Critics of foreign aid say that it **a** creates DVC dependency, **b** contributes to the growth of bureaucracies and centralized economic control, and **c** is ineffective because of corruption and mismanagement.

10. Rising energy prices, declining export prices, depreciation of the dollar, the unproductive use of borrowed funds, and concern about DVCs' creditworthiness combined to create a DVC debt crisis in the 1980s. External debt problems of many DVCs remain serious and hinder growth.

11. Economists suggest that DVCs can make future progress by establishing the rule of law, opening their economies to international trade, controlling population growth, encouraging foreign direct investment, building human capital, making peace with neighbours, establishing independent central banks, establishing realistic exchange rates, and privatizing state industries. The IACs can help in this process by directing foreign aid to the neediest nations, reducing tariffs and import quotas, providing debt relief, allowing more low-skilled immigration, and discouraging arms sales to the DVCs.

TERMS AND CONCEPTS

industrially advanced countries (IACs)
developing countries (DVCs)
demographic transition view
underemployment
brain drain
capital flight
infrastructure
capital-saving technology

capital-using technology
the will to develop
capricious universe view
land reform
vicious circle of poverty
World Bank
direct foreign investment

STUDY QUESTIONS

1. What are the characteristics of a developing nation? List the two basic avenues of economic growth available to such a nation. State and explain obstacles that DVCs face in breaking the poverty barrier. Use the "vicious circle of poverty" concept to outline steps a DVC might take to initiate economic development.

2. Explain how the absolute per-capita income gap between rich and poor nations might increase, even though per-capita income (or output) is growing faster in DVCs than in IACs.

3. **KEY QUESTION** *Assume a DVC and an IAC presently have real per-capita outputs of $500 and $5,000, respectively. If both nations have a 3 percent increase in their real per-capita outputs, by how much will the per-capita output gap change?*

4. Discuss and evaluate:
   a. "The path to economic development has been clearly blazed by American capitalism. It is only for the DVCs to follow this trail."
   b. "The problem with the DVCs is that income is too equally distributed. Economic inequality promotes saving, and saving is a prerequisite of investment. Therefore, greater inequality in the income distribution of the DVCs would be a spur to capital accumulation and growth."
   c. "The core of economic development involves changing human beings more than it does altering a nation's physical environment."
   d. "The foreign aid of the IACs is a sham. In reality it represents neocolonialism—a means by which the DVCs can be nominally free in a political sense but remain totally subservient in an economic sense."
   e. "The biggest obstacle facing poor nations in their quest for development is the lack of capital goods."

5. Studies indicate that, in general, landlocked countries tend to have lower per-capita income levels than surrounding nations that are bordered by oceans and seas. Why do you think this is the case? Use Global Perspective 22-1 to identify a major exception to this generalization.

6. **KEY QUESTION** *Contrast the "demographic transition view" of population growth with the traditional view that slower population growth is a prerequisite for rising living standards in the DVCs.*

7. **KEY QUESTION** *Because real capital is supposed to earn a higher return where it is scarce, how do you explain the fact that most international investment flows to the IACs (where capital is relatively abundant) rather than to the DVCs (where capital is very scarce)?*

8. Do you think that the nature of the problems the DVCs face require governmentally directed as opposed to a private-enterprise-directed development process? Explain why or why not.

9. How did the DVC debt crisis of the 1980s come about? How did it get resolved?

10. What have been the trends relating to government-provided foreign aid versus private capital flows to the DVCs in the 1990s? Why do you think these trends are occurring?

11. What types of products do the DVCs typically export? How do these exports relate to the law of comparative advantage?

12. Do you think that IACs such as Canada should open their doors wider to immigration of low-skilled DVC workers to help the DVCs develop? Do you think that it is appropriate for students from DVC nations to stay in IAC nations to work and build careers?

13. KEY QUESTION *Use Figure 22-2 (changing the box labels as necessary) to explain rapid economic growth in a country such as South Korea or Chile. What factors other than those contained in the figure might contribute to that growth?*

14. **(The Last Word)** Explain how civil wars, population growth, and public policy decisions have contributed to periodic famines in Africa.

15. WEB-BASED QUESTION **Group of 77—Promoting the Developing World** The Group of 77 (G-77) http://www.g77.org/ was established in 1964 by 77 developing countries. The Group of 77 promotes the collective economic interests of the developing world. What are the group's current developmental activities? What are the highlights in the latest Group of 77 Journal www.g77.org/Journal/message.htm?

16. WEB-BASED QUESTION **The World Bank Group—What's Hot in Development Economics** The major objective of the World Bank Group www.worldbank.org/ is to assist developing countries in achieving economic growth. What are three legs of the World Bank's development stool? What are the five agencies that make up the World Bank Group? Which one is the most influential? Go to the Development Economics section of the Topics in Development area and read the current research findings in What's Hot in Development Economics? What are the problems or opportunities, and what is the World Bank doing about them?

Transition Economies: Russia and China

TWO OF THE MOST PROFOUND ECONOMIC EVENTS of the past two decades are the collapse of communism in the Soviet Union and the rapid emergence of the market system in China. Russia (which emerged from the breakup of the Soviet Union) and China are perhaps the world's most significant developing economies: together they constitute 20 percent of the world's surface area and 24 percent of the world's population.

In this final chapter, first we briefly look at the Marxian (communist) ideology, which gave rise to the command economies. Then we examine the institutions and techniques of central planning common to both the Soviet Union and pre-reform China. Next, we discuss the coordination and incentive problems that central planning created. Finally, our attention turns to Russia and China's transitions to market economies.

IN THIS CHAPTER YOU WILL LEARN:

The ideology behind command economies.

•

Economic problems of centralized economies.

•

The contributing factors that led to the collapse of the Soviet economy.

•

About market reforms in China.

The Big Picture

IN 1989 THE SOVIET UNION BROKE UP, AND with it the world saw the end of one of the largest centralized economies that ever existed. China began its slow transformation to a market economy in the late 1970s. As the millennium turns, China and the various parts of the ex-Soviet Union seemed headed towards an economy dominated by markets.

As you read this chapter, keep the following points in mind:

- The main feature of a centrally planned economy is state ownership.
- The two major drawbacks to a centrally planned economy are coordination and incentive problems.
- Declining economic growth caused the Soviet economy to collapse.
- Although still beset by problems, the Chinese economy has grown rapidly since it undertook market reform. ■

IDEOLOGY AND INSTITUTIONS

To understand the command economies of the Soviet Union (prior to its collapse) and China (prior to market reforms), we must look back at the Marxian ideology that gave rise to central planning. Russia and China each have a unique history, but both nations established command economies following communist revolutions based on the ideas of Karl Marx. These revolutions established the Communist Party as the dominant force in political and economic life. The Russian revolution of 1917 resulted in a communist dictatorship under Vladimir Lenin and, later, Joseph Stalin and others. The Chinese revolution of 1947 led to a communist dictatorship under Mao Zedong. At the heart of the communist ideology was belief in state (or communal) ownership of capital and land.

The Communist Party in the Soviet Union and China viewed itself as the representative of the *proletariat* (the working class) and the *peasantry*. Based on Marxist-Leninist and Marxist-Maoist doctrines, the communists envisioned their systems as the inevitable successor to capitalism, a system they believed was plagued by internal contradictions resulting from the private ownership of capital and land. To communists, the market system was chaotic, unstable, and inequitable. Markets bred inflation, unemployment, discrimination, and an unfair distribution of income. In contrast, the communists viewed central planning of the economy

as a way to rationally organize the economy's resources, meet basic human needs, achieve macroeconomic stability, provide greater equality, and end exploitation of labour by capitalists.

Marxists believed in a **labour theory of value**, which is the idea that the value of any good is determined solely by the amount of labour required for its production. Because of the capitalist institution of private property, Marxists argue, capitalists own the machinery and equipment necessary for production in an industrial society. The working class owns no such capital goods and therefore is dependent on capitalists for employment and its livelihood. Workers lack bargaining power because capitalists can dismiss labour agitators and replace them from the large "reserve army of the unemployed." Capitalists exploit workers by paying them a wage far below the value of workers' production. That is, capitalists can and will expropriate the remaining fruits of workers' labour as profit, or what Marx termed **surplus value**. While all value comes from labour, in the capitalist system labour does not receive all value. In the communist planned economic system, the state as an agency of the working class would extract surplus value and distribute it in large part through subsidies for public or quasi-public goods (for example, education, transportation, health care, and housing).

The function of communism was to overthrow capitalism and replace it with a classless society void of human exploitation. The Communist Party viewed itself as the vanguard of the working class and peasantry, and its actions were held to be in keeping with the goals of those groups. In reality, the Communist Party was a strong, one-party dictatorship that often pursued the interests of its party members.

STATE OWNERSHIP AND CENTRAL PLANNING

Two major institutional characteristics of the pre-reform and precollapse economies of Russia and China were (1) state (government) ownership of property resources and (2) authoritarian central planning.

State Ownership

State ownership meant that the Soviet and Chinese governments owned all land, natural resources, transportation facilities, communication networks, the banking system, and virtually all industry. Most retail and wholesale enterprises and most urban housing were also government owned. Many farms were state-owned; most, however, were government collective farms, essentially cooperatives to which the state assigned land.

Central Economic Planning

Central economic planning meant that the two nations had centralized "command" economies functioning according to a detailed economic plan. Both economies were government-directed rather than market-directed. Choices that are made through the market in Canada and other market economies were made by bureaucratic decisions in the Soviet Union and China. Through the central five-year or seven-year plan (and its many subsets), the governments attempted to coordinate all economic activities of the economy as if they were parts of a large enterprise directed from their central headquarters.

Planning Goals and Techniques

Although central planning was far more complete in the Soviet Union than in China, each nation relied on direction from the central government. Several generalizations describe the functioning of central planning in both countries.

Industrialization (and Rural Development in China)

The former Soviet Union was dedicated to the task of rapid industrialization, economic growth, and military strength. These goals were achieved through extensive investment in heavy industry (such as steel, chemicals, and machine tools) and the allocation to the military of a large percentage of domestic output. In China, emphasis was also on rural development; for example, small-scale industries were scattered throughout the rural areas. But in both countries, the plans greatly neglected consumer goods industries and the distribution and service sectors.

Resource Overcommitment

In their efforts to increase total output (GDP), both the Soviet Union and China often overcommitted their economy's available resources. As a result, not every planning target could be achieved. In particular, the production of consumer goods suffered since planning priorities emphasized heavy industry, rural development, and the military.

Resource Mobilization

Both the Soviet Union and China initially achieved industrialization and economic growth through the mobilization of labour, capital, and raw materials. In the early years of planning there was substantial surplus labour in agriculture, which the central plans reallocated to industrial production. Similarly, both China and the Soviet Union induced or coerced a larger proportion of the population into the labour force. These countries achieved growth mainly by adding inputs rather than by using fixed amounts of inputs more productively. In the 1930s and again in the early post-World War II era, this strategy produced higher growth rates than those in Canada, the United States, and other industrialized nations.

Allocation by Directives

Central planners directed the allocation of inputs among industries and firms, thereby determining the composition of output. Planning directives were substituted for the market system as an allocative mechanism.

Government Price Setting

Government, not the forces of supply and demand, set resource and product prices. Planners seldom changed the prices of consumer goods, and as a matter of social policy, the prices of "necessities" such as housing and food were set at low levels. Rents on housing in the Soviet Union, for example, averaged only 3 percent of income and did not change between

1928 and 1992. Government also determined resource prices and the prices of each firm's output. Such prices were used primarily as accounting devices to gauge a firm's progress in meeting its production goals. The emphases of the various five- or seven-year plans were on the quantity of output, not on the cost or price of output.

Self-Sufficiency The Soviet Union and China each viewed itself as a single socialist nation, surrounded by hostile capitalist countries. Moreover, neither communist country trusted the other. They each maintained a strong military presence along their common border, and they vied for supremacy of influence among the developing countries. Because of the hostility they perceived around them, the central plan in each country stressed economic self-sufficiency. Each country greatly restricted trade with western nations, and neither country established easy convertibility between their respective currencies and those of other countries. The Soviet Union and China traded largely among other communist nations such as East Germany, Poland, Hungary, Cuba, North Korea, and Vietnam.

Passive Macroeconomic Policies Both the Soviet and prereform Chinese economies were quantity-directed systems in which money and prices played only a limited role in resource allocation. Monetary policy (changes in the money supply and interest rates) and fiscal policy (changes in government spending and taxes) were passive rather than active. Historically, unemployment—but not underemployment—was quite low, partly the result of ambitious planning targets and the various admonitions and "educational" campaigns to promote work. But low unemployment perhaps had more to do with overstaffing (managers could not fire redundant workers) and a lack of interest in cost-minimization (gross output was the overriding objective). It also had to do with the massive, highly labour-intensive, public works projects that both nations used to build infrastructure and glorify the socialist state.

Both countries primarily used direct government price setting as the primary device to control the price level. By simply not allowing prices to go up, both nations repressed any inflationary pressures. These price controls, however, created rising shortages of consumer goods.

PROBLEMS WITH CENTRAL PLANNING

Central planning was fraught with difficulties that ultimately led to the collapse of the Soviet economy and to the market reforms in China.

The Coordination Problem

As you have learned, the market system is a powerful organizing force that coordinates millions of individual decisions by consumers, resource suppliers, and businesses. In so doing, it promotes the efficient use of scarce resources. It is not easy to substitute central planning as a coordinating mechanism; such planning produces a significant **coordination problem**.

Example: Suppose that an enterprise in Moscow or Beijing is producing men's shoes. Planners must establish a realistic production target for that enterprise and then make available all the necessary inputs—labour, electric power, leather, rubber, thread, nails, appropriate machinery, transportation—for the production and delivery of that product. When the product is not as simple a one as shoes but a more complex one such as farm tractors, the planners' allocation problem are greatly compounded.

Because the outputs of many industries are inputs to other industries, the failure of any single industry to fulfil its output target will cause a chain reaction of adverse repercussions. If iron mines, for want of machinery or labour or transportation, do not supply the steel industry with the required inputs of iron ore, the steel mills will be unable to fulfil the input needs of the many industries dependent on steel. These steel-using industries (such as automobile, tractor, and transportation) will be unable to fulfil their planned production goals. Eventually the bottleneck chain reaction spreads to all firms using steel components as inputs.

The problem of centrally coordinating economic activity becomes more difficult as the economy grows. Early planning under Stalin in the late 1930s and 1940s and Mao in China in the 1950s resembled the highly focused planning of capitalist nations in directing resources to the effort to fight World War II. The Communist Party established a few key production goals and directed resources towards fulfilling those goals regardless of costs or consumer welfare. But the past success of such "campaign planning" in the Soviet Union and China resulted in increasing complexity. Products and production processes became more sophisticated, and the number of industries for which to plan increased. Planning techniques that worked for a simple economy became inadequate and inefficient as these economies grew. Bottlenecks and production stoppages occurred with alarming regularity.

A lack of adequate success indicators adds to the coordination problem in central planning. Market economies have a single, comprehensive success indicator: profit. Profit or loss measures each firm's success or failure. Profit depends on consumer demand, production efficiency, and product quality. In contrast, the major success indicator of the Soviet and prereform China economies was a quantitative production target assigned by the central planners. Production costs, product quality, and product mix become secondary considerations. Managers and workers often sacrificed product quality since they were awarded bonuses for meeting quantitative, not qualitative, targets. If meeting production goals meant sloppy assembly work, so be it.

In fact, it is difficult at best for planners to assign quantitative production targets without unintentionally producing ridiculous distortions in output. If the production target for an enterprise manufacturing nails is specified in terms of weight (tonnes of nails), the producer will tend to produce all large nails. But if its target is a quantity (thousands of nails), it will be motivated to use available inputs to produce all small nails. The problem is that the economy needs *both* large and small nails.

The Incentive Problem

In the capitalist system, profits and losses not only signal success and failure, they also act as incentives for firms to increase or decrease production. If there is a product shortage, its price and profitability increase and producers are motivated to expand production. Conversely, a product surplus means falling prices and profits and a reduction in output. Improved product quality and better production techniques are sought because of their profitability. Improved job skills and greater work effort by labour mean higher money incomes, which can be translated into a higher standard of living.

These actions and adjustments do not occur under central planning; there is an **incentive problem**. Central planners determined the output mix of the Soviet Union and the prereform China. When they misjudged how many automobiles, furniture, underwear, and chickens were wanted at the government-determined prices, there were persistent shortages and surpluses of those products. But since the managers who oversaw the production of these goods were rewarded for meeting their assigned production goals, they had no incentive to adjust production in response to product shortages or surpluses. And they did not have changes in prices and profitability to signal that more or less of certain products was desired. Thus, in the Soviet Union and China many products were unavailable or in short supply while other overproduced goods sat for months and years in warehouses.

The centrally planned system also lacked entrepreneurship. In market systems, the large potential monetary rewards to innovators is a stimulus to technological advancement. Moreover, firms that improve their products or production processes profit, while those that do not eventually suffer losses. Communist central planning does not allow the profit motive and does not reward innovation and enterprise.

The route for getting ahead in the centrally planned economies of the Soviet Union and China was by movement up the political hierarchy of the Communist Party. Moving up the hierarchy meant better housing, better access to health care, and the right to shop in special stores. Meeting planning targets and skilfully manoeuvring through the minefields of party politics measured success in "business." But a definition of success based solely on political savvy is not conducive to technological advance, which is often disruptive to existing products, production methods, and organizational structures.

Indeed, in both the Soviet Union and prereform China, innovation was often resisted. Enterprises were essentially government-owned monopolies. As a result, there was no private gain to managers or workers for improving product quality or developing more efficient production techniques. Enterprise managers and workers actually resisted government-imposed innovations because higher and sometimes unrealistic production targets usually accompanied them.

Innovation also lagged because of a lack of competition. There were no new startup firms, driven by the profit motive, to introduce better products, superior managerial techniques, or more efficient production methods. Similarly, the goal of economic self-sufficiency isolated Soviet and Chinese enterprises from import competition. Over an extended period, enterprises produced the same products with the same techniques, even as both the products and techniques became increasingly obsolete by world standards.

Finally, individual workers lacked motivation to work hard because there were few material incentives. Because of the low priority assigned to consumer goods in the production plans, only a limited array of inferior products and services was available to consumers. While hard work might result in promotions and bonuses, the increase in money income did not translate into a proportionate increase in real income. Why work hard for additional money if there is nothing to buy with the money you earn? As a Soviet worker once lamented to a western journalist: "The government pretends to pay us and we pretend to work."

23-1

QUICK REVIEW

- Marxian ideology is based on the labour theory of value and views capitalism as a system that expropriates surplus value from workers.

- The main features of the former Soviet economy and the prereform Chinese economy were state ownership of property resources and central economic planning.

- Central plans in the Soviet Union and China were characterized by by **a** an emphasis on rapid industrialization, rural development (in China), and military power; **b** resource overcommitment; **c** growth through the use of more inputs rather than greater efficiency; **d** resource allocation by government directives rather than markets; **e** government price determination; **f** an emphasis on economic self-sufficiency; and **g** passive monetary and fiscal policies.

- Two major problems of central planning are the **a** difficulty of coordinating inputs and outputs and **b** problem of fostering incentives, including those that cause technological advance.

COLLAPSE OF THE SOVIET ECONOMY

The general problems of central planning contributed to market reform in China and the collapse of the Soviet economy. Let's consider Russia first, then China.

In 1991, the Soviet Union broke into several newly independent states, the largest of which is the Russian Republic. The immediate reason for the collapse was political: a clumsy, failed attempt of old-line communists to wrest control of the government. (The failed military coup led to the ascendancy of Boris Yeltsin in Russia and independence of the former republics of the Soviet Union.) But behind the collapse of the Soviet Union were a number of economic problems, some stemming directly from the failures of central planning.

Declining Growth

Soviet economic growth in the 1950s and 1960s (at least as measured by questionable Soviet statistics) was quite impressive: The economy grew at roughly a 5 to 6 percent annual rate. But growth fell to 2 to 3 percent annually in the 1970s and declined to less than 2 percent in the mid-1980s. In the last year or two before the system broke down, real output was falling sharply.

Poor Product Quality

Further evidence of failure was the poor quality of Soviet goods. In such vital manufacturing sectors as computers and machine tools, Soviet technology lagged some 7 to 12 years behind advanced industrial nations.

It lagged even more in consumer goods, which were of notoriously poor quality and limited assortment. Durable goods such as automobiles, large household appliances, and consumer electronics were primitive by world standards. Also, widespread shortages of basic goods, interminable shopper lines, black markets, and corruption in product distribution characterized the consumer sector.

Lack of Consumer Goods

Not only were consumer goods of poor quality, they were also in short supply. In the early decades of Soviet Communism, the government established a "social contract" with its citizens to the effect that, by enduring the consumer sacrifices associated with rapid industrialization and growth, the population would be rewarded with consumer abundance in the future. The failure of the system to meet such expectations contributed to frustration and deteriorating morale among consumers and workers. The rewards of past sacrifices simply never materialized.

Large Military Burden

Large Soviet military expenditures of 15 to 20 percent of domestic output absorbed great quantities of resources that otherwise would have been available for the development and production of consumer and capital goods. The government's policy during the Cold War era was to channel superior management and the best scientists and engineers to defence and space research, which adversely affected technological progress and the quality (and thus productivity) of capital in the civilian sector.

Agricultural Drag

By standards of the market economies, agriculture in the Soviet Union was a monument to inefficiency and a drag on economic growth. This sector used about 30 percent of the labour force and roughly one-fourth of annual investment. Furthermore, output per worker was only 10 to 25 percent of the level in industrially advanced nations. The low productivity of Soviet agriculture was attributable to many factors: relative scarcity of good land, erratic weather patterns and growing seasons, serious errors in planning and administration, and perhaps most important, a lack of an effective incentive system.

Once a major exporter of grain and other agricultural products, the Soviet Union became one the world's largest importers of farm goods. This reliance on imports seriously drained the foreign currency reserves that the leadership might otherwise have used to import western capital goods and technology.

THE RUSSIAN TRANSITION TO A MARKET SYSTEM

The former Soviet republics, and particularly Russia, have committed themselves to making the transition to a market economy. There has been dramatic reform in the Russian economy since 1992, when Boris Yeltsin replaced Mikhail Gorbachev as Russia's leader.

Privatization

Private property rights have been established to encourage entrepreneurship. Much of the existing government property—housing, factories, machinery, equipment, and farmland—has been *privatized*, meaning transferred to private owners. Many new firms have formed and developed. Since 1992 more than two-thirds of former state-owned enterprises have been privatized: 90 percent of small companies are now privately owned, and 80 percent of service-sector companies are private.

The privatization process involved two phases. In the first phase, the government gave vouchers, each with a designated monetary value, to 40 million Russian citizens. Recipients could then pool these vouchers to purchase enterprises. The second phase, begun in 1994, allowed state enterprises to be purchased for cash. This enabled foreign investors to buy Russian enterprises and provided much-needed direct investment from abroad to those enterprises.

Land reform, on the other hand, has progressed more slowly. Although Boris Yeltsin decreed in 1996 that Russian peasants could buy and sell land, it will take many years to develop a functional market for farmland. Farmers, who have worked for decades on collective farms, in general fear the uncertainties and potential problems that might accompany privatization and free markets.

Price Reform

Unlike competitive market prices, the prices the Soviet government established bore no relationship to the economic value of either products or resources. In a competitive market system, the price of a product equals (at the margin) the value that consumers place on that good (the marginal benefit) and the value of the resources used in its production (the marginal cost). When free markets achieve this equality for all goods and services, the economy's scarce resources are being used efficiently to satisfy consumer wants.

But in the Soviet economy, government fixed both input and output prices and in many instances did not change those prices for many years. Because input prices did not measure the relative scarcities of resources, it was impossible for a firm to minimize real production costs. With fixed prices, it is impossible to produce a unit of a particular product in such a way as to minimize the sacrifice of alternative goods.

Example: High energy prices have caused firms in market economies to reduce energy use per unit of output. But the government under-priced such energy in the former Soviet Union (the world's largest producer of energy), so its industries used two or three times as much energy per unit of output as leading industrial countries.

Historically, not only was energy priced far below its true price, so too were many basic consumer goods. The Soviet rationale for these low prices was to ensure that everyone could afford such goods. As Figure 23-1 shows, this pricing policy helps explain the chronic product shortages

and long lines that had frustrated Soviet consumers. The perfectly inelastic supply curve S_1 reflects the fixed output of, say, shoes that the central plan provided. The demand curve D_1 slopes downward as it would in a market economy. In view of S_1, the equilibrium price would be P_a. But in an effort to make shoes accessible to those with lower incomes, the government fixed the price at P_f.

The result was that not everyone who wanted shoes at P_f could obtain them. At P_f the quantity demanded Q_f was substantially greater than the quantity supplied Q_a, so there was a shortage of shoes and other consumer goods priced below their market equilibrium. This explains the long lines of consumers and the empty shelves the rest of the world saw in television news clips. It also explains the black markets in which goods were sold at much higher prices than those fixed by government.

The task, then, was to remove these price controls. In January 1992, the government decontrolled about 90 percent of all prices. The international value of the ruble (the Russian currency) also was decontrolled, that is, allowed to float to the value determined by demand and supply. As a result, domestic prices immediately surged and the international value of the Russian ruble sank.

The decontrol of prices, however, did have several positive effects. In terms of Figure 23-1, the decontrol at first raised prices rapidly, here from P_f to P_a. There simply was no mechanism for firms to expand the amount of output for sale in response to the price increases. But with privatization, the higher prices signalled profit opportunities to enterprises and thus a positive supply response. The relevant supply curve then took on its more familiar upward slope as in S_2, and equilibrium output increased from Q_a to Q_e. Equilibrium price moved downward from P_a to P_e. More generally, prices began to more closely reflect the marginal cost to the Russian economy of producing goods, which helped reallocate resources to where they were best suited to meet consumer wants.

Promotion of Competition

As we have seen, the industrial sector of the former Soviet Union consisted of large state-owned enterprises. Single-firm "industries" produced about 30 to 40 percent of total industrial output.

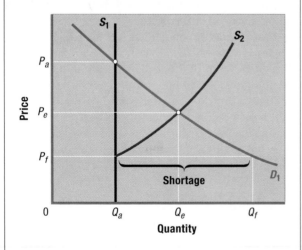

FIGURE 23-1   The effects of centrally planned prices

Central planners in the Soviet Union established below-equilibrium prices such as P_f on many basic consumer goods to allow low-income persons to buy them. But in fact, at such low prices quantity demanded (here Q_f) exceeded quantity supplied (set by planners at Q_a). This shortage meant that many consumers could not obtain such goods. The removal of government price setting at first increased price from P_f to P_a. But with privatization in Russia, the higher price stimulated greater output along supply curve S_2. Price therefore settled at P_e while output jumped from Q_a to Q_e.

When several enterprises produced a product, the planning process coordinated their actions to create a cartel. In short, most production took place under monopoly or near-monopoly conditions.

Russian reformers realize that an efficient market economy requires the dismantling of these public monopolies and the creation of antitrust laws to sustain competition. But only limited "de-monopolization" has accompanied privatization thus far. Private monopolies rather than public monopolies now reign in several industries. Joint ventures between Russia and foreign companies are one avenue for increasing competition, and Russian legislation has recently opened the door for foreign firms to invest directly in Russia. *(Key Question 5)*

Joining the World Economy

The Soviet economy was largely isolated from the world economy for 75 years. A key step in the transition to a market economy is to open the economy to international trade and finance. Russia has had some success in this endeavour; for example, it has made the ruble a fully convertible currency. This means that the ruble is acceptable in exchange for other currencies. The plunging value of the ruble (from 90 rubles = $1 in 1992 to 5,800 rubles = $1 in 1997) was obviously detrimental to Russia's world trade. But recently the international value of the ruble has stabilized, which has helped Russia increase its volume of international trade and finance.

Price-Level Stabilization

The transition to free markets brought with it hyperinflation. The decontrol of prices in January 1992 tripled and quadrupled prices almost overnight. Also, Russian households had stored huge amounts of currency and deposits at saving banks during years of waiting for scarce consumer goods to become more abundant. This so-called "ruble overhang" helped fuel inflation once prices were decontrolled and privatization began to deliver consumer goods to the marketplace.

But the most important source of inflation was the large government deficits financed by increases in the money supply. The deficits in turn had many roots. Privatization of state enterprises caused the government to lose those profits, an important source of revenue. The uncertainties

inherent in the transition led to general disorder and widespread tax evasion. To ease enterprise losses incurred during the transition, the government extended massive subsidy credits (financed by printing new money) to both industry and agriculture. Finally, the government also increased pensions and welfare benefits by printing money.

Russia's economic reforms, however, have created an independent central bank that has implemented an anti-inflationary monetary policy that has paid off in a swift decline in the rate of inflation. As shown in column 3 in Table 23-1, inflation declined from 1353 percent in 1992 to 14 percent in 1997. This decline has increased investor confidence in the stability of the Russian government and has been a major factor in the stabilization of the international value of the ruble. *(Key Question 6)*

Major Problems

Along with the successes and difficulties we just noted, the Russian transition to the market system has encountered two other significant problems:

Falling Output and Living Standards Thus far, the transition to capitalism in Russia has not paid off in rising real output and an improved standard of living for the great majority of Russians. Real output began to fall in the 1980s, but its decline accelerated during the reforms. Column 2 in Table 23-1 documents recent declines. Note, however,

TABLE 23-1 Real GDP growth and inflation in Russia, 1991-1997

(1) Year	(2) Growth of real GDP (percent)	(3) Rate of inflation (percent)
1991	−13	93
1992	−19	1,353
1993	−12	896
1994	−15	302
1995	− 4	190
1996	− 6	22
1997*	+ 1	14

*Estimate
Source: International Monetary Fund and Russian authorities.

that the fall in real GDP bottomed out in 1992 at 19 percent. Declines of real output of this magnitude resemble those associated with the Great Depression in Canada.

Causes of these declines include the (1) rapid inflation, which created an uncertain environment for borrowing and investing, (2) unravelling of Russia's international trade relationships with former communist-bloc nations of eastern Europe, (3) bankruptcy and closing of many former state-owned enterprises that could not survive in a market environment, and (4) massive reallocation of resources required by the reforms and the major reduction in government spending on the military.

Because real output equals real income, declining real output has meant declines in Russian living standards. Farmers, government employees, and pensioners have been hard hit, and many workers have had to accept deep real wage cuts to keep their jobs. Some workers are owed large amounts of "back pay" because of the inability of their employers to make wage payments. At least 30,000 scientists have left Russia to work in other nations.

Russian authorities, however, believe that the decline in real output has reached an end. Real output increased by 1 percent in 1997 and is expected to rise by about that same amount in 1998.

Inequality and Social Costs   Economic inequality has increased during the transition. While many people have become impoverished, a wealthy class of "new Russians" has emerged. Many of these people have gained their wealth through entrepreneurship. Others have prospered as executives, managers, and scientists in the newly privatized industries. Still others, however, have enriched themselves via corruption and illegal activities. The major disruptions, swift changes, and lack of regulatory oversight that accompanied the transition have created major opportunities for organized crime to expand and flourish.

Considerable friction between gainers and losers, the growth of organized crime, and "crony capitalism" fuels public doubts as to the desirability of a market economy. Greater economic freedom has also brought greater economic insecurity; medical and educational services have deteriorated, and school enrolments have declined. Alcoholism, historically high in Russia, has increased sharply, and life expectancy of Russian men declined from 65 in 1988 to 57 in 1997.

Future Prospects

A remaining concern about the transition to markets in Russia is the weakness of government in enforcing its laws, including the collection of taxes owed by enterprises and political subdivisions. Widespread tax evasion results in declining tax revenues, enlarged budget deficits, and the potential for financial instability. Declining tax revenues further weaken the government's ability to enforce tax laws, so a kind of vicious circle could continue until another political and economic collapse results. Declining tax revenues also cripple the central government's ability to perform other basic functions, such as maintaining law and order, providing regulatory oversight of banks and security markets, and providing a social safety net for its citizens. Pessimists point out that a government borrowing crisis, coupled with, say, a collapse of the Russia, banking system, might plunge Russia into another depression. That could lead to the abandonment of capitalistic reforms and even an end to democracy.

The more likely scenario, however, is that Russia will eventually succeed in creating a vibrant market economy. The most severe economic dislocations in the form of inflation and a declining real output seem to have ended. Economists who closely monitor the progress of Russia believe that its transition from central planning to markets might span another decade or so but that the market reforms are now largely irreversible and that another economic collapse is highly unlikely. In this view, although Russia is still far from being an advanced market economy, the nation is on a path to achieving one of the truly amazing economic transitions in world history.

23-2
QUICK REVIEW

- The former Soviet economy collapsed under pressure of declining economic growth, poor product quality, a lack of consumer goods, a large military burden, and agricultural inefficiency.

- Russia has committed itself to becoming a capitalistic market economy. Ingredients in its transition from central planning to markets include **a** creating private property and property rights, **b** removing domestic price controls, **c** promoting competition, **d** opening the economy to international trade and finance, **e** ending inflation.

- Russia's transition to markets has been accompanied by declining output and living standards, increasing income inequality, and social costs such as corruption, organized crime, increasing alcoholism, and reduced life expectancy.

- Although Russia still faces difficult economic times, it has made substantial progress in its move from communism to capitalism.

MARKET REFORMS IN CHINA

China has taken a different path than Russia in its transition to a market economy. Russia pursued a "shock therapy" approach to reform in 1992, attempting to achieve "irreversibility" of its reforms through a rapid and radical transformation to private property and free markets. China's market reforms began far earlier—in 1978—in a piecemeal, experimental, and gradual manner. In 1992 Russia concluded that its political apparatus, the Communist Party in particular, was an obstacle to economic reform; political reform or democratization preceded economic reform. China, in contrast, has sought economic reform under the strong direction of its Communist Party. China's view is that the upsetting of the political system would generate endless debate, competition for power, and ultimate stagnation and failure for its economic reforms. Unlike Russia, China believes that communist dictatorship and markets are compatible. China has protected the existence and development of its state-owned enterprises while simultaneously encouraging the creation of competing private enterprises.

Although China's GDP per capita is only $620 compared to Russia's $2,240, China has instituted its market reforms without suffering the economic depression that confronted Russia. In fact, China has achieved a 9 percent annual growth of real output over the past two decades (as compared to typical growth rates of 2 to 5 percent for most advanced economies).

Market reforms in China began in 1978 under the leadership of Deng Xiaoping, the successor to Mao Zedong. Deng did not share Mao's utopian vision of an eventual communist economy in which people would work for the glory of the community and monetary incentives would play only a minor role. Instead, Deng recognized that the profit incentives of a market economy could increase China's living standard. But he also realized that only a gradual transition to such an economy could preserve the Communist Party's political control over China. Many Chinese critics of Deng derisively called him "a capitalist roader," implying that he was setting China on the road towards capitalism. In retrospect, they were at least partly right.

Agricultural and Rural Reform

Market reform in China began in agriculture in 1978, at which time nearly 70 percent of the Chinese labour force was rural. The key elements of the 1978–84 reforms were the leasing of land to individual farmers ("decollectivization") and the establishment of a *two-track price system*. For the first time, individual farmers were allowed to lease government-owned land (for 15-year periods). Under the dual price system, farmers had to sell a prescribed amount of farm output to the government at a set price but could sell any surplus in markets at market-determined prices. Farmers were eventually allowed to sell increasing portions of their output at market-determined prices rather than at lower government-determined prices. In 1978 farmers sold only 8 percent of their commodities in competitive markets, but by 1990 that share had increased to 80 percent.

Decollectivization and price reform greatly strengthened production incentives and swiftly moved the Chinese economy towards market-based agriculture. Responding to the profit motive, individual farmers boosted their productivity by substituting tools for labour, shifting crops towards more valuable commodities, and farming previously untilled land. Agricultural output in China rose dramatically throughout the 1980s. Equally important, the greater productivity in agriculture released labour resources to a growing number of privately owned rural manufacturing firms called **township and village enterprises**.

Reform of Urban Industries

The success of reforms in agriculture led the central government to extend the reforms to the **state-**

owned enterprises (SOEs) in urban areas. These enterprises were granted more authority to determine the quantity and variety of their outputs, to make their own employment decisions, and to retain much of their profits. (Previously, they had to send the bulk of their profits to the central government.) The government also extended the two-track system of prices to nonagricultural products. SOEs were allowed to buy increasing portions of their inputs at market prices rather than at government-set prices. They were also allowed to sell increasing portions of their outputs at market prices as opposed to being forced to sell output to the government at fixed prices. The share of output sold at market prices rather than at government-set prices rose from 12 percent in 1980 to 66 percent in 1987.

Furthermore, the Chinese government encouraged the formation of nonstate enterprises called **urban collectives**—enterprises owned jointly by managers and their workforces. Like town and village enterprises, these nonstate firms were *not* subject to the directives of the central plan, so they were far more capable than SOEs of gauging and meeting consumer wants. The urban collectives experienced explosive growth of output and employment, some of it at the expense of SOEs. Also, the competition among these nonstate enterprises and the SOEs spurred productivity advance and innovation in many of the SOEs.

Special Economic Zones

In 1980 China created **special economic zones** (SEZs) open to foreign investment, private ownership, and international trade. Located in coastal regions, these special zones attracted increasing amounts of foreign capital (particularly from Hong Kong). They also significantly increased Chinese exports. As the successes of the SEZs became apparent, China increased their number and scope. The SEZs in China's southern provinces, in particular, became booming enclaves of "near-capitalism." The success of the SEZs relative to other regions in China eventually undercut support for central planning.

Development of Supporting Institutions

The reforms in China also included the building of institutions to facilitate the market system and its macroeconomic control. Specific examples: First,

the Chinese government established the Bank of China as the central bank and gave it the power to regulate the banking system and control the money supply to avoid inflation. Second, China replaced the system of "profit transfers" from state enterprises to the central government with an *enterprise tax system*. Third, it established a so-called "swap market" in which Chinese enterprises could trade foreign currency as needed to conduct international business. Finally, it developed a stock market for the exchange of the shares of newly created stockholder-owned corporations.

Transformation of the SOEs

In the 1990s Chinese reform turned to making state-owned enterprises more "corporate-like." The idea was to replace Communist Party operatives with professional managers who were independent of the central government. The government also redirected the goals of such enterprises away from social objectives (providing employment, housing, health care, and day care) and towards economic objectives (producing high-quality goods that people desire). This partial *"corporatization"* of state-enterprises, however, exposed the inefficiencies of the SOEs. In the competitive rather than state-directed environment, many SOEs found that they were producing the wrong goods, in the wrong amounts, using the wrong combinations of inputs. In short, thousands of SOEs simply were inefficient and unprofitable.

After Deng's death in the mid-1990s, leadership of China passed to Jiang Zemin. In 1997 Jiang and the Communist Party called for consolidation of the major SOEs into 1,000 large enterprises. These SOEs will issue stock and become shareholder-owned corporations. The idea is to make the firms' management responsive to the shareholders. The government, however, will hold the controlling share of stock ownership in these 1,000 corporations. All the other 300,000 state-owned enterprises will be sold to private individuals (or groups) or, if they have no value, will be allowed to go bankrupt.

OUTCOMES AND PROSPECTS

Economic reform in China has achieved impressive results, but is still incomplete.

Positive Outcomes of Reform

China's economic growth rate in the past two decades is among the highest recorded for any country during any period of world history; it has averaged nearly 9 percent annually since the beginning of reforms in 1978. That means that real output and real income have quadrupled in less than two decades. About 40 percent of this growth has resulted from increased capital. Expanded output and income has boosted domestic saving and investment. The expansion of capital goods has in turn further increased productivity, output, and income. The rising income has attracted more direct foreign investment. (Growth rates for recent years are shown in column 2, Table 23-2.)

A rapid expansion of China's international trade has accompanied the expansion of real output. Chinese exports rose from $5 billion in 1978 to more than $160 billion in 1996. These exports have provided the foreign currency needed to import consumer goods and capital goods. Imports of capital goods from industrially advanced countries have brought with them the highly advanced technology that is embodied within, for example, factory design, industrial machinery, office equipment, and telecommunications systems.

During the period of reform, China's real GDP and real income have grown much more rapidly than China's population. Per-capita income has increased at a very high annual rate of 8 percent since 1980. This is noteworthy because China's

population has expanded by 14 million a year (despite a policy that encourages "one child" per family). Per-capita income in China is now $620 annually based on exchange rates. But since the prices of many basic items in China are still low, Chinese per-capita purchasing power is estimated to be nearly $3,000.

The growth of per-capita income in China has resulted from increased use of capital, improved technology, and shifts of labour away from lower-productivity towards higher-productivity uses. One such shift of employment has been from agriculture towards rural and urban manufacturing. Another such shift has been from state-owned enterprises towards private firms. Both shifts have raised the productivity of Chinese workers. And because these employment shifts have been gradual, they have not produced widespread unemployment. Currently, China's unemployment rate is about 7 percent, although there is substantial underemployment in many regions.

Problems

China still faces some significant economic problems in its transition to the market system.

Incomplete Property Rights After the initial surges in the 1980s, productivity growth in agriculture has stagnated. A possible reason may be that property rights are incomplete. The Communist Party has opposed privatization of farmland, fearing a reversion to the wealthy landlord system it fought to abolish. Instead, the government policy has been to lease land for 15-year periods. But without ownership rights, many farmers are reluctant to invest in farm equipment and capital improvements on the land. The return on such investment is dependent on the assurance of having land to farm. Thus, further capital investment in Chinese agriculture may be dependent on the right to buy and sell land.

Macroeconomic Instability At times investment booms in China have resulted in too much spending relative to production capacity. The result has been occasional periods of 15 to 25 percent annual rates of inflation. (See column 3 in Table 23-2 for recent Chinese inflation rates.) China is confronting this problem by giving its central bank more power so that when appropriate the bank

TABLE 23-2 Real GDP growth and inflation in China, 1991-1997

(1) Year	(2) Growth of real GDP (percent)	(3) Rate of inflation (percent)
1991	9	3
1992	14	5
1993	13	12
1994	12	22
1995	10	15
1996	9	5
1997*	9	2

*Estimate
Source: International Monetary Fund and Chinese authorities.

can damp down investment spending by raising interest rates. Nevertheless, the financial and monetary control systems in China are still weak and inadequate. One potential problem is that many unprofitable SOEs owe colossal sums of money on loans made by the Chinese state-owned banks (a recent estimate is $96 billion). Because most of these loans are not collectable, there is a danger that China will need to bail out the banks to keep them in operation. If China (through its central bank) simply prints additional money to accomplish this bail-out, renewed inflation could result.

Integration into the Global Economy   China still has much work to do to fully integrate its economy into the world's system of international finance and trade. For example, China is not a member of the World Trade Organization, the successor to GATT, and it still has very high tariffs on many imported goods and restrictions on foreign ownership. In addition, China's record of protecting intellectual property rights such as copyrights, trademarks, and patents is very poor. Unauthorized copying of computer software, movie videos, and compact disks has been a major source of trade friction between China and developed nations.

Geographically Uneven Development   Finally, there is great regional unevenness in China's economic development. This fact is even more apparent now that the former British colony of Hong Kong is part of China. Hong Kong is a wealthy capitalist economy with per-capita income of about $22,000. The standard of living is also relatively high in China's southern provinces and China's coastal cities, although not nearly as high as in Hong Kong. In fact, people living in these special economic zones have been the major beneficiaries of China's rapid growth. In contrast, the majority of people living elsewhere in China have very low incomes. Despite its tremendous growth since 1978, China's per-person income level, on average, suggests that it continues to be a relatively low-income developing country. *(Key Question 8)*

23-3
QUICK REVIEW

- Market reform began earlier in China (1978) than in Russia (1992) and involves gradualism rather than "shock therapy."

- Key elements of China's economic reform are decollectivization of agriculture, establishment of township and village enterprises, price reform, establishment of privately owned urban enterprises, creation of special economic zones, development of support and control institutions, and "corporatization" of state-owned enterprises.

- Since the beginning of market reform in 1978, China's real output and per-capita income have grown at average annual rates of 9 percent and 8 percent, respectively.

- China's economy still faces problems of incomplete property rights, periodic inflation, lack of full integration with the world economy, and great unevenness in regional development.

CONCLUSION

Clearly, Russia and China have taken different paths in their transitions to market systems. It may seem that China's path of dictatorship and gradualism is superior economically (political realities aside) to Russia's path of democracy and swift transformation to capitalism. While Russia has suffered years of declining output and income, China has experienced very high rates of economic growth. But we must not be too hasty in reaching this conclusion. The disorder arising from Russia's abrupt transition to democracy and capitalism may be behind it, placing Russia in a stronger position than China to succeed in the future. The present "forced order" in China via the Communist Party may or may not last. History suggests that *economic* freedom usually creates demands for *political* freedom: free speech, freedom of peaceful assembly, freedom to organize political parties, free elections, and so on. Are China's communist leaders willing and able to design a gradual path towards political freedom? Or is China's period of disorder still to come? We have no answers for these questions. We simply note, in the words of a well-known sage: "the times they are a-changin."[1]

---

[1] Bob Dylan song lyrics from *The Times They Are A-Changin* (1963).

In
The Media

Nervous Kremlin to rein in the ruble

Hoping worst is over, Russia lops three zeros from currency

BY STEVE LIESMAN
THE WALL STREET JOURNAL

MOSCOW—Russia will take a leap of faith tomorrow when it lops three zeros off the much-maligned ruble, banking on an end to the currency's long decline.

The ruble, which trades at about 5,960 to the U.S. dollar, will be valued at around 5.96 when the new year begins.

Since January, 1991, the ruble has tumbled from 25 to the dollar. But most of the dive came in the first four years of reform, as the government waffled on policy and pumped rubles into the economy to prop up Soviet industries.

Since the central bank and the government agreed to control the money supply in 1995, gaining control over inflation, the currency's decline has been more modest. After drops of about 19 per cent in 1995 and 1996, the ruble will measure its best postreform performance this year, posting a 6-per-cent decline against the dollar.

With $18-billion (U.S.) in reserves, a trade surplus and foreign investment, the central bank says it can support the ruble.

Such figures are lost on most average Russians. After six years of economic change and a government that has bungled reforms, Russians harbour distrust. "There

will absolutely be inflation; that's what usually happens with these things," said Olga Loseva, a 40-year-old teacher in Moscow who lives on $30 a month.

In 1991, then-president Mikhail Gorbachev withdrew all 50- and 100-ruble notes and gave people three days to convert their money into smaller bills. In 1993, President Boris Yeltsin withdrew all Soviet-era rubles and allowed only $35 worth to be exchanged. Chaos reigned.

This time, Russians believe they will be hurt. The talk is that a loaf of bread, which sells for 2,800 rubles, will be rounded up and redenominated to three rubles, up about 10 per cent. Some currency traders have reported pressure on the ruble as Russians converted rubles into dollars.

Anders Aslund, with the Carnegie Endowment for International Peace in Washington, said the history of such reforms is mixed. In Poland, it led to minor inflation. In Ukraine, there was none. Russia should see the normal January inflationary increase, which accompanies the gift-giving season, come a little earlier this year. "If you're changing the price tags, you might as well increase them while you're at it," he said.

In about a dozen stores in Moscow, no price increases were

evident. A shop named Gifts had already set out both old and new prices. A set of Russian-made wine glasses that sells for 222,000 rubles will convert to 222 rubles.

"The prices will be exactly the same," insisted Vitaly Kirienov, director of a nearby jewelry store. "There is a lot of competition, so we can't just raise prices." Competition will determine whether the change works by limiting shop owners from rounding prices higher.

Peter Derby, president of Dialog Bank, a Russian-U.S. institution, said it isn't the government or the central bank that will hurt average Russians. This time, he says, they will do it to themselves out of fear. With little reason for redenomination to push prices higher, he said, those who move into dollars will end up paying a 2-percent to 4-per-cent commission.

The most important issue is a psychological one for big Russian currency traders and foreign and domestic institutions, Mr. Derby said. "The question is whether it's easier to go from six to seven rubles than from 6,000 to 7,000."

Source: *Globe and Mail*, December 31, 1997, p. B6. Reprinted by permission of the *Wall Street Journal* © 1997, Dow Jones Company, Inc.

THE STORY IN BRIEF

Russia lops three zeros off its currency, the ruble. It is hoped that this move will mark the beginning of both currency and price stability.

THE ECONOMICS BEHIND THE STORY

- Since the breakup of the Soviet Union, the value of the ruble dropped on international markets. The primary reason for the decline was the rapid expansion of the money supply that led to inflation. The value of the ruble fell from 25 rubles to the U.S. dollar, to 5,960 rubles to the U.S. dollar.

- In January 1998 Russian monetary authorities lopped three zeros off the ruble. Many residents feared inflation, but simply lopping zeros off would

not in itself generate inflation. Given a significant amount of competition, it is unlikely many merchants would "round off" to the next highest number.

- What actions brought inflation under control in Russia? ■

The
Last Word

I THINK EVERYTHING WILL BE OK.

A Russian baked-goods company is successfully making the difficult transition to capitalism.

MOSCOW (AP)—IN SOVIET TIMES, A MOVIE might have had a heroine much like Lyudmila Korilkova. She would be dressed in a white smock, her dark hair tufting out from behind a scarf, the tools of industrial production in her hands.

"I love my job very much," she would say. "Otherwise, I would not have stayed here for 40 years." Actually, Korilkova—in the smock and scarf, a pastry bag in her hand—said those words just the other day. More amazing still, she seemed to mean them. Maybe it had something to do with the fact that on January 1, her factory doubled her salary.

In today's Russian economy, Korilkova is a lucky woman. She works for a baked-goods company, Bolshevik, which has weathered the transition to a market economy and under new French management appears poised on the brink of success. Last year, Bolshevik's production increased for the first time in eight years. The improvement was modest—3 percent—but it comes close to mirroring national statistics that suggest the worst years of Russia's economic transition may be in the past.

You can see this at a company like Bolshevik, which has betrayed its name and wholeheartedly joined the capitalist mainstream. Siou and Company, as it was originally called, was founded by a French couple in Moscow in 1855. By the late 19th century, it was the biggest cookie baker in Russia. It acquired its current name in 1924, when it was nationalized by the new Bolshevik (communist) government. Even now, a statue of Bolshevik leader Vladimir Lenin stands watch over the court-

yard of the landmark brick factory. By the late 1980s, Bolshevik was turning out 78,000 tons of cookies, cakes and other baked goods a year, as dictated by central planners. Quality was poor, factory workers now say, and production methods archaic.

In 1992, after the collapse of the Soviet Union, Bolshevik was privatized. In 1994, the French yogurt-maker Groupe Danone bought a 59 percent stake. In 1996, with sales slumping 14 percent a year, Danone brought in a Franco-Russian manager, Jacques Ioffe, to turn things around. A former physicist from St. Petersburg, Ioffe emigrated to France in 1977, went to business school and wound up managing a publishing company in Paris. Fluent in Russian, French and English, he had the credentials Danone was looking for.

"Danone said, 'Look, we've got a big company, we don't know what to do with it, we don't understand what they're saying,'" Ioffe recalled during an interview in his office, which is decorated with photos of Paris and little French and Russian flags. The biggest problem he found at Bolshevik was one of mentality. The Russian managers, while well meaning, simply couldn't grasp the idea of a market economy. There was no sales department, no marketing department, and the idea of basing production plans on sales was still foreign.

Today, all that is changing. The new marketing department recently unveiled its first billboard, just outside the factory gates. Television commercials will follow in June. And while Bolshevik now produces only half as much as it did a decade ago, it is producing what the market wants. Ioffe has set a goal of 20 percent growth for 1998. "Before, the quality lacked," said Svetlana Gritskova, who has worked at Bolshevik for 20 years and is in charge of assembling cakes for special orders. Now, she said, quality is much better. Plus, "our production is more versatile."

A few yards away, Korilkova decorated cakes, squeezing pink icing out of a pastry bag to form delicate flowers. Although her methods rely on classic—and simple—French tools, she pointed approvingly to modern mixers and refrigerators nearby. "We've become better

technically equipped," she said. "Before, the state showed little concern for equipment to make our lives easier." Nor did it do what her current bosses have done: raise her monthly salary from $250 to $500. Others may fret, but Korilkova is now optimistic about the future of Russia.

"Yes," she said. "I think everything will be OK." ■

Source: "Russia's Economy May Be Past Worst," Associated Press, January 25, 1998. Printed by permission of the Associated Press.

CHAPTER SUMMARY

1. The labour theory of value is a central principle of Marxian ideology. Capitalists, as property owners, allegedly expropriate most of labour's value as profits, or surplus value. The supposed solution was for the workers and peasants to take control of all production processes through their representative: the Communist Party.

2. Virtually complete state ownership of property resources, collective farming, and central planning were the major features of the Soviet economy and the prereform Chinese economy.

3. Characteristics of Soviet and Chinese central planning included **a** emphasis on industrialization, rural development (in China), and military strength; **b** overcommitment of resources through the central plans; **c** allocation of resources by bureaucracy rather than market decisions; **d** government price setting; **e** economic self-sufficiency; and **f** passive macroeconomic policies.

4. Central planners in the Soviet Union and China faced a coordination problem, which was the difficulty of achieving internal consistency in plans to avoid bottlenecks and the chain reaction of production failures that they cause. The more complex their economies became, the greater became the problem of coordinating inputs and outputs.

5. Central planners also faced a difficult incentive problem. Without private property, entrepreneurship, and availability of consumer goods, it proved difficult if not impossible to achieve efficiency, promote innovation, and induce hard work.

6. Along with the difficulties of central planning, the collapse of the Soviet economy resulted from a diminishing growth rate, limited and shoddy consumer goods, a large military burden, and stagnation of agriculture.

7. The key elements of the Russian transition to capitalism were privatizing firms, establishing market-based prices, promoting greater competition, liberalizing international trade and finance, and ending rapid inflation. Russia's transition to capitalism has not been easy. Output and income have declined, income inequality has increased, and social problems such as crime and alcoholism have worsened. Nevertheless, Russia has succeeded in making its reforms largely irreversible, and its output and income are now expected to rise.

8. Market reform in China has differed from reform in Russia in several ways: **a** it began earlier than in Russia (1978 compared to 1992); **b** it was not precipitated by collapse of the political system, as was true in Russia; **c** it has used a gradual approach, not "shock therapy"; **d** it has been directed by the Communist Party, not by anticommunist reformers; and **e** it only recently has begun the process of privatizing state-owned enterprises, whereas Russia has privatized most of its industry.

9. China's market reforms began with leasing of farmland and allowing farmers to sell increasing amounts of their output at market-determined rather than state-determined prices. Subsequent reforms included the establishment of township and village enterprises and urban collectives (both are types of private enterprises) and the setting up of special enterprise zones open to international trade and direct foreign investment. More recently, China's reforms have involved development of support and control institutions for the market system and the corporatization of state-owned enterprises, in some cases via issuance of stock.

10. China's reforms have generated two decades of rapid economic growth, with real GDP rising by 9 percent annually and per-capita income rising by 8 percent annually. Nevertheless, this growth has been very uneven geographically and at times has been accompanied by rapid inflation. To continue its success, China may have to end prohibitions against ownership of land, integrate its economy more fully with the international system of trade and finance, and privatize state industries.

TERMS AND CONCEPTS

labour theory of value
surplus value
state ownership
central economic planning
coordination problem

incentive problem
township and village enterprises
state-owned enterprises
urban collectives
special economic zones

STUDY QUESTIONS

1. Compare the economic ideology of the former Soviet Union and prereform China with that of the capitalist economies as to the **a** source and role of profits, **b** ownership of capital, and **c** best method of allocating resources.

2. What does the term "central economic planning" mean? Describe the coordination problem that central planners in the Soviet Union and prereform China faced. Explain how a planning failure can cause a chain reaction of additional failures.

3. Why were new product introductions and the use of new methods of production so uncommon in the Soviet Union and prereform China compared to such capitalist economies as the United States?

4. What factors contributed to the collapse of the Soviet economy?

5. KEY QUESTION *Use a supply and demand diagram to explain why persistent shortages of many consumer goods occurred under central planning in the Soviet Union and in prereform China. Why were black markets common in each country?*

6. KEY QUESTION *What are the major components of economic reform in Russia? What is meant when these reforms are described as "shock therapy"? How successful has Russia been thus far in its reforms?*

7. In what general respects have Chinese economic reforms differed from those of Russia? Do you believe that these differences account for China's higher growth rate? Why?

8. KEY QUESTION *Relate each of the following items to the success of market reform in China:* **a** *leasing farm land,* **b** *price reform,* **c** *private rural and urban enterprises,* **d** *special economic zones, and* **e** *corporatization of state-owned enterprises.*

9. What progress has China achieved in its transition to a market economy? What problems remain?

10. Do you think that China's economic reforms will eventually result in the demise of the Communist Party in China? Explain your answer.

11. "Paradoxically, Russia's disorder may provide a firmer base for future growth than China's order." Do you agree or disagree? Explain.

12. **(The Last Word)** Why was "marketing" a foreign concept to managers such as those of the baked-goods enterprise discussed in this chapter's Last Word? Why do you think the quality of the baked goods produced in this enterprise has increased?

13. WEB-BASED QUESTION **Russia's Transition to a Market Economy—Today's Business Headlines** Russia Today www.russiatoday.com/rtoday/business/business.html provides weekday business headlines about

Russia. Review the Russian business headlines for the past two weeks. Identify which are related to its transition to a market economy (e.g., increased company profit) and which are nontransition-related (e.g., cold weather depletes heating-oil stocks). What portion of the transition-related headlines are reporting difficulties? What portion are describing success stories?

14. **WEB-BASED QUESTION** **China and Hong Kong—Beyond 1997** On July 1, 1997, Hong Kong, the world's fourth-largest trading entity, entered a new phase of its existence as Asia's business hub. After a 14-year transition period, its status changed from that of a Dependent Territory of Britain to that of a Special Administration Region of China. How is Hong Kong's capitalist system supposed to survive the control of China's Communist Party? Visit the South China Morning Post www.scmp.com/ for your answers.

Glossary

Ability-to-pay principle The idea that those who have greater income (or wealth) should pay a greater proportion of it as taxes than those who have less income (or wealth).

Abstraction Elimination of irrelevant and noneconomic facts to obtain an *economic principle*.

Actual budget A listing of amounts spent by the federal government (to purchase goods and services and for *transfer payments*) and the amounts of tax revenue collected by it in any (fiscal) year.

Actual deficit The size of the federal government's *budget deficit* actually recorded in any particular year.

Actual investment The amount that *firms* do invest; equal to *planned investment* plus *unplanned investment*.

Actual reserves The funds that a bank has on deposit at the Bank of Canada (plus its *vault cash*).

Adaptive expectations theory The idea that people determine their expectations about future events (for example, inflation) on the basis of past and present events (rates of inflation) and only change their expectations as events unfold.

Adjustable pegs The device used in the *Bretton Woods system* to alter *exchange rates* in an orderly way to eliminate persistent payments deficits and surpluses. Each nation defined its monetary unit in terms of (pegged it to) gold or the dollar, kept the *rage of exchange* for its money stable in the short run, and adjusted its rate in the long run when faced with international payments disequilibrium.

Adverse selection problem A problem arising when information known to one party to a contract is not known to the other party, causing the latter to incur major costs. Example: Individuals who have the poorest health are more likely to buy health insurance.

Advertising A seller's activities in communicating its message about its product to potential buyers.

Affirmative action Policies and programs that establish targets of increased employment and promotion for women and minorities.

Aggregate demand A schedule or curve that shows the total quantity of goods and services demanded (purchased) at different *price levels*.

Aggregate demand-aggregate supply model The macroeconomic model that uses *aggregate demand* and *aggregate supply* to determine and explain the *price level* and the real *domestic output*.

Aggregate expenditures The total amount spent for final goods and services in the economy.

Aggregate expenditures-domestic output approach Determination of the equilibrium gross domestic product by finding the real GDP at which aggregate expenditures equal *domestic output*.

Aggregate expenditures schedule A schedule or curve showing the total amount spent for final goods and services at different levels of GDP.

Aggregate supply A schedule or curve showing the total quantity of goods and services supplied (produced) at different *price levels*.

Aggregation Combining individual units or data into one unit or number. For example, all prices of individual goods and services are combined into a *price level*, or all units of output are aggregated into *real gross domestic product*.

Agricultural Stabilization Board The federal agency established in 1958 to support the following commodities at not less than 90 percent of their average price over the previous five years, with adjustments according to production costs: cattle, hogs, and sheep; industrial milk and cream; and oats and barley not produced on the Prairies (where the *Canadian Wheat Board* has jurisdiction).

Allocative efficiency The apportionment of resources among firms and industries to obtain the production of the products most wanted by society (consumers); the output of each product at which its *marginal cost* and *price* or *marginal benefit* are equal.

American Federation of Labor (AFL) The American organization of affiliated *craft unions* formed in 1886.

Anti-combines (*See* Combines Investigation Act.)

Anti-Inflation Board The federal agency established in 1975 (and disbanded in 1979) to administer the government's inflation control program.

Applied economics (*See* Policy economics.)

Appreciation (of the dollar) An increase in the value of the dollar relative to the currency of another nation so that a dollar buys a larger amount of the foreign currency and thus of foreign goods.

"Asian tigers" The newly industrialized and rapidly growing nations of Hong Kong, Singapore, South Korea, and Taiwan.

Asset Anything of monetary value owned by a firm or individual.

Asymmetric information A situation where one party to a market transaction has much more information about a product or service than the other; the result may be an under- or overallocation of resources.

Authoritarian capitalism An economic system in which property resources are privately owned and government extensively directs and controls the economy.

Average fixed cost A firm's total *fixed cost* divided by output (the quantity of product produced).

Average product The total output produced per unit of a resource employed (*total product* divided by the quantity of that employed resource).

Average revenue Total revenue from the sale of a product divided by the quantity of the product sold (demanded); equal to the price at which the product is sold when all units of the product are sold at the same price.

Average tax rate Total tax paid divided by total (taxable) income, as a percentage.

Average propensity to consume Fraction (or percentage) of *disposable income* that households plan to spend for consumer goods and services; consumption divided by *disposable income*.

Average propensity to save Fraction (or percentage) of *disposable income* that households save; *saving* divided by *disposable income*.

Average tax rate Total tax paid divided by total (taxable) income, as a percentage.

Balanced budget multiplier The extent to which an equal change in government spending and taxes changes equilibrium gross domestic product; always has a value of 1, since it is equal to the amount of the equal changes in G and T.

Balance of payments (*See* International balance of payments).

Balance of payments deficit The amount by which the sum of the *balance on current account* and the *balance on the capital account* is negative in a year.

Balance on current account The exports of goods and services of a nation less its imports of goods and services plus its *net investment income* and *net transfers* in a year.

Balance on goods and services (*See* Balance of trade.)

Balance on the capital account The *capital inflows* of a nation less its *capital outflows*.

Balance sheet A statement of the *assets*, *liabilities*, and *net worth* of a firm or individual at some given time.

Bank rate The interest rate that the Bank of Canada charges on advances (*normally* very short-term loans) made to the chartered banks.

Bankers' bank A bank that accepts the deposits of and makes loans to *chartered banks*; in Canada, the Bank of Canada.

Barter The exchange of one good or service for another good or service.

Base year The year with which other years are compared when an index is constructed; for example, the base year for a *price index*.

Benefit-cost analysis Comparing the *marginal benefits* of a government project or program with the *marginal costs* to decide whether to employ resources in that project or program, and to what extent.

Benefit-reduction rate The percentage of any increase in earned income by which subsidy benefits in a *negative income tax* plan are reduced.

Bond A financial device through which a borrower (a firm or government) is obligated to pay the principle and interest on a loan at a specific date in the future.

Brain drain The emigration of highly educated, highly skilled workers from a country.

Break-even income The level of *disposable income* at which *households* plan to consume (spend) all their income and to save none of it; also denotes that level of earned income at which subsidy payments become zero in an income transfer program.

Bretton Wood system The international monetary system developed after World War II in which *adjustable pegs* were employed, the *International Monetary Fund* helped to stabilize foreign exchange rates, and gold and the dollar were used as *international monetary reserves*.

Budget deficit The amount by which the expenditures of the federal government exceed its revenues in any year.

Budget surplus The amount by which the revenues of the federal government exceed its expenditures in any year.

Built-in stabilizer A mechanism that increases government's budget deficit (or reduces its surplus) during a recession and increases government's budget surplus (or reduces its deficit) during inflation without any action by policymakers; the tax system is one such mechanism.

Business cycle Recurring increases and decreases in the level of economic activity over periods of years. Consists of peak, recession, trough, and recovery phases.

Business firm (*See* Firm.)

Canada Assistance Plan The federal Act under which the federal government makes funds available to the provinces for their programs of assistance to disabled, handicapped, unemployed who are not entitled to unemployment insurance benefits, and other needy persons.

Canada Deposit Insurance Corporation Federal Crown Corporation that, for a fee payable by the chartered banks and federally chartered trust companies, insures their customers' deposits up to a limit of $60,000 per customer per bank or trust company.

Canada Labour Code The federal law of 1970 that consolidated previous legislation regulating employment practices, labour standards, and so on, in the federal jurisdiction.

Canada Pension Plan The compulsory, contributory, earnings-related federal pension plan that covers most employed members of the labour force between the ages of 18 and 65, and payable at the latter age; it came into effect in 1965; there is transferability between the Plan and the Quebec Pension Plan, which applies to the people of that province.

Canada-United States Free Trade Agreement (FTA) An accord that came into effect on January 1, 1989, to eliminate all *tariffs* between the two countries over the following ten years.

Canadian Congress of Labour (CCL) The federation of *industrial unions* formed in 1940 and affiliated with the *Congress of Industrial Organizations*; amalgamated into *Canadian Labour Congress* in 1956.

Canadian International Development Agency (CIDA) The federal agency responsible for the operation and administration of Canada's international development assistance programs of approximately $2.5 billion a year.

Canadian Labour Congress (CLC) The largest federation of *labour unions* in Canada, with 3 million members in international and national unions; founded in 1956 on the amalgamation of the *Canadian Congress of Labour* and the *Trades and Labour Congress of Canada*.

Canadian Payments Association The federal agency set up in 1982 to provide for *cheque clearing*.

Canadian Wheat Board Federal Crown Corporation established in 1935, which does not own or operate grain-handling facilities but has complete control over the way western wheat is marketed and the price at which it is sold. The Board also acquired complete control of the supplies of all Prairie coarse grains in 1949.

Capital Human-made resources (buildings, machinery, and equipment) used to produce goods and services; goods that do not directly satisfy human wants; also called capital goods.

Capital account The section of a nation's *international balance of payments* statement in which are recorded the foreign purchases of assets in Canada (producing money *capital inflows*) and Canadian purchases of assets abroad (producing money *capital outflows* of that nation).

Capital account deficit A negative *balance on the capital account*.

Capital account surplus A positive *balance on the capital account*.

Capital consumption allowances Estimate of the amount of *capital* worn out or used up (consumed) in producing the *gross domestic product*; depreciation.

Capital flight The transfer of savings from developing countries to industrially advanced countries to avoid government expropriation, taxation, and high rates of inflation or to realize better investment opportunities.

Capital gain The gain realized when securities or properties are sold for a price greater than the price paid for them.

Capital goods (*See* Capital.)

Capital inflow The expenditures made by the residents of foreign nations to purchase real and financial capital from the residents of a nation.

Capital-intensive commodity A product that requires a relatively large amount of *capital* to produce.

Capitalism (*See* Pure capitalism.)

Capital outflow The expenditures made by the residents of a nation to purchase real and financial capital from the residents of foreign nations.

Capital-saving technological advance An improvement in *technology* that permits a greater quantity of a product to be produced with a specific amount of *capital* (or permits the same amount of the product to be produced with a smaller amount of capital).

Capital stock The total available *capital* in a nation.

Capital-using technological advance An improvement in *technology* that requires the use of a greater amount of *capital* to produce a specific quantity of a product.

Causation A relationship in which the occurrence of one or more events brings about another event.

Central bank A bank whose chief function is the control of the nation's *money supply*; in Canada, the Bank of Canada.

Central economic planning Government determination of the objectives of the economy and how resources will be directed to attain those objectives.

***Ceteris paribus* assumption** (*See* "Other things equal" assumption.)

Change in demand A change in the *quantity demanded* of a good or service at every price; a shift of the *demand curve* to the left or right.

Change in supply A change in the *quantity supplied* of a good or service at every price; a shift of the *supply curve* to the left or right.

Chartered bank One of the multibranched, privately owned, commercial, financial intermediaries that have received charters by Act of Parliament and that alone, with Quebec Savings Banks, may call themselves "banks"; and which accept *demand deposits*.

Chartered banking system All *chartered banks* as a group.

Checkoff The deduction by an employer of union dues from the pay of workers and the transfer of the amount deducted to a *labour union*.

Chequable deposit Any deposit in a *chartered bank* or other financial intermediary (trust company, credit union, etc.) against which a cheque may be written and which deposit, if it is in a bank, is thus part of the *M1* money supply.

Cheque clearing The process by which funds are transferred from the *chequing accounts* of the writers of cheques to the *chequing accounts* of the recipients of the cheques; also called the "collection" of cheques.

Chequing account A *demand deposit* in a chartered bank.

Circular flow model The flow of resources from *households* to *firms* and of products from firms to households. These flows are accompanied by reverse flows of money from firms to households and from households to firms.

Civilian labour force Persons 15 years of age and older who are not residents of the Yukon or the Northwest Territories, who are not in institutions or the armed forces, and who are employed for a wage or salary, seeking such employment, or self-employed for gain.

Classical economics The macroeconomic generalizations accepted by most economists before the 1930s that led to the conclusion that a capitalistic economy was self-regulating and therefore would usually employ its resources fully.

Closed economy An economy that neither exports nor imports goods and services.

Coincidence of wants A situation in which the good or service that one trader desires to obtain is the same as that which another trader desires to give up, and an item that the second trader wishes to acquire is the same as that which the first trader desires to surrender.

COLA (*See* Cost-of-living adjustment.)

Combines Investigation Act The federal Act, first passed in 1910, whose avowed aim is to prevent agreements to lessen competition unduly; amended and renamed the Competition Act in June 1986.

Command economy An economic system (method of organization) in which property resources are publicly owned and government uses *central economic planning* to direct and coordinate economic activities.

Commercial bank (*See* Chartered bank.)

Communism (*See* Command economy.)

Comparative advantage A lower relative or comparative cost than another producer.

Competing goods (*See* Substitute goods.)

Competition The presence in a market of a large number of independent buyers and sellers competing with one another and the freedom of buyers and sellers to enter and leave the market.

Complementary goods Products and services that are used together; when the price of one falls the demand for the other increases (and conversely).

Complex multiplier The *multiplier* that exists when changes in the *gross domestic product* change *net taxes* and *imports*, as well as *saving*.

Conglomerate combination A group of *plants* owned by a single *firm* and engaged at one or more stages in the production of different products (of products that do not compete with each other).

Congress of Industrial Organizations (CIO) The organization of affiliated *Industrial unions* formed in the United States in 1936.

Consumer goods Products and services that satisfy human wants directly.

Consumer price index (CPI) An index that measures the prices of a fixed "market basket" of some 600 goods and services bought by a "typical" consumer.

Consumer sovereignty Determination by consumers of the types and quantities of goods and services that will be produced with the scarce resources of the economy; consumer direction of production through their dollar votes.

Consumption of fixed capital Estimate of the amount of *capital* worn out or used up (consumed) in producing the *gross domestic product*; also called depreciation.

Consumption schedule A schedule showing the amounts *households* plan to spend for *consumer goods* at different levels of *disposable income*.

Contractionary fiscal policy A decrease in *government expenditures* for goods and services, an increase in *net taxes*, or some combination of the two, for the purpose of decreasing *aggregate demand* and thus controlling inflation.

Coordination failure A situation in which people do not reach a mutually beneficial outcome because they lack some way to jointly coordinate their actions; a possible cause of macroeconomic instability.

Corporate income tax A tax levied on the net income (profit) of corporations.

Corporation A legal entity ("person") chartered by a province or the federal government that is distinct and separate from the individuals who own it.

Correlation A systematic and dependable association between two sets of data (two kinds of events); does not necessarily indicate causation.

Cost-of-living adjustment (COLA) An automatic increase in the incomes (wages) of workers when inflation occurs; guaranteed by a collective bargaining contract between firms and workers.

Cost-push inflation Increases in the price level (inflation) resulting from an increase in resource costs (for example, higher wage rates and raw material prices)

and hence in *per-unit production costs*; inflation caused by reductions in *aggregate supply*.

Cost ratio An equality showing the number of units of two products that can be produced with the same resources; the cost ratio 1 corn = 3 olives shows that the resources required to produce 3 units of olives must be shifted to corn production to produce a unit of corn.

Craft union A *labour union* that limits its membership to workers with a particular skill (craft).

Credit An accounting item that increases the value of an asset (such as the foreign money owned by the residents of a nation).

Credit union An association of persons who have a common tie (such as being employees of the same firm or members of the same labour union) that sells shares to (accepts deposits from) its members and makes loans to them.

Crowding model of occupational discrimination A model of labour markets suggesting that *occupational discrimination* has kept many women and minorities out of high-paying occupations and forced them into a limited number of low-paying occupations.

Crowding-out effect A rise in interest rates and a resulting decrease in *planned investment* caused by the federal government's increased borrowing in the money market.

Currency Coins and paper money.

Currency appreciation (*See* Exchange rate appreciation.)

Currency depreciation (*See* Exchange rate depreciation.)

Current account The section in a nation's *international balance of payments* that records its exports and imports of goods and services, its *net investment income*, and its *net transfers*.

Customary economy (*See* Traditional economy.)

Cyclically adjusted budget What the budget balance would be for the total government sector if the economy were operating at an average or cyclically adjusted level of activity.

Cyclically adjusted deficit The budget deficit that would have occurred even though the economy was operating at an average or cyclically adjusted level of activity.

Cyclical unemployment A type of *unemployment* caused by insufficient total spending (or by insufficient *aggregate demand*).

Cyclically balanced budget The quality of government expenditures and *net tax collections* over the course of a *business cycle*; deficits incurred during periods of recession are offset by surpluses obtained during periods of prosperity (inflation).

Debit An accounting item that decreases the value of an asset (such as the foreign money owned by the residents of a nation).

Deduction Reasoning from assumptions to conclusions; a method of reasoning that first develops a hypothesis (an assumption) and then tests the hypothesis with economic facts.

Deflating Finding the *real gross domestic product* by decreasing the dollar value of the GDP for a year in which prices were higher than in the *base year*.

Deflation A decline in the economy's *price level*.

Demand A schedule showing the amounts of a good or service buyers (or a buyer) wish to purchase at various prices during some time period.

Demand curve A curve illustrating *demand*.

Demand deposit A deposit in a *chartered bank* against which cheques may be written; a *chequable deposit*.

Demand-deposit multiplier (*See* Monetary multiplier.)

Demand factor (in growth) The increase in the level of *aggregate demand* that brings about the *economic growth* made possible by an increase in the production potential of the economy.

Demand management The use of *fiscal policy* and *monetary policy* to increase or decrease *aggregate demand*.

Demand-pull inflation Increases in the price level (inflation) resulting from an excess of demand over output at the existing price level, caused by an increase in *aggregate demand*.

Dependent variable A variable that changes as a consequence of a change in some other (independent) variable; the "effect" or outcome.

Depository institutions Firms that accept the deposits of *money* of the public (businesses and persons); *chartered banks*, and other *financial intermediaries*.

Depreciation (*See* Capital consumption allowance.)

Depreciation (of the dollar) A decrease in the value of the dollar relative to another currency so that a dollar buys a smaller amount of the foreign currency and therefore of foreign goods.

Derived demand The demand for a resource that depends on the demand for the products it can be used to produce.

Desired reserves The amount of vault cash each chartered bank chooses to keep on hand for daily transaction. This amount includes reserves held at the Bank of Canada for cheque settlements among the chartered banks.

Determinants of aggregate demand Factors such as consumption spending, *investment*, government spending, and *net exports* that, if they change, shift the *aggregate demand curve*.

Determinants of aggregate supply Factors such as input prices, *productivity*, and the legal-institutional environment that, if they change, shift the *aggregate supply curve*.

Determinants of demand Factors other than its price that determine the quantities demanded of a good or service.

Determinants of supply Factors other than its price that determine the quantities supplied of a good or service.

Devaluation A decrease in the governmentally defined value of a currency.

DI (*See* Disposable income.)

Developing countries Many countries of Africa, Asia, and Latin America that are characterized by a lack of capital goods, use of nonadvanced technologies, low literacy rates, high unemployment, rapid population growth, and labour forces heavily committed to agriculture.

Differentiated product A product that differs physically or in some other way from the similar products produced by other *firms*; a product such that buyers are *not* indifferent to the seller from whom they purchase it when the price charged by all sellers is the same.

Direct foreign investment The building of new factories (or the purchase of existing capital) in a particular nation by corporations of other nations.

Direct relationship The relationship between two variables that change in the same direction, for example, product price and quantity supplied.

Discouraged workers Employees who have left the *labour force* because they have not been able to find employment.

Discrimination According individuals or groups inferior treatment in hiring, occupational access, education and training, promotion, wage rates, or working conditions, even though they have the same abilities, education and skills, and work experience as other workers.

Discretionary fiscal policy Deliberate changes in taxes (tax rates) and government spending by Parliament to promote full employment, price stability, and economic growth.

Diseconomies of scale Increase in the *average total cost* of producing a product as the *firm* expands the size of its *plant* (its output) in the *long run*.

Disinflation A reduction in the rate of *inflation*.

Disposable income *Personal income* less personal taxes; income available for *personal consumption expenditures* and *personal saving*.

Dissaving Spending for consumer goods and services in excess of *disposable income*; the amount by which *personal consumption expenditures* exceed disposable income.

Dividends Payments by a corporation of all or part of its profit to its stockholders (the corporate owners).

Division of labour Dividing the work required to produce a product into a number of different tasks that are performed by different workers; *specialization* of workers.

Dollar votes The "votes" that consumers and entrepreneurs cast for the production of consumer and capital goods, respectively, when they purchase them in product and resource markets.

Domestic capital formation Addition to a nation's stock of *capital* by saving and investing part of its own domestic output.

Domestic output *Gross* (or net) *domestic product*; the total output of final goods and services produced in the economy.

Domestic price The price of a good or service within a country, determined by domestic demand and supply.

Double taxation The taxation of both corporate net income (profits) and the *dividends* paid from this net income when they become the personal income of households.

Dumping The sale of products below cost in a foreign country or below the prices charged at home.

Durable good A consumer good with an expected life (use) of three or more years.

Dynamic efficiency The development over time of more efficient (less costly) techniques of producing existing products and of improved products; technological progress.

E-cash Electronic money; an entry (usable as money) stored in a computer or a stored-value card ("smart card").

Earnings The money income received by a worker; equal to the *wage* (rate) multiplied by the amount of time worked.

Easy money policy Bank of Canada actions to increase the *money supply* to lower interest rates and expand *real GDP*.

Economic analysis Deriving *economic principles* from relevant economic facts.

Economic cost A payment that must be made to obtain and retain the services of a *resource*; the income a firm must provide to a resource supplier to attract the resource away from an alternative use; equal to the quantity of other products that cannot be produced when resources are instead used to make a particular product.

Economic efficiency Obtaining the socially optimal amounts of goods and services using minimum necessary resources; entails both *productive efficiency* and *allocative efficiency*.

Economic growth (1) An outward shift in the *production possibilities curve* that results from an increase in resource supplies or quality or an improvement in *technology*; (2) an increase either in real output (*gross domestic product*) or in real output per capita.

Economic integration Cooperation among and the complete or partial unification of the economies of different nations; the elimination of barriers to trade among these nations; the bringing together of the markets in each of the separate economies to form one large (a common) market.

Economic law (*See* Economic principle.)

Economic model A simplified picture of economic reality; an abstract generalization.

Economic perspective A viewpoint that envisions individuals and institutions making rational decisions by comparing the marginal benefits and marginal costs associated with their actions.

Economic policy A course of action intended to correct or avoid a problem.

Economic principle A widely accepted generalization about the economic behaviour of individuals and institutions.

Economic profit The *total revenue* of a firm less all its *economic costs*; also called "pure profit" and "above normal profit."

Economic regulation (*See* Industrial regulation.)

Economic rent The price paid for the use of land and other natural resources, the supply of which is fixed (*perfectly inelastic*).

Economic resources The *land, labour, capital*, and *entrepreneurial ability* that are used in the production of goods and services; productive agents; factors of production.

Economics The social science dealing with the use of scarce resources to obtain the maximum satisfaction of society's virtually unlimited material wants.

Economic theory Deriving *economic principles* from relevant economic facts; an *economic principle.*

Economic system A particular set of institutional arrangements and a coordinating mechanism for solving the economizing problem; a method of organizing an economy; of which the *market economy, command economy,* and *traditional economy* are three general types.

Economies of scale Reductions in the *average total cost* of producing a product as the firm expands the size of plant (its output) in the *long run*; the economies of mass production.

Economizing problem The choices necessitated because society's material wants for goods and services are unlimited but the *resources* available to satisfy these wants are limited (scarce).

Efficiency factors (in growth) The capacity of an economy to combine resources effectively to achieve growth of real output that the *supply factors* (of growth) make possible.

Efficient allocation of resources That allocation of the resources of an economy among the production of different products that leads to the maximum satisfaction of the wants of consumers; producing the socially optimal mix of output with society's scarce resources.

Employment insurance The insurance program that in Canada is financed by compulsory contributions from employers and employees and from the general tax revenues of the federal government with benefits (income) made available to insured workers who are unable to find jobs.

Employment rate The percentage of the *civilian labour force* employed at any time.

Entrepreneurial ability The human resources that combine the other resources to produce a product, make nonroutine decisions, innovate, and bear risks.

Equation of exchange $MV = PQ$, in which M is the supply of money, v is the *velocity of money*, p is the *price level*, and Q is the physical volume of *final goods and services* produced.

Equilibrium real domestic output The *gross domestic product* at which the total quantity of final goods and services purchased (*aggregate expenditures*) is equal to the total quantity of final goods and services produced (the real domestic output); the real domestic output at which *aggregate demand curve* intersects the *aggregate supply curve.*

Equilibrium price The *price* in a competitive market at which the *quantity demanded* and the *quantity supplied* are equal; where there is neither a shortage nor a surplus; and where there is no tendency for price to rise or fall.

Equilibrium price level The price level at which the *aggregate demand curve* intersects the *aggregate supply curve.*

Equilibrium quantity The quantity demanded and supplied at the equilibrium price in a competitive market.

European Union (EU) An association of European nations initiated in 1958 that has eliminated tariffs and import quotas that existed among them, established common tariffs for goods imported from outside the member nations, allowed the free movement of labour and capital among them, and created other common economic policies.

Excess reserves The amount by which a chartered bank's *actual reserves* exceed its *desired reserves*; actual reserves minus desired reserves.

Exchange control (*See* Foreign exchange control.)

Exchange rate The *rate of exchange* of one nation's currency for another nation's currency.

Exchange rate application An increase in the value of a nation's currency in foreign exchange markets; an increase in the *rate of exchange* for foreign currencies.

Exchange rate depreciation A decrease in the value of a nation's currency in foreign exchange markets; a decrease in the *rate of exchange* for foreign currencies.

Exchange rate determinant Any factor other than the *rate of exchange* that determines a currency's demand and supply in the *foreign exchange market.*

Excise tax A tax levied on the production of a specific product or on the quantity of the product purchased.

Exclusion principle The ability to exclude those who do not pay for a product from receiving its benefits.

Exhaustive expenditure An expenditure by government resulting directly in the employment of *economic resources* and in the absorption by government of the goods and services those resources produce; a *government purchase.*

Expanding industry An industry whose firms earn *economic profits* and experience an increase in output as new firms enter the industry.

Expansionary fiscal policy An increase in *government expenditures* for goods and services, a decrease in *net taxes*, or some combination of the two for the purpose of increasing *aggregate demand* and expanding real output.

Expectations The anticipations of consumers, firms, and others about future economic conditions.

Expected rate of return The increase in profit a firm anticipates it will obtain by purchasing capital (or engaging in research and development), expressed as a percentage of the total cost of the investment (or R&D) activity.

Expenditure approach The method that adds all expenditures made for *final goods and services* to measure the *gross domestic product*.

Expenditures-output approach (*See* Aggregate expenditures-domestic output approach.)

Export controls The limitation or prohibition of the export of certain products on the basis of foreign policy or national security objectives.

Exports Goods and services produced in a nation and sold to customers in other nations.

Export subsidies Government payments to domestic producers to enable them to reduce the *price* of a good or service to foreign buyers.

Export supply curve An upsloping curve showing the amount of a product domestic firms will export at each *world price* above the *domestic price*.

Export transactions A sale of a good or service that increases the amount of foreign currency flowing to the citizens, firms, and governments of a nation.

External benefit (*See* Spillover benefit.)

External cost (*See* Spillover cost.)

External debt Private or public debt owed to foreign citizens, firms, and institutions.

Externality (*See* Spillover.)

Face value The dollar or cents value stamped on a coin.

Factors of production *Economic resources: land, capital, labour,* and *entrepreneurial ability.*

Fallacy of composition Incorrectly reasoning that what is true for the individual (or part) is necessarily true for the group (or whole).

Fallacy of limited decisions The false notion that there are a limited number of economic decisions to be made so that, if government makes more decisions, there will be fewer private decisions to render.

Feedback effects (or monetary policy) The effects that a change in the money supply will have (because it affects the interest rate, planned investment, and the equilibrium GDP) on the demand for money, which is itself directly related to the GDP.

Fiat money Anything that is *money* because government has decreed it to be money.

Final goods and services Goods and services that have been purchased for final use and not for resale or further processing or manufacturing.

Financial capital (*See* Money capital.)

Financial intermediary A *chartered bank* or other financial institution (trust or mortgage loan company, credit union, *caisse populaire*), which uses the funds (savings) deposited with it to make loans (for consumption or investment).

Firm An organization that employs resources to produce a good or service for profit and owns and operates one or more *plants*.

Fiscal policy Changes in government spending and tax collections designed to achieve a full-employment and noninflationary domestic output; also called *discretionary fiscal policy*.

Five fundamental economic questions The five questions that every economy must answer: how much to produce, what to produce, how to produce it, how to divide the total output, and how to ensure economic flexibility.

Fixed cost Any cost which in total does not change when the *firm* changes its output; the cost of *fixed resources*.

Fixed exchange rate A *rate of exchange* that is set in some way and hence prevented from rising or falling with changes in currency supply and demand.

Flexible exchange rate A *rate of exchange* determined by the international demand for and supply of a nation's money; a rate free to rise or fall (to float).

Floating exchange rate (*See* Flexible exchange rate.)

Foreign competition (*See* Import competition.)

Foreign exchange control The control a government may exercise over the quantity of foreign currency demanded by its citizens and firms and over the *rates of exchange* in order to limit its *outpayments* to its *inpayments* (to eliminate a *payments deficit*).

Foreign exchange market A market in which the money (currency) of one nation can be used to purchase (can be exchanged for) the money of another nation.

Foreign exchange rate (*See* Rate of exchange.)

Foreign trade effect The inverse relationship between the *net exports* of an economy and its price level relative to foreign price levels.

45-degree line A line along which the value of *GDP* (measured horizontally) is equal to the value of *aggregate expenditures* (measured vertically).

Fractional reserve A *reserve ratio* that is less than 100 percent of the deposit liabilities of *chartered bank*.

Freedom of choice The freedom of owners of property resources to employ or dispose of them as they see fit, of workers to enter any line of work for which they are qualified, and of consumers to spend their incomes in a manner that they think is appropriate.

Freedom of enterprise The freedom of *firms* to obtain economic resources, to use these resources to produce products of the firm's own choosing, and to sell their products in markets of their choice.

Free-rider problem The inability of potential providers of an economically desirable but indivisible good or service to obtain payment from those who benefit, because the *exclusion principle* is not applicable.

Free trade The absence of artificial (government-imposed) barriers to trade among individuals and firms in different nations.

Frictional unemployment A type of unemployment caused by workers voluntarily changing jobs and by temporary layoffs; unemployed workers between jobs.

Full employment (1) Use of all available resources to produce want-satisfying goods and services. (2) The situation when the *unemployment rate* is equal to the *full-employment unemployment rate* and there is *frictional* and *structural* but no *cyclical unemployment* (and the *real output* of the economy equals its *potential real output*).

Full-employment budget A comparison of the government expenditures and tax collections that would occur if the economy operated at *full employment* throughout the year.

Full-employment unemployment rate The *unemployment rate* at which there is no *cyclical unemployment* of the *labour force*; equal to about 7.5 percent in Canada because some *frictional* and *structural unemployment* is unavoidable.

Full production Employment of available resources so that the maximum amount of (or total value of) goods and services is produced; occurs when both *productive efficiency* and *allocative efficiency* are realized.

Functional distribution of income The manner in which *national income* is divided among the functions performed to earn it (or the kinds of resources provided to earn it); the division of national income into wages and salaries, proprietors' income, corporate profits, interest, and rent.

Functional finance The use of *fiscal policy* to achieve a noninflationary full employment *gross domestic product* without regard to the effect on the *public debt*.

G-7 Nations A group of seven major industrial nations (the United States, Japan, Germany, United Kingdom, France, Italy, and Canada) whose leaders meet regularly to discuss common economic problems and try to coordinate economic policies. (Recently has also include Russia, making it unofficially the G-8.)

Gains from trade The extra output that trading partners obtain through specialization of production and exchange of goods and services.

GDP (*See* Gross domestic product.)

GDP deflator The *price index* found by dividing *nominal GDP* by *real GDP*; a price index used to adjust money (or nominal) GDP to real GDP.

GDP gap The amount by which actual *gross domestic product* falls below potential *gross domestic product*.

General Agreement on Tariffs and Trade (GATT) The international agreement reached in 1947 in which 23 nations agreed to give equal and nondiscriminatory treatment to the other nations, to reduce tariff rates by multinational negotiations, and to eliminate *import quotas*. Now includes most nations and has become the *World Trade Organization*.

Generalization Statement of the nature of the relation between two or more sets of facts.

Gold standard A historical system of fixed exchange rates in which nations defined their currency in terms of gold, maintained a fixed relationship between their stock of gold and their money supplies, and allowed gold to be freely exported and imported.

Government purchases Disbursements of money by government for which government receives a currently produced good or service in return; the expenditures of all governments in the economy for *final goods and services*.

Government transfer payment The disbursement of money (or goods and services) by government for which government receives no currently produced good or service in return.

Gross domestic product (GDP) The total market value of all *final goods and services* produced annually within the boundaries of Canada, whether by Canadian or foreign-supplied resources.

Gross private domestic investment Expenditures for newly produced *capital goods* (such as machinery, equipment, tools, and buildings) and for additions to inventories.

Guaranteed annual income The minimum income a family (or individual) would receive if a *negative income tax* were to be adopted.

Guaranteed Income Supplement A 1966 amendment to the *Old Age Security Act* provides for the payment of a full supplement to pensioners with no other income and a partial supplement to those with other, but still low, income.

Guiding function of prices The ability of price changes to bring about changes in the quantities of products and resources demanded and supplied.

Horizontal axis The "left-right" or "west-east" axis on a graph or grid.

Horizontal combination A group of *plants* in the same stage of production that are owned by a single *firm*.

Household An economic unit (of one or more persons) that provides the economy with resources and uses the income received to purchase goods and services that satisfy material wants.

Human capital The accumulation of prior investments in education, training, health, and other factors that increase productivity.

Human-capital investment Any expenditure undertaken to improve the education, skills, health, or mobility of workers, with an expectation of greater productivity and thus a positive return on the investment.

Hyperinflation A very rapid rise in the price level.

Hypothesis A tentative, untested economic principle.

IMF (*See* International Monetary Fund.)

Import competition The competition that domestic firms encounter from the products and services of foreign producers.

Import demand curve A downsloping curve showing the amount of a product that an economy will import at each *world price* below the *domestic price*.

Import quota A limit imposed by a nation on the quantity (or total value) of a good that may be imported during some period of time.

Imports Spending by individuals, *firms*, and governments for goods and services produced in foreign nations.

Import transaction The purchase of a good or service that decreases the amount of foreign money held by citizens, firms, and governments of a nation.

Income approach The method that adds all the income generated by the production of *final goods and services* to measure the *gross domestic product*.

Income effect A change in the price of a product changes a consumer's *real income* (*purchasing power*) and thus the quantity of the product purchased.

Income inequality The unequal distribution of an economy's total income among persons or families.

Income-maintenance system Government programs designed to eliminate poverty and reduce inequality in the distribution of income.

Increase in demand An increase in the *quantity demanded* of a good or service at every price; a shift of the *demand curve* to the right.

Increase in supply An increase in the *quantity supplied* of a good or service at every price; a shift in the *supply curve* to the right.

Independent goods Products or services for which there is no relationship between the price of one and the demand for the other; when the price of one rises or falls, the demand for the other remains constant.

Independent variable The variable causing a change in some other (dependent) variable.

Indirect business taxes Such taxes as *sales*, *excise*, and business *property taxes*, licence fees, and *tariffs* that firms treat as costs of producing a product and pass on (in whole or in part) to buyers by charging higher prices.

Individual demand The demand schedule or *demand curve* of a single buyer.

Individual supply The supply schedule or *supply curve* of a single seller.

Induction A method of reasoning that proceeds from facts to *generalization*.

Industrially advanced countries High-income countries such as Canada, the United States, Japan, and the nations of western Europe that have highly developed *market economies* based on large stocks of technologically advanced capital goods and skilled labour forces.

Industrial policy Any policy by which government takes a direct and active role in promoting specific firms or industries for purposes of expanding their output and achieving economic growth; called "technology policy" when its goal is to promote technological advance.

Industrial regulation The older and more traditional type of regulation in which government is concerned with the prices charged and the services provided the public in specific industries; in contrast to *social regulation*.

Industrial union A *labour union* that accepts as members all workers employed in a particular industry (or by a particular firm).

Industry A group of (one or more) *firms* that produce identical or similar products.

Inferior good A good or service whose consumption declines as income rises (and conversely), price remaining constant.

Inflating Determining real *gross domestic product* by increasing the dollar value of the nominal *gross domestic product* produced in a year in which prices are lower than in a *base year*.

Inflation A rise in the general level of prices in an economy.

Inflation premium The component of the *nominal interest rate* that reflects anticipated inflation.

Inflationary expectations The belief of workers, firms, and consumers that substantial inflation will occur in the future.

Inflationary gap The amount by which the equilibrium GDP exceeds full employment GDP.

Infrastructure The capital goods usually provided by the *public sector* for the use of its citizens and firms (for example, highways, bridges, transit systems, wastewater treatment facilities, municipal water systems, and airports).

Injection An addition of spending to the income-expenditure stream; *investment, government purchases,* and *net exports.*

In-kind investment (*See* Nonfinancial investment.)

Innovation The first commercially successful introduction of a new product, the use of a new method of production, or the creation of a new form of business organization.

In payments The receipts of its own or foreign money that individuals, firms, and governments of one nation obtain from the sale of goods and services abroad, or as investment income, *remittances*, and *capitals inflows* from abroad.

Insider-outsider theory The hypothesis that nominal wages are inflexible downward because firms are aware that workers ("insiders") who retain employment during recession may refuse to work cooperatively with previously unemployed workers ("outsiders") who offer to work for less than the current wage.

Interest The payment made for the use of money (of borrowed funds).

Interest income Payments of income to those who supply the economy with *capital.*

Interest rate The annual rate at which interest is paid; a percentage of the borrowed amount.

Interest-rate effect The tendency for increases in the *price level* to increase the demand for money, raise interest rates, and, as a result, reduce total spending in the economy (and the reverse for price level decreases).

Intermediate goods Products that are purchased for resale or further processing or manufacturing.

Internally held public debt *Public debt* owed to citizens, firms, and institutions of the same nation issuing the debt.

International balance of payments A summary of all the transactions that took place between the individuals, firms, and government unit of one nation and those in all other nations during a year.

International balance of payments deficit (*See* Balance of payments deficit.)

International balance of payments surplus (*See* Balance of payments surplus.)

International Bank for Reconstruction and Development (*See* World Bank.)

International gold standard (*See* Gold standard.)

International Monetary Fund (IMF) The international association of nations that was formed after World War II to make loans of foreign monies to nations with temporary *payments deficits* and, until the early 1970s, to administer the *adjustable pegs*; it now mainly makes loans to nations facing possible defaults on private and government loans.

International monetary reserves The foreign currencies and such assets as gold a nation may use to settle a *payments deficit.*

International value of the dollar The price that must be paid in foreign currency (money) to obtain one Canadian dollar.

Intrinsic value The market value of the metal within a coin.

Inventories Goods that have been produced but are still unsold.

Inverse relationship The relationship between two variables that change in opposite directions, for example, product price and quantity demanded.

Investment Spending for the production and accumulation of *capital* and additions to inventories.

Investment goods Same as *capital.*

Investment schedule A curve or schedule that shows the amounts firms plan to invest at various possible values of *real gross domestic product.*

Investment-demand curve A curve that shows the amount of *investment* demanded by an economy at a series of *real interest rates*.

Investment in human capital (*See* Human-capital investment.)

Invisible hand The tendency of firms and resource suppliers seeking to further their own self-interests in competitive markets to also promote the interest of society as a whole.

Keynesian economics The macroeconomic generalizations that lead to the conclusion that a capitalistic economy is characterized by macroeconomic instability and that *fiscal policy* and *monetary policy* can be used to promote *full employment*, *price-level stability*, and *economic growth*.

Keynesianism The philosophical, ideological, and analytical views pertaining to *Keynesian economics*.

Labour The physical and mental talents and efforts of people that are used to produce goods and services.

Labour force Persons 15 years of age and older who are not in institutions and who are employed or are unemployed (and seeking work).

Labour force participation rate The percentage of the working-age population that is actually in the *labour force*.

Labour-intensive commodity A product requiring a relatively large amount of *labour* to produce.

Labour productivity Total output divided by the quantity of labour employed to produce it; the *average product* of labour or output per worker per hour.

Labour theory of value The Marxian idea that the economic value of any commodity is determined solely by the amount of labour required to produce it.

Labour union A group of workers organized to advance the interests of the group (to increase wages, shorten the hours worked, improve working conditions, and so on).

Laffer curve A curve showing the relationship between tax rates and the tax revenues of government and on which there is a tax rate (between zero and 100 percent) where tax revenues are a maximum.

Laissez faire capitalism (*See* Pure capitalism.)

Land Natural resources ("free gifts of nature") used to produce goods and services.

Land-intensive commodity A product requiring a relatively large amount of land to produce.

Law of demand The principle that, other things equal, an increase in a product's price will reduce the quantity of it demanded; and conversely for a decrease in price.

Law of increasing opportunity costs As the production of a good increases, the *opportunity cost* of producing an additional unit rises.

Law of supply The principle that, other things equal, an increase in the price of a product will increase the quantity of it supplied; and conversely for a price decrease.

Leakage (1) A withdrawal of potential spending from the income-expenditures stream via *saving*, tax payments, or *imports*. (2) A withdrawal that reduces the lending potential of the banking system.

Leakages-injections approach Determination of the equilibrium *gross domestic product* by finding the real GDP at which *leakages* are equal to *injections*.

Least-cost combination of resources The quantity of each resource a firm must employ in order to produce a particular output at the lowest total cost.

Legal tender Anything that government says must be accepted in payment of a debt.

Lending potential of an individual chartered bank The amount by which a single bank can safely increase the *money supply* by making new loans to (or buying securities from) the public; equal to the bank's excess reserves.

Lending potential of the banking system The amount by which the banking system can increase the money supply by making new loans to (or buying securities from) the public; equal to the *excess reserves* of the banking system multiplied by the *monetary multiplier*.

Liability A debt with a monetary value; an amount owed by a firm or an individual.

Limited liability Restriction of the maximum loss to a predetermined amount for the owners (stockholders) of a *corporation*, the maximum loss is the amount they paid for their shares of stock.

Limited-liability company An unincorporated business whose owners are protected by *limited liability*.

Liquidity *Money* or things that can be quickly and easily converted into money with little or no loss of purchasing power.

Long run (1) In *microeconomics*, a period of time long enough to enable producers of a product to change the quantities of all the resources they employ; period in which all resources and costs are variable and no resources or costs are fixed. (2) In *microeconomics*, a period sufficiently long for *nominal wages* and other input prices to change in response to a change in the nation's *price level*.

Long-run aggregate supply curve The *aggregate supply curve* associated with a time period in which input prices (especially *nominal wages*) are fully responsive to changes in the *price level*.

Lump-sum tax A tax that is a constant amount (the tax revenue of government is the same) at all levels of GDP.

M1 The narrowly defined *money supply*; the *currency* (coins and *paper money*) and *demand deposits* in *chartered banks* not owned by the federal government or banks.

M2 Includes, in addition to M1, Canadian dollar personal savings deposits and nonpersonal notice deposits at chartered banks.

M2+ Includes, in addition to M2, deposits at trust and mortgage loan companies, and deposits and shares at *caisses populaires* and credit unions.

Macroeconomics The part of economics concerned with the economy as a whole; with such major aggregates as the household, business, and governmental sectors; and with measures of the total economy.

Managed floating exchange rate An *exchange rate* that is allowed to change (float) as a result of changes in currency supply and demand but at times is altered (managed) by governments via their buying and selling of particular currencies.

Marginal analysis The comparison or marginal ("extra" or "additional") benefits and marginal costs, usually for decision making.

Marginal benefit The extra (additional) benefit of consuming one more unit of some good or service; the change in total benefit when one more unit is consumed.

Marginal cost The extra (additional) cost of producing one more unit of output; equal to the change in *total cost* divided by the change in output (and in the short run to the change in total *variable cost* divided by the change in output).

Marginal propensity to consume The fraction of any change in *disposable income* spent for *consumer goods*; equal to the change in consumption divided by the change in disposable income.

Marginal propensity to import The fraction of any change in income (*gross domestic product*) spent for imported goods and services; equal to the change in *imports* divided by the change in income.

Marginal propensity to save The fraction of any change in *disposable income* that households save; equal to the change in *saving* divided by the change in disposable income.

Marginal tax rate The tax rate paid on each additional dollar of income.

Marginal utility The extra *utility* a consumer obtains from the consumption of one additional unit of a good or service; equal to the change in total utility divided by the change in the quantity consumed.

Market Any institution or mechanism that brings together buyers (demanders) and sellers (suppliers) of a particular good or service.

Market demand (*See* Total demand.)

Market economy An economy in which only the private decisions of consumers, resource suppliers, and firms determine how resources are allocated; the market system.

Market failure The failure of a market to bring about the allocation of resources that best satisfies the wants of society. In particular, the over- or underallocation of resources to the production of a particular good or service because of *spillovers* or informational problems and because markets fail to provide desired *public goods*.

Market socialism An *economic system* (method of organization) in which property resources are publicly owned *and* markets and prices are used to direct and coordinate economic activities.

Market system All the product and resource markets of a *market economy* and the relationships among them; a method that allows the prices determined in these markets to allocate the economy's scarce resources and to communicate and coordinate the decisions made by consumers, firms, and resource suppliers.

Medium of exchange Items sellers generally accept and buyers generally use to pay for a good or service; *money*; a convenient means of exchanging goods and services without engaging in *barter*.

Microeconomics The part of economics concerned with such individual units as *industries, firms,* and *households*; and with individual markets, particular prices, and specific goods and services.

Minimum wage The lowest *wage* employers may legally pay for an hour of work.

Mixed capitalism An economy in which both government and private decisions determine how resources are allocated.

Monetarism The macroeconomic view that the main cause of changes in aggregate output and the price level are fluctuations in the *money supply*; advocates a *monetary rule*.

Monetary multiplier The multiple of its *excess reserves* by which the banking system can expand *demand deposits* and thus the *money supply* by making new loans (or buying securities); and equal to one divided by the *desired reserve ratio*.

Monetary policy A central bank's changing of the *money supply* to influence interest rates and assist the economy in achieving a full-employment, noninflationary level of total output.

Monetary rule The rule suggested by *monetarism*; the *money supply* should be expanded each year at the same annual rate as the potential rate of growth of the *real gross domestic product*; the supply of money should be increased steadily at from 3 to 5 percent per year.

Money Any item that is generally acceptable to sellers in exchange for goods and services.

Money capital Money available to purchase *capital*.

Money income (*See* Nominal income.)

Money interest rate The *nominal interest rate*; the interest rate that includes an *inflationary premium* (if any).

Money market The market in which the demand for and the supply of money determine the *interest rate* (or the level of interest rates) in the economy.

Money supply Narrowly defined, *M1*; more broadly defined, *M2* and *M2+*.

Money wage (*See* Nominal wage.)

Money wage rate (*See* Nominal wage.)

Monopoly A market structure in which the number of sellers is so small that each seller is able to influence the total supply and the price of the good or service. (Also see *Pure monopoly*.)

Most-favoured-action (MFN) status An agreement by Canada to allow some other nation's *exports* into Canada at the lowest tariff level levied by Canada, then or at any later time.

Multinational corporation A firm that owns production facilities in other countries and produces and sells its product abroad.

Multiple counting Wrongly including the value of *intermediate goods* in the *gross domestic product*; counting the same good or service more than once.

Multiplier The ratio of a change in the *equilibrium GDP* to the change in *investment* or in any other component of *aggregate expenditures* or *aggregate demand*; the number by which a change in any component of aggregate expenditures or aggregate demand must be multiplied to find the resulting change in the equilibrium GDP.

Multiplier effect The effect on equilibrium GDP of a change in *aggregate expenditures* or *aggregate demand* (caused by a change in the *consumption schedule, investment, government expenditures*, or *net exports*).

Mutually exclusive goals Two or more goals that conflict and cannot be achieved simultaneously.

National Policy Sir John A. Macdonald's 1879 policy of high tariff protection for Canadian (Ontario and Quebec) secondary manufacturers.

National income Total income earned by resource suppliers for their contributions to *gross national product*; equal to the gross domestic product minus *nonincome charges*, minus *net foreign factor income*.

National income accounting The techniques used to measure the overall production of the economy and other related variables for the nation as a whole.

Natural monopoly An industry in which *economies of scale* are so great the product can be produced by one firm at a lower average total cost than if the product were produced by more than one firm.

Natural rate hypothesis The idea that the economy is stable in the long run at the *natural rate of unemployment*; views the long-run *Phillips Curve* as vertical at the *natural rate of unemployment*.

Natural rate of unemployment The *full-employment unemployment rate*; the unemployment rate occurring when there is no cyclical unemployment and the economy is achieving its potential output; the unemployment rate at which actual inflation equals expected inflation.

Near-money Financial assets, the most important of which are saving, term, and notice deposits in chartered banks, trust companies, credit unions, and other savings institutions, that are not a medium of exchange but can be readily converted into money.

Negative income tax The proposal to subsidize families and individuals with money payments when their incomes fall below a *guaranteed (annual) income*; the negative tax would decrease as earned income increases (*see* Benefit-reduction rate).

Negative relationship (*See* Inverse relationship.)

Net domestic product *Gross domestic product* less the part of the year's output that is needed to replace the *capital goods* worn out in producing the output; the nation's total output available for consumption or additions to the *capital stock*.

Net export effect The idea that the impact of a change in *monetary policy* or *fiscal policy* will be strengthened or weakened by the consequent change in *net exports*; the change in net exports occurs because of changes in real interest rates, which affect exchange rates.

Net exports *Exports* minus *imports*.

Net foreign factor income Payments by a nation of resource income to the rest of the world minus receipts of resource income from the rest of the world.

Net investment income The interest and dividend income received by the residents of a nation from residents of other nations less the interest and dividend payments made by the residents of that nation to the residents of other nations.

Net taxes The taxes collected by government less *government transfer payments*.

Net transfers The personal and government transfer payments made by one nation to residents of foreign nations, less the personal and government transfer payments received from residents of foreign nations.

Net worth The total *assets* less the total *liabilities* of a firm or an individual; the claims of the owners of a firm against its total assets.

New classical economics The theory that, although unanticipated price level changes may create macroeconomic instability in the short run, the economy is stable at the full-employment level of domestic output in the long run because prices and wages adjustment automatically correct movements away from the full employment, noninflationary output.

Nominal gross domestic product (GDP) The *GDP* measured in terms of the price level at the time of measurement (unadjusted for *inflation*).

Nominal income The number of dollars received by an individual or group for its resources during some period of time.

Nominal interest rate The interest rate expressed in terms of annual amounts currently charged for interest and not adjusted for inflation.

Nominal wage The amount of money received by a worker per unit of time (hour, day, etc.); money wage.

Nondiscretionary fiscal policy (*See* Built-in stabilizer).

Nondurable good A *consumer good* with an expected life (use) of less than three years.

Nonexhaustive expenditure An expenditure by government that does not result directly in the employment of economic resources or the production of goods and service; see *Government transfer payment*.

Nonfinancial investment An investment that does not require *households* to save a part of their money incomes;

but which uses surplus (unproductive) labour to build *capital goods*.

Nonincome charges *Capital consumption allowance* and *indirect business taxes*; amounts subtracted from *GDP* (along with *net investment income* from non-residents) in determining *national income*.

Nonincome determinants of consumption and saving All influences on *consumption* and *saving* other than the level of *GDP*.

Noninterest determinants of investment All influences on the level of investment spending other than the *interest rate*.

Noninvestment transaction An expenditure for stocks, bonds, or second-hand *capital goods*.

Nonmarket transactions The production of goods and services excluded in the measurement of the *gross domestic product* because they are not bought and sold.

Nonprice competition The means other than decreasing the prices of their products that *firms* employ to increase the sale of their products; and that includes *product differentiation*, advertising, and sales promotion activities.

Nonproduction transaction The purchase and sale of any item that is not a currently produced good or service.

Nontariff barriers All barriers other than *protective tariffs* that nations erect to impede international trade: include *import quotas*, licensing requirements, unreasonable product-quality standards, unnecessary red tape in customs procedures, and so on.

Normal good A good or service whose consumption increases when income increases and falls when income decreases, price remaining constant.

Normal profit The payment made by a firm to obtain and retain *entrepreneurial ability*; the minimum income entrepreneurial ability must receive to induce it to perform entrepreneurial functions for a firm.

Normative economics The part of economics involving value judgements about what the economy should be like; concerned with which economic goals and policies should be implemented.

North American Free Trade Agreement (NAFTA) A 1993 agreement establishing, over a 15-year period, a free trade zone composed of Canada, Mexico, and the United States.

Occupational discrimination The form of discrimination that excludes women from certain occupations and the higher wages paid workers in these occupations.

Official reserves (*See* Official international reserves.)

Official international reserves The international monetary assets owned by the federal government and held in its behalf by the Bank of Canada in the Exchange Fund Account.

Okun's Law The generalization that any one percentage point rise in the *unemployment rate* above the *full-employment unemployment rate* will increase the GDP gap by 2 percent of the *potential output* (GDP) of the economy.

Old Age Security Act The 1951 federal Act, as subsequently amended, by which a pension is payable to every person aged 65 and older provided the person has resided in Canada for ten years immediately preceding the approval of an application for pension; in addition a *Guaranteed Income Supplement* may be paid; the pension is payable in addition to the *Canada Pension*.

Oligopoly A market structure in which a few firms sell either a *standardized* or *differentiated product*, into which entry is difficult, in which the firm has limited control over product price because of *mutual interdependence* (except when there is collusion among firms), and in which there is typically *nonprice competition*.

OPEC An acronym for the *Organization of Petroleum Exporting Countries*.

Open economy An economy that exports and imports goods and services.

Open-market operations The buying and selling of Canadian government bonds by the Bank of Canada for purposes of carrying out *monetary policy*.

Opportunity cost The amount of other products that must be forgone or sacrificed to produce a unit of a product.

Organization of Petroleum Exporting Nations (OPEC) The cartel formed in 1970 by 13 oil-producing countries to control the price and quantity of crude oil exported by its members, and that accounts for a large proportion of the world's export of oil.

Other things equal assumption The assumption that factors other than those being considered are held constant.

Outpayments The expenditures of its own or foreign currency that the individuals, firms, and governments of one nation make to purchase goods and services, for *remittances*, as investment income, and *capital outflows* abroad.

Overnight loans rate The interest rate chartered banks, investment dealers, and other financial market participants borrow and lend funds for one day.

Paper money Pieces of paper used as a *medium of exchange*; in Canada, Bank of Canada notes.

Partnership An unincorporated firm owned and operated by two or more persons.

Patent An exclusive right to inventors to produce and sell a new product or machine for a set period of time.

Payments deficit (*See* Balance of payments deficit.)

Payments surplus (*See* Balance of payments surplus.)

Per-capita GDP *Gross domestic product* (GDP) per person; the average GDP of a population.

Per-capita income A nation's total income per person; the average income of a population.

Perfect inelastic supply A change in price results in no change in the *quantity supplied* of a product or resource; the *quantity supplied* is the same at all prices.

Personal consumption expenditures The expenditures of *households* for *durable* and *nondurable consumer goods* and services.

Personal distribution of income The manner in which the economy's *personal* or *disposable income* is divided among different income classes or different households.

Personal income The earned and unearned income available to resource suppliers and others before the payment of *personal income taxes*.

Personal income tax A tax levied on the taxable income of individuals, households, and unincorporated firms.

Personal saving The *personal income* of households less *personal taxes* and *personal consumption expenditures*; *disposable income* not spent for *consumer goods*.

Per-unit production cost The average production cost of a particular level of output; total input cost divided by units of output.

Phillips Curve A curve showing the relationship between the *unemployment rate* (on the horizontal axis) and the annual rate of increase in the *price level* (on the vertical axis).

Planned economy An economy in which government determines how resources are allocated.

Planned investment The amount that *firms* plan or intend to invest.

Plant A physical establishment that performs one or more functions in the production, fabrication, and distribution of goods and services.

Policy economics The formulation of courses of action to bring about desired economic outcomes or to prevent undesired occurrences.

Political business cycle The alleged tendency of Parliament to destabilize the economy by reducing taxes and increasing government expenditures before elections and to raise taxes and lower expenditures after elections.

Positive economics The analysis of facts or data to establish scientific generalizations about economic behaviour.

Positive relationship Direct relationship between two variables.

Post hoc, ergo propter hoc **fallacy** Incorrectly reasoning that when one event precedes another the first event must have caused the second event.

Potential output The real output (*GDP*) an economy can produce when it fully employs its available resources.

Premature inflation A type of inflation that sometimes occurs before the economy has reached *full employment*.

Price The amount of money needed to buy a particular good, service, or resource.

Price index An index number that shows how the weighted average price of a "market basket" of goods changes through time.

Price leadership An informal method that firms in an *oligopoly* may employ to set the price of their product: one firm (the leader) is the first to announce a change in price and the other firms (the followers) soon announce identical or similar changes.

Price level The weighted average of the prices of all the final goods and services produced in an economy.

Price level surprises Unanticipated changes in the price level.

Price-level stability A steadiness of the price-level from one period to the next; zero or low annual inflation; also called "price stability."

Price-wage flexibility Changes in the *prices* of products and in the *wages* paid to workers; the ability of prices and wages to rise or fall.

Price war Successive and continued decreases in the prices charged by the firms in an oligopolistic industry; each firm lowers its price below rivals' prices, hoping to increase it sales and revenues at its rivals' expense.

Prime interest rate The *interest rate* banks charge their most credit-worthy borrowers—for example, large corporations with excellent financing credentials.

Principal-agent problem A conflict of interest that occurs when agents (workers or managers) pursue their own objectives to the detriment of the principal's (stockholders) goals.

Private good A good or service subject to the *exclusion principle* and that is provided by privately owned firms to consumers who are willing to pay for it.

Private property The right of private persons and firms to obtain, own, control, employ, dispose of, and bequeath *land*, *capital*, and other property.

Private sector The *households* and business *firms* of the economy.

Production possibilities curve A curve showing the different combinations of two goods or services that can be produced in a *full-employment, full-production* economy where the available supplies of resources and technology are fixed.

Productive efficiency The production of a good in the least costly way; occurs when production takes place at the output at which *average total cost* is a minimum and at which *marginal product* per dollar's worth of input is the same for all inputs.

Productivity A measure of average output or real output per unit of input. For example, the productivity of labour may be determined by dividing real output by hours of work.

Productivity slowdown The decline in the rate at which *labour productivity* in Canada has increased in recent decades.

Product differentiation Physical or other differences between the products of different *firms* that result in individual buyers preferring (so long as the price charged by all sellers is the same) the product of one *firm* to the products of the other *firms*.

Product market A market in which products are sold by *firms* and bought by *households*.

Profit The return to the resource entrepreneurial ability (*see* Normal profit); *total revenue* minus *total cost* (*see* Economic profit).

Profit sharing plan A compensation device through which workers receive part of their pay in the form of a share of their employer's profit (if any).

Progressive tax A tax whose *average tax rate* increases as the taxpayer's income increases and decreases as the taxpayer's income decreases.

Property tax A tax on the value of property (*capital*, *land*, stocks and bonds, and other *assets*) owned by *firms* and *households*.

Proportional tax A tax whose *average tax rate* remains constant as the taxpayer's income increases or decreases.

Proprietor's income The net income of the owners of unincorporated firms (proprietorships and partnerships).

Protective tariff A *tariff* designed to shield domestic producers of a good or service from the competition of foreign producers.

Public debt The total amount owed by the federal government to the owners of government securities; equal to the sum of past government *budget deficits* less government *budget surpluses.*

Public finance The branch of economics that analyzes government revenues and expenditures.

Public good A good or service that is indivisible and to which the *exclusion principle* does not apply; a good or service with these characteristics provided by government.

Public sector The part of the economy that contains all government entities; government.

Purchasing power The amount of goods and services that a monetary unit of income can buy.

Purchasing power parity The idea that exchange rates between nations equate the purchasing power of various currencies; exchange rates between any two nations adjust to reflect the price level differences between the countries.

Pure capitalism An economic system in which property resources are privately owned and markets and prices are used to direct and coordinate economic activities.

Pure monopoly A *market* in which one *firm* sells a unique product (one for which there are no close substitutes), into which entry is blocked, in which the *firm* has considerable control over the price at which the product sells, and in which *nonprice competition* may or may not be found.

Pure rate of interest An essentially risk-free, long-term interest rate that is free of the influence of market imperfections.

Quantity demanded The amount of a good or service buyers (or a buyer) desire to purchase at a particular price during some period.

Quantity supplied The amount of a good or service producers (or a producer) offer to sell at a particular price during some period.

Quasi-public good A good or service to which the *exclusion principle* could apply, but that has such a large *spillover benefit* that government sponsors its production to prevent an underallocation of resources.

R&D Research and development activities undertaken to bring about *technological advance.*

Ratchet effect The tendency for the *price level* to rise when *aggregate demand increases,* but not fall when aggregate demand declines.

Rate of exchange The price paid in one's own money to acquire one unit of a foreign currency; the rate at which the money of one nation is exchanged for the money of another nation.

Rate of return The gain in net revenue divided by the cost of an investment or an *R&D* expenditure; expressed as a percentage.

Rational expectations theory The hypothesis that firms and households expect monetary and fiscal policies to have certain effects on the economy and (in pursuit of their own self-interests) take actions that make these policies ineffective.

Rationing function of prices The ability of market forces in a competitive market to equalize *quantity demanded* and *quantity supplied* and to eliminate shortages and surpluses via changes in prices.

Real-balances effect (*See* Wealth effect.)

Real business cycle theory A theory that *business cycles* result from changes in technology and resource availability, which affect *productivity* and thus increase or decrease *long-run aggregate supply.*

Real capital (*See* Capital.)

Real gross domestic product (GDP) *Gross domestic product* adjusted for inflation; gross domestic product in a year divided by the *GDP deflator* for that year, expressed as a decimal.

Real GDP (*See* Real gross domestic product.)

Real income The amount of goods and services that can be purchased with *nominal income* during some period of time; nominal income adjusted for inflation.

Real interest rate The interest rate expressed in dollars of constant value (adjusted for *inflation*); and equal to the *nominal interest rate* less the expected rate of inflation.

Real wage The amount of goods and services a worker can purchase with his or her *nominal wage*; the purchasing power of the nominal wage.

Recession A period of declining real GDP, accompanied by lower real income and higher unemployment.

Recessionary gap The amount by which equilibrium GDP falls short of full employment GDP.

Refinancing the public debt Paying owners of maturing government securities with money obtained by selling new securities or with new securities.

Regressive tax A tax whose *average tax rate* decreases as the taxpayer's income increases and increases as the taxpayer's income decreases.

Remittance A gift or grant; a payment for which no good or service is received in return; the funds sent by workers who have legally or illegally entered a foreign nation to their families in the nations from which they have migrated.

Resource market A market in which *households* sell and *firms* buy resources or the services of resources.

Retiring the public debt Reducing the size of the *public debt* by paying money to owners of maturing Government of Canada securities.

Revaluation An increase in the governmentally defined value of its currency relative to other nations' currencies.

Revenue tariff A *tariff* designed to produce income for the federal government.

Roundabout production The construction and use of *capital* to aid in the production of *consumer goods*.

Rule of 70 A method for determining the number of years it will take for some measure to double, given its annual percentage increase. Example: To determine the number of years it will take for the *price level* to double, divide 70 by the annual rate of *inflation*.

Sales tax A tax levied on the cost (at retail) of a broad group of products.

Saving Disposable income not spent for consumer goods; equal to *disposable income* minus *personal consumption expenditures*.

Savings deposit A deposit that is interest-bearing and that can normally be withdrawn by the depositor at any time.

Saving schedule A schedule that shows the amounts *households* plan to save (plan not to spend for *consumer goods*), at different levels of *disposable income*.

Say's law The largely discredited macroeconomic generalization that the production of goods and services (supply) creates an equal *demand* for these goods and service.

Scarce resources The limited quantities of *land, capital, labour,* and *entrepreneurial ability* that are never sufficient to satisfy the virtually unlimited material wants of humans.

Seasonal variations Increases and decreases in the level of economic activity within a single year, caused by a change in the season.

Secular trend Long-term tendency; change in some variable over a very long period of years.

Self-interest That which each firm, property owner, worker, and consumer believes is best for itself and seeks to obtain.

Seniority The length of time a worker has been employed absolutely or relative to other workers; may be used to determine which workers will be laid off when there is insufficient work for them all, and who will be rehired when more work becomes available.

Separation of ownership and control The fact that different groups of people own a *corporation* (the stockholders) and manage it (the directors and officers).

Service An (intangible) act or use for which a consumer, firm, or government is willing to pay.

Shirking Actions by workers to increase their *utility* or well-being by neglecting or evading work.

Shortage The amount by which the *quantity demanded* of a product exceeds the *quantity supplied* at a particular (below-equilibrium) price.

Short run (1) In macroeconomics, a period in which nominal wages and other input prices to not change in response to a change in the price level. (2) In microeconomics, a period of time in which producers are able to change the quantity of some but not all of the resources they employ; a period in which some resources (usually plant) are fixed and some are variable.

Short-run aggregate supply curve An aggregate supply curve relevant to a time period in which input prices (particularly *nominal wages*) do not change in response to changes in the *price level*.

Simple multiplier The *multiplier* in an economy in which government collects no *net taxes*, there are no *imports*, and *investment* is independent of the level of income; equal to one divided by the *marginal propensity to save*.

Slope of a line The ratio of the vertical change (the rise or fall) to the horizontal change (the run) between any two points on a line. The slope of an upward sloping line is positive, reflecting a direct relationship between two variables; the slope of a downward sloping line is negative, reflecting an inverse relationship between two variables.

Social accounting (*See* National income accounting.)

Social regulation The newer and different type of regulation in which government is concerned with the conditions under which goods and services are produced, their physical characteristics, and the impact of their production on society; in contrast to *industrial regulation*.

Sole proprietorship An unincorporated *firm* owned and operated by one person.

Special economic zones Regions of China open to foreign investment, private ownership, and relatively free international trade.

Specialization The use of the resources of an individual, a firm, a region, or a nation to produce one or a few goods and services.

Speculation The activity of buying or selling with the motive of later reselling or rebuying for profit.

Spillover A benefit or cost from production or consumption, accruing without compensation to nonbuyers and nonsellers of the product (see *Spillover benefit* and *spillover cost*).

Spillover benefit A benefit obtained without compensation by third parties from the production or consumption of sellers or buyers. Example: A beekeeper benefits when a neighbouring farmer plants clover.

Spillover costs A cost imposed without compensation on third parties by the production or consumption of sellers or buyers. Example: A manufacturer dumps toxic chemicals into a river, killing the fish sought by sport fishers.

Stagflation Inflation accompanied by stagnation in the rate of growth of output and an increase in unemployment in the economy; simultaneous increases in the *price level* and the *unemployment rate*.

Standardized product A product such that buyers are indifferent to the seller from whom they purchase it so long as the price charged by all sellers is the same; a product such that all units of the product are perfect substitutes for each other (are identical).

State-owned enterprises Businesses that are owned by government; the major types of enterprises in Russia and China before their transitions to the market system.

Stock (corporate) An ownership share in a corporation.

Store of value An *asset* set aside for future use; one of the three functions of *money*.

Strategic trade policy The use of trade barriers to reduce the risk inherent in product development by domestic firms, particularly that involving advanced technology.

Structural deficit The extent to which the federal government's expenditures exceed its tax revenues when the economy is at full employment (or the extent to which its current expenditures exceed the projected tax revenues that would accrue if the economy were at full employment); also known as a full-employment budget deficit.

Structural unemployment Unemployment of workers whose skills are not demanded by employers, they lack sufficient skill to obtain employment, or they cannot easily move to locations where jobs are available.

Subsidy A payment of funds (or goods and services) by a government, firm, or household for which it receives no good or service in return; when made by a government, it is a *government transfer payment*.

Substitute goods Products or services that can be used in place of each other. When the price of one falls the demand for the other falls, and conversely with an increase of price.

Substitution effect (1) A change in the price of a *consumer good* changes the relative expensiveness of that good and hence changes the consumer's willingness to buy it rather than other goods. (2) The effect of a change in the price of a *resource* on the quantity of the resource employed by a firm, assuming no change in its output.

Superior good (*See* Normal good.)

Supply A schedule showing the amounts of a good or service sellers (or a seller) will offer at various prices during some period.

Supply curve A curve illustrating *supply*.

Supply factor (in growth) An increase in the availability of a resource, an improvement in its quality, or an expansion of technological knowledge that makes it possible for an economy to produce a greater output of goods and services.

Supply shock An event that increased production costs, decreases *aggregate supply*, reduces *real GDP*, and increases *unemployment*.

Supply-side economics A view of macroeconomics that emphasizes the role of costs and *aggregate supply* in explaining *inflation*, *unemployment*, and *economic growth*.

Surplus The amount by which the *quantity supplied* of a product exceeds the *quantity demanded* at a specific (above-equilibrium) price.

Surplus value A Marxian term; the amount by which the value of a worker's daily output exceeds his daily wage; the output of workers appropriated by capitalists as profit.

Switching Government of Canada deposits Action of Bank of Canada to increase (decrease) backing for *money supply* by switching government deposits from (to) itself to (from) the *chartered banks*.

Tariff A tax imposed by a nation on an imported good.

Tax An involuntary payment of money (or goods and services) to a government by a *household* or *firm* for which the household or firm receives no good or service directly in return.

Tax incidence The person or group who ends up paying a tax.

Technology The body of knowledge and techniques that can be used to produce goods and services from *economic resources*.

Technological advance New and better goods and services and new and better ways of producing or distributing them.

Terms of trade The rate at which units of one product can be exchanged for units of another product; the price of a good or service; the amount of one good or service that must be give up to obtain one unit of another good or service.

Tight money policy Bank of Canada actions that contract, or restrict, the growth of the nation's *money supply* for the purpose of reducing or eliminating inflation.

Till money (*See* Vault cash.)

Token money Coins having a *face value* greater than their *intrinsic value*.

Total cost The sum of *fixed cost* and *variable cost*.

Total demand The demand schedule or the *demand curve* of all buyers of a good or service; also called market demand.

Total demand for money The sum of the *transactions demand for money* and the *asset demand for money*.

Total spending The total amount buyers of goods and services spend or plan to spend; also called *aggregate expenditures*.

Total supply The supply schedule or the supply curve of all sellers of a good or service; also called market supply.

Trade balance The export of goods (or goods and services) of a nation less its imports of goods (or goods and services).

Trade bloc A group of nations that lower or abolish trade barriers among members. Examples include the *European Union* and the nations of the *North American Free Trade Agreement*.

Trade controls *Tariffs, export subsidies, import quotas,* and other means a nation may employ to reduce *imports* and expand *exports*.

Trade deficit The amount by which a nation's *imports* of goods (or goods and services) exceed its *exports* of goods (or goods and services).

Tradeoffs The sacrifice of some or all of one economic goal, good, or service to achieve some other goal, good, or service.

Trade surplus The amount by which a nation's exports of goods (or goods and services) exceed its imports of goods (or goods and services).

Trades and Labour Congress of Canada (TLC) The federation of *craft unions* formed in 1886 and affiliated with the *American Federation of Labor*; amalgamated into the *Canadian Labour Congress* in 1956.

Trading possibilities line A line that shows the different combinations of two products an economy is able to obtain (consume) when it specializes in the production of one product and trades (exports) it to obtain the other product.

Traditional economy An economic system in which traditions and customs determine how the economy will use its scarce resources.

Transactions demand for money The amount of money people want to hold for use as a *medium of exchange* (to make payments), and which varies directly with the *nominal GDP*.

Transfer payment A payment of *money* (or goods and services) by a government to a *household* or *firm* for which the payer receives no good or service directly in return.

Unanticipated inflation Increases in the price level (*inflation*) at a rate greater than expected.

Underemployment (1) Failure to produce the maximum amount of goods and services that can be produced from the resources employed; failure to achieve *full production*. (2) A situation in which workers are employed in positions requiring less than the amount of education and skill than they have.

Undistributed corporate profits After-tax corporate profits not distributed as dividends to stockholders; corporate or business saving; also called retained earnings.

Unemployment Failure to use all available *economic resources* to produce goods and services; failure of the economy to fully employ its *labour force*.

Unemployment compensation (*See* Employment insurance.)

Unemployment insurance (*See* Employment insurance.)

Unemployment rate The percentage of the *labour force* unemployed at any time.

Unit labour cost Labour costs per unit of output; total labour cost divided by total output; also equal to the *nominal wage rate* divided by the *average product of* labour.

Unit of account A standard unit in which prices can be stated and the value of goods and services can be compared; one of the three functions of *money*.

Unlimited liability Absence of any limits on the maximum amount that an individual (usually a business owner) may become legally required to pay.

Unlimited wants The insatiable desire of consumers for goods and services that will give them satisfaction or *utility*.

Unplanned investment Actual investment less *planned investment*; increases or decreases in the *inventories* of firms resulting from production greater than sales.

Urban collectives Chinese enterprises jointly owned by their managers and their workforces, located in urban areas.

Uruguay Round The eighth and most recent round of trade negotiations under *GATT* (now the *World Trade Organization*).

Utility The want-satisfying power of a good or service; the satisfaction or pleasure a consumer obtains from the consumption of a good or service (or from the consumption of a collection of goods and services).

Value added The value of the product sold by a *firm* less the value of the products (materials) purchased and used by the firm to produce the product.

Value judgement Opinion of what is desirable or undesirable; belief regarding what ought or ought not to be (regarding what is right or just and wrong or unjust).

Value of money The quantity of goods and services for which a unit of money (a dollar) can be exchanged; the purchasing power of a unit of money; the reciprocal of the *price level*.

Variable cost A cost that in total increases when the firm increases its output and decreases when it reduces its output.

Vault cash The *currency* a bank has in its vault and cash drawers.

Velocity The number of times per year the average dollar in the *money supply* is spent for *final goods and services*; nominal GDP divided by the money supply.

Vertical axis The "up-down" or "north-south" axis on a graph or grid.

Vertical combination A group of *plants* engaged in different stages of the production of a final product and owned by a single *firm*.

Vertical intercept The point at which a line meets the vertical axis of a graph.

Vicious circle of poverty A problem common in some developing countries in which their low per-capita incomes are an obstacle to realizing the levels of saving and investment requisite to acceptable rates of economic growth.

Voluntary export restrictions Voluntary limitations by countries or firms of their exports to a particular foreign nation to avoid enactment of formal trade barriers by that nation.

Wage The price paid for the use or services of *labour* per unit of time (per hour, per day, and so on).

Wage rate (*See* Wage.)

Wealth effect The tendency for increases (decreases) in the price level to lower (raise) the real value (or purchasing power) of financial assets with fixed money values; and, as a result, to reduce (expand) total spending in the economy.

"Will to develop" Wanting economic growth strongly enough to change from old to new ways of doing things.

World Bank A bank that lends (and guarantees loans) to developing nations to assist them in increasing their *capital stock* and thus to achieve economic growth; formally, the International Bank for Reconstruction and Development.

World price The international market price of a good or service, determined by world demand and supply.

World Trade Organization An organization established in 1994 to replace *GATT* to oversee the provisions of the *Uruguay Round* and resolve any disputes stemming therefrom.